HINDI GRAMMAR REFERENCE AND TUTOR

All-in-One

With Transliteration

Worth it's weight in Gold

A Handy Hindi Tutor, Grammar Guide plus a Vast Reference Book

Prof. Ratnakar Narale

Ratnakar

PUSTAK BHARATI

TORONTO, CANADA

Author :
Dr. Ratnakar Narale, Ph.D (IIT), Ph.D. (Kalidas Hindi Univ.)
Prof. Hindi, Ryerson University, Toronto

Title : **Hindi Grammar Reference and Tutor All-in-One.**
A Handy Hindi Grammar Guide, Tutor plus a Vast Reference Book with transliteration.

A Handy Hindi Tutor, Grammar Guide plus a Vast Reference Book is All-in-One ocean of essential information, This book is designed for all levels of learning and reference. It is conveniently Transliterated for the benefit of new users. It has unique Charts, Tables, Flowcharts, Golden Rules, Conjugations of Hindi Verbs, Case Inflections all possible noun types and every element of grammar you would ever need to know, but may not find elsewhere. It is enriched with Chhand Sutras and much more. A must for Hindi students and scholars, this book is one of its kind, worth its Weight in Gold. The question is not, "can you afford to buy it," the question is "can you afford not to buy this priceless book?"

Published by :
Pustak Bharati (Books-India)
Division of PC PLUS Ltd.

Published For :
Hindi Hindi Research Institute, Toronto

ISBN 978-1-989416-95-2
90000
9 781989 416952

Copyright ©2024
ISBN 978-1-989416-95-2 (Soft Cover)
ISBN 978-1-989416-94-5 (Hard Cover)

© All rights reserved. No part of this book may be copied, reproduced or utilised in any manner or by any means, computerised, e-mail, scanning, photocopying or by recording in any information storage and retrieval system, without the permission in writing from Prof. Ratnakar Narale.

INDEX

anukramaṇikā

अनुक्रमणिका

INTRODUCTION
प्रतिष्ठापन

Hindi is by far the most poetic and florid language in the world. It is the glorious literature written by the immortal poets that attracts the learners to the Hindi language. It is the profound but poetic sweetness and the melodic nature Hindi language that makes its learning so very interesting.

Unique Charts and Tablesare key tools in this book. One of them you will find on the back cover of this book, in the form of the 'Chart of Hindi Alphabet.' Unique is the technique of depicting the *māheśhvarāṇi sūtrāṇi.*

Included in this book are several Transliterated Dictionaries. For the first time ever you will find a systematically laid out huge listing of nearly 2000 Chhand sūtras in this book in the chapter called *Chhand-ratnakar*, a handy reference work for the poets and poetry and prosody lovers.

I have tried to make this book easy, unique and useful as possible. Nevertheless, I beg the readers to forgive me for any errors, omissions or imperfections that they may find. I hope the new as well as the learned readers, will find this book interesting and useful. ॐ तत् सत्।

-Ratnakar

KNOW THIS BEFORE YOU BEGIN

1. The word Grammar (*vyākaraṇa* व्याकरण) comes from the root verb vāk (√वाक्) which is the process of analysis. It is one of the six limbs of the Veda.
2. Vyakran is also called *Shabdānushāsana* (शब्दानुशासन).
3. In any society, the langauge comes first and then in order to make it systematic, coordinate it according to set of rules, the grammar is developed.
4. Grammar shows the pure form of the language.
5. The four considerations in the study of Grammar is i. the letters, ii. the words, iii. The sentences and iv. their construction.
6. Hindi is written in the Devanagari Script (देवनागरी लिपि).
7. Hindi is a Phonetic Language. Unlike English, here rather than writing the spellings of the words the symbols for the spoken sounds of the letters of the word are written.
8. The original sound of a spoken letter is called a Vanrn (वर्ण).
9. A systematic table of the strings of the root Varnas forms the Chart of Alphabet (वर्णमाला).
10. Hindi is derived from the Sanskrit Language.
11. In Hindi each letter, divisible as well as indivisible, is loosely called an Akshara (अक्षर, √क्षर् + अच्, नञ् तत्पुरुष समास). However, in Sanskrit the word Akshara (अ–क्षर) means only the letter that is not-divisible.

PREVIEW GLIMPSE AT THE GENERAL HINDI GRAMMAR KEYS

REMARKS ON HINDI LANGUAGE :

1. Hindi is a Phonetic Language.
2. Hindi words do not have arbitrarily fixed spellings like the English words.
3. Words of any language can be written in Hindi, solely based on their spoken sounds, not the fixed spellings.
4. Hindi is 'WOSIWOW' language. In Hindi 'What One Says Is What One Writes.'
5. Hindi is an Agglutinative language. All inflections of verbs and nouns are constructed by fixed predetermined suffixes appended to the noun or verb stems.
6. Hindi is an Inflected language. All Nouns, Pronouns and Adjectives inflect into Cases affected by Genders and Numbers.
7. Hindi does not use any definate articles such as *a, an, the* of the English language. e.g. a house, an egg and the sun. In Hindi it will simply be house, egg and sun.
8. Impersonal Pronouns are not used in Hindi. e.g. (English). **It** is summer now = (Hindi) now is summer. *ab garmee hai* अब गरमी है
9. Most of the English pre-positions are post-positions in Hindi.
10. Hindi makes extensive use of Passive Construction.

LAURELS

1. Hindi is, not the oldest, but most well known among the fourteen Indian daughters of the Royal Old Mother Sanskrit.
2. More than two-billion people in the world have some interest in Hindi.
3. Hindi is the National Language of India.
4. Hindi is the most suited language for Indian Song Lyrics.
5. Hindi is very rich in classical as well as non-classical literature.
6. Hindi's Avadhi and Vraj dilects are the sweet versions for poetic Hindi. The sweetest example of such writing is *Ramacharitmanas* of Tulsidas.
7. As Hindi comes from the Sanskrit, a language rich in word power. There may be many Hindi words for each English word.

DARTS

1. Hindi is probably the world's language most littered with English and other non-Hindi words.
2. The Bollywood Hindi Film Industry and the modern Hindi Lexicograhpers, inspired by Oxford, are the biggest promoters of hybridization of Hindi with English words.
3. Modern Hindi Dictionaries have more English words (or English words with a Hindi twist), than they have Hindi words in them.
4. As a short cut, in Hindi writing the half vowels *n* न्, *m* म्, hard *n* ण्, and the vowels *ng* ङ and *ny* ञ, are plainly replaced with a Nasal Dot.
5. As a short cut, the Half Consonants are more than often replace by writing Full Consonants with the (*halant*) Slash Sigh. e.g. उच्च्च for उच्च
6. Consonants *'v'* व and *'b'* ब; *'y'* य and *'j'* ज; *'s'* स and *'sh'* श are intermixed at will. e.g. '*vinā* ' विना could be '*binā*' बिना and '*Yashoda*' यशोदा could be '*Jasoda*' जसोदा
7. The Sanskrit vowel sounds of 'a' ॅ in the word 'bat' and 'o' ॉ in the word 'bottle' are dropped in Hindi Alphabet. Thus, these sounds are approximately written and spoken, e.g. E. bat = H. bait, E. bottle = H. *botal* बोतल, E. Officer = H. *afsar* अफसर, .. etc.
8. Many foreign words are distorted with a Hindi Twist, such as McDonald = *Makdānal* मकडानल, Russia = *Roos* रूस, Tomato = *tamātar* टमाटर, August = *Agast* अगस्त, bomb = *bum* बम, Captain = कप्तान *kaptān,* .. etc.
9. Spoken Hindi is not only loaded with English words, the grammar is very loosely used.
10. Sometimes proper Hindi is too Nasal. Thus, in spoken language, few Nasals are omitted to make it more palatable. e.g. (English) Small little girls are there, is (Hindi) grammatically *'<u>chhoteen</u> <u>chhoteen</u> ladkiyān haĩ'* छोटीं छोटीं लडकियाँ हैं in spoken Hindi it may be *'<u>chhotee</u> <u>chhotee</u> ladkiyā haĩ'* छोटी छोटी लडकिया हैं
11. Even though the **<u>Gender is one Single most important aspect of the Hindi Language</u>**, there are no logical rules for determining whether a noun is Masculine or Feminine. In addition, a noun may have some masculine words

and some feminine words, arbitrarily. e.g. Book = M. *granth* ग्रंथ; F. *kitāb* किताब, F. *pustak* पुस्तक

12. Too many exceptions to the rules of pluralization. Besides being a daughter of the Grand Old mother Sanskrit, Hindi's own vocab is so poor, that it has to use non-Hindi words, that too proudly on the excuse of being most "absorptive" and modern language.
13. Hindi's verb vocabulary is so scanty, that most of the nouns have to be converted into verbs by adding the intransitive infinitive suffix "honā होना" or transitive infinitive suffix "karna करना" to the nouns. eg. to rain = *barish honā,* to work = *kām karnā,* etc.
14. Hindi is universally taught through pre-made sentences, without understanding the Hindi Grammar. Hindi Teachers or Hindi Learning Books do not bothers to teach **"how to make your own Hindi sentences."**

A. AN OVERVIEW OF HINDI GRAMMATICAL ASPECTS :

1. Nouns :

1. Common Nouns — e.g. E. Man = H. *ādmī* आदमी
2. Proper Nouns — e.g. E. Mike = H. *māik* माइक
3. Abstract Nouns — e.g. E. Pity = *kripā* कृपा
4. Collective Nouns — e.g. E. People = H. *log* लोग

2. Persons :

1. First Person — e.g. E. I, we = H. *maĩ* मैं, *hum* हम
2. Second Person — e.g. E. You = H. *āp* आप
3. Third Person — e.g. E. He = H. *vah* वह

3. Genders :

4. Masculine
5. Feminine

4. Numbers :

1. Singular
2. Plural

5. Cases :

1. Nominative Case e.g. E. a boy = H. *ladkā* लडका
2. Accusative Case e.g. E. to a boy = H. *ladke ko* लड़के को
3. Instrumental Case e.g. E. by a boy = H. *ladke se* लड़के से
4. Dative Case e.g. E. to a boy = H. *ladke ko* लड़के को
5. Ablative Case e.g. E. from a boy = H. *ladke se* लड़के से
6. Possessive or Genitive Case e.g. E. of a boy = H. *ladke kā* लडके का
7. Locative Case e.g. E. in a boy = H. *ladke men* लड़के में
8. Vocative Case e.g. E. O boy! = H. *ladke!* लड़के!

6. Adjectives :

1. Descriptive Adjectives e.g. E. a big boy = H. *badā ladkā* बड़ा लडका
2. Quantitative Adjectives e.g. E. some milk = H. *thods doodh* थोड़ा दूध
3. Numeral Adjectives

Definite Numeral Adjective e.g. E. one boy = H. *ek ladkā* एक लडका

Indefinite Numeral Adjective e.g. E. all boys = H. *sāre ladke* सारे लडके

Distributive Numeral Adjective e.g. E. each boy = H. *har ladkā* हर लडका

Ordinal Numeral Adjective e.g. E. first boy = H. *pahilā ladkā* पहिला लडका

4. Demonstrative Adjectives e.g. E. such boy = H. *aisā ladkā* ऐसा लडका
5. Interrogative Adjective e.g. E. which boy? = H. *kaisā ladkā?* कैसा लडका
6. Comparative Adjective e.g. E. taller boy = H. *ucchatar ladkā* उच्चतर लडका
7. Superlative Adjective e.g. E. tallest boy = H. *ucchatam ladkā* उच्चतम लडका

7. Pronouns :

1. Personal Pronouns e.g. E. <u>He</u> is a boy = H. *<u>vah</u> ladkā hai* वह लडका है
2. Possessive or Pronominal Pronouns

   e.g. E. <u>My</u> book = H. *<u>meree</u> kitāb* मेरी किताब
3. Impersonal Pronouns e.g. E. I, we = H. *maĩ, hum* मैं, हम
4. Interrogative Pronouns e.g. E. <u>Who</u> is there? = H. *<u>kaun</u> hai?* कौन है
5. Compound Personal Pronouns e.g. E. I myself = H. *maĩ khud* मैं ख़ुद

6. Demonstrative Pronouns e.g. E. These boys = H. *ye ladke* ये लडके
7. Indefinite Pronouns e.g. E. One day = H. *ek din* एक दिन
8. Reciprocal Pronouns e.g. E. to <u>each other</u> = H. <u>*ek doosre*</u> *ko* एक दूसरे को
9. Relative Pronouns e.g. E. The boy who = H. *jo jadkā* जो लडका

8. Verbs :

1. Intransitive Verbs
2. Transitive Verbs
3. Causative Verbs
4. Super Causative Verbs

9. Moods :

1. Imperative Mood
2. Potential Mood
3. Desiderative Mood
4. Assertive

10. Adverbs :

1. Adverbs of Time e.g. E. now = H. *ab* अब
2. Adverbs of Frequency e.g. E. twice = H. *dubārā* दुबारा
3. Adverbs of Place e.g. E. Stay <u>here</u> = H. <u>*yahān*</u> *rahiye* यहां रहिये
4. Adverb of Manner e.g. E. walk <u>slowly</u> = H. <u>*dheere*</u> *chaliye* धीरे चलिये
5. Adverb of Degree e.g. E. very fast = H. *bahut tez* बहुत तेज़
6. Adverb of Assertion e.g. E. certainly = H. *zaroor* ज़रूर
7. Adverb of Negation e.g. E. don't = H. *mat* मत
8. Adverb of Reason e.g. E. because = H. *kyonki* क्योंकि
9. Adverb of Interrogation e.g. E. why? = H. *kyon?* क्यों ?

11. Conjunctions :

Copulative Conjunctions e.g. E. and = H. *aur* और
Adversative Conjunctions e.g. E. but = H. *magar* मगर
Correlative Conjunction e.g. E. if...then = H. *yadi...to* यदि...तो
Compound Conjunctions e.g. E. In order that = H. *tāki* ताकि

12. Infinitive :

1. Active Infinitive e.g. E. to eat = H. *khānā* खाना

2. Passive Infinitive e.g. E. be eaten = H. *khāyā jānā* खाया जाना

13. Participles :

1. Present Participle e.g. E. doing = H. *kartā huā* करता हुआ
2. Past Participle e.g. E. done = H. *kiyā, kiyā huāa* किया, किया हुआ
3. Future Participle

   e.g. E. worth doing = H. *karaniya, kārya, kartavya* करणीय, कार्य, कर्तव्य

14. Tenses :

1. Present Tense

   i. Habitual Present Tense : e.g. E. I do = H. *mai̐ kartā hū̐* मैं करता हूँ

   ii. Continuous Present Tense :e.g. E. I am doing = H. *mai̐ kar rahā hū̐* मैं कर रहा हूँ

2. Past Tense

   i. Habitual Past Tense : e.g. E. I used to do = H. *mai̐ kartā thā* मैं करता था

   ii. Continuous Past Tense :

   e.g. E. I was doing = H. *mai̐ kar rahā thā* मैं कर रहा था

3. Future Tense

   i. Simple Future Tense :

   e.g. E. I will do, I shall do = H. *mai̐ karoongā* मैं करूंगा

   ii. Continuous Present Tense :

   e.g. I will be doing = *mai̐ kartā rahū̐gā* मैं करता रहूँगा

4. Perfect Tense

   i. Simple Intransitive Perfect Tense

   e.g. E. I did walk (I walked 5 km.) = H. *mai̐ 5 km. chalā* मैं चला

   ii. Present Intransitive Perfect Tense

   e.g. E. I have walked 5km. = H. *mai̐ 5 km. chalā hū̐* मैं चला हूँ

   iii. Past Intransitive Perfect Tense

   e.g. E. I had walked = H. *mai̐ chalā thā* मैं चला था

   iv. Future Intransitive Perfect Tense

   e.g. E. I will have walked = H. *mai̐ chalā hū̐gā* मैं चला हूँगा

   v. Simple Transitive Perfect Tense : e.g. E. I did = H. *mai̐ne kiyā* मैंने किया

   vi. Present Transitive Perfect Tense :

e.g. E. I am doing = H. *maiँne kiyā hai* मैंने किया है

vii. Past Transitive Perfect Tense : e.g. E. I do = H. *maiँne kiyā thā* मैंने किया था

viii. Future Transitive Perfect Tense :

e.g. E. I am doing = H. *maiँne kiyā hogā* मैंने किया होगा

15. Gerunds :

1. Present Participle Gerund e.g. while eating. *khāte hue.* खाते हुए
2. Verbal Noun Gerund e.g. eating *khānā.* खाना
3. Infinitive Gerund e.g. to eat, for eating *khāne.* खाने के लिये(

16. Participles :

1. Present Active Participles e.g. doing. *karte hue.* करते हुए
2. Past Passive Participles e.g. done. *kiyā huā.* किया हुआ
3. Future Potential Partici.

e.g. doable. *kārya, karniya, kartavya* कार्य, करणीय, कर्तव्य

17. Prepositions (prefixes) and Post-positions (suffixes):

1. Prepositions :
   (i) 32 Sanskrit prefixes,
   (ii) 6 Urdu prefixes,
   (iii) 4 Hindi's own prefixes.

3. Post-positions :

(i) Verb suffixes,
(ii) Substantive suffixes

18. Voices :

4. Active Voice e.g I love you. *maiँ āpse pyār kartā hūँ.* मैं आपसे प्यार करता हूँ
5. Passive Voice e.g. I have love for you, You are loved by me. *mujhe āpse pyār hai.* मुझे आपसे प्यार है

B. **<u>ON HINDI PHONICS</u>** :

1. HINDI ALPHABET :

1. The Chart of written and spoken Hindi Alphabet is arranged according to the Sounds created with the regulated passage of air through the Vocal System including the lungs, vocal cord, wind pipes, throat, tongue, pallet,

teeth and lips.

2. In the Chart of Alphabet, the Vowels come first and then the Consonants.
3. There are 13 basic vowel sounds in the Hindi Alphabet.
4. There are four Simple Vowels or Short Vowels. From the four simple vowels, other nine Compound Vowels or Long Vowels are produced.
5. Vowel sounds can be written in their Character Shapes or as Vowel Signs.
6. Vowel Characters can be written and spoken independently.
7. A Vowel Sign is used only when the vowel is attached to a consonant.
8. For the 13 basic vowel sounds there are 13 basic vowel signs.
9. Vowel signs are attached to the left, right over or under the consonant characters.
10. There are 33 simple Consonant sounds in the Alphabet.
11. The consonants are written and spoken as a half character or a full character.
12. The Half Consonants are used together with the Full Consonants to produce the Compound Consonant sounds.
13. First 25 consonants are classified into Five Classes of 5 consonants each. The First Class is Guttural Consonants (spoken with the aid the Throat), second is Palatal Consonants (spoken with the aid the Palate), the third is Cerebral Consonants (spoken with the aid Cerebrum), the fourth is Dental (spoken with the aid the Teeth), and the fifth is Labial (spoken with the aid the Lips).
14. The last Consonant from each of the Five Classes is called Nasal Consonant (spoken with the aid of the nose).
15. Pronunciation of the Palatal Consonants and the Dental Consonants need special care.
16. The difference between and among the pronunciation of the consonants *k* क and *kh* ख, *g* ग and gh घ, *c* च and *chh* छ, palatal *t* ट and *th* ठ, palatal *d* ड and *dh* ढ, dental *t* त and *th* थ, dental *d* द and *dh* ध needs to be understood very cautiously. They are new to the English speaking tongue.

2. HINDI WORDS :

1. If the word ends in a consonant with a short vowel, that last consonant is pronounced as a half consonant. e.g. Rāma = *Rām* राम

2. In Hindi words, when two or more consonants come consecutively in a row, the last consonant is written as Full Consonant and the rest are written as Half Consonants, and spoken likewise.

3. HINDI SENTENCES :

1. Hindi sentences are often spoken with emphatic tones stressed on specific or desired words or word parts.

C. RESEARCH IN HINDI MORPHOLOGY :

Please see the lessons on i. Ratnakar's Ten Noble Truths, ii. Ratnakar's Brain Surgery of Hindi Grammar, and iii. Ratnakar's X-Ray Vision of Hindi Syntax.

1. HINDI SYNTAX :

1. Hindi is a SOV (subject-object-verb) Language, while English is SVO (subject-verb-object) language.
2. Normally, the Hindi sentences start with the Subject or its Pronoun.
3. Normally, the Hindi sentences terminate with the Verb appended with the Mode, Gender, Tense and Auxiliary verb.
4. The Object is placed within the sentence.
5. If there is Adjective, it is placed before the Object.
6. If there is Adverb, it is placed before the Verb.
7. If there is a Time Element (e.g. yesterday, tomorrow, today, now), it may be placed even before the Subject.

2. HINDI GENDERS :

1. Gender is **the single most important**, delicate and tricky aspect of the Hindi language.
2. There are only two Genders in Hindi, Masculine Noun and Feminine Noun. The Neuter Gender of the Sanskrit language is dropped in Hindi language.
3. All Nouns and Pronouns are tagged Masculine or Feminine.
4. A Masculine Noun can be converted into its Feminine form.
5. A Feminine Noun can be converted into its Masculine form.
6. The Adjectives and Verbs do not have Gender of their own.
7. The Adjectives take Gender from the Noun or Pronoun they qualify.
8. The Verbs take Gender from either the Subject or the Object, depending on the Tense of the sentence.
9. Adverbs do not take any Gender or number.

3. HINDI NUMBER :

1. Number is another tricky property of the Hindi words.
2. There are Two Numbers in Hindi language, Singular Number and Plural Number. The Dual Number of Sanskrit language is omitted in the Hindi language.

3. A Singular word can be converted into its Plural Form.
4. A Plural Word can be converted into its Singular Form.
5. The Nouns of the Subject and Object, the Pronouns, the Adjectives and the Verb terminations take Number.
6. The Singular Masculine Noun that ends in long *'ā आ,'* the *'ā आ'* is changed to *'e'* ए in plural.
7. The Singular Feminine Noun that ends in long *'ā आ,' 'en एँ'* is added to it in plural.
8. The Singular Feminine Noun that ends in a consonant, *'en एँ'* is added to it in plural.
9. The Singular Feminine Noun that ends in long *'ee ई,'* the *'ee ई'* is changed to *'iyān इयाँ'* in plural.
10. For most other nouns, the Singular form does not change when pluralized.

4. HINDI NOUNS :

1. Nouns are either Tangible or Intangible.
2. Nouns are Masculine or Feminine.
3. Nouns are Singular or Plural
4. Nouns take Adjectives.
5. The Adjectives agree with their Nouns in Gender and Number.
6. Some Nouns can be converted into Adjectives and Verbs.

5. HINDI PRONOUNS :

1. All Nouns can be represented by Pronouns.
2. Pronouns are Masculine or Feminine.
3. Pronouns are Singular or Plural.
4. Pronouns take Adjectives.
5. The Adjectives agree with the attached Pronoun in Gender and Number.

6. HINDI ADJECTIVES :

1. The Adjectives do not have their own Gender or Number
2. Adjective agree with the Gender and Number of the Noun or Pronoun it qualifies.
3. All Numerals are treated as adjectives.
4. An Adjective can be converted into a Noun.

7. HINDI ADVERBS :

1. The Adverb qualifies a verb, adjective or another adverb.

2. Adverb comes before the verb, adjective or the adverb it qualifies.
3. Adverbs do not take Gender.
4. Adverbs do not take Number.
5. Some adverbs can be used as Adverbs as well as Adjectives.

8. HINDI CASES :

1. Hindi utilizes Eight Cases. Hindi people like the word 'Kārak' for Cases (vibhakti).
2. The Case Affixes are pre-positions in English, in Hindi they are post-positions.
3. In active voice, Nominative Case is used for Subject of the sentence. E. Roy = H. Roy राय
4. In Nominative case, the subject takes no Termination in all tenses except in the Transitive Perfect Tense.
5. In Nominative Case, the Subject of the Transitive Perfect Tense takes (*ne* ने) Terminator suffix. e.g. E. Roy = H. Roy ne राय ने
6. Accusative case is used for the Object of the sentence.
7. The object of the Accusative Case takes (*ko* को) Terminator suffix. e.g. E. to Roy = H. Roy ko राय को
8. The Accusative Case Terminator (*ko* को) is not always actually used in the sentence, but is understood to be there.
9. The Case Terminator for both the Instrumental and the Ablative cases is (*se* से). e.g. i. E. With Roy = H. Roy se राय से; ii. E. From Roy = H. Roy se राय से
10. Similar to Accusative Case, the Case Terminator for the Dative Case is also (*ko* को). e.g. E. to Roy = H. Roy ko राय को
11. In Dative Case, the Terminator (ko को) is always used.
12. The Possessive Case Terminator is (*kā* का). e.g. E. of Roy = H. *Roy kā* राय का
13. Only the Possessive Case Terminator (*kā* का) is Gender and Number sensitive.
14. The Possessive Case Terminator (*kā* का) agrees with the Gender and Number of the object.
15. The Locative Case Terminators are i. meँ में. e.g. E. In Roy = H. *Roy men* राय में and ii. *par* पर. e.g.E. On Roy = H. *Roy par* राय पर

16. The Vocative Case is modified form of the Nominative Case.
17. If a Noun is Masculine and Singular and it ends in *'ā'* आ, then this last vowel *'ā* आ' changes to *'e'* ए when any Case Terminator is attached to that noun.
18. But, if the Noun is Plural, then suffix *'on'* ओं is added to that Plural Noun, before attaching any Case Terminator.

9. HINDI PREPOSITIONS :

1. All Case pre-positions in the English syntax become post-positions in Hindi syntax. However, the Possessive Case is exception.

10. HINDI PERSONS :

1. Like English, there are three persons in Hindi.
2. The Speaker (I or we) of the sentence, is the First Person.
3. The person to whom the First Person is talking is the Second Person.
4. The person, place or thing which the speaker is referring, is the Third Person.
5. The Imperative sentence is always aimed at the Second Person.
6. The Second Person can be referred in Hindi in three ways, viz. i. Less respect or closeness (*tuu* तू), ii. equality (*tum* तुम) and iii. respectful use (*āp* आप).

11. HINDI TERMS OF RESPECT :

1. Use of Plural forms of the Pronouns and Verb Suffixes, in place of their Singular forms, impart expression of respect.

12. HINDI VERBS :

1. The verbs are Gender and Number sensitive.
2. In all tenses, except Transitive Perfect tense, the Verb agrees with the Gender and Number of the Subject.
3. In Transitive Perfect Tense the Verb agrees with the gender and Number of the Object.
4. In English many nouns are verbs also (e.g. rain, snow). In Hindi many nouns can be converted into verbs. To convert an Intransitive (Hindi or foreign language verb) into a Hindi verb, attach the verb *'ho* हो*'* to it, and then use this compound phrase as a verb. To convert a Transitive (Hindi or foreign language verb) into Hindi verb, attach the verb *'kar* कर*'* to it, and then use this compound phrase as a verb.
5. A Hindi verb stem can be converted into an Infinitive, a Verbal Noun or a

Gerund simply by attaching suffix *'nā* ना*'* to the verb stem.

6. The verbs 'take, give, do and drink' are Irregular Verbs in Imperative Mood.
7. The verb 'go' is Irregular in Perfect tense.

13. HINDI PARTICIPLES :

1. A Hindi Past Participle can be used as an adjective or as a verb of a Perfect Tense.
2. In Hindi, the Future Participle is formed in three ways, but one of these three types is more popular for each verb.

14. HINDI PRESENT TENSE :

1. If the Subject in a Hindi sentence is First Person Singular, Masculine or Feminine, the sentence normally terminates with *'hū̃'* हूँ
2. If the Subject in a Hindi sentence is Second or Third Person Singular, Masculine or Feminine, the sentence normally terminates with *'hai'* है
3. If the Subject in a Hindi sentence is Plural, Masculine or Feminine, the sentence normally terminates with *'haĩ'* हैं
4. If the Subject in a Hindi sentence is Honorific Second Person Singular or Plural, Masculine or Feminine, the sentence normally terminates with *'haĩ'* हैं
5. If an English sentence has 'was' or 'had' in it, the corresponding Hindi sentence will end in *'thā'* था (masculine singular), *'thī'* थी (feminine singular), or *'the'* थे (masculine plural), or *'thī̃'* थीं (feminine plural) terminator.

15. HINDI PAST TENSE :

1. If the Subject in a Hindi sentence is Singular Masculine, the sentence normally terminates with *'thā'* था
2. If the Subject in a Hindi sentence is Singular Feminine, the sentence normally terminates with *'thī'* थी
3. If the Subject in a Hindi sentence is Plural Masculine, the sentence normally terminates with *'the'* थे
4. If the Subject in a Hindi sentence is Feminine Plural, the sentence could be terminated with *'the'* थे or *'thī̃'* थीं

16. HINDI FUTURE TENSE :

1. If the Subject in a Hindi sentence is First Person Singular, Masculine, the

sentence normally terminates with *'hū̐gā'* हूँगा

2. If the Subject in a Hindi sentence is First Person Singular, Feminine, the sentence normally terminates with *'hū̐gee'* हूँगी
3. If the Subject in a Hindi sentence is Second or Third Person Singular, Masculine, the sentence normally terminates with *'egā'* एगा
4. If the Subject in a Hindi sentence is Second or Third Person Singular, Feminine, the sentence normally terminates with *'egee'* एगी
5. If the Subject in a Hindi sentence is First, Second or Third Person Plural, Masculine, the sentence normally terminates with *'enge'* एंगे
6. If the Subject in a Hindi sentence is First, Second or Third Person Plural, Feminine, the sentence normally terminates with *'enge* एंगे*'* but could be ended with *'engee* एंगी*'*
7. If the Subject in a Hindi sentence is Honorific Second Person, Singular, Feminine, the sentence normally terminates with *'enge* एंगे*'* but could be ended with *'engee* एंगी*'*

17. HINDI PERFECT TENSE :

1. In all four Hindi Intransitive Perfect tenses, the verb agrees with the Subject.
2. In all four Hindi Transitive Perfect tenses, the verb agrees with the Object.
3. The sentence of a Hindi Simple Perfect tense normally terminates with a Past Participle used as verb.
4. The Transitive Perfect tense with Singular Object normally terminates with *'hai* है*'*
5. Transitive Perfect tense with Plural Object normally terminates with *'hai̐* हैं*'*
6. The Future Perfect tense is not much used in Hindi, but it normally terminates like a corresponding Future Tense.
7. The verb 'go' is Irregular Verbs in Perfect tense.

18. NEGATIVE MOOD :

1. A Negative Mood is created by pre-positioning *'nahin* नहीं*'* before the verb.
2. The Negative Imperative Mood is created by placing *'mat* मत*'* before the verb.

19. INTERROGATIVE MOOD :

1. The Interrogative Mood can simply created by attaching the *'kyā* क्या*'* at the

beginning or at the end of the sentence. Here the *'kyā क्या'* represents just a question mark.

2. This *'kyā क्या'* if placed anywhere 'within' the sentence, then this *'kyā क्या'* means 'what?'

20. IMPERATIVE MOOD :

1. The Imperative Mood indicates a request or an order, but when it is used with the Honorific Pronoun *'āp आप,'* it only means request.
2. The Honorific Imperative Suffix *'iye इये'* includes the property of 'please,' therefore with the use of '*āp* आप' addition of 'please' *(kripayā कृपया)* is not necessary.
3. In Hindi the Imperative Mood is spoken in three manners : i. as an order to a person of lower level or close relationship, ii. as an order or a request to a person of same level, and iii. as a request to a respectable person. I first case, the verb stem without any suffix is used as an Imperative verb e.g. Don't eat! *mat khā* मत खा. In second case, suffix *'o'* ओ is added to the verb stem to make an Imperative verb e.g. Don't eat. *mat khao* मत खाओ. In third case, suffix *'iye'* इये is added to the verb stem to make an honorific Imperative verb e.g. Please do not eat. *mat khāiye* मत खाइये.

21. POTENTIAL MOOD

1. In Hindi, many times simply the Future Tense is used to speak in Potential Mood.
2. A Passive construction is preferred over the Active Voice for speaking in Potential Mood.
3. The verbs 'take, give, do and drink' are Irregular Verbs in Imperative Mood

22. VOICES :

The Passive Voice is quite common in Hindi speaking.

22. EMPHASIS :

The expressions of Emphasis and Punctuation of word endings are common in Hindi speech.

CHAPTER 1

THE HINDI ORTHOGRAPHY

हिंदी वर्ण विन्यास

(i) Varṇa (वर्ण) :

Representation of the sounds of Hindi by written letters (वर्ण) or symblos (चिह्न) is Hindi Orthography. Varṇa (वर्ण) is the original basic (*mūla* मूल) indivisible (*akṣara* अ-क्षर, अक्षर) sound which can be represented by written symbol or **letter**.

(ia) **Basic Root** Varṇa (मूल वर्ण) : a (अ), i (इ), u (उ); ri (ऋ); k (क्), kh (ख्), g (ग्) .. etc.

(ib) **Compound Varṇa** (संयुक्त वर्ण) : ā (अ+अ = आ), ī (इ+इ = ई), ū (उ+उ = ऊ); e (अ+इ = ए), ai (अ+अ+इ = ऐ), o (अ+उ = ओ), au (अ+अ+उ = औ), ka (क्+अ = क), kā (क्+अ+अ = का), ki (क्+इ = कि), kī (क्+इ+इ = की), ku (क्+उ = कु), kū (क्+उ+उ = कू), ke (क्+अ+इ = के), kai (क्+अ+अ+इ = कै), ko (क्+अ+उ = को), kau (क्+अ+अ+उ = कौ), kri (क्+ऋ = कृ), kṝ (क्+ऋ+ऋ = कॄ), ki (क्+क = क्क), ki (च्+च = च्च), etc. The Union of the similar letters such as अ+अ, अ+आ, इ+इ, इ+ई, उ+उ, उ+ऊ, etc. is referred as **sandhi yukta varna (संधियुक्त वर्ण)** and the union of dissimilar letters such as अ+इ=ए, अ+उ=ओ, आ+ए=ऐ, आ+ओ=औ, क्+व=क्व, च्+य=च्य, etc. is called **compound varna (संयुक्त वर्ण)**.

(ii) Shabda (शब्द) :

Shabda is a **word** composed of basic (मूल) or compound (*samyukta* संयुक्त) letters (वर्ण). Such as : In the word Rāma (राम), r+a+a m+a, the compound letter rā (रा) is composed of basic Varṇas r+a+a (र्+अ+अ) and compound letter म is made of Varṇas ma (म्+अ).

(iii). Varṇamālā (वर्णमाला) :

In Hindi the Alphabet is called *Varṇamālā* (वर्णमाला), the chart (माला) of String of Varṇas (वर्ण). The Hindi Varnamlā is composed of 4 original + 9 compound = 13 Vowels (*svara* स्वर) and 34 original Consonants (*mūla vyañjana* मूल व्यंजन).

(3a) 13 Vowels (*svar* स्वर) and 47 Consonants (*vyañjan* व्यंजन) :

1. **Root Vowels :** There are 4 **Original Root Vowels :**

a (अ), i (इ), u (उ) and ri (ऋ);

2. **Dipthongs :** There are 9 **Compound Vowels** (Dipthongs *mishra-svar* मिश्र-स्वर) :

ā (अ+अ = आ), ī (इ+इ = ई), ū (उ+उ = ऊ); e (अ+इ = ए), ai (अ+अ+इ = ऐ), o (अ+उ = ओ), au (अ+अ+उ = औ), ṁ (अं), ah (अ:);

3. **Class Consonants :** There are 25 **Class** (*varga* वर्ग) **Consonants** : (shown as full consontnat for ease of understanding)

	Class	Hard Consonants	Soft Consonants	Nasal Consonants
i.	k Class :	ka (क), kha (ख),	ga (ग), gha (घ),	ṅa (ङ)
ii.	ch Class :	ca (च), chha (छ),	ja (ज), jha (झ),	ñ (ञ)
iii.	ṭ Class :	ṭa (ट), ṭha (ठ),	ḍa (ड), ḍha (ढ),	ṇa (ण)
iv.	t Class :	ta (त), tha (थ),	da (द), dha (ध),	na (न) and
v.	p Class :	pa (प), pha (फ),	ba (ब), bha (भ),	ma (म)

The first two letteers in each of the 5 class-consonants are **Hard** (*kaṭhor* कठोर) consonants, the next two letters are **Soft** (*mridu* मृदु) consonants and the last consonant is **Nasal** (*anunāsik* अनुनासिक) consonant. Please see the back cover of the book for a clear picture.

An original consonant without added vowel a (अ) is called Half (*ardha* अर्ध) Consonant and a consonant with added inherant vowel a (अ) is Full (पूर्ण) Consonant. The next 4 characters य्, र्, ल्, व् are semi-consonsnts or semi-vowels अन्तस्थ (*antastha*). The remaining four characters श्, ष्, स्, ह् are the ऊष्म 'warm breath characters' (*uṣhma*) of which the first three श्, ष्, स् are called 'sibilants (स्-युक्त उच्चार).' The fourth ह् is the aspirate (breath Character).

NOTE : In Devanagari Alphabet there are three more vowels ṝ (ॠ), lri (ऌ) and ḹ (ॡ) as well as one more consonant ḷ (ळ). In Hindi these four letters are not used. In fact, the nasal consonants ṅ (ङ) and ñ (ञ) are also rarely or never used in Hindi writing.

THE HINDI ALPHABET

हिंदी वर्णमाला

THE HINDI HALF-CONSONANTS

हिंदी के अर्ध व्यंजन

Half Consonant = the Root Consonant without a vowel*

क् क्‍	ख् ख्‍	ग् ग्‍	घ् घ्‍	ङ्
k	kh	g	gh	ṅ
च् च्‍	छ्	ज् ज्‍	झ् झ्‍	ञ् ञ्‍
ch	chh	j	jh, z	ñ
ट्	ठ्	ड्	ढ्	ण् ण्‍
ṭ	ṭh	ḍ	ḍh	ṇ
त् त्‍	थ् थ्‍	द्	ध् ध्‍	न् न्‍
t	th	d	dh	n
प् प्‍	फ् फ्‍	ब् ब्‍	भ् भ्‍	म् म्‍
p	ph, f	b	bh	m
य् य्‍	र्	ल् ल्‍	व् व्‍	
y	r	l	v, w	
श् श्‍	ष् ष्‍	स् स्‍	ह् ह्‍	
śh	ṣh	s	h	

* **NOTE :** The short slant (्) attached at the foot of a consonant (to nullify the default vowel a (अ) from that consonant) is called halant (हलंत). A Consonant with halant is a Haf letter.

Hindi Full Consonants with vowel a (अ) added as default vowel

क	ख	ग	घ	ङ	**1 - the Gutterals** (see below)
ka	kha	ga	gha	ṅa	
च	छ	ज	झ	ञ	**2 - the Palatals**
cha*	chha	ja	jha	ña	
ट	ठ	ड	ढ	ण	**3 - the Cerebrals**
ṭa	ṭha	ḍa	ḍha	ṇa	
त	थ	द	ध	न	**4 - the Dentals**
ta	tha	da	dha	na	
प	फ	ब	भ	म	**5 - the Labials**
pa	pha	ba	bha	ma	

य	र	ल	व	श	ष	स	ह
ya	ra	la	va	śha	ṣha	sa	ha

NOTES :

1. In order to refer any consonant letter by its name in Hindi, suffix *kār* (कार) is added to that letter. e.g. a-kār (अकार), ā-kār (आकार), k-kār (ककार), kha-kar (खकार), .. etc. The letter r (र) is referred as r-kār (रकार) or ref (रेफ).
2. In order to refer any word by its end letter, suffix *kārānt* (कारांन्त) is added to that letter. e.g. a-kārānt (अकारान्त) word, ā-kārānt (आकारान्त) word, k-kārānt (ककारान्त) word, kha-karānt (खकारान्त) word, .. etc.

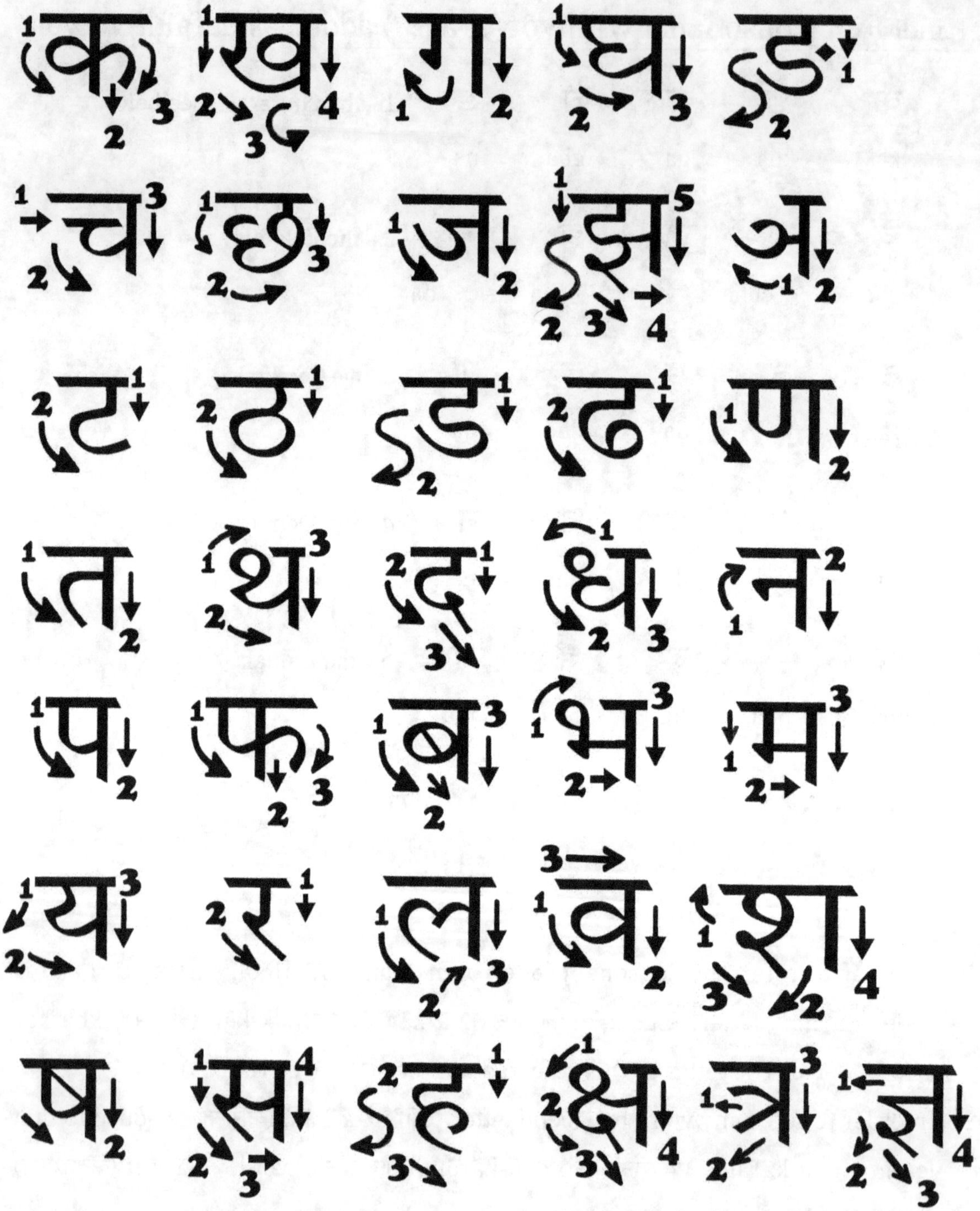
क ख ग घ ङ
च छ ज झ ञ
ट ठ ड ढ ण
त थ द ध न
प फ ब भ म
य र ल व श
ष स ह क्ष त्र ज्ञ

CHARACTERS GROUPED
ACCORDING TO THE SHAPE for EASY LEARNING

अ a	आ ā	ओ o	औ au	अं ṁ	अँ m̐	अः ḥ
इ i	ई ī	उ u	ऊ ū	ऋ ṛ	ए e	ऐ ai
व va	ब ba	क ka		ऌ ḷ		
प pa	ष ṣa	फ pha				
त ta	न na	ग ga	म ma	भ bha	ण ṇa	
च ća	ज ja	ञ ña	ल la		ॡ lṝ	
घ gha	ध dha	छ ćha				
य ya	थ tha					
ट ṭa	ठ ṭha	ढ ḍha	द da			
ड ḍa	ङ ṅa	झ jha	ह ha		इ i	ई ī
र ra	स sa	ख kha	श śa			

Short, Long and Saturated Vowel mātrās

In Hindi *mātrā* is also called मत्त, मत्ता, कला or कल..

(1) Short vowels अ, इ, उ, ऋ, लृ *a, i, u, ri, lri*

(2) Long vowels आ, ई, ऊ, ॠ, ए, ऐ, ओ, औ, ॡ *ā, ī, ū, rí, e, ai, o, au, lrí*

(3) Simple vowels अ, आ, इ, ई, उ, ऊ, ऋ, ॠ, लृ, ॡ *a, ā, i, ī, u, ū, ri, rí, lri, lrí*

(4) Dipthongs ए, ऐ, ओ औ *e, ai, o, au*

(5) Pluta vowels ऽ

a. **Short** (*laghu or hrasva* लघु, ह्रस्व) **Vowels are those which take one unit** (मात्रा) **of time to pronounce it.** Short vowels अ, इ, उ, ऋ *a, i, u, ri*

b. **Long** (*dīrgha orguru* दीर्घ, गुरु) **Vowels take two units of time to pronounce.**

(1) Long vowel आ = short vowel अ + short vowel अ

(2) Long vowel ई = short vowel इ + short vowel इ

(3) Long vowel ऊ = short vowel उ + short vowel उ

(4) Long vowel ए = short vowel अ + short vowel इ

(5) Long vowel ऐ = short vowel अ + short vowel अ + short vowel इ

(6) Long vowel ओ = short vowel अ + short vowel उ

(7) Long vowel औ = short vowel अ + short vowel अ + short vowel उ

c. **Saturated** (*pluta* प्लुत) **Vowels are those which take more than two units of time to pronounce it.**

The extended expressions such as vowel आऽऽ (raऽऽ) in the word राऽऽऽम or ओऽऽ (oऽऽ) in the word ओऽऽऽम् are pluta vowels. Pluta mātrās are more used in music.

NOTE : As a consonant can not be pronounced without sdding at least vowel a (अ), the *mātrā* of the *halant* consonant is counted half. e.g. mahat (महत्) 1+1+1.5=2.5 *mātrās.*

एक मात्रं भवेध्रस्वं द्विमात्रं दीर्घमुच्यते ।
त्रिमात्रं तु प्लुतं ज्ञेयं व्यञ्जनं चार्धमात्रकम् ।।

ORGANS of PONOUNCIATION

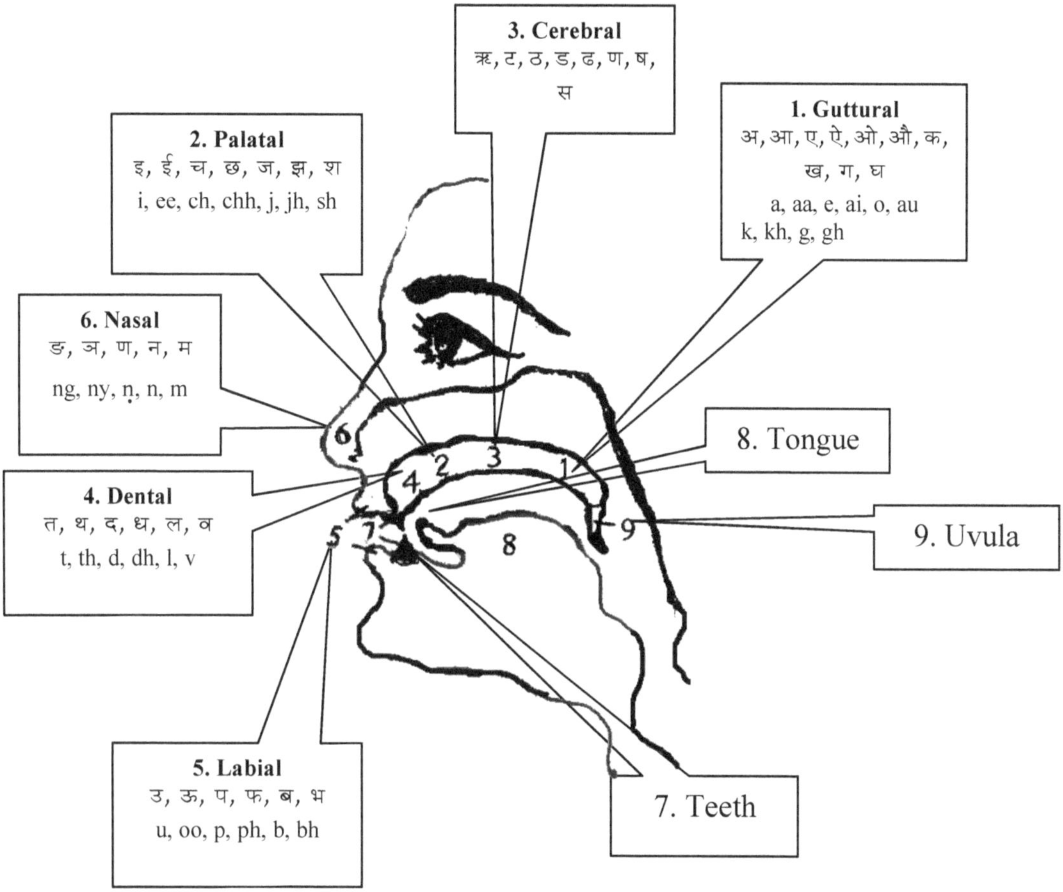

(1) Guttural	कण्ठ्य	*(kaṇṭhya)*	=	with throat
(2) Palatal	तालव्य	*(tālavya)*	=	with palate
(3) Cerebral	मूर्धन्य	*(mūrdhanya)*	=	with cerebrum
(4) Dental	दन्त्य	*(dantya)*	=	with teeth
(5) Labial	ओष्ठ्य	*(oṣhṭhya)*	=	with lips
(6) Nasal	अनुनासिक	*(anunāsik)*	=	with nose

(1) THE VOWELS :

Vowel	Stands for	Sounds like	As in	Pronunciation
a	(अ)	A	American	Guttural
ā	(आ)	a	car	Guttural
i	(इ)	I	India	Palatal
ī	(ई)	ee	peel	Palatal
u	(उ)	u	pull	Labial
ū	(ऊ)	oo	pool	Labial
ri	(ऋ)	ri, ru	ring, crucial	Cerebral
rí	(ॠ)	rī, rū		Cerebral
lri	(ऌ)	lri, lru		Dental
lrí	(ॡ)	lrī, lrū		Dental
e	(ए)	e	grey	Guttural+Palatal
ai	(ऐ)	ai	aisle	Guttural+Palatal
o	(ओ)	o	go	Guttural+Labial
au	(औ)	au	gauge	Guttural+Labial

(2) THE SEMIVOWELS :

ḿ	(अं)	ã		nasal
:	(अ:)	half-h		breath

(3) THE CONSONANTS :

Consonant	Stands for	Sounds like	As in	Pronunciation
k	(क्)	k	kit	Guttural
kh	(ख्)	kh	khyber	Guttural
g	(ग्)	g	god	Guttural
gh	(घ्)	gh	ghost	Guttural
ṅ	(ङ्)	n	ring	Guttural
ch	(च्)	ch	rich	Palatal
chh	(छ्)	chh	ch with breath	Palatal

j	(ज्)	j	jug	Palatal
jh	(झ्)	dgeh	zoo	Palatal
ñ	(ञ्)	n	hinge	Palatal
ṭ	(ट्)	t	cuṭ	Cerebral
ṭh	(ठ्)	th	ṭ with breath	Cerebral
ḍ	(ड्)	d	red	Cerebral
ḍh	(ढ्)	dh	adhere	Cerebral
ṇ	(ण्)	n	band	Cerebral
t	(त्)	t	(soft t)	Dental
th	(थ्)	th	path	Dental
d	(द्)	th	other	Dental
dh	(ध्)	dh	Buddha	Dental
n	(न्)	n	no	Dental
p	(प्)	p	cup	Labial
ph	(फ्)	ph, f	photo	Labial
b	(ब्)	b	rub	Labial
bh	(भ्)	bh	abhore	Labial
m	(म्)	m	mug	Labial
y	(य्)	y	yes	Palatal
r	(र्)	r	rub	Cerebral
l	(ल्, ऌ)	l	love	Dental
v	(व्)	v, w	wave	Dental + Labial
ś́h	(श्)	sh	shoot	Palatal
ṣh	(ष्)	sh	should	Cerebral
s	(स्)	s	sun	Dental
h	(ह्)	h	hug	Guttural
ḷ	(ळ्)	soft l		Cerebral

Pronunciation

(1) GUTTURALS are अ, आ, क्, ख्, ग्, घ्, ङ्, ह्: *(a, ā,, k, kh, g, gh, ṅ, h).*

They are pronounced from the **throat**

(2) PALATALS are इ, ई, च्, छ्, ज्, झ्, ञ्, य्, श् *i, ī, ch, chh, j, jh, ñ, y, śh.*

They are pronounced from the **palate**

(3) CEREBRALS are ऋ, ॠ, ट्, ठ्, ड्, ढ्, ण्, र्, ष् *ri rī, ṭ, ṭh, ḍ, ḍh, ṇ, r, ṣh.*

They are pronounced from the **roof of the mouth**

(4) DENTALS are लृ, (लॄ), त्, थ्, द्, ध्, न्, ल्, स् *lri, (lrī), t, th, d, dh, n, l, s.*

They are pronounced from the **teeth**

(5) LABIALS are उ, ऊ, प्, फ्, ब्, भ्, म् *u, ū, p, ph, b, bh, m.*

They are pronounced from the **lips.** Character व *v* is dental-labial; ए, ऐ *e, ai* are guttural-palatal, ओ, औ *o, au* are guttural-labials and व *v* is dental-labial.

(6) THE **HARD** CONSONANTS

The first two consonants from each class (क्, ख्; च्, छ्; ट्, ठ्; त्, थ्; प्, फ् *k, kh, ch, chh, ṭ, ṭh, t, th, p, ph*) and three sibilants (श्, ष्, स् *śh, ṣh, s*) are Hard Consonants (*kaṭhor vyañjan* कठोर व्यंजन).

(7) THE **SOFT** CONSONANTS

The rest of the consonants, namely, the last three consonants from each class (ग्, घ्, ङ्; ज्, ज्, ञ्; ड्, ढ्, ण्; द्, ध्, न्; ब्, भ्, म् *g, gh, ṅ, j, jh, ñ, ḍ, ḍh, ṇ, d, dh, n, b, bh, m*), the semi-vowels (य्, र्, ल्, व् *y, r, l, v*) and the aspirate (ह् *h*) are Soft Consonants (*mridu vyañjan* मृदु व्यंजन).

(8) THE **NASAL** CONSONANTS

The last character from each of the five classes ṅ, ñ, ṇ, n, m (ङ्, ञ्, ण्, न्, म्), are the Nasal Consonants (*anunāsik* अनुनासिक).

THE **ANUSVĀRA** AND **THE VISARGA**

अनुस्वार और विसर्ग

Anusvāra (ं) and *visarga* (:) are two more sounds in Hindi. The *anuswār* (अनुस्वार) is the modification of nasal consonants ङ्, ञ्, ण्, न्, म् and अं (*ṅ, ñ, ṇ, n, m, m̃*). The *visarga* (विसर्ग) is the modified form of consonant स्, र् or ह् (*s* or *r*) and it sounds like consonant ह्. The *anusvār* and *visarga* are counted among the consonants, but even though they are not counted as separate characters, they are sometimes treated as semi-vowels. Together they are called *Āyogavāha* (आयोगवाह).

THE **ANUSVĀRA and VISARGA**

अं	अँ	अः
aṁ	*a̐*	*a*

1. Anusvāra (अनुस्वार)

1. Bindi (ं):

Anusvāra is the Nasal dot (*bindī* बिंदी or *bindu* बिंदु) placed over a consonant to indicate its Nasal pronunciation. This dot is an abbriviated Nasal form of the short letter m̃ (अं). However, within a word, the sound of the anusvāra is determined by the class (*varga* वर्ग) of the letter that comes after the letter that has anusvāra over it. The sound of the Nasal consonant at the end of that class is the sound of that *anusvāra*. e.g.

m̃ (अं), m (म्); ma (म), ṅ (ङ्), ñ (ञ्), ṇ (ण्), n (न्), na (न)

1. paṅka (पंक) = pa+ṅ+ka (प+ङ्+क)   2. paṅkha (पंख) = pa+ṅ+kha (प+ङ्+ख)

3. aṅga (अंग) = a+ṅ+ga (अ+ङ्+ग)   4. saṅgha (संघ) = sa+ṅ+gha (स+ङ्+घ)

5. pañcha (पंच) = pa+ñ+cha (प+ञ्+च)   6. añchara (अंछर) = a+ñ+chha+ra (अ+ञ्+छ+र)

7. rañja (रंज) = ra+ñ+ja (र+ञ्+ज)   8. jhañjhaṭa (झंझट) = jha+ñ+jha+ṭa (झ+ञ्+झ+ट)

9. chaṅṭa (चंट) = cha+ṅ +ṭa (च+ण्+ट)   10. chaṅḍa (चंड) = cha+ṅ +ḍa (च+ण्+ड)

11. kaṅṭha (चंट) = ka+ṅ +ṭha (क+ण्+ठ)   12. chaṅḍha (चंढ) = cha+ṅ +ḍha (च+ण्+ढ)

13. anta (अंत) = a+n+ta (अ+न्+त)   14. pantha (पंथ) = pa+n+tha (प+न्+थ)

15. nanda (नंद) = na+n+da (न+न्+द)   16. andha (अंध) = a+n+dha (अ+न्+ध)

17. sampad (संपद्) = sa+m+pa+d (स+म्+प+द्)

18. samphala (संफल) = sa+m+pha+la (स+म्+फ+ल)

19. ambara (अंबर) = a+m+ba+ra (अ+म्+ब+र)   20. ambha (अंभ) = a+m+bha (अ+म्+भ)

However, when a non-class consant appears after the anusvāra, the sound of that anusvāra is simply as **m̃ (अं)**. e.g.

1.	ya (य)	sam̃yama (संयम)	=	sa+m̃+ya+ma (स+अं+य+म)
2.	ra (र)	sam̃rakshaṇa (संरक्षण)	=	sa+m̃+ra+ksha+ṇa (स+अं+र+क्ष+ण)
3.	la (ल)	sam̃lagna (संलग्न)	=	sa+m̃+la+g+na (स+अं+ल+ग्+न)
4.	va (व)	sam̃vat (संवत्)	=	sa+m̃+va+t (स+अं+व+त्)
5.	sha (श)	sam̃shaya (संशय)	=	sa+m̃+sha+ya (स+अं+श+य)
6.	sa (स)	sam̃sada (संसद)	=	sa+m̃+sa+da (स+अं+स+द)
7.	ha (ह)	sam̃hata (संहत)	=	sa+m̃+ha+ta (स+अं+ह+त)

Some other examples : कंस, दंश, ध्वंस, मंसब, वंश, शंसन, संस्कृत, संयत, हंस.

2. Chandra Bindi (ँ) :

Chandra Bindi ँ is another form of the *anusvāra* used in Hindi and Sanskrit evolved (*tadbhava* तद्‌भव) words to indicate either short or ṁ (अं) sound as in the words dhaṁsan (धँसन) piercing, Bhaṁvar (भँवर worldly ocean), saṁvar (सँवर prepardness), etc. or also a long āṁ (आँ) sound as in the words mā̐ (माँ) mother, sā̐njh (साँझ evening), yahā̐ (यहाँ here), etc.

2. Visarga (विसर्ग)

Visarga is the expression of aspiration or breath, represented by the symbol of " : " like the colon (:) sign of English punctuation, which sounds like letter h (ह्), but short in length. It may come within a word or at the end of a word. e.g. *duḥkha* (दु:ख) pain, *chhaḥ* छ: (six), *atah* अत: (thus).

The visagra has its own sound like short h (ह्), but at the same time, this h (ह्) sound is also influenced by its preeceding vowel. e.g.

1. a (अ) - rāmaha (राम:) Rama
2. ā (आ) - mālāhā (माला:) garlands
3. i (इ) - kavihi (कवि:) Poet
4. ī (ई) - nadīhī (नदी:) to the Rivers
5. u (उ) - guruhu (गुरु:) Teacher
6. ū (ऊ) - vadhūhū (वधू:) bride
7. e (ए) - kavehe (कवे:) of the poet
8. ai (ऐ) - devaihi (देवै:) by the Gods
9. o (ओ) - guroho (गुरो:) of the guru
10. au (औ) - guahu (गौ:) cow

Flaps and Underdots (प्रहार, नुक्ता)

Flaps : In Hindustānī Hindi, letters with softer sound in between r (r) and ḍ (ड) are indicated with a dot under them. They are classed as flaps. e.g. उड़ना (*uḍanā* to fly), कीड़ा (*kīḍā* worm), खड़ा (*khaḍā* standing), पीड़ा (*pīḍā* pain), लड़ना (*laḍanā* to fight), सड़ना (*saḍanā* to rot), etc.

Under Dots : In Hindustani Hindi, the words that are taken from Arabic, Persian or Urdū languages, may contain a letter with slightly varied sound than its Devanagari counterpart, which is written with an underdot (नुक्ता) below that letter. e.g. kạ (क़), khạ (ख़), gạ (ग़), jạ (ज़), fạ (फ़), in the words क़दर, ख़र, ग़म, ज़बर, फ़ख़र, etc.

Doubling (द्वित्व)

When two similar consonants come together, the first letter is written as a half consonant and the second letter as full letter. They are written in two ways. e.g.

kk	chch	ṭṭ	ṭṭh	ḍḍ	dd	nn	ll
क्क क्क;	च्च च्च	ट्ट ट्ट;	ट्ठ ट्ठ;	ड्ड ड्ड,	द्द द्द;	न्न न्न;	ल्ल ल्ल

Accepted Impurity (स्वीकार्य अशुद्धि)

Many Hindi compounded consonants with letter h (h) are often written incorrectly, but they are generally accepted. e.g.

Pure		Impure	
āhlād	(आह्लाद)	as ālhād	(आल्हाद)
āhvān	(आह्वान)	as āvhān	(आव्हान)
brahma	(ब्रह्म) as	bramha	(ब्रम्ह)
chihna	(चिह्न)	as chinha	(चिन्ह)
madhyāhna	(मध्याह्न)	as madhyānha	(मध्यान्ह), etc.

VOWEL SIGNS

स्वरों के मात्रा चिह्न

In Hindi any vowel can be written in its letter forms or in its vowel sign or vowel symbol (मात्रा) form. I have formulated four rules for using the vowels.

1. When a word begins with any vowel, that initial vowel must be wtitten in its letter form. e.g. ab (अब) now.
2. When a vowel comes after a consonant, that following vowel must be attached to that consonant in its vowel sign form. e.g. mātā (माता) mother.
3. When two vowels come on row in any word, the second vowel must be written in its letter form. e.g. āīnā (आईना) mirror, bhāī (भाई) brother, parāī (पराई) stranger.
4. Only one vowel (not more than one vowels) can be attached to any consonant.

WRITING HINDI VOWEL SIGNS (मात्रा)

Vowels	अ	आ	इ	ई	उ	ऊ	ऋ	ए	ऐ	ओ	औ
Signs		ा	ि	ी	ु	ू	ृ	े	ै	ो	ौ
Sound	a	ā	i	ī	u	ū	ri	e	ai	o	au
		aa		ee		oo	ri	é			

ā i ī u ū ri é ai o au

पा	पि	पी	पु	पू	पृ	पे	पै	पो	पौ
pā, paa	pi	pī, pee	pu	pū, poo	pri	pé	pai	po	pau

अ a	आ ā ा	इ i ि	ई ī ी	उ u ु	ऊ ū ू	ऋ ṛ ृ
ए e े	ऐ ai ै	ओ o ो	औ au ौ	अं m̃ ं	अँ m̐ ँ	अः ḥ ः

NOTES : It is generally said that the letter a (अ) has no vowel sign, but it not quite correct. The vowel sign for vowel a (अ) is (ा) which is normally inherant in the Hindi full consonants and is not perceived by lame eyes. e.g.

The root consonant p is (ट) to which vowel a (अ) is added in its vowel sign form (ा) and thus p + a = pa (ट + ा + = प). But, in this consonant प, people think vowel a (अ) has no vowel sign (मात्रा). Compound consonant pā (पा) is written as p+a+a (ट + ा + ा = पा). In this pā (ट +ा+ा =पा) there are two ा ा signs representing a + a, but people think there is only one vowel sign (ा) representing vowel ā (आ).

In consonants ख, ग, घ, च, ज, झ, ञ, ण, त, थ, ध, न, प, ब, भ, म, य, ल, व, श, ष, स the inherant or default vowl sigh (ा) can be easily seen by us, but in remaining letters क, ङ, छ, ट, ठ, ड, ढ, द, फ, र, ह this matra is not visible to a layman, but it is still existing there.

VOWEL SIGNS, EXAMPLES :

जितना, जीतना, मृत, चिंता, जूता, कुछ, वैसा, औंधा, दिया, दीया, बेकारी, सूखा, सुखी, भेद, मैं, भिक्षा, ज्ञानी, सुंदरता, कोका कोला, महानता, सुख दुःख, चूहा, ज्ञानयोग, भारतीय, अमरीकन, पौराणिक

jitnā (as much), jītanā (to win), mrit (dead), chintā (worry), jūtā (shoe), kuchh (some), vaisā (like that), aundhā (face down), diyā (gave), dīyā (lamp), bekārī (unemployment), sūkhā (dry), sukhī (happy), bhed (difference), maiँ (I), bhikshā (alms), jñānī (knowledgable), sundartā (beauty), kokā kolā (coke), mahānatā (greatness), sukh duhkh (happyness and sorrow), chūhā (mouse), jñānayoga (yoga of knowledge), bhāratīya (Indian), amarīkan (American), paurāṇik (ancient).

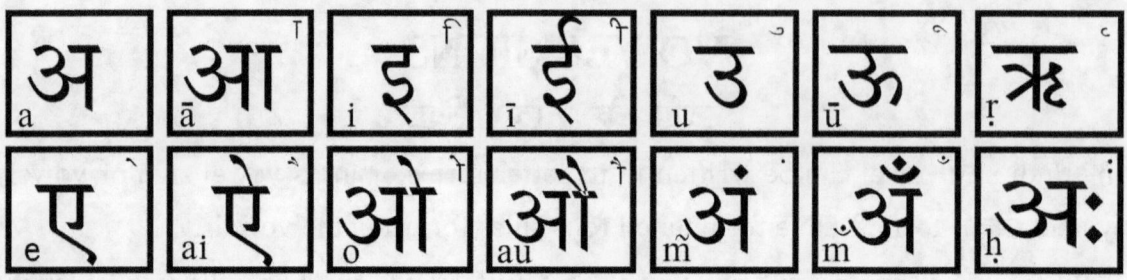

CHART OF VOWEL-SIGNS APPLICATION

अ	आ	इ	ई	उ	ऊ	ऋ	ॠ	ए	ऐ	ओ	औ
	ा	ि	ी	ु	ू	ृ	ॄ	े	ै	ो	ौ
	ā	i	ī	u	ū	ri	rī́	e	ai	o	au
क	का	कि	की	कु	कू	कृ	कॄ	के	कै	को	कौ
क्ष	क्षा	क्षि	क्षी	क्षु	क्षू	क्षृ	क्षॄ	क्षे	क्षै	क्षो	क्षौ
ख	खा	खि	खी	खु	खू	खृ	खॄ	खे	खै	खो	खौ
ग	गा	गि	गी	गु	गू	गृ	गॄ	गे	गै	गो	गौ
घ	घा	घि	घी	घु	घू	घृ	घॄ	घे	घै	घो	घौ
ङ	ङा	ङि	ङी	ङु	ङू	–	–	ङे	ङै	ङो	ङौ
च	चा	चि	ची	चु	चू	चृ	चॄ	चे	चै	चो	चौ
छ	छा	छि	छी	छु	छू	छृ	छॄ	छे	छै	छो	छौ
ज	जा	जि	जी	जु	जू	जृ	जॄ	जे	जै	जो	जौ
ज्ञ	ज्ञा	ज्ञि	ज्ञी	ज्ञु	ज्ञू	–	–	ज्ञे	ज्ञै	ज्ञो	ज्ञौ
झ	झा	झि	झी	झु	झू	झृ	झॄ	झे	झै	झो	झौ
ञ	ञा	ञि	ञी	ञु	ञू	–		ञे	ञै	ञो	ञौ
ट	टा	टि	टी	टु	टू	टृ	टॄ	टे	टै	टो	टौ
ठ	ठा	ठि	ठी	ठु	ठू	ठृ	ठॄ	ठे	ठै	ठो	ठौ
ड	डा	डि	डी	डु	डू	डृ	–	डे	डै	डो	डौ
ढ	ढा	ढि	ढी	ढु	ढू	ढृ	–	ढे	ढै	ढो	ढौ
ण	णा	णि	णी	णु	णू	णृ	–	णे	णै	णो	णौ
त	ता	ति	ती	तु	तू	तृ	तॄ	ते	तै	तो	तौ
थ	था	थि	थी	थु	थू	थृ	थॄ	थे	थै	थो	थौ
द	दा	दि	दी	दु	दू	दृ	दॄ	दे	दै	दो	दौ
ध	धा	धि	धी	धु	धू	धृ	धॄ	धे	धै	धो	धौ
न	ना	नि	नी	नु	नू	नृ	नॄ	ने	नै	नो	नौ
प	पा	पि	पी	पु	पू	पृ	पॄ	पे	पै	पो	पौ
फ	फा	फि	फी	फु	फू	फृ	–	फे	फै	फो	फौ
ब	बा	बि	बी	बु	बू	बृ	बॄ	बे	बै	बो	बौ
भ	भा	भि	भी	भु	भू	भृ	भॄ	भे	भै	भो	भौ

म	मा	मि	मी	मु	मू	मृ	मॄ	मे	मै	मो	मौ
य	या	यि	यी	यु	यू	यृ	–	ये	यै	यो	यौ
र	रा	रि	री	रु*	रू*	–	–	रे	रै	रो	रौ
ल	ला	लि	ली	लु	लू	लृ	लॄ	ले	लै	लो	लौ
व	वा	वि	वी	वु	वू	वृ	वॄ	वे	वै	वो	वौ
श	शा	शि	शी	शु	शू	शृ	शॄ	शे	शै	शो	शौ
ष	षा	षि	षी	षु	षू	षृ	–	षे	षै	षो	षौ
स	सा	सि	सी	सु	सू	सृ	सॄ	से	सै	सो	सौ
ह	हा	हि	ही	हु	हू	हृ	–	हे	है	हो	हौ

*** NOTE the special mātrā for letters रु and रू**

Organs of Pronunciation and Speech Efforts
उच्चारण अवयव और वाणी क्रिया

As seen earlier in the diagram for "Organs of Pronunciation," the vocal organs such as the lips, teeth, tongue, palate, head, throat and vocal cord are responsible for speaking words. At the same time, in order to use the speech organs to utter sounds of the vowels and consonants, our internal and external efforts are other components required for speech.

1. Internal Efforts :

a. **Open Mouth** (*vivritta* विवृत्त) : The letters which need mouth to be open to speak them. e.g. a (अ), ā (आ).

b. **Partial Open Moutn** (*īṣhat vivritta* ईषत् विवृत्त) : The letters which need mouth to be partially open to speak them. e.g. ya (य), ra (र), la (ल), va (व)

c. **Uvular or Labial Touch** : (*īṣhat vivritta* ईषत् विवृत्त) : The letters which need a touch (*sparśha* स्पर्श) of tongue or lower lip with other parts of mouth. In this class all 25 class consonants from a (अ) to ma (म) and vowels i (इ), ī (ई), u (उ), ū (ऊ) are included.

d. **Partial Uvular Touch** (*īṣhat spriṣhṭa* ईषत् स्पृष्ट) : The letters which need touch or friction of tongue with particular parts of throat. In this category characters śha (श), ṣha (ष), sa (स), ha (ह) and vowels e (ए), ai (ऐ), o (ओ), au (औ) are included. As the pronunciation of these letters need friction of tongue, they are called *uṣhma varṇa* (ऊष्म वर्ण warm breath).

2. External Efforts :

a. **Voice** (*ghoṣha* घोष) : The letters which need vibration (*kampan* कम्पन) of the vocal cord come in theis category. They include the 3rd, 4th and 5th consonants of the first four classes (ग घ ङ; ज झ ञ, ड ढ ण, द ध न) as well as it includes the consonants ya, ra, la, va (य, र ल, व) and all vowels.

b. **Breath** (*śhvāsa* श्वास) : The letters which do not need vibration of the vocla cord but they need the flow of breath in stead. This class has the letters other than the above mentioned characters. They include 1st and 2nd consonants of the first four classes (क ख, च छ, ज झ, ट ठ, त थ) and the *uṣhma* varṇnas श ष स ह.

(b1) Short Breath (*alpaprāṇa* अल्पप्राण) : The letters that need partial flow of breath (*prāṇa* प्राण) fall in this category. They include all vowels and the 1st, 2nd and 5th consonants of all five classes (क ख ङ, च छ ञ, ट ठ ण, त थ न, प फ म).

(b2) Long Breath (*mahāprāṇa* महाप्राण) : The letters that need added use of the sound of letter h (ह) come oin this category. They are 2nd and 4th consonants of all five classes, such as ख घ, छ झ, ठ ढ, थ ध, फ भ and the consonants श ष स ह.

Effect of Compound Consonants
संयुक्त वर्ण का आघात

Within a word, if a Compound Consonanr (संयुक्त वर्ण) comes after any Short Vowel (लघु स्वर), that Short Vowel is considered a Long Vowel (दीर्घ स्वर) as a result of the impact (आघात) of the Compound Consonant (व्यंजनाघात, वर्णाघात) on the short vowel.

e.g. The short vowel इ in the word नित्य is considered as long vowel ई as a result of the impact (आघात) of the next compound consonant त्य. Some writers think this is not a वर्णाघात, it is a स्वराघात.

More Examples :

सत्य (3 mātrā, स 2 + त्य 1 = 3), सिद्ध (3 mātrā, सि 2 = द्ध 1 = 3), स्तुत्य (3 mātrā, स्तु 2 + त्य 1 = 3), संत = सन्त, सन्त (3 mātrā, स 2 + न्त 1 = 3), सिंधु, सिन्धु (3 mātrā, स्वि 2 + न्धु 1 = 3), सुंदर = सुन्दर (4 mātrā, सु 2 + न्द 1 + र 1 = 4)

However, when the coumpund character comes after a long vowel, it has no effect (आघात) on the long vowel. Such as :

साध्य (3 mātrā), सीत्कार (5 mātrā), सूक्ति (3 mātrā), सेव्य (3 mātrā), सैन्य (3 mātrā), सौख्य (3 mātrā), संख्या (4 mātrā), सांख्य (3 mātrā), etc.

When a Visarga (ivasaga|) comes after a short vowel, that short vowel is considered as a long vowel. e.g. थिती: (1+2=3 मात्रा), गुरु: (1+2=3 मात्रा), राम: (2+2=4 मात्रा), नर: (1+2=3 मात्रा), etc.

EXCEPTIONS (अपवाद) :

1. In Hindi, there are words such as कन्हैया (*kanhaiyā* 5 mātrā), where the compound consonant न्है has no effect (आघात) on the short vowel अ of the letter क.
2. The letters with *chandrabindī* are also considered and spoken as short vowels. e.g. हँसी (3 mātrā).
3. The last short vowel at the end of a line of poetry can be considered as a long vowel. किमकुर्वत सञ्जय। Here, the word सञ्जय at the end of the line has (2+1+2=5 mātrā).

THE SOUND-FORMULAS FROM SHIVA

māheśhvarāṇi sūtrāṇi

महेश्वर के सूत्र

Following 14 character strings, in the form of sounds chords, were first produced by Lord Śiva from his *damru* drum :

1. अइउण्	2. ऋलृक्	3. एओङ्
4. ऐऔच्	5. हयवरट्	6. लण्
7. ञमङणनम्	8. झभञ्	9. घढधष्
10. जबगडदश्	11. खफछठथचटतव्	12. कपय्
13. शषसर्	14. हल्	

The last character of each equation string is always a consonant.

These characters are grouped into several strings (प्रत्याहार) according to their assigned attributes (सङ्केत). e.g. अण् प्रत्याहार means the characters अ, इ, उ of the first सूत्र अइउण्, i.e. all characters except the last character of that *sūtra.*

प्रत्याहार

1. अक् – अ इ उ ऋ लृ (the vowels *a, i, u, ri, lri*)
2. अच् – स्वर all the vowels (अ – औ)
3. अट् – स्वर (अ – औ) + य, र, व ह all vowels + consonants *y, r, v, h*
4. अण् – स्वर + य, र ल व ह all vowels + semi-vowels *y, r, l, v* + the aspirate *h*
5. अल् – वर्ण all characters (अ – ह)
6. अश् – all vowels and soft consonants (अ–औ, ग्–ङ्, ज्–ञ्, ड्–ण्, द्–न्, ब्–म्, य्–व्, ह)
7. एङ् – vewels *e* and *o* (ए, ओ)
8. एच् – vewels *e, ai, o, au* (ए, ऐ, ओ, औ)
9. ऐच् – vewels *ai* and *au* (ऐ, औ)
10. खर् – hard consonants (क् ख् च् छ् ट् ठ् त् थ् प् फ् श् ष् स्)
11 जश् – the third consonant from each class : *g, j, ḍ, d, b* (ग्, ज्, ड्, द्, ब्)
12. झज् – the consonants *jh,* and *bh* (झ्, भ्)
13. झर् – sibilants + class consonants - nasals (क्–घ्, च्–झ्, ट्–ढ्, त्–ध् प्–भ् + श्, ष्, स्)
14. झल् – consonants other than semi-vowels and nasals क्–घ्, च्–झ्, ट्–ढ्, त्–ध्– प्–भ्, य्–ह्
15. झश् – the third and fourth class consonants (ग्, घ्, ज्, झ्, ड्, ढ्, द्, ध्, ब्, भ्)
16. झष् – the fourth consonant from each calss *gh, jh, ḍh, dh, bh* (घ, झ, ढ, ध, भ)
17. यण् – अन्तस्थ वर्ण (य् र् ल् व् consonants *y r l* and *v*)
18. यय् – all consonants other than *śh ṣh s h* (श् ष् स् ह् = उष्म अक्षर)
19. यर् – all consonants other than *h* ह् (क् – स्)
20. शल् – the *ūṣhma* consonants *śh, ṣh, s,* and *h* (श, ष, स, ह = ऊष्म)
21. हल् – व्यञ्जन (all consonants क् – ह्)
22. हश् – मृदुव्यञ्जन (soft consonants ग्–ङ्, ज्–ञ्, ड्–ण्, द्–न्, ब्–म्, य्–व्, ह्)

इत्यादि प्रत्याहार हैं

Māheśhvarāṇi Sūtrāṇi

महेश्वर के चौदह सूत्र

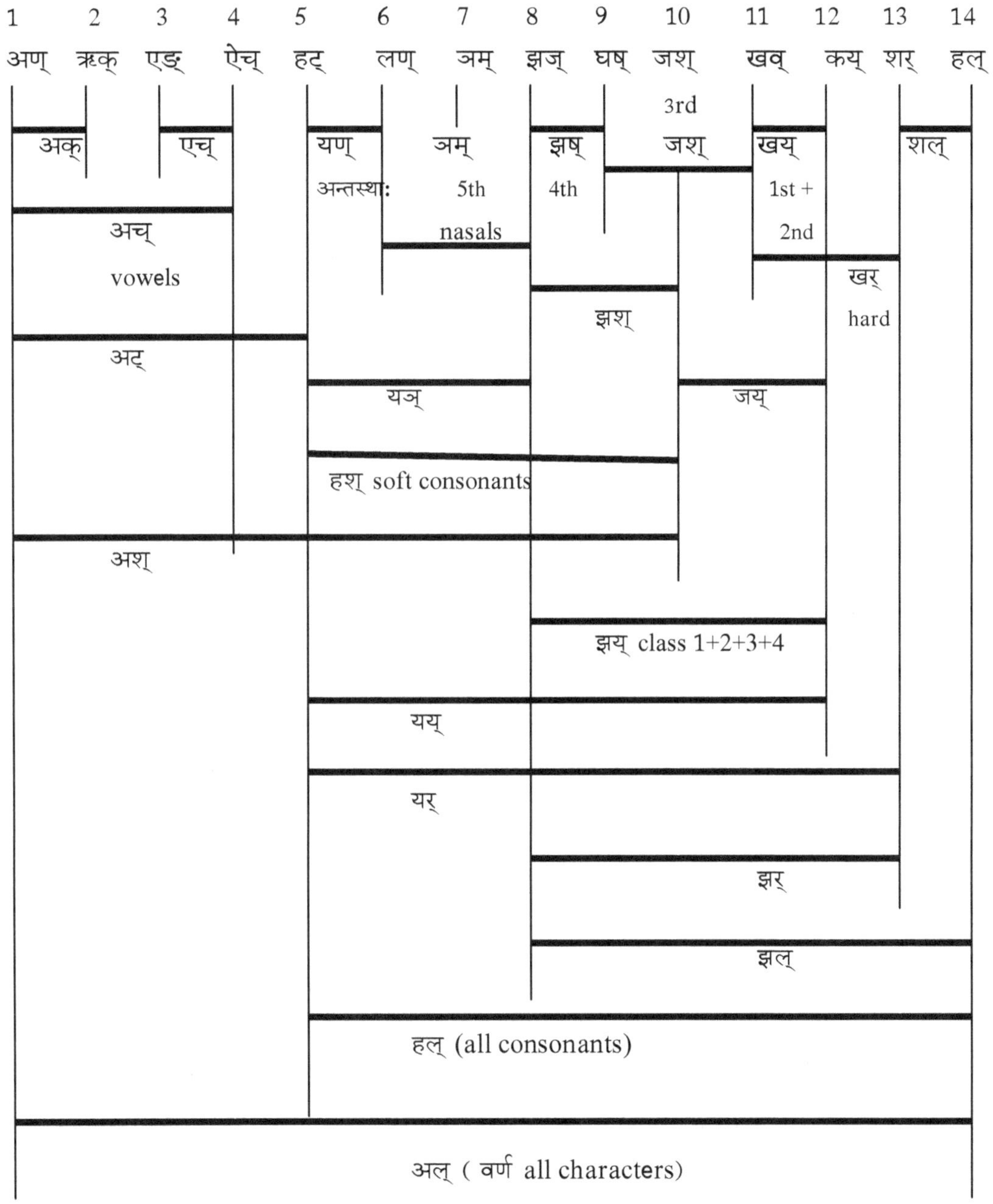

Designed by Ratnakar Narale

HALANT
हलंत

As we can see from the Māheśhvarāṇl Sūtrāṇi (महेश्वर के चौदह सूत्र), the हल् characters (वर्ण) are all 33 pure consonants (व्यंजन). The अद् characters are all vowels (स्वर), and all vowels plus consonants together are called the अल् characyers.

The हल् state means the pure oroginal condition of a consonant without adding even the default inherant vowel अ to it. This हल् state of a consonant is indicated by attaching a small slant mark (्) at the bottom of that character. e.g. pa is प and only pure consonant p without its default inherant vowel अ is ꠲ or प्. This प् called हल ending (अंत) प or हलंत प.

Similarly,

क, ख, ग, घ,. ङ, च, छ, ज, झ, ञ, ट, ठ, ड, ढ, ण, त, थ, द, ध, न, प, फ, ब, भ, म, य, र, ल, व, श, ष, स, ह These are considered as **Full Consonants**.

Without their default vowel अ the same letters look like -

क्, ख्, ग्, घ्,. ङ्, च्, छ्, ज्, झ्, ञ्, ट्, ठ्, ड्, ढ्, ण्, त्, थ्, द्, ध्, न्, प्, फ्, ब्, भ्, म्, य्, र्, ल्, व्, श्, ष्, स्, ह्. These consonants are now considered as **Half Consonants**.

The function of this halant mark (्) is to nullify or cancel the inherant vowel अ from the full consonant.

THEREFORE :

The full consonant Pa प, is half ꠲ plus vowel sign (मात्रा) ा for letter अ. And, the compound consonant Pā (Paa) पा, is half ꠲ plus two vowel signs ाा for two letters अअ.

Those who do not see or do not realize or do not understend that the letter प has vowel mātrā ा for letter अ is already built in and then in order to write leter पा, one extre mātrā ा for second letter अ is added. Thus, the mātrā for vowel अ is ा and the vowel mātrā for letter आ is two ा ा signs. Hope you get it.

OTHER IMPORTANT GRAMMATICAL TERMS

1. **अक्षर** *akṣhar* (अ–क्षर) : A character or a word that can not be subdivided into fractions or its components. e.g. अ, इ, उ, ऋ, ॐ
2. **अव्यय** *avyay*: A word that does not change with number, gender or case. e.g. नहीं, हाँ, मत, बहुत, etc.
3. **आख्यात** *ākhyāt*: A word that is either a noun, pronoun, adjective or verb.
4. **ऊष्म** *ūṣhma* : The non-class consonants श, ष, स ह *śha, ṣha, sa, h.*
5. **गुण** *guṇa* : The vowels अ, ए, ओ *a, e, o*
6. **वृद्धि** *vriddhi* : The vowels आ, ऐ, औ *ā, ai, au*
7. **उपाधा** *upādhā* : The character that comes before the last character.
8. **सम्प्रसारण** samprasāraṇ : Comming of इ, उ, ऋ, लृ *i, u, ri, lri* in place of य, व, र, ल *ya, va, ra, la*
9. **टि** *ṭi*: The group of characters from the last vowel to the end character of the word.
10. **प्रातिपादिक** *prātipādika*: A meaningful word, other than a verb-root itself or a suffix itself.
11. **सुप्** *sup* : A suffix that attaches to a substantive (प्रातिपादिक *prātipādika*). There are Twenty-One (21) सुप् *sup* suffixes namely : सि, औ, जस्, अम्, औ, शस्, टा, भ्याम्, भिस्, ङे, भ्याम्, भ्यस्, ङसि, भ्याम्, भ्यस्, ङस् ओस्, आम्, ङि, ओस्, सुप् । *si, au, jas, am, au, śhas, ṭā, bhyām, bhis, ṅge, bhyām, bhyas, ṅgsi, bhyām, bhyas, ṅgs, os, ām, ṅgi, os, sup.*
12. **तिङ्** *tiṅ* : A suffix that attaches to a verb root. There are Eighteen (18) तिङ् *tiṅ* suffixes namely : तिप्, तः, झि, सिप्, थः, थ, मिप्, वः, मः, त, आताम्, झ, थाः, आथाम्, ध्वम्, इट्, वहि, महिङ् । *tip, ta, jhi, sip, tha, tha, mip, va, ma, ta, ātām, jha, thā, āthām,*

dhvam, iṭ, vahi, mahiṅ.

13. **पद** pad : A word formed with the addition of a सुप् *sup* or a तिङ् *tiṅ* suffix.

14. **सर्वनामस्थान** *sarvanāmasthān* : The case suffixes of सु, औ, जस्, अम्, औट् *su, au, jas, am, auṭ* that attach to any masculine or feminine word.

15. **भ** *bha* : A substantive that has taken a suffix that starts with य *ya* or a vowel.

16. **घु** *ghu* : The verbs √दा, √धा √*dā*, √*dhā* (not the verb √दाप् √*dāp*).

17. **घ** *gha* : The comparative suffixes तरम्, तरप् *taram, parap*

18. **विभाषा, विकल्प** *vibhāṣhā, vikalpa* : A possibility of being or not being.

19. **निष्ठा** *niṣhṭhā* : The suffixes क्त, क्तवतु *kta, ktavatu*

20. **संयोग** *saṁyoga* : Joining of two (or more) consonants without any vowel between them.

21. **प्रगृह्य** *pragrihya* : A Dual Number word ending in ई, ऊ, or ए *ī, ū,* or *e.*

22. **सत्** *sat* : The शतृ, शानच् *ś́hatri, ś́hānach* suffixes.

23. **विप्सा** *vipsā* : Repetation of a word.

24. **स्पर्श** *sparś́ha* : The class consonants from क to म *k* to *m.*

25. **लुक्** *luk* : The disappearance (लोप) of a suffix.

26. While writing a poetic work the discreet poets make sure that :

1. Their work begins with an auspicious letter (*ś́hubh akshar* शुभ अक्षर). The auspicious letters are क, ख, ग, घ, च, छ, ज, ड. The inauspicious letters are ङ, झ, ञ, ट, ठ, त्र, ण, थ, फ. The letters त, प, झ, ह, र, भ, ष are also to be avoided if possible.

2. The prudent poets also make sure that their works begin with an auspicious word which stands for the crux of the work. e.g. The Rig Veda begins with the word अग्नि. Agni being the chief deity of the Veda. Similarly, the Bhagavadgītā begins with work धर्म and the Rāmrakṣhā with the word श्री.

KNOW THIS BEFORE YOU CONTINUE

Ratnakar's Golden Rules :

1. When a word begins with a vowel, that initial vowel must be written in its letter form. e.g. अब, आज, इतना, ईश, उधर, ऊन, एक, ऐसा, ओज, औषध
2. Within a word, when two vowels come in a row, the second vowel must be written in its letter form. e.g. उऋण, अऋजु, आइये, आइए, आईना, ऐशोआराम, कुआँ, कूआँ, हाउस, ताई, ताऊ
3. In any word when a vowel comes after a consonant, that following vowel must be written in its vowel sign form attached to the preceding consonant. e.g. अकारण, काल, लीला, राम, सीता, राधा, हनुमान, हाईवे, हाईस्कूल
4. In any word, when two or more consonants come in a row the last consonant of such group must be written as a full character and the remaining consonants on its left side must be written as half-consonants. e.g. अग्नि, अस्तु, कल्याण, तत्त्व, रक्त, वस्तु, परिस्थिति, उज्ज्वल, एक्स्पेस, एक्स्प्लोजन
5. In a word, when two consonants come in a row and one of them is र, the possibilities are (i) the first letter is र, (ii) the second letter is र, (iii) both letters are र. In thosecases :

(i) When the first letter is र, that letter र is a half letter according to the rule 4 above, . This half र is to be written as a symbol ॅ above the second consonant. e.g. कर्‌म कर्म, तर्‌क तर्क, गर्‌दभ गर्दभ, गर्‌भ, गर्भ, पर्‌व पर्व, पर्‌वत पर्वत, कीर्‌ति कीर्ति

(ii) When the second letter is र, that letter र is a full character, according to the rule 4 above. Whe this full letter र comes after any letter that is ending with vertical line (खड़ीपाई), it should be written with the slant line symbol ⸝ attached to the verticle line of that consonant. This small little slant line symbol ⸝ of full letter र is so powerful that it converts the attached full consonant into a half consonant, even if that consonant looks like full in shape. e.g. वज्‌र वज्र, वक्‌र वक्र, समग्‌र समग्र, प्‌रकाश प्रकाश, प्‌रिय प्रिय, नम्‌र नम्र, शस्‌त्‌र शस्त्र, श्‌री श्री, स्‌त्‌री स्त्री,

क्‌र क्र, ख्‌र ख्र, ग्‌र ग्र, घ्‌र घ्र, च्‌र च्र, ज्‌र ज्र, झ्‌र झ्र, त्‌र त्र, थ्‌र थ्र, द्‌र द्र, ध्‌र ध्र, न्‌र न्र, प्‌र प्र, फ्‌र फ्र, ब्‌र ब्र, भ्‌र भ्र, म्‌र म्र, ल्‌र लर, व्‌र व्र, श्‌र श्र, स्‌र स्र, ह्‌र ह्र.

However, when the first letter (such as ट ठ ड ढ छ) which does not have the ending verticla line (खड़ीपाई), in that case the full र is written as ^ under the ट ठ ड ढ छ characters. e.g. ट्र ठ्र ड्र ढ्र छ्र.

iii. When the first and second both characters are letters र्र, in that case the firsr र् is half letter (ॅ रेफ) written over the second full letter र. e.g. छर्‌रा छर्रा, थर्‌राना, थर्राना, बर्‌रान बर्राना.

COMMON DEVANAGARI COMPOUND CHARACTERS

Help of many Sanskrit words is taken for wider scope of examples.

(1) Character k (क् क)

क k पक्व, पक्‌व (*pakva* ripened), क्लीब, क्‌लीब, (*klība* weakness) क्लेद क्‌लेद (*kleda* wettness), वाक्य, वाक्‌य (*vākya* speech), रक्त, रक्‌त (*raktam* blood), रुक्मिणी, रुक्‌मिणी (*rukmiṇī*), क्वचित्, क्‌वचित् (*kvachit* sometimes)

(2) Character kh (ख् ख)

ख kh ख्याति ख्‌याति (*khyāti* fame), आख्या आख्‌या (*ākhyā* saying), सख्य सख्‌य (*sakhya* friendship)

(3) Characters g and gh (ग् ग ; घ् घ)

ग g; घ gh ग्लानि ग्‌लानि (*glāni* downfall), अग्नि अग्‌नि (*agni* fire), भाग्य भाग्‌य (*bhāgya* fortune), भग्न भग्‌न (*bhagna* broken), विघ्न विघ्‌न (*vighna* obstacle)

(4) Characters ṅ (ङ्)

ङ् ṅ ङ्क ṅka ङ्क्त ṅkta ङ्ख ṅkha ङ्ग ṅga

ङ्घ ṅgha ङ्म ṅma ङ्ल ṅla ङ्क्ष ṅkṣha ङ्क्ष्व ṅkṣhva

लङ्का लङ्‌का (*laṅkā* Sri Lanka), पङ्क्ति पङ्‌क्ति पङ्‌क्‌ति (*paṅkti* line, row), शङ्ख शङ्‌ख (*śhaṅkha* conchshell), रङ्ग रङ्‌ग (*raṅga* colour), सङ्घ सङ्‌घ (*saṅgha* group), वाङ्मय् वाङ्‌मय (*vāṅmaya* literature), आङ्ल आङ्‌ल (*āṅla* English), काङ्क्षा काङ्‌क्षा (*kāṅkṣhā* desire), भुङ्क्ष्व (*bhuṅkṣhva* please enjoy)

(5) Characters ch and chh (च् च ; छ्)

च ch ; छ् chh — अच्युत अच्‌युत (*achyuta* Krishna), अवाच्य अवाच्‌य (*avāchya* unspeakable), सुवाच्य सुवाच्‌य (*suvāchya* well said), उच्छ्वास उच्‌छ्‌वास (*uchchhavās* breath)

(6) Characters j and ñ (ज् ज ; झ् झ ; ञ् ञ)

ज j ; झ jh ; ञ ñ — राज्य राज्‌य (*rājya* kingdom), सज्ज सज्‌ज (*sajja* ready), उज्ज्वल उज्‌ज्‌वल (*ujjval* bright), ज्योति ज्‌योति (*jyoti* light), प्रोझ्य प्रोझ्‌य (*projhya* leaving), पञ्च पञ्‌च (*pañcha* five), भञ्जन भञ्‌जन (*bhañjanam* destruction), वाञ्छा वाञ्‌छा (*vāñchhā* desire)

(7) Characters ṭ, ṭh (ट्, ठ्)

ट् ṭ ; ठ् ṭh — पट्टक पट्‌टक (*paṭṭak* plate), पट्टन पट्‌टन (*paṭṭan* town), कण्ठ्य कण्‌ठ्‌य (*kaṇṭhya* guttural)

(8) Character ḍ, ḍh (ड्, ढ्)

ड् ḍ ; ढ् ḍh — उड्डयन उड्‌डयन (*uḍḍayan* flight), उड्डित (*uḍḍita* flown), चकृढ्वे (*chakriḍhve* you all had done)

(9) Character ṇ (ण्, ण)

ण ṇ — पाण्डव पाण्‌डव (*pāṇḍava*), कण्ठ कण्‌ठ (*kaṇṭha* throat), कण्टक कण्‌टक (*kaṇṭak* thorn), षण्मास षण्‌मास (*ṣhaṇmāsa* six-months)

(10) Characters t, th and dh (त् त ; थ् थ ; ध् ध)

त t ; थ th ; ध dh — सत्कार सत्‌कार (*satkār* honour), दुग्ध दुग्‌ध (*dughda* milk), रत्नाकर रत्‌नाकर (*ratnākar* ocean), उत्पात उत्‌पात (*utpāt* rise), आत्मा आत्‌मा (*ātmā* soul), सत्य सत्‌य (*satya* truth), त्याग त्‌याग (*tyāg* sacrifice), त्वरा त्‌वरा (*tvarā* rush); तथ्य तथ्‌य (*tathyam* reality); बाध्य बाध्‌य (*bādhya* binding)

(11) Character n (न्, न)

न n — आनन्द आनन्‌द (*ānand* joy), अन्न अन्‌न (*anna* food), जन्म जन्‌म (*janma* birth), अन्य अन्‌य (*anya* other), अन्वय अन्‌वय (*anvay* relation), भिन्न भिन्‌न (*bhinna* different),

वन्दन वन्‌दन *(vandan* salute*)*, बन्धन बन्‌धन *(bandhan* bondage*)*, पान्थ पान्‌थ *(pāntha* traveller*)*

(12) Characters p, ph (प् प्‍ ; फ् फ्‍)

प्‍ p ; फ्‍ ph

समाप्त समाप्‌त *(samāpta* ended*)*, अप्सरा अप्‌सरा *(apsarā* celestial maid*)*, स्वप्न स्वप्‌न *(svapna* dream*)*, रूप्यक रुप्‌यक *(rūpyak* Rupee*)*.

(13) Characters b, bh and m (ब् ब्‍ ; भ् भ्‍ ; म् म्‍)

ब्‍ b ; भ्‍ bh ; म्‍ m

शब्द शब्‌द *(śhabda* word), शैब्य शैब्‌य *(śhaibya)*, सभ्य सभ्‌य *(sabhya* gentle*)*, सम्पदा सम्‌पदा *(sampadā* wealth*)*, सम्यक् सम्‌यक् *(samyak* right*)*, धृष्ट ध्‌ऋष्‌ट *(dhrișhța* courageous*)*, अम्ल अम्‌ल *(amla* sour*)*

(14) Characters y and l (य् य्‍ ; ल् ल्‍)

य्‍ y ; ल्‍ l

शय्या शय्‌या *(śhayyā* bed*)*, उल्का उल्‌का *(ulkā* meteor*)*, उल्लेख उल्‌लेख *(ullekha* reference*)*, अल्प अल्‌प *(alpa,* short*)*, कल्याण कल्‌याण *(kalyāņ* benefit*)*, वल्गना वल्‌गना *(valganā* chatter*)*

(15) Character v (व् व्‍)

व्‍ v

व्यय व्‌यय *(vyaya* expense*)*, व्यायाम व्‌यायाम *(vyāyāma* exercise*)*, व्योम व्‌योम *(vyoma* sky*)*, व्यूढ व्‌यूढ *(vyūḍha,* arranged*)*, व्यङ्ग व्‌यंग *(vyanga* deformity*)*, व्यवसाय व्‌यवसाय *(vyavasāy* business*)*

(16) Chararacter śh (श् श्‍ श्‍)

श्‍ श्‍ śh

विश्वास विश्‍वास विश्‌वास *(viśhvās* trust*)*, निश्चय निश्‍चय निश्‌चय *(nișhchay* firm resolution*)*, पश्चात् पश्‍चात् पश्‌चात् *(paśhchāt* after*)*, काश्मीर काश्‌मीर *(kāśhmīra)*, अवश्य अवश्‌य *(avaśhya* certainly*)*, अश्मक अश्‌मक *(aśhmak* stone*)*, विश्लेषण *(viśhleșhaņ* analysis*)*, *other compounds* शृति, वृश्चिक, प्रश्न, आश्रय, श्लाघ, विश्व, etc.

श्च, शृ, श्‍च, श्न, श्र, श्ल, श्व

(17) Character șh (ष् ष्‍)

ष्‍ ș

अष्ट अष्‌ट *(așhța* eight*)*, इष्ट इष्‌ट *(ișhța* desired*)*, कष्ट कष्‌ट *(kașhțam* trouble*)*,

आविष्कार आविष्‌कार *(āvishkār* discovery*)*, मनुष्य मनुष्‌य *(manushya*, man*)*, पुष्प पुष्‌प *(pushpa* flower*)*, उष्मा उष्‌मा *(ushmā* heat*)*, ओष्ठ ओष्‌ठ *(oshtha* lip*)*, उष्ण उष्‌ण *(ushna* hot*)*, कृष्ण कृष्‌ण *(krishna)*, बाष्प बाष्‌प *(bāshpa* vapour*)*, भविष्य भविष्‌य *(bhavishya* future*)*

(18) Character s (स्‌ ‍स्)

स् s   तस्कर *(taskar* thief*)*, अस्तु अस्‌तु *(astu* let it be*)*, स्थिति स्‌थिति *(sthiti* state*)*, स्फटिक स्‌फटिक *(sphatik* crystal*)*, स्नायु स्‌नायु *(snāyu*, muscle*)*, स्पष्ट स्‌पष्‌ट *(spashta* clear*)*, अस्य अस्‌य *(asya* of this*)*, हास्य *(hāsya* laughter*)*, स्मित *(smita* a smile*)*, स्वत: स्‌वत: *(svata* oneself*)*, स्वदेश स्‌वदेश *(svadeśha* motherland*)*, स्वागत *(svāgat* welcome*)*, स्कन्द स्‌कन्‌द *(skand)*, स्मृति स्‌मृति *(smriti* memory*)*

(19) Character h (ह्‌ ह)

ह h   हृ hri   ह्ण hṇa   ह्न hna   ह्य hya

ह्म hma   ह्र hra   ह्ल hla   ह्व hva

हृदय ह्‌ऋदय *(hriday* heart*)*, बाह्य बाह्‌य *(bāhya* external*)*, ब्रह्म ब्‌रह्‌म *(brahma* Brahma*)*, आह्लाद आह्‌लाद *(āhlād* joy*)*, गृह्णाति गृह्‌णाति *(grihnāti* he takes*)*, ह्रस्व ह्‌रस्‌व *(hrasva* short*)* चिह्न चिह्‌न *(chihna* sign*)*, वह्नि वह्‌नि *(vahni* fire*)*, जिह्वा जिह्‌वा (*jihvā* tongue)

SPECIAL
DEVANAGARI COMPOUND CHARACTERS

क्त क्त   kta

Characters क्‌ + त can be written as क्त *(kta)*, but there is a special single character क्त for this purpose. e.g. रक्त रक्त *(rakta* blood*)*, भक्ति भक्ति *(bhakti* devotion*)*, वक्ता वक्ता *(vaktā* speaker*)*, युक्त युक्त *(yukta* equipped*)*

द्द dda　　द्घ dgha　　द्ध ddha　　द्ग dga

द्भ dbha　　द्य dya　　द्म dma　　द्व dva

Character *da* (द्) has following common compounds

1. d + da = dda → द् + द = द्द (उद्देश *uddeśh* objective, तद्दान *taddāna* that charity)
2. d + dha = ddha → द् + ध = द्ध (युद्ध *yuddha* war, बुद्धि *buddhi* thinking)
3. d + ga = dga → द् + ग = द्ग (उद्गम *udgam* rise, भगवद्गीता *bhagavadgītā*)
4. d + bha = dbha → द् + भ = द्भ (सद्भाव *sadbhāv* goodness; उद्भव *udbhav* rise)
5. d + ya = dya written as : द् + य = द्य (आद्य *ādya* first; द्यूत *dyūta,* gambling)
6. d + ma = dma written as : द् + म = द्म (पद्म *padma* lotus, छद्मी *chhadmī* cunning)
7. d + va = dva written as : द् + व = द्व (द्वंद्व *dvandva* duality, विद्वान् *vidvān* learned)

LETTER ra र

Letter ra (र) forms following two groups of compounds:

(A) As said above, **when full-consonant र (ra) comes after any half-consonant,**

Thet full-consonant र (ra) is written as a slanted line (⸝) attached to that half-consonant.

क्र kra　　ग्र gra　　श्र śhra　　त्र tra

1. k + ra (क् + र = क्र) चक्र *chakra* wheel, क्रान्ति *krānti* revolution, क्रोध *krodha* anger, क्रिया *kriyā* deed, क्रूर: *krūra* cruel, क्रेता *kretā* buyer.
2. g + ra (ग् + र = ग्र) अग्र *agra* tip, अग्रेसर *agresar* leader, ग्राम *grām* village, ग्रीवा *grīvā* neck.

3. d + ra (द् + र = द्र) भद्र *bhadra* gentle, सुभद्रा *subhadrā,* द्रविड *draviḍa,* द्रोण *droṇa,* द्रोह *droha* treachery, द्रुम *druma* tree

4. śh + ra (श् + र = श् + र = श्र) श्रद्धा *śhraddhā* faith, विश्रांति *viśhrānti* rest, श्री *śhrī* divine, श्रेष्ठ *śhreṣhṭha* superior, श्रोता *śhrotā* listner, श्रुत *śhruta* heard

5. t + ra (त् + र = त्र) यन्त्र *yantra* machine, रात्रि *rātri* night, पत्र *patra* leaf, त्रेता *tretā* saviour, त्रिधा *tridhā* in three ways.

ट्र tra ड्र ḍra स्र sra स्त्र stra

6. ṭ or ḍ + ra (ट्र, ड्र) : उष्ट्र उष्ट्र *uṣhṭra* camel, राष्ट्र: राष्ट्र *rāṣhṭra* country, पौण्ड्र पौण्ड्र *pauṇḍra* (Bhima's conch shell).

7. s + ra (स् + र = स्र) सहस्र सहस्र *sahasra* thousand, स्रोत स्रोत *srot* flown, स्राव स्राव *srāva* a flow

8. s+ t + ra (स्+त्+र = स्त्र) स्त्री स्त्री *strī* woman, अस्त्र अस्त्र *astra* weapon, वस्त्र वस्त्र *vastra* cloth, सहस्र, शास्त्र

(B) When <u>half-consonant र् (r)</u> comes before any consonant, it is written as (ि) above the following full consonant.

र्क rka र्प rpa

9. र् + प = (र्प); अर्क: अर्क *arka* sun, सर्ग सर्ग *sarga* the creation, अर्चना अर्चना *archanā* worship, वार्ता वार्ता *vārtā* news, सर्प सर्प *sarpa* snake, कर्म कर्म *karma* deed, कार्य कार्य *kārya* duty

Character *ta and na* (त्, न्) makes following common compounds

त्त tta त्त्व ttva न्न nna

1. t + ta = tta (त्+त = त्त, त्त) उत्तम *uttam* best, सत्ता *sattā* jurisdiction, सत्त्व *sattava* truth.

2. n + na = nna (न्+न = न्न) खिन्न *khinna* sad

3. h + ma = hma (ह्+म = ह्म) ब्रह्मा *brahmā* the Creator, ब्रह्माण्ड *brahmaṇḍa* universe

4. h + ya = hya (ह्+य = ह्य) बाह्य *bāhya* external, गुह्य *guhya* secret

MORE WORDS WITH COMPOUND CHARACTERS

क् क्क, क्क (वुक्कति, वुक्कति वुक्कति *vukkati,* he barks), क्ख (कक्खति *kakkhati* he laughs, कक्खट *kakkhaṭa* hard), क्च (त्वक्चैव *tvakchaiva* skin also), क्त (उक्त *ukta* said), क्त्य (भक्त्या *bhaktyā* with devotion), क्त्र (वक्त्र *vaktra,* mouth), क्त्व (उक्त्वा *uktvā* having said), क्न (शक्नोमि *śhaknomi,* I am able), क्प (पृथक्पृथक् *prithak-prithak* separately), क्म (रुक्मिणी *rukmiṇī*), क्य (वाक्य *vākya* speech), क्र (क्रम *kram* order), क्ल (क्लान्त *klānt* tired), क्लृ (क्लृप्ति *klripti* invention), क्व (क्वचित् *kvachit* sometimes), क्श (प्राक्शरीरविमोक्षण *prāk-śharīra-vimokṣhaṇa* before death), क्ष (क्षमा *kṣhamā,* forgiveness), क्स (ऋक्साम *rik-sām* Rigveda and Sāmveda)

क्ष् क्ष्म्य (सौक्ष्म्य *saukṣhmya* minuteness), क्ष्य (समीक्ष्य *samīkṣhya* having seen), क्ष्व (*Ikṣhvāku* इक्ष्वाकु)

ख् ख्य (सांख्य *sāṅkhya*)

ग् ग्द (वाग्देवी *vāg-devī* Sarasvatī), ग्ध (दुग्ध *dugdha* milk), ग्न (अग्नि *agni* fire), ग्प (वाग्पटु *vāgpaṭu* elouquent), ग्भ (पृथग्भाव *prithag-bhāv* different nature), ग्भ्य (लिग्भ्याम् *ligbhyām* for two writers), जग्मु: (*jagmuh* they went), ग्य (भाग्य *bhāgya* luck), ग्र (ग्रसन *grasan* eating), ग्ल (ग्लानि *glāni* downfall), ग्व (पृथग्विधा *prithagvidhā* differently), ग्व्य (सम्यग्व्यवस्थित *samyag-vyavasthita* properly established)

घ् घ्न (विघ्न *vighna* obstacle), घ्न्य (अघ्न्य *aghnya* not to be killed), घ्य (अर्घ्य *arghya* holy), घ्र (घ्राण *ghrāṇ* nose), घ्व (लघ्वाशी *laghvāśhī* moderate eater)

ङ् ङ्क (अङ्क *aṅka* body), ङ्क्त (भुङ्क्ते *bhuṅkte* he eats), ङ्क्थ (भुङ्क्थ *bhuṅgtha* you all enjoy), ङ्ख (शङ्ख *śhaṅkha* conch-shell), ङ्ग (गङ्गा *gaṅgā*), ङ्ग (सङ्गीत *saṅgīt* music), ङ्घ (सङ्घ *saṅgha*

attachment), ङ्ध्व (भुङ्ध्वे *bhuṅgdhve* you all enjoy), ङ्म (वाङ्मय *vāṅgmaya* literature), ङ्क्ष (काङ्क्षामि *kāṅkṣhāmi* I desire), ङ्भ्य (प्राङ्भ्याम् *prāṅgbhyām* for two Easterners)

च् च्च (उच्चैः *uchcha,* loudly), च्छ (इच्छा *ichchhā,* desire), च्छृ (उच्छृङ्खल *uchchhriṅkhal* un-restrained), युद्धाच्छ्रेय (*yuddhāchchhreya* better than war), च्य (अच्युत *achyut* Krishna), उच्यते *uchyate* it is called), च्वि (*chvi* existance of non-existant)

छ् छ्य (छ्यवते *chhyavate* he approaches), छ्र (यच्छ्रेय *yachchhreya* that which is better), उच्छ्रित (*uchchhrit* raised), उच्छ्वास *uchchhvās* exhalation)

ज् ज्ज (सज्ज *sajja* ready), ज्ज्य (तज्ज्योति *tajjyoti* that light), ज्ज्ञ (तज्ज्ञात्वा *tajjñātvā* knowing that), ज्य (राज्य *rājya* kingdom), ज्र (वज्र *vajra* thunderboalt), ज्व (ज्वाला *jwālā* flame)

ञ् ञ्च (पञ्च *pañch* five), ञ्छ (वाञ्छा *vañchhā* desire), ञ्ज (सञ्जय *sañjay*), ञ्ज्य (युञ्ज्याद्योग *yuñjādyoga* should practice yoga), ञ्झ (उञ्झति *uñjhati* he lets it go), ञ्ज्म (भुञ्ज्म *bhuñjma* we all enjoy), ञ्ज्व (भुञ्ज्व *bhuñjva* we both enjoy), ञ्श्र (पश्यञ्श्रुण्वन् *paśhyañ-śhruṇvan* while seeing and hearing), ञ्श्व (स्वपञ्श्वसन् *svapañśhvasan* sleeping and breething)

ट् ट्ट (पट्टिका *paṭṭikā,* plate), ष्ट्र (राष्ट्र *rāṣhtra* country), ष्ट्व (दृष्ट्वा *drṣhṭvā,* seeing)

ड् ड्ड (उड्डयते *uḍḍayate* he flies), ड्भ्य (राड्भ्याम् *rāḍbhyām* for two kings), ड्य (ईड्य *īdya* glorified)

ढ् ढ्य (आढ्य *āḍḍhya* wealthy)

ण् ण्ट (कण्टक *kaṇṭaka* thorn), ण्ठ (वैकुण्ठ *vaikuṇṭha* heaven), ण्ड (पाण्डव *pāṇḍav),* ण्ढ (षण्ढ *ṣhaṇḍha* impotant), ण्ड्र (पौण्ड्र *pauṇḍra*), ण्ण (विषण्ण *vṣhaṇṇa* dejected), ण्म (षण्मास *ṣhaṇ-māsa six*-months), ण्य (कार्पण्य *kārpaṇya* pity)

त् त्क (तत्काल *tatkāl,* that time), त्कृ (अभिभवात्कृष्ण *abhibhavāt-krishṇa!* O Krishna! from the rise of), त्क्र (कामात्क्रोध: *kāmātkrodha* anger from desire), त्क्ष (अन्यत्क्षत्रियस्य *anyat-kṣhatriyasya* anything else for a warrior), त्च (भयात्च *bhayātcha* and from the fear), त्त (सत्ता *sattā* power), त्य (भयात्त्यजेत् *bhayāt-tyajet* let go out of fear), त्त्र (तत्त्रय *tat-traya* those three), त्त्व (तत्त्व *tattva* principle), त्थ (अश्वत्थामा *aśhvatthāmā*), त्न (रत्नाकर *ratnākar* ocean), त्प (तत्पर *tatpara* that supreme), तात्पर्य (*tātparya* morale), त्प्र (तत्प्राप्य *tatprāpya* having attained that), त्म (आत्मा *ātmā* soul), त्म्य (महात्म्य *mahātmya* greatness), त्य (त्यक्त्वा *tyaktvā* having renounced), त्र (धर्मक्षेत्र *dharmakṣhetra* righteous place), त्र्य (रात्र्यागमैं *rātryāgame* at night), त्व (त्वम् *tvam* you), त्स (उत्साह *utsāha* encouragement), त्स्थ (पश्यत्स्थितान् *paśhyatsthitān* he saw the standing ones), त्स्न (कृत्स्न *kritsna* all), त्स्म (सम्मोहात्स्मृतिविभ्रम *sammohātsmriti-vibhrama* loss of thinking as a result of delusion) त्स्य (प्रतियोत्स्यामि *pratiyotsyāmi* I will defend) त्स्व (परधर्मात्स्वनुष्ठितात् *para-dharmāt-svanuṣhṭhitāt* than performed other's duty)

थ् मथ्नाति (*mathnāti* he churns), थ्य (तथ्य *tathya* truth); मिथ्या *mithyā* false)

द् द्ग (उद्गार *udgār* exclamation), द्ग्र (असद्ग्राह *asadgrāha* misunderstanding), द्घ (उद्घाटन *udghāṭan* inauguration), द्द (उद्देश *uddeśha* objective), द्द्य (महद्द्युतिकर *mahad-dyutikar,* sun), द्द्र (अन्यद्द्रष्टुमिच्छसि *anyad-draṣhṭum-ichchhasi* whatever else you wish to see), द्ध (युद्ध *yuddha* war), द्ध्य (युद्ध्यस्व *yuddhyasva* please fight), द्ध्व (बुद्ध्वा *buddhvā* having known) द्ब (स्मृतिभ्रंशाद्बुद्धिनाश: *smriti-bhramśhād-buddhi-nāśha* misunderstanding due to confusion), द्ब्र (तस्माद्ब्रह्मणि *tasmād-brahmaṇi* therefore in the brahma), द्भ (सद्भाव *sad-bhāv* righteousness), द्भ्य (भगवद्भ्याम् *bhagavadbhyām* for two gods), द्म (पद्म *padma,* lotus), द्य (पद्य *padya* song), द्र (द्रुपद *drupada*), द्व (द्वंद्व, द्वन्द्व *dvandva* duality), द्व्य (अव्यक्ताद्व्यक्तय *avyaktād-vyaktaya,* the manifest emerged from the unmanifest)

ध् ध्न (बध्नाति *badhnāti* it binds), ध्म (दध्मौ *dadhmau* he blew), ध्य (ध्यान *dhyāna* meditation), ध्र (ध्रुव *dhruva* unmoving), ध्व (ध्वज *dhvaj* flag)

न् न्क (समवेतान्कुरून् *samavetān-kurūn* to the assembled Kurus), न्ग (अश्नन्गाच्छन् *aśhnan-gachchhan* eating and going), न्त (णिजन्त *ṇijanta* causative), न्त (अन्त *anta* end), न्त्य (व्यथयन्त्येते *vyathayantyete* these do bother), न्त्र्य (आमन्त्र्य *āmantrya* having invited), न्थ (मन्थन *manthan* churning), न्त्र (यन्त्र *yantra* machine), न्त्व (सान्त्वना *sāntvanā* consolation), न्त्स्य (भन्त्स्यति *bhantsyati* he will tie), न्द (आनन्द *ānanda* joy), न्द्र (इन्द्रिय *indriya* organ), न्द्व (द्वन्द्वम् *dvandvam* duality), न्द्ध (रुन्द्धाम् *runddhām* he should resist), अरुन्द्ध्वम् (*arunddhvam* you all had resisted), न्द्ध्य (रुन्द्ध्यताम् *runddhyātām* may they stop), न्ध (अन्ध *andha* blind), अरुन्ध्महि (*arundhmahi* we all had resisted), विन्ध्यन्तः (*vindhyantaḥ* lacking), अरुन्ध्वहि (*arundhvahi* we two had resisted), न्न (अन्न *anna* food), न्प (स्थितान्पार्थः *sthitān-pārtha* Arjuna to the seated ones), न्प्र (प्राणान्प्राणेषु *prāṇān-prāṇeṣhu* breath in the breaths), न्ब (सर्वान्बन्धून् *sarvān-bandhūn* to all brothers), न्ब्र (तान्ब्रवीमि *tān-bravīmi* I tell about them), न्भ (भवान्भिष्म *bhavān-bhīṣhma* you Bhīshma), न्भ्य (खन्भ्याम् *khanbhyām* for two lame men), न्भ्र (मातुलान्भ्रातॄन् *mātulān-bhratrṫn* to uncles and brothers), न्म (जन्म *janma* birth), न्य (अन्य *anya,* other), न्र (अस्मिन्रणे *asmin-raṇe* on this battlefield), न्व (अन्वय *anvay* following), न्व्य (भगवन्व्यक्ति *bhagavan-vyakti* O Lord! Your Personifiction), न्स (तान्समीक्ष्य *tān-samīkṣhya* having seen them), न्स्य (बुद्धिमान्स्यात् *buddhimān-syāt* he will be wise), न्स्व (धार्तराष्ट्रान्स्वबान्धवान् *dhārtarāṣhṭrān-sva-bāndhavān,* to our brother Kauravas), न्ह (सञ्जनयन्हर्षम् *sañjanayan-harṣham,* while increasing the joy)

प् प्त (पर्याप्त *paryāpta* limited), प्त्व (लोलुप्त्व *loluptva* eagerness), प्न, प्न (स्वप्न *svapna* sleep, dream), प्म (पाप्म *pāpma* wicked), प्य (अवाप्य *avāpya* having obtained), प्र (प्रति *prati* towards), म्प्ल (सम्प्लुतोदक *samplutodak* full of water), प्ल (प्लुत *pluta* flooded), प्स (अप्सु *apsu* in the water), प्स्य (अवाप्स्यसि *avāpsyasi* you will attain)

ब् ब्द (शब्द *s'habda* sound), ब्ध (लब्ध *labdha* attained), ब्ध्व (लब्ध्वा *labdhvā* having), ब्भ्य (गुब्भ्याम् *gubbhyām* for tow defenders), ब्य (शैब्य *s'haibya*), ब्र (ब्रह्म *brahma*)

भ् भ्य (अभ्यास *abhyās* study), भ्र (भ्रम *bhram* delusion), भ्वादि (*bhvādi* bhū etc.)

म् म्न (धृष्टद्युम्न *dhrishṭadyumna*), म्प (विकम्प *vikampa* trembling), म्फ (गुम्फित *gumphit* intertwined), म्ब (अम्बा *anbā* mother), म्भ (अम्भसि *ambhasi* in the water), म्भ्य (पुम्भ्याम् *pumbhyām* for two persons), म्म (सम्मान *sammān* respect), म्य (रम्य *ramya* enchanting), म्र (म्रियते *mriyate* it dies)

य् य्य (त्वय्युपपद्यते *tvayyupapadyate* it befits you)

र् र्क (अर्क *arka* sun), र्क्ष्य (सूर्क्ष्यिष्यति *sūrkṣhiṣhyati* he will disrespect), र्ख (मूर्ख *mūrkha* foolish) र्ग (वर्ग *varga* class), र्ग्भ्य (ऊर्ग्भ्याम् *ūrgbhyām* with two languages), र्ग्य (अस्वर्ग्य *asvargya* un-heavenly), र्घ्य (अर्घ्य *arghya* offering) र्च (अर्चना *archanā* worship), र्च्य (अभ्यर्च *abhyarcha* salute), र्च्छ (मूर्च्छति *mūrchchhati* it coagulates), र्ज (भीमार्जुनौ *bhīmārjunau* of Bhima and Arjuna), र्ज्य (वर्ज्य *varjya* without), र्ज्व (वदनैर्ज्वलद्भिः *vadanairjvaladbi* with balzing mouths), र्झ (झर्झरा *jharjharā* prostitute), र्ण (वर्ण *varṇa* a class), र्ण्य (आकर्ण्य *ākarṇya,* hearing), र्त (धार्तराष्ट्र *dhārtarāṣhṭra* Kaurava), र्त्त (आर्त्त *ārtta* afflicted) र्त्म (वर्त्मनि *vartmani* on the path), र्त्य (मर्त्य *martya* dying), र्थ (अर्थ *artha* meaning), र्द (जनार्दन *janārdan* Kriṣhṇa), र्ध (अर्ध *ardha* half), र्ध्न (मूर्ध्नि *mūrdhni* in the head), र्ध्न्य (मूर्ध्न्याधायात्मन *mūrdhnyādhāyātman* having fixed in one's head), र्ध्र (मृत्युर्ध्रुवम् *mrityurdhruvam* death is certain), र्ध्व (ऊर्ध्व *ūrdhva* up), र्न (निराशीर्निर्मम *nirāsīrnirmama* indifferent and selfless), र्प (सर्प *sarpa* snake), र्ब (दुर्बुद्धि *dur-buddhi,* wicked), र्ब्र (हविर्ब्रह्माग्नौ *havirbrhmāgnau* offering in the fire of brahma), र्भ (दर्भ *darbha* grass), र्म (कर्म *karma* deed), र्म्य (धर्म्यात् *dharmyāt* than the righteous), र्य (शौर्य *s'haurya* bravery), र्ल (चिकीर्षुर्लोकसंग्रह *chikīrṣhur-lokasangraha* desirous of people), र्व (सर्व *sarva* all), र्व्य (बुद्धिर्व्यतितरिष्यति *buddhirvyatitariṣhyati* mind will transcend), र्श (स्पर्श *spars'ha* contact), र्ष (हर्ष *harṣha* joy), र्ष्ण (वार्ष्णेय *vārṣhṇeya* Shri Krishna), र्ह (अर्हः *arha* worthy),

र्ज्ञ (प्रकृतेर्ज्ञानवानपि *prikriterjñānavānapi* the wise also - with his own nature)

ल् ल्क (वल्कल *valkala* bark), ल्ग (वल्गना *valganā* chatter), ल्प (अल्प *alpa* short), उल्बेन (*ulbena* with umblical cord), प्रगल्भ (*pragalbha* proud), ल्म (कल्मष *kalmaṣha* sin), ल्य (शल्य *śhalya* thorn), ल्ल (श्रद्धावाँल्लभते *śhraddhāvām̐l-labhate* the faithful person attains), ल्व (बिल्व *bilva* the Bel tree)

व् व्य (व्याघ्र *vyāghra* tiger), व्र (व्रत *vrata* austerity)

श् श्च (आश्चर्य *āśhcharya* wonder), श्छ (भ्रष्टश्छिन्न *bhraṣhṭśhchhinna* broken and spoiled), श्न (अश्नामि *aśhnāmi* I eat), श्म (कश्मल *kaśhmal* delusion), श्य (पश्य *paśhya* see), श्र (श्री *śhrī* divine), श्व, श्व (अश्व, अश्व *aśhva* horse), श्ल (अश्लील *aśhlīl* obscene)

ष् ष्क (निष्काम *niṣhkām* without desire), ष्कृ (निष्कृति *niṣhkriti* fruitless act), ष्ट (अष्ट *aṣhṭa* eight), ष्टय (द्वेष्टयकुशलम् *dveṣhṭya-kuśhal* he hates non-pleasent), ष्ट्र (राष्ट्र *rāṣhṭra* country), ष्ट्व (दृष्ट्वा *driṣhṭvā* seeing), ष्ठ (पृष्ठ *priṣṭha* surface), ष्ण (कृष्ण *kriṣhṇa* black), ष्प (पुष्प *puṣhpa* flower), ष्प्र (दुष्प्राप *duṣhprāpa* difficult to attain), ष्ण्य (औष्ण्य *auṣhṇya* warmth), ष्म (भीष्म *bhīṣhma*), ष्य (मनुष्य *manuṣhya* man), ष्व (कुरुष्व *kuruṣhva* do)

स् स्क (स्कन्द *skand* chapter), स्ख (स्खलति *skhalati* it falls), स्ज् (भ्रस्ज् *bhrasj* to roast), स्त (अस्त *asta* setting), स्त्य (प्राणान्स्त्यक्त्वा *prāṇānstyaktvā* having renounced their lives), स्त्र (स्त्रंसते *sram̐sate* it falls), स्त्रोत (*srota* flow), स्त्र (स्त्री *strī* woman), स्त्व (कुतस्त्वा *kutastvā* from where did you?), स्थ (स्थान *sthāna* place), स्न (स्नान *snāna* bath), स्प (स्पर्श *sparśha* contact), स्फ (विस्फोट *visphoṭa* explosion), स्म (तस्मात् *tasmāt* therefore), स्म्य (गिरामस्म्येकमक्षर *girām-asmyekam-akṣhara* among the syllables I am the syllable of Om), स्य (अस्य *asya* its), स्र (सहस्र *sahasra* thousand), स्व (स्वत: *svatah* oneself), स्स (हिनस्सि *hinassi* you kill)

ह् हृ (हृदय *hridaya* heart), हृष्यति (*hrṣhyati* he enjoys), ह्ण (गृह्णाति *grhṇāti* he takes), ह्न (वह्नि *vahni* fire), ह्म (ब्रह्मा *brahmā*), ह्य (दह्यते *dahyate* it burns), ह्र (जिह्रेति *jihreti* she blushes), ह्ल (प्रह्लाद *prahlād*), ह्व (जुह्वति *juhvati* he performs offering)

CHAPTER 2

SANDHI संधि

1. COMPOUNDING OF HINDI VOWELS

RATNAKAR'S CHART FOR VOWEL SANDHI RULES

When two vowels come together, they are mathematically added into a single long vowel.

First vowel	+ Second vowel	=	Result, a long vowel
1 अ, आ	+ अ, आ	=	आ
अ, आ	+ इ, ई	=	ए
अ, आ	+ उ, ऊ	=	ओ
अ, आ	+ ऋ, ॠ	=	अर्
अ, आ	+ ए, ऐ	=	ऐ
अ, आ	+ ओ	=	औ
2 इ, ई	+ अ, आ, उ, ऊ, ए, ऐ, ओ, औ	=	य, या, यु, यू, ये, यै, यो. यौ
इ, ई	+ इ, ई	=	ई, ई
3 उ, ऊ	+ अ, आ, इ, ई, ए, ऐ, ओ, औ	=	व, वा, वि, वी, वे, वै, वो, वौ
4 ऋ	+ अ, आ, इ, ई, ए, ऐ, ओ, औ	=	अर् + अ, आ, इ, ई, ए, ऐ, ओ, औ = अर्, अर, अरा, अरि, अरी, अरे, अरो, अरै, अरौ
5 ए	+ अ, आ, इ, ई, उ, ऊ, ए, ऐ, ओ, औ	=	अय् + अ, आ, इ, ई, उ, ऊ, ए, ऐ, ओ, औ = अय्, अय, अया, अयि, अयी, अये, अयो, अयै, अयौ
ऐ	+ अ, आ, इ, ई, उ, ऊ, ए, ऐ, ओ, औ	=	आय् + अ, आ, इ, ई, उ, ऊ, ए, ऐ, ओ, आ = आय्, आय, आया, आयि, आयी, आये, आयो, आयै, आयौ
6 ओ	+ अ, आ, इ, ई, उ, ऊ, ए, ऐ, ओ, औ	=	अव् + अ, आ, इ, ई, उ, ऊ, ए, ऐ, ओ, औ = अव्, अव, अवा, अवि, अवी, अवे, अवो, अवै, अवौ
औ	+ अ, आ, इ, ई, उ, ऊ, ए, ऐ, ओ, औ	=	आव् + अ, आ, इ, ई, उ, ऊ, ए, ऐ, ओ, औ = आव्, आव, आवा, आवि, आवी, आवे, आवो, आवै, आवौ

SANSKRIT VOWEL SANDHI CHART

अ	इ	उ	ण्	ऋ	लृ	क्

अ	इ	उ

अ	आ	इ	ई	उ	ऊ	ऋ

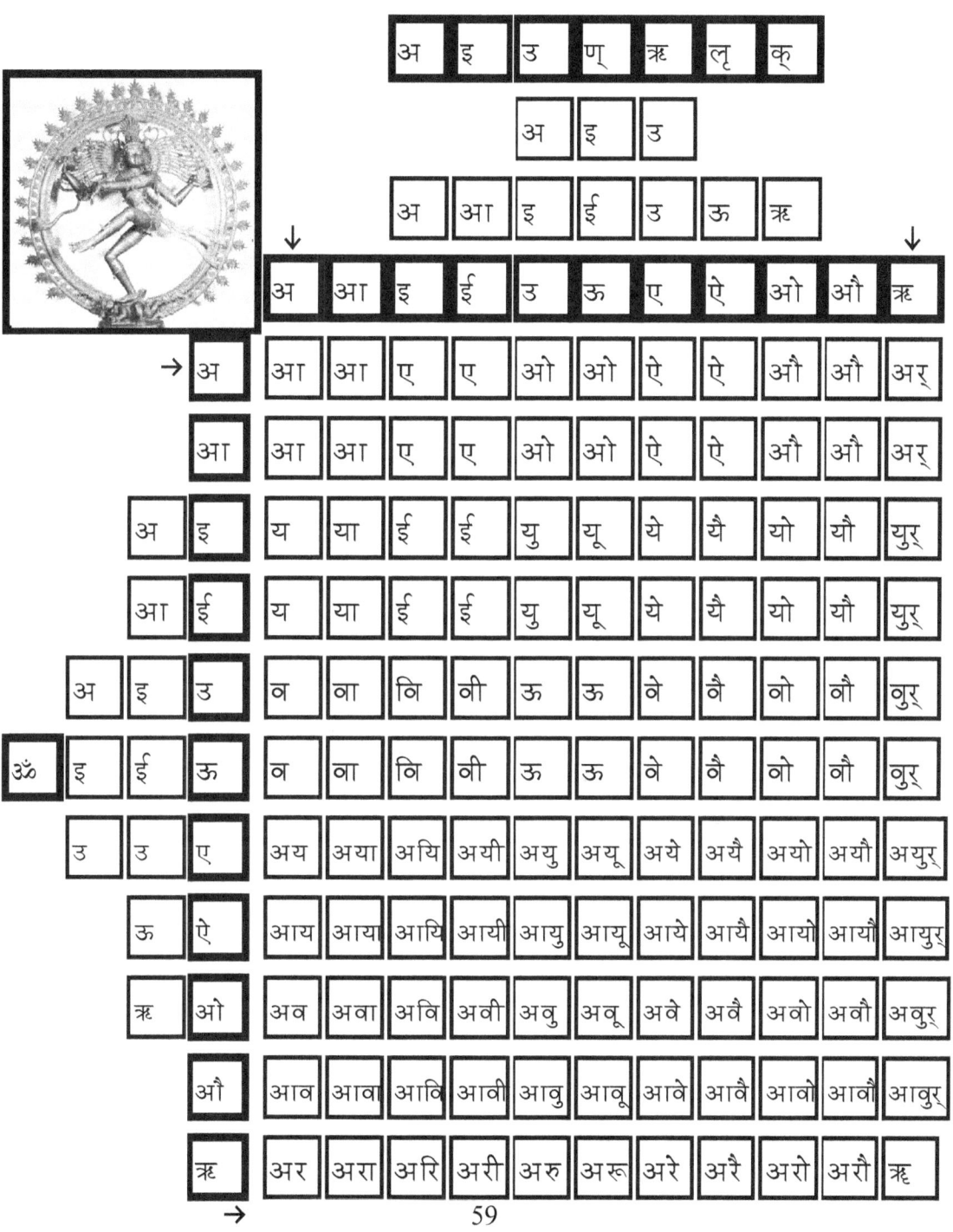

				अ	आ	इ	ई	उ	ऊ	ए	ऐ	ओ	औ	ऋ
			अ	आ	आ	ए	ए	ओ	ओ	ऐ	ऐ	औ	औ	अर्
			आ	आ	आ	ए	ए	ओ	ओ	ऐ	ऐ	औ	औ	अर्
		अ	इ	य	या	ई	ई	यु	यू	ये	यै	यो	यौ	युर्
		आ	ई	य	या	ई	ई	यु	यू	ये	यै	यो	यौ	युर्
	अ	इ	उ	व	वा	वि	वी	ऊ	ऊ	वे	वै	वो	वौ	वुर्
ॐ	इ	ई	ऊ	व	वा	वि	वी	ऊ	ऊ	वे	वै	वो	वौ	वुर्
	उ	उ	ए	अय	अया	अयि	अयी	अयु	अयू	अये	अयै	अयो	अयौ	अयुर्
		ऊ	ऐ	आय	आया	आयि	आयी	आयु	आयू	आये	आयै	आयो	आयौ	आयुर्
		ऋ	ओ	अव	अवा	अवि	अवी	अवु	अवू	अवे	अवै	अवो	अवौ	अवुर्
			औ	आव	आवा	आवि	आवी	आवु	आवू	आवे	आवै	आवो	आवौ	आवुर्
			ऋ	अर	अरा	अरि	अरी	अरु	अरू	अरे	अरै	अरो	अरौ	ऋ

1. COMPOUNDING A VOWEL WITH THE NEXT VOWEL

उपरोक्त सूत्रों के शास्त्रोक्त उदारहण :

अ	+	अ	=	आ	वात	(अ)	+	(अ)	अयन	=	वातायन
अ	+	आ	=	आ	हिम	(अ)	+	(आ)	आलय	=	हिमालय
अ	+	इ	=	ए	देव	(अ)	+	(इ)	इन्द्र	=	देवेन्द्र
अ	+	ई	=	ए	परम	(अ)	+	(ई)	ईश्वर	=	परमेश्वर
अ	+	उ	=	ओ	चन्द्र	(अ)	+	(उ)	उदय	=	चन्द्रोदय
अ	+	ऊ	=	ओ	प्र	(अ)	+	(ऊ)	ऊढ	=	प्रौढ
अ	+	ऋ	=	अर्	सप्त	(अ)	+	(ऋ)	ऋषि	=	सप्तर्षि
अ	+	ए	=	ऐ	एक	(अ)	+	(ए)	एक	=	एकैक
अ	+	ऐ	=	ऐ	देव	(अ)	+	(ऐ)	ऐश्वर्य	=	देवैश्वर्य
अ	+	ओ	=	औ	जल	(अ)	+	(ओ)	ओघ	=	जलौघ
अ	+	औ	=	औ	जन	(अ)	+	(औ)	औदार्य	=	जनौदार्य
आ	+	अ	=	आ	विद्या	(आ)	+	(अ)	अर्थी	=	विद्यार्थी
आ	+	आ	=	आ	विद्या	(आ)	+	(आ)	आलय	=	विद्यालय
आ	+	इ	=	ए	यथा	(आ)	+	(इ)	इच्छा	=	यथेच्छा
आ	+	ई	=	ए	रमा	(आ)	+	(ई)	ईश	=	रमेश
आ	+	उ	=	ओ	महा	(आ)	+	(उ)	उत्सव	=	महोत्सव
आ	+	ऊ	=	ओ	महा	(आ)	+	(ऊ)	ऊरु	=	महोरु
आ	+	ऋ	=	अर्	महा	(आ)	+	(ऋ)	ऋषि	=	महर्षि
आ	+	ए	=	ऐ	सदा	(आ)	+	(ए)	एव	=	सदैव
आ	+	ऐ	=	ऐ	प्रजा	(आ)	+	(ऐ)	ऐक्य	=	प्रजैक्य
आ	+	ओ	=	औ	गंगा	(आ)	+	(ओ)	ओघ	=	गंगौघ
आ	+	औ	=	औ	विद्या	(आ)	+	(औ)	औत्सुक्य	=	विद्यौत्सुक्य
इ	+	अ	=	य	यदि	(इ)	+	(अ)	अपि	=	यद्यपि

इ	+	आ	=	या	इति	(इ)	+	(आ)	आदि	=	इत्यादि
इ	+	इ	=	ई	रवि	(इ)	+	(इ)	इन्द्र	=	रवीन्द्र
इ	+	ई	=	ई	कवि	(इ)	+	(ई)	ईश्वर	=	कविश्वर
इ	+	उ	=	यु	अति	(इ)	+	(उ)	उत्तम	=	अत्युत्तम
इ	+	ऊ	=	यू	प्रति	(इ)	+	(ऊ)	ऊह	=	प्रत्यूह
इ	+	ऋ	=	युर्	अति	(इ)	+	(ऋ)	ऋद्धि	=	अत्युर्द्धि
इ	+	ए	=	ये	प्रति	(इ)	+	(ए)	एक	=	प्रत्येक
इ	+	ऐ	=	यै	प्रति	(इ)	+	(ऐ)	ऐरावत	=	प्रत्यैरावत
इ	+	ओ	=	यो	दधि	(इ)	+	(ओ)	ओदन	=	दध्योदन
इ	+	औ	=	यौ	दधि	(इ)	+	(औ)	औषध	=	दध्यौषध
ई	+	अ	=	य	नदी	(ई)	+	(अ)	अम्बु	=	नद्यम्बु
ई	+	आ	=	या	देवी	(ई)	+	(आ)	आज्ञा	=	देव्याज्ञा
ई	+	इ	=	ई	जननी	(ई)	+	(इ)	इच्छा	=	जननीच्छा
ई	+	ई	=	ई	काली	(ई)	+	(ई)	ईश्वरी	=	कालीश्वरी
ई	+	उ	=	यु	सुधी	(ई)	+	(उ)	उपास्य	=	सुध्युपास्य
ई	+	ऊ	=	यू	अवी	(ई)	+	(ऊ)	ऊर्णा	=	अव्यूर्णा
ई	+	ऋ	=	युर्	महती	(ई)	+	(ऋ)	ऋक्षी	=	महर्त्युक्षी
ई	+	ए	=	ये	गोपी	(ई)	+	(ए)	एषा	=	गोप्येषा
ई	+	ऐ	=	यै	गौरी	(ई)	+	(ऐ)	ऐश्वर्य	=	गौर्यैश्वर्य
ई	+	ओ	=	यो	नारी	(ई)	+	(ओ)	औत्कर्ष	=	नार्योत्कर्ष
ई	+	औ	=	यौ	वाणी	(ई)	+	(औ)	औचित्य	=	वाण्यौचित्य
उ	+	अ	=	व	मनु	(उ)	+	(अ)	अन्तर	=	मन्वन्तर
उ	+	आ	=	व	गुरु	(उ)	+	(आ)	आदेश	=	गुर्वादेश
उ	+	इ	=	वि	अनु	(उ)	+	(इ)	इत	=	अन्वित
उ	+	ई	=	वी	ऋतु	(उ)	+	(ई)	ईश्वर	=	ऋत्वीश्वर

उ	+	उ	=	ऊ	गुरु	(उ)	+	(उ)	उपदेश	=	गुरूपदेश
उ	+	ऊ	=	ऊ	चमू	(उ)	+	(ऊ)	ऊहिनी	=	चमूहिनी
उ	+	ऋ	=	वृ	मधु	(उ)	+	(ऋ)	ऋते	=	मध्वृते
उ	+	ए	=	वे	अनु	(उ)	+	(ए)	एषण	=	अन्वेषण
उ	+	ऐ	=	वै	साधु	(उ)	+	(ऐ)	ऐक्य	=	साध्वैक्य
उ	+	ओ	=	वो	गुरु	(उ)	+	(ओ)	ओज	=	गुर्वोज
उ	+	औ	=	वौ	मधु	(उ)	+	(औ)	औषधि	=	मध्वौषधि
ऊ	+	अ	=	व	शरयू	(ऊ)	+	(अ)	अम्बु	=	शरय्वम्बु
ऊ	+	आ	=	व	अमू	(ऊ)	+	(आ)	आसते	=	अम्वासते
ऊ	+	इ	=	वि	बन्धू	(ऊ)	+	(इ)	इमौ	=	बन्ध्विमौ
ऊ	+	ई	=	वी	वधू	(ऊ)	+	(ई)	ईक्षण	=	वध्वीक्षण
ऊ	+	उ	=	ऊ	वधू	(ऊ)	+	(उ)	उत्सव	=	वधूत्सव
ऊ	+	ऊ	=	ऊ	वधू	(ऊ)	+	(ऊ)	ऊहा	=	वधूहा
ऊ	+	ऋ	=	वृ	वधू	(ऊ)	+	(ऋ)	ऋक्थ	=	वध्वृक्थ
ऊ	+	ए	=	वे	कण्डू	(ऊ)	+	(ए)	एषणा	=	कण्वेषणा
ऊ	+	ऐ	=	वै	वधू	(ऊ)	+	(ऐ)	ऐश्वर्य	=	वध्वैश्वर्य
ऊ	+	ओ	=	वो	वधू	(ऊ)	+	(ओ)	ओक	=	वध्वोक
ऊ	+	औ	=	वौ	यवागू	(ऊ)	+	(औ)	औष्ण्य	=	यवाग्वौष्ण्य
ऋ	+	अ	=	र	मातृ	(ऋ)	+	(अ)	अंश	=	मात्रंश
ऋ	+	आ	=	रा	पितृ	(ऋ)	+	(आ)	आदेश	=	पित्रादेश
ऋ	+	इ	=	रि	भ्रातृ	(ऋ)	+	(इ)	इच्छा	=	भ्रात्रिच्छा
ऋ	+	ई	=	री	सवितृ	(ऋ)	+	(ई)	ईश	=	सवित्रीश
ऋ	+	उ	=	रु	कर्तृ	(ऋ)	+	(उ)	उत्तम	=	कर्त्रुत्तम
ऋ	+	ऊ	=	रू	नप्तृ	(ऋ)	+	(ऊ)	ऊडा	=	नप्त्रूडा
ऋ	+	ऋ	=	ॠ	धातृ	(ऋ)	+	(ऋ)	ऋण	=	धातॄण

ऋ	+	ए	=	रे	गन्तृ	(ऋ)	+	(ए)	एध	=	गन्त्रेध
ऋ	+	ऐ	=	रै	नेतृ	(ऋ)	+	(ऐ)	ऐश्वर्य	=	नेत्रैश्वर्य
ऋ	+	ओ	=	रो	वक्तृ	(ऋ)	+	(ओ)	ओज	=	वक्त्रोज
ऋ	+	औ	=	रौ	भर्तृ	(ऋ)	+	(औ)	औदार्य	=	भर्त्रौदार्य
ए	+	अ	=	अय	ने	(ए)	+	(अ)	अन	=	नयन
ए	+	आ	=	अया	ते	(ए)	+	(आ)	आगत	=	तयागत
ए	+	इ	=	अयि	शे	(ए)	+	(इ)	इत	=	शयित
ए	+	ई	=	अयी	ते	(ए)	+	(ई)	ईर्षा	=	तयीर्षा
ए	+	उ	=	अयु	मे	(ए)	+	(उ)	उपदेश	=	मयुपदेश
ए	+	ऊ	=	अयू	ये	(ए)	+	(ऊ)	ऊह	=	ययूह
ए	+	ऋ	=	अयुर्	के	(ए)	+	(ऋ)	ऋच्र्छति	=	कयुर्छति
ए	+	ए	=	अये	ते	(ए)	+	(ए)	एते	=	तयेते
ए	+	ऐ	=	अयै	ते	(ए)	+	(ऐ)	ऐश्वर्य	=	तयैश्वर्य
ए	+	ओ	=	अयो	गृहे	(ए)	+	(ओ)	ओकण	=	गृहयोकण
ए	+	औ	=	अयौ	ते	(ए)	+	(औ)	औषधि	=	तयौषधि
ऐ	+	अ	=	आय	गै	(ऐ)	+	(अ)	अन	=	गायन
ऐ	+	आ	=	आया	तस्मै	(ऐ)	+	(आ)	आदेश	=	तस्मायादेश
ऐ	+	इ	=	आयि	एतस्मै	(ऐ)	+	(इ)	इमानि	=	एतस्मायिमानि
ऐ	+	ई	=	आयी	स्त्रियै	(ऐ)	+	(ई)	ईडा	=	स्त्रियायीडा
ऐ	+	उ	=	आयु	श्रियै	(ऐ)	+	(उ)	उद्यत	=	श्रियायुद्यत
ऐ	+	ऊ	=	आयू	कस्मै	(ऐ)	+	(ऊ)	ऊर्ज	=	कस्मायूर्ज
ऐ	+	ऋ	=	आयुर्	यस्मै	(ऐ)	+	(ऋ)	ऋण	=	यस्मायुर्ण
ऐ	+	ए	=	आये	एतस्मै	(ऐ)	+	(ए)	एव	=	एतस्मायेव
ऐ	+	ऐ	=	आयै	कस्मै	(ऐ)	+	(ऐ)	ऐश्वर्य	=	कस्मायैश्वर्य
ऐ	+	ओ	=	आयो	कस्यै	(ऐ)	+	(ओ)	ओज	=	कस्यायोज

ऐ + औ	=	आयौ	अस्यै	(ऐ)	+	(औ)	औचित्य	=	अस्यायौचित्य
ओ + अ	=	अव	यो	(ओ)	+	(अ)	अयन	=	यवन
ओ + आ	=	अवा	साधो	(ओ)	+	(आ)	आगच्छ	=	साधवागच्छ
ओ + इ	=	अवि	विष्णो	(ओ)	+	(इ)	इति	=	विष्णविति
ओ + ई	=	अवी	गो	(ओ)	+	(ई)	ईश्वर	=	गवीश्वर
ओ + उ	=	अवु	नो	(ओ)	+	(उ)	उद्योग	=	नवुद्योग
ओ + ऊ	=	अवू	गुरो	(ओ)	+	(ऊ)	ऊनयतु	=	गुरवुनयतु
ओ + ऋ	=	अवुर्	विष्णो	(ओ)	+	(ऋ)	ऋच्छतु	=	विष्णवुर्च्छतु
ओ + ए	=	अवे	गो	(ओ)	+	(ए)	एषणा	=	गवेषणा
ओ + ऐ	=	अवै	भानो	(ओ)	+	(ऐ)	ऐशानी	=	भानवैशानी
ओ + ओ	=	अवो	गो	(ओ)	+	(ओ)	ओक	=	गवोक
ओ + औ	=	अवौ	मधो	(ओ)	+	(औ)	औखतु	=	मधवौखतु
औ + अ	=	आव	पौ	(औ)	+	(अ)	अन	=	पवन
औ + आ	=	आवा	रात्रौ	(औ)	+	(आ)	आगत	=	रात्रावागत
औ + इ	=	आवि	पुत्रौ	(औ)	+	(इ)	इमौ	=	पुत्राविमौ
औ + ई	=	आवी	तौ	(औ)	+	(ई)	ईश्वरौ	=	तावीश्वरौ
औ + उ	=	आवु	गुरौ	(औ)	+	(उ)	उक्त	=	गुरावुक्त
औ + ऊ	=	आवू	रुग्णौ	(औ)	+	(ऊ)	ऊर्जयतु	=	रुग्णावूर्जयतु
औ + ऋ	=	आवुर्	तौ	(औ)	+	(ऋ)	ऋषी	=	तावुर्षी
औ + ए	=	आवे	कौ	(औ)	+	(ए)	एतौ	=	कावेतौ
औ + ऐ	=	आवै	द्वौ	(औ)	+	(ऐ)	ऐतिहासिका	=	द्वावैतिहासिकौ
औ + ओ	=	आवो	एतौ	(औ)	+	(ओ)	ओकसी	=	एतावोकसी
औ + औ	=	आवौ	गौ	(औ)	+	(औ)	औ	=	गावौ

(1) PANINI'S SUTRAS FOR VOWEL SANDHI

(1) अकः सवर्णे दीर्घः *akaḥ savarṇe dīrghaḥ* (6:1:101)

When a short or long vowel comes after a short or long vowel of the same kind, both of thes two vowels are replaced with a long vowel of the same kind.

(2) (i) अदेङ्गुणः *adeṅguṇaḥ,* (ii) आद्गुणः *ādguṇaḥ* (6:1:87)

(a) When vowel अ or आ (a or ā) is followed by vowel इ or ई (i or ī), vowel ए (e) comes in their place. (b) When vowel अ or आ (a or ā) is followed by vowel उ or ऊ (u or ū), vowel ओ (o) comes in their place. (c) When vowel अ or आ (a or ā) is followed by vowel ऋ or ॠ (ri or rí), syllable अर् (ar) comes in their place. (d) When vowel अ or आ (a or ā) is followed by vowel ऌ (lri), syllable अल् (al) comes in their place.

(3) (i) वृद्धिरेचि *vriddhirechi* (6:1:88), (ii) वृद्धिरादैच् *vriddhirādaich* (1:1:1)

(a) When vowel अ or आ (a or ā) is followed by vowel ए or ऐ (e or ai), vowel ऐ (ai) comes in their place. (b) When vowel अ or आ (a or ā) is followed by vowel ओ or औ (o or au), vowel औ (au) comes in their place.

(4) इकोयणचि *ikoyaṇachi* (6:1:77)

(a) When vowel इ or ई (i or ī) is followed by any vowel other than vowel इ or ई (i or ī), consonant य् (y) comes in the place of vowel इ or ई (i or ī). (b) When vowel उ or ऊ (u or ū) is followed by any vowel other than vowel उ or ऊ (u or ū), consonant व् (v) comes in the place of vowel उ or ऊ (u or ū). (c) When vowel ऋ or ॠ (ri or rí) is followed by any vowel other than vowel ऋ or ॠ (ri or rí), consonant र् (r) comes in the place of vowel ऋ or ॠ (ri or rí).

(5) एचोऽयवायावः *echo'yavāyāvaḥ* (6:1:78)

When vowel ए, ऐ, ओ or औ (*e, ai, o, au*) is followed by any vowel, other then - (i) syllable

अय् (ay) comes in the place of vowel ए (e); (ii) syllable आय् (āy) comes in the place of vowel ऐ (ai); (iii) syllable अव् (av) comes in the place of vowel ओ (o); (v) syllable आव् (āv) comes in the place of vowel औ (au).

(5) लोप: शाकल्यस्य *lopaḥ śhākalyasya* (8:5:19)

(a) When consonant य् or व् (y or v) at the end of a word is preceeded by vowel अ or आ (a or ā) and followed by any vowel, the consonant य् or व् (y or v) may optionally be deleted (लोप:). (b) And, then, if two vowels come next to each other as a result of this deletion (लोप:) of the consonant or visarga, these two vowels do not again join in a svara-sandhi.

(6) वान्तो यि प्रत्यये *vānto yi pratyaye* (6:1:79)

(a) When vowel ओ or औ (o or au) is followed by any suffix beginning with consonant य् (y), then syllable अव् or आव् (av or āv) comes in place of ओ or औ (o or au) respectively.

(7) एङः पदान्तादति *eṅgaḥ padāntādati* (6:1:109)

When vowel ए or ओ (a or o), that comes at the end of a substantive or verb, is followed by vowel अ (a), then vowel ए or ओ (a or o) remain it it's original form (पूर्वरूपम्) and the vowel अ (a) is changed to an *avagraha* ऽ (').

(8) ईदूदेद् द्विचवनं प्रगृह्यम् *īdūded-dvivachanam pragrihyam* (1:1:11)

When a word, in it's dual number, ends in vowel ई, ऊ or ए (ī, ū or e) and is followed by any vowel (of the following dual word), then the vowel ई, ऊ or ए (ī, ū or e) remains unchanged.

2. COMPOUNDING A CONSONANT WITH THE NEXT VOWEL

(1) **Rule of 3rd consonant :** If a consonant from any of the five classes (k, ch, ṭ, t, p, क्, च्, ट्, त, प्), other than the nasal consonants, is followed by a vowel, this class consonant is replaced with the third consonant from that class. (This third consonant then conjugates with the vowel that comes after it). e.g.

क् + उ	=	ग् + उ	= गु	→	सम्यक्	+ उभयोः	=	सम्यगुभयोः (Gītā 5.4)
त् + अ	=	द् + अ	= द	→	तत्	+ अस्माकम्	=	तदस्माकम् (Gītā1.10)
त् + ऋ	=	द् + ऋ	= दृ	→	एतत्	+ ऋतम्	=	एतदृतम् (Gītā 10.14)
त् + ॐ	=	द् + ॐ	= दोम्	→	तस्मात्	+ ओम्	=	तस्मादोम् (Gītā 1.22)

(2) **Conjugation of the word ending in n (न्) :** When a word ending in n (न्) is preceeded by any short vowel and is followed by any vowel, the ending n (न्) is doubled and becomes nn (न्न्) e.g.

अनिच्छन्	+ अपि	=	अनिच्छन्नपि (Gītā 3.36)
पश्यन्	+ आत्मनि	=	पश्यन्नात्मनि। (Gītā 6.20)
विषीदन्	+ इदम्	=	विषीदन्निदम् (Gītā 1.27)
गृह्णन्	+ उन्मिषन्	=	गृह्णन्नुन्मिषन्। (Gītā 5.9)
युञ्जन्	+ एवम्	=	युञ्जन्नेवम्। (Gītā 6.15)

3. COMPOUNDING A CONSONANT WITH THE FOLLOWING CONSONANT

(3) **Rule of 3rd consonant :** When a consonant, other than a nasal consonant, comes after a hard consonant from any of the five classes (namely, k, ch, ṭ, t, p, क्, च्, ट्, त्, प्), then this hard consonant is replaced by the third consonant from that same class (or optionally by the nasal consonant from that class). e.g.

क् + ब	=	ग् + ब	= ग्ब	→	पृथक् + बालाः	=	पृथग्बालाः (Gītā 5.4)
क् + म	=	ङ् + म	= ङ्म	→	ईदृक् + मम	=	ईदृङ्मम (Gītā 11.49)
त् + ग	=	द् + ग	= द्ग	→	यत् + गत्वा	=	यद्गत्वा (Gītā 15.6)
त् + द	=	द् + द	= द्द	→	विद्यात् + दुःखं	=	विद्याद्दुःखं (Gītā 6.23)
त् + ध	=	द् + ध	= द्ध	→	बुद्धियोगात् + धनञ्जय	=	बुद्धियोगाद्धनञ्जय (Gita 2.49)
त् + भ	=	द् + भ	= द्भ	→	क्रोधात् + भवति	=	क्रोधाद्भवति (Gītā 2.63)

त् + य = द् + य = द्य → अपनुद्यात् + यत् = अपनुद्याद्यत् (Gītā 2.8)
त् + र = द् + र = द्र → यत् + राज्यम् = यद्राज्यम् (Gītā 1.45)
त् + व = द् + व = द्व → एतत् + विद्मः = एतद्विद्मः (Gītā 2.6)
त् + ह = द् + ह = द्ध → धर्म्यात् + हि = धर्म्याद्धि (Gītā 2.31)

(4) The Rule of Same Order Consonant : When any consonant from t (त्) class (t, th, d, dh, n त्, थ्, द्, ध्, न्), is followed by any consonant from ch (च्) class (ch, chh, j, jh, ñ च्, छ्, ज्, झ्, ञ्), then that consonant from t (त्) class is replaced by the consonant of same order from the ch (च्) class. e.g.

त् + च = च् + च = च्च → आश्चर्यवत् + च = आश्चर्यवच्च (Gītā 2.29)
त् + ज = ज् + ज = ज्ज → स्यात् + जनार्दन = स्याज्जनार्दन (Gītā 1.36)

* When a consonant from t (त्) class (t, th, d, dh, n त्, थ्, द्, ध्, न्), is followed by consonant śh (श्), then that consonant from the t (त्) class (t, th, d, dh, n त्, थ्, द्, ध्, न्), is replaced by the consonant of same order from the ch (च्) class (ch, chh, j, jh, ñ च्, छ्, ज्, झ्, ञ्).

And the following consonant śh (श्) is optionally replaced by consonant chh (छ्)

त् + श = च् + छ = च्छ → यत् + शोकम् = यच्छोकम् (Gītā 2.8)
त् + श्र = च् + छ्र = च्छ्र → युद्धात् + श्रेयः = युद्धाच्छ्रेयः (Gītā 2.31)

* However, When consonant t (त्) or d (द्) is followed by consonant l (ल्), then that consonant t (त्) or d (द्) is replaced by consonant l (ल्) e.g.

त् + ल = ल् + ल = ल्ल → भुवनात् + लोकाः = भुवनाल्लोकाः (Gita 8.16)

(5) Nasal Inflections : If a consonant, other than a nasal consonant, from any class (k, ch, ṭ, t, p क, च, ट, त प), is followed by a nasal consonant, then this class consonant is optionally replaced by the nasal consonant from the same class.

त् + न = न् + न = न्न → तस्मात् + न = तस्मान्न (Gītā 1.37)
त् + म = न् + म = न्म → तत् + मैं = तन्मैं (Gītā 1.46)
द् + म = न् + म = न्म → सुहृद् + मित्रम् = सुहृन्मित्रम् (Gītā 6.9)

(6) म् becomes a nasal dot (अनुस्वार) : When a word ending in letter m (म्) is followed by a word starting with any consonant, then that end-letter m (म्) becomes a nasal dot, and that is placed over the character that is before m (म्). e.g.

पाण्डवानीकम् व्यूढम् = पाण्डवानीकं व्यूढम्। (Gītā 1.2)

* But, when a word ending in letter m (म्) is at the end of the sentence, that letter m (म्) remains unchanged.

पश्यैतां पाण्डुपुत्राणामाचार्य महतीं चमूम्।।25।। (Gītā 1.3)

पर्याप्तं त्विदमेतेषां बलं भीमाभिरक्षितम्।।26।। (Gītā 1.10)

(7) Change of n (न्) to ṇ (ण्) at the end of a word :

(a) When letter n (न्) within or at the end of a word is preceded by letter ri, rí, r or ṣh (ऋ, ॠ, र्, ष्); and

(b) between this n (न्) and the preceding ri, rí, r or ṣh (ऋ, ॠ, र्, ष्), even if any vowel, an anusvāra, a consonant from class k (क्) or a consonant from class p (प्) or letter y, r, v or h (य्, र्, व् ह्) comes,

(c) in all these cases, this n (न्) changes to ṇ (ण्). e.g.

द्रुपदपुत्रेण	→ त् + र् + ए + न	= त् + र् + ए + ण	=	त्रेण (Gītā 1.3)
शरीरिण:	→ र् + इ + न:	= र् + इ + ण:	=	रिण: (Gītā 2.18)
कर्मणा	→ र् + म् + अ + न् + आ	= र् + म् + अ + ण् + आ	=	र्मणा (Gītā 3.20)

(8) Change of s (स्) to ṣh (ष्) at the end of a word : If a vowel other than *a* or *ā* (अ, आ) or any consonant from the class *k* (क) or the letter *r* (र्) comes after a word ending in a case suffix such as *saḥ, sā, sām, si, su, syati, syate, syanti, syāmi, sye, sva, etc.* (स: सा, साम्, सि, सु, स्यति, स्यते, स्यन्ति, स्यामि, स्ये, स्व), then, in all these cases, the *s* (स्) in these suffixes changes to *ṣh* (ष्)

एष: (Gītā 3.10) एषा (Gītā 2.39) एतेषाम् (Gītā 1.10) करोषि (Gītā 9.27)
अयनेषु (Gītā 1.11) परिशुष्यति (Gītā 1.29) कथयिष्यन्ति (Gītā 2.34) विशिष्यते (Gītā 7.17)
कथयिष्यामि (Gītā 10.19) हनिष्ये (Gītā 16.14) कुरुष्व (Gītā 9.27)

(2) PANINI'S SUTRAS FOR CONSONANT SANDHI

(1) स्तोः श्चुना श्चुः *stoḥ śhchunā śhchuḥ* (8 :4 :40)

When a consonant of class त (t) is followed by consonant श् or स् (śh or s), the consonant of the class त (त्, थ्, द्, ध्, न् t, th, d, dh, n) is replaced with corresponding consonant from the class च (च्, छ्, ज्, झ्, ञ् ch, chh, j, jh, ñ).

(2) शात् *śhāt* (8 :4 :44)

If consonant श् (śh) is followed by a consonant from the class त (t), the class त (t) consonant is not changed to class च (ch).

(3) ष्टुना ष्टुः *ṣhṭunā ṣhṭuḥ* (8 :4 :41)

When consanant स् (s) or a consonant of class त (t) is followed by consonant of class त (t), the consonant स् (s) changes to consonant ष् (ṣh), and consonant of the class त (त्, थ्, द्, ध्, न् t, th, d, dh, n) changes to the corresponding consonant of the class ट (ट्, ठ्, ड्, ढ्, ण् ṭ, ṭh, ḍ, ḍh, ṇ).

(4) न पदान्ताट्टोरनाम् *na padāntāṭṭoranām* (8 :4 :42)

When consonant from class ट् (ṭ) at the end of a word is followed by a word beginning with consonant स् (s) or a consonant from class त् (t), the स् (s) does not change to ष् (ṣh), and the consonant from class त् (t) does not change to the corresponding consonant from class ट् (ṭ).

(5) तोः षिः *toḥ ṣhiḥ* (8 :4 :43)

When consonant from class त् (t) at the end of a word is followed by a word beginning with consonant ष् (ṣh), the consonant from class त् (t) does not change to the corresponding consonant from class ट् (ṭ).

(6) झलां जशोऽन्ते *jhalām jaśho'nte* (8 :2 :49)

When a word that ends in a *jhal* झल् (the 1st, 2nd, 3rd, 4th class consonants and the *uṣhma* sibilant consonants श्, ष, स् *śh, ṣh, s,* i.e. any consonant other than य्, र, ल, व्, ङ्, ञ्, ण्,

न्, म् y, r, l, v, ṅ, ñ, ṇ, n, m), is followed by any character, the *jhal* changes to *jaśh* जश् (the third consonant of it's class, i.e. ग, ज, ड, द, ब g, j, ḍ, d, b).

(7) झलां जश् झशि *jhalām jaśh jhaśhi* (8 :4 :53)

When a word (substantive or verb) that ends in a *jhal* झल् (the 1st, 2nd, 3rd, 4th class consonants and the *uṣhma* consonants श्, ष, स्, ह् *śh, ṣh, s, h,* i.e. any consonant other than य्, र, ल, व्, ङ्, ञ्, ण्, न्, म् y, r, l, v, ṅ, ñ, ṇ, n, m), is followed by a *jhaśh* झश् (the 3rd and 4th class consonants i.e. ग, घ, ज, झ, ड, ढ, द, ध, ब, भ g, gh, j, jh, ḍ, ḍh, d, dh, b, bh), then the *jhal* झल् changes to *jaśh* जश् (the third consonant of it's class, i.e. ग, ज, ड, द, ब g, j, ḍ, d, b).

(8) यरोऽनुनासिकेऽनुनासिको वा *yaro'nunāsike'nunāsiko vā* (8 :4 :45)

When a word (substantive or verb) that ends in a *yar* यर् (any consonant other than ह् h), if followed by a nasal consonant (5th class consonant ङ्, ञ्, ण्, न्, म् ṅ, ñ, ṇ, n, or m), then the *yar* यर् changes to it's corresponding nasal consonant.

(9) तोर्लि *torli* (8 :4 :60)

When consonant from class त् (t) at the end of a word is followed by a word beginning with consonant ल् (l), the त् (t) also changes to ल् (l). However, if न् (n) is followed by ल् (l), the न् (n) changes to nasal लँ (ँ).

(10) उदः स्थास्तम्भो पूर्वस्य *udaḥ sthāstambho pūrvasya* (8 :4 :61)

When the prefix उत् (ut) is followed by verb root √sthā √स्था or √stambh √स्तम्भ्, the स् (s) of √sthā √स्था or √stambh √स्तम्भ् changes to थ् (th) and this थ् (th) gets deleted. If a consonant from class त् (t) at the end of a word is followed by a word beginning with consonant ल् (l), the त् (t) also changes to ल् (l). However, if न् (n) is followed by ल् (l), the न् (n) changes to nasal लँ (ँ).

(11) झरो झरि सवर्णे *jharo jhari savarṇe* (8 :4 :65)

When a consonant is followed by a *jhar* झर् (sibilants + class consonants - nasals क्-घ्, च्-झ्, ट्-ढ्, त्-ध् प्-भ् + श्, ष्, स्), the *jhar* झर् is optionally deleted.

(12) खरि च *khari cha* (8 :4 :55)

When any consonant other than a *jhal* झल् (the 1st, 2nd, 3rd, 4th class consonants and the *ushma* consonants श्, ष, स्, ह् *śh, ṣh, s, h,* i.e. any consonant other than य्, र, ल, व्, ङ्, ञ्, ण्, न्, म् y, r, l, v, ṅ, ñ, ṇ, n, m), is followe by a *khar* खर् (the 1st and 2nd class consonants क् ख् च् छ् ट् ठ् त् थ् प् फ् *k, kh, ch, chh, ṭ, ṭh, t, th, p, ph*), then the *jhal* झल् changes to *char* चर् (the 1st consonant of it's class).

(13) वाऽवसाने *vā'vasāne* (8 :4 :56)

When any consonant *jhal* झल् (the 1st, 2nd, 3rd, 4th class consonants and the *ushma* consonants श्, ष, स्, ह् *śh, ṣh, s, h,* i.e. any consonant other than य्, र, ल, व्, ङ्, ञ्, ण्, न्, म् y, r, l, v, ṅ, ñ, ṇ, n, m), is not followed by any character, the *jhal* झल् changes to the 1st or optionally the 3rd character of it's class.

(14) झयो होऽन्यतरस्याम् *jhayo ho'nyatarasyām* (8 :4 :62)

When any consonant *jhay* झय् (any class consonant other than the 5th nasal characters) is followed by ह् h, then optionally the *jhay* झय् changes to the 4th character of its class (घ्, झ्, ढ, ध्, भ् gh, jh, ḍh, dh, bh). i.e. any consonant other than य्, र, ल, व्, ङ्, ञ्, ण्, न्, म् y, r, l, v, ṅ, ñ, ṇ, n, or m, - is not followed by any character, the *jhal* झल् changes to the 1st or optionally the 3rd character of it's class.

(15) शश्छोऽटि *śhaśhchhoṭi* (8 :4 :63)

When any consonant *jhal* झल् (the 1st, 2nd, 3rd, 4th class consonants and the *ushma* consonants श्, ष, स्, ह् *śh, ṣh, s, h,* i.e. any consonant other than य्, र, ल, व्, ङ्, ञ्, ण्, न्, म् y, r, l, v, ṅ, ñ, ṇ, n, m), is followed by श् *śh,* the श् *śh* changes to छ् *chh.*

And, if this श् *śh* is followed by an *aṭ* अट् (any vowel or य् र्, व, ह् *y, r, v, h*), then optionally, according to the Sutra 1 and 12 given above, consonant च् *ch* is attached before that छ् *chh.*

(16) मोऽनुस्वारः *mo'nusvāraḥ* (8 :3 :23)

When a word ending in म् m is followed by a word beginning with a consonant, the म् m is changed to the nasal dot (ं).

However, When a word ending in म् m is followed by a word beginning with a vowel, then the म् m is not changed to the nasal dot. The vowel will join the म् m.

(17) नश्चापदान्तस्य झलि *naśhchāpadāntasya jhali* (8 :3 :24)

When a word ending in म् m is followed by a *jhal* झल् (the 1st, 2nd, 3rd, 4th class consonants and the *uṣhma* consonants श्, ष, स्, ह् *śh, ṣh, s, h,* i.e. any consonant other than य्, र, ल, व्, ङ्, ञ्, ण्, न्, म् y, r, l, v, ṅ, ñ, ṇ, n, m), then the म् m is changed to the nasal dot.

(18) अनुस्वारस्य ययि परसवर्णः *anusvārasya yayi parasavarṇaḥ* (8 :4 :58)

Within a word, when the anusvāra nasal dot (ं) is followed by a यय् *yay* (any consonant other than the uṣhma श्, ष्, स् ह् śh, ṣh, s, h), the anusvāra nasal dot is changed to parasvarṇa (the 5th nasal letter of the same class as the यय् *yay* letter following the nasal dot).

(19) वा पदान्तस्य *vā padāntasya* (8 :4 :59)

In a sentence, when the anusvāra nasal dot (ं) at the end of a word is followed by a word beginning with a यय् *yay* (any consonant other than the uṣhma श्, ष्, स् ह् śh, ṣh, s, h), the anusvāra nasal dot is changed to parasvarṇa (the 5th nasal letter of the same class as the यय् *yay* letter following the nasal dot) and these two words join in a sandhi.

(20) नश्छव्यप्रशान् *naśhchvyapraśhān* (8 :3 :7)

Other than the word प्रशान् *praśhān*, when any other word ending in consonant न् n is followed by a छव् chhav (च्, छ्, ट्, ठ्, त्, थ् ch, chh, ṭ, ṭh, t, th) and the छव् chhav is followed by an अम् am (any vowel or य, र्, ल्, व, ङ्, ञ्, ण्, न्, म् y, r, l, v, ṅ, ñ, ṇ, n, m), then the न् n at end of that word is changed to स् s and joins with the following word in a sandhi.

(21) ङसि धुट् *ṅgasi dhuṭ* (8:3:29)

If ङ् ṅ is followed by स् s, then धुट् dhuṭ (ट् ṭ) comes between the ङ् ṅ and स् s.

(22) नश्च *naśhcha* (8 :3 :30)

When स् s comes after letter ङ् ṅ, then optionally dhuṭ (त् t) comes between स् s and ङ् ṅ.

(23) ङ्णोः कुक्टुक्शरि *ṅgaṇoḥ kukṭukśhari* (8 :3 :28)

When शर् śhar (श्, ष्, स् śh, ṣh, s) comes between ङ् ṅ and ण् ṇ, then optionally letter letter क् k or ट् ṭ) comes and forms sandhi.

(24) ङमो ह्रस्वादचि ङमुण् नित्यम् *ṅgmo hrasvādchiṅgmuṇ nityam* (8:3:32)

When ङ्, ण् or न् ṅ, ṇ, or n comes after a vowel and any vowel comes after this ङ्, ण् or न् ṅ, ṇ, or n, then the ङ्, ण् or न् ṅ, ṇ, or n becomes double.

(25) शि तुक् *śhi tuk* (8 :3 :31)

When न् n at the end of a word is followed by consonant श् śh, then तुक् tuk (त् t) is optionally added between that न् n and श् śh.

(26) छे च *chhe cha* (6 :1 :72)

When छ् chh comes after a short vowel, then त् t comes between छ् chh and the short vowel and this त् t change to च् ch, according to the sūtra # 1 given above.

(27) दीर्घात् *dīrghāt* (6 :1 :74)

When छ् chh comes after a long vowel, then त् t comes between छ् chh and the short vowel and this त् t change to च् ch, according to the sūtra # 1 given above.

(28) पदान्ताद्वा *padāntādvā* (6 :1 :75)

When छ् chh comes after a word ending in a long vowel, then त् t is added to the छ् chh and and this त् t changes to च् ch, according to the sūtra # 1 given above.

(29) आङ्माङोश्च *āṅgmāṅgośhcha* (6 :1 :73)

When छ् chh comes after आङ् āṅg (आ ā) and माङ् māṅg (मा mā), then त् t is prefixed to the छ् chh and and this त् t changes to च् ch, according to the sūtra # 1 given above.

COMPOUNDING DEVANAGARI CONSONANTS

+	क	ख	ग	घ	च	छ	ज	झ	ट	ठ	ड	ढ	ण	त	थ	द
क्	क्क	क्ख	क्ग	क्घ	क्च	क्छ	क्ज	क्झ	क्ट	क्ठ	क्ड	क्ढ	ल्ण	क्त	क्थ	क्द
ख्	ख्क	ख्ख	ख्ग	ख्घ	ख्च	ख्छ	ख्ज	ख्झ	ख्ट	ख्ठ	ख्ड	डढ	ख्ण	ख्त	ख्थ	ख्द
ग्	ग्क	ग्ख	ग्ग	ग्घ	ग्च	ग्छ	ग्ज	ग्झ	ग्ट	ग्ठ	ग्ड	ग्ढ	ग्ण	ग्त	ग्थ	ग्द
घ्	घ्क	घ्ख	घ्ग	घ्घ	घ्च	घ्छ	घ्ज	घ्झ	घ्ट	घ्ठ	घ्ड	घ्ढ	घ्ण	घ्त	घ्थ	घ्द
ङ्	ङ्क	ङ्ख	ङ्ग	ङ्घ	ङ्च	ङ्छ	ङ्ज	ङ्झ	ङ्ट	ङ्ठ	ङ्ड	ङ्ढ	ङ्ण	ङ्त	ङ्थ	ङ्द
च्	च्क	च्ख	च्ग	च्घ	च्च	च्छ	च्ज	च्झ	च्ट	च्ठ	च्ड	च्ढ	च्ण	च्त	च्थ	च्द
छ्	छ्क	छ्ख	छ्ग	छ्घ	छ्च	छ्छ	छ्ज	छ्झ	छ्ट	छ्ठ	छ्ड	छ्ढ	छ्ण	छ्त	छ्थ	छ्द
ज्	ज्क	ज्ख	ज्ग	ज्घ	ज्च	ज्छ	ज्ज	ज्झ	ज्ट	ज्ठ	ज्ड	ज्ढ	ज्ण	ज्त	ज्थ	ज्द
झ्	झ्क	झ्ख	झ्ग	झ्घ	झ्च	झ्छ	झ्ज	झ्झ	झ्ट	झ्ठ	झ्ड	झ्ढ	झ्ण	झ्त	झ्थ	झ्द
ञ्	ञ्क	ञ्ख	ञ्ग	ञ्घ	ञ्च	ञ्छ	ञ्ज	ञ्झ	ञ्ट	ञ्ठ	ञ्ड	ञ्ढ	ञ्ण	ञ्त	ञ्थ	ञ्द
ट्	ट्क	ट्ख	ट्ग	ट्घ	ट्च	ट्छ	ट्ज	ट्झ	ट्ट	ट्ठ	ट्ड	ट्ढ	ट्ण	ट्त	ट्थ	ट्द
ठ्	ठ्क	ठ्ख	ठ्ग	ठ्घ	ठ्च	ठ्छ	ठ्ज	ठ्झ	ठ्ट	ठ्ठ	ठ्ड	ठ्ढ	ठ्ण	ठ्त	ठ्थ	ठ्द
ड्	ड्क	ड्ख	ड्ग	ड्घ	ड्च	ड्छ	ड्ज	ड्झ	ड्ट	ड्ठ	ड्ड	ड्ढ	ड्ण	ड्त	ड्थ	ड्द
ढ्	ढ्क	ढ्ख	ढ्ग	ढ्घ	ढ्च	ढ्छ	ढ्ज	ढ्झ	ढ्ट	ढ्ठ	ढ्ड	ढ्ढ	ढ्ण	ढ्त	ढ्थ	ढ्द
ण्	ण्क	ण्ख	ण्ग	ण्घ	ण्च	ण्छ	ण्ज	ण्झ	ण्ट	ण्ठ	ण्ड	ण्ढ	ण्ण	ण्त	ण्थ	ण्द
त्	त्क	त्ख	द्ग	द्घ	च्च	छ्छ	ज्ज	झ्झ	द्ट	द्ठ	द्ड	द्ढ	द्ण	त्त	त्थ	द्द
थ्	थ्क	थ्ख	ध्ग	ध्घ	थ्च	थ्छ	थ्ज	थ्झ	थ्ट	थ्ठ	थ्ड	थ्ढ	थ्ण	थ्त	थ्थ	ध्द
द्	द्क	द्ख	द्ग	द्घ	च्च	छ्छ	ज्ज	झ्झ	द्ट	द्ठ	द्ड	द्ढ	द्ण	त्त	त्थ	द्द
ध्	ध्क	ध्ख	ध्ग	ध्घ	ध्च	ध्छ	ध्ज	ध्झ	ध्ट	ध्ठ	ध्ड	ध्ढ	ध्ण	ध्त	ध्थ	ध्द
न्	न्क	न्ख	न्ग	न्घ	ञ्च	ञ्छ	ञ्ज	ञ्झ	ण्ट	ण्ठ	ण्ड	ण्ढ	ण्ण	न्त	न्थ	न्द
प्	प्क	प्ख	प्ग	प्घ	प्च	प्छ	प्ज	प्झ	प्ट	प्ठ	प्ड	प्ढ	प्ण	प्त	प्थ	प्द
फ्	फ्क	फ्ख	फ्ग	फ्घ	फ्च	फ्छ	फ्ज	फ्झ	फ्ट	फ्ठ	फ्ड	फ्ढ	फ्ण	फ्त	फ्थ	फ्द

ब्	ब्क	ब्ख	ब्ग	ब्घ	ब्च	ब्छ	ब्ज	ब्झ	ब्ट	ब्ठ	ब्ड	ब्ढ	ब्ण	ब्त	ब्थ	ब्द
भ्	भ्क	भ्ख	भ्ग	भ्घ	भ्च	भ्छ	भ्ज	भ्झ	भ्ट	भ्ठ	भ्ड	भ्ढ	भ्ण	भ्त	भ्थ	भ्द
म्	ङ्क	ङ्ख	ङ्ग	ङ्घ	ङ्च	ङ्छ	ङ्ज	ङ्झ	म्ट	म्ठ	म्ड	म्ढ	म्ण	म्त	म्थ	म्द
य्	य्क	य्ख	य्ग	य्घ	य्च	य्छ	य्ज	य्झ	य्ट	य्ठ	य्ड	य्ढ	य्ण	य्त	य्थ	य्द
र्	र्क	र्ख	र्ग	र्घ	र्च	र्छ	र्ज	र्झ	र्ट	र्ठ	र्ड	र्ढ	र्ण	र्त	र्थ	र्द
ल्	ल्क	ल्ख	ल्ग	ल्घ	ल्च	ल्छ	ल्ज	ल्झ	ल्ट	ल्ठ	ल्ड	ल्ढ	ल्ण	ल्त	ल्थ	ल्द
व्	व्क	व्ख	व्ग	व्घ	व्च	व्छ	व्ज	व्झ	व्ट	व्ठ	व्ड	व्ढ	व्ण	व्त	व्थ	व्द
श्	श्क	श्ख	श्ग	श्घ	श्च	श्छ	श्ज	श्झ	श्ट	श्ठ	श्ड	श्ढ	श्ण	श्त	श्थ	श्द
ष्	ष्क	ष्ख	ष्ग	ष्घ	ष्च	ष्छ	ष्ज	ष्झ	ष्ट	ष्ठ	ष्ड	ष्ढ	ष्ण	ष्त	ष्थ	ष्द
स्	स्क	स्ख	स्ग	स्घ	स्च	स्छ	स्ज	स्झ	स्ट	स्ठ	स्ड	स्ढ	स्ण	स्त	स्थ	स्द
ह्	ह्क	ह्ख	ह्ग	ह्घ	ह्च	ह्छ	ह्ज	ह्झ	ह्ट	ह्ठ	ह्ड	ह्ढ	ह्ण	ह्त	ह्थ	ह्द

+	ध	न	प	फ	ब	भ	म	य	र	ल	व	श	ष	स	ह
क्	क्ध	क्न	ग्प	ग्फ	ग्ब	ग्भ	क्म	क्य	क्र	क्ल	क्व	क्श	क्ष	क्स	ख
ख्	ख्ध	ख्न	ख्प	ख्फ	ख्ब	ख्भ	ख्म	ख्य	ख्र	ख्ल	ख्व	ख्श	ख्ष	ख्स	ख्ख
ग्	ग्ध	ग्न	ग्प	ग्फ	ग्ब	ग्भ	ग्म	ग्य	ग्र	ग्ल	ग्व	ग्श	ग्ष	ग्स	घ
घ्	घ्ध	घ्न	घ्प	घ्फ	घ्ब	घ्भ	घ्म	घ्य	घ्र	घ्ल	घ्व	घ्श	घ्ष	घ्स	घ्ह
ङ्	ङ्ध	ङ्न	ङ्प	ङ्फ	ङ्ब	ङ्भ	ङ्म	ङ्य	ङ्र	ङ्ल	ङ्व	ङ्श	ङ्क्ष	ङ्स	ङ्घ
च्	च्ध	च्न	ज्प	ज्फ	च्ब	च्भ	च्म	च्य	च्र	च्ल	च्व	च्श	च्ष	च्त	छ
छ्	छ्ध	छ्न	छ्प	छ्फ	छ्ब	छ्भ	छ्म	छ्य	छ्र	छ्ल	छ्व	छ्श	छ्ष	छ्स	छ्छ
ज्	ज्ध	ज्न	ज्प	ज्फ	ज्ब	ज्भ	ज्म	ज्य	ज्र	ज्ल	ज्व	ज्श	ज्ष	ज्स	ज्झ
झ्	झ्ध	झ्न	झ्प	झ्फ	झ्ब	झ्भ	झ्म	झ्य	झ्र	झ्ल	झ्व	झ्श	झ्ष	झ्स	झ्झ
ञ्	ञ्ध	ञ्न	ञ्प	ञ्फ	ञ्ब	ञ्भ	ञ्म	ञ्य	ञ्र	ञ्ल	ञ्व	ञ्श	ञ्ष	ञ्स	ञ्ह
ट्	ट्ध	ट्ण	ट्प	ट्फ	ट्ब	ट्भ	ट्म	ट्य	ट्र	ट्ल	ट्व	ट्श	ट्ष	ट्स	ठ
ठ्	ठ्ध	ठ्ण	ठ्प	ठ्फ	ठ्ब	ठ्भ	ठ्म	ठ्य	ठ्र	ठ्ल	ठ्व	ठ्श	ठ्ष	ठ्स	ठ्ह
ड्	ड्ध	ड्ण	ड्प	ड्फ	ड्ब	ड्भ	ड्म	ड्य	ड्र	ड्ल	ड्व	ड्श	ड्ष	ड्स	ढ
ढ्	ढ्ध	ढ्ण	ढ्प	ढ्फ	ढ्ब	ढ्भ	ढ्म	ढ्य	ढ्र	ढ्ल	ढ्व	ढ्श	ढ्ष	ढ्स	ढ्ह

ण्	ण्ध	ण्ण	ण्प	ण्फ	ण्ब	ण्भ	ण्म	ण्य	ण्र	ण्ल	ण्व	ण्श	ण्ष	ण्स	ण्ह
त्	द्ध	त्न	त्प	त्फ	द्ब	द्भ	त्म	त्य	त्र	त्ल	त्व	त्श	त्ष	त्स	थ
थ्	थ्ध	थ्न	ध्प	ध्फ	थ्ब	थ्भ	थ्म	थ्य	थ्र	थ्ल	थ्व	थ्श	थ्ष	थ्स	थ्थ
द्	द्ध	द्न	द्प	द्फ	द्ब	द्भ	द्ज	द्झ	द्र	द्ल	द्व	द्श	द्ष	द्स	ध्ह
ध्	ध्ध	ध्न	ध्प	ध्फ	ध्ब	ध्भ	ध्म	ध्य	ध्र	ध्ल	ध्व	ध्श	ध्ष	ध्स	ध्ध
न्	न्ध	न्न	न्प	न्फ	न्ब	न्भ	न्म	न्य	न्र	न्ल	न्व	ञ्श	ञ्ष	न्स	न्ह
प्	प्ध	प्न	प्प	प्फ	प्ब	प्भ	प्म	प्य	प्र	प्ल	प्व	प्श	प्ष	प्स	प्ह
फ्	फ्फ	फ्न	फ्प	फ्फ	फ्ब	फ्भ	फ्म	फ्य	फ्र	फ्ल	फ्ब	फ्श	फ्ष	फ्स	फ्ह
ब्	ब्ध	ब्न	ब्प	ब्फ	ब्ब	ब्भ	ब्म	ब्य	ब्र	ब्ल	ब्व	ब्श	ब्ष	ब्स	भ
भ्	भ्ध	भ्न	भ्प	भ्फ	भ्ब	भ्भ	भ्म	भ्य	भ्र	भ्ल	भ्ब	भ्श	भ्ष	भ्स	भ्ह
म्	म्ध	म्न	म्प	म्फ	म्ब	म्भ	म्म	म्य	म्र	म्ल	म्व	म्श	म्ष	म्स	म्ह
य्	य्ध	य्न	य्प	य्फ	य्ब	य्भ	य्म	य्य	य्र	य्ल	य्व	य्श	य्ष	य्स	य्ह
र्	र्ध	र्न	र्प	र्फ	र्ब	र्भ	र्म	र्य	र्र	र्ल	र्व	र्श	र्ष	र्स	र्ह
ल्	ल्ध	ल्न	ल्प	ल्फ	ल्ब	ल्भ	ल्म	ल्य	ल्र	ल्ल	ल्व	ल्श	ल्ष	ल्स	ल्ह
व्	व्ध	व्न	व्प	व्फ	व्ब	व्भ	व्म	व्य	व्र	व्ल	व्व	व्श	व्ष	व्स	व्ह
श्	श्ध	श्न	श्प	श्फ	श्ब	श्भ	श्म	श्य	श्र	श्ल	श्व	श्श	श्ष	श्स	श्ह
ष्	ष्क	ष्ख	ष्प	ष्फ	ष्ब	ष्भ	ष्म	ष्य	ष्र	ष्ल	ष्व	ष्श	ष्ष	ष्स	ष्थ
स्	स्ध	स्न	स्प	स्फ	स्ब	स्भ	स्म	स्य	स्र	स्ल	स्व	स्श	स्ष	स्स	स्ह
ह्	ह्ध	ह्न	ह्प	ह्फ	ह्ब	ह्भ	ह्म	ह्य	ह्र	ह्ल	ह्व	ह्श	ह्ष	ह्स	ह्ह

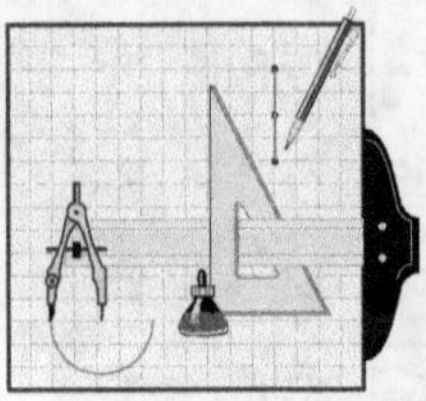

CONJUGATION WITH A VISARGA (:)
विसर्गसन्धि

RATNAKAR'S UNIQUE FLOWCHART FOR VISARGA SANDHI

Before the visarga	the visarga	After the visarga	The result
1. एष: स:	:	other than अ	**visarga is deleted**
↓			
2. Any character	:	त, थ	**visarga becomes स्**
↓			
3. any other character	:	च, छ	**visarga becomes श्**
↓			
4. any chcharacter	:	ट, ठ	**visarge becomes ष्**
↓		श, ष्, स	**visarge becomes श् . स्**
5. any other ch.	:	any hard character	**visarga remains**
↓			
6. आ	:	any other ch.	**visarga is deleted**
↓			
7. अ	:	अ	**(अ + :) become ओऽ**
↓			
8. अ	:	other vowel	**visarga is deleted**
↓			
9. अ	:	soft consonant	**visarga becomes ओ**
↓			
10. other vowel	:	any character	**visarga becomes र्**

EXAMPLES OF THE ABOVE TEN RULES ARE GIVEN BELOW :

1. एषः क्रोधः → एष क्रोधः (Gītā 3.37)
   एषः रजोगुणः → एष रजोगुणः (Gītā 3.37)
   एषः तु → एष तु (Gītā 10.40)
   सः शब्दः → स शब्दः (Gītā 1.13)
   सः कौन्तेयः → स कौन्तेयः (Gītā 1.27)
2. सौमदत्तिः तथा → सौमदत्तिस्तथा (Gītā 1.2)
   शब्दः तुमुलः → शब्दस्तुमुलः (Gītā 1.13)
   शिष्यः ते → शिष्यस्ते (Gītā 2.6)
3. पाण्डवाः च → पाण्डवाश्च (Gītā 1.1)
   विराटः च → विराटश्च (Gītā 1.4)
   विभ्रष्टः छिन्न → विभ्रष्टश्छिन्न (Gītā 6.38)
4. रामः टीकते → रामष्टीकते
   रामः ठक्कुरः → रामष्ठक्कुरः
5. चेकितानः काशिराजः → चेकितानः काशिराजः (Gītā 1.5)
   मामकाः पाण्डवाः → मामकाः पाण्डवाः (Gītā 1.1)
   योगेश्वरः कृष्णः → योगेश्वरः कृष्णः (Gītā 18.78)
6. समवेताः युयुत्सवः → समवेता युयुत्सवः (Gītā 1.1)
   शूराः महेश्वासाः → शूरा महेश्वासाः (Gītā 1.3)
   गुणाः गुणेषु → गुणा गुणेषु (Gītā 3.28)
7. तुमुलः अभवत् → तुमुलोऽभवत् (Gītā 1.13)
   शाश्वतः अयम् → शाश्वतोऽयम् (Gītā 2.20)
   सः अमृतत्त्वाय कल्पते → सोऽमृतत्त्वाय कल्पते (Gītā 2.15)
8. यः एनम् → य एनम् (Gītā 2.19)
   अतः ऊर्ध्वम् → अत ऊर्ध्वम् (Gītā 12.8)
   अव्ययः ईश्वरः → अव्यय ईश्वरः (Gītā 15.17)
9. श्रेयः भोक्तुम् → श्रेयो भोक्तुम् (Gītā 2.5)
   पार्थः धनुर्धरः → पार्थो धनुर्धरः (Gītā 18.78)
   विजयः भूतिः → विजयो भूतिः (Gītā 18.78)

10. मुनि: उच्यते → मुनिरुच्यते (Gītā 2.56)
दोषै: एतै: → दोषैरेतै: (Gītā 1.43)
सेनयो: उभयो: → सेनयोरुभयो: (Gītā 1.21)
स्थितधी: मुनि: → स्थितधीर्मुनि: (Gītā 2.56)
भू: मा → भूर्मा (Gītā 2.47)
उभयो: मध्ये → उभयोर्मध्ये (Gītā 1.21)

NOTES :

(1) Once any *sandhi* rule is applied between two words, those two words do not conjugate again with any of the other *sandhi* rule.

e.g. In विक्रान्त: उत्तमौजा: (Gītā 1.6), विक्रान्त: and उत्तमौजा: are conjugated into विक्रान्त उत्तमौजा: with rule 9. Now विक्रान्त उत्तमौजा: CAN NOT again be conjugated into विक्रान्तोत्तमौजा: using the *sandhi* rule अ + उ = ओ, with rule 10.1

(2) The visarga before श, ष or स (*śha, ṣha or sa*), either stays or is optionally changed to श्, ष्, स् respectively.

Difference between Sandhi and Samāsa

1. In Sandhi (संधि), the end leter of the first word changes and merges into the first letter of the next word when two words are joined together to render a compound meaning. e.g. यदि + अपि = यद्यपि, मन: + बल = मनोबल
2. In samāsa (समास), when two words are joined together to produce a compound word, the Case suffix (*vibhakti* विभक्ति) of each word is dropped, other than in *aluk* (अलुक) Samāsa, e.g. युधि + स्थिर = युधिष्ठिर. Sometimes the end character of the first word is also changed or dropped. e.g. राजन् = कुमार – राजकुमार. In Samāsa, the न् of राजन् is dropped.

(3) PANINI'S SUTRAS FOR VISARGA SANDHI

(All these rules are summarized in the simple Ratnakar's Flow Chart shown above)

(1) ससजुषो रुः *sasajuṣho ruḥ* (8 :2 :66)

If visarga (स् s) at the end of a word is preceeded by any vowel other than अ, आ (a, ā) and followed by a vowel or a soft or a nasal consonant, the the visarga becomes र् (r).

(2) खरवसानयोर्विसर्जनीयः *kharavasānayorvisarjanīyaḥ* (8 :3 :15)

If visarga is followed by nothing or by a खर *khar* (a hard consonant), then the visarga stays.

(3) वा शरि *vā śhari* (8 :3 :36)

If visarga (स् s) at the end of a word is followed by शर् *śhar* (श्, ष्, स् śh, ṣh, s), then optionally the visarga becomes the following शर् *śhar* letter, and forms sandhi between the two words.

(4) शर्परे विसर्जनीयः *śharpare visarjanīyaḥ* (8 :3 :35)

When the visarga (स् s) at the end of a word is followed by त् or थ् *t* or *th* and if a शर् *śhar* (श्, ष्, स् śh, ṣh, s) comes after this त् or थ् *t* or *th,* then this visarga stays.

(5) इणः षः *iṇaḥ ṣhaḥ* (8 :3 :39)

If इण् *iṇ* (any vowel other than अ a, and य्, र्, ल्, व्, ह् y, r, l, v, h) comes before visarga, and the visarga is followed by क्, ख्, प् or फ् *k, kh, p* or *ph*, then the ष् ṣh comes in place of the visarga.

(6) नमस्पुरसोर्गत्योः *namaspurasorgatyoḥ* (8 :3 :40)

If the visarga of the word नमः or पुरः *namaḥ* or *puraḥ* is followed by a consonant of the k-class or p-class, then the visarga becomes स् s.

(7) इदुदुपधस्य चाप्रत्ययस्य *idudupadhasya chāpratyayasya* (8 :3 :41)

If the letter before the last visarga of a word has vowel इ or उ *e* or *u* and the visarga is followed by a word beginning with a consonant of k-class or p-class, then the this visarga becomes ष् *ṣh.* This rule does not apply if this visarga belongs to a suffix.

(6) इसुसोः सामर्थ्ये *isusoḥ sāmarthye* (8 :3 :44)

When the sandhi is possible, the visarga after इस् and उस् (*is* and *us*) becomes ष् *ṣh* when a letter from k-class or p-class comes after the visarga.

(7) नित्यं समासेऽनुत्तरपदस्थस्य *nityam samāse'nuttarapadasthasya* (8 :3 :45)

When the samās is possible, the visarga after इस् and उस् (*is* and *us*) becomes ष् *ṣh* when a word beginning with k-class or p-class comes after such visarga.

(8) अतो रोरप्लुतादप्लुते *ato roraplutādaplute* (6 :1 :111)

When visarga comes after a word ending in vowel अ (*a*), and a word beginning with vowel अ a comes after the visarga, then अः अ (a: a) becomes ओऽ o'. This is according to the svara sandhi sutra #7 given above.

(9) हशि च *haśhi cha* (6 :1 :114)

When visarga comes after a word ending in vowel अ (*a*) and a word beginning with a हश् *haṣh* (a soft consonant, य, र्, ल, व, or ह् *y, r, l, v*, or *h*) comes after the visarga, then the अः हश् (a: *haṣh*) becomes ओऽ हश् *haṣh.* This is also according to the svara sandhi sutra #7 given above.

(10) ढ्रलोपे पूर्वस्य दीर्घोऽणः *dhralope pūrvasya dīrgho'ṇaḥ* (6 :13:110)

When the letter ढ् or र् *ḍha* or *r* at the end of a word has अण् *aṇ* (short vowel अ, इ or उ *a, i* or *u*) before it, and a word beginning with ढ् or र् *ḍha* or *r* comes after it, then this अण् *aṇ* short vowel becomes long.

(11) एतत्तदोः सुलोपोऽकोरनञ्-समासे हलि *etattadoḥ sulopo'koranañ-samāse hali* (6 :1 :132)

When any letter other than vowel अ (*a*) comes after the word एषः or सः *eṣhaḥ* or *saḥ,* the visarga is deleted. In नञ्-समास *nañ-samāsa.* When any consonant comes after the word एषः, एषकः, सः or एषकः *eṣhaḥ, eṣhakaḥ, saḥ* or *eṣhakaḥ,* the visarga is not deleted.

(12) सोऽचि लोपे चेत्पादपूरणम् *so'chi lope chedpādapūraṇam* (6 :1 :134)

If एषः *eṣhaḥ* is a filler word after सः *saḥ* in a shloka, the visarga of सः *saḥ* is deleted and स and एषः *sa* and *eṣḥ* form sandhi सैषः *saiṣhaḥ.*

CHAPTER 3
COMPOUND WORDS
sāmāsa
समास

When TWO or MORE related words are joined together with a **logical defination** to form a single MEANINGFUL word, they forms a *sāmāsik-śhabda* (सामासिकशब्द compound word). अनेकपदानाम् तार्किकम् एकीभवनं समासः।

On the other hand, when TWO words are joined together purely with grammatical rules, to form a single word, it is called a *sandhi* (सन्धि) betweeb two words.

The word *samāsa* comes from ←ind◦ *sam* (सम् equal, even) + par◦ 4√*as* (√अस् to be, unite, aggregate, combine, join, connect, compound). समसनं समासः।
Eight main *samāsas* are briefly explained below, with examples from the Gītā.

A *samāsa* can be formed in five ways. कृत्तद्धितसमासैकशेषसनाद्यन्तधातवः पञ्च वृत्तयः।

(1) By adding suffix to a verbal root;
(2) By attaching suffix to a noun stem;
(3) By joining simpler noun stems into a single word;
(4) By merging two or more nouns with a single stem;
(5) By adding desiderative or other affixes to roots.

NOTE : Before forming a *samasa* between two (or more) words, the words being compounded should generally be first rendered in their original forms, removing the case, gender, number or any other suffixes attached to them. The case, gender, number or any other suffixes are added to the compound word, after forming a *samāsa.*

SAMASA CLASSIFICATION

समास का वर्गीकरण

(A) विशेष-समास (तत्पुरुष-बहुव्रीहि-द्वंद्व-अव्ययीभावादि संज्ञा से युक्त जो है वह विशेष-समास)

(i) तत्पुरुष-समास (प्रायः उत्तरपद प्रधान वाला तत्पुरुष-समास होता है)

(a) सामान्य-समास (सामान्यरूप से पदों में विभक्ति का सम्बन्ध होता है)

(1) प्रथमा-तत्पुरुष-समास (e.g. सर्व आरम्भ, सर्वारम्भ Gītā 12.16)

(2) द्वितीया-तत्पुरुष-समास (e.g. मद्भाव को आगत, मद्भावमागत Gītā 4.10)

(3) तृतीया-तत्पुरुष-समास (e.g. योग से युक्त, योगयुक्त Gītā 5.6)

(4) चतुर्थी-तत्पुरुष-समास (मोक्ष के लिए परायण, मोक्षपरायण Gītā 5.28)

(5) पंचमी-तत्पुरुष-समास (योग से भ्रष्ट, योगभ्रष्ट Gītā 6.41)

(6) षष्ठीत-त्पुरुष-समास (धर्मयुक्त-कर्मों का क्षेत्र, धर्मक्षेत्रम् Gītā 1.1)

(7) सप्तमी-तत्पुरुष-समास (योग में स्थ (स्थित) वह, योगस्थ Gītā 2.48)

(b) कर्मधारय-समास (समानाधिकरण तत्पुरुष वाला कर्मधारय-समास)

(1) जहाँ पूर्वपद विशेष हो वह कर्मधारय-समास (महान् इष्वास, महेष्वास Gītā 1.4)

(2) जहाँ उत्तर पद विशेष हो वह कर्मधारय-समास (रथों में उत्तम, रथोत्तम Gītā 1.24)

(3) जहाँ उभय पद विशेष हों वह कर्मधारय-समास (आगम अपायी, आगमापायी Gītā 2.14)

(4) जहाँ पूर्वपद उपमान हो वह कर्मधारय-समास (सिंह जैसा नाद, सिंहनाद Gītā 1.12)

(5) जहाँ उत्तरपद उपमान हो वह कर्मधारय-समास (नरों में पुङ्गव समान, नरपुङ्गव Gītā 1.5)

(6) जहाँ पूर्वपद अवधारणा हो वह कर्मधारय-समास (ज्ञान ही असि जहाँ, ज्ञानासि Gītā 4.42)

(7) जहाँ पूर्वपद सम्भावना हो वह कर्मधारय-समास (संसार समान सागर, संसारसागर Gītā 12.7)

(8) जहाँ मध्यमपद का लोप हो वह -कर्मधारय-समास (सत्त्व से संशुद्धि, सत्त्वसंशुद्धिः Gītā 16.1)

(9) मयूरव्यंसकादि का कर्मधारय-समास (निवृत्त या निरुद्ध हो वात जहाँ, निवात Gītā 6.19)

(c) द्विगु-समास (सांख्यवाचक सुबन्ते से होने वाला द्विगु-समास)

(1) समाहार-द्विगु-समास (त्रय विधाओं का समाहार, त्रिविध Gītā 16.21)

(2) तद्धित अर्थ का द्विगु-समास (त्रिगुणों में उत्पन्न विषय, त्रैगुण्यविषयाः Gītā 2.45)

(3) उत्तरपद-द्विगु-समास (लोकों का त्रय, लोकत्रय Gītā 11.20)

(d) नञ्-तत्पुरुष-समास (धर्म नहीं जहाँ, अधर्म Gītā 1.40)

(ii) बहुव्रीहि-समास (अन्य पद प्रधान वाला बहुव्रीहि समास)

(a) सामान्य-बहुव्रीहि-समास (सामान्यरूप से पदों में विभक्ति का सम्बन्ध)

(1) द्वितीया-बहुव्रीहि-समास (दु:ख और सुख दोनों समान जिसे, समदु:खसुखम् Gītā 2.15)

(2) तृतीया-बहुव्रीहि-समास (जीत लिए हैं इन्द्रिय जिसने वह, जितेन्द्रिय Gītā 5.7)

(3) चतुर्थी-बहुव्रीहि-समास (मैंने आश्रय दिया जिसे वह, मद्व्यपाश्रय Gītā 18.56)

(4) पञ्चमी-बहुव्रीहि-समास (जिसमें से रस गया है वह, गतरसम् Gītā 17.10)

(5) षष्ठी-बहुव्रीहि-समास (महान जिसका आत्मा वह, महात्मा Gītā 7.19)

(6) सप्तमी-बहुव्रीहि-समास (जिसमें श्रद्धा नहीं वह, श्रद्धाविरहितम् Gītā 17.13)

(b) विशेष-बहुव्रीहि-समास (पदों में वशेष रूप से सम्बन्ध)

(1) व्यधिकरण-बहुव्रीहि-समास (पाणियों में शस्त्र जिनके, शस्त्रपाणय: Gītā 1.46)

(2) संख्योत्तरपद-बहुव्रीहि-समास (मन छठा भाग है जिनका वे, मन:षष्ठानि Gītā 15.7)

(3) संख्योभयपद-बहुव्रीहि-समास (द्वे वा त्रि का समाहार वाला, द्वित्राणि)

(4) सह-बहुव्रीहि-समास (गद्गद गति के साथ, सगद्गदम् Gītā 11.35)

(5) नञ्-बहुव्रीहि-समास (नहीं होता च्युत जो, अच्युत Gītā 1.21)

(iii) द्वंद्व-समास (उभयपदप्रधान: द्वंद्व-समास)

(a) इतरेतर-द्वंद्व-समास (दो अयवा अनेक पदों के समाहार वाला)

(1) द्विपद-द्वंद्व-समास (सुघोष और मणिपुष्पक, सुघोषमणिपुष्पकौ Gītā 1.16)

(2) बहुपद-द्वंद्व-समास (पणव आनक और गोमुख च, पणवानकगोमुखा: Gītā 1.13)

(b) समाहार-द्वंद्व-समास (संज्ञाओं अथवा परिभाषाओं के समाहार वाला)

(1) समाहार-द्वंद्व-समास (गुणों का और कर्मों का समाहार जिनमें, गुणकर्मसु Gītā 13.14)

(1) नित्यसमाहार-द्वंद्व-समास (पाणि और पाद का समाहार, पाणिपादम् Gītā 13.14)

(iv) अव्ययीभाव-तत्पुरुष-समास (अव्यय सुबन्त से समाहित अव्ययीभाव-समास)

(1) जहाँ पूर्वपद अव्यय हो वह तत्पुरुष-समास (जैसा भाग हो वैसा, यथाभागम्, Gītā 1.11)

(2) उत्तरपद जहाँ अव्यय हो वह अव्ययीभाव-समास (सहस्त्र वार करना, सहस्त्रकृत्व Gītā 11.39)

(B) केवल-समास: (तत्पुरुष-बहुव्रीहि-द्वंद्व-अव्ययीभावादि संज्ञाओं से विनिमुक्त जो वह केवल-समास)

(1) अलुक-समास (युधि स्थिर, युधिष्ठिर, Gītā 1.16)

(2) प्रादि-समास (प्रभाव Gītā 11.43)

(3) उपपद-समास (उपपद नामक कोई संज्ञा जहाँ प्र का भाव है, मम यजी = मद्याजी Gītā 9.34)

SAMASA RULES WITH EXAMPLES

परस्पर अन्वित सुबन्तों का समास होता है.
प्राय: तिङ्गतों का समास नहीं होता है.

1. **Tatpurusha samāsa** (tat॰ तत्पुरुष समास), the Determinative or Dependent Compound :

   In this *samāsa*, the last component-word is primary (प्रधान) and the other words are secondary (गौण). Therefore, the case, number and gender of the last word dictate the case, number and gender of the entire composite word. (परस्य यल्लिङ्गं तद्भवति द्वंद्वस्य तत्पुरुषस्य च - pāṇini, *aṣhṭādhyāyī* 2: 4.26).

e.g. *dharmakṣhetre* धर्मक्षेत्रे n॰ loc॰ sing॰ *dharmasya kṣhetre* धर्मस्य क्षेत्रे on sacred land. (Gītā 1,1)
dharma-mayam धर्ममयम् (the sacred, righteous) pos॰ sing॰ ←m॰ *dharma* धर्म (righteousness) *kṣhetre* क्षेत्रे (on the land) loc॰ sing॰ ←n॰ *kṣhetr* (the field).

(i) Generally, the compound words of which last component is a Past Passive Participle, such as *gata* गत, *mrita* मृत, *atíta* अतीत, *sthita* स्थित, *rata* रत, *āsakta* आसक्त, *prāpta* प्राप्त, *mukta* मुक्त, *stha* स्थ, *etc.*, come under *tatpuruṣha-samāsa.*

(ii) The *karmadhāraya* and *dvigu samāsas* are subdivisions of the *tatpuruṣha-samāsa.*

2. **Bahuvrīhi samāsa** (bah॰ बहुव्रीहि समास), the Attributive or Relative Compound :

   In this *samāsa*, any one component is not primary. The whole compound word is an epithet (adjective) of an element outside of the compound itself. (अन्यपदप्रधान: बहुव्रीहि:। अन्यपदार्थे बहुव्रीहि:। pāṇini, 2: 2: 24).

Bhīmārjaunasamāḥ भीमार्जुनसमा: nom॰ pl॰ ←adj॰ *bhīmārjaunasama, bhīmasya arjaunasya vā samaḥ yaḥ saḥ* भीमार्जुनसम, भीमस्य अर्जुनस्य वा सम: य: स:। (he who is equal to *bhīma* or *arjauna*). The adjective in this *samāsa* is an epithet of some third person, (other than *bhīma* and *arjauna*), who is not mentioned in the *samāsa.*

3. **Dvandva samāsa** (द्वन्द्व समास), the Dual or Aggregative Compound.

In this *samāsa*, all component words have equal importance and they are connected together with an ind◦ copulative conjunction *cha* च (and). Though this *samāsa* is a simple aggregation of individual nouns. The case, number and gender of the whole *samāsa* is usually attached to the last element only (similar to tat◦), keeping the rest in stem form. (परवत्-लिङ्गं द्वन्द्व-तत्पुरुषयोः pāṇini, 2: 4.26) This *samasa* must always consist of words which, if uncompounded, will have same case-declensions.

e.g. *paṇavānakagomukhā:* पणवानकगोमुखाः (Gītā 1.13) ←*paṇavāḥ cha ānakāḥ cha gomukhāḥ cha* पणवाः च आनकाः च गोमुखाः च *(paṇavas and anakas and gomukhas)* ←m◦ *paṇava* पणव (cymbal) + m◦ *ānaka* आनक (drum) + *gomukha* गोमुख (horn).

(i) As there are always two or more individual word elements in this *samāsa*, it is usually in dual or plural form. However, when it denotes a single collective noun, it is in singular neuter gender.

(ii) When more than two singular words are aggregated together, only the last element is pluraled and the compound word then assumes the gender of the last element. e.g. *harṣhāmarṣhabhayodvegaiḥ,* हर्षामर्षभयोद्वेगैः Instrumental case, (*harṣheṇa cha āmarṣheṇa cha bhayena cha udvegena cha* हर्षेण च आमर्षेण च भयेन च उद्वेगेन च). However, in a plural *dvanva* word, each individual element could be plural too, but not necessarily..

e.g. *kaṭvamlalavaṇātyuṣhṇatīkṣhṇarūkṣhavidāhinaḥ* कट्वम्ललवणात्युष्णतीक्ष्णरूक्षविदाहिनः। *kaṭvaḥ cha amlāḥ cha lavaṇāḥ cha atyuṣhṇāḥ cha tīkṣhṇāḥ cha rūkṣhāḥ cha vidāhinaḥ cha* कट्वः च अम्लाः च लवणाः च अति-उष्णाः च तीक्ष्णाः च रूक्षाः च विदाहिनः च। (Gītā 17.9)

(iii) When words are aggregated, the इकारान्त, ईकारान्त word should be kept first, the rest anywhere. eg. हरिः and चन्द्रः हरिश्चन्द्र, not चन्द्रहरिः। When there are many इकारान्त words, at least one इकारान्त word kept first, the rest anywhere. e.g. रामः हरिः गुरुः हरिगुरुरामाः। Generally, the words starting with any vowel, and ending with vowel अ should be kept first. e.g. इन्द्रः इन्दुः अग्निः वायुः = इन्द्विन्द्रग्निवायवः। The word that has less characters should come first. हरिः केशवः, हरिकेशवौ। Normally, the **feminine name** should come first then masculine name. e.g. सीतारामौ, राधाकृष्णौ।

4. **Dvigu samāsa** (द्विगु समास), the Numeral or Collective Compound (dvigu∘)

   In this *samāsa*, the first element is a numerical adjective (संख्या-विशेषणम्) and the entire compound word is a singular collective noun. (द्विगुरेकवचनम्। pāṇini, *ashṭādhyāyī* 2: 4.1)

e.g. *navadvāra* नवद्वार (the aggregate of nine gates) ←num∘ adj∘ *nava* (nine) + m∘ *dvāra* (gate) Gītā 5.13. Note: This *samāsa* is always in singular number collective noun.

5. **Karmadhāraya samāsa** (कर्मधारय समास), Appositional Compound (karmadhāray∘)

   In this *samāsa*, usually there are two component words and they are always in Nominative (1st) case. The first element is a usually an adjective (विशेषणम्) and the second word is a substantive (विशेष्यम्). Sometimes there are three words, where the middle word physically does not exist but is only understood. eg. *svabhāva* स्वभाव (the inherent nature) ←adj∘ *sva* स्व (inherent) + substantive *bhāva* भाव (nature)

6. **Prādi samāsa** (प्रादि समास)

   If the first word is an adjective-prefix indicating such meanings as- much, extreme, more, improper, opposite, etc. (प्र–, अति–, उद्–, अधि, अनु, अव–, निः–, वि, परि–, e.g. प्रगत, अत्यन्त, उद्गत, अधिक, अनुचित, अवकृष्ट, निर्गत, विपरीत, परिक्लान्त) then the *samasa* is known as प्रादि समास. It is also used for expressing an opposite circumstance, e.g. prefix adj∘ *vi* वि (opposite) + substantive *sama* सम (normal circumstance) (Gītā 2.2)

The *dvigu samāsa* and the *karmadhāraya samāsa* are subdivisions of the *tatpuruṣha-samāsa* (द्विगुकर्मधारयौ तत्पुरुषभेदौ).

7. **Avyayībhāva samāsa** (अव्ययीभाव समास) Adverbial Compound:

In this *samāsa*, the first word is indeclinable, it is the primary term and the whole compound word is an indeclinable adverb. (अनव्ययम् अव्ययं भवति). Sometimes, however, the first word is a noun-stem and the last word is indeclinable. e.g. in◦ *yathābhāgam* यथाभागम् (as appointed) ← in◦ *yathā* यथा (as) + m◦ *bhāgam* भागम् (appointment).

Note: (नञ्-समास:) A word with the negative prefix *nañ* नञ् is not an *ayayibhāva.* It forms negative-tat◦ *samāsa* (e.g. *aparyāpta*) or negative-bah◦ *samāsa* (e.g. *achyuta*).

8. **Aluk samāsa** (अलुक् समास) In this *samāsa,* the case-affixes (विभक्तिप्रत्यय) of the member words are not dropped, they remain intact in the compound word.

e.g. *yudhiṣṭhiraḥ* युधिष्ठिर: ← *yudhi* युधि + *sthiraḥ* स्थिर: ← locative of noun *yudh* (in the battle) + nom◦ adj◦ *shtiraḥ* (stable). युधिष्ठिर: ←युधि + स्थिर: ←युध् सप्तमी + वि◦ स्थिर:

THUS (mostly) :

पूर्वपदार्थप्रधानोऽव्ययीभाव: उत्तरपदार्थप्रधानस्तत्पुरुष:।
अन्यपदार्थप्रधानो बहुव्रीहि: उभयपदार्थप्रधानो द्वंद्व:।।

(i) In an Avayībhāva samāsa (अव्ययीभाव समास:), its first member is dominant; in a Tatpuruṣha samāsa (तत्पुरुषसमास:), its last member is dominant.

(ii) In Bahuvrīhi samāsa (बहुव्रीहि समास) no single word is dominating. It points to a thing different from the individual meanings of any of its component members.

(iii) In a Dvandva samāsa (द्वंद्व समास), all words are equally dominating, and the meanings of all its members are have same importance.

WORD ETYMOLOGY
शब्द व्युत्पत्ति

According to the etymology or the derivation (व्युत्पत्ति) of the words, are grouped in three types.

1. Words of **Accepted Origin** (रूढ़ शब्द) : The words that are not derived from other words are classified in this group. e.g. हाथ, पैर, लाल, जल्दी, etc.
2. Words **formed by Uunion of Words** (यौगिक शब्द) : The words that formed with the union of two or more words are classified in this group. e.g. दिनरात (दिन+रात, खानपान (खान+पान), खानापीना (खाना+पीना), राजकन्या (राजन्+कन्या), etc.
3. Words of **Accepted Union** (योगारूढ़ शब्द) : The intended meaning of the word that is formed by union of two words are classified in this group. e.g. नीलकण्ठ (नील+कण्ठ = शिवजी), जलद (जल+द =बादल), रत्नाकर (रत्न+आकर = समुद्र), etc.

WORD ORIGIN
शब्द उत्पत्ति

Based on the origin (उत्पत्ति), the words are grouped in four types.

1. Words of **Same Script and Pronunciation** (तत्सम शब्द) : The words originated from Sanskrit language that are taken "as they are" are classified in this group. e.g. जगत्, अग्नि, सूर्य, चंद्र, etc.
2. Words **Evolved from Sanskrit** (तद्भव शब्द) : The words which are derived from original Sanskrit words are classified in this group. e.g. जग, आग, सूरज, चाँद, etc.
3. Words **Originated from Native Languages** (देशज) : The words which are originated from the native language are classified in this group. e.g. खरा, बरोबर, चंगा, बाड़ी, etc.
4. Words **Taken from Foreign Languages** (विदेशी शब्द) : The words which are derived from any of the foreigh languages such as Arabic, Persian, Turkish, English, Urdu, etc. are classified in this group. e.g. जफ़ा, दफ़ा, मुहब्बत, प्याला, कार, etc.

CHAPTER 4
THE HINDI NUMERALS
हिंदी संख्या

In Hindi, the numerals (*saṁkhyā, aṅka* संख्या, अङ्क) are used as adjectives (*viśheṣhaṇa* विशेषण) as well as substantives (*viśheṣhya* विशेष्य). The numerals from 1 to 18 are adjectives, but they can be used as substantives too.

The numerals may be expressed in two ways, namely

(1) Expressive of numbers (*saṅkhyāvāchaka* संख्यावाचक) e.g. one (*eka* एक), two (*dvi, do* द्वि, दो), three (*tri or tīn* त्रि, तीन), four (*chatur or chār* चतुर्, चार), five (*pañcha or pāñcha* पञ्च, पाँच), six (*ṣhaṣh* षष्), seven (*sapta or sāt* सप्त, सात), eight (*aṣhṭa or āṭh* अष्ट, आठ), nine (*nava or nau* नव, नौ), ten (*daśha* दश), eleven (*ekādaśha* एकादश) .. etc.

(2) Sequence indicating (*kramavāchakā* क्रमवाचक) e.g. 1st (*prathama* प्रथम), 2nd (*dvitīya* द्वितीय), 3rd (*tritīya* तृतीय), 4th (*chaturtha* चतुर्थ), 5th (*pañchama* पञ्चम), 6th (*ṣhaṣhṭha* षष्ठ), 7th (*saptama* सप्तम), 8th (*aṣhṭama* अष्टम), 9th (*navama* नवम), 10th (*daśhama* दशम), 11th (*ekādaśha* एकादश) .. etc.

In masculine gender, they end with अ (*akārānta* अकारान्त) and in feminine gender, with आ (*ākārānta* आकारान्त) or ई (*īkārānta* ईकारान्त).

The suffix that converts a number into a sequence indicating numeral is called पूरणप्रत्यय *pūraṇa-pratyaya.*

HINDI NUMERALS

Hindi - (English)	Sound	Sequencial Ûmavaacak
० - (0)	शून्य (śūnya)	
१ - (1)	एक (ek)	पहला (pahalā) 1st
२ - (2)	दो (do)	दूसरा (dūsara) 2nd
३ - (3)	तीन (tīn)	तीसरा (tīsarā) 3rd
४ - (4)	चार (cār)	चौथा (cauthā) 4th
५ - (5)	पांच (pāṅc)	पाँचवाँ (pāṅcavāṃ) 5th
६ - (6)	छह (chah)	छठा (chaṭhā) 6th
७ - (7)	सात (sāt)	सातवाँ (sātavāṃ) 7th
८ - (8)	आठ (āṭh)	आठवाँ()āṭhavāṃ) 8ht
९ - ()9)	नौ (nau)	नौवाँ (nauvāṃ) 9th
१० - (10)	दस (das)	दसवाँ (dasavāṃ) 10th
११ - (11)	ग्यारह (gyārah)	ग्यारहवाँ (gyārahavāṃ)
१२ - (12)	बारह (bārah)	बारहवाँ (bārahavāṃ)
१३ - (13)	तेरह (tērah)	तेरहवाँ (tērahavāṃ)
१४ - (14)	चौदह (caudah)	चौदहवाँ (caudahavāṃ)
१५ - (15)	पंद्रह (paṅdrah)	पंद्रहवाँ (paṅdrahavāṃ)
१६ - (16)	सोलह (solah)	सोलहवाँsolahavāṃ)

१७ - (17)	सत्रह् (satrah)	सत्रहवाँ) satrahavāṃ)
१८ - (18)	अठारह (aṭhārah)	अठारहवाँ) aṭhārahavāṃ)
१९ - (19)	उन्नीस (unnīs)	उन्नीसवाँ) unnīsavāṃ)
२० - (20)	बीस (bīs)	बीसवाँ) bīsavāṃ)
२१ - (21)	इक्कीस (ikkīs)	इक्कीसवाँ (ikkīsvaṅ)
२२ - (22)	बाईस (bāīs)	बाईसवाँ (bāīsvaṅ)
२३ - (23)	तेईस (tēīs)	तेईसवाँ (tēīsvaṅ)
२४ - (24)	चौबीस (chaubīs)	चौबीसवाँ (chaubīsvaṅ)
२५ - (25)	पच्चीस (paccīs)	पच्चीसवाँ (paccīsvaṅ)
२६ - (26)	छब्बीस (chabbī)	छब्बीसवाँ (chabbīvaṅ)
२७ - (27)	सत्ताईस (sattāīs)	सत्ताईसवाँ (sattāīsvaṅ)
२८ - (28)	अट्ठाईस (aṭṭhāīs)	अट्ठाईसवाँ (aṭṭhāīsvaṅ)
२९ - (29)	उनतीस (unatīs)	उनतीसवाँ (unatīsvaṅ)
३० - (30)	तीस (tīs)	तीसवाँ (tīs)
३१ - (31)	इकतीस (ikatīs)	इकतीसवाँ (ikatīsvaṅ)
३२ - (32)	बत्तीस (battīs)	बत्तीसवाँ (battīsvaṅ)
३३ - (33)	तैंतीस (taiṃtīs)	तैंतीसवाँ (taiṃtīsvaṅ)
३४ - (34)	चौंतीस (cauṃtīs)	चौंतीसवाँ (cauṃtīsvaṅ)
३५ - (35)	पैंतीस (paiṃtīs)	पैंतीसवाँ (paiṃtīsvaṅ)
३६ - (36)	छत्तीस (chattīs)	छत्तीसवाँ (chattīsvaṅ)

३७ - (37)	सैंतीस (saiṃtīs)	सैंतीसवाँ (saiṃtīsvaṅ)
३८ - (38)	अड़तीस (aṛatīs)	अड़तीसवाँ (aṛatīsvaṅ)
३९ - (39)	उनतालीस (unatālīs)	उनतालीसवाँ (unatālīsvaṅ)
४० - (40)	चालीस (cālīs)	चालीसवाँ (cālīsvaṅ)
४१ - (41)	इकतालीस (ikatālīs)	इकतालीसवाँ (ikatālīsavaṅ)
४२ - (42)	बयालीस (bayālīs)	बयालीसवाँ (bayālīsvaṅ)
४३ - (43)	तैंतालीस (taiṃtālīs)	तैंतालीसवाँ (taiṃtālīsvaṅ)
४४ - (44)	चौंतालीस (cauṃtālīs)	चौंतालीसवाँ (cauṃtālīsvaṅ)
४५ - (45)	पैंतालीस (paiṃtālīs)	पैंतालीसवाँ (paiṃtālīsvaṅ)
४६ - (46)	छियालीस (chiyālīs)	छियालीसवाँ (chiyālīsvaṅ)
४७ - (47)	सैंतालीस (saiṃtālīs)	सैंतालीसवाँ (saiṃtālīsvaṅ)
४८ - (48)	अड़तालीस (aṛatālīs)	अड़तालीसवाँ (aṛatālīsvaṅ)
४९ - (49)	उनचास (unacās)	उनचासवाँ (unacāsvaṅ)
५० - (50)	पचास (pacās)	पचासवाँ (pacāsvaṅ)
५१ - (51)	इक्याबन (ikyāvan)	इक्यावनवाँ (ikyābanvaṅ)
५२ - (52)	बावन (bāvan)	बावनवाँ (bāvanvaṅ)
५३ - (53)	तिरेपन (tirēpan)	तिरेपन (tirēpanvaṅ)
५४ - (54)	चौबन (cauvan)	चौवनवाँ (caubanvaṅ)
५५ - (55)	पचपन (pacapan)	पचपनवाँ (pacapanvaṅ)
५६ - (56)	छप्पन (chappan)	छप्पनवाँ (chappanvaṅ)

५७ - (57)	सत्तावन (sattāvan)	सत्तावनवाँ (sattāvanvaṅ)
५८ - (58)	अट्ठावन (aṭṭhāvan)	अट्ठावनवाँ (aṭṭhāvanvaṅ)
५९ - (59)	उनसठ (unasaṭh)	उनसठवाँ (unasaṭhvaṅ)
६० - (60)	साठ (sāṭh)	साठवाँ (sāṭhvaṅ)
६१ - (61)	इकसठ (ikasaṭh)	इकसठवाँ (ikasaṭhvaṅ)
६२ - (62)	बासठ (bāsaṭh)	बासठवाँ (bāsaṭhvaṅ)
६३ - (63)	तिरसठ (tirasaṭh)	तिरसठवाँ (tirasaṭhvaṅ)
६४ - (64)	चौंसठ (cauṃsaṭh)	चौंसठवाँ (cauṃsaṭhvaṅ)
६५ - (65)	पैंसठ (paiṃsaṭh)	पैंसठवाँ (paiṃsaṭhvaṅ)
६६ - (66)	छियासठ (chiyāsaṭh)	छियासठवाँ (chiyāsaṭhvaṅ)
६७ - (67)	सड़सठ (saṛasaṭh)	सड़सठवाँ (saṛasaṭhvaṅ)
६८ - (68)	अड़सठ (aṛasaṭh)	अड़सठवाँ (aṛasaṭhvaṅ)
६९ - (69)	उनहत्तर (unahattar)	उनहत्तरवाँ (unahattarvaṅ)
७० - (70)	सत्तर (sattar)	सत्तरवाँ (sattarvaṅ)
७१ - (71)	इकहत्तर (ikahattar)	इकहत्तरवाँ (ikahattarvaṅ)
७२ - (72)	बहत्तर (bahattar)	बहत्तरवाँ (bahattarvaṅ)
७३ - (73)	तिहत्तर (tihattar)	तिहत्तरवाँ (tihattarvaṅ)
७४ - (74)	चौहत्तर (cauhattar)	चौहत्तरवाँ (cauhattarvaṅ)
७५ - (75)	पचहत्तर (pacahattar)	पचहत्तरवाँ (pacahattarvaṅ)
७६ - (76)	छिहत्तर (chihattar)	छिहत्तरवाँ (chihattarvaṅ)

७७ - (77)	सतहत्तर (satahattar)	सतहत्तरवाँ (satahattarvaṅ)
७८ - (78)	अठहत्तर (aṭhahattar)	अठहत्तरवाँ (aṭhahattarvaṅ)
७९ - (79)	उनासी (unāsī)	उनासीवाँ (unāsīvaṅ)
८० - (80)	अस्सी (assī)	अस्सीवाँ (assīvaṅ)
८१ - (81)	इक्यासी (ikyāsī)	इक्यासीवाँ (ikyāsīvaṅ)
८२ - (82)	बयासी (bayāsī)	बयासीवाँ (bayāsīvaṅ)
८३ - (83)	तिरासी (tirāsī)	तिरासीवाँ (tirāsīvaṅ)
८४ - (84)	चौरासी (caurāsī)	चौरासीवाँ (caurāsīvaṅ)
८५ - (85)	पचासी (pacāsī)	पचासीवाँ (pacāsīvaṅ)
८६ - (86)	छियासी (chiyāsī)	छियासीवाँ (chiyāsīvaṅ)
८७ - (87)	सतासी (satāsī)	सतासीवाँ (satāsīvaṅ)
८८ - (88)	अठासी (aṭhāsī)	अठासीवाँ (aṭhāsīvaṅ)
८९ - (89)	नवासी (navāsī)	नवासीवाँ (navāsīvaṅ)
९० - (90)	नब्बे (nabbē)	नब्बेवाँ (nabbēvaṅ)
९१ - (91)	इक्यानबे (ikyānabē)	इक्यानबेवाँ (ikyānabēvaṅ)
९२ - (92)	बानवे (bānavē)	बानवेवाँ (bānavē)
९३ - (93)	तिरानवे (tirānavē)	तिरानवेवाँ (tirānavēvaṅ)
९४ - (94)	चौरानवे (caurānavē)	चौरानवेवाँ (caurānavēvaṅ)
९५ - (95)	पचानवे (pacānavē)	पचानवेवाँ (pacānavēvaṅ)
९६ - (96)	छियानवे (chiyānavē)	छियानवेवाँ (chiyānavēvaṅ)

९७ - (97)	सत्तानवे (sattānavē)	सत्तानवेवाँ (sattānavēvaṅ)
९८ - (98)	अट्ठानवे (aṭṭhānavē)	अट्ठानवेवाँ (aṭṭhānavēvaṅ)
९९ - (99)	निन्यानवे (ninyānavē)	निन्यानवेवाँ (ninyānavēvaṅ)
१०० - (100)	सौ (sau)	सौवाँ (sauvaṅ)
१,००० - (1,000)	हज़ार (hazār)	हज़ारवाँ (hazāravaṅ)
१०,००० - (10,000)	दस हज़ार (das hazār)	
१,००,००० (100,000 / 1 lakh)	लाख (lākh)	एक लाखवाँ (lākhvaṅ)
१०,००,००० (1 million / 10 lakh)	दस लाख (das lākh)	दस लाखवाँ (das lākhvaṅ)
१००,००,००० (10 million / 1 crore)	करोड़ (karoṛ)	एक करोड़वाँ (karoṛvaṅ)
१०,००,००,००० (100 million / 10 crore)	दस करोड़ (das karoṛ)	दस करोड़वाँ (das karoṛvaṅ)

HINDI NUMERALS FROM 0 TO 99

	0	1	2	3	4	5	6	7	8	9
0	०	१	२	३	४	५	६	७	८	९
1	१०	११	१२	१३	१४	१५	१६	१७	१८	१९
2	२०	२१	२२	२३	२४	२५	२६	२७	२८	२९
3	३०	३१	३२	३३	३४	३५	३६	३७	३८	३९
4	४०	४१	४२	४३	४४	४५	४६	४७	४८	४९
5	५०	५१	५२	५३	५४	५५	५६	५७	५८	५९
6	६०	६१	६२	६३	६४	६५	६६	६७	६८	६९
7	७०	७१	७२	७३	७४	७५	७६	७७	७८	७९
8	८०	८१	८२	८३	८४	८५	८६	८७	८८	८९
9	९०	९१	९२	९३	९४	९५	९६	९७	९८	९९

SOME LARGE NUMBERS

1	इक, एक	*ik, ek*	
10	दश, दस	*das, dash*	
100	शत, एकशत	*ś́hata, ekś́hata*	
1000	सहस्त्र	*sahasra*	
10,000	अयुत	*ayuta*	
100,000	लक्ष, लाख	*lakṣha, lākh*	
1000,000	नियुत	*prayuta*	Million
10,000,000	कोटि, करोड़	*koṭi, karod*	
100,000,000	अर्बुद	*arbuda*	
1,000,000,000	वृन्द, महार्बुद	*vrinda, mahārbuda*	Billion
10,000,000,000	खर्व	*kharva*	
100,000,000,000	निखर्व, नील	*nikharva, nīl*	
1,000,000,000,000	शंख	*ś́haṅkha*	Trillion
10,000,000,000,000	पद्म	*padma*	
100,000,000,000,000	सागर	*sāgara*	
1,000,000,000,000,000	अत्यन्त	*atyanta*	Zillion
10,000,000,000,000,000	मध्यम	*madhyama*	
100,000,000,000,000,000	परार्ध	*parārdha*	
1,000,000,000,000,000,000	प्रपरार्ध	*parparārdha*	
Infinity	अनन्त	*anant*	

FRACTIONS AND DECIMALS
अपूर्णांक और दशांश

1/4	(।)	0.25	Quarter	पाव, चौथाई	*pāv, chauthāī*
1/3		0.33	One Third	तिहाई	*tihāī*
1/2	(।।)	0.50	Half	अर्ध, आधा	*ardha, ādhā*
3/4	(।।।)	0.75	Three Quarters	पौन, पौना	*paun, paunā*
1¼	(१।)	1.25	One and Quarter	सवा	*savā*
1/½	(१।।)	1.50	One and Half	डेढ़	*ḍeḍh*
1¾	(१।।।)	1.75	One and Three-Quarters	पौने दो	*paune do*
2½	(२।।)	2.5	Two and Half	अढ़ाई	*aḍhāī*
5¾	(५।।।)	5.75	Five and Three Quarters	पाँच पूर्णांक तीन बटे चार	

0.25	Quarter (¼)	शून्य दशमलव पच्चीस	*śhunya dashamlav pacchīs*
1.25	One and Quarter	एक दशमलव पच्चीस	*ek dashamlav pacchīs*
2.5	Two and Half	दो दशमलव पच्चास	*do daśhamlav pachās*

¼	One Quarter	एक बटा चार (चौथाई)	*ek baṭā chār(chauthāī)*
½	One Half	एक बटा दो	*ek baṭā do*
¾	Three Quarters	तीन बटा चार	*tīn baṭā chār*
⅓	One Third	एक बटा तीन (तिहाई)	*ek baṭā tīn (tihāī)*
⅔	Two one-thirds	दो बटा तीन (दो तिहाई)	*do baṭā tīn (do tihāī)*
⅛	One Eighth	एक बटा आठ	*ek baṭā āṭh*
⅜	Three Eighths	तीन बटा आठ	*tīn baṭā āṭh*
⅝	Five Eighths	पाँच बटा आठ	*pǎ̃ch baṭā āṭh*
⅞	Seven Eighths	सात बटा आठ	*sāt baṭā āṭh*

ORDINAL NUMBERS
क्रम वाचक संख्या

1st	पहला	*pahlā*	=	अव्वल *avval,* आद्य *ādya,* आदिम *ādim,*
2nd	दूसरा	*dūsrā*	=	द्वितीया *dvitīya,* दूजा *dūjā*
3rd	तीसरा	*tīsrā*	=	तृतीय *tritīya,* तीजा *tījā,*
4th	चौथा	*chauthā*	=	चतुर्थ *chaturtha*
5th	पाँचवाँ	*pāñchvā̃*	=	पंचम *pañchama*
6th	छठा	*chhaṭhā*	=	षष्ठ *ṣhaṣhṭha,* छहवाँ *chhavavā̃,*
7th	सातवाँ	*sātvā̃*	=	सप्तम *saptam*
8th	आठवाँ	*āṭhavā̃*	=	अष्टम *aṣhṭam*
9th	नवाँ	*navā̃*	=	नवम *navam*
10th	दसवाँ	*dasvā̃*	=	दशम *saśham*

MULTIPLICATIVE NUMBERS
आवृत्ति वाचक संख्या

Tow times, Double	दुगुना, दूना, दोगुना, द्विगुण	*dugunā, dūnā, dogunā, dviguṇa*
Three times, Triple	तिगुना , त्रिगुण	*tigunā, triguṇa*
Four times, Quadruple	चौगुना	*chaugunā*
Five times	पचगुना	*pachgunā*
Six times	छगुना	*chhagunā*
seven times	सतगुना	*satgunā*
Eight times	अठगुना	*aṭhgunā*
Nine times	नौगुना	*naugunā*
Ten times	दसगुना	*dasgunā*

CHAPTER 5

STUDENTS' TRANSLITERETED ENGLISH-HINDI DICTIONARY

1. ENGLISH WORDS WITH A HINDI TWIST

Following is a list of English words twisted (mispronounced) and commonly used in Hindi as Hindi words. These Hinglish words have now entered the modern Hindi Dictionaries and are used by Hindi speakers.

English Word = Accepted as Hindi Word

Academy = *akādamī* अकादमी
Acre = *ekaḍ* एकड़
Agenda = *aigaṇḍā* ऐजंडा
Alcohol = *alkohal* अलकोहल
Algebra = *Aljebrā* अलजेबरा
Aluminum = *alyumīniyam* अल्युमीनियम
America = *Amrikā* अमरीका
April = *Aprel* अप्रेल
Arrowroot = *ārāroṭ* आरारोट
Asthma = *asthamā* अस्थमा
Attorney = *aṭārnī* अटार्नी
August = *Agast* अगस्त
Avoid = *awāyaḍ* अवायड
Biscuit = *biskuṭ* बिस्कुट
Boil = *bwāil* ब्वाइल
Bomb = *bum* बम
Bottle = *botal* बोतल
Brush = *brush, burus* ब्रुश, बुरुस
Budget = *bajaṭ* बजट
Bugle = *bigul* बिगुल
Calendar = *kalendar* कलेंडर
Canada = *Kaneḍā* कनेडा
Cartridge = *kātrūs* कारतूस
Ceuuent = *karent* करेंट
China = *Chīn* चीन
Christial = *Krischiyan* क्रिश्चियन
Coal = *kolā, koylā* कोला, कोयला
Colony = *kalonī* कलोनी
Command = *kamān* कमान
Criminal = *krimanal* क्रिमनल
Dacoit = *dakait* दकैत
December = *Disambar* दिसंबर
Delivery = *dilavarī* डिलवरी
Dowry = *ḍāurī* डाउरी
Enamel = *ināmil* इनामिल
Engine = *injan* इंजन
English = *angrezī* अंग्रेजी
Father (church) = *pādrī* पादरी
February = *Farwarī* फरवरी
Film = *filam* फिलम
Flannel = *falālain* फलालैन
Garage = *gairej* गैरेज
Gazette = *gajaṭ* गजट
Geography = *jyography* ज्योग्राफी
Geometry = *jyometry* ज्योमेट्री
Glass = *gilās* गिलास
Guyana = *guyānā* गुयाना
Hospital = *aspatāl* अस्पताल
Hostel = *hosṭal* होस्टल
Hotel= *hoṭal* होटल

Insurance = *inshorence* इन्शोरेंस
Invoice = *invāyas* इन्वायस
Iron = *āyaran* आयरन
Italic = *itailik* इटैलिक
January = *Janwarī* जनवरी
Jewller = *jwelar* ज्वेलर
Join = *jyoin* ज्वाइन
Joint = *vwāint* ज्वाइंट
Kerosene = *kirāsan* किरासन
Kettle = *ketlī* केतली
Kitchen = *Kichin* किचिन
Long-cloth = *lanklāṭ* लंकलाट
May = *maī* मई
McDonald = *makḍānal* मकडानल
Mercury = *markarī* मरकरी
Middle = *midil* मिडिल
Minute = *minaṭ* मिनट
Mixture = *mikchar* मिक्चर
Model = *modal* मोडल
Monopoly = *manopālī* मनोपाली
Motel = *moṭal* मोटल
Movie = *mūvī* मूवी
Nigative = *negativ* नेगेटिव
Novel = *nāval* नावल
November = *Navambar* नवंबर
Nylon = *nāilon* नाइलोन
Oblige = *ublige* उब्लाइज
October = *Aktubar* अक्तूबर
Officer = *afsar* अफसर
Oil = *āyal* आयल
Orderly = *ardalī* अरदली
Ottawa = *Oṭāwā* ओटावा
Pantaloon = *patlūn* पतलून
Parket = *mārkiṭ* मार्किट
Pencil = *pensal* पेंसल
Period = *piriyad* पिरियड
Pistol = *pistal, pistaul* पिस्टल, पिस्तौल
Plaster = *palastar* पलस्तर
Platoon = *palṭan* पलटन
Pocket = *pakiṭ* पाकिट
Police = *pulis* पुलिस
Polish = *pālis* पालिस
Powder = *pāudar* पाउडर
Puncture = *panchar* पंचर
Pure = *pyor* प्योर
Quarter = *quater* क्वाटर
Question = *queschan* क्वेश्चन
Radar = *rāḍār* राडार
Raspberry = *rasbharī* रसभरी
Receipt = *rasīd* रसीद
Record = *rikard* रिकार्ड
Recruit = *rangrūṭ* रंगरूट
Report = *rapaṭ* रपट
Restauranr = *restarā̃* रेस्तराँ
Rubber = *rabaḍ* रबड़
Russia = *Rūs* रूस
Sandalwood = *sandal* संदल
Science = *sāīns* साईंस
Second = *sekinḍ* सेकंडि
Section = *seksan* सेक्सन
Sentry = *santrī* संतरी
September = *sitambar* सितंबर
Stable = *astabal* अस्तबल
Store = *stor* स्टोर
Table = *ṭebil, ṭebul* टेबिल, टेबुल
Tablet = *tableṭ* टबलेट
Tank = *ṭankī* टंकी
Tarpulin = *tirpāl* तिरपाल
Telephone= *teliphūn* टेलीफून
Theory = *thyorī* थ्योरी
Ticket = ṭikaṭ टिकट
Token = *ṭoken* टोकेन
Tomato = *ṭamāṭar* टमाटर
Tragedy = *trāsadī* त्रासदी
Twil = *tuil* टुइल
Urgent = *arjent* अरजेंट
Verandah = *barāmadā* बरामदा
Via = *vāyā* वाया
Vitamin = *viṭāmin* विटामिन
Viva = *vāivā* वाइवा
Warden = *wārden* वार्डेन

2. HINDI LEARNRS'
Transliterated
ENGLISH-HINDI DICTIONARY

PLEASE NOTE : As this Dictionary is constructed for the use of Hindi Learners, (i) gender of each noun is shown to help the new users; (ii) Transliteration is given according to phonetic rules, to produce proper Hindi pronunciation of each syllable; (iii) While giving Hindi meanings, only popular & easy Hindi words chosen (eg◦ Water has many Hindi names, eg◦ अम्बु, अम्भस, आप, उद, उदक, जल, जीवन, तोय, नीर, पय, पानी, पुष्कर, वारि, सलिल, क्षीर, .. etc. but only पानी and जल are given in this Dictionary); and (iv) for Hindi meanings, instead of giving definitions, only a single Hindi word or phrase is give.

In order to obtain the verb-stems for making tenses, just remove the *nā* (ना) attached at the end of the Verbal-noun / Infinitive and then attach the tense suffixe to this verb-stem. For Examples: (1) Infinitive *pīnā* पीना = to drink, (2) removing the *nā* (ना) gives you the verb *pī* (पी) = drink, (3) attach required tense suffix to this verb-stem *pī* (पी) + ***tā*** *hū̃* (**ता** हूँ) = *pītā hū̃* (पीता हूँ), and thus (4) *maĩ pānī pītā hū̃* = मैं पानी पीता हूँ = I drink water, (5) *maĩ pānī pī* ***rahā*** *hū̃* = मैं पानी पी रहा हूँ = I am drinking water ...and so on. (See Table 18, for making your own sentences from the verb-stems)

KEY : v◦ = Verbal-noun / Infinitiv, adj◦ = Adjective, av◦ = adverb, f◦ = feminine, m◦ = masculine, * = Transitive action.

A

Abandon (v◦) *tyāgnā, chhoḍnā* त्यागना, छोड़ना*

Abbreviated (adj◦) *sanksḥipta* संक्षिप्त

Abbreviation (m◦) *sanksḥep* संक्षेप

Abdomen (m◦) *udar, peṭ* उदर, पेट

Abduction (m◦) *apaharaṇ, bhagānā* अपहरण, भगाना

Abide (v◦) *sahanā, bardāśht karnā* सहना, बर्दाश्त करना*

Ability (f◦) *kṣhamatā,* (m◦) *sāmarthya* क्षमता, सामर्थ्य

Able (adj◦) *sakṣham, samartha, kābil* सक्षम, समर्थ, काबिल

Abnormal (adj◦) *asāmānya, alag* असामान्य, अलग

Abode (m◦) *ghar, āvās* घर, आवास

Abolish (v◦) *samāpta karnā, ukhāḍnā* समाप्त करना, उखाड़ना*

Abortion (m◦) *garbhapāt* गर्भपात

Abortive (adj◦) *niṣhphal* निष्फल

About (av◦) 1. *karīb, ās-pās, lagbhag* करीब, आसपास, लगभग (about ten k.m. = *lagbhag das k.m.*); 2. *ke bāre mẽ* के बारे में (a book about India = *bhārat ke bāre mẽ kitāb*)

Above (av◦) *ūpar* ऊपर

Abroad (m◦) *pardeśha* परदेश

Abrupt (adj◦) *ākasmik* आकस्मिक

Abruptly (av∘) *ekāek, ekdam, achānak* एकाएक, एकदम, अचानक

Absence (f∘) *anupasthiti, gairhājirī* अनुपस्थिति, गैरहाजिरी

Absent (adj∘) *anupasthit, gairhājir* अनुपस्थित, गैरहाजिर

Absolutely (av∘) *bilkul* बिलकुल

Absorption (m∘) *śhoṣhaṇ* शोषण

Abstinence (f∘) *parhez, tyāg* परहेज़, त्याग

Absurd (adj∘) *asaṅgat, betukā* असंगत, बेतुका

Abundant (adj∘) *prachur, adhik, bahut* प्रचुर, अधिक, बहुत

Abuse (m∘) *durupayog* दुरुपयोग

Accept (v∘) *kabūl karnā, mānanā* कबूल करना, मानना*

Acceptance (m∘) *svīkār, svikriti manzurī* स्वीकार, स्वीकृति, मंज़ूरी

Accident (f∘) *durghaṭnā* दुर्घटना

Accidental (adj∘) *ākasmik* आकस्मिक

Accomodation, place (m∘) *āvās* आवास (a place of accomodation for today = *āj ke āvās ke liye jagah*)

Accomplishment (f∘) *safaltā, prāpti, upalabdhi* सफलता, प्राप्ति, उपलब्धि

According (prep∘) *ke anusār* के अनुसार

Account (m∘) *hisāb* हिसाब

Accountant (m∘) *munīm* मुनीम

Accumulated (adj∘) *ikaṭṭhā, jamā, sañchit* इकट्ठा, जमा, संचित

Accurate (adj∘) *sahī, śhuddha* सही, शुद्ध

Ache (m∘) *dard, pīḍā, vednā, śhūl* दर्द, पीड़ा, वेदना, शूल

Achieve (v∘) *pānā, prāpta karnā* पाना, प्राप्त करना*

Acid (m∘) *tezāb, amla* तेज़ाब, अम्ल

Acknowledge (v∘) *mānanā, kabūl karnā, svīkār karnā* मानना. कबूल करना, स्वीकार करना*

Acknowledgement (f∘) *kabūlī, svīkār, svīkriti* कबूली, स्वीकार, स्वीकृति

Acquaintance (m∘) *parichay,* (f∘) *jānakārī* परिचय, जानकारी

Acquire (v∘) *pānā, prāpta karnā* पाना, प्राप्त करना*

Acronym (m∘) *saṅkṣhep* संक्षेप

Across (av∘) *ke pār* के पार

Act (m∘) *kām, kārya, karma* काम, कार्य, कर्म

Act (v∘) *karnā* करना*

Acting (m∘) *abhinay* अभिनय

Action (f∘) *kriyā, kām* क्रिया, काम

Active (adj∘) *sakrīya, furtīlā, chapal* सक्रीय, फुरतीला, चपल

Activity (f∘) *kriyā, kām* क्रिया, काम

Actor (m∘ f∘) *kalākār* कलाकार

Actual (adj∘) *aslī, sach* असली, सच

Actuality (f∘) *aslīyat, sachāī, satyatā* असलीयत, सचाई, सत्यता

Acute (adj∘) *ghor, tez, tīkṣhṇa, prakhar* घोर, तेज़, तीक्ष्ण, प्रखर

Adamant (adj∘) *aṭal, driḍha; ziddī, aḍiyal* अटल, दृढ़; जिद्दी, अड़ियल

Add (v∘) *milānā, joḍnā, kul karnā* मिलाना, जोड़ना, कुल करना*

Addict (adj∘) *āsakt, vyasanī, laṭṭū* आसक्त, व्यसनी, लट्टू

Addiction (f∘) *āsakti, naśhā,* (m∘) *vyasan* आसक्ति, नशा, व्यसन,

Addictive (adj∘) *mādk, naśhīlā* मादक, नशीला

Address (m∘) *patā* पता (my address in Delhi = *merā Dillī kā patā*)

Adequate (adj∘) *kāfī* काफी

Adhere (v∘) *juḍnā, chipaknā, sāth lagnā* जुड़ना, चिपकना, साथ लगना

Adhesive (m∘) *gond* गोंद

Adjective (m◦) *vis'heshaṇ* विशेषण

Adjoin (v◦) *joḍnā, milānā, lagānā* जोड़ना, मिलाना, लगाना*

Adjust (v◦) *anukūl honā; ṭhīk karnā** अनुकूल होना; ठीक करना*

Adjustment (m◦) *sudhār* सुधार

Administration (m◦) *s'hāsan* शासन

Admiration (f◦) *stuti, pras'hansā* स्तुति, प्रशंसा

Admire (v◦) *stuti karnā* स्तुति करना*

Admission (m◦) *dākhilā* दाखिला (the admission charge is ten Rupees = *dākhile kā shulk das Rupaye hai*)

Adoration (m◦) *prem;* (f◦) *pūjā, bhakti* प्रेम, पूजा, भक्ति

Adulteration (f◦) *milāvaṭ* मिलावट

Advance (f◦) *pes'hgī* पेशगी (please give ten Rupees as advance = *pes'hgī ke das Rupaye dījiye*)

Advance (v◦) *āge baḍhanā* आगे बढ़ना

Advancement (f◦) *pragati, unnati* (m◦) *vikās, utkarṣha* प्रगति, उन्नति, विकास, उत्कर्ष (India's advancement in 2007 = *2007 mẽ Bhārat kī pragati*)

Advantage (m◦) *lābh,* (f◦) *suvidhā* लाभ, सुविधा

Adventure (m◦) *sāhas* साहस

Adventurous (adj◦) *sāhasī* साहसी

Adverb (m◦) *kriyāvis'heṣhaṇ* क्रियाविशेषण

Advertisement (f◦) *ghoṣhaṇā;* (m◦) *vigyāpan* घोषणा; विज्ञापन

Advice (m◦) *upades'h* उपदेश

Advise (v◦) *upades'ha denā* उपदेश देना*

Affection (m◦) *lagāv, pyār, prem* लगाव, प्यार, प्रेम

Affluence (f◦) *amīrī, samriiddhi* अमीरी, समृद्धि

Affluent (adj◦) *amīr, samriddha* अमीर, समृद्ध

Afraid (adj◦) *ḍarā, bhayabhīta, trast* डरा (डरा हुआ), भयभीत, त्रस्त

After (av◦) *bād, bād mẽ, fir, pīchhe* बाद, बाद में, फिर, पीछे

Afternoon (f◦) *dopahar* दोपहर

Afterwards (av◦) *fir, bād mẽ* फिर, बाद में

Again (av◦) *punaḥ, fir, fir se, aur bhī* पुन:, फिर, फिर से, और भी

Again and again (av◦) *bārambār* बारंबार

Against (av◦) *pratikūl, viparīt, viruddha* प्रतिकूल, विपरति, विरुद्ध

Age (f◦) *umar, āyu* उमर, आयु

Agenda (m◦) *kāryakram* कार्यक्रम

Agent (m◦) *munīm; sādhan* मुनीम; साधन

Aggravation (m◦) *bhaḍkāv* भड़काव

Aggressive (adj◦) *ākramak* आक्रमक

Agile (adj◦) *chapal, chañchal* चपल, चंचल

Ago (av◦) *pahale* पहले

Agree (v◦) *kabūl karnā, mānanā* कबूल करना, मानना*

Agriculture (f◦) *khetī* खेती

Ahead (av◦) *āge* आगे

Aid (f◦) *madad, sahāyatā* मदद, सहायता

Aim (m◦) *dhyeya, hetu, lakṣhya* ध्येय, हेतु, लक्ष्य

Air (f◦) *havā* हवा

Airconditioned (adj◦) *vātānukūlit* वातानुकूलित

Airmail (f◦) *havāī ḍāk* हवाई डाक

Airplane (m◦) *vimān* विमान

Airport (m◦) *havāī aḍḍā* हवाई अड्डा

Alarm (f◦) *pukār, sūchanā* पुकार, सूचना

Albeit (conj◦) *yadyapi* यद्यपि

Alcoholic drink (f◦) *s'harāb* शराब

Alert (adj◦) *sāvadhān, sajag* सावधान, सजग

Algebra (m◦) *bījgaṇit* बीजगणित

Alien (adj◦) *pardesī* परदेसी

Alike (adj∘) *samānm, sama* समान, सम

Alive (adj∘) *sajīv, jīvita* सजीव, जीवित

All (adj∘) *sab, pūrā, pūrṇa, sārā, kul, sarva* सब, पूरा, पूर्ण, सारा, कुल, सर्व

All along (av∘) *nirantar, lagātār, sadā* निरंतर, लगातार, सदा

All around (av∘) *sab or se* सब ओर से

All at once (av∘) *ekadam, yakāyak* एकदम, यकायक

All of a sudden (av∘) *akasmāt, ekadam* अकस्मात्, एकदम

All over (av∘) *pūrṇa rūp se, sarvatra* पूर्ण रूप से, सर्वत्र

All right (av∘) *ṭhīk* ठीक

Alley (f∘) *galī* गली

Alliance (f∘) *sandhi, samjhautā* संधि, समझौता

Alligation (m∘) *ārop* आरोप

Alligator (m∘) *ghaḍiyāl* घड़ियाल

Allocate (v∘) *bā̃ṭanā* बाँटना*

Allow (v∘) *mānanā, anumodan denā* मानना, अनुमोदन देना*

Allowance (m∘) *bhattā, mujrā, dalālī, chhūt;* भत्ता, मुजरा, दलाली, छूट

Almighty (m∘) *sarvaśhaktimān* सर्वशक्तिमान्

Almond (f∘) *bādām* बादाम

Almost (av∘) *lagabhag, takrīban, prāyaḥ* लगभग, तकरीबन, प्राय:

Alone (adj∘) *akelā* अकेला (av∘) *akele,* अकेले

Along (av∘) *barābar, sāthsāth* बराबर, साथसाथ

Alphabet (f∘) *varṇamālā* वर्णमाला

Already (av∘) *pahale se* पहले से

Also (av∘) *aur, bhī, sivāy* ओर, भी, सिवाय

Alter (v∘) *badalnā* बदलना*

Alternately (av∘) *pārī pārī se* पारी पारी से, *yathākram* यथाक्रम

Although (av∘) *hālāki, yadyapi* हालाकि, यद्यपि

Altogether (av∘) *kul, sarvathā* कुल, सर्वथा

Always (av∘) *sadā, hameśhā* सदा, हमेशा

Am (v∘) *hū̃* हूँ

Amature (adj∘) *anipuṇ* अनिपुण

Amaze (v∘) *chakit honā, chakit karnā** चकित होना, चकित करना*

Amazement (m∘) *achambhā, āśhcharya, vismay, tājjub* अचंभा, आश्चर्य, विस्मय, ताज्जुब

Amazing (adj∘) *adbhut* अद्भुत

Ambiguous (m∘) *aspaṣhṭa* अस्पष्ट

Ambition (f∘) *ichhā, abhilāṣhā, abhilāśhā* इच्छा, आकांक्षा, अभिलाशा

Amen (inter∘) *tathāstu, bhavatu* तथास्तु, भवतु

Amiable (adj∘) *pyārā, ramaṇīya* प्यारा, रमणीय

Amicable (adj∘) *mitravat, suhrid* मित्रवत्, सुहृद्

Amid (prep∘) *bīch mẽ, sāth mẽ* बीच में, साथ में

Amity (m∘) *bandhutva, mitratā* बंधुत्व, मित्रता

Ammunition (f∘) *yuddha sāmagrī* युद्ध सामग्री

Amnesty (m∘) *kṣhamā dān* क्षमा दान

Among (av∘) *bīch mẽ* बीच में

Amoral (adj∘) *adharmī* अधर्मी

Amorous (adj∘) *rasik, kāmuk* रसिक, कामुक

Amount (f∘) *rakam, tādād* रकम, तादाद

Amplification (m∘) *vistār, vriddhi* विस्तार, वृद्धि

Analysia (m∘) *viśhleṣhaṇ* विश्लेषण

Anarchy (f∘) *arājaktā* अराजकता

Ancestor (m∘) *purkhā, pitar* पुरखा, पितर

Anchor (m∘) *laṅgar* लंगर

Ancient (adj∘) *purānā, prāchīn* पुराना, प्राचीन

And (con∘) *aur* और

Angel (m∘) *devadūt,* (f∘) *apsarā* देवदूत, अप्सरा

Anger (m∘) *krodh, gussā* क्रोध, गुस्सा

Angle (m∘) *konā, koṇa* कोना, कोण

Angry (adj∘) *nārāz* नाराज़

Anguish (m∘) *dukh, santāp;* (f∘) *vednā* दुख, संताप; वेदना

Animal (m∘) *jānvar, paśhu, jantu* जानवर, पशु, जंतु

Animosity (f∘) *śhatrutā* शत्रुता

Annihilate (v∘) *miṭānā* मिटाना*

Anniversary (f∘) *sālgirāh* सालगिराह

Announcement (f∘) *ghoṣhaṇa, sūchanā,* (m∘) *vigyāpan* घोषणा, सूचना, विज्ञापन

Annoy (v∘) *dukhānā* दुखाना*

Annoyance (f∘) *pareśhānī* परेशानी

Annual (adj∘) *vārṣhik* वार्षिक

Anonymous (adj∘) *gumnām* गुमनाम

Another (adj∘) *dūsrā* दूसरा

Answer (m∘) *jawāb, uttar* जवाब, उत्तर

Answer (v∘) *jawāb denā* जवाब देना*

Ant (f∘) *chīṇṭī* चींटी

Anthem (m∘) *stutigān* स्तुतिगान

Anticipate (v∘) *āśhā karnā* आशा करना*

Antique (adj∘) *purānā, prāchīn* पुराना, प्राचीन

Antonym (m∘) *viruddhārthī śhabda* विरुद्धार्थी शब्द

Any (av∘) *kuchh, koī, koī bhī* कुछ, कोई, कोई भी

Anybody (pr∘) *koī bhī* कोई भी

Anyhow (av∘) *kisī tarah se* किसी तरह से

Anything (av∘) *kuchh bhī* कुछ भी

Anyway (av∘) *kisī tarah se* किसी तरह से

Anywhere (av∘) *kahīँ bhī* कहीं भी

Apart (av∘) *alag, prithak, bhinna* अलग, पृथक्, भिन्न

Apex (f∘) *choṭī,* (m∘) *śhikhar* चोटी, शिखर

Apology (m∘) *kṣhamā yāchanā* क्षमा याचना

Apparent (adj∘) *prakaṭ, spaṣhṭa* प्रकट, स्पष्ट

Appear (v∘) *dikhnā* दिखना

Append (v∘) *joḍnā, milānā* जोड़ना, मिलाना*

Appetite (f∘) *bhūkh* भूख

Applaud (v∘) *tālī bajānā* ताली बजाना*

Applause (f∘) *stuti* स्तुति

Apple (m∘) *seb* सेब

Application (f∘) *prārthanāpatra* प्रार्थनापत्र

Appoint (v∘) *niyukta karnā* नियुक्त करना*

Appointment (f∘) *niyukti* नियुक्ति

Appreciation (m∘) *mūlyāṅkan* मूल्यांकन

Approach (m∘) *kī or jānā* की ओर जाना

Approval (m∘) *Anaumāedna* (f∘) *svīkṛti* अनुमोदन, स्वीकृति

Approximately (av∘) *takrīban* तकरीबन

Aquatic (adj∘) *jalchar* ज लचर

Arch (f∘) *kamān* कमान

Archaeology (m∘) *purātattva* पुरातत्त्व

Architect (m∘) *śhilpakār* शिल्पकार

Architecture (m∘) *śhilpavidyā* शिल्पविद्या

Ardent (adj∘) *prakhar* प्रखर

Are (v∘) *haiँ* हैं

Arguement (m∘) *vivād, tark* विवाद, तर्क

Aristocrat (adj∘) *kulīn* कुलीन

Arithmatic (m∘) *gaṇit, aṅkgaṇit* गणित, अंकगणित

Arm (m∘) *hāth, bāhu, bhujā* हाथ, बाहु, भुजा

Aroma (m∘) *sugandh* सुगंध

Around (av∘) *chārōँ or, samīp, bāharī or* चारों ओर, समीप, बाहरी ओर

Arrange (v◦) *rachanā* रचना*

Arrangement (f◦) *rachanā* रचना

Arrival (m◦) आना, पहुँचना

Arrive (v◦) *ānā, pahūnchanā* आना, पहुँचना

Arrogant (adj◦) *haṭhī, ahamkārī* हठी, अहंकारी

Arrow (m◦) *tīr, bāṇ* तीर, बाण

Art (f◦) *kalā, kārīgarī* कला, कारीगरी

Artful (adj◦) *chatur* चतुर

Artificial (adj◦) *kritrim, banāvaṭī* कृत्रिम, बनावटी

Artisan (m◦) *kārīgar* कारीगर

As (av◦) *yathā, jis tarah se* यथा, जिस तरह से

As far as (av◦) *jab tak, jahā̃ tak* जब तक, जहाँ तक

As if (av◦) *jaise* जेसे

As though (av◦) *jaise* जेसे

As well as (av◦) *bhī* भी

Ascetic (m◦) *yogī, tapasvī* योगी, तपस्वी

Ash (f◦) *rakṣhā, rākh* रक्षा, राख

Ashamed (adj◦) *lajjit* लज्जित

Aside (av◦) *ek or* एक ओर

Ask (v◦) *pūchhanā* पूछना*

Asleep (adj◦) *nidrit, soyā* निद्रित, सोया

Assassin (m◦) *htyāra, ghātak* हत्यारा, घातक

Assembly (f◦) *sabhā, maṇḍlī* सभा, मंडली

Assention (f◦) *anumati, svīkriti* अनुमति, स्वीकृति

Assets (f◦) *pū̃jī, sampati* पूँजी, संपति

Assignment (f◦) *niyukti* नियुक्ति

Assistance (m◦) *sahārā* (f◦) *madad* सहारा, मदद

Association (f◦) *sabhā, pasiṣhad* सभा, परिषद्

Assult (m◦) *dhāvā* (f◦) *chaḍhāī* धावा, चढ़ाई

Assumption (f◦) *kalpanā* कल्पना

Assurance (m◦) *viśhvās, bīmā* विश्वास, बीमा

Asthma (m◦) *damā* दमा

Astonishment (m◦) *āśhcharya, achambhā* आश्चर्य, अचम्भा

Astrology (m◦) *jyotiṣh* ज्योतिष

Astronomy (f◦) *khagol vidyā* खगोल विद्या

Asylum (m◦) *āśhraya, śharaṇ* आश्रय, शरण

At (prep◦) *mẽ, se, pās, or* में, से, पास, ओर

At any time (av◦) *kabhī bhī* कभी भी

At last (av◦) *ant mẽ, ākhir* अंत में, आखिर

At least (av◦) *kam se kam* कम से कम

At night *(av◦) rāt mẽ* रात में

At once (av◦) *turant, ekadam* तुरंत, एकदम

At one time (av◦) *ekadā, ek bār* एकदा, एक बार

At present (av◦) *ab, abhī, āj, hāl mẽ* अब, अभी, आज, हाल में

At the same time (av◦) *sāth sāth, sāth hī* साथ साथ, साथ ही

At this time (av◦) *ab, abhī* अब, अभी

At what time (av◦) *kab* कब

Atheist (adj◦) *nāstik* नास्तिक

Atmosphere (m◦) *vātāvaraṇ* वातावरण

Atom (m◦) *aṇu, paramāṇu* अणु, परमाणु

Attach (v◦) *bāndhanā, joḍnā* बाँधना, जोड़ना*

Attain (v◦) *pānā, prāpta karanā* पाना, प्राप्त करना*

Attempt (m◦) *prayatna* प्रयत्न, *yatna* यत्न

Attempt (v◦) *prayatna karanā* प्रयत्न करना*

Attention (m◦) *dhyān* ध्यान

Attentive (adj◦) *sāvadhān* सावधान

Attitude (f◦) *vṛtti* वृत्ति

Attraction (m◦) *ākarṣhaṇ, lubhāv, moha* आकर्षण, लुभाव, मोह

Attractive (adj∘) *ākarṣhak, lubhāvanā, mohak* आकर्षक, लुभावना, मोहक

Attribute (m∘) *guṇa, dharma* गुण, धर्म

Auction (m∘) *nīlām* नीलाम

Audience (m∘) *śhrotāgaṇa* श्रोतागण

Auspicious (adj∘) *śhubha, maṅgal* शुभ, मंगल

Authentic (adj∘) *sachchā* सच्चा

Author (m∘) *lekhak* लेखक

Authority (m∘) *adhikār* अधिकार

Autobiography (m∘) *ātmacharitra* आत्मचरित्र

Autumn (m∘) *śharad ritu* शरद् ऋतु

Available (adj∘) *sulabh, sugam* सुलभ, सुगम

Avarage (m∘) *ausat* औसत

Awake (v∘) *jāganā* जागना

Award (m∘) *Pāritoshak* पारितोषक

Aware (adj∘) *sachet, sajag* सचेत, सजग

Away (av∘) *dūr* दूर

Aweful (adj∘) *bhayaṅkar* भयंकर

Ax (f∘) *kulhāḍī* कुल्हाड़ी

B

Babble (f∘) *bakbak. bakvād, gappa* बकबक, बकवाद, गप्प

Babble (v∘) *baḍbaḍānā* बड़बड़ाना

Baboon (m∘) *laṅgūr* लंगूर

Bachelor (adj∘) 1. (single) *avivāhit, chhaḍā* अविवाहित, छड़ा; 2. (graduate) *snātak* स्नातक

Back (f∘) *pīṭh* पीठ

Backbone (f∘) *rīḍh* रीढ़

Background (f∘) *pārśhvabhūmi* पार्श्वभूमी

Backing (m∘) *āśhray, sahārā, samarthan, anumodan* आश्रय, सहारा, समर्थन, अनुमोदन

Backward (adj∘) *pichhaḍa* पिछड़ा

Backwards (av∘) *pichhalī or, pīchhe* पिछली ओर, पीछे

Bad (adj∘) *burā, kharāb* बुरा, खराब

Badly (av∘) *burī tarah se* बुरी तरह से

Baffle (v∘) *ghabaḍānā* घबड़ाना

Bag (m∘) *thailā* थैला

Balance (m∘) *tarājū* तराजू

Balance (v∘) *taulnā* त ौलना*

Bald (m∘) *gañjā* गंजा

Ball (f∘) *gend* गेंद

Balloon (m∘) *gubbārā* गुब्बारा

Balm (m∘) *malham* मलहम

Bamboo (m∘) *bā̃s* बाँस

Banana (m∘) *kelā* केला

Band (m∘) *bandhan, tasmā, paṭṭā, peṭī* बंधन, तस्मा, पट्टा, पेटी

Bangle (f∘) *chūḍī* चूड़ी

Banyan (m∘) *bargad* बरगद

Bar (m∘) *ḍaṇḍā, chhaḍ* डंडा, छड़

Barbaric (adj∘) *jaṅglī, asabhya* जंगली, असभ्य

Barber (m∘) *nāī, hajjām* नाई, हज्जाम

Bare (adj∘) *naṅgā, khālī* नंगा, खाली

Bark (v∘) *bhŏknā* भोंकना

Barn (m∘) *khalihān* खलिहान

Barrel (m∘) *pīpā, kaṭharā* पीपा, कठरा

Base, foundation (m∘) *mūl*, (f∘) *nī̃va* मूल, नींव

Base, lowly (adj∘) *nīch, kamīnā* नीच, कमीना

Basil (f∘) *tulsī* तुलसी

Basis (m∘) *mūl, ādhār* मूल, आधार

Basket (f∘) *ṭokrī, ḍaliyā* टोकरी, डलिया

Bat (m◦) *chamgādaḍ* चमगादड़

Bat, sport (m◦) *ballā* बल्ला

Bathe (v◦) *nahānā* नहाना

Battle (f◦) *yuddha, laḍāī* लड़ाई

Battlefield (f◦) *raṇabhūmi* रणभूमि

Be (v◦) *rahanā, honā* रहना, होना*

Be born (v◦) *janma lenā* जन्म लेना

Bead (m◦) *maṇī* मणी

Beak (f◦) *choṅch* चोंच

Beans (f◦) *sem* सेम

Bear (m◦) *bhālū, rīchh* भालू, रीछ

Bear (v◦) *sahnā* सहना*

Beard (f◦) *dāḍhī* दाढ़ी

Beast (m◦) *paśhu* पशु

Beat (v◦) *pīṭnā, mārnā* पीटना, मारना*

Beautiful (adj◦) *sundar, suśhobhit* सुंदर, सुशोभित

Beautify (v◦) *sajānā* सजाना*

Beauty (f◦) *sundartā, śhobhā* सूंदरता, शोभा

Beaver (m◦) *udbilāv* उदबिलाव

Because (av◦) *kyoṅki, is kāraṇ se* क्योंकि, इस कारण से

Becoming (adj◦) *uchit, yogya* उचित, योग्य

Bed (m◦) *bistar* बिस्तर

Bedroom (m◦) *śhayanāgār* शयनागार

Bee (f◦) *makkhī, bhramar* मक्खी, भ्रमर

Beet (m◦) *chukandar* चुकन्दर

Before (av◦) *āge, sāmne, pahle* आगे, सामने, पहले

Before, time-place (av◦) *pahale, pūrva* पहले, पुर्व

Beg (v◦) *yāchanā karanā* याचना करना*

Beggar (m◦) *bhikhārī, mangtā* भिखारी, मंगता

Behaviour (m◦) *ācharaṇ* आचरण

Behead (v◦) *katal karnā* कतल करना*

Behind (av◦) *pīchhe* पीछे

Behold (v◦) *dekhanā* देखना*

Being (m◦) *jīv, prāṇī* जीव, प्राणी

Belch (v◦) *ḍakārnā, oknā* डकारना, ओकना

Believe (v◦) *viśhvās karnā* विश्वास करना*

Bell (f◦) *ghaṇṭī* घंटी

Bellybutton (f◦) *nābhī* नाभी

Beloved (m◦) *priya, pyārā* प्रिय, प्यारा

Below *(av◦) nīche* नीचे

Belt (m◦) *peṭī* पेटी

Bend (v◦) *jhuknā, jhukānā** झुकना; झुकाना*

Beneath (av◦) *nīche* नीचे

Benediction (m◦) *āśhīrvād* आशीर्वाद

Benefactor (m◦) *dātā, hitkārī* दाता, हितकारी

Benefit (m◦) *lābh, hit* लाभ, हित

Benevolence (f◦) *dayā, kripā* दया, कृपा

Bent (adj◦) *jhukā* झुका

Beside (prep◦) *nikaṭ, pās* निकट, पास

Besides (av◦) *sivāy* सिवाय

Best (adj◦) *uttam, śhreṣhṭha* उत्तम, श्रेष्ठ

Bet (m◦) *dāँv, paṇ, bājī* दाँव, पण, बाजी

Better (adj◦) *baḍhiyā* बढिया

Between (prep◦) *bīch meँ* बीच में

Beverage (m◦) *peya* पेय

Beyond (prep◦) *pār* पार

Bi fold (adj◦) *do parat* दो परत

Bias (m◦) *pakṣhapāt* पक्षपात

Bible (m◦) *Iñjīl* इञ्जील

Bibliography (f◦) *grantha-sūchī* ग्रंथ-सूची

Bicycle (m∘) *sāyakil* सायकील

Bide (v∘) *ṭharnā, rahnā* ठहरना, रहना

Big (adj∘) *baḍā* बड़ा

Bill (f∘) *parchī* परची

Billingual (adj∘) *do bhāṣhī* दो भाषी

Bin (f∘) *khattī, ṭokrī* खत्ती, टोकरी

Bind (v∘) *bāndhanā* बाँधना*

Binding (m∘) *bandhan* बंधन

Binocular (m∘) *dūrbīn* दूरबीन

Biography (m∘) *jīvanī* जीवनी

Biology (m∘) *prāṇiśhāstra* प्राणीशास्त्र

Bird (m∘) *pakṣhi, pañchhī* पक्षी, पंछी

Birth (m∘) *janma, janam* जन्म, जनम

Bite, cut (v∘) *kāṭanā* काटना*

Bitter (adj∘) *kaṭu, tītā* कटु, तीता

Bittergourd (m∘) *karelā* करेला

Black (adj∘) *kālā* काला

Blacksmith (m∘) *luhār* लुहार

Blame (v∘) *doṣh lagānā* दोष लगाना*

Blank (adj∘) *khālī, korā, śhūnya, rīkt* खाली, कोरा, शून्य, रीक्त (blank space = खाली स्थान; ∘ papar = कोरा कागज़; ∘ expression = शून्य चेहरा, ∘ account = रिक्त खाता)

Blanket (m∘) *kambal* कंबल

Blast (m∘) *dhamākā, visphot* धमाका, विस्फोट

Blaze (v∘) *bhaḍaknā, jalnā* भड़कना, जलना

Bleed (v∘) *khūn bahanā* खून बहना

Blemish (m∘) *dhabbā, dāg* धब्ब, दाग

Blessing (m∘) *vardān, kripā* वरदान, कृपा

Blind (adj∘) *andhā* अंधा

Blink (v∘) *ṭimṭimāna* टिमटिमाना

Bliss (m∘) *kripā* कृपा

Blister (m∘) *chhālā, fafolā* छाला, फफोला

Blizzard (m∘) *tūfān* तूफ़ान

Blob (m∘) *chhīṭā* छींटा

Block (m∘) *avarodh, pratirodh, rok* अवरोध, प्रतिरोध, रोक

Blockade (m∘) *nākabandī, gherāo* नाकाबंदी, घेराव

Blood (m∘) *khūn, rakt* खून, रक्त

Bloom (m∘) *bahār* बहार

Blossom (v∘) *khilanā* खिलना

Blot (m∘) *dhabbā, dāg* धब्बा, दाग

Blotch (m∘) *dhabbā, dāg* धब्बा, दाग

Blow (m∘) *āghāt, dhakkā, vār, prahār* आघात, धक्का, वार, प्रहार

Blow (v∘) *fū̃knā* फूँकना*

Blue (adj∘) *nīlā* नीला

Bluff (m∘) *jhā̃sā, dhaū̃s* झाँसा, धौंस

Blunder (m∘) *baḍī galtī* बड़ी गलती

Blunt (adj∘) *rūkhā, atīkṣhṇa* रूखा, अतीक्ष्ण

Blur (adj∘) *aspaṣhṭa, dhundhalā* अस्पष्ट, धूँधला

Blush (f∘) *lālimā* लालिमा

Board (m∘) *takhtā, faṭṭa* तख्ता, फट्टा

Boast (v∘) *ḍīng mārnā* डींग मारना*

Boat (f∘) *nāv, naukā, kiśhtī, jahāz* नाव, नौका, किश्ती, जहाज

Body (m∘) *śharīr, deh* शरीर, देह

Boil (v∘) *ubalnā, ubālanā** उबलना, उबालना*

Bold (adj∘) *nidar, sāhsal; baeoarma* निडर, साहसी; बेशरम

Bomb (m∘) *bam, barūd golā* बम, बारूद गोला

Bombard (m∘) *bambārī karnā, golābārI karnā* बमबारी करना, गोलाबारी करना

Bombay (f∘) *Mumbaī* मुंबई

Bondage (f∘) *dāsatā, gulāmī* दासता, गुलामी

Bone (f∘) *haḍḍī* हड्डी

Book (f∘) *kitāb, paustak* किताब, पुस्तक

Boon (m∘) *vardāb* वरदान

Boost (m∘) *baḍhāvā* बढ़ावा

Boot (m∘) *jūtā* जूता

Booze (f∘) *s̀harāb, dārū* शराब, दारू

Bore (adj∘) *ubāne vālā* उबाने वाला

Borrow (v∘) *udhār lenā* उधार लेना*

Borrowed (adj∘) *udhār* उधार

Bosom (f∘) *chhātī* छाती

Boss (m∘) *mālik* मालिक

Botany (m∘) *vanaspati s̀hastra* वनस्पति शास्त्र

Both (adj∘) *dono̐* दोनों

Bother (v∘) *taṅg karnā, pares̀hān karnā* तंग करना, परेशान करना*

Bottle (f∘) *s̀hīs̀hī* शीशी

Bottom (m∘) *tal* तल

Bounce (v∘) *uchhalnā; uchhālnā** उछलना, उछालना*

Boundry (f∘) *sīmā, sarhad* सीमा, सरहद

Bow (m∘) *dhanuṣh* धनुष

Bow (v∘) *jhuknā* झुकना

Bowl (m∘) *kaṭorā* कटोरा

Box (m∘) *baksā, ḍibbā, sandūk* बक्सा, ड़िब्बा, संदूक

Boy (m∘) *laḍakā, bālak* लड़का, बालक

Boycott (m∘) *bahiṣhkār* बहिष्कार

Brag (v∘) *dīṅg mārnā, s̀hekhī baghārnā* डींग मारना, शेखी बघारना*

Brain (m∘) *dimāg, magaz* दिमाग, मगज़

Branch (f∘) *ḍālī, s̀hakhā, ṭahnī* डाली, शाखा, टहनी

Brave (adj∘) *bahādur* बहादुर

Bread (f∘) *roṭī* रोटी

Break (v∘) *ṭūṭanā, toḍanā** टूटना, तोड़ना*

Breakfast (m∘) *nās̀htā* नाश्ता

Breath (m∘) *sā̐s* साँस

Breathless (adj∘) *bedam* बेदम

Breeze (f∘) *mand havā* मंद हवा

Bribe (f∘) *ris̀hvat, ghūs* रिश्वत, घूस

Brick (f∘) *īṅṭ* ईंट

Bride (f∘) *dūlhan, vadhū* दूल्हन, वधू

Bridge (m∘) *pul, setu* पुल, सेतु

Brief (adj∘) *alpa, saṅkṣhipta* अल्प, संक्षिप्त

Bright (adj∘) *tez, chamkīlā* तेज़, चमकीला

Brilliant (adj∘) *prakhar, prabhāvī* प्रखर, प्रभावी

Brim (m∘) *kinārā* किनारा

Bring (v∘) *lānā* लाना*

Brink (m∘) *kinārā, sirā* किनारा, सिरा

Brisk (adj∘) *tez, furtilā* तेज़, फुरतीला

Brittle (adj∘) *bhaṅgur, kurkurā* भंगुर, कुरकुरा

Broad (adj∘) *chauḍā* चौड़ा

Broke (adj∘) *kaṅgāk; ṭūṭā* कंगाल, टूटा (He is broke = *vah kaṅgāl hai;* The glass broke = *gilās ṭūṭā*)

Broker (m∘) *dalāl* दलाल

Brokerage (f∘) *dalālī* दलाली

Bronze (m∘) *kā̐sā* काँसा

Broom (m∘) *jhaḍū, buhārī* झाड़ू, बुहारी

Brother (m∘) *bhāī, bhaiyā* भाई, भैया

Brother-in-law (m∘) *sālā, dewar* साला, देवर

Brown (adj∘) *bhūrā* भूरा

Brush (m∘) *kūchī, tūkikā* कुची, तूलिका

Bucket (f∘) *bālṭī* बाल्टी

Bud (f∘) *kalī* कली

Buffalo (f∘) *bhains* भैंस

Bug (m∘) *kīḍā* कीड़ा

Building (f∘) *imārat, bhavan* इमारत, भवन

Bunch (m∘) *guchhā* गुच्छा

Bundle (f∘) *poṭlī* पोटली

Bungalow (m∘) *banglā* बंगला

Burden (m∘) *bhār* भार

Bureaucracy (f∘) *daftarśhāhī, naukarśhāhī* दफ्तरशाही, नौकरशाही

Burglar (m∘) *sendhmār* सेंधमार

Burglary (f∘) *sendhmārī* सेंधमारी

Burial (m∘) *dafan* दफ़न

Burn (v∘) *jalnā, jalānā** जलना, जलाना*

Burp (m∘) *ḍakār* डकार

Burrow (m∘) *bil* बिल

Burst (m∘) *visphoṭ* विस्फोट

Bury (av∘) *dafnānā, gāḍnā* दफनाना, गाड़ना

Bush (f∘) *jhāḍī* झाड़ी

Busy (adj∘) *vyasta* व्यस्त

But (av∘) *kintu, magar, lekin, to bhī* किंतु, मगर, लेकिन, तो भी

Butter (m∘) *makkhan* मक्खन

Butterfly (f∘) *titalī* तितली

Buttock (m∘) *chūtaḍ, nitamb* चूतड़, नितंब

Buy (v∘) *kharīdanā* खरीदना*

Buzz (f∘) *bhinbhināhaṭ* भिनभिनाहट

By (prep∘) *pās, samīp* पास, समीप

By day (av∘) *din meṅ, savere* दिन में, सवेरे

By night (av∘) *rāt meṅ* रात में

Bypass (m∘) *upa-mārg* उपमार्ग

C

Cabbage (f∘) *band-gobhī* बंदगोभी

Cable (f∘) *tār* तार

Cafe (m∘) *jalpāngriha* जलपानगृह

Cage (m∘) *piñjarā* पिंजरा

Cajole (v∘) *fuslānā* फुसलाना*

Calamity (m∘) *sankaṭ* (f∘) *vipatti* संकट, विपत्ति

Calcium (m∘) *chūnā* चूना

Calculation (m∘) *hisāb* हिसाब

Calcutta (m∘) *kolkātā* कोलकाता

Calf (m∘) *bachhaḍā* बछड़ा

Call (v∘) *bulānā* बुलाना*

Calm (adj∘) *śhānt* शांत; (f∘) *śhānti* शांति

Camel (m∘) *ūṅṭ* ऊँट

Camp (m∘) *śhivir* शिविर

Campaign (m∘) *abhiyān* अभियान

Can (m∘) *dibba, ṭīn* डिब्बा, टीन

Canal (m∘) *nahar* नहर

Cancel (v∘) *radd karnā* रद्द करना*

Candid (adj∘) *spaṣhṭa* स्पष्ट

Candidate (m∘) *ummidvār* उम्मीदवार

Candle (f∘) *mombattī* मोमबत्ती

Cane (f∘) *chhaḍī* छड़ी

Cannon (f∘) *top* तोप

Canoe (f∘) *ḍongī* डोंगी

Cap (f∘) *ṭopī* टोपी

Capability (f∘) *kṣhamatā* क्षमता

Capacity (f∘) *kṣhamatā* क्षमता

Capital (f∘) *rājdhānī* राजधानी

Capitalism (m∘) *pūñjīvād* पूँजीवाद

Capsize (v∘) *ḍūbnā* डूबना

Captivated (adj∘) *mugdha, mohit* मुग्ध, मोहित

Capture (v∘) *pakaḍnā* पकड़ना*

Car (f∘) *gāḍī* गाड़ी

Cardamom (f∘) *ilāyachī* इलायची

Care (f∘) *parvāh, dekhbhāl* परवाह, देखभाल

Career (m∘) *peśhā* पेशा

Careful (adj∘) *sāvadhān* सावधान

Careless (adj∘) *lāparvāh* लापरवाह

Caretaker (m∘) *rakhavālā* रखवाला

Carpenter (m∘) *baḍhaī* बढ़ई

Carpet (f∘) *darī* दरी

Carrot (m∘) *gājar* गाजर

Carry (v∘) *ḍhonā* ढोना*

Carry away (v∘) *le jānā* ले जाना*

Case (f∘) *ghaṭnā, māmalā, viṣhay, samasyā, mukadmā* घटना, मामला, विषय, समस्या, मुकदमा

Cash (adj∘) *nakad, rokaḍ* नकद, रोकड़

Cashew (m∘) *kājū* काजू

Cast (v∘) *fẽknā* फेंकना*

Caste (f∘) *jāti* जाति

Castle (m∘) *kīlā, durg* कीला, दुर्ग

Casual (adj∘) *anaupacharik* अनौपचारिक

Cat (f∘) *billī* बिल्ली

Catch (v∘) *pakaḍnā* पकड़ना*

Catsup (f∘) *chaṭnī* चटनी

Cattle (m∘) *ḍhor* ढोर

Caugh (f∘) *khā̃sī* खाँसी

Cauliflower (f∘) *fūlgobhī* फूलगोभी

Cause (m∘) *kāraṇ* कारण

Caustic (adj∘) *dāhak, tīkhā* दाहक, तीखा

Caution (f∘) *sāvadhānī* सावधानी

Cautious (adj∘) *sāvadhān* सावधान

Cave (f∘) *gufā, kandar* गुफा, कन्दर

Celebrate (v∘) *manānā* मनाना*

Cell-phone जंगम-दूरवाणी (f∘) *jaṅgama-dūravāṇī*

Centenary (f∘) *śhatābdī* शताब्दी

Central (adj∘) *kendrīya, madhya* केन्द्रीय, मध्य

Century (f∘) *śhatābdī* शताब्दी

Ceremony (m∘) *samāroh* समारोह

Certainly (av∘) *avaśhya, nischit* अवश्य, निश्चित

Certainty (m∘) *niśhchay* निश्चय

Certificate (m∘) *pramāṇ-patra* प्रमाण-पत्र

Chain (f∘) *jañjīr* जंजीर

Chair (f∘) *kurasī* कुरसी

Chairman (m∘) *sabhāpati, adhyakṣha* सभापति, अध्यक्ष

Chalk (f∘) *khaḍiyā* खड़िया

Challange (f∘) *chunautī* चुनौती

Chamber (m∘) *kamrā, kakṣha* कमरा, कक्ष

Chance (m∘) *sambhāvanā, maukā* संभावना (possibility), मौका (opportunity)

Change (m∘) *badal, parivartan; rejgārī, chhuṭṭā* बदल, परिवर्तन; रेजगारी, छुट्टा (I changed my name = *maĩ ne apnā nām badlā*; Take change for a Dollar = *ek dālar kī rejgārī lījiye, chhuṭṭā lījiye*)

Change (v∘) *badalnā* बदलना

Chaos (m∘) *uljhan* उलझन

Chapter (m∘) *pāṭh, adhyāy* पाठ, अध्याय

Chariot (m∘) *rath* रथ

Charm (m∘) *ākarṣhaṇ, jādū, moha* आकर्षण, जादू, मोह

Chat (f∘) *gapśhap* गपशप

Chatter (f∘) *bakvās, kiṭkiṭ* बकवास, किटकिट

Cheap (adj∘) *sastā* सस्ता

Cheat (v∘) *ṭhagānā* ठगाना*

Check (v∘) *jā̃chanā* जाँचना*

Cheek (m∘) *gāl* गाल

Cheer (m∘) *jayghoṣh, vāhvāhī* जयघोष, वाहवाही

Cheerful (adj∘) *prasanna* प्रसन्न

Cheerless (adj∘) *khinna, udās* खिन्न, उदास

Cheese (m∘) *panīr* पनीर

Cheetah (m∘) *chītā* चीता

Chemical (m∘) *rasāyan* रसायन

Chemistry (m∘) *rasāyan-śhāstra* रसायनशास्त्र

Chess (f∘) *śhatrañj* शतरंज

Chest (f∘) *chhātī* छाती

Chew (v∘) *chabānā* चबाना*

Chicken (f∘) *muragī,* (m∘) *muragā* मुर्गी, मुर्गा

Chief (m∘) *mukhiyā* मुखिया, *mukhya* मुख्य

Child (m∘) *bachchā, bālak* बच्चा, बालक

Chill (f∘) *siharan* सिहरन

Chilly (f∘) *mirchī* मिरची

Chin (f∘) *thuḍḍī* ठुड्डी

Chisel (f∘) *chhenī* छेनी

Choice (m∘) *chunāv, varaṇ* चुनाव, वरण

Choke (v∘) *ghuṭnā* घुटना

Choose (v∘) *chunanā* चुनना*

Chop (v∘) *kāṭnā* काटना*

Christ (m∘) *īsā masīh* ईसा मसीह

Christian (adj∘) *īsāī* ईसाई

Chronicle (m∘) *itihās* इतिहास

Chronology (m∘) *kālkram* कालक्रम

Chubby (adj∘) *gol-maṭol* गोल-मटोल

Chum (m∘) *dost* दोस्त

Chunk (m∘) *ṭukḍā* टुकड़ा

Church (m∘) *girjāghar* गिरजाघर

Churn (v∘) *mathnā* मथना*

Churner (f∘) *mathnī* मथनी

Cinamon (f∘) *dālchīnī* दालचीनी

Circle (m∘) *gol, vritta* गोल, वृत्त

Circumference (f∘) *paridhi* परिधि

Circumstance (f∘) *paristhiti* परिस्थिति

Citizen (m∘) *nāgarik* नागरिक

City (m∘) *nagar, śhahar* नगर, शहर

Civilization (f∘) *sabhyatā* सभ्यता

Claim (m∘) *adhikār* अधिकार

Claim (v∘) *dāvā karnā* दावा करना*

Clamour (m∘) *śhor, hohallā* शोर, होहल्ला

Clamp (m∘) *śhikañjā* शिकंजा

Clap (v∘) *tālī bajanā* ताली बजाना*

Clarified-butter (m∘) *ghee* घी

Clarify (m∘) *spaṣhṭa karnā* स्पष्ट करना

Clarity (f∘) *spaṣhṭtā* स्पष्टता

Clash (f∘) *ṭakkar* टक्कर

Class (m∘) *kakṣhā* कक्षा

Classification (m∘) *vargīkaraṇ* वर्गीकरण

Claw (m∘) *pañjā, chaṅgul* पंजा, चंगुल

Clean (adj∘) *sāf, svachha* साफ़, स्वच्छ

Clean (v∘) *sāf-karanā* साफ करना*

Cleanliness (f∘) *svachhatā* स्वच्छता

Clear (adj∘) *spaṣhṭa* स्पष्ट

Clearly (av∘) *sāf-sāf* साफ़-साफ़

Clerk (m∘) *munīm* मुनीम

Cliant (m∘) *grāhak* ग्राहक

Cliff (f∘) *chaṭṭān* चट्टान

Climate (m∘) *vātāvaraṇ* वातावरण

Climax (f∘) *parākāṣhṭhā* पराकाष्ठा

Climb (v∘) *chaḍhanā* चढ़ना

Cling (v∘) *chipaknā, lipaṭnā* चिपकना, लिपटना

Cloak (m∘) *labādā* लबादा

Clock, watch (f∘) *ghaḍī* घड़ी

Close (adj∘) *najadīk, samīp* नजदीक, समीप

Close (av∘) *pād mẽ* पास में

Closed (adj∘) *band* बंद

Clot (m∘) *thakkā* थक्का

Cloth (m∘) *kapaḍā* कपड़ा

Cloud (m∘) *bādal* बादल

Clove (f∘) *lauaṅg* लौंग

Clown (m∘) *viduṣhak* विदुषक

Club (m∘) *mudgar* मुदगर

Clue (m∘) *saṅket* संकेत

Clumsy (adj∘) *beḍaul, beḍhaṅgā* बेडौल, बेढंगा

Cluster (m∘) *guchhā* गुच्छा

Clutch (m∘) *śhikañjā, pakaḍ, chaṅgul* शिकंजा, पकड़, चंगुल

Clutter (f∘) *astavyastatā* अस्तव्यस्तता

Coagulate (v∘) *jamanā* जमना

Coal (m∘) *koylā* कोयला

Coarse (adj∘) *ghaṭiyā* घटिया

Coast (m∘) *samudrataṭ* समुद्रतट

Coax (v∘) *fusalānā* फुसलाना*

Cob (m∘) *bhuṭṭā* भुट्टा

Cobra (m∘) *nāg* नाग

Cock (m∘) *murgā* मुर्गा

Cock-eyed (adj∘) *bewakūf* बेवकूफ़

Cockroach (m∘) *tilchaṭṭā* तिलचट्टा

Coconut (m∘) *nāriyal* नारियल

Coffee (m∘) *kahavā* कहवा

Coin (m∘) *sikkā* सिक्का

Coincidence (m∘) *sañjog* संजोग

Cold (adj∘) *ṭhaṇḍā, śhītal* ठंडा, शीतल

Cold (f∘) *sardī, ṭhaṇḍak* सर्दी, ठंडक

Collapse (v∘) *girnā* गिरना

Colleague (m∘) *sahayogī* सहयोगी

Collection (m∘) *saṅgraha* संग्रह

College (m∘) *vidyālay* विद्यालय

Collide (v∘) *ṭakrānā* टकराना

Collision (f∘) *ṭakkar* टक्कर

Colour (m∘) *raṅg* रंग

Colour (v∘) *raṅgānā* रँगाना*

Column (m∘) *khambhā, stambh* खंबा, स्तंभ

Comb (f∘) *kaṅghā* कंघा

Combat (f∘) *laḍāī* लड़ाई

Combat (v∘) *laḍnā* लड़ना*

Combine (v∘) *milānā* मिलाना*

Come (v∘) *ānā* आना

Comfort (m∘) *ārām, chain* आराम, चैन

Comfortable (adj∘) *sukhdāyak* सुखदायक

Comical (f∘) *hāsyamay* हास्यमय

Command (m∘) *adhikār; ādeśh, hukma* अधिकार; आदेश, हुक्म

Comment (f∘) *ṭippaṇī* टिप्पणी

Commentary (f∘) *ṭīkā* टीका

Commerce (m∘) *vāṇijja* वाणिज्य

Commission (m∘) *baṭṭā* (f∘) *dalālī* बट्टा, दलाली

Committee (f∘) *samiti* समिति

Common (adj∘) *sādhāraṇ* साधारण

Commonwealth (m∘) *rājyasaṅgha* राज्यसंघ

Commotion (m∘) *śhorgul* शोरगुल

Communal (adj∘) *sāmudāyik* सामुदायिक

Communication (m∘) *sañcharaṇ* संचरण

Communism (m∘) *sāmyavād* साम्यवाद

Community (m∘) *samāj* समाज

Companion (m∘) *sāthī* साथी

Comparable (adj∘) *tulya, samān* तुल्य, समान

Compare (v∘) *tulnā karnā* तुलना करना*

Comparison (f∘) *tulnā* तुलना

Compass (m∘) *kutubnumā* कुतुबनुमा

Compassion (f∘) *dayā* दया

Compatible (adj∘) *anukūl* अनुकूल

Compatriot (m∘) *hamvatan* हमवतन

Compel (v∘) *bādhya karnā, majbūr karnā* बाध्य करना, मजबूर करना*

Compete (v∘) *spardhā karnā* स्पर्धा करना*

Competition (f∘) *spardhā, mukābalā, hoḍ* स्पर्धा, मुकाबला, होड़

Competitor (m∘) *pratiyogī* प्रतियोगी

Compilation (m∘) *saṅkalan* संकलन

Complain (v∘) *śhikāyat karnā* शिकायत करना*

Complaint (f∘) *śhikāyat* शिकायत

Complementary (m∘) *pūrak* पूरक

Complete (adj∘) *purṇa* पूर्ण

Complete (v∘) *purṇa karnā* पूर्ण करना*

Complex (adj∘) *jaṭil* जटिल

Complexion (m∘) *raṅg-rūp* रंग-रूप

Complicated (adj∘) *jaṭil* जटिल

Component (m∘) *avayava, ghaṭak* अवयव, घटक

Compose (v∘) *rachanā* रचना*

Composition (f∘) *rachanā* रचना

Compound (m∘) *miśhraṇ* मिश्रण

Compress (v∘) *ṭhū̃sanā* ठूँसना*

Compromise (f∘) *sulah* सुलह

Compulsion (m∘) *dabāv, majabūrī* दबाव, मजबूरी

Compulsory (adj∘) *āvaśhyak, anivārya* आवश्यक, अनिवार्य

Computer (m∘) *saṅgaṇak* संगणक

Comred (m∘) *sāthī* साथी

Con (v∘) *ṭhagnā* ठगना*

Concede (v∘) *kabūl karnā* कबूल करना*

Conceit (m∘) *ghamaṇḍ, ahamkār* घमंड, अहंकार

Concentration (f∘) *ekāgratā* एकाग्रता

Conception (f∘) *dhāraṇā* धारणा

Concern (f∘) *chintā* चिंता

Concerted (adj∘) *saṅgaṭhit* संगठित

Concession (f∘) *chhūṭ, riyāyat* छूट, रियायत

Concise (adj∘) *saṅkṣhipta* संक्षिप्त

Conclude (v∘) *nirṇay lenā* निर्णय लेना*

Conclusion (m∘) *niṣkarṣha* निष्कर्ष

Condemn (v∘) *nindā karnā* निंदा करना*

Condensed (adj∘) *ghana* घन

Condiment (m∘) *masālā* मसला

Condition (f∘) *sthiti, avasthā* स्थिति, अवस्था

Condolence (m∘) *śhok* शोक

Conduct (m∘) *ācharaṇ* आचरण

Conduction (m∘) *pravāh* प्रवाह

Conductive (adj∘) *sahāyak* सहायक

Conductor (m∘) *sañchālak* संचालक

Cone (m∘) *śhanku* शंकु

Confederation (m∘) *mahāsangha* महासंघ

Confer (v∘) *pradān karnā* प्रदान करना*

Confess (m∘) *kabūl karnā* कबूल करना*

Confession (m∘) *svīkār*, (f∘) *kabuīlī* स्वीकार, कबूली

Confidence (m∘) *bharosā* भरोसा

Confident (adj∘) *viśhvasta* विश्वस्त

Confidential (adj∘) *gopanīya* गोपनीय

Confirmation (m∘) *pakkā karnā* पक्का करना

Confiscate (v∘) *kabjā karnā* कब्जा करना*

Conflict (m∘) *sangharṣha, matabhed* संघर्ष, मतभेद

Conform (m∘) *pālan karnā* पालन करना

Confound (v∘) *gaḍbaḍānā* गड़बड़ाना

Confront (v∘) *sāmanā karnā* सामना करना

Confuse (v∘) *gaḍbaḍānā* गड़बड़ाना

Confusion (f∘) *gaḍbaḍa* गड़बड़

Congestion (f∘) *bhīḍ* भीड़

Congratulation (m∘) *badhāī, abhinandan* बधाई, अभिनंदन

Congress (m∘) *sammelan* संम्मेलन

Conjunction (m∘) *joḍ* जोड़

Connect (v∘) *joḍnā* जोड़ना*

Connection (m∘) *sambandha, joḍ* संबंध, जोड़

Conquer (v∘) *jītnā* जीतना*

Conquest (f∘) *jīt* जीत

Conscious (adj∘) *satark* सतर्क

Consciousness (f∘) *chetnā* चेतना

Consecutive (adj∘) *Lagātār* लगातार

Consensus (f∘) *sarvānumati* सर्वानुमति

Consent (f∘) *anumati* अनुमति

Consequence (m∘) *pariṇām* परिणाम

Conservative (adj∘) *rūḍhivādī* रूढीवादी

Consider (v∘) *lihāz karnā* लिहाज़ करना*

Considerable (adj∘) *kāfī* काफी

Consideration (m∘) *lihāz* लिहाज़

Consign (v∘) *saũpanā* सौंपना*

Consistent (adj∘) *niyamit* नियमित

Consolation (f∘) *dilāsā* दिलासा

Console (v∘) *idlāsā denā* दिलासा देना*

Consolidation (f∘) *chakbandī* चकबंदी

Consonant (m∘) *vyañjan* व्यंजन

Conspiracy (m∘) *ṣhaḍyantra* षड्यंत्र

Constable (m∘) *sipāhī* सिपाही

Constant (adj∘) *sthir, aṭal* स्थिर, अटल

Constantly (av∘) *nitya, nirantar, lagātār* नित्य, निरंतर, लगातार

Constipation (m∘) *kabj* कब्ज

Constituent (m∘) *ghaṭak, avayav* घटक, अवयव

Constitution (m∘) *saṁvidhān* संविधान

Consul (m∘) *dūt* दूत

Consulate (m∘) *dūtāvās* दूतावास

Consumer (m∘) *upa-bhoktā* उपभोक्ता

Consumption (m∘) *upa-bhog* उपभोग

Contact (m∘) *sparśha, sampark* स्पर्श, संपर्क

Container (m∘) *pātra* पात्र

Contamination (m∘) *dūshaṇ* दूषण

Contemporary (adj∘) *samakalīn* समकालीन

Contempt (m∘) *apamān* अपमान

Contension (m∘) *jhagḍā, saṅgharṣha* झगड़ा, संघर्ष

Content (adj∘) *santuṣhṭa* संतुष्ट

Contest (f∘) *spardhā* स्पर्धा

Context (m∘) *sandarbha* संदर्भ

Continent (m∘) *khaṇḍa* खंड

Contingent (adj∘) *sambhāvit* संभावित

Continue (v∘) *jārī rakhanā* जारी रखना*

Continuity (f∘) *akhaṇḍtā* अखंडता

Continuous (adj∘) *akhaṇḍ* अखंड

Contract (m∘) *ikrār* इकरार

Contractor (m∘) *ṭhekedār* ठेकेदार

Contrary (adj∘) *viparīt* विपरीत

Contrast (m∘) *vaiṣhamya* वैषम्य

Contribution (m∘) *yogdān* योगदान

Control (m∘) *niyantraṇ* नियंत्रण

Controversy (m∘) *vād* वाद

Convenience (f∘) *suvidhā* सुविधा

Convenient (adj∘) *upa-yukta* उपयुक्त

Convention (m∘) *sammelan,* (f∘) *sabhā* सम्मेलन, सभा

Conversation (m∘) *vārtālāp* (f∘) *bātchīt* वार्तालाप, बातचीत

Conversion (m∘) *parivartan* परिवर्तन

Convert (v∘) *badalnā, badak karnā** बदलना; बदल करना*

Convice (m∘) *aparādhī, doṣhī* अपराधी, दोषी

Cook (v∘) *pakānā* पकाना*

Cool (adj∘) *ṭhaṇḍā* ठंडा

Cooperation (m∘) *sahayog* सहयोग

Copper (m∘) *tāmā* तामा

Copy (f∘) *nakal* नकल

Copy (v∘) *nakal karnā* नकल करना*

Cord (m∘) *tār,* (f∘) *ḍorī* तार, ड़ोरी

Coriander (m∘) *dhaniyā* धनिया

Corn (f∘) *makkī* मक्की

Corner (m∘) *konā, nukkaḍ* कोना, नुक्कड़

Corporation (m∘) *nigam* निगम

Corpse (f∘) *lāśh* लाश

Correct (adj∘) *ṭhīk karnā, sahī karnā* ठीक करना, सही करना

Correct (adj∘) *ṭhīk, sahī* ठीक, सही

Correction (f∘) *śhuddhi* शुद्धि

Corrugated (adj∘) *lahardār* लहरदार

Corrupt (adj∘) *beīmān* बेईमान

Corrupt (adj∘) *bhraṣṭa* भ्रष्ट

Corruption (m∘) *bhrāṣhṭāchār* भ्रष्टाचार

Cosmatics (m∘) *saundarya prasādhan* सौंदर्य प्रसाधन

Cosmos (m∘) *brahmānd* ब्रह्मांड

Cost (m∘) *dām,* (f∘) *kīmat* दाम, कीमत

Costly (adj∘) *mahaṅgā* महंगा

Costume (m∘) *pośhāk* पोशाक

Cot (f∘) *khaṭiyā* खटिया

Cottage (f∘) *kuṭiyā* कुटिया

Cotton (f∘) *ruī, kapās* रुई, कपास

Couch (m∘) *palaṅg* पलंग

Could (v∘) *saknā* सकना

Council (f∘) *pariṣhad* परिषद्

Counsel (f∘) *salāh* सलाह

Counsel (v∘) *samjhānā, suljhānā* समझाना, सुलझाना*

Count (v◦) *ginanā* गिनना*

Country (m◦) *deśh* देश

Countryman (m◦) *hamvatan* हमवतन

Couple (m◦) *yugma, joḍa* युग्म, जोड़ा

Courage (m◦) *sāhas* साहस

Court (f◦) *kachaharī, nyāyālay* कचहरी, न्यायालय

Courtious (adj◦) *bhadra, śhiṣhṭa* भद्र, शिष्ट

Courtsy (m◦) *saujanya, śhiṣhṭāchār* सौजन्य, शिष्टाचार

Cousult (v◦) *salāh lenā* सलाह लेना*

Cousultation (f◦) *salāh* सलाह

Cover (m◦) *ḍhakkan, āvaraṇ* ढक्कन, आवरण

Cover (v◦) *ḍhakanā* ढकना*

Covert (adj◦) *gupta* गुप्त

Covet (v◦) *lalchānā* ललचाना

Cow (f◦) *gāy, gau* गाय, गो

Coward (adj◦) *ḍarpok* ड़रपोक

Crab (m◦) *kekḍā* केकड़ा

Crack (f◦) *darār, chīr* दरार, चीर

Cradle (m◦) *palnā* पालना

Craft (f◦) *kalā* कला

Cram (v◦) *ṭhū̃snā* ठूँसना*

Cramp (f◦) *śhūl, aĩṭhan* शूल, ऐंठन

Crane (m◦) *bagulā, sāras* बगुला, सारस

Crank (adj◦) *jhakkī* झक्की

Crash (m◦) *ṭakkar* टक्कर

Crave (v◦) *tarasnā* तरसना

Crease (f◦) *chunnaṭ, tah* चुन्नट, तह

Creation (f◦) *utpatti, sṛṣhṭi* उत्पत्ति; सृष्टि

Creative (adj◦) *utpādak* उत्पादक

Creativity (m◦) *utpādan* उत्पादन

Creator (m◦) *kartā* कर्ता

Creature (m◦) *prāṇī, jīv* प्राणी, जीव

Credible (adj◦) *viśhvasanīya* विश्वसनीय

Credit (f◦) *pratīti* प्रतीति

Creditor (m◦) *lendār, mahājan. riṇadātā* लेनदार, महाजन, ऋणदाता

Credulity (m◦) *bholāpan* भोलापन

Creduluous (adj◦) *bhola-bhālā* भोला-भाला

Creed (m◦) *pantha, dharma* पंथ, धर्म

Creek (m◦) *nālā* नाला

Creep (v◦) *reṅgnā* रेंगना

Creeper (f◦) *latā, bel* लता, बेल

Cremation (m◦) *dahan* दहन

Crime (m◦) *aprādh* अपराध

Criminal (m◦) *aparādhī* अपराधी

Crimson (adj◦) *kirmijī* किरमिजी

Crinkle (f◦) *chunnaṭ* चुन्नट

Cripple (m◦) *apaṅg* अपंग

Crippled (adj◦) *lūlā* लूला

Crisis (m◦) *saṅkaṭ* संकट

Crisp (adj◦) *kurkurā, khastā* कुरकुरा, खस्ता

Critic (m◦) *ṭīkākār, nindak* टीकाकार, निंदक

Criticism (f◦) *nindā, ālochanā* निंदा, आलोचना

Crocodile (m◦) *magar-machchha, ghaḍiyāl* मगरमच्छ, घड़ियाल

Crook (m◦) *dhūrta* धूर्त

Crooked (adj◦) *kapaṭī, beīmān* कपटी, बेईमान

Crop (f◦) *fasal* फ़सल

Cross (v◦) *pār karanā* पार करना*

Cross, the (f◦) *sūlī* सूली

Crow (m◦) *kauā* कौआ

Crowd (f◦) *bhīḍ* भीड़

Cruel (adj◦) *rrūr, nirday* क्रूर, निर्दय

Cruelty (f◦) *krūratā* क्रुरता

Crush (v◦) *kuchalnā* कुचलना*

Cry (m◦) *ronā, chīkhanā* रोना, चीखना

Cry (v◦) *ronā* रोना

Crystal (m◦) *billor, sphaṭik* बिल्लोर, स्फटिक

Cube (m◦) *ghana* घन

Cubic (adj◦) *ghanākār* घनाकार

Cuckoo (f◦) *koyal* कोयल

Cucumber (m◦) *khīrā, kakḍī* खीरा, ककड़ी

Cud (f◦) *jugālī* जुगाली

Cue (m◦) *saṅkei, iśhārā* संकेत, इशारा

Culmination (f◦) *parākaṣhṭhā* पराकाष्ठा

Culprit (m◦) *doṣhī, aprādhī* दोषी, अपराधी

Cultivation (f◦) *khetī, jutāī* खेती, जुताई

Cultural (adj◦) *sānskritik* सांस्कृतिक

Culture (f◦) *sanskriti* संस्कृति

Culvert (m◦) *nālā* नाला

Cumbersome (adj◦) *kaṭhin, bhārī* कठिन, भारी

Cumulative (adj◦) *sañchit* संचित

Cunbustible (adj◦) *jwālāgrahī* ज्वालाग्रही

Cunning (adj◦) *dhūrta, chatur* धूर्त, चतुर

Cup (m◦) *pyālā, gilās* प्याल, गिलास

Curable (adj◦) *sādhya* साध्य

Curd (m◦) *dahī* दही

Cure (m◦) *ilāj, upchār* इलाज, उपचार

Curiosity (m◦) *kutuhal* कुतुहल

Curious (adj◦) *utsuk* उत्सुक

Curl (v◦) *muḍnā, moḍnā** मुडना, मोड़ना*

Curly (adj◦) *ghuṅgharālā* घुंघराला

Currency (f◦) *mudrā* मुद्रा

Current (adj◦) *vartamān, prachalit* वर्तमान, प्रचलित

Current (m◦) *pravāha* प्रवाह

Curriculum (m◦) *pāṭhyakram* पाठ्यक्रम

Curry (f◦) *sabjī* सब्जी

Curse (m◦) *śhāp* शाप

Curtail (v◦) *ghaṭāna* घटाना*

Curtain (m◦) *pardā* परदा

Curve (m◦) *ghumāv, moḍ* घुमाव, मोड़

Curved (adj◦) *vakra* वक्र

Cushion (f◦) *gaddī* गद्दी

Custard apple (m◦) *sītāfal* सीताफल

Custodian (m◦) *rakṣhak* रक्षक

Custody (f◦) *hirāsat* हिरासत

Customer (m◦) *grāhak* ग्राहक

Cut, bite (v◦) *kāṭnā* काटना*

Cute (adj◦) *sundar* सुंदर

Cycle (m◦) *krama* क्रम

Cyclone (m◦) *bavaṇḍar, chakravāt* बवंडर, चक्रवात

Cymbal (m◦) *mañjīrā* मंजीरा

D

Dad, Daddy (m◦) *pitājī* पिताजी

Daggar (f◦) *kaṭār, chhurā* कटार, छुरा

Daily (adj◦) *dainik* दैनिका

Daily (av◦) *pratidin, nitya, roz* प्रतिदिन, नित्य, रोज़

Dairy (m◦) *dugdhālay* दुग्धालय

Dall (f◦) *guḍiyā* गुड़िया

Dam (m◦) *bāndh* बाँध

Damage (m◦) *nuksān, hāni* नुक़्सान, हानि

Damnation (f◦) *tabāhī* तबाही

Damp (adj◦) *nam, sīlā* नम, सीला

Dampness (f◦) *namī, sīlan* नमी, सीलन

Dance (m◦) *nāch, nritya* नाच, नृत्य

Dance (v◦) *nāchanā* नाचना

Dancer (f◦) *nartakī* नर्तकी

Danger (m◦) *dhokhā, khatra, sankaṭ* धोखा, ख़तरा, संकट

Dangerous (adj◦) *khatarnāk* ख़तरनाक

Dangle (v◦) *laṭaknā, jhūlnā* लटकना, झूलना

Dare (m◦) *chunautī* चुनौती

Daring (adj◦) *sāhasī, nidar* साहसी, निडर

Dark (adj◦) *gaḍhā; kālā* गाढ़ा; काला

Dark (m◦) *andherā* अँधेरा

Darling (adj◦) *priya, pyārā* प्रिय, प्यारा

Dash (v◦) *jhapaṭnā* झपटना

Date (f◦) *tithi, tārīkh* तिथि, तारीख

Daughter (f◦) *laḍkī, beṭī* लड़की, बेटी

Daughter-in-law (f◦) *bahū* बहू

Dawn (m◦) *saverā* सवेरा

Day (m◦) *vār, din* वार, दिन

Day after tomorrow(av◦) *parsõ* परसों

Day before yesterday (av◦) *parsõ* परसों

Dead (adj◦) *mrit, arā* मृत, मरा, मरा हुआ

Deadly (adj◦) *ghātak* घातक

Deaf (adj◦) *bahrā, badhir* बहरा, बधिर

Deal (m◦) *samjhautā* समझौता

Deal (v◦) *nipaṭnā* निपटना*

Dealing (m◦) *vyavahār* व्यवहार

Dear (adj◦) *pyāra, priya* प्यारा, प्रिय

Dearth (f◦) *kamī* कमी

Death (m◦) *mrityua* (f◦) *maut* मृत्यु, मौत

Debacle (f◦) *hār* हार

Debanture (m◦) *riṇapatra* ऋणपत्र

Debate (m◦) *vād-ivād* वाद-विवाद

Debris (m◦) *malvā* मलवा

Debt (m◦) *riṇ, udhār, karj* ऋण, उधार, कर्ज

Decade (m◦) *daśhak* दशक

Decay (m◦) hrās, (f◦) *avanati* अवनति, ह्रास

Decay (v◦) *saḍnā* सड़ना

Deceased (adj◦) *mrit, arā* मृत, मरा हुआ

Deceit (m◦) *dhokhā, beīmāmī* धोखा, बेईमानी

Deceive (v◦) *dhokhā denā* धोखा देना*

December (m◦) *disambar* दिसंबर

Decency (m◦) *ṣhiṣhṭāchār* शिष्टाचार

Decent (adj◦) *śhiṣhṭa, uchit* शिष्ट, उचित

Deception (m◦) *dhokhebāzī* धोखेबाज़ी

Deceptive (adj◦) *dhokhebāz* धोखेबाज़

Decide (m◦) *inaśhchay karnā* निश्चय करना

Decimal (adj◦) *daśhamlav* दशमलव

Decision (m◦) *nirṇay* निर्णय

Decisive (adj◦) *nirṇayātmak* निर्णयात्मक

Declaration (f◦) *ghoṣaṇā* घोषणा

Declare (v◦) *ghoṣhit karna* घोषित करना*

Decline (f◦) *avanati,* (m◦) *kṣhaya* अवनति, क्षय

Decline, decrease (v◦) *ghaṭnā* घटना

Decompose (v◦) *saḍnā, galnā* सड़ना, गलना

Decor (f◦) *sajāvaṭ* सजावट

Decorate (f◦) *sajānā* सजाना

Decoration (f◦) *sajāvaṭ* सजावट

Decorativen (f∘) *sajāvaṭī* सजावटी

Decoy (m∘) *fām̐sā* फाँसा

Decrease (v∘) *ghaṭnā* घटना

Dedication (m∘) *samarpaṇ* समर्पण

Deduct (m∘) *kamī karnā* कमी करना

Deduction (f∘) *kamī, kaṭautī* कमी, कटौती

Deed (m∘) *kārya, kām* कार्य, काम

Deep (adj∘) *gahrā* गहरा

Deer (m∘) *harin* हरिन

Defame (f∘) *badnāmī* बदनामी

Defeat (v∘) *hranā, jītnā* हराना, जीतना*

Defect (m∘) *doṣh* (f∘) *kharābī* दोष, खराबी

Defence (f∘) *rakṣhā* रक्षा

Defend (v∘) *rakṣha karnā* रक्षा करना*

Defer (v∘) *sthagit larnā* स्थगित करना*

Defiance (m∘) *virodh, iṅkār* विरोध, इनकार

Deficiency (f∘) *kamī, abhāv* कमी, अभाव

Deficit (m∘) *kamī, ghāṭā* कमी, घाटा

Definite (adj∘) *pakkā, nischit* पक्का, निश्चित

Definition (f∘) *vyākhyā* व्याख्या

Deformation (m∘) *bigāḍ,* (f∘) *vikṛti* बिगाड़, विकृति

Defraud (v∘) *ṭhagnā* ठगना*

Defunct (adj∘) *anupayukta* अनुपयुक्त

Deity (f∘) *devatā* देवता

Dejected (adj∘) *māyūs, nirāśh* मायूस, निराश

Dejection (f∘) *nirāśhā, māyūsī* निराशा, मायूसी

Delay (f∘) *derī* देरी

Delhi (f∘) *Dillī* दिल्ली

Delicate (adj∘) *nājuk* नाजुक

Delicious (adj∘) *svādiṣṭa* स्वादिष्ट

Delight (f∘) *prasannatā* प्रसन्नता

Deluge (f∘) *bāḍh* बाढ़

Delusion (f∘) *bhrānti* भ्रांति

Demand (f∘) *māṅg* माँग

Demand (v∘) *māṅgnā* माँगना*

Demeanour (m∘) *bartāv* बरताव

Demise (m∘) *mrityu,* (f∘) *maut* मृत्यु, मौत

Democracy (m∘) *loktantra* लोकतंत्र

Demolish (v∘) *girānā* गिराना*

Demon (m∘) *rākṣhas* राक्षस

Demonstrate (v∘) *dikhānā* दिखाना*

Demonstration (m∘) *pradarśhan* प्रदर्शन

Demotion (f∘) *padāvnati* पदावनति

Den (f∘) *gufā, mānd* गुफा, माँद

Dense (adj∘) *gāḍhā, ghana* गाढ़ा, घन

Density (m∘) *ghanatva* घनत्व

Dent (m∘) *pichkā* पिचका

Dentist (m∘) *dant-vaidya* दंत-वैद्य

Deny (v∘) *nakārnā* नकारना*

Depart (v∘) *prasthān karnā, jānā* प्रस्थान करना, जाना

Department (m∘) *vibhāg* विभाग

Departure (m∘) *prasthān* प्रस्थान

Depend (v∘) *bharosā karnā* भरोसा करना*

Dependent (adj∘) *āśhrit* आश्रित

Deplorable (adj∘) *nindanīya* निंदनीय

Deplore (v∘) *nindā karnā* निंदा करना*

Deposit (f∘) *jamā rakam* जमा रकम

Deposit (v∘) *jamā karnā* जमा करना*

Depot (m∘) *gudām* गुदाम

Depression (f∘) *udāsī* उदासी

Depth (f∘) *gaharāī* गहराई

Descend (v∘) *utarnā* उतरना

Describe (v∘) *varṇan karnā* वर्णन करना*

Description (m∘) *varṇan* वर्णन

Desert (m∘) *registān* रेगिस्तान

Deserve (v∘) *lāyak honā* लायक होना

Design (f∘) *yojnā, rūpreṣhā* योजना, रूपरेषा

Designation (m∘) *pad* पद

Desirable (adj∘) *iṣhṭa* इष्ट

Desire, want (f∘) *chāh, ichhā* चाह, इच्छा

Desire, want (v∘) *chāhanā* चाहना*

Desk, table (m∘) *mez* मेज़

Despair (f∘) *inarāśhā* निराशा

Desperate (adj∘) *uddaṇḍ, nirāśh* उद्दंड, निराश

Despise (v∘) *tiraskār karnā* तिरस्कार करना*

Despite (prep∘) *ke bāvajūd* के बावजूद

Despondent (adj∘) *udās* उदास

Destination (m∘) *lakṣhya* लक्ष्य

Destiny (m∘) *niyati, bhāgya* नियति, भाग्य

Destroy (v∘) *naṣṭa karnā* नष्ट करना*

Destruction (m∘) *vināśh* विनाश

Destructive (adj∘) *nāśhkārī* नाशकारी

Detach (v∘) *alag karnā* अलग करना*

Detail (m∘) *byorā* ब्योरा

Detariorate (v∘) *kṣhaya honā* क्षय होना

Detarioration (m∘) *kṣhaya* क्षय

Detect (v∘) *patā lagānā* पता लगाना*

Detective (m∘) *jāsūs* जासूस

Detention (f∘) *kaid* कै़द

Determination (m∘) *saṅkalpa* संकल्प

Determine (v∘) *nischay karnā* निश्चय करना*

Deterrent (f∘) *bādhā* बाधा

Detest (v∘) *ghriṇā karnā* घृणा करना*

Detestation (f∘) *ghriṇa* घृणा

Detonation (m∘) *visphoṭ* विस्फोट

Detriment (f∘) *hāni* हानि

Devastation (f∘) *tabāhī* तबाही

Develop (v∘) *baḍhānā* बढ़ाना*

Development (m∘) *vikās* विकास

Deviate (v∘) *haṭnā* हटना

Device (f∘) *yukti, sādhan* युक्ति, साधन

Devil (m∘) *duṣhṭātmā* दुष्टात्मा

Devious (adj∘) *beīmān* बेईमान

Devoid (adj∘) *rahit* रहित

Devote (v∘) *arpit karnā* अर्पित करना*

Devotee (m∘) *bhakta* भक्त

Devotion (f∘) *bhakti* भक्ति

Devour (v∘) *nigalnā* निगलना*

Devout (adj∘) *śhraddhālu* श्रद्धालु

Dew (f∘) *os* ओस

Dexterity (f∘) *nipuṇatā* निपुणता

Dexterous (adj∘) *nipuṇ* निपुण

Diabetes (m∘) *madhumeh* मधुमेह

Diagram (m∘) *ākriti* आकृति

Dialogue (m∘) *sambhāṣhaṇ, vārtālāp* संभाषण, वार्तालाप

Diameter (m∘) *vyās* व्यास

Diamond, gem (m∘) *hīrā* हीरा

Diarrhoea (f∘) *dast* दस्त

Diary (f∘) *dainikī* दैनिकी

Dice (m∘) *pāsā* पासा

Dictator (m∘) *tānāśhāh* तानाशाह

Dictionary (m∘) *śhabda kośh* शब्दकोश

Die (v∘) *maranā* मरना

Diet (f∘) *pathya* पथ्य

Difference (m∘) *antar, bhinnatā* अंतर, भिन्नता

Different (adj∘) *bhinna, alag* भिन्न, अलग

Difficult (adj∘) *kaṭhin* कठिन

Difficulty (f∘) *kaṭhināī* कठिनाई

Dig (v∘) *khodnā* खोदना*

Digest (v∘) *pachānā* पचाना*

Digest, summary (m∘) *sārāṁśha* सारांश

Digestion (m∘) *pachan* पचन

Digit (m∘) *aṅk* अंक

Dignity (f∘) *pratiṣhṭhā, mān* प्रतिष्ठा, मान

Dilemma (f∘) *duvidhā* दुविधा

Diligent (adj∘) *sāvadhān* सावधान

Dilly-dally (v∘) *hichakichānā* हिचकिचाना

Dilute (adj∘) *patlā* पतला

Dim (adj∘) *dhundhalā* धुँधला

Dimension (m∘) *āyām* आयाम

Diminish (v∘) *ghaṭnā, kam honā* घटना, कम होना

Dine (v∘) *bhojan karnā* भोजन करना*

Dinghy (f∘) *ḍoṅgī* डोंगी

Dinner (m∘) *bhojan* भोजन

Dip (v∘) *ḍubonā* डुबोना*

Diploma (m∘) *pramāṇ-patra* प्रमाण-पत्र

Diplomacy (f∘) *kūṭnīti* कूटनीति

Dire (adj∘) *bhayaṅkar* भयंकर

Direct (adj∘) *sīdhā* सीधा

Direction (f∘) *diśhā* दिशा

Director (m∘) *nirdeśhak, digdarśhak* निर्देशक, दिग्दर्शक

Directory (f∘) *sūchī* सूची

Disappear (v∘) *gāyab honā, adriśhya honā* गायब होना, अदृश्य होना

Disappointment (f∘) *nirāśhā* निराशा

Disapprove (v∘) *nākārnā* नाकारना*

Disarmed (adj∘) *nihatthā* निहत्था

Disassociation (f∘) *asahamati* असहमति

Disaster (f∘) *durghaṭnā, āfat* दुर्घटना, आफ़त

Disbelief (m∘) *aviśhvās* अविश्वास

Discard (v∘) *tyāgnā* त्यागना*

Discern (v∘) *jānanā* जानना*

Disciple (m∘) *anuyāyī* अनुयायी

Discipline (m∘) *anuśhāsan* अनुशासन

Disclose (v∘) *prakaṭ karnā* प्रकट करना*

Discomfort (f∘) *asuvidhā* असुविधा

Disconcert (f∘) *gaḍbaḍ* गड़बड़

Disconnected (adj∘) *alag, prithak* अलग, पृथक्

Discord (f∘) *asahamati* असहमति

Discount (f∘) *chhūṭ, kaṭautī* छूट, कटौती

Discouraged (adj∘) *hatotsāhit* हतोत्साहित

Discourse (m∘) *pravachan* प्रवचन

Discourteous (adj∘) *abhadra, aśhiṣhṭa* अभद्र, अशिष्ट

Discover (v∘) *patā lagānā* पता लगाना*

Discovery (m∘) *khoj* खोज

Discreet (adj∘) *satark, sāvadhān* सतर्क, सावधान

Discrepancy (m∘) *antar* अंतर

Discretion (m∘) *vivek* विवेक

Discrimanation (m∘) *bhedbhāva* भेदभाव

Discriminate (v∘) *bhed karnā* भेद करना*

Discus (m∘) *vichār-ivamars'ha* विचार-विमर्श

Disease (m∘) *rog, bīmārī* रोग, बीमारी

Disengage (v∘) *chhuḍānā* छुड़ाना*

Disgrace (f∘) *badnāmī* बदनामी

Disgruntled (adj∘) *nārāz* नाराज़

Disguise (m∘) *svāṅg* स्वाँग

Disgust (m∘) *khed,* (f∘) *jugupsā* खेद, जुगुप्सा

Dish (f∘) *thālī* थाली

Dishonest (adj∘) *beīmān, dhokhebāz* बेईमान, धोखेबाज़

Dishonour (m∘) *badnāmī* बदनामी

Disillusion (m∘) *bhram* भ्रम

Dislike (f∘) *nāpasandgī* नापसंदगी

Disloyal (adj∘) *namakharām* नमकहराम

Dismay (m∘) *udveg* उद्वेग

Dismiss (v∘) *barkhāst karnā* बरखास्त करना*

Disobey (v∘) *āgyā bhaṅg karnā* आज्ञा भंग करना*

Disorder (f∘) *gaḍbaḍī* गड़बड़ी

Disparity (f∘) *asamānatā* असमानता

Dispatch (v∘) *bhejnā* भेजना*

Dispensary (m∘) *davākhānā* दवाखाना

Dispersion (m∘) *vitaraṇ* वितरण

Display (m∘) *pradars'han* प्रदर्शन

Display (v∘) *dikhāna* दिखाना*

Displeasure (f∘) *nārāzagī* नाराज़गी

Disposition (f∘) *chitta-vritti* चित्त-वृत्ति

Dispute (m∘) *mata-bhed* मत-भेद

Disregard (f∘) *upekṣhā* उपेक्षा

Disrepute (f∘) *badnāmī* बदनामी

Disrespect (m∘) *anādar* अनादर

Disrupt (v∘) *bhaṅg karnā* भंग करना*

Dissatisfaction (f∘) *nārāzgī* नाराज़गी

Disseration (m∘) *prabandh* प्रबंध

Dissimilar (adj∘) *asamān* असमान

Dissolve (v∘) *ghulnā, gholnā** घुलना, घोलना*

Dissuade (v∘) *parāvritta karnā* परावृत्त करना*

Distance (f∘) *dūrī* दूरी

Distant (adj∘) *dUr kā* दूर का

Distinct (adj∘) *spaṣhṭa* स्पष्ट

Distortion (f∘) *vikriti* विकृति

Distraction (m∘) *vighna* विघ्न

Distress (f∘) *pīḍā* पीड़ा

Distribution (m∘) *vitaraṇ* वितरण

District (m∘) *zilā* ज़िला

Distrust (m∘) *s'haṅkā* शंका

Disturbance (f∘) *as'hānti* अशांति

Dive (m∘) *gotā* गोता

Diverse (adj∘) *vividh* विविध

Diversity (f∘) *vividhatā* विविधता

Divesion (m∘) *vibhājan* विभाजन

Divide (v∘) *vibhājan karnā* विभाजन करना*

Divine (adj∘) *daivī* दैवी

Divinity (f∘) *devatā* देवता

Divisive (adj∘) *vibhājak* विभाजक

Divorce (m∘) *talāk* तलाक

Dizzy (adj∘) *chakrāyā huā* चकराया हुआ

Do (v∘) *karanā* करना*

Do not (va∘) *mat* मत

Doctor (m∘) *vaidya* वैद्य

Document (m∘) *kāgjhāt, dastāvez* कागज़ात, दस्तावेज़

Documentry (m∘) *vṛtta-chitra* वृत्त-चित्र

Dodge (v∘) *vār bachānā* वार बचाना∗
Doe (f∘) *hariṇī* हरिणी
Dog (m∘) *kuttā* कुत्ता
Dogma (m∘) *haṭhadharma* हठधर्म
Dominion (m∘) *svāmitva* स्वामित्व
Don't (va∘) *mat* मत
Donate (v∘) *dān denā* दान देना∗
Donation (m∘) *dān* दान
Donkey (m∘) *gadhā* गधा
Donor (m∘) *dātā* दाता
Don't (av∘) *mat* मत
Door (m∘) *darawājhā* दरवाज़ा
Dot (f∘) *bindī,* (m∘) *bindu* बिंदी, बिंदु
Double (adj∘) *duguṇā* दुगुना
Doubt (m∘) *sandeha* संदेह
Doubtful (adj∘) *sandigdha* संदिग्ध
Doubtless (adj∘) *asandigdha* असंदिग्ध
Dove (m∘) *kabūtar* कबूतर
Down (av∘) *nīche* नीचे
Doze (v∘) *ūṅghanā, jhapkī lenā** ऊँघना, झपकी लेना∗
Dozen (m∘) *darjan* दर्जन
Drab (adj∘) *niras* निरस
Drag (v∘) *ghasīṭnā* घसीटना∗
Drain (f∘) *nālī* नाली
Drama (m∘) *nāṭak* नाटक
Draw (v∘) *nikālanā* निकालना∗
Dream (m∘) *sapnā* सपना
Drench (v∘) *bhigonā* भिगोना∗
Dress (m∘) *pośhāk* पोशाक
Drink (m∘) *pāna* पान, *peya* पेय
Drink (v∘) *pīnā* पीना∗
Drip (v∘) *ṭapkanā* टपकना
Drive (v∘) *chalānā* चलाना∗
Driver (m∘) *hchālak* चालक
Drizzle (f∘) *fuhār* फुहार
Droop (v∘) *jhuknā* झुकना
Drop (m∘) *būnd* बूँद
Drug (f∘) *davā* दवा
Drum (m∘) *tablā* तबला
Drunk (adj∘) *madhośh* मदहोश
Dry (adj∘) *sūkhā* सूखा
Dry (v∘) *sūkhanā, sukhānā** सूखना, सुखाना∗
Duck (m∘) *batakh* बतख
Due (adj∘) *deya* देय
Duel (m∘) *dvandva* द्वंद्व
Dull (adj∘) *mand, sust* मंद, सुस्त
Dumb (adj∘) *gūṅgā* गूँगा
Dung (m∘) *gobar* गोबर
Duplicate (f∘) *pratikriti* प्रतिकृति
Duplicity (m∘) *chhal* छल
Dust (f∘) *dhūl* धूल
Duty (m∘) *kartavya, farz* कर्तव्य, फ़र्ज़
Dye, paint (v∘) *raṅgānā* रँगाना∗
Dynasty (m∘) *rājvaṁśha* राजवंश
Dysentry (m∘) *pechiśh* पेचिश

E

Each (adj∘) *pratyek, har ek* प्रत्येक, हर एक
Eager (adj∘) *utsuk, ātur* उत्सुक, आतुर
Eagle (m∘) *chīl, bāz* चील, बाज़

Ear (m◦) *kān* कान

Early (av◦) *pahale, jaldī* पहले, जल्दी

Earn (v◦) *kamānā* कमाना*

Earnest (adj◦) *gambhīr* गंभीर

Earning (f◦) *kamāī* कमाई

Earth (f◦) *zamīn, dhartī, prithvī* ज़मीन, घरती, पृथ्वी

Earthquake (m◦) *bhūkamp* भूकंप

Ease (f◦) *āsānī* आसानी

East (f◦) *pūrva, pūrab* पूर्व, पूरब

Easy (adj◦) *āsān, saral* आसान, सरल

Eat (v◦) *khānā* खाना*

Eccentric (adj◦) *sankī, jhakkī* सनकी, झक्की

Echo (m◦) *gūñj* गूँज

Eclipse (m◦) *grahaṇ* ग्रहण

Economic (adj◦) *ārthik* आर्थिक

Economics (m◦) *arthaśhastra* अर्थशास्त्र

Economy (f◦) *kifāyat* किफ़ायत

Eczema (m◦) *charma rog* चर्म रोग

Edge (m◦) *kinārā* किनारा

Edible (adj◦) *khādya* खाद्य

Edifice (m◦) *prāsād, bhavan* प्रासाद, भवन

Edit (v◦) *sampādan karnā* संपादन करना*

Edition (m◦) *sanskaraṇ* संस्करण

Editor (m◦) *sampādak* संपादक

Editorial (m◦) *sampādakīya* संपादकीय

Education (f◦) *ṣhikṣhā* शिक्षा

Eecology (m◦) *paryāvaraṇ* पर्यावरण

Eemerge (v◦) *ubharnā* उभरना

Effect (m◦) *prabhāv, asar, pariṇām* प्रभाव, असर, परिणाम

Effective (adj◦) *prabhāvī* प्रभावी

Efficiency (f◦) *kṣhamatā* क्षमता

Efficient (m◦) *sakṣham* सक्षम

Effort (m◦) *prayās, prayatna* प्रयास, प्रयत्न

Egg (m◦) *aṇḍā* अंडा

Eggplant (m◦) *baigan* बैगन

Ego (m◦) *ahamkār* अहंकार

Egocentric (adj◦) *ahamkārī* अहंकारी

Eight (adj◦) *āṭh* आठ

Eighteen (adj◦) *aṭhārah* अठारह

Eighty (adj◦) *assī* अस्सी

Either (pron◦) *do mẽ se ek* दो में से एक

Elaboration (m◦) *vistār* विस्तार

Elapse (v◦) *guzarnā, bītnā* गुज़रना, बीतना

Elastic (adj◦) *lachīlā* लचीला

Elbow (f◦) *kuhanī* कुहनी

Elder (adj◦) *jyeṣhṭha* ज्येष्ठ

Elderly (adj◦) *adheḍ* अधेड़

Eldest (adj◦) *agraj* अग्रज

Elect (v◦) *chunanā* चुनना*

Election (m◦) *chunāv* चुनाव

Electricity (f◦) *bijlī, vidyut* बिजली, विद्युत

Elegant (adj◦) *lalit* ललित

Elegible (m◦) *upayukta, yogya* उपयुक्त, योग्य

Element (m◦) *tattva* तत्त्व

Elementary (adj◦) *prārambhik* प्रारंभिक

Elemiante (v◦) *haṭānā* हटाना*

Elemination (m◦) *haṭāv, lop* हटाव, लोप

Elephant (m◦) *hāthī* हाथी

Eleven (adj◦) *gyārah* ग्यारह

Ellipse (m◦) *aṇḍākār* अंडाकार

Elocution (m∘) *vaktritva* वक्तृत्व

Elongate (v∘) *baḍhnā, baḍhānā** बढ़ना, बढ़ाना*

Elongation (m∘) *baḍhāv, vriddhi* बढ़ाव, वृद्धि

Eloquent (adj∘) *vākpaṭu* वाक्पटु

Else (av∘) *anyathā* अन्यथा

Elsewhere (av∘) *anyatra, aur kahī̐* अन्यत्र, और कहीं

Emanate (v∘) *nikalnā* निकलना

Emancipation (f∘) *mukti* मुक्ति

Embargo (f∘) *rok* रोक

Embark (v∘) *savār honāī* सवार होना*

Embassy (m∘) *dūtāvās* दूतावास

Embelish (v∘) *sajānā* सजाना*

Emblem (m∘) *pratīk, chihna* प्रतीक, चिह्न

Embrace (v∘) *gale lagānā* गले लगाना*

Embracement (f∘) *lajjā* लज्जा

Embryo (m∘) *bhrūṇa* भ्रूण

Emergency (m∘) *āpatkāl* आपतकाल

Emigrant (adj∘) *āvāsī* आवासी

Emigration (m∘) *āvās* आवास

Emission (m∘) *nissaraṇ* निस्सरण

Emotion (m∘) *manobhāv* मनोभाव

Empathy (f∘) *sahānubhūti* सहानुभूति

Emperor (m∘) *mahārajā* महाराजा

Emphasis (m∘) *mahattva* महत्त्व

Empire (m∘) *sāmrājya* साम्राज्य

Employment (f∘) *naukarī, kam* नौकरी, काम

Empty (adj∘) *khālī* खाली

Encircle (v∘) *ghernā* घेरना*

Encore (int∘) *mukarrar* मुकर्रर

Encounter (f∘) *muṭhbheḍ* मुठभेड़

Encouragement (m∘) *protsāhan* प्रोत्साहन

Encyclopedia (m∘) *viśhvakośh* विश्वकोश

End (m∘) *ant, sirā, chhor* अंत, सिरा, छोर

End (v∘) *samāpta karnā* समाप्त करना*

Endavour (m∘) *prayās* प्रयास

Endless (adj∘) *anthīn* अंतहीन

Endorsement (m∘) *samarthan* समर्थन

Endurance (f∘) *sahanśhakti* सहनशक्ति

Endure (v∘) *sahanā* सहना*

Enemy (m∘) *ṣhatru, duṣhman* शत्रु, दुष्मन

Energetic (adj∘) *utsāhī* उत्साही

Enfold (v∘) *lapeṭnā* लपेटना*

Enforce (v∘) *lāgu karnā* लागु करना*

Engage (v∘) *lagānā* लगाना*

Engagement (f∘) *sagāī* सगाई

Engine (m∘) *piñjan* ईंजन

Engineer (m∘) *abhiyantā* अभियंता

English (adj∘) *aṅgrezī* अंग्रेज़ी

Engrave (v∘) *kurednā* कुरेदना*

Engrossed (adj∘) *tallin* तल्लीन

Engrossment (f∘) *tallinatā* तल्लीनता

Enhance (v∘) *baḍhanā, aḍhānā** बढ़ना, बढ़ाना*

Enjoin (v∘) *lāgū karnā* लागू करना*

Enjoy (v∘) *lābh uṭhānā* लाभ उठाना*

Enlarge (v∘) *baḍhnā, adhānā** बढ़ना, बढ़ाना*

Enlighten (v∘) *prabuddha karnā* प्रबुद्ध करना*

Enlist (v∘) *bhartī karnā* भरती करना*

Enlistment (f∘) *bhartī* भरती

Enmity (m∘) *vair, bair* वैर, बैर

Enormous (adj∘) *viśhāl* विशाल

Enough (av◦) *bas, kāfī* बस, काफी

Enrichment (f◦) *samriddhī* समृद्धि

Ensure (v◦) *niśhchit karnā* निश्चित करना*

Enter (v◦) *praveśh karanā* प्रवेश करना*

Enterprise (m◦) *udyam* उद्यम

Entertain (v◦) *bahalānā* बहलाना*

Entertainment (m◦) *manorañjan* मनोरंजन

Enthusiasm (m◦) *utsāh, umaṅg* उत्साह, उमंग

Entice (v◦) *fuslānā* फुसलाना*

Entire (m◦) *sab, sampurṇa* सब, संपूर्ण

Entirely (av◦) *purī tarah se* पुरी तरह से

Entrance, door (m◦) *dvār* द्वार

Entry (m◦) *praveśh* प्रवेश

Enumerate (v◦) *ginanā* गिनना*

Envelop (m◦) *lifāfā* लिफ़ाफ़ा

Environment (m◦) *vātāvaraṇ* वातावरण

Envoy (m◦) *dūt* दूत

Envy (m◦) *īrṣhā, jalan* ईर्ष्या, जलन

Epic (m◦) *mahākāvya* महाकाव्य

Epidemic (f◦) *mahāmārī* महामारी

Epigram (m◦) *subhāṣhit, sūkti* सुभाषित, सूक्ति

Epilogue (m◦) *upasaṁhār* उपसंहार

Episode (m◦) *vrittānt* वृत्तांत

Epithet (f◦) *upādhi* उपाधि

Epoch (m◦) *yug, kāl* युग, काल

Equal (adj◦) *barābar, samān* बराबर, समान

Equality (f◦) *samānatā* समानता

Equanimity (f◦) *samabuddhi* समबुद्धि

Equation (m◦) *samīkaraṇ, sutra* समीकरण, सूत्र

Equator (f◦) *bhūmadhya rekhā* भूमध्य रेखा

Equidistant (adj◦) *samadūrastha* समदूरस्थ

Equilateral (m◦) *samabhuja* समभुज

Equilibrium (m◦) *santulan* संतुलन

Equipment (m◦) *pukaraṇ, sāmān* उपकरण, सामान

Equipped (adj◦) *sajja* सज्ज

Equitanle (adj◦) *uchit* उचित

Equivalent (adj◦) *barābar, samatulya* बराबर, समतुल्य

Era (m◦) *saṁvat, yug* संवत्, युग

Erase (v◦) *miṭānā* मिटाना*

Erratic (adj◦) *matvālā* मतवाला

Erroneous (adj◦) *galat* ग़लत

Error (f◦) *galatī, bhūl* गलती, भूल

Erudite (adj◦) *paṇḍit* पंडित

Escalate (v◦) *baḍhanā, aḍhānā** बढ़ना, बढ़ाना*

Escalator (f◦) *sīḍhī* सीढ़ी

Escape (v◦) *bhāgnā* भागना

Especial (adj◦) *viśhiṣhṭa* विशिष्ट

Espionage (f◦) *jāsūsī* जासूसी

Essay (m◦) *nibandh* निबंध

Essence (m◦) *sār, tattva* सार, तत्त्व

Establish (v◦) *sthāpan karnā* स्थापन करना*

Estate (f◦) *jāgīr, jāyadād* जागीर, जायदाद

Estimate (m◦) *anumān, andāz* अनुमान, अंदाज

Eternal (adj◦) *nitya* नित्य

Eternally (av◦) *nitya, sadā, nirantar* नित्य, सदा, निरंतर

Ethic (f◦) *nīti* नीति

Ethics (m◦) *nītiśhastra* नीतिशास्त्र

Ethnic (adj◦) *jātīy* जातीय

Etiquate (m◦) *ṣhiṣhṭāchār* शिष्टाचार

Evade (v◦) *ṭālnā* टालना*

Evaluation (m∘) *mūlyāṅkan* मूल्यांकन

Evaporation (m∘) *bāṣhpan* बाष्पन

Evaquation (m∘) *khālī karnā* खाली करना

Eve (f∘) *pūrvasandhyā* पूर्वसंध्या

Even (adj∘) *sama, ekrūp* सम, एकरूप

Even (av∘) *fir bhī* फिर भी

Even if, even though (av∘) *yadyapi* यद्यपि

Evening (f∘) *sandhyā, śhām* संध्या, शाम

Event (f∘) *ghaṭnā* घटना

Ever (av∘) *sarvadā* सर्वदा

Every (av∘) *pratyek, har ek* प्रत्येक, हर एक

Everyday (av∘) *pratidin, roj* प्रतिदिन, रोज

Everytime (av∘) *yadā-yadā, jab-jab, jaba bhī, hameśhā* यदा-यदा, जब-जब, जब भी, हमेशा

Everywhere (av∘) *sarvatr, sabhī jagah* सर्वत्र, सभी जगह

Evidence (m∘) *pramāṇ, gavāhī* प्रमाण, गवाही

Evil (adj∘) *pāpī, duṣhṭa* पापी, दुष्ट

Evolution (m∘) *vikās* विकास

Evolve (v∘) *vikasit honā* विकसित होना

Exact (adj∘) *ṭhīk-ṭhīk* ठीक-ठीक

Exaggeration (f∘) *atiśhayokti* अतिशयोक्ति

Examination (f∘) *parīkṣhā* परीक्षा

Examine (v∘) *parakhnā, jā̃chnā* परखना, जाँचना*

Example (m∘) *namūnā, udāharaṇ* नमूना, उदाहरण

Excavation (m∘) *khodnā* खोदना

Exceed (v∘) *adhik honā* अधिक होना

Excellence (f∘) *śhreṣhṭhatā* श्रेष्ठता

Excellent (adj∘) *uttam* उत्तम

Excellently (av∘) *uttam rūp se* उत्तम रूप से

Except (av∘) *atirikta, sivāy* अतिरिक्त, सिवाय

Exception (m∘) *apvād* अपवाद

Excess (f∘) *adhiktā* अधिकता

Exchange (v∘) *badalnā* बदलना*

Excitement (m∘) *uttejan* उत्तेजन

Exclamation (m∘) *chitkār* चित्कार

Excrement (f∘) *viṣhṭhā, mal* विष्ठा, मल

Excuse (m∘) *bahānā, māfī* बहाना, माफ़ी

Execution (f∘) 1. *fā̃nsī* (death verdict) फाँसी; 2. *amal* (obey an order) अमल

Executive (m∘) *prabandhak* प्रबंधक

Exemption (f∘) *chhūṭ, māfī* छूट, माफ़ी

Exercise (m∘) *vyāyām,* (f∘) *kasrat* कसरत

Exist (v∘) *rahnā, honā* रहना, होना

Expedient (adj∘) *hitkar* हितकर

Expedition (m∘) *abhiyān* अभियान

Expel (v∘) *nikālnā* निकालना*

Expenditure (m∘) *kharchā* खर्चा

Experience (m∘) *anubhav* अनुभव

Experient (m∘) *prayog* प्रयोग

Expert (adj∘) *nipuṇ* निपुण

Expire (v∘) *samāpta honā* समाप्त होना

Explain (v∘) *samajhānā* समझाना*

Explicit (adj∘) *spaṣhṭa* स्पष्ट

Exploration (f∘) *khoj* खोज

Explosion (m∘) *sphoṭ* स्फोट

Explosive (adj∘) *sphoṭak* स्फोटक

Export (f∘) *niryāt* निर्यात

Expose (v∘) *dikhānā* दिखाना*

Exposure (m∘) *pradarśhan* प्रदर्शन

Expression (f∘) *abhivyakti* अभिव्यक्ति

Extend (v॰) *failānā* फैलाना*

Extension (m॰) *vistār* विस्तार

Extensive (adj॰) *vistīrṇa* विस्तीर्ण

Extensively (av॰) *vistār se* विस्तार से

Extent (m॰) *had* हद

Exterior (adj॰) *bāharī* बाहरी

External (adj॰) *bāhya* बाह्य

Extince (adj॰) *lupta* लुप्त

Extinguish (v॰) *būjhnā, bujhānā** बूझना, बुझाना*

Extra (adj॰) *adhik* अधिक

Extract (adj॰) *sār* सार

Extraordinary (adj॰) *asādhāraṇ* असाधारण

Extravagent (adj॰) *fizūlkharchī* फ़िज़ूलखर्ची

Extreme (adj॰) *param, charam* परम, चरम

Extremist (m॰) *ugravādī* उग्रवादी

Eye (f॰) *ā̃nkh* आँख

Eyeball (f॰) *putalī* पुतली

Eyebrow (f॰) *bhõha* भौंह

Eyeglasses (m॰) *chaśhmā,* (f॰) *ainak* चश्मा, ऐनक

Eyelid (f॰) *palak* पलक

F

Fable (f॰) *laghukathā, nītikathā* लघुकथा, नीतिकथा

Fabric (m॰) *kapḍā* कपड़ा

Fabricate (v॰) *taiyār karnā* तैयार करना*

Fabulous (adj॰) *bahut achhā* बहुत अच्छा

Face (m॰) *cheharā* चेहरा

Facet (m॰) *pahalu* पहलू

Facial (adj॰) *maukhik* मौखिक

Facility (f॰) *suvidhā* सुविधा

Facinating (adj॰) *ākarṣhak* आकर्षक

Facination (m॰) *ākarṣhaṇ* आकर्षण

Fact (m॰) *tathya* तथ्य

Faction (m॰) *dal* दल

Factor (m॰) *ghaṭak* घटक

Factory (m॰) *kārkhānā* कारखाना

Faculty (m॰) *vibhāg* विभाग

Fad (f॰) *jhak* झक

Fade (v॰) *murjhānā* मुरझाना

Failure (f॰) *asafalatā* असफलता

Faint (adj॰) *dhũdhalā, aspaṣhṭa* धुँधला, अस्पष्ट

Fair (adj॰) *suhāvanā* सुहावना

Fair (m॰) *melā* मेला

Fairy (f॰) *parī* परी

Faith (f॰) *śhraddhā, niṣhṭhā* श्रद्धा, निष्ठा

Fake (adj॰) *kālī, naklī* जाली, नकली

Falcon (m॰) *bāj* बाज

Fall (v॰) *giranā* गिरना

Fallacy (f॰) *bhrānti* भ्रान्ति

False (adj॰) *jhūṭhā, galat* झूठा, गलत

Falsely (av॰) *jhūṭhī tarah se, mithyā rūp mẽ* झूठी तरह से, मिथ्या रूप में

Falter (v॰) *hichkichānā, gaḍbaḍānā* हिचकिचाना, गड़बड़ाना

Fame (f॰) *prasiddhi, kīrti* प्रसिद्धि, कीर्ति

Famed (adj॰) *prasiddha* प्रसिद्ध

Familiar (adj॰) *parichit* परिचित

Family (m॰) *parīwār* परिवार

Famine (m॰) *akāl* अकाल

Famous (adj॰) *prasiddha* प्रसिद्ध

Fan (f॰) *paṅkhā* पंखा

Fanatic (adj∘) *kattar* कट्टर

Fantastic (adj∘) *ajīb, vilakṣhaṇ, asāmānya* अजीब, विलक्षण, असामान्य

Fantasy (f∘) *kalpanā* कल्पना

Far (av∘) *dūr* दूर

Farce (m∘) *svāṅg, nāṭak* स्वाँग, नाटक

Fare (m∘) *kirāyā, bhāḍā* किराया, भाड़ा

Farewell (m∘) *alvidā* अलविदा

Farm (m∘) *khet* खेत

Farmer (m∘) *kisān* किसान

Fashion (f∘) *śhailī* शैली

Fashionable (adj∘) *śhaukin* शौकिन

Fast (adj∘) *tez* तेज़

Fast (m∘) *upvās, anśhan* उपवास, अनशन

Fasten (v∘) *bāndhanā* बाँधना*

Fat (adj∘) *moṭa* मोटा

Fat (f∘) *charbī* चरबी

Father (m∘) *pitā* पिता

Father-in-law (m∘) *sasur* ससुर

Fault (m∘) *doṣh, aparādh* दोष, अपराध

Faulty (adj∘) *doṣhī, aparādhī* दोषी, अपराधी

Favour (f∘) *sahāyatā* सहायता

Favourable (adj∘) *anukūl* अनुकूल

Favoutite (adj∘) *pyāra, pasand* प्यारा, पसंद

Fear (m∘) *ḍar, bhay* डर, भय

Fear (v∘) *ḍarnā* डरना

Feast (f∘) *dāvat* दावत

Feat (m∘) *kartab, kamāl* करतब, कमाल

Feather (m∘) *paṅkh* पंख

Feature (m∘) *lakṣhaṇ* लक्षण

February (m∘) *farvarī* फ़रवरी

Fed up (adj∘) *ūbā huā* ऊबा हुआ

Federation (m∘) *saṅghaṭan* संघटन

Fee (m∘) *fīs, śhulk* फ़ीस, शुल्क

Feed (m∘) *khānā, chārā* खाना, चारा

Feed (v∘) *khilānā* खिलाना*

Feel (m∘) *anubhav* अनुभव

Feel (v∘) *mahasūs karnā* महसूस करना*

Feeling (f∘) *bhāvanā* भावना

Fellow (m∘) *sāthī* साथी

Female (f∘) *mādā, nārī* मादा, नारी

Ferocious (adj∘) *krūr, khū̃khār* क्रूर, खूँखार

Fertile (adj∘) *upajāū* उपजाऊ

Fertilizer (m∘) *khād* खाद

Fervent (adj∘) *jośhīlā* जोशीला

Fervour (m∘) *jośh* जोश

Festival (m∘) *utsav, tyauhār* उत्सव, त्यौहार

Fever (m∘) *bukhār, jwar* बुखार, ज्वर

Few (adj∘) *kuchh, thoḍā sā* कुछ, थोड़ा सा

Fez (f∘) *ṭopī* टोपी

Fiance (f∘) *maṅgetar* मँगेतर

Fib (m∘) *jhūṭh* झूठ

Fibre (m∘) *tantu* तंतु

Fickle (adj∘) *asthir* अस्थिर

Fiction (m∘) *upanyās* उपन्यास

Fictitious (adj∘) *kālpanik* काल्पनिक

Fiddle (f∘) *belā* बेला

Fidelity (f∘) *īmāndārī* ईमानदारी

Field (m∘) *khet, maidān* खेत, मैदान

Fierce (adj∘) *ugra, tīvra* उग्र, तीव्र

Fifteen (adj∘) *pandraha* पंद्रह

Fifth (adj∘) *pā̐chavā̐* पाँचवाँ

Fig (m∘) *añjīr* अंजीर

Fighre (f∘) *ākriti,* (m∘) *aṅka* आकृति, अंक

Fight (f∘) *laḍāī* लड़ाई

Fight (v∘) *laḍanā* लड़ना

Fill (v∘) *bharnā* भरना

Filling (f∘) *bharāī* भराई

Filth (f∘) *gandagī, mail* गंदगी, मैल

Final (adj∘) *antim* अंतिम

Finale (m∘) *samāpan* समापन

Finance (m∘) *pūñjī* पूँजी

Find (v∘) *pānā; dhūndhanā* पाना, ढूँढ़ना*

Fine (adj∘) *umdā* उम्दा

Fine (m∘) *juramānā* जुरमाना

Finger (f∘) *uṅglī* उँगली

Fire (f∘) *āg,* (m∘) *agni* आग, अग्नि

Firefly (m∘) *juganu* जुगनु

Firework (f∘) *ātiśhbāzī* आतिशबाज़ी

Firm (adj∘) *pakkā, mazbūt* पक्का, मज़बूत

First (adj∘) *pratham, pahalā* प्रथम, पहला

Fish (f∘) *machhalī* मछली

Fisherman (m∘) *machhuā* मछुआ

Fissure (f∘) *darār* दरार

Fist (f∘) *muṭṭhī* मुठ्ठी

Fit (adj∘) *lāyak, upayukta, uchit, yogya, anukūl* लायक, उपयुक्त, उचित, योग्य, अनुकूल

Fit (f∘) *mūrchhā,* (m∘) *daurā* मूर्छा, दौरा

Fitness (f∘) *yogyatā* योग्यता

Five (adj∘) *pā̐ch* पाँच

Fix (v∘) *ṭhīk karanā* ठीक करना*

Fixation (f∘) *sthirtā* स्थिरता

Fixture (m∘) *jaḍī hī vastu* जड़ी हुई वस्तु

Flabbergasted (adj∘) *bhau̐chakkā* भौंचक्का

Flag (m∘) *jhaṇḍā* झंडा

Flagrant (adj∘) *lajjājanak* लज्जाजनक

Flair (f∘) *śhailī* शैली

Flake (f∘) *pāpḍī, parat* पापड़ी, परत

Flamboyant (adj∘) *ākarṣhak* आकर्षक

Flame (f∘) *lapaṭ, jwālā* लपट, ज्वाला

Flamingo (m∘) *marāl* मराल

Flammable (adj∘) *jwālāgrahī* ज्वालाग्रही

Flap (f∘) *faḍfadāhaṭ* फड़फड़ाहट

Flap (m∘) *pallā* पल्ला

Flap (v∘) *faḍfaḍnā* फड़फड़ना

Flash (f∘) *chamak* चमक

Flat (adj∘) 1. *samtal, sapāṭ* (flat surface) समतल, सपाट; 2. *niras, fīkā* (flat drink) निरस, फीका; 3. *besurā* (flat voice) बेसुरा

Flattering (f∘) *chāplūsī* चापलूसी

Flavour (m∘) *svād, sugandh* स्वाद, सुगंध

Flaw (m∘) *aib, doṣh, truṭi* ऐब, दोष, तृटि

Flee (v∘) *bhāg jānā* भाग जाना

Fleece (f∘) *ūn* ऊन

Fleet (f∘) *nau-senā* नौ-सेना

Flesh (m∘) *mā̐s, gośhṭ* मांस, गोश्त

Flexible (adj∘) *lachilā, parivartanśhīl* लचीला, परिवर्तनशील

Flicker(v∘) *ṭimṭimānā* टिमटिमाना

Flight (f∘) *uḍān* उड़ान

Flimsy (adj∘) *kamzor* कमज़ोर

Flip (v.) *palaṭnā, palaṭānā** पलटना, पलटाना*

Flirt (f.) *iṣhkbāzī* इष्कबाज़ी

Float (v.) *tirnā* तिरना

Flock (m.) *jhuṇḍ* झुंड

Flood (f.) *bāḍh* बाढ़

Floor (f.) 1. *zamīn, farśh* (sit on floor) ज़मीन, फर्श; 2. satah, manzil (live on 2nd floor) सतह, मंझिल

Flour (m.) *āṭā* आटा

Flow (f.) *dhārā*, (m.) *pravāh* धारा, प्रवाह

Flow (v.) *bahanā* बहना

Flower (m.) *fūl* फूल

Fluctuation (m.) *chaḍhāv-utār* चढ़ाव-उतार

Fluid (m.) *drava* द्रव

Flute (f.) *bā̐surī, murlī* बाँसुरी, मुरली

Flutter (v.) *maṇḍarānā* मँडराना

Fly (m.) *makkhī* मक्खी

Fly (v.) *uḍanā, uḍānā** उड़ना, उड़ाना*

Foam (m.) *jhāg, fen* झाग, फेन

Focus (m.) *kendra bindu* केन्द्र बिंदु

Fodder (m.) *chārā* चारा

Foe (m.) *śhatru, duṣhman* शत्रु, दुष्मन

Foetus (m.) *bhrūṇa, garbha* भ्रूण, गर्भ

Fog (m.) *kohrā* कोहरा

Fold (f.) *tah* तह

Fold (v.) *tahānā, moḍnā* तहाना, मोड़ना*

Folk (m.) *log* लोग

Follow (f.) 1. *anusaraṇ karnā* (follow a mentor) अनुसरण करना 2. *pīchhe jānā* (follow to catch) पीछे जाना 3. *samaznā* (understand) समझना

Following (adj.) 1. *aglā* (next) अगला; 2. *nimna-* (given below) निम्न-

Folly (f.) *mūrkhatā* मूर्खता

Fond (adj.) *priya* प्रिय

Fondle (v.) *dulārnā* दुलारना*

Food (m.) *ahār, bhojan* आहार, भोजन

Fool (m.) *bewakūf, mūrkh* बेवकूफ़, मूर्ख

Foolish (adj.) *mūrkha* मूर्ख

Foot (m.) *charaṇ* चरण

Foot (m.) *pair, pā̐v* पैर, पाँव

Footnote (f.) *pād-ṭippaṇī* पाद-टिप्पणी

For (prep.) *ke liye* के लिये

Forbid (v.) *manā karnā* मना करना*

Force (f.) *śhakti* (m.) *bal* शक्ति, बल

Forceps (m.) *chimṭā* चिमटा

Forcibly (av.) *balapūrvak, jor se* बलपुर्वक, जोर से

Fore (adj.) *aglā, āge kā* अगला, आगे का

Forecast (f.) *pūrva-sūchanā* पूर्वसूचना

Forefather (f.) *pūrvaj* पूर्वज

Forefinger (f.) *tarjanī* तर्जनी

Forehead (m.) *lalāṭ, māthā* ललाट, माथा

Foreigh (m.) *videśh* विदेश

Foremost (adj.) *sabse pahalā* सबसे पहला

Forename (m.) *pahalā nām* पहला नाम

Foresight (f.) *dūr-dṛṣhṭi* दूरदृष्टि

Forest (m.) *jaṅgal* जंगल

Forever (av.) *sadā, sarvadā* सदा, सर्वदा

Forge (v.) *nakal karnā* नकल करना*

Forgery (f.) *nakal, jālsāzī* नकल, जालसाज़ी

Forget (v.) *bhūlnā* भूलना*

Forgive (v.) *māf karnā* माफ करना*

Fork (m.) *kā̐ṭā* (knife & fork) काँटा

Form (m∘) *rūp* रूप

Form (v∘) *rūp denā* रूप देना*

Formal (adj∘) *aupachārik* औपचारिक

Formality (m∘) *śhishṭāchār* शिष्टाचार

Format (m∘) *rūprekā* रूपरेखा

Formation (m∘) *nirmāṇ* निर्माण

Former (adj∘) *pahlā, pūrva* पहला, पूर्व

Formerly (av∘) *pahle* पहले

Formidable (adj∘) *ajeya* अजेय

Formula (m∘) *sūtra, samīkaraṇ* सूत्र, समीकरण

Forsake (v∘) *tyāgnā* त्यागना*

Fort (m∘) *kīlā, gaḍh* कीला, गढ़

Forthcoming (adj∘) *āgāmī* आगामी

Forthright (adj∘) *kharā, spashṭa* खरा, स्पष्ट

Forthwith (av∘) *turant, jhaṭ se* तुरंत, झट से

Fortniht (m∘) *pakhvāḍā* पखवाड़ा

Fortress (m∘) *kīlā, gaḍhī* कीला, गढ़ी

Fortunately (av∘) *daivayog se* देवयोग से

Fortune (f∘) *takdīr* तकदीर (m∘) *bhāgya* भाग्य

Fortutide (m∘) *sāhas* साहस

Forty (adj∘) *chālīs* चालीस

Forward (av∘) *āge* आगे

Foul (adj∘) *gandā* गंदा

Foundation (m∘) *nīv, buniyād* नीव, बुनियाद

Founder (f∘) *saṁsthāpak* संस्थापक

Fountain (m∘) *favvārā* फव्वारा

Four (adj∘) *four* चार

Fourteen (adj∘) *chaudah* चौदह

Fowl (m∘) *murgā,* (f∘) *murgī* मुर्गा, मुर्गी

Fox (f∘) *lomḍī* लोमड़ी

Fraction (m∘) *aṁśha, hissā* अंश, हिस्सा

Free (v∘) *chhoḍnā* छोड़ना

Frequency (f∘) *āvritti* आवृत्ति

Frequently (av∘) *punaḥ-punaḥ, bārambār* पुन: पुन:, बारंबार

Friction (f∘) *ragaḍ* रगड़

Friday (m∘) *śhukravār* शुक्रवार

Friend (m∘) *mitra, dost* मित्र, दोस्त

Friendship (f∘) *dosti* दोस्ती

Frightful (adj∘) *ḍarāvanā* डरावना

Frog (m∘) *menḍhak* मेंढक

From (prep∘) *se* से

Front (m∘) *moharā* मोहरा

Frsh (adj∘) *tāzā, nayā* ताज़ा, नया

Fruit (m∘) *fal* फल

Fruitful (adj∘) *safal* सफल

Frustration (m∘) *nirutsāh* निरुत्साह

Fry (v∘) *talnā, bhūnanā* तलना, भूनना*

Frying-pan (m∘) *kaḍāhī* कड़ाही

Fuel (m∘) *īndhan* ईंधन

Fully (av∘) Fully (av∘) *bilkul, purī tarah se* बिलकुल, पुरी तरह से

Fumes (m∘) *dhuँā,* (f∘) *bhāp* धूँआ, भाप

Fun (m∘) *ānand* आनंद

Function (m∘) 1. (event) *samāroh;* समारोह, 2. (duty) *kāra* कार्य

Fund (f∘) *dhanrāśhi* धनराशि

Fundamental (adj∘) *mūlbhūt* मूलभूत

Fundamentalism (m∘) *rūḍhivād* रूढ़िवाद

Funds (m∘) *nidhi, koṣh* निधि, कोष

Funnel (f∘) *kīp,* (m∘) *choṅgā* कीप, चोंगा

Funny (adj◦) *hāsya-janak* हास्यजनक

Furious (adj◦) *krodhit* क्रोधित

Furnace (f◦) *bhaṭṭī* भट्टी

Further (av◦) *āge, āge kī or* आगे, आगे की ओर

Fury (m◦) *unmād* उन्माद

Fuss (f◦) *ghabarāhaṭ* घबराहट

Futile (adj◦) *vyartha* व्यर्थ

Fuzzy (aj) *aspaṣhṭa* अस्पष्ट

G

Gadget (m◦) *auzār* औज़ार

Gain (m◦) *lābh* लाभ

Gain (v◦) *pānā* पाना*

Gala (m◦) *ānandotsav* आनंदोत्सव

Gallant (adj◦) *bahādur* बहादुर

Gallows (f◦) *sūlī* सूली

Gambit (f◦) *pahlī chāl* पहली चाल

Garden (m◦) *bagīchā* बगीचा

Garland (m◦) *hār* (f◦) *mālā* हार, माला

Garlic (m◦) *lahasun* लहसुन

Garment (m◦) *vastra, kapḍe* वस्त्र, कपड़े

Gas (m◦) *vāyu, peṭrol* वायु, पेट्रोल

Gash (m◦) *ghāv* घाव

Gate (m◦) *fāṭak, dvār* फाटक, द्वार

Gather (v◦) *ikaṭṭhā honā, ikaṭṭhā karnā** इकट्ठा होना, इकट्ठा करना*

Gathering (m◦) *jamāv* जमाव

Gauge (m◦) *māp* माप

Gear (m◦) 1. *dā̃tedār chakra* (machine gear) दाँतेदार चक्र 2. *sāmān* (sport gear) सामान

Gem (m◦) *maṇi, ratna* मणि, रत्न

Gemini (f◦) *mithun rāśhi* मिथुन राशि

Geneology (f◦) *vaṁśhāvalī* वंशावली

General (adj◦) *sāmānya, ām* सामान्य, आम

Generality (f◦) *sāmānyatā* समान्यता

Generation (f◦) *utpatti* (production) उत्पत्ति; 2. *pīḍhī* (age group) पीढ़ी

Generosity (f◦) *udārtā* उदारता

Genesis (m◦) *prārambha* प्रारंभ

Genius (f◦) *pratibhā* प्रतिभा

Genocide (m◦) *jātisaṁhār* जातिसंहार

Gentle (adj◦) *saumya, śhānt* सौम्य, शांत

Gentleman (m◦) *sajjan* सज्जन

Geography (m◦) *bhūgol* भूगोल

Geology (m◦) *bhūmiśhāstra* भूमिशास्त्र

Geometry (f◦) *bhūmiti* भूमिति

Geophysics (m◦) *bhautikī* भौतिकी

Germ (m◦) *jīvāṇu* जीवाणु

Germinate (v◦) *uganā* उगना

Gesture (m◦) *bhāv* भाव

Get (v◦) *pānā* पाना*

Ghost (m◦) *bhūt* भूत

Giant (adj◦) *viśhāl* विशाल

Gift (f◦) *bheṭ̃* (m◦) *upahār* भेंट, उपहार

Gigantic (adj◦) *bhīmakāy* भीमकाय

Ginger (f◦) *adarak* अदरक

Girl (f◦) *laḍakī* लड़की

Give (v◦) *denā* देना*

Glad (adj◦) *khuśh* खुश

Gladly (av◦) *khuśhī se* खुशी से

Glance (m∘) *jhalak* झलक

Gland (f∘) *granthi* ग्रंथि

Glass, (m∘) 1. *śhiśhā, kā̃ch* शीशा, काँच; 2. (tumbler) *pyālā* प्याला

Glasses (m∘) *chaṣhmā* चष्मा

Glide (v∘) *fisalnā* फिसलना

Glimpse (f∘) *jhalak* झलक

Glitter (f∘) *chamak* चमक

Glitter (v∘) *chamaknā* चमकना

Global (adj∘) *jāgatik* जागतिक

Gloom (f∘) *udāsī* उदासी

Glorification (f∘) *stuti* स्तुति

Glory (f∘) *kīrti* कीर्ति

Glossary (f∘) *artha sūchī* अर्थ सूची

Glossy (adj∘) *chiknā* चिकना

Glove (m∘) *dastānā* दस्ताना

Glow (f∘) *chamak, tez* चमक, तेज़

Glow (v∘) *chamaknā* चमकना

Glue (f∘) *sares* सरेस

Glue (v∘) *chipakānā* चिपकाना*

Gnat (m∘) *ḍā̃s* डाँस

Go (v∘) *jānā* जाना

Goad (m∘) *aṅkuśh* अंकुश

Goal (m∘) *dhyeya, lakṣhya* ध्येय, लक्ष्य

Goat (f∘) *bakarī, (m∘) bakrā* बकरी, बकरा

God (m∘) *bhagwān* भगवान्

Goddess (f∘) *devī* देवी

Gold (m∘) *sonā* सोना

Goldsmith (m∘) *sunār* सुनार

Good (adj∘) *achchhā* अच्छा

Goodbye (m∘) *alvidā, ṭāṭā* अलविदा, टाटा

Goodness (f∘) *achchhāī* अच्छाई

Goose (f∘) *haṁsanī* हंसनी

Gorgeous (adj∘) *śhāndār* शानदार

Gossip (f∘) *gap* गप

Gourd (m∘) *kaddū, peṭhā* कद्दू, पेठा

Government (f∘) *sarkār* सरकार

Governor (m∘) *rājyapāl* राज्यपाल

Gown (m∘) *chogā* चोगा

Grab (v∘) *pakaḍnā* पकड़ना*

Grace (f∘) *kripā* कृपा, कृपादृष्टि

Graceful (adj∘) *manoram* मनोरम

Gracious (adj∘) *udār* उदार

Grade (f∘) *śhreṇī* श्रेणी

Gradual (adj∘) *kramik* क्रमिक

Graduate (m∘) *snātak* स्नातक

Graft (f∘) *kalam* कलम

Grain (m∘) *dānā, kaṇ, ravā* दाना, कण, रवा

Gram, chickpea (m∘) *chanā* चना

Grammar (m∘) *vyākaraṇ* व्याकरण

Grand (adj∘) *bhavya, śhāndār* भव्य, शानदार

Granddaughter (f∘) *potī* पोती

Grandeur (m∘) *vaibhav* (f∘) *śhān* वैभव, शान

Grandfather (m∘) *nānā, dādā* नाना, दादा

Grandmother (m∘) *nānī, dādī* नानी, दादी

Grandson (m∘) *potā* पोता

Grant (v∘) *anumati denā* अनुमति देना

Grape (m∘) *aṅgūr* अंगूर

Grass (f∘) *ghās* घास

Grass (f∘) *ghās* घास

Grasshopper (m∘) *ṭiḍḍhā* टिड्डा

Grating (f∘) *jālī* जाली

Gratitude (f∘) *kritaguatā* कृतज्ञता

Gratuity (m∘) *inām* इनाम

Grave (adj∘) *gambhīr* गंभीर

Grave (f∘) *kabr* कब्र

Gravel (f∘) *bajrī* बजरी

Gravity (m∘) *gurutvākarṣhaṇ* गुरुत्वाकर्षण

Gravy (f∘) *tarī* तरी

Graze (v∘) *charnā* चरना

Grease (f∘) *charbī* चरबी

Greasy (adj∘) *fisalnā* फिसलना

Great (adj∘) *kbaḍā, mahān* बड़ा, महान

Greed (f∘) *lālach* लालच

Green (adj∘) *harā* हरा

Greeting (m∘) *abhinandan* अभिनंदन

Grey (adj∘) *dhūsar* धूसर

Grid (m∘) *jālā* जाला

Grief (m∘) *s̒hok, santāp* शोक, संताप

Grievance (f∘) *s̒hikāyat* शिकायत

Grind (v∘) *pīsanā* पीसना*

Grip (f∘) *pakaḍ* पकड़

Grocery *kirānā* किराना

Groom (m∘) *dūlhā* दूल्हा

Groove (m∘) *khā̃chā* (f∘) *nālī* खाँचा, नाली

Grotesque (adj∘) *betukā* बेतुका

Ground (m∘) *maidān* (f∘) *zamīn* मैदान, ज़मीन

Group (m∘) *samūha, saṅgha* समूह, संघ

Grow (v∘) *ugnā, baḍhna;, baḍhānā** उगना, बढ़ना; बढ़ाना*

Growth (m∘) *vikās,* (f∘) *vriddhi* विकास, वृद्धि

Grumble (v∘) *bhunbhunānā* भुनभुनाना*

Grumpy (adj∘) *badmizāj* बदमिज़ाज

Gtuesome (adj∘) *bībhatsa* बीभत्स

Guarantee (f∘) *zamānat* ज़मानत

Guarantor (m∘) *zāmin* ज़ामिन

Guard (m∘) *pahredār, santrī* पहरेदार, संतरी

Guard (v∘) *pahrā denā* पहरा देना*

Guardian (m∘) *rakṣhak* रक्षक

Guava (m∘) *amrūd* अमरूद

Guess (m∘) *anumān, andāzā* अनुमान, अंदाज़ा

Guest (m∘) *mehmān, atithi* मेहमान, अतिथि

Guidance (m∘) *upades̒h* उपदेश

Guide (m∘) *mārga-dars̒hak* मार्गदर्शक

Guilt (m∘) *doṣh, aparādh* दोष, अपराध

Guilty (adj∘) *doṣhī, aparādhī* दोषी, अपराधी

Gulp (v∘) *nigalnā* निगलना*

Gum, on teeth (m∘) *masūḍā* मसूड़ा

Gumnasuim (f∘) *vyāyāma-s̒hālā* व्यायामशाला

Gun (f∘) *bandūk, top* बंदूक, तोप

Gust (m∘) *jhõkā* झोंका

Gut (f∘) *ā̃ta* आँत

Gutter (f∘) *nālī* नाली

Guy (m∘) *ādmī* आदमी

Gymnastics (m∘) *kasrat* कसरत

H

Habit (f∘) *ādat* आदत

Habitat (m∘) *āvās* आवास

Habiyual (adj∘) *niyamit* नियमित

Had (v∘) *thā, thī, the* था, थी, थे

Hag (f∘) *chuḍail* चुड़ैल

Haggard (adj∘) *mariyal* मरियल

Hair (m∘) *bāl* बाल

Half (adj∘) *ādhā* आधा

Hall (m∘) *narak* नरक

Halt (v∘) *ruknā* रुकना

Halve (v∘) *adhiyānā* अधियाना*

Hamdle (m∘) *dastā* (f∘) *muṭh* दस्ता, मुठ

Hamlet (m∘) *purvā, gāँv* पुरवा, गाँव

Hammer (m∘) *hathauḍā* हथौड़ा

Hand (m∘) *hāth* हाथ

Handcuff (f∘) *hathkaḍī* हथकड़ी

Handicap (f∘) *vikalāṅgtā* विकलांगता

Handicapped (adj∘) *vikalāṅg* विकलांग

Handicraft (f∘) *dastkārī* दस्तकारी

Handkerchief (m∘) *rumāl* रुमाल

Handloom (m∘) *hath-karghā* हथ-करघा

Handy (adj∘) *suvidhā-janak* सुविधाजनक

Hang (v∘) *laṭaknā, laṭakānā** लटकना, लटकाना*

Hanker (v∘) *lalchānā* ललचाना

Haphazzard (adj∘) *avyavasthit* अव्यवस्थित

Happen, have (v∘) *honā* होना

Happily (av∘) *khuśhī se* खुशी से

Happy (adj∘) *khuśh, prasanna* खुश, प्रसन्न

Harass (v∘) *satānā* सताना

Harbinger (m∘) *agradūt* अग्रदूत

Harbour (m∘) *bandargāh* बंदरगाह

Hard (adj∘) *kaḍā, kaṭhin* कड़ा, कठिन

Hare (m∘) *kharagośh* खरगोश

Harsh (adj∘) *kaṭhor* कठोर

Harvest (f∘) *fasal* फसल

Harvest (v∘) *fasal kāṭnā* फसल काटना*

Has (v∘) *hai, haiँ* है, हैं

Hashish (m∘) *gāँjā* गाँजा

Hassle (f∘) *pareśhānī* परेशानी

Haste (f∘) *jaldī* जल्दी

Hastily (av∘) *jaldī se* जल्दी से

Hat (f∘ m∘) *ṭopī, ṭop* टोपी, टोप

Hatchet (f∘) *kulhāḍī* कुल्हाड़ी

Hatred (f∘) *ghriṇā* घृणा

Have (v∘) *hai, haiँ, pās honā* है, हैं, पास होना

Head (m∘) *sir* सिर

Health (m∘) *svāsthya* स्वास्थ्य

Healthy (adj∘) *svastha* स्वस्थ

Heap (f∘) *rāśhi, ḍher* राशि, ढेर

Hear (v∘) *sunanā* सुनना*

Heart (m∘) *dil* दिल

Hearty (adj∘) *hārdik* हार्दिक

Heat (f∘) *garamī* गरमी

Heaven (m∘) *svarg* स्वर्ग

Heavy (adj∘) *bhārī* भारी

Hedge (m∘) *bāḍā* बाड़ा

Hedgehog (f∘) *sāhī* साही

Heed (v∘) *dhyān denā* ध्यान देना*

Heel (f∘) *eḍī* एडी

Hefty (adj∘) *bhārī* भारी

Heifer (f∘) *bachhiyā* बछिया

Height (adj∘) *ūchāī* ऊँचाई

Heighten (v∘) *baḍhānā* बढ़ाना*

Heir (m∘) *vāris* वारिस

Help (f∘) *madad* मदद

Hemisphere (m∘) *ardhavritta* अर्धवृत्त

Hen (m∘) *murgī* मुर्गी

Hence (av∘) *ab se* अब से

Her (prep∘) *uskā* उसका

Herdly (av∘) *muśhkil se* मुश्किल से

Here (av∘) *yahā̃* यहाँ

Here and there (av∘) *idhar-udhar, jahā̃-tahā̃, yahā̃-vahā̃* इधर-उधर, जहाँ-तहाँ, यहाँ-वहाँ

Hereafter (av∘) *is ke bād* इसके बाद

Hermit (m∘) *yati, riṣhi* यति, ऋषि

Hero (m∘) *nāyak* नायक

Hero (m∘) *vīr, bahādur* वीर, बहादुर

Heroin (f∘) *nāyikā* नायिका

Hesitate (v∘) *hichakichānā* हिचकिचाना

Hexagon (m∘) *shaṭkoṇa* षट्कोण

Hhurdle (f∘) *bādhā* बाधा

Hide (f∘) *chamḍī* चमड़ी

Hide (v∘) *chhupnā, chhupānā** छुपना, छुपाना*

Hierarchy (m∘) *padānukram* पदानुक्रम

High (adj∘) *uccha, ūchā* उच्च, ऊँचा

Highly (av∘) *bahut, kāfī* बहुत, काफी

Hill (f∘) *pahāḍī* पहाड़ी

Him (m∘) *usko* उसको

Hinge (m∘) *kabzā* कब्ज़ा

Hint (m∘) *iṣhārā, saṅket* इषारा, संकेत

Hippo (m∘) *kariyād* करियाद

Hire (v∘) *bhaḍe se lenā* भाड़े से लेना

His (m∘) *uskā* उसका

History (m∘) *itihās* इतिहास

Hit (v∘) *māranā* मारना*

Hive (m∘) *chhattā* छत्ता

Hobby (m∘) *śhauk* शौक

Hoe (f∘) *kudālī* कुदाली

Hog (m∘) *sūar* सूअर

Hold, catch (v∘) *pakaḍanā* पकड़ना

Hole (m∘) *chhed* (f∘) *surākh* छेद, सुराख़

Holiday (f∘) *chhuṭṭī* छुट्टी

Hollow (adj∘) *khokhlā, polā* खोखला, पोला

Holy (adj∘) *pavitra* पवित्र

Homage (f∘) *śhraddhāñjali* श्रद्धांजलि

Home, house (m∘) *ghar* घर

Homely (adj∘) *gharelu* घरेलु

Homicide (f∘) *nar-hatyā* नरहत्या

Homogeneous (adj∘) *ek-rūp* एकरूप

Honest (adj∘) *īmāndār, nek* ईमानदार, नेक

Honesty (f∘) *īmānadārī, nekī* ईमानदारी, नेकी

Honey (m∘) *śhahad, madhu* शहद, मधु

Honey, darling (adj∘) (f∘) *gorī, sakhī* गोरी, सखी; (m∘) *piyā, sanam* पिया, सनम

Honour (m∘) *sammān, ādar* सम्मान, आदर

Honourable (adj∘) *ādarṇīya* आदरणीय

Hoof (m∘) *khur* खुर

Hooligan (m∘) *guṇḍā* गुंडा

Hope (f∘) *āśhā* आशा

Horizon (m∘) *kṣhitij* क्षितिज

Horizontal (adj∘) *samatal, sapāṭ* समतल, सपाट

Horn (m∘) *siṅg* सिंग

Horoscope (f∘) *janmakuṇḍalī* जन्मकुंडली

Horrendous (adj∘) *bhayānak* भयानक

Horrible (adj∘) *bhayānak* भयानक

Horrific (adj∘) *bhayānak* भयानक

Horror (f∘) *jugupsā* जुगुप्सा

Horse (m∘) *ghoḍā* घोड़ा

Horsepower (f∘) *aśhvaśhakti* अश्वशक्ति

Hospital (m∘) *davākhānā* दवाखाना

Hospitality (m∘) *atithi-satkār* अतिथि-सत्कार

Host (m∘) *mezbān* मेज़बान

Hostel (m∘) *chhātrāvās* छात्रावास

Hot (adj∘) *garam* गरम

Hothead (adj∘) *tunak-mizāz* तुनकमिज़ाज़

Hour (m∘) *ghaṇṭā* घंटा

House (m∘) *ghar* घर

How (av∘) *kis tarah se, kaise* किस तरह से, कैसे

How else (av∘) *aur kaise, nahīँ to kaise* ओर कैसे, नहीं तो कैसे

However (av∘) *fir bhī, kintu* फिर भी, किंतु

Hrru (f∘) *jaldī* जल्दी

Hug (v∘) *gale lagānā* गले लगाना*

Huge (adj∘) *viśhāl* विशाल

Hum (v∘) *gunagunānā* गुनगुनाना

Human (m∘) *mānava* मानव

Humane (adj∘) *dyāmaya* दयामय

Humanity (f∘) *mānav jāti* मानव जाति

Humble (adj∘) *namra* नम्र

Humility (f∘) *namratā* नम्रता

Humour (m∘) *vinod* विनोद

Hump (m∘) *kubaḍ* कूबड़

Humudity (f∘) *sīlan* सीलन

Hundred (adj∘) *sau* सौ

Hunger (f∘) *bhūkh* भूख

Hungry (adj∘) *bhūkhā* भूखा

Hunt (v∘) *śhikār karnā* शिकार करना*

Hunter (m∘) *śhikārī* शिकारी

Hurt (adj∘) *dukhī* दुखी

Hurt (v∘) *dukhānā* दुखाना*

Husband (m∘) *pati* पति

Husk (m∘) *bhūsā* भूसा

Hut (f∘) *kuṭiyā* कुटिया

Hybrid (adj∘) *saṅkar* संकर

Hyena (m∘) *lakaḍbaghā* लकड़बग्घा

Hygine (f∘) *safāī* सफाई

Hymn (m∘) *śhlok* श्लोक

Hypocrisy (m∘) *pākhaṇḍ* पाखंड

Hysteria (m∘) *unmād* उन्माद

I

I (pron∘) *maīँ* मैं

Ice (f∘) *baraf* बरफ

Idea (f∘) *kalpanā* कल्पना

Ideal (adj∘) *ādarśha* आदर्श

Identical (adj∘) *samān* समान

Identity (f∘) *pahachān* पहचान

Ideology (f∘) *vichārdhārā* विचारधारा

Idiom (m∘) *muhāvrā* मुहावरा

Idiot (adj∘) *mūrkha* मूर्ख

Idle (adj∘) *bekār* बेकार

Idly (av∘) *ālasya se, vrithā* आलस्य से, वृथा

Idol (f∘) *mūrti* मूर्ति

If (av◦) *agar, yadi* अगर, यदि

If not (av◦) *nahī̃ to, anyathā* नहीं तो, अन्यथा)

Ignite (v◦) *sulgānā* सुलगाना*

Ignomity (f◦) *badnāmī* बदनामी

Ignorance (m◦) *agyān* अज्ञान

Ignorant (adj◦) *agyānī* अज्ञानी

Ignorantly (av◦) *ajgyānatā se* अज्ञानता से

Ignore (v◦) *upekṣhā karnā* उपेक्षा करना*

Iiem (m◦) *chīz* चीज़

Iiicit (adj◦) *avaidh* अवैध

Iindefinite (adj◦) *aniśhchit* अनिश्चित

Iinteresting (adj◦) *dilchasp* दिलचस्प

Iivasion (m◦) *ākramaṇ, hamlā, dhāvā* आक्रमण, हमला, धावा

Ill (adj◦) *bīmār* बीमार

Illegal (adj◦) *avaidh* अवैध

Illegitimate (adj◦) *avaidh* अवैध

Illiterate (adj◦) *anpaḍh, nirakṣhar* अनपढ़, निरक्षर

Illness (f◦) *bīmārī* बीमारी

Illuminate (v◦) *prakāśhit larnā* प्रकाशित करना*

Illusion (f◦) *māyā, bhrānti* माया, भ्रांति

Illustration (m◦) *udāharaṇ* उदाहरण

Illustrious (m◦) *prasiddha* प्रसिद्ध

Image (f◦) *pratimā, mūrti* प्रतिमा, मूर्ति

Imagination (f◦) *kalpanā* कल्पना

Imagine (v◦) *kalpanā karnā* कल्पना करना*

Imbecile (adj◦) *mūrkha* मूर्ख

Imitate (v◦) *nakal karnā* नकल करना*

Imitattion (f◦) *nakal* नकल

Immaculate (adj◦) *truṭīhīn* त्रुटीहीन

Immature (adj◦) *kacchā* कच्चा

Immediately (av◦) *tatkāl, turant, tabhī* तत्काल, तुरंत, तभी

Immense (adj◦) *viśhāl* विशाल

Immerse (v◦) *ḍubonā* डुबोना*

Immigrant (m◦) *āpravāsī* आप्रवासी

Immigration (m◦) *āpravās* आप्रवास

Immobile (adj◦) *achal, sthir* अचल, स्थिर

Immoral (adj◦) *anaitik* अनैतीक

Immortal (adj◦) *amar* अमर

Immune (adj◦) *mukta* मुक्त

Immunity (f◦) *mukti* मुक्ति

Impact (m◦) *asar, prabhāv* असर, प्रभाव

Impaired (adj◦) *durbal* दुर्बल

Impartial (adj◦) *taṭastha* तटस्थ

Impatient (adj◦) *ātur, utāvlā* आतुर, उतावला

Impediment (f◦) *aḍchan* अड़चन

Imperfect (adj◦) *adhūrā* अधूरा

Imperialism (m◦) *sāmrājya-vād* साम्राज्यवाद

Impervious (m◦) *abhedya* अभेद्य

Impetus (m◦) *preraṇā* प्रेरणा

Implement (m◦) *aujār, upakaraṇ* औजार, उपकरण

Implement (v◦) *lagu karnā* लागु करना

Implication (m◦) *āśhay* आशय

Implore (v◦) *prārthanā karnā* प्रार्थना करना*

Import (f◦) *āyāt* आयात

Important (adj◦) *mahattvapūrṇa* महत्त्वपूर्ण

Imposter (m◦) *ḍhoṅgī, pākhaṇḍī* ढोंगी, पाखंडी

Impotent (adj◦) *napunsak* नपुंसक

Impregnable (adj◦) *abhedya* अभेद्य

Impression (f∘) *chhāp* छाप

Impressive (adj∘) *prabhāvī* प्रभावी

Improper (adj∘) *anuchit* अनुचित

Improperly (av∘) *anuchitatā se* अनुचितता से

Improve (v∘) *sudhārnā* सुधारना*

Impulse (m∘) *āveg,* (f∘) *prerṇā* आवेग, प्रेरणा

Impure (adj∘) *aśhuddha* अशुद्ध

Imsolent (adj∘) *badtamīz* बदतमीज़

In (prep∘) *mẽ* में

In a short time (av∘) *tabhī, usī vakta* तभी, उसी वक्त

In front of (av∘) *āge, sāmane* आगे, सामने

In the morning (av∘) *savere* सवेरे

Inability (f∘) *aśhakti* अशक्ति

Inaccessible (adj∘) *agamya* अगम्य

Inaccurate (adj∘) *galat* ग़लत

Inadequate (adj∘) *aparyāpta* अपर्याप्त

Inadvertantly (av∘) *anjāne mẽ* अनजाने में

Inappropriate (adj∘) *anuchit* अनुचित

Inasmuch as (conj∘) *kyõki, chũki* क्योंकि, चूँकि

Inauguration (m∘) *udghāṭan* उद्घाटन

Incapable (adj∘) *asamartha* असमर्थ

Incarnation (m∘) *avatār* अवतार

Incentive (m∘) *protsāhan* प्रोत्साहन

Inception (f∘) *śhuruāt* शुरुआत

Incessant (adj∘) *nirantar* निरंतर

Incessantly (av∘) *nirantar, lagātār* निरंतर, लगातार

Incident (f∘) *ghaṭnā* घटना

Incite (v∘) *bhaḍkānā* भड़काना*

Inclination (m∘) *jhukāv* झुकाव

Incline (v∘) *jhukānā* झुकाना*

Include (v∘) *sāth milānā* साथ मिलाना*

Inclusion (m∘) *samāveśh* समावेश

Inclusive (adj∘) *sammilit* संमिलित

Income (f∘) *āya, āmadānī* आय, आमदानी

Incompetent (adj∘) *akṣham* अक्षम

Incomplete (adj∘) *adhūrā* अधूरा

Incongruous (adj∘) *bemel* बेमेल

Inconsistent (adj∘) *bemel* बेमेल

Inconspicuous (adj∘) *nagaṇya* नगण्य

Incorrect (adj∘) *galat* ग़लत

Increase (f∘) *vṛddhi, baḍhat* वृद्धि, बढ़त

Increase (v∘) *baḍhnā, baḍhānā** बढ़ना, बढ़ाना*

Incredible (adj∘) *aviśhvasanīya* अविश्वसनीय

Incursion (m∘) *ākramaṇ* आक्रमण

Indebted (adj∘) *ābhārī, riṇī* आभारी, ऋणी

Indecision (f∘) *hichkichāhaṭ* हिचकिचाहट

Indecisive (adj∘) *aniśhchit* अनिश्चित

Indeed (av∘) *vastutaḥ, sachamuch* वस्तुत:, सचमुच

Indefinitely (av∘) *hameśhā ke liye* हमेशा के लिये

Independent (adj∘) *āzād* आज़ाद

Index (m∘) *suchak* (f∘) *suchī* सूचक, सूची

India (m∘) *bhārat, hindustān* भारत, हिंदुस्थान

Indian (m∘) *bhāratīya* भारतीय

Indicate (v∘) *dikhānā* दिखाना*

Indicator (m∘) *saṅket, lakṣhaṇ* संकेत, लक्षण

Indifferent (adj∘) *taṭastha* तटस्थ

Indigenous (m∘) *deśhī, desī* देशी, देसी

Indigestion (m∘) *apachan, badhazmī* अपचन, बदहज़मी

Indirect (adj∘) *apratyakṣha* अप्रत्यक्ष

Inference (m∘) *anumān* अनुमान

Infertile (adj∘) *bāñjh* बांझ

Infiltration (f∘) *ghuspaiṭh* घुसपैठ

Infinite (adj∘) *anant* अनंत

Inflame (v∘) *bhaḍkānā* भड़काना*

Inflammable (adj∘) *dāhya* दाह्य

Inflammation (f∘) *sūjan* सूजन

Inflexible (adj∘) *kaḍā, kaṭhor* कड़ा, कठोर

Infliction (f∘) *pīḍā* पीड़ा

Influence (m∘) *prabhāv* प्रभाव

Influencial (adj∘) *prabhāvī* प्रभावी

Information (f∘) *sūchanā, khabar, jānakārī* सूचना, खबर, जानकारी

Infrastructure (m∘) *ḍhācha* ढाचा

Infringement (m∘) *ākramaṇ* आक्रमण

Ingenuity (f∘) *kuśhaltā* कुशलता

Ingredient (m∘) *ghaṭak* घटक

Input (m∘) *yogdān* योगदान

Inquiry (f∘) *pūchhtāchh* पूछताछ

Insane (adj∘) *pāgal* पागल

Insect (m∘) *kīḍā* कीड़ा

Insecure (adj∘) *asurakṣhit* असुरक्षित

Insert (v∘) *ghuseḍnā* घुसेड़ना*

Inside (av∘) *bhītar* भीतर

Insignificant (adj∘) *nagaṇya* नगण्य

Insipid (adj∘) *fikā* फीका

Insist (v∘) *āgraha karnā* आग्रह करना*

Inspect (v∘) *parakhanā* परखना*

Inspection (m∘) *parīkṣhaṇ* परीक्षण

Inspector (m∘) *parīkṣhak* परीक्षक

Inspiration (f∘) *preraṇā* प्रेरणा

Inspire (v∘) *prerit karnā* प्रेरित करना*

Integration (m∘) *ekīkaraṇ* एकीकरण

Integrity (f∘) *ektā* एकता

Intellect (f∘) *buddhi* बुद्धि

Intelligence (f∘) *buddhi* बुद्धि

Intense (adj∘) *tīvra* तीव्र

Intent (m∘) *hetu* हेतु

Intention (m∘) *hetu, irādā* हेतु, इरादा

Intercourse (m∘) *samāgam* समागम

Interest (m∘) *ruchi, dilchaspī* रुचि, दिलचस्पी

Interim (adj∘) *antarim* अंतरिम

Interior (m∘) *bhītarī bhāg* भीतरी भाग

Interlock (v∘) *gū̃thanā* गूँथना*

Intermediate (adj∘) *mādhyamik* माध्यमिक

Intermission (m∘) *madhyāntar* मध्यांतर

Intermittent (adj∘) *savirām* सविराम

Internal (adj∘) *āntarik* आंतरिक

International (adj∘) *antar-rāṣhṭrīya* अंतर्राष्ट्रीय

Interpretation (f∘) *vyākhyā* व्याख्या

Interrogate (v∘) *praśhna krnā* प्रश्न करना*

Interrupt (v∘) *bādhā ḍālnā* बाधा डालना*

Interruption (f∘) *bādhā* बाधा

Intersection (m∘) *chaurāhā* चौराहा

Interval (m∘) *madhyāntar* मध्यांतर

Interview (f∘) *bheṭ̃, mulākat* भेंट, मुलाकत

Intestine (f∘) *ā̃t* आँत

Intimate (adj∘) *ghaniṣhṭha* घनिष्ट

Intimate (v∘) *sūchit karnā* सूचित करना*

Intimidate (v∘) *darānā, dhamkānā* डराना, धमकाना*

Intimidation (f∘) *dhamkī* धमकी

Into (prep◦) *ke bhītar* के भीतर

Intolerable (adj◦) *asahanīya* असहनीय

Intoxication (m◦) *naśhā* नशा

Intrepid (adj◦) *sāhasī* साहसी

Intricate (adj◦) *jaṭil* जटिल

Intrigue (m◦) *ṣhaḍyantra* षडयंत्र

Intrinsic (adj◦) *āntarik* आंतरिक

Introduce (v◦) *kprastut karnā* प्रस्तुत करना*

Introduction (m◦) *parichay* (f◦) *prastāvanā* परिचय, प्रस्तावना

Introductory (adj◦) *prārambhik* प्रारंभिक

Intrusion (m◦) *ākramaṇ* आक्रमण

Intuition (f◦) *sahajbuddhi* सहजबुद्धि

Invalid (adj◦) *agrāhya* अग्राह्य

Invariable (adj◦) *sthir* स्थिर

Invencible (adj◦) *ajay, ajeya* अजय, अजेय

Invention (m◦) *āviṣhkār* आविष्कार

Inverse (adj◦) *ulṭā* उल्टा

Investigate (v◦) *khoj karnā* खोज करना*

Investigation (f◦) *khoj* खोज

Investment (f◦) *pū̃jī* पूँजी

Invisible (adj◦) *agochar* अगोचर

Involve (v◦) *śhāmil honā* शामिल होना

Invonvenience (f◦) *asuvidhā* असुविधा

Inward (adj◦) *bhītarī* भीतरी

Ire (m◦) *krodh* क्रोध

Iron (f◦) *istarī;* (m◦) *lohā* इस्तरी; लोहा

Irony (f◦) *viḍambanā* विडंबना

Irrational (adj◦) *tarkhīn* तर्कहीन

Irregular (adj◦) *aniyamit* अनियमित

Irrelevant (adj◦) *asaṅgat* असंगत

Irrigation (f◦) *sĩchāī* सींचाई

Is (v◦) *hai* है

Island (m◦) *dvīp* द्वीप

Isolate (v◦) *alag karnā* अलग करना*

Issue (m◦) 1. *viṣhay* (subject) विषय; 2. (publication) *prachālan* प्रचालन 3. (child) (f◦) *santān* संतान

It (pron◦) *yah* यह

Itch (f◦) *khujlī* खुजली

Itself (pron◦) *svayam* स्वयं

Ivitation (m◦) *āmantraṇ* आमंत्रण

J

Jab (m◦) *mukkā, ghūsā, dhakkā* मुक्का, घूसा, धक्का

Jackel (m◦) *siyār, gīdaḍ* सियार, गीदड़

Jacket (f◦) *mirjaī* मिरजई

Jackfruit (m◦) *kaṭhal* कटहल

Jaelousy (f◦) *īrṣhā, ḍāh* ईर्ष्या, डाह

Jagged (adj◦) *dā̃tedār* दाँतेदार

Jail (m◦) *kārāgār,* (f◦) *kaid* कारागार, कैद

January (m◦) *janavarī* जनवरी

Jar (m◦) *bartan* बरतन

Jasmine (f◦) *chamelī* चमेली

Jaundice (m◦) *pīliyā* पीलिया

Javelin (m◦) *bhālā* भाला

Jaw (m◦) *jabḍā* जबड़ा

Jay bird (m◦) *bulbul* बुलबुल

Jeopardy (m◦) *saṅkaṭ* संकट

Jerk (adj◦) *mūrkha* मूर्ख

Jerk (m◦) *jhaṭkā* झटका

Jet (f∘) *dhārā* धारा

Jew (m∘) *yahūdī* यहूदी

Jewel (m∘) *ratna, jawāhar* रत्न, जवाहर

Jingle (f∘) *chhanchhanāhaṭ* छनछनाहट

Jinx (m∘) *abhiśhāp* अभिशाप

Jjmble (m∘) *gaḍbaḍjhālā* गड़बड़झाला

Job (f∘) *anukarī* (m∘) *kām* नौकरी, काम

Join (v∘) *juḍnā, joḍnā** जुड़ना, जोड़ना*

Joint (m∘) *joḍ* जोड़

Joke (m∘) *mazāk* मज़ाक

Joker (m∘) *vidushak* विदुषक

Jolly (adj∘) *ānandit* आनंदित

Jolt (m∘) *jhaṭkā, dhakkā* झटका, धक्का

Journey (f∘) *yātrā,* (m∘) *safar* यात्रा, सफर

Joy (m∘) *harsha,* (f∘) *khuśhī* हर्ष, खुशी

Jubilant (adj∘) *ullāsit* उल्लासित

Jubilation (m∘) *ullās* उल्लास

Judge (m∘) *nyāyādhīśh* न्यायाधीश

Judgement (m∘) *nyāya* न्याय

Judicial (adj∘) *adālatī* अदालती

Judiciary, court (f∘) *adālat* अदालत

Judisdiction (f∘) *sīmā* सीमा

Jug (f∘) *surāhī, ghaḍā* सुराही, घड़ा

Juggling (f∘) *bāzīgarī* बाज़ीगरी

Juice (m∘) *ras* रस

Juicy (adj∘) *rasdār* रसदार

July (m∘) *julāī* जुलाई

Jumbo (adj∘) *viśhal* विशाल

Jump (v∘) *kūdanā* कूदना

Junction (m∘) *sandhi-sthān* संधि-स्थान

Juncture (m∘) *ghaṭnāchakra* घटनाचक्र

Junior (adj∘) *chhoṭa, avar* छोटा, अवर

Junk (m∘) *kūḍā-karkaṭ* कूड़ा-करकट

Jupitor (m∘) *brihaspati* बृहस्पति

Jury (m∘) *pañch* पंच

Just (av∘) 1. (now) *abhī-abhī, turant* अभी-अभी, तुरंत 2. (only) *keval* केवल 3. (fair) *vaidh, uchit* वैध, उचित

Justice (m∘) *nyāy, insāf* न्याय, इंसाफ़

Justification (m∘) *samarthan* समर्थन

Juvenile (m∘) *kiśhor, taruṇ* किशोर, तरुण

Juxtapose (v∘) *lagānā* लगाना*

K

Keen (adj∘) *utkaṭ* उत्कट

Keep (v∘) *rakhanā* रखना*

Keeper (m∘) *rakhavālā* रखवाला

Kernel (f∘) *garī* गरी

Kerosene (m∘) *miṭṭī kā tel* मिट्टी का तेल

Kettle (f∘) *ketali* केतली

Key (f∘) *chābī* चाबी

Kick (f∘) *ṭhokar* ठोकर

Kick (v∘) *ṭhokar māranā* ठोकर मारना*

Kid (m∘) *bacchā, bāl* बच्चा, बाल

Kidnap (m∘) *apaharaṇ* अपहरण

Kidney (m∘) *gurdā* गुरदा

Kill (v∘) *māranā* मारना*

Kiln (f∘) *bhaṭṭī* भट्टी

Kin (m∘) *riśhtedār* रिश्तेदार

Kind (adj∘) *dayālu* दयालु

Kind (m∘) *prakār* (f∘) *jāti* प्रकार, जाति

Kindle (v◦) *uksānā* उकसाना*

Kindness (f◦) *dayā* दया

King (m◦) *rājā* राजा

Kingdom (m◦) *rājya* राज्य

Kink (m◦) *bal* बल

Kinship (m◦) *riśhtā* रिश्ता

Kiss (m◦) *chumban* चुंबन

Kitchen (f◦) *rasoī* रसोई

Kite (f◦) 1. *pataṅg* पतंग, 2. (bird) *chīl* चील

Knack (f◦) *kalā* कला

Knapsack (m◦) *thailā* थैला

Knee (m◦) *ghuṭnā* घुटना

Kneed (v◦) *gū̃dhanā* गूँधना*

Kneel (v◦) *ghuṭne ṭeknā* घुटने टेकना*

Knife (f◦) *chhurī* छुरी (m◦) *chāku* चाकु

Knit (v◦) *bunanā* बुनना*

Knob (m◦) *muṭh* मुठ

Knock (f◦) *khaṭkhaṭāhaṭ* खटखटाहट

Knock (v◦) *khaṭkhaṭānā* खटखटाना

Knot (f◦) *gā̃ṭh* गाँठ

Know (v◦) *jānanā* जानना*

Knowledge (m◦) *gyān, bodh* ज्ञान, बोध

L

Label (f◦) *chippī* चिप्पी

Laboratory (f◦) *prayogśhālā* प्रयोगशाला

Labour (f◦) *mehnat* मेहनत

Labourer (m◦) *majdūr* मजदूर

Lace (f◦) *fītā, jālī* फ़ीता, जाली

Lack (f◦) *kamī* कमी

Lad (m◦) *laḍkā, bālak* लड़का, बालक

Ladder (f◦) *sīḍhī* सीढ़ी

Ladle (f◦) *kaḍchī* कडछी

Lady (f◦) *strī, aurat, mahilā* स्त्री, औरत, महिला

Lagoon (m◦) *jhīl* झील

Lake (m◦) *jhīl, sarovar* झील, सरोवर

Lamb (m◦) *memnā* मेमना

Lame (adj◦) *laṅgḍā* लँगड़ा

Lamp (m◦) *dīyā* दीया

Language (f◦) *bhāṣhā* भाषा

Lap (f◦) *god* गोद

Lapse (f◦) *bhūl, chūk* भूल, चूक

Lard (f◦) *charbī* चरबी

Large (adj◦) *baḍā, viśhāl* बड़ा, विशाल

Last (adj◦) *antim, ākharī* अंतिम, आखरी

Last (v◦) *ṭiknā* टिकना

Latch (f◦) *chiṭkanī* चिटकनी

Late (adj◦) 1. (time) *der kā* देर का 2. (passed away) *mṛt* मृत

Lately (av◦) *ājakal* आजकल

Later (av◦) *bād me̐, fir* बाद में, फिर

Laugh (f◦) *haṅsī* हँसी

laugh (v◦) *hãsanā* हँसना

Law (m◦) *kānūn* कानून

Lawyer (m◦) *vakīl* वकील

Lazy (adj◦) *ālasī* आलसी

Lead (m◦) *sīsā* सीसा

Lead (v◦) *āge rahnā* आगे रहना

Leader (m◦) *netā* नेता

Leading (adj◦) *mukhya* मुख्य

Leaf (m◦) *pattā* पत्ता

League (m◦) *saṅgh* संघ

Lean (adj◦) *dublā-patlā* दुबला-पतला

Leap (v◦) *kūdna* कूदना

Learn (v◦) *sīkhnā* सीखना*

Lease (m◦) *izārā* इज़ारा

Least (pron◦) *kam se kam* कम से कम

Leave (f◦) *chhuṭṭī* छुट्टी

Leave (v◦) *chale jānā* चले जाना

Lecture (m◦) *bhāṣhaṇ* भाषण

Left (adj◦) *bā̃yā* बाँया

Leg (f◦) *ṭāṅg* टांग; (m◦) *pair* पैर

Legal (adj◦) *vaidh, kānūnī* वैध, कानूनी

Legend (f◦) *dantakathā* दंतकथा

Legible (adj◦) *suvācchya* सुवाच्य

Legislature (f◦) *vidhansabhā* विधानसभा

Legitimate (adj◦) *vaigh* वैध

Leisure (f◦) *fursat* फ़ुरसत

Lemon (m◦) *nīmbū* नींबू

Lend (v◦) *udhār denā* उधार देना*

Length (f◦) *lambāī* लंबाई

Lengthy (adj◦) *lambā* लंबा

Leniecy (f◦) *udārtā* उदारता

Lenient (adj◦) *udār, saumya* उदार, सौम्य

Lentil (m◦) *masūr* मसूर

Leopard (m◦) *chītā* चीता, *tenduā* तेंदुआ

Less (adj◦) *kam* कम

Lessen (m◦) *kam hona, kam karnā** कम होना, कम करना*

Lesson (m◦) *pāṭh* पाठ

Lethargy (m◦) *ālas* आलस

Letter 1. (m◦ alphabet) *akṣhar* अक्षर 2. (f◦ mail) *hiṭṭhī* चिठ्ठी

Level (adj◦) *samtal, sapāṭ* समतल, सपाट

Level (m◦) *star* स्तर

Levy (m◦) *kar* कर

Liability (m◦) *uttardāyītva* उत्तरदायीत्व

Liable (adj◦) *uttardāyī* उत्तरदायी

Liar (adj◦) *jhūṭhā* झूठा

Liberal (adj◦) *udār* उदार

Liberate (v◦) *mukta karnā* मुक्त करना*

Liberation (f◦) *mukti* मुक्ति

Liberty (f◦) *mukti, svātantrya* मुक्ति, स्वातंत्र्य

Libra (f◦) *tulā raśhi* तुला राशि

Library (m◦) *pustakālay* पुस्तकालय

Licence (f◦) *anumati* अनुमति

Lick (v◦) *chāṭnā* चाटना*

Lid (m◦) *ḍhakanā* ढकना

Lie (v◦) 1. (speaking) *jhuṭh bolnā* झूठ बोलना* 2. (rest) *leṭnā* लेटना

Life (m◦) *prāṇ jīvan* प्राण, जीवन

Lift (v◦) *uṭhānā* उठाना*

Ligament (m◦) *snāyu* स्नायु

Light (adj◦) 1. (weight) *halkā* हलका 2. (colour) *phīkā* फीका

Light (m◦) *prakāśh, rośhanī* प्रकाश, रोशनी

Lightning (f◦) *bijlī* बिजली

Like (adj◦) *samān* समान

Like (v◦) *chāhanā* चाहना*

Like that (av◦) *vaise* वैसे

Like this (av◦) *aise* ऐसे

Like what (av◦) *kaise* कैसे

Likely (adj∘) *sambhāvya* संभाव्य

Likelyhood (f∘) *sambhāvanā* संभावना

Likewise (av∘) *bhī, vaise hī* भी, वैसे ही

Lily (f∘) *kumudinī* कुमुदिनी

Lime (m∘) 1. (fruit) *nimbū* निंबू 2. (chemical) *chūnā* चूना

Limit (f∘) *sīmā* सीमा

Limited (adj∘) *sīmit* सीमित

Limp (v∘) *langḍānā* लँगड़ाना

Line (f∘) *rekhā, katār* रेखा, कतार

Lining (m∘) *astar* अस्तर

Link (f∘) *kaḍī* कड़ी

Lint (m∘) *fāhā* फाहा

Lion (m∘) *sher, simha* शेर, सिंह

Lioness (f∘) *sheranī, simhanī* शेरनी, सिंहनी

Lip (m∘) *oṭh* ओठ

Liquid (m∘) *drav* द्रव

Liquidation (m∘) *diwālā* दिवाला

Liquor (f∘) *sharāb, madya* शराब, मद्य

List (f∘) *sūchī, tālikā* सूची, तालिका

Listen (v∘) *sunanā* सुनना*

Literacy (f∘) *sākṣhartā* साक्षरता

Literal (adj∘) *shābdik* शाब्दिक

Little (adj∘) *chhoṭā* छोटा

Little (av∘) *kiñchit, jarā* किंचित्, जरा

Little finger (f∘) *kanakī* कनीका

Live (adj∘) *jīvit, zindā* जीवित, ज़िंदा

Live (v∘) *jīnā* जीना

Lively (adj∘) *furtīlā* फ़ुरतीला

Livelyhood (f∘) *jīvikā* जीविका

Liver (m∘) *kalejā* कलेजा

Living (adj∘) *jīvit, zindā* जीवित, ज़िंदा

Living (f∘) *jīvikā* जीविका

Lizard (f∘) *chipakalī* छिपकली

Load (m∘) *bhār* भार

Loan (m∘) *karj, riṇ* कर्ज, ऋण

Local (adj∘) *sthānik* स्थानिक

Locality (m∘) *muhallā, ilākā* मुहल्ला, इलाका

Locate (v∘) *patā lagānā* पता लगाना*

Location (m∘) *sthān, jagah* स्थान, जगह

Lock (m∘) *tālā* ताला

Locust (f∘) *ṭiddī* टिड्डी

Loft (f∘) *aṭārī* अटारी

Lofty (adj∘) *aleshān* अलेशान

Logic (m∘) *tark* तर्क

Logo (m∘) *pratīk-chihna* प्रतीक-चिह्न

Loitering (f∘) *maṭargashtī, āwārāgardī* मटरगश्ती, आवरागर्दी

London (m∘) *Landan* लंदन

Lone (adj∘) *akelā* अकेला

Lonely (adj∘) *akelā* अकेला

Lonesome (adj∘) *akelā, sūnā* अकेला, सूना

Long (adj∘) *lambā* लंबा

Look (v∘) *dekhnā* देखना*

Loom (m∘) *karghā* करघा

Loose (adj∘) *ḍhīlā* ढीला

Lopsided (adj∘) *ektarfā* एकतरफ़ा

Lord (m∘) *mālik, swāmī* मालिक, स्वामी

Lose (v∘) *khonā* खोना*

Loss (m∘) *nuksān* नुकसान

Lost (adj∘) *khoyā huā* खोया हुआ

Lot (adj∘) *bahut* बहुत

Lotus (m∘) *kamal* कमल

Loud (adj∘) *śhor vālā* शोर वाला

Louse (f∘) *jūṅ* जूँ

Lovable (adj∘) *pyārā* प्यारा

Love (m∘) *pyār, sneha* प्यार, स्नेह

Love (v∘) *pyār karanā* प्यार करना*

Lovely (adj∘) *pyārā, sundar* प्यारा, सुंदर

Lover (m∘ f∘) *premī, premikā* प्रेमी, प्रेमिका

Low (adj∘) *nīchā* नीचा

Loyal (adj∘) *īmāndār* ईमानदार

Lucid (adj∘) *subodh* सुबोध

Lucious (adj∘) *sumadhur* सुमधुर

Luck (m∘) *bhāgya, bhāg* भाग्य, भाग

Luckily (av∘) *bhāgyavaśha, saubhāgya se* भाग्यवश, सोभाग्य से

Lucky (adj∘) *bhāgyaśhālī* भाग्यशाली

Lucrative (adj∘) *fāyademand* फायदेमंद

Lump (m∘) *ḍhelā* ढेला

Lunatic (adj∘) *pāgal* पागल

Lung (m∘) *fefaḍā* फेफड़ा

Lure (m∘) *pralobhan* प्रलोभन

Lust (f∘) *lālsā* लालसा

Luxuriant (adj∘) *prachur* प्रचुर

Luxury (m∘) *vilās* विलास

Lyric (f∘) *kavitā* कविता

M

Machine (m∘) *yantra* यंत्र

Mad (adj∘) *pāgal* पागल

Madam (f∘) *mahilā* महिला

Madium (adj∘) *madhyam* मध्यम

Madium (m∘) *mādhyam* माध्यम

Magazine (f∘) *patrikā* पत्रिका

Magic (f∘) *jādū* जादू

Magician (m∘) *jādūgar* जादूगर

Magnet (m∘) *chumbak* चुंबक

Magnificient (adj∘) *śhāndār* शानदार

Magnify (v∘) *baḍhānā* बढ़ाना*

Magnitude (f∘) *mahattā* महत्ता

Maid (f∘) *dāsī* दासी

Mail (f∘) *ḍāk* डाक

Mailman (m∘) *ḍākiyā* डाकिया

Main (adj∘) *mukhya* मुख्य

Maize, corn (m∘) *makkā* मक्का

Major (adj∘) *mukhya* मुख्य

Majority (m∘) *bahumata* बहुमत

Make (v∘) *banānā* बनाना*

Maker (m∘) *kartā* कर्ता

Male (adj∘) *nar* नर

Malice (m∘) *dveṣh* द्वेष

Malign (v∘) *nindā karnā* निंदा करना*

Mammoth (adj∘) *viśhāl* विशाल

Man (m∘) *ādmī* आदमी

Management (m∘) *vyavasthā* व्यवस्था

Manager (m∘) *vyavasthāpak* व्यवस्थापक

Mane (m∘) *ayāl, kesar* अयाल, केसर

Mango (m∘) *ām* आम

Mania (f∘) *sanak* सनक

Mankind (f∘) *mānava jāti* मानव जाति

Manner (f◦) *rīti, ḍhaṅg* रीति, ढंग

Mansion (f◦) *havelī, koṭhī* हवेली, कोठी

Manslaughter (f◦) *narhatyā* नरहत्या

Manufacture (m◦) *utpādan* उत्पादन

Manure (m◦) *khād, gobar* खाद, गोबर

Many (pron◦) *kaī* कई

Map (m◦) *nakśhā* नक्शा

Mar (v◦) *bigāḍnā* बिगाड़ना*

Marble (m◦) *saṅgamaramar* संगमरमर

March (m◦) *julūs, prayāṇ* जुलूस, प्रयाण

Margin (m◦) *kinārā* किनारा

Maritime (adj◦) *samudrī* समुद्री

Mark (m◦) *niśhān* निशान

Market (m◦) *bāzār* बाज़ार

Marquee (m◦) *śhāmiyānā* शामियाना

Marriage (m◦) *vivāha,* (f◦) *śhadī* विवाह, शादी

Marrow (f◦) *majjā* मज्जा

Marry (v◦) *vivāh-śhadī karnā* विवाह-शादी करना*

Mars (m◦) *maṅgal* मंगल

Martyr (m◦) *śhahīd* शहीद

Marvel (m◦) *chamatkār* चमत्कार

Marvelous (adj◦) *chamatkārik* चमत्कारिक

Mascara (m◦) *añjan* अंजन

Mask (m◦) *nakāb* नक़ाब

Massacre (f◦) *katal* कतल

Massage (f◦) *māliśh* मालिश

Massiah (m◦) *masīh* मसीह

Massive (adj◦) *mahākāy* महाकाय

Master (m◦) *swāmī* स्वामी

Mat (f◦) *chaṭāī* चटाई

Match (f◦) *spardhā* स्पर्धा

Matchbox (f◦) *māchis* माचिस

Mate (m◦ f◦) *sāthī* साथी

Material (m◦) *sāmān* सामान

Materialism (m◦) *bhautikvād* भौतिकवाद

Maternal uncle (m◦) *māmā* मामा

Mathematics (m◦) *gaṇit* गणित

Matter (m◦) *viṣhay,* (f◦) *bāt* विषय, बात

Mattress (f◦) *gaddī* गद्दी

Mattress (m◦) *gaddā* गद्दा

Mature (adj◦) *pakva, prauḍh* पक्व, प्रौढ़

Maximum (m◦) *adhiktam* अधिकतम

May, month (m◦) *amī* मई

Maybe (av◦) *śhāyad* शायद

Maze (f◦) *bhūl-bhulaiyā* भूल-भुलैया

Me (pron◦) *mujhe* मुझे

Meal (m◦) *bhojan* भोजन

Mean (adj◦) *ghaṭiyā* घटिया

Meaning (m◦) *arth, matalab* अर्थ, मतलब

Means (m◦) *upāy* उपाय

Measles (f◦) *chechak* चेचक

Measure (m◦) *upāy* उपाय

Measure (v◦) *nāpanā* नापमा*

Measurement (m◦) *nāp* नाप

Meat (m◦) *mā̃s* मांस

Medal (m◦) *padak* पदक

Meddling (m◦) *hastakṣhep* हस्तक्षेप

Media (m◦) *mādhyam* माध्यम

Medication (f◦) *davāī, auṣhadhī* दवाई, औषधि

Medicine (f◦) *davāī, auṣhadhī* दवाई, औषधि

Medicine (m∘) *aushadh* औषध
Medoicre (adj∘) *māmulī* मामुली
Meet (v∘) *milanā* मिलना
Meeting (f∘) *sabhā* सभा
Melancholy (f∘) *udāsī* उदासी
Melody (f∘) *dhun* धुन
Melon (m∘) *kharbūzā* खरबूज़ा
Melt (v∘) *pighalanā* पिघलना
Melt (v∘) *pighalnā,ghulnā* पिघलना, घुलना
Member (m∘) *sadsya* सदस्य
Membrane (f∘) *jhilli* झिल्ली
Memento (f∘) *yādgār* यदगार
Memorable (adj∘) *smaranīya* स्मरणीय
Memorandum (f∘) *gyāpikā* ज्ञापिका
Memorial (m∘) *smārak* स्मारक
Memory (f∘) *yād, smriti* याद, स्मृति
Menace (m∘) *sankaṭ* संकट
Menawhile (av∘) *itne mẽ* इतने में
Mend (v∘) *ṭhīk karnā* ठीक करना*
Mental (adj∘) *mānasik* मानसिक
Mentality (f∘) *manovritti* मनोवृत्ति
Merchandise (m∘) *māl* माल
Merchant (m∘) *vyāpārī, saudāgar* व्यापारी, सौदागर
Merciful (adj∘) *dayāvān* दयावान
Mercury, liquid(m∘) *pārā* पारा
Mercury, planet (m∘) *budh* बुध
Mercy (f∘) *dayā* दया
Mere (adj∘) *keval* केवल
Merely (av∘) *keval, sirf* केवल, सिर्फ
Merge (v∘) *ek honā* एक होना

Merit (m∘) *guṇ* गुण
Meritorious (adj∘) *sarāhanīya* सराहनीय
Merry (adj∘) *ānandit* आनंदित
Mesh (f∘) *jālī* जाली
Message (m∘) *sandeśh* संदेश
Metal (f∘) *dhātu* धातु
Metaphor (m∘) *rūpak* रूपक
Meteor (f∘) *ulkā* उल्का
Method (m∘) *tarīkā,* (f∘) *rīti* तरीका, रीति
Meticulous (adj∘) *dhyānpūrvak* ध्यानपूर्वक
Microbe (m∘) *jīvāṇu* जीवाणु
Midday (f∘) *dopahar* दोपहर
Middle (m∘) *madhya, bīch* मध्य, बीच
Middle finger (f∘) *madhyamā* मध्यमा
Middleman (m∘) *dalāl* दलाल
Midst (m∘) *bīch mẽ* बीच में
Might (m∘) *bal,* (f∘) *śhakti* बल, शक्ति
Mild (adj∘) *saumya* सौम्य
Mile (m∘) *mīl* मील
Militant (adj∘) *laḍākū* लड़ाकू
Military (f∘) *senā* सेना
Milk (m∘) *dūdh* दूध
Milkmaid (f∘) *gwālin* ग्वालिन
Milkman (m∘) *gwālā* ग्वाला
Mill (m∘) *kārkhānā* कारखाना
Mill (v∘) *pīsnā* पीसना*
Millionaire (m∘) *lakhpati* लखपति
Mimic (v∘) *nakal utārnā* नकल उतारना*
Mind (m∘) *man* मन
Mindful (adj∘) *sāvadhān* सावधान

Mine (f◦) *khadān* खदान

Mine (pron◦ m◦ f◦) *merā, merī* मेरा, मेरी

Mineral (adj◦) *khanij* खनिज

Minimum (adj◦) *kma se kam* कम से कम

Minister (m◦) *mantri* मंत्री

Ministry (m◦) *mantrālay* मंत्रालय

Minor (adj◦) *gauṇ* गौण

Mint (f◦ money) *ṭaksāl* टकसाल; (m◦ plant) *pudīnā* पुदीना

Minute (adj◦) *sūkṣhma* सूक्ष्म

Miracle (m◦) *chamatkār* चमत्कार

Mire (m◦) *kichaḍ* कीचड़

Mirror (m◦) *āīnā* आईना

Miscellaneous (adj◦) *fuṭkar* फुटकर

Mischief (f◦) *śharārat* शरारत

Mischievous (adj◦) *śharāratī* शरारती

Miscreant (m◦) *badmāśh* बदमाश

Miser (adj◦) *kañjūs* कंजूस

Miserable (adj◦) *dayanīya* दयनीय

Misery (f◦) *durdaśhā* दुर्दशा

Misfortune (m◦) *durbhāgya* दुर्भाग्य

Misgiving (m◦) *sandeha* संदेह

Misguided (adj◦) *bahkāyā* बहकाया

Mishap (f◦) *durghaṭnā* दुर्घटना

Miss (v◦) *chūknā* चूकना*

Mist (m◦) *kuhrā* कुहरा

Mistake (f◦) *galtī, bhūl* ग़लती, भूल

Mistrust (m◦) *aviśhvās* अविश्वास

Misuse (m◦) *durupayog* दुरुपयोग

Mix (v◦) *milnā, milānā** मिलना, मिलाना*

Mixture (m◦) *miśhraṇ* मिश्रण

Moan (v◦) *krāhnā* कराहना

Mob (f◦) *bhīḍ* भीड़

Mockery (f◦) *upahās* उपहास

Mode (f◦) *rīti* रीति. (m◦) *ḍhaṅg, tarīkā* ढंग, तरीका

Modern (adj◦) *ādhunik* आधुनिक

Modest (adj◦) *sādhāraṇ* साधारण

Modification (m◦) *parivartan, badal* परिवर्तन, बदल

Moist (adj◦) *gīlā, nam* गीला, नम

Moisture (f◦) *namī, sīl* नमी, सील

Molar (f◦) *dāḍh* दाढ़

Mole (m◦) *til* तिल

Molecule (m◦) *aṇu* अणु

Molestaion (f◦) *chheḍkhānī* छेड़खानी

Moment (m◦) *pal, kṣhaṇ* पल, क्षण

Momentary (adj◦) *kṣhaṇik* क्षणिक

Momentum (m◦) *saṁveg* संवेग

Monarch (m◦) *rājā* राजा

Monday (m◦) *somwār* सोमवार

Money (m◦) *paise* पैसे

Mongoose (m◦) *nevlā* नेवला

Monitor (m◦) *nirīkṣhak* निरीक्षक

Monk (m◦) *bhikṣhu* भिक्षु

Monkey (m◦) *bandar* बंदर

Monopoly (m◦) *ekādhikār* एकाधिकार

Monotonous (adj◦) *eksurā* एकसुरा

Monster (m◦) *rākṣhas* राक्षस

Month (m◦) *mahīnā* महीना

Monument (m◦) *smārak* स्मारक

Mood (f◦) *manaḥsthiti* मन:स्थिति

Moon (m∘) *chandra, chā̃d* चंद्र, चाँद

Moral (adj∘) *naitik* नैतिक

Morality (f∘) *naitiktā* नैतिकता

More (adj∘) *jyādā* ज्यादा

More (av∘) *adhikatā se* अधिकता से

Moreover (av∘) *is se adhik, sivāy* इससे अधिक, सिवाय

Morning (m∘) *saverā* सवेरा

Mortal (m∘) *naśhvar* नश्वर

Mortgage (m∘) *girvī* गिरवी

Mosquito (m∘) *machchhar* मच्छर

Most (pron∘) *sabse adhik* सबसे अधिक

Mostly (av∘) *prāyaḥ. bahudhā* प्राय:, बहुधा

Moth (m∘) *pataṅg* पतंग

Mother (f∘) *māṅ* माँ

Mother-in-law (f∘) *sās* सास

Motion (f∘) *gati, chāl* गति, चाल

Mountain (m∘) *pahāḍ* पहाड़, *parvat* पर्वत

Mouse (m∘) *chūhā* चूहा

Mouth (m∘) *mũh* मुँह

Move (v∘) *hilnā, hilānā** हिलना, हिलाना*

Movement (f∘) *gati-vidhi* गतिविधि

Movie (f∘) *filam* फिलम

Movie (m∘) *chalachitra* चलचित्र

Much (av∘) *bahut, jyādā* बहुत, ज्यादा

Mule (m∘) *khacchar* खच्चर

Multiplication (m∘) *guṇā* गुणा

Mumble (v∘) *budbudānā, fusfusānā* बुदबुदाना, फुसफुसाना

Murder (m∘) *khūn,* (f∘) *hatyā* खून, हत्या

Murmer (v∘) *budbudānā, fusfusānā* बुदबुदाना, फुसफुसाना

Muscle (f∘) *peśhī* पेशी

Museum (m∘) *saṅgrahālay, ajāyabghar* संग्रहालय, अजायबघर

Music (m∘) *saṅgīt* संगीत

Musician (av∘) *saṅgītakār* संगीतकार

Must (av∘) *avaśhya* अवश्य

Mustache (f∘) *mūchh* मूछ

Mute (adj∘) *gūṅgā* गूँगा

Mutually (av∘) *paraspar* परस्पर

Myself (pron∘) *apne āp* अपने आप

Mysterious (adj∘) *rahasyamay* रहस्यमय

Mystery (m∘) *rahasya* रहस्य

Mythology (m∘) *purāṇaśhāstra* पुराणशास्त्र

N

Nab (v∘) *jhapaṭnā* झपटना*

Nag (adj∘) *jhagaḍālū, fasādī* झगड़ालू, फ़सादी

Nail, 1. on finger (m∘) *nākhūn* नाखून 2. to hammer (f∘) *kīl* कील

Naive (adj∘) *bholā* भोला

Naked (adj∘) *naṅgā, khulā* नंगा, खुला

Name (m∘) *nām* नाम

Namely (av∘) *yānī, arthāt* यानी, अर्थात

Nap (f∘) *jhapkī* झपकी

Narration (m∘) *vivaraṇ, varṇan* विवरण, वर्णन

Narrow (adj∘) *patlā, saṅkuchit* पतला, संकुचित

Nasty (adj∘) *gandā* गंदा

Nation (m∘) *deśh, rāṣhṭra, kaum* देश, राष्ट्र, कौम

National (adj∘) *rāṣhtrīya* राष्ट्रीय

Nationality (f∘) *nāgrīktā* नागरीकता

Nationalization (m∘) *rāṣhṭrīyakaraṇ* राष्ट्रीयकरण

Native (adj∘) *desī* देसी

Native (m◦) *nivāsī* निवासी

Natural (adj◦) *naisargik* नैसर्गिक

Nature (f◦) *prakriti, srishti* प्रकृति, सृष्टि

Naughty (adj◦) *naṭkhaṭ, śharārtī* नटखट, शरारती

Nauseate (v◦) *machalnā* मचलना

Navel (f◦) *nābhī* नाभी

Navigation (m◦) *sanchālan* संचालन

Navy (f◦) *nau-senā* नौसेना

Near (adj◦) *nikaṭ, samīp* निकट, समीप

Nearly (av◦) *lagbhag* लगभग

Neat (adj◦) *sāf-suthrā* साफ-सुथरा

Necessary (adj◦) *zarūrī, āvaśhyak* ज़रूरी, आवश्यक

Neck (f◦) *gardan* गर्दन

Necklace (m◦) *hār* हार

Nectat (m◦) *śhahad, makrand* शहद, मकरंद

Need (f◦) *zarūrat, āvaśhyaktā* ज़रूरत, आवश्यकता

Needle (f◦) *sūī, salāī* सूई, सलाई

Needy (adj◦) *zarūratmand* ज़रूरतमंद

Negative (adj◦) *riṇ, nakārātmak* ऋण, नकारात्मक

Neglect (f◦) *upekṣhā* उपेक्षा

Neglect (v◦) *dhyān na denā* ध्यान न देना*

Negligence (f◦) *lāparvāhī* लापरवाही

Negligent (adj◦) *lāparvāh* लापरवाह

Negotiation (m◦) *vinimay* विनिमय

Neigh (v◦) *hinhinānā* हिनहिनाना

Neighbor (m◦) *paḍosī* पड़ोसी

Neighborly (adj◦) *milansār* मिलनसार

Neighbour (m◦) *paḍosī* पड़ोसी

Neither (pron◦) *do me̐ se ek bhī nahī̐* दो में से एक भी नहीं

Nephew (m◦) *bhatijā, bhā̐jā* भतीजा, भाँजा

Nepotism (f◦) *āpsī laḍāī* आपसी लड़ाई

Neptune (m◦) *varuṇ* वरुण

Nerve (f◦) *nas, snāyu* नस, स्नायु

Nervous (adj◦) *ghabḍāyā huā* घबड़ाया हुआ

Nest (m◦) *gho̐salā* घोंसला

Net (m◦) *jāl* जाल

Neutral (adj◦) *taṭastha* तटस्थ

Never (av◦) *kabhī nahī̐* कभी नहीं

Nevertheless (av◦) *tathāpi* तथापि

News (m◦) *samāchār* (f◦) *khabar* समाचार, खबर

Newspaper (m◦) *akhbār* अखबार

Next (adj◦) *aglā* अगला

Nibble (v◦) *kutarnā* कुतरना*

Nice (adj◦) *bahut acchhā* बहुत अच्छा

Nickname (m◦) *upanām* उपनाम

Niece (f◦) *bhatījī, bhā̐jī* भतीजी, भाँजी

Night (f◦) *rāt* रात

Nightfall (f◦) *sandhyā, śhām* संध्या, शाम

Nightingale (f◦) *bulbul* बुलबुल

Nil (m◦) *kuchh nahī̐* कुछ नहीं

Nimble (adj◦) *furtīlā* फुरतीला

Nine (adj◦) *nau* नौ

Nineteen (adj◦) *unnīs* उन्नीस

Ninety (adj◦) *nabbe* नब्बे

Ninth (adj◦) *nauvā̐* नौवाँ

Nipple (m◦) *stanāgra* स्तनाग्र

Nitwit (m◦) *mūrkha, buddhū* मूर्ख, बुद्धू

No (av◦) *na, nahī̐* न, नहीं

Nobility (f◦) *kulīnatā* कुलीनता

Noble (adj◦) *kulīn* कुलीन

Nobody (pron∘) *koī nahī̐* कोई नहीं

Nocturnal (adj∘) *niśhāchar* निशाचर

Noise (m∘) *śhor* शोर

Nomad (adj∘) *āwārā* आवारा

Nominal (adj∘) *nāmamātra* नाममात्र

Nomination (m∘) *nāmā̇nkan* नामांकन

None (pron∘) *koī bhī nahī̐* कोई भी नहीं

Nose (m∘) *nāk* नाक

Not (av∘) *nahī̐, na* नहीं, न

Not at all (av∘) *bilakul nahī̐* बिलकुल नहीं

Notice (f∘) *sūchanā* सूचना

Notification (f∘) *sūchanā* सूचना

Notify (v∘) *sūchanā denā* सूचना देना*

Novel (m∘) *upanyās* उपन्यास

Now (av∘) *ab* अब

Now a days (av∘) *ājakal* आजकल

Now and then (av∘) *kabhī-kabhī* कभी कभी

Nowhere (av∘) *kahī̐ nahī̐* कहीं नहीं

Nurse (f∘) *parichārikā* परिचारिका

Nutmeg (m∘) *jāyfal* जायफल

Nutrition (m∘) *āhār* आहार

Nymph (f∘) *apsarā* अप्सरा

O

O' Clock (m∘) *baje* बजे

Oasis (m∘) *marudyān* मरुद्यान

Oath (f∘) *śhapath* शपथ

Obese (adj∘) *bahut moṭā* बहुत मोटा

Obey (v∘) *kahanā mānanā* कहना मानना*

Object (f∘) *vastu, chīz* वस्तु, चीज़

Objection (m∘) *etrāz* (f∘) *āpatti* एतराज़, आपत्ति

Objective (m∘) *hetu, dhyeya, uddeśhya* हेतु, ध्येय, उद्देश्य

Obligation (m∘) *dāyitva* दायित्व

Oblique (m∘) *ṭeḍhā, tirchhā* टेढ़ा, तिरछा

Obliterate (v∘) *miṭānā* मिटाना*

Oblong (m∘) *āyat* आयत

Obscene (adj∘) *aśhlīl* अश्लील

Obscure (adj∘) *aprasiddha* अप्रसिद्ध

Observation (m∘) *nirīkṣhaṇ* निरीक्षण

Observatory (m∘) *vedhaśhālā* वेधशाला

Observe (v∘) *inirīkṣhaṇ karnā* निरीक्षण करना*

Obsession (f∘) *dhun* धुन

Obsolete (adj∘) *aprachalit* अप्रचलित

Obstacle (f∘) *bādhā* बाधा

Obstinate (adj∘) *ziddī* ज़िद्दी

Obstruct (v∘) *bādhā ḍalnā* बाधा डालना*

Obstruction (f∘) *bādhā, vighna* बाधा, विघ्न

Obtain (v∘) *pānā* पाना*

Obvious (adj∘) *suspaṣhṭ, prakaṭ* सुस्पष्ट, प्रकट

Occasion (m∘) *avsar* अवसर

Occupation (m∘) *dhandhā* धंधा

Occupy (v∘) *rahnā* रहना

Occur (v∘) *honā* होना

Occurence (f∘) *ghaṭnā* घटना

Ocean (m∘) *samudra, sāgar* समुद्र, सागर

Octagon (m∘) *aṣhṭabhuj* अष्टभुज

Octave (m∘) *aṣhṭak* अष्टक

October (m∘) *aktūbar* अक्तूबर

Odd (adj∘) *anūṭhā, vichitra* अनूठा, विचित्र

Odor (m∘) *gandh, mahak* गंध, महक

Of (pron◦) *kā, kī, ke, rā, rī re* का, की के, रा, री, रे

Off (adj◦) *band* बंद

Offence (m◦) *aparādh* अपराध

Offensive (adj◦) *ghātak* घातक

Offensive (m◦) *hamlā* हमला

Offer (m◦) *prastāv* प्रस्ताव

Offer (v◦) *arpaṇ karnā* अर्पण करना*

Office (m◦) *kāryālay, daftar* कार्यालय, दफ्तर

Officer (m◦) *adhikārī* अधिकारी

Official (adj◦) *sarkārī* सरकारी

Offspring (f◦) *santān* संतान

Often (av◦) *bārambār, aksar* बारंबार, अक्सर

Oil (m◦) *tel* तेल

Ok (aj◦ av◦) *ṭhīk* ठीक, ठीक है

Okra (f◦) *bhiṇḍī* भिंडी

Old (adj◦) *purānā, būḍhā* पुराना, बूढ़ा

Old lady (f◦) *buḍhiyā* बुढ़िया

Old man (m◦) *vṛddha* वृद्ध

Omen (m◦) *sagun* सगुन

Omission (f◦) *bhūl* भूल

Omit (v◦) *choḍnā* छोड़ना*

Omnipotent (adj◦) *sarvaśhaktimān* सर्वशक्तिमान

Omniscient (adj◦) *sarvagya* सर्वज्ञ

On (m◦) *-par, ūpar* -पर, ऊपर

On both sides (av◦) *donõ taraf se* दोनों तरफ से

On the contrary (av◦) *dūsarī or* दूसरी ओर

Once (av◦) *ek bār* एक बार

One (adj◦) *ek* एक

Oneself (pron◦) *svayam* स्वयं

Onion (m◦) *pyāz* प्याज़

Only (av◦) *kewal, sirf* केवल, सिर्फ

Onset (m◦) *ārambha* आरंभ

Onslaught (m◦) *hamlā, chaḍhāī* हमला, चढ़ाई

Onto (prep◦) *-par* -पर

Onus (m◦) *dāyitva* दायित्व

Onward (av◦) *āge* आगे

Oodient (adj◦) *āgyākārī* आज्ञाकारी

Ooze (v◦) *ṭapaknā, risnā* टपकना, रिसना

Opaque (adj◦) *apārdarśhī* अपारदर्शी

Open (adj◦) *khulā* खुला

Open (v◦) *kholanā* खोलना*

Opening (m◦) 1. (aparture) *chhidra* छिद्र; 2. (opportunity) *avsar* अवसर; 3. (way out) *mārga* मार्ग; 4. (unveiling) *ārambha* आरंभ

Openly (av◦) *khule ām, spaṣhṭa* खुलेआम, स्पष्ट

Operate (v◦) *chalānā* चलाना*

Operation (f◦) *kārvāī* कारवाई

Operational (adj◦) *chālū, lāgū* चालू, लागू

Operator (m◦) *chālak* चालक

Opinion (f◦) *rāy* राय

Opium (m◦) *afīm* अफ़ीम

Opponent (m◦) *pratispardhī* प्रतिस्पर्धी

Opportune (adj◦) *upayukta* उपयुक्त

Opportunist (m◦) *avasarvādī* अवसरवादी

Opportunity (m◦) *maukā* मौका

Oppose (v◦) *virodh karnā* विरोध करना*

Opposite (adj◦) *viruddha* विरुद्ध

Opposition (m◦) *virodh* विरोध

Oppress (v◦) *satānā* सताना*

Oppression (m◦) *atyāchār* अत्याचार

Oppulent (adj∘) *samriddha* समृद्ध

Optimist (m∘) *āśhāvādī* आशावादी

Option (m∘) *vikalp* विकल्प

Or (av∘) *athawā, yā* अथवा, या

Oral (adj∘) *zabānī* ज़बानी

Orange (adj∘) *santrā* संतरा

Orange (m∘) *santrā* संतरा

Orator (m∘) *vaktā* वक्ता

Orchard (m∘f∘) *falavāṭikā* फलवाटिका

Order (m∘) *hukum, ādeśh* (f∘) *āgyā* हुकुम, आदेश, अज्ञा

Order (v∘) *āgyā denā* आज्ञा देना*

Ordinary (adj∘) *sādā, sādhāraṇ* सादा, साधारण

Ore (m∘) *khanij* खनिज

Organ (m∘) *avayav, aṅg* अवयव, अंग

Organism (m∘) *jīv* जीव

Organization (f∘) *sansthā* संस्था

Origin (m∘) *udgam* उद्गम

Original (adj∘) *ādim, mūl* आदिम, मूल

Ornament (m∘) *gahnā, ābhūṣhaṇ, alaṅkār* गहना, आभूषण, अलंकार

Orphan (adj∘) *anāth* अनाथ

Orthodox (adj∘) *rūḍhivādī* रूढ़िवादी

Ostination (m∘) *āḍambar, pākhaṇḍ* आडंबर, पाखंड

Ostrich (m∘) *śhuturmurg* शुतुरमुर्ग

Other (pron∘) *dūsrā* दूसरा

Otherwise (av∘) *athvā, anyathā* अथवा, अन्यथा

Oulandish (adj∘) *ajīb* अजीब

Our (pron∘) *apnā* अपना

Ourselves (pron∘) *ham apne āp* हम अपने आप

Out (av∘) *bāhar* बाहर

Outbreak (m∘) *prakop* प्रकोप

Outcome (m∘) *fal, natījā* फल, नतीजा

Outcome (m∘) *pariṇām, natījā* परिणाम, नतीजा

Outdated (adj∘) *aprachalit* अप्रचलित

Outer (adj∘) *bāharī* बाहरी

Outfit (m∘) *pośhāk* पोशाक

Outlaw (adj∘) *bahiṣhkrit* बहिष्कृत

Outlay (m∘) *kharch, vyay* खर्च, व्यय

Outlet (m∘) *dvār* द्वार

Outline (m∘) *khākā* ख़ाका

Outlook (m∘) *driṣhṭikoṇ* दृष्टिकोण

Out-of-date (adj∘) *aprachalit* अप्रचलित

Outpost (m∘) *nākā* नाका

Outrage (m∘) *gussā* गुस्सा

Outrageous (adj∘) *nindanīya* निंदनीय

Outset (m∘) *prārambha* प्रारंभ

Outside (adj∘) *bāhar* बाहर

Outsider (adj∘) *bāharī* बाहरी

Outstanding (adj∘) *achhā* अच्छा

Outwards (av∘) *bāhar kī or* बाहर की ओर

Oval (m∘) *aṇḍākritī* अंडाकृति

Oven (f∘) *bhaṭṭī* भट्टी

Over (av∘) *ūpar* ऊपर

Overall (adj∘) *kul milākar* कुल मिलाकर

Overbaring (adj∘) *uddhat* उद्धत

Overcome (v∘) *jītnā* जीतना*

Overhaul (f∘) *marammat* मरम्मत

Overnight (av∘) *rāt-bhar* रातभर

Overpower (v∘) *kābu meṅ lānā* काबू में लाना*

Overt (adj∘) *gupta* गुप्त

Overturn (v∘) *ulaṭnā* उलटना

Owe (v∘) *riṇī honā* ऋणी होना

Owl (m∘) *ullū* उल्लू

Own (pron∘) *apnā, nijī* अपना, निजी

Owner (m∘) *swāmī, mālīk* स्वामी, मालिक

Ox (m∘) *bail* बैल

Oxygen (m∘) *prāṇvāyu* प्राणवायु

P

Pace (m∘) *gatī* (motion) गति

Pacify (v∘) *śhānt karnā* शांत करना*

Pack (f∘) 1. (bundle) *poṭlī* पोटली, 2. (group) *jhuṇḍ, samūh* झुंड, समूह

Package, box (m∘) *ḍabbā* डब्बा

Packet (f∘) *poṭlī* पोटली

Pact (m∘) *samjhautā, karār* (f∘) *sandhi* समझौता, करार, संधि

Pad (f∘) *gaddī* गद्दी

Paddy (m∘) *dhān* धान

Page (v∘) *pukārnā* पुकारना*

Page, book (m∘) *priṣhṭha* पृष्ठ

Paint (m∘) *raṅg* रँग

Painter (m∘) *raṅgwālā* रंगवाला

Pair (m∘ f∘) *joḍā, joḍī* जोड़ा, जोड़ी

Pal (m∘) *sāthī* साथी

Palace (m∘) *raj-mahal* राजमहल

Palatable (adj∘) *svādiṣhṭa* स्वादिष्ट

Palate (f∘) *tālu* तालु

Pale (adj∘) *fīkā, nistej* फीका, निस्तेज

Palm, hand (m∘) *kartal* करतल

Palm, tree (m∘) *tāḍ* ताड़

Palpitation (f∘) *ḍhaḍkan* धड़कन

Pamper (v∘) *laḍ karnā* लाड़ करना*

Pan (m∘) *bartan* बरतन

Pandemonium (m∘) *hullaḍ* हुल्लड़

Panic (f∘) *bhagdaḍ, tahalkā* भगदड़, तहलका

Panther (m∘) *tenduā* तेंदुआ

Pants (f∘) *patlūn* पतलून

Papaya (m∘) *papītā* पपीता

Paper (m∘) *kāgaja* कागज

Paper, news (m∘) *akhabār* अखबार

Parable (f∘) *nītikathā* नीतिकथा

Parade (m∘) *julūs* जुलूस

Paradise (m∘) *svarg* स्वर्ग

Paradox (m∘) *virodhābhās* विरोधाभास

Paragraph (m∘) *anucchhed* अनुच्छेद

Parallel (adj∘) *ksamānāntar* समानांतर

Paralyse (v∘) *bala-hīn karnā* बलहीन करना*

Paralysis (m∘) *lakvā* लकवा

Paramount (adj∘) *sarvocchya* सर्वोच्च

Paranoid (adj∘) *aviśhvāsū* अविश्वासू

Paraphernalia (m∘) *sāmagrī* सामग्री

Parch (v∘) *jhulasnā, sūkhnā* झुलसना, सूखना

Pardon (f∘) *kṣhamā, māfī* क्षमा, माफ़ी

Pardon (m∘) *kṣhmā karnā, māf karnā* क्षमा करना, माफ़ करना

Parent (m∘) *mātā-pitā* माता–पिता

Pariah (m∘) *achhūt* अछूत

Parity (f∘) *samānatā* समानता

Park (m∘) *udyān* उद्यान

Parliament (f∘) *saṅsad* संसद

Parody (f∘) *nakal* नकल

Parrot (m∘) *totā* तोता

Parson (m∘) *pādrī* पादरी

Part (m∘) *bhāg, hissā* भाग, हिस्सा

Part (v∘) *alag honā* अलग होना

Participate (v∘) *bhāg lenā* भाग लेना*

Partner (m∘) *sāthī* साथी

Partridge (m∘) *tītar* तीतर

Pass (v∘) 1. (go) *guzarnā* गुज़रना; 2. (success) *uttirṇa honā* उत्तीर्ण होना; 3. (time) *bītanā* बीतना; 4. (give) *denā* देना*; 5. (law) *anumodit karnā* अनुमोदित करना*; 6. (excrete) *visarjit karnā* विसर्जित करना*

Passage (m∘) *rastā, mārg* रस्ता, मार्ग

Passenger (m∘) *yātrī, musāfir* यात्री, मुसाफिर

Passion (m∘) *manobhāv* मनोभाव

Past (adj∘) *pichhlā* पिछला

Past (m∘) *bhūtkāl* भूतकाल

Paste (v∘) *chipkānā* चिपकाना*

Pasture (m∘) *charāgāh* चरागाह

Pat (v∘) *thapthapānā* थपथपाना*

Patch (m∘) *paivand* पैवंद

Paternal uncle (m∘) *chāchā* चाचा

Path (m∘) *rastā* रस्ता

Pathetic (adj∘) *dayanīya* दयनीय

Pathology (m∘) *rog vigyān* रोग विज्ञान

Patience (f∘) *sahanśhakti* सहनशक्ति

Patient (m∘) *rogī, marīz* रोगी, मरीज़

Patriot (m∘) *deśhbhakta* देशभक्त

Patriotism (f∘) *deśhbhakti* देशभक्ति

Patrol (f∘) *gaśhta* गश्त

Patron (m∘) *āśhrayadātā* आश्रयदाता

Patronage (m∘) *āsgray* आश्रय

Pattern (m∘) *ḍhaṅg* ढंग

Paucity (m∘) *abhāv* अभाव

Pauper (m∘) *kaṅgāl* कंगाल

Pause (m∘) *virām* विराम

Pavillion (m∘) *maṇḍap* मंडप

Paw (m∘) *pañjā* पंजा

Pea (m∘) *maṭar* मटर

Peace (f∘) *śhānti* शांति

Peaceful (adj∘) *śhānt* शांत

Peach (m∘) *āḍū* आड़ू

Peacock (m∘) *mor* मोर

Peahen (f∘) *mornī* मोरनी

Peak (f∘) *choṭī* चोटी

Peanut (f∘) *mūnfgali* मूँगफली

Pear (f∘) *nāśhapātī* नाशपाती

Pearl (m∘) *motī* मोती

Peasant (m∘) *kisān* किसान

Peciliar (m∘) *viśheṣha* विशेष

Peculiarity (f∘) *viśheṣhatā* विशेषता

Peek (v∘) *jhā̃knā* झाँकना*

Peel (m∘) *chhilakā* छिलका

Peel (v∘) *cIlanā* छीलना*

Peer (m∘) *sāthī* साथी

Peg (f∘) *khū̃ṭī* खूँटी

Pen (f∘) *kalam* कलम

Penalty (m∘) *daṇḍ* (f∘) *sazā* दंड, सज़ा

Penance (f∘) *tapasyā* तपस्या

Pencil (f∘) *lekhanī* लेखनी

Pendulum (m◦) *lolak* लोलक

Penetrate (v◦) *ghusnā, ghusānā** घुसना, घुसाना*

Penitentiary (m◦) *kārāgār* कारागार

Penitration (m◦) *praveśh* प्रवेश

Penniless (adj◦) *kaṅgāl* कंगाल

Pension (f◦) *sevāvritti* सेवावृत्ति

Pentagon (m◦) *pañchabhuj* पंचभुज

Penultimate (adj◦) *upāntya* उपान्त्य

Penury (m◦) *garībī* गरीबी

People (m◦) *log* लोग

Perceive (v◦) *dekhnā* देखना*

Percent (adj◦) *pratiśhat* प्रतिशत

Perceptible (adj◦) *gochar* गोचर

Perception (m◦) *bodh* बोध

Perfect (adj◦) *paripūrṇa* परिपूर्ण

Perfection (m◦) *paripūrṇatā* परिपूर्णता

Perform (v◦) *krnā* करना*

Performance (m◦) *kārya* कार्य

Perfume (m◦) *itra* इत्र

Perhaps (av◦) *kadāchit, śhāyad* कदाचित्, शायद

Peril (m◦) *khatrā* खतरा

Perimeter (f◦) *paridhi* परिधि

Period (m◦) *kāl, avadhi* काल, अवधि

Periodic (adj◦) *āvartī* आवर्ती

Periphery (m◦) *kinārā* किनारा

Perish (v◦) *naṣhṭa honā* नष्ट होना

Permanent (adj◦) *sthir, sthāyī* स्थिर, स्थायी

Permision (f◦) *ijāzat* इजाज़त

Permission (f◦) *anumati, ijāzat* अनुमति, इजाज़त

Permit (f◦) *anumati* अनुमति

Permit (v◦) *anumati denā* अनुमति देना*

Perpendicular (adj◦) *lamb* लंब

Perpetual (adj◦) *anant* अनंत

Perplexed (adj◦) *hairān* हैरान

Persecute (v◦) *satānā* सताना*

Persecution (m◦) *atyāchār* अत्याचार

Person (f◦) *vyakti* व्यक्ति

Personality (m◦) *vyaktitva* व्यक्तित्व

Perspiration (m◦) *pasīnā* पसीना

Persuade (v◦) *rāzī karnā* राज़ी करना*

Perturb (v◦) *ghabrānā* घबराना

Pervade (v◦) *failnā* फैलना

Pessimism (m◦) *nirāśhā-vād* निराशावाद

Pessimist (m◦) *nirāśhā-vādī* निराशावादी

Pest (m◦) *vināśhī* विनाशी

Pester (v◦) *satānā* सताना*

Pestilence (f◦) *mahamārī* महामारी

Petal (f◦) *paṅkhaḍī* पँखड़ी

Pharmact (m◦) *auṣhadhālay* औषधालय

Phase (f◦) *avasthā, sthiti* अवस्था, स्थिति

Pheasant (m◦) *titar* तीतर

Phenomenal (adj◦) *asādhāraṇ* असाधारण

Philosopher (m◦) *tattvagya* तत्त्वज्ञ

Philosophy (m◦) *darśhan-śhāstra* दर्शन शास्त्र

Phone (m◦) *dūrabhāṣh* दूरभाष

Phoney (adj◦) *naklī* नकली

Photograoh (m◦) *chhāyāchitra* छायाचित्र

Phrase (m◦) *padbandha* पदबंध

Physica (m◦) *bhautik-śhastra* भौतिक शास्त्र

Physical (m◦) *bhautik* भौतिक

Pick (v◦) *uṭhānā, chunanā* उठाना*, चुनना*

Pickle (m◦) *achār* अचार

Pictorial (adj◦) *sachitra* सचित्र

Picture (m◦) *chitra* चित्र

Piece (m◦) *ṭukḍā* टुकड़ा

Pierce (v◦) *bhednā* भेदना*

Pig (m◦) *sūar* सूअर

Pigeon (m◦) *kabūtar* कबूतर

Pigment (m◦) *raṅg* रंग

Pile (f◦) *ḍher, rāśhi* ढेर, राशि

Pilgrim (m◦) *tīrthyātrī* तीर्थयात्री

Pill (f◦) *golī* गोली

Pillage (f◦) *lūṭmār* लूटमार

Pillar (m◦) *khambhā* खंभा

Pillow (m◦) *takiyā* तकिया

Pimple (f◦) *funsī* फुंसी

Pin (f◦) *mekh* मेख

Pine (m◦) *devadār* देवदार

Pineapple (f◦) *anannās* अनन्नास

Pink (adj◦) *gulābī* गुलाबी

Pinnacle (m◦) *śhikhar* शिखर

Pioneer (adj◦) *aguā* अगुआ

Pious (adj◦) *pavitra* पवित्र

Pipe (m◦) *nal,* (f◦) *nalī* नल, नली

Pit (m◦) *gaḍḍhā* गड्ढा

Pitch (m◦) *sur* सुर

Pitcher (f◦) *surāhī* सुराही

Pity (m◦) *taras* (f◦) *dayā* तरस, दया

Pivot (f◦) *dhurī* धुरी

Place (m◦) *sthān, jagah* स्थान, जगह

Place (v◦) *rakhnā* रखना*

Plague (f◦) *mahāmārī* महामारी

Plain (adj◦) *sādā, saral* सादा, सरल

Plan (f◦) *yijnā* योजना

Plane (m◦) *havāī jahāz* हवाई जहाज़

Planet (m◦) *graha* ग्रह

Plank (m◦) *takhtā* तख्ता

Plant (m◦) *paudhā* पौधा

Plantation (m◦) *bāg, bagīchā* बाग, बगीचा

Plate, dish (f◦) *thālī* थाली

Platform (m◦) *chabūtarā* चबूतरा

Play (m◦) 1. (game) *khel, krīḍā* खेल, क्रीड़ा; 2. (drama) *nāṭak* नाटक

Play (v◦) *khelnā* खेलना

Playback Singer (m◦) *pārshva-gāyak* पार्श्वगायक

Player (m◦) *khilāḍī* खिलाड़ी

Pleasant (adj◦) *ramaṇīya* रामणीय

Please (v◦) *khuśh karnā* खुश करना*

Pleasure (m◦) *sukh, ānand* सुख, आनंद

Pledge (f◦) *partigyā* प्रतिज्ञा

Plenty (adj◦) *prachur, bahut* प्रचुर, बहुत

Pliars (m◦) *jamūr* जमूर

Plot (m◦) 1. (land) *bhūmi-khaṇḍ* भूमिखंड; 2. (scheme) *ṣhaḍyantra* षडयंत्र; 2. (story) *kathā-vastu* कथावस्तु

Plough (m◦) *hal* हल

Pluck (v◦) *ukhāḍnā* उखाड़ना*

Plum (m◦) *ber* बेर

Plumet (v◦) *girnā* गिरना

Plump (adj◦) *gol-maṭol* गोल-मटोल

Plunder (v◦) *lūṭnā* लूटना*

Plunge (v◦) 1. (sink) *ḍūbnā* डूबना* 2. (pierce) *ghuseḍnā* घुसेड़ना*

Plural (m◦) *bahuvachan* बहुवचन

Plus (prep◦) *aur* और

Plush (f◦) *makhamal* मखमल

Pocket (f◦) *jeb* जेब

Pocket money (m◦) *jeb kharch* जेब खर्च

Pod (f◦) *falī* फली

Podium (m◦) *mañch* मंच

Poem (f◦) *kavitā* कविता

Poet (m◦) *kavi* कवि

Poetry (m◦) *kāvya* काव्य

Point (m◦) 1. (tip) *nok* नोक; 2. (dot) *bindu* बिंदु; 3. (place) *sthān* स्थान; 4. (moment) *kṣhaṇa* क्षण; 1. (item) *pad* पद

Pointless (adj◦) *vyartha* व्यर्थ

Poison (m◦) *viṣh, zahar* विष, ज़हर

Poke (v◦) *kurednā* कुरेदना*

Pole (m◦) 1. (North or South) *dhruva* ध्रुव 2. (a post) *khambhā* खंभा

Police (m◦) *pulis* पुलिस

Police Station (m◦) *thānā* थाना

Polish (f◦) *chamak* चमक

Polish (v◦) *chamkānā* चमकाना*

Polite (adj◦) *namra, śhiṣhṭa* नम्र, शिष्ट

Politics (f◦) *rājnīti* राजनीति

Poll (m◦) *chunāv* चुनाव

Pollen (m◦) *parāg* पराग

Pollution (m◦) *pradūṣhaṇ* प्रदूषण

Pomegranate (m◦) *anār* अनार

Pomp (m◦) *āḍambar* आडंबर

Pond (m◦) *tālāb* तालाब

Ponytail (f◦) *choṭi* चोटी

Pool (m◦) *pokhar* पोखर

Poor (adj◦) *garīb* गरीब

Poppy (f◦) *khaskhas* खसखस

Popular (adj◦) *lokpriya* लोकप्रिय

Population (f◦) *ābādī* आबादी

Porcupine (f◦) *sāhī* साही

Pore (m◦) *chhed* छेद

Porridge (m◦) *daliyā* दलिया

Port (m◦) *bandargāh* बंदरगाह

Portion (m◦) *bhāg, hissā* भाग, हिस्सा

Portray (v◦) *dikhānā* दिखाना*

Position (f◦) *sthiti* स्थिति

Possess (v◦) *pās honā* पास होना

Possession (f◦) *jāyadād* जायदाद

Possibility (f◦) *sambhāvanā* संभावना

Possible (adj◦) *sambhav* संभव

Possibly (av◦) *kadāchit*, sambhavataḥ कदाचित्, संभवत:

Post 1. (mail) (f◦) *ḍāk* डाक; 2. (pole) *khambhā* खंभा 3. (designation) *pad* पद

Post office (m◦) *ḍākghar* डाकघर

Postman (m◦) *ḍākiyā* डाकिया

Post-mortem (f◦) *śhav-parīkṣhā* शव-परीक्षा

Postpone (v◦) *sthagit karnā* स्थगित करना*

Posture (f◦) *mudrā* मुद्रा

Pot (m◦) *baratan* बरतन

Potato (m◦) *ālu* आलु

Potential (adj◦) *sambhāvya* संभाव्य

Potter (m◦) *kumhār* कुम्हार

Pouch (f∘) *thailī* थैली

Pour (v∘) *ḍālnā, bahānā* डालना*, बहाना*

Poverty (f∘) *garībī* गरीबी

Powder (m∘) *chūrṇa* चूर्ण

Power (f∘) *śhakti* शक्ति

Powerful (adj∘) *śhaktiśhālī* शक्तिशाली

Powerless (adj∘) *śhaktihīn* शक्तिहीन

Practice (m∘) 1. (experience) *abhyās* अभ्यास, 2. (work) *vyavahār* व्यवसाय

Praise (f∘) *stuti, sarāhnā* स्तुति, सराहना

Praise (v∘) *sarāhnā* सराहना*

Prank (f∘) *śharārat* शरारत

Prawn (m∘) *jhiṅgā* झिंगा

Prayer (f∘) *prārthanā* प्रार्थना

Precarious (adj∘) *khatarnāk* खतरनाक

Precaution (f∘) *sāvadhānī* सावधानी

Precious (adj∘) *kimtī* कीमती

Precise (adj∘) *ṭhīk-ṭhīk* ठीक-ठीक

Predicate (m∘) *vidheya* विधेय

Prediction (f∘) *bhaviṣhya-vāṇī* भविष्यवाणी

Predominant (adj∘) *prabal* प्रबल

Preface (f∘) *prastāvanā* प्रस्तावना

Preference (f∘) *pasand* पसंद

Prefix (m∘) *upasarg* उपसर्ग

Pregnant (adj∘) *garbhavati* गर्भवति

Prejudice (m∘) *pakṣhapāt* पक्षपात

Preliminary (adj∘) *prārambhik* प्रारंभिक

Premises (m∘) *bhavan* भवन

Preparation (f∘) *taiyārī* तैयारी

Prepare (v∘) *banānā* बनाना*

Prescription (m∘) *nuskhā* नुसख़ा

Presence (f∘) *upasthiti* उपस्थिति

Present (adj∘) *upasthit, vartamān, vidyamān* उपस्थित, वर्तमान, विद्यमान

Present (f∘) *bheṅṭ,* (m∘) *upahār* भेंट, उपहार

Present (v∘) *prastut karnā* प्रस्तुत करना*

Preserve (v∘) *surakṣhit rakhnā* सुरक्षित रखना*

President (m∘) *sabhāpati, rāṣhṭrapati* सभापति, राष्ट्रपति

Press (m∘) *chhāpkhānā* छापखाना

Press (v∘) *dabānā* दबाना*

Pressure (m∘) *dabāv* दबाव

Prestige (f∘) *pratiṣhṭhā* प्रतिष्ठा

Presumption (f∘) *parikalpanā* परिकल्पना

Pretence (f∘) *bahānebāzī* बहानेबाज़ी

Pretend (v∘) *ḍhoṅg rachnā* ढोंग रचना*

Pretension (m∘) *svāṅg* स्वाँग

Pretext (m∘) *bahānā* बहाना

Pretty (adj∘) *manoram* मनोरम

Pretty (av∘) *kāfī* काफ़ी

Prevelent (adj∘) *prachalit* प्रचलित

Prevent (v∘) *roknā* रोकना*

Prevention (f∘) *rok, nivāraṇ* रोक, निवारण

Preview (m∘) *pūrvadarśhan* पूर्वदर्शन

Previous (adj∘) *pūrva* पूर्व

Prey (m∘) *śhikār* शिकार

Price (m∘) *dām* (f∘) kīmat दाम, कीमत

Prickle (m∘) *kāṅṭā* काँटा

Pricy (adj∘) *kīmatī* कीमती

Pride (m∘) *abhimān; ghamaṇḍ* अभिमान, घमंड

Priest (m∘) *pujārī, purohit* पुजारी, पुरोहित

Primary (adj◦) *prāthamik* प्राथमिक

Prime (adj◦) *mukhya* मुख्य

Primitive (adj◦) *ādim* आदिम

Prince (m◦) *rājkumār* राजकुमार

Princess (f◦) *rājkumārī* राजकुमारी

Principal (m◦) *pradhān, mukhya* प्रधान, मुख्य

Principle (m◦) *tattva* तत्त्व

Print (m◦) *mudraṇ* मुद्रण

Print (v◦) *chhāpnā* छापना*

Prior (adj◦) *pūrva* पूर्व

Priority (f◦) *agratā* अग्रता

Prison (f◦) *kaid* कैद

Prisoner (m◦) *kaidī* कैदी

Privacy (f◦) *ekāntatā* एकांतता

Private (adj◦) *nijī, vyaktigat* निजी, व्यक्तिगत

Privilage (f◦) *suvidhā* सुविधा

Prize (m◦) *inām, puraskār* इनाम, पुरस्कार

Pro (adj◦) *peśhevar* पेशेवर

Probability (f◦) *sambhāvanā* संभावना

Probably (av◦) *kadāchit* कदाचित्

Probihition (m◦) *niṣhedh, rok* निषेध, रोक

Problem (f◦) *samasyā* समस्या

Procedure (f◦) *rīti, paddhati* रीति, पद्धति

Proceed (v◦) *āge jānā, baḍhnā* आगे जाना, बढ़ना

Process (f◦) *ppakriyā, vidhi* प्रक्रिया, विधि

Procession (m◦) *julūs* जुलूस

Proclamation (f◦) *ghoṣhaṇā* घोषणा

Procrastinate (v◦) *ṭālnā* टालना*

Procrastination (f◦) *ṭāl-maṭol* टाल-मटोल

Procrastinator (m◦) *dīrghasūtrī* दीर्घसूत्री

Produce (m◦) *utpādan, nirmiti* उत्पादन, निर्मिति

Produce (v◦) *paidā karnā* पैदा करना*

Producer (m◦) *nirmātā* निर्माता

Product (m◦) *utpādan, upaj* उत्पादन, उपज

Production (m◦) *nirmāṇ* (f◦) *nirmiti, upaj* निर्माण, निर्मिति, उपज

Productivity (f◦) *utpādaktā* उत्पादकता

Profess (v◦) *dāvā karnā* दावा करना*

Profession (m◦) *dhandhā, jīvikā* धंधा, जीविका

Professional (adj◦) *vyavasāyik, nipuṇ* व्यवसायिक, निपुण

Professor(m◦) *adhyāpak* अध्यापक

Proficient (adj◦) *nipuṇ. kuśhal* निपुण, कुशल

Profit (m◦) *lābh, fāyadā* लाभ, फ़ायदा

Profitable (adj◦) *lābhdāyak* लाभदायक

Profound (adj◦) *gahrā, gahan* गहरा, गहन

Profuse (adj◦) *prachur* प्रचुर

Progeny (f◦) *santān* संतान

Program (m◦) *kāryakram* कार्यक्रम

Progress (f◦) *pragati* प्रगति

Prohibit (v◦) *roknā* रोकना

Project (m◦) *yojnā* योजना

Prolong (v◦) *baḍhānā* बढ़ाना*

Prominent (adj◦) *prasiddha* प्रसिद्ध

Promise (m◦) *pratigyā, vādā, vachan* प्रतिज्ञा, वादा, वचन

Promise (v◦) *pratigyā karnā, vādā karnā, vachan denā* प्रतिज्ञा करना, वादा करना, वचन देना*

Promote (v◦) *pragati karnā, prachār karnā* प्रगति करना, प्रचार करना*

Promoter (m◦) *prachārak* प्रचारक

Promotion (f◦) *pragati, prachār* प्रगति, प्रचार

Prone (adj◦) *grahaṇśhīl, bhedya* ग्रहणशील, भेद्य

Prong (m◦) *kẫṭā, śhūl* काँटा, शूल

Pronoun (m◦) *sarvanām* सर्वनाम

Pronounce (v◦) *kahnā* कहना*

Pronunciation (m◦) *ucchār* उच्चार

Proof (m◦) *prāmāṇ, sabūta* प्रमाण, सबूत

Propagate (v◦) *prasār karnā* प्रसार करना*

Propagation (m◦) *prasār* प्रसार

Propel (v◦) *ghakelnā* धकेलना*

Proper (adj◦) *yathārtha, uchit, samyak* यथार्थ, उचित, सम्यक्

Properly (av◦) *samyak, ṭhīk se* सम्यक्, ठीक से

Property (m◦) *jāyadād, sampatti, daulat* जायदाद, संपत्ति, दौलत

Prophesy (f◦) *bhaviṣhyavāṇī* भविष्यवाणी

Proponent (adj◦) *samarthak* समर्थक

Proportion (m◦) *pramāṇ, anupāt* प्रमाण, अनुपात

Proportional (adj◦) *pramāṇbaddha* प्रमाणबद्ध

Proposal (m◦) *prastāv, sujhāv* प्रस्ताव, सुझाव

Propose (v◦) *prastut karnā, sujhānā* प्रस्तुत करना*, सुझाना*

Proposition (m◦) *prastāv, sujhāv* प्रस्ताव, सुझाव

Proprietor (m◦) *mālik, swāmī* मालिक, स्वामी

Prosaic (adj◦) *ubāū, nīras* उबाऊ, नीरस

Prose (m◦) *gadya* गद्य

Prosecute (v◦) *kārvāī chalānā* कारवाई चलाना*

Prosecution (f◦) *kārvāī* कारवाई

Prospect (m◦) *sambhāvanā* संभावना

Prosper (v◦) *samriddha honā* समृद्ध होना

Prosperity (f◦) *samriddhi* समृद्धि

Prosperous (adj◦) *samriddha* समृद्ध

Prostitute (f◦) *veśhyā* वेश्या

Protect (v◦) *rakṣhā karanā* रक्षा करना*

Protection (m◦) *saṁrakṣhaṇ* (f◦) *rakṣhā* संरक्षण, रक्षा

Protector (adj◦) *rakṣhak* रक्षक

Protest (m◦) *virodh* विरोध

Protest (v◦) *virodh karnā* विरोध करना*

Proud (adj◦) *abhimānī; ghamaṇḍī* अभिमानी; घमंडी

Prove (m◦) *siddha karnā* सिद्ध करना

Proven (adj◦) *siddha* सिद्ध

Proverb (f◦) *kahāvat* कहावत

Provide (m◦) *pradān karnā, uualabdha karnā* प्रदान करना, उपलब्ध करना

Providence (m◦) *vidhātā, īśhvar* विधाता, ईश्वर

Province (m◦) *pradeśh, prānt* प्रदेश, प्रांत

Provincial (adj◦) *prādeśhik* प्रादेशिक

Provision (m◦) *prabandh* प्रबंध

Provisional (adj◦) *kām-chalāū* काम-चलाऊ

Proviso (f◦) *śhart* शर्त

Provocate (v◦) *uksānā, bhaḍkānā* उकसाना, भड़काना*

Provocation (m◦) *uksāva, bhaḍkāva* उकसाव, भड़काव

Prowess (m◦) *parākram* पराक्रम

Prpaganda (m◦) *duṣhprachār* दुष्प्रचार

Psalm (m◦) *stotra* स्तोत्र

Pseudo (adj◦) *chhadma* छद्म

Pseudomym (m◦) *upanām* उपनाम

Psychic (adj◦) *mānasik* मानसिक

Psychology (m◦) *manovigyān* मनोविज्ञान

Psychopath (m◦) *manovikārī* मनोविकारी

Pub (f◦) *madhuśhālā* मधुशाला

Public (adj◦) *ām, sārvajanik* आम, सार्वजनिक

Publication (m∘) *prakāśhan* प्रकाशन

Publicity (f∘) *prasiddhi* प्रसिद्धि

Publish (m∘) *prakāśhiy karnā* प्रकाशित करना

Published (adj∘) *prakāśhit* प्रकाशित

Publisher (m∘) *prakāśhak* प्रकाशक

Pucker (v∘) *sikuḍnā* सिकुड़ना

Pudding (m∘) *haluā* हलुआ

Puddle (m∘) *pokhari, gaḍhī* पोखरी, गड़ही

Puff (m∘) *jhõkā* झोंका

Puff (v∘) *fūlnā* फूलना

Puke (f∘) *ulṭī* उलटी

Puke (v∘) *ulṭī karnā* उलटी करना*

Pull (m∘) *khĩchāv, ghasīṭā* खींचाव, घसीटा

Pull (v∘) *khīñchanā, ghasīṭnā* खींचना, घसीटना*

Pully (f∘) *ghirnī* घिरनी

Pulp (m∘) *gūdā, lugdī* गूदा, लुगदी

Pulsate (m∘) *dhaḍknā* धड़कना

Pulsation (m∘) *dhaḍkan* धड़कन

Pulse (f∘) 1. (vein) *nāḍī, nabz* नाड़ी, नब्ज़ 2. (cereal) *dāl* दाल

Pump (m∘) *pichkārī* पिचकारी

Pumpkin (m∘) *kaddu, sītāfal* कद्दु, सीताफल

Punch (c∘) *mukkā mārnā, ghũsā mārnā* मुक्का मारना, घूँसा मारना

Punch (m∘) *mukkā, ghũsā* मुक्का, घूँसा

Punctual (adj∘) *niyamit* नियमित

Puncture (m∘) *chhed* छेद

Puncture (v∘) *chhed karnā* छेद करना*

Pungent (adj∘) *tīkhā, tikta* तीखा, तिक्त

Punish (v∘) *daṇḍa denā* दंड देना*

Punish (v∘) *sajzā denā* सज़ा देना*

Punishment (f∘) *sajā* सज़ा

Punitive (adj∘) *kaṭhor* कठोर

Puny (m∘) *chhoṭā, nikrishṭa* छोटा, निकृष्ट

Pupil (m∘) *vidyārthi, chhatra, śhishya* विद्यार्थी, छात्र, शिष्य

Puppet (f∘) *kaṭhputlī* कठपुतली

Puppy, pup (adj∘) *pillā* पिल्ला

Purchase (m∘) *kharidārī* खरीदारी

Purchase (v∘) *kharīdnā* खरीदना*

Pure (m∘) *śhuddha* शुद्ध

Purification (f∘) *śhuddhi* शुद्धि

Purify (v∘) *śhuddha karnā* शुद्ध करना*

Purple (adj∘) *jāmunī,baingani* जामुनी, बैंगनी

Purpose (m∘) *irādā, hetu* इरादा, हेतु

Purr (v∘) *ghurghurānā* घुरघुराना

Purse (m∘) *baṭuā* बटुआ

Pursue (m∘) 1. (∘ a person) *pīchhā karna* पीछा करना. 2. (∘ a thing) *lage rahnā* लगे रहना

Pursuit (m∘) 1. (going after) *pīchhā* पीछा 2. (activity) *dhandhā, lakshya* धंधा, लक्ष्य

Pus (m∘) *mavād* मवाद

Push (m∘) *dhakkā, ṭhelā* धक्का, ठेला

Push (v∘) *dhakelnā* धकेलना*

Put, keep (v∘) *rakhnā* रखना*

Putrify (v∘) *saḍnā* सड़ना

Putty (m∘) *puṭīn* पुटीन

Puzzle (f∘) *pahelī* पहेली

Pyre (f∘) *chitā* चिता

Python (m∘) *ajgar* अजगर

Q

Quack (adj◦) *nim-hakīm* निम-हकीम

Quadrilateral (m◦) *chaturbhuj* चतुर्भुज

Quadruped (f◦) *chaupāī* चौपाई

Quagmire (f◦) *daldal* दलदल

Quail (f◦) *bater* बटेर

Quake (m◦) *kamp* कंप

Qualification (f◦) *yogyatā* योग्यता

Qualified (adj◦) *yogya* योग्य

Quality (m◦) *yogyatā, guṇ* योग्यता, गुण

Qualm (f◦) *śhaṅkā* शंका

Quandry (f◦) *uljhan* उलझन

Quantity (m◦) *pramāṇ, mātrā* प्रमाण, मात्रा

Quarrel (m◦) *jhagḍā* झगड़ा

Quarrel (v◦) *jhagaḍnā*, laḍnā* झगड़ना*, लड़ना

Quarry (f◦) *khadān* खदान

Quarter (adj◦) *chauthāī* चौथाई

Quarterly (adj◦) *timāhī* तिमाही

Queen (f◦) *rānī* रानी

Queer (adj◦) *asādhāraṇ* असाधारण

Query (m◦) *praśhna* प्रश्न

Quest (f◦) *talāśh, khoj* तलाश, खोज

Question (m◦) *praśhna* प्रश्न

Question (m◦) *praśhna pūchhnā* प्रश्न पूछना

Questionaire (f◦) *praśhnāvalī* प्रश्नावली

Queue (m◦) *katār, paṅkti* कतार, पंक्ति

Quick (adj◦) *chañchal* चंचल

Quickly (av◦) *jhaṭ se, turant* झट से, तुरंत

Quiet (adj◦) *śhānt* शांत

Quietly (av◦) *śhānti se* शांति से

Quietness (m◦) *śhānti* शांति

Quilt (f◦) *rajāī* रजाई

Quit (v◦) *tyāgnā, chhoḍnā* त्यागना, छोड़ना*

Quiver (m◦) *tarkas* तरकस

Quiver (v◦) *thartharnā* थरथरना

Quotation (m◦) *uddharaṇ* उद्धरण

R

Rabbit (m◦) *khargośh* खरगोश

Race (f◦) 1. (sport) *pratiyogitā* प्रतियोगिता, 2. (class) *jāti* जाति

Racial (adj◦) *jātīya* जातीय

Racism (m◦) *jativād* जातिवाद

Racket, noise (m◦) *hallā* हल्ला

Radiant (adj◦) *chamakdār* चमकदार

Radiation (m◦) *tāp* ताप

Radical, basic (adj◦) *mūlbhūt* मूलभूत

Radical, view (m◦) *ugravādī* उग्रवादी

Radio (f◦) *ākāśhavāṇī* आकाशवाणी

Radish (f◦) *mūlī* मूली

Radius (f◦) *trijyā* त्रिज्या

Rag (m◦) *faṭā kapḍā, lattā, chithaḍā* फटा कपड़ा, लत्ता, चिथड़ा

Rag (v◦) *taṅg karnā* तंग करना*

Rage (f◦) *hiṁsā* हिंसा

Raid (m◦) *dhāvā, chhāpā* धावा, छापा

Rail (f◦) *relgāḍī* रेलगाड़ी

Railing (m◦) *jaṅglā* जंगला

Rain (f◦) *bāriṣh, varṣhā* बारिष, वर्षा

Rain (v◦) *barasnā* बरसना

Rainbow (m◦) *indra-dhanuṣha* इंद्रधनुष

Rainy (adj◦) *barsātī* बरसाती

Raise (f∘) *badhotrī* बढोतरी

Raise (v∘) *ūpar uṭhānā* ऊपर उठाना*

Raisin (m∘) *kiśhmiśh* किशमिश

Ram (m∘) *bheḍā, meḍhā* भेड़ा, मेढ़ा

Ramp (f∘) *ḍhalān* ढलान

Rampage (m∘) *krodh* क्रोध

Range (f∘) *paṅkti* पंक्ति

Rank (m∘) *star, darzā* स्तर, दर्ज़ा

Ransom (f∘) *firautī* फिरौती

Rant (v∘) *baknā* बकना

Rap (v∘) *khaṭkhaṭānā* खटखटाना*

Rape (m∘) *balātkār* बलात्कार

Rapid (adj∘) *tez, śhīghra* तेज़. शीघ्र

Raply (m∘) *jawāb, uttar* जवाब, उत्तर

Rare (adj∘) *viral* विरल

Rarely (av∘) *kvachit, viral* क्वचित्, विरल

Raspberry (f∘) *rasbharī* रसभरी

Rat (m∘) *chūhā* चूहा

Rate (m∘) *dar* दर

Rate, speed (f∘) *gati* गति

Rather (av∘) *balki* बल्कि

Ratio (m∘) *anupāt, pramāṇ* अनुपात, प्रमाण

Rational (adj∘) *samajhdār* समझदार

Rattle (m∘) *khaḍkhaḍānā* खड़खड़ाना

Ravage (v∘) *ujāḍnā* उजाड़ना*

Ravine (f∘) *ghāṭī* घाटी

Ravishing (adj∘) *mohak* मोहक

Raw (adj∘) *kacchā* कच्चा

Raw (adj∘) *kachchā* कच्चा

Ray (m∘) *kiraṇ* किरण

Raze (v∘) *miṭānā* मिटाना*

Razor (m∘) *ustarā* उस्तरा

Re (pref∘) *fir se* फिर से

Reach (f∘) *pahũch* पहुँच

Reach (v∘) *pahũchanā* पहुँचना

Reaction (f∘) *pratikriyā* प्रतिक्रिया

Read (v∘) *paḍhanā* पढ़ना*

Reader (m∘) *pāṭhak* पाठक

Ready (adj∘) *taiyār* तैयार

Real (adj∘) *aslī* असली

Reality (f∘) *aslīyat* असलीयत

Realization (f∘) *anubhūti* अनुभूति

Really (av∘) *vastutaḥ* वस्तुत:

Reap (v∘) *fasal kāṭnā* फसल काटना*

Rear (m∘) *pichhvāḍā* पिछवाड़ा

Rear (v∘) *poshaṇ karnā* पोषण करना*

Reason (m∘) *kāraṇ, hetu* कारण, हेतु

Reason (v∘) *tark karnā* तर्क करना*

Reasonable (adj∘) *yathochit* यथोचित

Reassurance (m∘) *āśhvāsan* आश्वासन

Rebate (f∘) *chhūṭ* छूट

Rebel (m∘) *bāgī, vidrohī* बाग़ी, विद्रोही

Rebellion (f∘) *bagāvat* बग़ावत

Rebound (v∘) *ṭakrā kar lauṭnā* टकरा कर लौटना

Rebuke (v∘) *ḍãṭnā* डाँटना*

Recede (v∘) *ghaṭnā, haṭnā* घटना, हटना

Receipt (f∘) *rasīd* रसीद

Receipt (f∘) *rasīd, pāvatī* रसीद, पावती

Receive (v∘) *pānā* पाना

Recent (adj∘) *nayā* नया

Recess (m◦) *madhyāvakāśh* मध्यावकाश

Recession (f◦) *avanati* अवनति

Reciprocal (adj◦) *pārasparik* पारस्परिक

Recital (m◦) *pāṭh* पाठ

Reckless (adj◦) *lāparvāh* लापरवाह

Recklessness (f◦) *lāparvāhī* लापरवाही

Recline (v◦) *leṭnā* लेटना

Reclusion (m◦) *ekānt* एकांत

Recognition (f◦) *kadar, mānyatā* क़दर, मान्यता

Recognize (v◦) *pahichān* पहिचान*

Recollect (v◦) *yād karnā* याद करना*

Recollection (f◦) *yād, smriti* याद, स्मृति

Recommendation (f◦) *sifāriśh* सिफ़ारिश

Reconing (f◦) *gintī* गिनती

Record (m◦) *lekh* लेख

Record (v◦) *likhnā* लिखना*

Recorded (adj◦) *likhit* लिखित

Recreation (m◦) *manorañjan* मानोरंजन

Recruit (m◦) *raṅgrūṭ* रंगरूट

Rectangle (m◦) *āyat* आयत

Rectum (m◦) *malāśhay* मलाशय

Recycling (f◦) *punarnirmiti* पुनर्निर्मिति

Red (adj◦) *lāl* लाल

Redemption (m◦) *uddhār* उद्धार

Red-handed (adj◦) *raṅge-hāth* रंगे-हाथ

Reduce (v◦) *ghaṭnā, ghaṭānā** घटना, घटाना*

Refliction (m◦) *prāvartan* परावर्तन

Reform (v◦) *sudhārnā* सुधारना*

Reformation (m◦) *sudhār* सुधार

Refrain (m◦) *dūr rahnā* दूर रहना

Refresh (v◦) *tāzā karnā* ताज़ा करना*

Refreshed (adj◦) *tarotāzā* तरोताज़ा

Refreshment (m◦) *jal-pān* जलपान

Refreshment (m◦) *nāśhtā* नाश्ता

Refuge (m◦) *śharaṇ* शरण

Refugee (m◦) *śharaṇārthī* शरणार्थी

Refund (v◦) *paise lauṭānā* पैसे लौटाना*

Refusal (m◦) *inkār* इनकार

Refuse (m◦) *kūḍā-karkaṭ* कूड़ा-करकट

Refuse (v◦) *inkār karnā* इनकार करना*

Region (m◦) *kṣhetra, vibhāg* क्षेत्र, विभाग

Register (f◦) *pañjikā* पंजिका

Register (v◦) *bhartī karna, likhānā* भरती करना, लिखाना*

Registration (m◦) *pañjīkaraṇ* पंजीकरण

Regret (m◦) *khed, dukh* खेद, दुख

Regret (v◦) *dukhī honā* दुखी होना

Regulation (m◦) *niyantraṇ* नियंत्रण

Rein (f◦) *bāgḍor* बागडोर

Reject (v◦) *nakārnā* नकारना*

Rejection (m◦) *nakār, asvīkriti* नकार, अस्वीकृति

Relation (m◦) *sambandh* संबंध

Relationship (m◦) *nātā, riśhtā* नाता, रिश्ता

Relative (m◦) *nātedār, riśhtedār* नातेदार, रिश्तेदार

Relax (v◦) *viśhrām karnā* विश्राम करना*

Release (v◦) *chhoḍnā* छोड़ना

Relevant (adj◦) *sambaddh, saṅgat* संबद्ध, संगत

Reliable (adj◦) *bharosemand* भरोसेमंद

Relief (m◦) *ārām* आराम

Religion (m◦) *dharma* धर्म

Religious (adj◦) *dhārmik* धार्मिक

Relinquish (v∘) *tyāgnā, chhoḍnā* त्यागना, छोड़ना*

Reluctance (f∘) *anichhā* अनिच्छ

Reluctant (adj∘) *anichhuk* अनिच्छुक

Remain (v∘) *bākī rahnā* बाक़ी रहना

Remainder (m∘) *bākI, śheṣh* बाक़ी, शेष

Remedy (m∘) *ilāj, upāy* इलाज, उपाय

Remember (v∘) *yād karnā* याद करना*

Remembrance (f∘) *yād,* (m∘) *smaraṇ* याद, स्मरण

Remind (v∘) *yād dilānā* याद दिलाना*

Remorse (m∘) *paschātāp, pachhatāvā* पश्चाताप, पछतावा

Remorse (v∘) *pachhatānā* पछताना

Remote (adj∘) *dūr kā* दूर का

Remove (v∘) *haṭānā* हटाना*

Renounce (v∘) *tyāgnā, chhoḍnā* त्यागना, छोड़ना*

Renovation (m∘) *punaruddhār* पुनरुद्धार

Repair (v∘) *ṭhīk karnā* ठीक करना*

Repeat (m∘) *dobārā karnā* दोबारा करना

Repeatedly (av∘) *bārambār, punaḥ-punaḥ* बारंबार, पुन: पुन:

Repeatedly (av∘) *bārbār* बारबार

Repeatition (f∘) *punarāvritti* पुनरावृत्ति

Repel (v∘) *radda karnā* रद्द करना*

Repent (v∘) *pachhatānā* पछताना

Repentance (m∘) *pachhatāvā* पछतावा

Repercusision (m∘) *pratighāt* प्रतिघात

Replacement (m∘) *badlā* बदला

Replete (adj∘) *paripūrṇa* परिपूर्ण

Report (m∘) *vrittānt, vivaraṇ* वृत्तांत, विवरण

Report (v∘) *vrittānt denā* वृत्तांत देना*

Representative (m∘) *pratinidhi* प्रतिनिधि

Reproach (m∘) *dhikkār* धिक्कार

Reproduce (m∘) *dobārā karnā* दोबारा करना

Republic (m∘) *gaṇatantra* गणतंत्र

Repulsion (f∘) *aruchi, ghriṇṇā* अरुचि, घृणा

Reputable (adj∘) *pratiṣhṭhit* प्रतिष्ठित

Reputation (m∘) *pratiṣhṭhā* प्रतिष्ठा

Request (m∘) *vinati, prārthanā* विनति, प्रार्थना

Request (v∘) *prārthanā karnā* प्रार्थना करना*

Require (v∘) *āvaśhyak honā* आवश्यक होना

Requirement (f∘) *āvaśhyaktā* आवश्यकता

Requisite (adj∘) *zarūrī* ज़रूरी

Research (m∘) *anusandhān* अनुसंधान

Resemblance (f∘) *samānatā* समानता

Resent (v∘) *nārāz honā* नाराज़ होना

Resentment (f∘) *nārāzgī* नाराज़गी

Reservation (m∘) *ārakṣhaṇ* आरक्षण

Reserved (adj∘) *ārakṣhit* आरक्षित

Reside (v∘) *rahanā* रहना

Residence (m∘) *nivās-sthān* निवास-स्थान

Resident (m∘) *nivāsī* निवासी

Residue (m∘) *avaśheṣh* अवशेष

Resignation (m∘) *istifā, pad-tyāg* इस्तिफ़ा, पदत्याग

Resist (v∘) *virodh karnā* विरोध करना*

Resistance (m∘) *virodh* विरोध

Resolution (m∘) *saṅkalp* संकल्प

Resourse (m∘) *upāy, sādhan* उपाय, साधन

Respect (m∘) *ādar, sammān* आदर, सम्मान

Respect (v∘) *ādar karnā* आदर करना*

Respite (m∘) *ārām* आराम

Respond (m∘) *uttar denā, javāb denā* उत्तर देना, जवाब

देना

Responsibility (f∘) *jimmedārī* जिम्मेदारी

Responsiblr (adj∘) *jimmedār* जिम्मेदार

Rest (m∘) *ārām* आराम

Rest (v∘) *ārāma karnā* आराम करना*

Restless (adj∘) *bechain* बेचैन

Restlessness (f∘) *bechainī* बेचैनी

Restoration (f∘) *marammat* मरम्मत

Restrain (v∘) *roknā* रोकना*

Restraint (m∘) *rok, niyantraṇ* रोक, नियंत्रण

Restricted (adj∘) *sīmiy* सीमित

Restriction (m∘) *pratibandh* प्रतिबंध

Retail (m∘) *khudrā* खुदरा

Retaliate (v∘) *badlā lenā* बदला लेना*

Retarded (adj∘) *mandbuddhi* मंदबुद्धि

Retirement (f∘) *nivritti* निवृत्ति

Retreat (v∘) *pīchhe haṭnā* पीछे हटना

Retribution (m∘) *daṇḍ* दंड

Return (v∘) *lauṭnā, lauṭānā** लौटना, लौटाना*

Reveal (v∘) *prakaṭ karnā* प्रकट करना*

Revenge (m∘) *badlā* बदला

Revere (v∘) *ādar krnā* आदर करना*

Reverence (m∘) *ādar* आदर

Reverse (adj∘) *ulṭā* उलटा

Review (m∘) *punar-parīkṣhaṇ* पुनर्परीक्षण

Revile (v∘) *gālī denā* गाली देना*

Revival (m∘) *punar-jīvan* पुनर्जीवन

Revoke (v∘) *radda karnā* रद्द करना*

Revolt (m∘) *vidroha* विद्रोह

Revolt (v∘) *vidroha karnā* विद्रोह करना*

Revolution (f∘) *krānti* क्रांति

Revolve (v∘) *ghūmnā* घूमना

Revolver (m∘) *tamañchā* तमंचा

Reward (m∘) *bakṣhis, inām* बक्षिस, इनाम

Rhino (m∘) *geṇḍā* गेंडा

Rhyme (f∘) *tuk* तुक

Rhythm (m∘) *lay* लय

Rib (f∘) *paslī* पसली

Ribbon (m∘) *fītā* फ़ीता

Rice (m∘) *chāval* चावल

Rich (adj∘) *dhanī, amīr* धनी, अमीर

Riddle (f∘) *pahelī* पहेली

Ride, drive (v∘) *chalānā* चलाना*

Ridicule (m∘) *uphās* उपहास

Rift (f∘) *darār* दरार

Right, direction (adj∘) *dāhinā* दाहिना

Right, proper (adj∘) *uchit* उचित

Rightly (av∘) *yathā -tathā, samyak* यथातथा, सम्यक्

Rigor (m∘) *saṁyam* संयम

Rind (m∘) *vhhilkā* छिलका

Ring (f∘) *aṅgūṭhī* अंगूठी

Ring finger (f∘) *anāmikā* अनामिका

Riot (m∘) *daṅgā* दंगा

Rip (v∘) *chīrnā* चीरना*

Ripe (adj∘) *pakā* पका

Ripen (v∘) *paknā* पकना

Ripple (f∘) *lahar* लहर

Rise (m∘) *chaḍhāv* चढ़ाव

Rise (v∘) *uṭhnā, uṭhānā** उठना, उठाना*

Risk (m∘) *khatrā* खतरा

Ritual (m◦) *karma-kāṇḍ* कर्मकांड

River (f◦) *nadī* नदी

Road (m◦) *rastā, mārg* रस्ता, मार्ग

Roam (v◦) *ghūmanā* घूमना

Roar (f◦) *garjanā, dahāḍī* गर्जना, दहाड़ी

Roar (v◦) *dahāḍī mārnā* दहाड़ी मारना*

Roast (v◦) *bhūnanā* भूनना*

Rob (v◦) *lūṭnā* लूटना*

Robust (adj◦) *mazbūt* मज़बूत

Rock (f◦) *chaṭṭān* चट्टान

Rod (m◦) *ḍaṇḍā* डंडा

Role (f◦) *bhūmikā* भूमिका

Role (f◦) *bhūmikā* भूमिका

Roll (v◦) *luḍhaknā* लुढ़कना*

Rolling pin (m◦) *belan* बेलन

Romantic (adj◦) *romāñchak* रोमांचक

Romantic (adj◦) *romāñchak* रोमांचक

Roof (m◦) *chhat* छत

Room (m◦) *kamarā* कमरा

Rooster (m◦) *murgā* मुर्गा

Root (f◦) *jaḍ* जड़

Rope (f◦) *rassī* रस्सी

Rose (m◦) *gulāb* गुलाब

Rot (v◦) *saḍanā* सड़ना

Rotate (v◦) *ghūmnā, ghumānā** घूमना, घुमाना

Rotation (m◦) *chakkar* चक्कर

Rough (ajm◦) 1. (not smooth) *khurdarā* खुरदरा, 2. (not final) *kacchā* कच्चा

Roughly (av◦) *lagbhag* लगभग

Round (adj◦) *gol* गोल

Row (f◦) *katār* कतार

Rowdy (m◦) *jhagḍālū* झगड़ालू

Rrliance (m◦) *bharosā* भरोसा

Rub (v◦) *ragaḍnā* रगड़ना*

Rubber (m◦) *rabaḍ* रबड़

Rubbish (m◦) *kūḍā* कूड़ा

Rude (adj◦) *kaṭhor* कठोर

Ruffian (m◦) *guṇḍā, badmāśh* गुंडा, बदमाश

Rug (m◦) *galīchā* ग़लीचा

Rugged (adj◦) *mazbūt* मज़बूत

Ruin (m◦) *nāśh* नाश

Ruin (v◦) *nashṭa karnā* नष्ट करना*

Rule (m◦) *niyam, kāydā* नियम, क़ायदा

Ruler, king (adj◦) *śhāsak* शासक

Rumble (m◦) *gaḍgaḍānā* गड़गड़ाना

Rumous (f◦) *afavāh* अफ़वाह

Run (v◦) *bhāganā, dauḍnā* भागना, दौड़ना

Rupee (m◦) *rupayā* रुपया

Rural (adj◦) *grāmīṇ* ग्रामीण

Rush (f◦) *haḍbaḍī* हडबड़ी

Rush (v◦) *jhapaṭnā* झपटना

Rust (m◦) *zaṅg* जंग

Ruthless (adj◦) *krūr, nirday* क्रूर, निर्दय

S

Sack (m◦) *thailā, borā* थैला, बोरा

Sacred (adj◦) *pavitra* पवित्र

Sacrifice (m◦) *tyāga* त्याग

Sad (adj◦) *dukhī, udās* दुखी, उदास

Saddle (m◦) *jīn* जीन

Safe (adj॰) *surakṣhit, salāmata* सुरक्षित, सलामत

Safeguard (f॰) *surakṣhā* सुरक्षा

Safety (f॰) *surakṣhā* सुरक्षा

Saffron (adj॰) *kesrī* केसरी

Saffron (m॰) *kesar* केसर

Sage (m॰) *muni* मुनि

Sagittariua (f॰) *dhanu rāśhi* धनु राशि

Sailor (m॰) *nāvik* नाविक

Saint (m॰) *sādhu* साधु

Sale (m॰) *bikrī* बिक्री

Saliva (f॰) *thūk* थूक

Salt (m॰) *namak* नमक

Salute (m॰) *naman* नमन

Salute (m॰) *salām, namaste* सलाम, नमस्ते

Salvation (m॰) *mokṣha,* (f॰) *mukti* मोक्ष, मुक्ति

Same (adj॰) *vahī, samān* वही, समान

Sample (m॰) *namūnā* नमूना

Sancity (f॰) *pavitratā* पवित्रता

Sanction (f॰) *anumati* अनुमति

Sanction (v॰) *anumati denā* अनुमति देना*

Sand (f॰) *ret, bālū* रेत, बालू

Sane (adj॰) *samajhdār* समझदार

Sanitation (f॰) *safāī* सफ़ाई

Sanity (m॰) *sanajhdārī* समझदारी

Saphire (m॰) *nīlam* नीलम

Sapling (m॰) *paudhā* पौधा

Sarcasm (m॰) *tānā* ताना

Satisfaction (m॰) *santoṣh* संतोष

Satisfactory (adj॰) *santoṣh janak* संतोष जनक

Satisfy (v॰) *santuṣhṭa karnā* संतुष्ट करना*

Saturday (m॰) *śhanivār* शनिवार

Saturn (m॰) *śhani* शनि

Sauce (f॰) *chaṭnī* चटनी

Savage (m॰) *jaṅglī* जंगली

Save (v॰) *bachānā* बचाना

Saving (f॰) *bachat* बचत

Savour (m॰) *svād* स्वाद

Savoury (adj॰) *svādiṣhṭa* स्वादिष्ट

Saw (f॰) *ārī* आरी

Say (v॰) *kahnā* कहना*

Saying (m॰) *vachan, kathan* वचन, कथन

Scab (m॰) *khuraṇḍ* खुरंड

Scaf (m॰) *dupaṭṭā* दुपट्टा

Scale (m॰) 1. (measure) *nāp, māp* नाप, माप; 2. (balance) *tarāzū* तराज़ू; 2. (coat) *kavach* कवच

Scam (m॰) *ghoṭālā* घोटाला

Scandal (m॰) *badnāmī* बदनामी

Scanty (adj॰) *alp, bahut thoḍā* अल्प, बहुत थोड़ा

Scar (m॰) *vraṇ, dāg, niśhan* व्रण, दाग, निशान

Scarce (adj॰) *durlabh* दुर्लभ

Scare (m॰) *āntak* आंतक

Scare (v॰) *ḍrānā* डराना*

Scarlet (adj॰) *sindūrī* सिंदूरी

Scary (m॰) *ḍarāvnā, bhayānak* डरावना, भयानक

Scathing (adj॰) *kaṭhor* कठोर

Scatter (v॰) *failānā, titar-bitar karnā, bikharāna* फैलाना, तितर-बितर करना, बिखराना*

Scenario (m॰) *driṣhya, paṭkathā* दृश्य, पटकथा

Scene (m॰) *driṣhya* दृश्य

Scenic (adj॰) *ramya* रम्य

Scent (m∘) *sugandh, mahak* सुगंध, महक

Sceptical (adj∘) *s'hankāyukta* शंकायुक्त

Schedule (f∘) *kārya-sūchī* कार्यसूची

Scheme (m∘) *yojnā* योजना

Scholar (m∘) *pandit, vidvān* पंडित, विद्वान

Scholarship (f∘) 1. (aid) *chhātravritti* छात्रवृत्ति; 2. (erudition) *pānditya, vidvattā* पांडित्य, विद्वत्ता

School (m∘) *vidyālaya,* (f∘) *pāthas'hālā* विद्यालय, पाठशाला

Science (m∘) *s'hāstra, vigyān* शास्त्र, विज्ञान

Scientific (adj∘) *s'hāstrīya, vaigyānik* शास्त्रीय, वैज्ञानिक

Scientist (m∘) *vaigyānik* वैज्ञानिक

Scissors (f∘) *kaiñchī* कैंची

Scold (v∘) *jhidaknā, dāṭnā* झिड़कना, डाँटना*

Scoop (m∘) *belchā* बेलचा

Scope (f∘) 1. (possibility) *guñjāis'h* गुंजाइश; 2. (range) *vistār* विस्तार

Scorch (v∘) *jhulsānā* झुलसाना*

Score (m∘) *hisāb* हिसाब

Score (v∘) *pānā* पाना*

Scorn (m∘) *apamān* अपमान

Scorpio (f∘) *vrischic rās'hi* वृश्चिक राशि

Scorpion (m∘) *bichchhu* बिच्छु

Scoundrel (adj∘) *badmās'h* बदमाश

Scramble (v∘) 1. (to crowl) *reṅgnā* रेंगना; 2. (to mix up) *milā denā* मिला देना*; 3. (to strugle) *chhīnā-jhaptī karnā* छीना-झपटी करना*

Scrap (m∘) *kūdā* कूड़ा

Scrape (v∘) *ragadnā, khurachnā* रगड़ना, खुरचना*

Scratch (f∘) *khujlī* खुजली

Scratch (v∘) *khurachnā, kurednā* खुरचना, कुरेदना*

Screen (m∘) *chitrapaṭ* चित्रपट

Screw (m∘) *pech* पेच

Screwdriver (m∘) *pechkas'h* पेचकश

Scribble (v∘) *ghasīṭnā* घसीटना*

Script (f∘) *paṭa-kathā* पटकथा

Scripture (m∘) *dharma-granth* धर्मग्रंथ

Scruple (f∘) *naitik saṅkoch* नैतिक संकोच

Scrupulous (adj∘) *īmāndār* ईमानदार

Scrutinize (v∘) *jāñch karnā* जाँच करना*

Scrutiny (f∘) *jāñch* जाँच

Scuffle (f∘) *hāthāpāī* हाथापाई

Sculptor (m∘) *mūrtikār* मूर्तिकार

Sculpture (f∘) *mūrtī* मूर्ति

Scum (m∘) *jhāg, fen* झाग, फेन

Scurry (v∘) *bhāgnā* भागना

Sea (m∘) *samudra, sāgar* समुद्र, सागर

Seal (f∘) *mohar* मोहर

Seam (f∘) *sīvan* सीवन

Search (m∘) *khoj, talās'h* खोज, तलाश

Search (v∘) *khojnā, ḍhūñḍhanā* खोजना, ढूँढना*

Season (m∘) *ritu, mausam* ऋतु, मौसम

Seasonal (adj∘) *mausamī* मौसमी

Seasoned (adj∘) *anubhavī* अनुभवी

Seat (m∘) *āsan, sthān* आसन, स्थान

Second (adj∘) *dūsrā* दूसरा

Secondary (m∘) *duyyam, gauṇ* दुय्यम, गौण

Secret (adj∘) *gopanīya, gupt* गोपनीय, गुप्त

Secret (m∘) *rahasya, bhed* रहस्य, भेद

Secretary (m∘) *sachiv* सचिव

Sect (m∘) *sampradāy* संप्रदाय

Section (m∘) *vibhāg, khaṇḍ* विभाग, खंड

Sector (m∘) *añchal, kṣhetra* अंचल, क्षेत्र

Secular (m∘) *dharma-nirapekṣha* धर्म-निरपेक्ष

Secure (adj∘) *surakṣhit* सुरक्षित

Secure (v∘) *pānā* पाना*

Security (f∘) *surakṣha* सुरक्षा

See (v∘) *dekhanā* देखना*

Seed (m∘) *bīj* बीज

Seek (v∘) *khojnā, dhũḍhanā* खोजना, ढूँढना*

Seep (v∘) *chūnā* चूना

Segment (m∘) *hissā, khaṇḍ* हिस्सा, खंड

Segregation (m∘) *prithakkaraṇ* पृथक्करण

Seige (f∘) *gherābandī* घेराबंदी

Seize (v∘) *chhīnanā* छीनना*

Seldom (adj∘) *kadāchit* कदाचित्

Select (v∘) *chunanā* चुनना*

Selection (m∘) *chunāv* चुनाव

Self (pref∘) *āp, ātma, svayam* आप, आत्म, स्वयं

Self-centered (m∘) *āp-matalabī* आप-मतलबी

Self-control (m∘) *ātma-saṁyam* आत्मसंयम

Self-defence (f∘) *ātma-rakṣhā* आत्मरक्षा

Self-inspired (m∘) *svayam-sfurta* स्वयं-स्फूर्त

Selfless (adj∘) *niḥsvārtha* निःस्वार्थ

Self-respect (m∘) *ātma-gaurav* आत्मगौरव

Self-sufficient (adj∘) *ātma-nirbhar* आत्म-निर्भर

Sell (v∘) *bechanā* बेचना*

Seller (m∘) *vikretā* विक्रेता

Semi (pref∘) *ardh-* अर्ध-

Semicolon (m∘) *ardha-virām* अर्धविराम

Seminar (m∘) *goṣhṭhī* गोष्ठी

Senate (f∘) *sanad* सनद

Send (v∘) *bhejanā* भेजना*

Senior (adj∘) *jyeṣhṭha* ज्येष्ठ

Senriment (f∘) *bhāvuktā* भावुकता

Sense (m∘) *hoś́h* होश

Senselass (adj∘) *behoś́h* बेहोश

Sensible (adj∘) *samajhdār* समझदार

Sensitive (maj) *bhāvuk* भावुक

Sentence (m∘) *vākya* वाक्य

Sentry (m∘) *paharedār* पहरेदार

Separate (adj∘) *alag* अलग

Separately (av∘) *alag se* अलग से

Separation (m∘) *prithakkaraṇ* पृथक्करण

Separete (v∘) *alag honā, alag karnā** अलग होना, अलग करना*

September (m∘) *sitambar* सितंबर

Sepulture (f∘) *samādhi* समाधि

Sequence (m∘) *kram* क्रम

Serial (adj∘) *kramik* क्रमिक

Series (f∘) *ś́hriṅkhalā* शृंखला

Serinity (f∘) *ś́hāntatā* शांतता

Serious (adj∘) *pgambhīr* गंभीर

Seriously (av∘) *gambhīrtā se* गंभीरता से

Seriousness (m∘) *gāmbhīrya* गांभीर्य

Sermon (m∘) *pravachan* प्रवचन

Serpent (m∘) *sarpa* सर्प

Serrated (adj∘) *dantur* दंतुर

Servant (m∘) *naukar* नौकर

Serve (v∘) *sevā karanā* सेवा करना*

Service (f∘) *naukarī, kām* नौकरी, काम

Sesame (m∘) *til* तिल

Set (m∘) *samucchay* समुच्चय

Set (v∘) *rachnā* रचना*

Settle, compromise (v∘) *nipaṭnā* निपटना

Settlement (m∘) *samjhautā, niptārā* समझौता, निपटारा

Seven (adj∘) *sāt* सात

Seventeen (adj∘) *satrah* सत्रह

Seventy (adj∘) *sattar* सत्तर

Sever (v∘) *kāṭnā* काटना*

Several (adj∘) *kaī* कई

Severally (av∘) *pṛthak* पृथक्

Severe (adj∘) *kaṭhor* कठोर

Sew (v∘) *sīnā* सीना*

Sewer (m∘) *nālā* नाला

Sex (m∘) *liṅg* लिंग

Sexual (adj∘) *laiṅgik* लैंगिक

Shabby (adj∘) *faṭe-hāl* फटेहाल

Shack (f∘) *kuṭiyā, jhom̐paḍī* कुटिया, झोंपड़ी

Shackle (f∘) *beḍī* बेड़ी

Shade (f∘) *chhām̐va, chhāyā* छाँव, छाया

Shadow (f∘) *parchhāī* परछाई

Shaft (m∘) *ḍaṇḍā* डंडा

Shake (v∘) *hilānā* हिलाना*

Shaky (adj∘) *kamzor* कमज़ोर

Shallow (adj∘) *uthlā, chhichhlā* उथला, छिछला

Shame (f∘) *lajjā, śharm* लज्जा, शर्म

Shape (f∘) *ākār, śhakal, ākritī* आकार, शकल, आकृति

Shapr (v∘) *ākār denā* आकार देना*

Share (m∘) *bhāg, hissā* भाग, हिस्सा

Share (v∘) *bām̐ṭnā* बाँटना*

Sharp (adj∘) *tez* तेज़

Shave (v∘) *hajāmat karnā* हजामत करना*

She (pron∘) *vah* वह

Shear (v∘) *kāṭnā* काटना*

Shears (f∘) *kaiñchī* कैंची

Sheep (f∘) *bheḍ* भेड़

Sheep (m∘ f∘) *bheḍ* भेड़

Sheet, bed sheet (f∘) *chādar* चादर

Shelf (f∘) *kapāṭ* कपाट

Shell (f∘) *sīp, sīpī* सीप, सीपी

Shelter (m∘) *āśhray* आश्रय

Shepherd (m∘) *gaḍeria* गडेरिया

Shieft (m∘) *badal* बदल

Shieft (v∘) *badalnā* बदलना*

Shield (m∘) *kavach, () ḍhāl* कवच, ढाल

Shimmer (v∘) *jhilmilānā* झिलमिलाना

Shine (v∘) *chamaknā, chamkānā** चमकना, चमकाना*

Shins (f∘) *chamak* चमक

Ship (m∘) *jahāz* जहाज़

Shirt (f∘) *kamīj,* (m∘) *kuratā* कमीज, कुर्ता

Shock (m∘) *dhakkā, sadmā* धक्का, सदमा

Shoe, boot (m∘) *jūtā* जूता

Shoot (v∘) *golī mārnā* गोली मारना*

Shop (f∘) *dukān* दुकान

Shore (m∘) *taṭ, kinārā* तट, किनारा

Short (adj∘) *chhoṭā, laghu* छोटा, लघु

Shortage (m∘) *abhāv* अभाव

Shortly (av∘) *turant* तुरंत

Shoulder (m∘) *kandhā, skand* कंधा, स्कंद

Shout (f∘) *pukār* पुकार

Shout (v◦) *pukārna*, chillānā* पुकारना*, चिल्लाना

Shovel (m◦) *belchā* बेलचा

Shovel (m◦) *fāvaḍā* फावड़ा

Show (m◦) *pradarśhan* प्रदर्शन

Show (v◦) *dikhānā* दिखाना*

Shower (f◦) *bauchhār;* (m◦) *fuhārā* बौछार, फुहारा

Shred (f◦) *dhajjī* धज्जी

Shred (v◦) *dhajjiyā̃ karnā* धज्जियाँ करना*

Shrewd (adj◦) *sayānā, samajhdār* सयाना, समझदार

Shrimp (m◦) *hjiṅgā* झिंगा

Shrine (f◦) *samādhi,* (m◦) *makbarā* समाधि, म्कबरा

Shrink (v◦) *sikuḍnā* सिकुड़ना

Shrivel (v◦) *kumhalānā* कुम्हलाना

Shroud (m◦) *kafan, ḍhaknā* कफ़न, ढकना

Shrub (f◦) *jhāḍī* झाड़ी

Shudder (v◦) *thartharānā* थरथराना

Shuffle (v◦) *phẽṭnā* फेंटना*

Shun (v◦) *bachnā* बचना

Shut (v◦) *band karnā* बंद करना*

Shutter (f◦) *jhilmilī* झिलमिली

Shy (adj◦) *lajjāyukta* लज्जायुक्त

Shy (v◦) *lājnā, saṅkoch karnā** लजाना, संकोच करना*

Sick (adj◦) *bīmār, asvastha* बीमार, अस्वस्थ

Sicken (v◦) *ūbānā* ऊबाना

Sickness (f◦) *bīmārī* बीमारी

Side (f◦) *bājū, bagal* बाजू, बगल

Sieve (f◦) *chalnī, chhalnī* चलनी, छलनी

Sift (v◦) *chhānanā* छानना*

Sigh (v◦) *āh bharnā* आह भरना*

Sight (m◦) *drishṭi* दृष्टि

Sign (m◦) *pratik, chihna* प्रतिक, चिह्न

Signal (m◦) *saṅket* संकेत

Signature (f◦) *hastākṣhar* हस्ताक्षर

Significance (m◦) *mahattva* महत्त्व

Silence (m◦) *maun* (f◦) *khāmośhī* मौन, ख़ामोशी

Silent (adj◦) *khāmośh, chup* ख़ामोश, चुप

Silently (av◦) *chupachāp* चुपचाप

Silk (m◦) *reśham* रेशम

Silky (adj◦) *reśhmī* रेशमी

Silly (adj◦) *bevakūf* बेवक़ूफ़

Silver (f◦) *chāndī* चाँदी

Similar (adj◦) *samān* समान

Similarly (av◦) *usī tarah se* उसी तरह से

Simile (f◦) *upamā* उपमा

Simmer (v◦) *ubalnā* उबलना

Simple (adj◦) *sādā, sādhāraṇ, saral* सादा, साधारण, सरल

Simplicity (f◦) *saraltā* सरलता

Simplify (v◦) *āsāna karnā* आसान करना*

Simultaneous (adj◦) *ek-kālik* एककालिक

Simultaneously (av◦) *sāth-sāth, ek sāth* साथ-साथ, एक साथ

Sin (m◦) *pāp* पाप

Since (m◦) 1. (from) *ke bād se* के बाद से, 2. (because) *kyõ kī* क्योंकि

Sing (v◦) *gānā* गाना*

Singe (v◦) *jhulasnā* झुलसना

Singer (f◦) *gāyikā* गायिका

Singer (m◦) *gāyak* गायक

Singer (m◦) *gāyak* गायक

Single (adj◦) *akelā* अकेला

Singular (adj◦) *ek-vachan* एक वचन

Sinister (adj∘) *kuṭil* कुटिल

Sink (v∘) *ḍūbnā, ḍubonā** डूबना, डुबोना*

Sip (v∘) *chuskī lenā* चुस्की लेना*

Sir (m∘) *mahoday, śhrimān* महोदय, श्रीमान

Siren (m∘) *bhõpū* भोंपू

Sister (f∘) *dīdī* दीदी

Sister-in-law (f∘) *sālī, bhābhī* साली, भाभी

Sit (v∘) *baiṭhanā* बैठना

Site (m∘) *sthān, jagah* स्थान, जगह

Situation (f∘) *sthiti, hālat* स्थिति, हालत

Six (adj∘) *chhah* छह

Sixteen (adj∘) *solah* सोलह

Sixty (adj∘) *sāṭh* साठ

Size (m∘) *ākār* आकार

Skeleton (m∘) *kaṅkāl* कंकाल

Sk etc.h (m∘) *khākā*, (f∘) *rūp-rekhā* खाका, रूपरेखा

Skid (v∘) *fisalnā* फिसलना

Skin (f∘) *chamaḍī, tvachā* चमड़ी, त्वचा

Skip (v∘) *fā̃dnā* फाँदना*

Skirmish (f∘) *muṭhbheḍ* मुठभेड़

Skirt (m∘) *ghāgrā* घागरा

Skull (f∘) *khopaḍī* खोपड़ी

Sky (m∘) *ākāśh* आकाश

Sky (m∘) *ākāśh, āsmān* आकाश, आसमान

Slab (f∘) *paṭrī* पटरी

Slack (f∘) *ḍhīl* ढील

Slam (v∘) *paṭaknā* पटकना*

Slander (f∘) *jhūṭhī nindā* झूठी निंदा

Slant (adj∘) *tirchhā* तिरछा

Slap (f∘) *thappaḍ* थप्पड़

Slap (v∘) *thappaḍ mārnā* थप्पड़ मारना*

Slash (v∘) *kāṭnā* काटना*

Slaughter (f∘) *hatyā* हत्या

Slave (m∘) *dād, gulām* दास, ग़ुलाम

Slay (v∘) *hatyā karnā* हत्या करना*

Sleek (adj∘) *chiknā-chupḍā* चिकना-चुपड़ा

Sleep (f∘) *nind* नींद

Sleep (v∘) sonā सोना

Sleeve (f∘) *bā̃h, āstīn* बाँह, आस्तीन

Slender (adj∘) *patlā* पतला

Slice (f∘) *phā̃k* फाँक

Slide (v∘) *khisaknā, fisalnā* खिसकना, फिसलना

Slight (adj∘) *kiñchit* किंचित

Slightly (av∘) *jarā* जरा

Slimber (f∘) *nīnd* नींद

Slip (v∘) *fisalnā* फिसलना

Slit (f∘) *chīr, darār* चीर, दरार

Slogan (m∘) *nārā* नारा

Slope (f∘) *ḍhalān* ढलान

Sloppy (adj∘) *lāparvāh* लापरवाह

Slot (m∘) *khā̃chā* खाँचा

Slow (adj∘) *mand* मंद

Slowly (av∘) *dhīre-dhīre* धीरे धीरे

Sluggish (adj∘) *sust* सुस्त

Slump (f∘) *mandī* मंदी

Smack (f∘) *thappaḍ*, (m∘) *tamāchā* थप्पड़, तमाचा

Small (adj∘) *chhoṭā* छोटा

Smallpox (m∘) *chechak* चेचक

Smart (adj∘) *hośhiyār* होशियार

Smash (f∘) *ṭakkar* टक्कर

Smash (v॰) *ṭakrānā* टकराना

Smear (v॰) *potnā* पोतना

Smell (f॰) *gandh* गंध

Smell (v॰) *sūṅghanā* सूँघना*

Smelt (v॰) *pighālnā* पिघालना*

Smile (f॰) *musakān* मुसकान

Smile (v॰) *musakarānā* मुसकराना

Smoke (m॰) *dhuā̃* धुआँ

Smoke (v॰) *bīḍī pīnā* बीड़ी पीना*

Smooth (adj॰) *chiknā* चिकना

Smoulder (v॰) *sulagnā* सुलगना

Smudge (m॰) *dhabbā, dāg* धब्बा, दाग

Snack (m॰) *nāśhtā* नाश्ता

Snail (m॰) *ghoṅghā* घोंघा

Snake (m॰) *sāṁp* साँप

Snap (v॰) *taḍaknā* तड़कना

Snare (m॰) *fandā, jāl* फंदा, जाल

Snarl (v॰) *gurrānā* गुर्राना

Snatch (v॰) *chhīnanā* छीनना*

Sneeze (f॰) *chhī̃k* छींक

Sneeze (v॰) *chhī̃knā* छींकना

Sniff (v॰) *sū̃ghanā* सूँघना*

Snip (v॰) *kāṭnā* काटना*

Snivel (v॰) *khījnā* खीजना*

Snoop (v॰) *nigāh rakhanā* निगाह रखना*

Snooty (adj॰) *dambhī* दंभी

Snooze (f॰) *jhapkī* झपकी

Snooze (v॰) *jhapkī lenā* झपकी लेना*

Snore (m॰) *kharraṭā* खर्राटा

Snore (v॰) *kharrāṭe bharnā* खर्राटे भरना*

Snot (m॰) *rẽṭ* रेंट

Snout (f॰) *sū̃ḍ* सूँड

Snow (f॰) *baraf* बरफ

Snow (v॰) 1. (falling) *baraf girnā* बरफ गिरना, 2. (removing) *baraf sāf karnā* बरफ साफ करना*

Snub (v॰) *ṭhukrānā* ठुकराना*

So (av॰) *tathā* तथा; (ादइ्) *itnā* इतना; (conj॰) *isliye* इसलिये

So long (av॰) *tab tak, jahā̃ tak* तब तक, जहाँ तक

So that (av॰) *yathā, isaliye ki, tāki* यथा, इसलिए कि, ताकि)

Soak (v॰) *tarbatar karnā, bhigonā* तरबतर करना, भिगोना*

Soap (f॰) *sābun* साबुन

Soar (v॰) *manḍarānā* मँडराना

Sob (v॰) *sisaknā* सिसकना

Sober (adj॰) *saumya* सौम्य

Sociable (adj॰) *milansār* मिलनसार

Social (adj॰) *sāmājik* सामाजिक

Socialism (m॰) *samājvād* समाजवाद

Society (m॰) *samāj* समाज

Sociology (m॰) *samāj-śhāstra* समाजशास्त्र

Sock (m॰) *mojā* मोजा

Soft (adj॰) *komal, naram, mulāyam* कोमल, नरम, मुलायम

Soggy (adj॰) *daldalī* दलदली

Soil (f॰) *miṭṭī* मिट्टी

Sojourn (v॰ m॰) *ruknā* रुकना

Solder (m॰) *ṭā̃kā* टाँका

Solder (v॰) *ṭā̃kā lagānā* टाँका लगाना*

Soldier (m॰) *jawān* जवान

Soldier (m॰) *sipāhī* (police), *sainik* (in army) सिपाही, सैनिक

Sole (adj॰) *akelā, ekmātra* अकेला, एकमात्र

Sole (m◦) *talavā* तलवा

Solicit (v◦) *māṅgnā* माँगना*

Solid (adj◦) *ṭhos, ghana* ठोस, घन

Solidarity (f◦) *ektā* एकता

Solitary (adj◦) *akelā* अकेला

Solitude (m◦) *akelāpan* अकेलापन

Solo (av◦) *akele* अकेले

Solution (m◦) 1. (liquid) *ghol* घोल, 2. (answer) *hal* हल

Solve (v◦) *hal nikālnā* हल निकालना*

Somber (adj◦) *khinna, udās* खिन्न, उदास

Some (pron◦) *kuchh, koī* कुछ, कोई

Somehow (av◦) *kisī na kisī prakar* किसी न किसी प्रकार

Somehow (av◦) *kisī tarah se* किसी तरह से

Somersault (f◦) *kalābāzī* कलाबाज़ी

Sometimes (av◦) *kabhī kabhī* कभी कभी

Somewhat (av◦) *kuchh-kuchh* कुछ-कुछ

Somewhere (av◦) *kahī̃* कहीं

Somnolent (adj◦) *nidrālu* निद्रालु

Son (m◦) *putra, beṭā* पुत्र, बेटा

Song (m◦) *gānā* गाना

Son-in-law (m◦) *dāmād* दामाद

Soon (av◦) *tatkāl* तत्काल

Soot (m◦) *kājal* काजल

Soothe (v◦) *śhānt karnā* शांत करना*

Sophisticated (adj◦) *kritrim* कृत्रिम

Sorcery (f◦) *tāntrīkī* तांत्रीकी

Sordid (adj◦) *faṭe-hāl* फटेहाल

Sore (adj◦) *dardīlā* दर्दीला

Sorry (adj◦) *dukhī* दुखी

Sort (m◦) *prakār, tarah* प्रकार, तरह

Sort (v◦) *chhā̃ṭnā* छाँटना*

Soul (m◦) *ātmā* आत्मा

Sound (adj◦) *achhā* अच्छा

Sound (f◦) *āwāz, dhvani* आवाज़, ध्वनि

Sour (adj◦) *khaṭṭā* खट्टा

Source (m◦) *udgam sthān* उद्गम स्थान

South (f◦) *dakṣhiṇ* दक्षिण

Souvenir (f◦) *smārikā* स्मारिका

Sow (v◦) *bonā* बोना*

Spacious (adj◦) *lambā-chauḍā* लंबा-चौड़ा

Spactator (m◦) *darśhak* दर्शक

Spade (m◦) *fāvaḍā* फावड़ा

Span (m◦) *failāv, vistār* फैलाव, विस्तार

Spanner (m◦) *jamūr* जमूर

Sparce (adj◦) *chhitrā* छितरा

Spare (adj◦) *khālī* खाली

Spare (v◦) *bachānā* बचाना*

Spark (f◦) *chiṅgārī* चिंगारी

Sparkle (f◦) *jhilmil* झिलमिल

Sparkle (v◦) *jhilmilānā* झिलमिलाना

Sparrow (f◦) *gauraiyā* गौरैया

Spasm (m◦) *daurā* (f◦) *aĩṭhan* दौरा, ऐंठन

Spate (f◦) *bāḍh* बाढ़

Spatter (v◦) *chhiḍaknā* छिड़कना*

Speak (v◦) *bolanā* बोलना

Speaker (m◦) *vaktā* वक्ता

Spear (m◦) *bhālā* भाला

Special (adj◦) *viśheṣh, khās* विशेष, खास

Speciality (f◦) *khāsīyat, viśheṣhtā* खासीयत, विशेषता

Species (f◦) *jāti* जाति

Specific (adj∘) *vis̒hiṣhṭa* विशिष्ट

Specimen (m∘) *namūnā* नमूना

Spectacle (m∘) *tamās̒hā* तमाशा

Spectacles (m∘) *chaṣhmā,* (f∘) *ainak* चष्मा, ऐनक

Spectacular (adj∘) *s̒hāndār* शानदार

Spectrum (m∘) *varṇakram* वर्णक्रम

Speculate (v∘) *aṭkal lagānā* अटकल लगाना*

Speculation (f∘) *aṭkal* अटकल

Speech (m∘) *bhāṣhaṇ* भाषण

Speed (f∘) *gati* गति

Speedily (av∘) *turant* तुरंत

Spellbound (adj∘) *mantramugdha* मंत्रमुग्ध

Spice (m∘) *masālā* मसाला

Spider (f∘) *makaḍī* मकड़ी

Spike (m∘) *kā̃ṭā, kīl* काँटा, कील

Spill (v∘) *chhalaknā* छलकना

Spin (v∘) *ghūmnā, ghumānā** घूमना, घुमाना*

Spinach (f∘) *pālak* पालक

Spindle (f∘) *dhurī* धुरी

Spine (f∘) *rīḍh* रीढ़

Spiral (adj∘) *golākār, kuṇḍlākār* गोलाकार, कुंडलाकार

Spire (m∘) *minār* मिनार

Spirit (m∘) 1. (soul) *ātmā* आत्मा, 2. (liquor) *s̒harāb* शराब

Spiritual (adj∘) *adhyātmik, dhārmik* अध्यात्मिक, धार्मिक

Spleen (f∘) *tillī* तिल्ली

Splendid (adj∘) *s̒hāndār* शानदार

Splendorous (adj∘) *s̒hāndār* शानदार

Splendour (f∘) *s̒hān* शान

Splinter (m∘) *kirach* किरच

Split (v∘) *chīrnā* चीरना*

Spoil (v∘) *bigaḍnā* बिगाड़ना

Spoke (m∘) *ārā* आरा

Spokesman (m∘) *pravaktā* प्रवक्ता

Spontaneous (adj∘) *svābhāvik* स्वाभाविक

Spontaneously (av∘) *svayam, āp hī* स्वयं, आप ही

Spool (f∘) *firkī, charkhī* फिरकी, चरख़ी

Spoon (m∘) *chammach, camchā* चम्मच, चमचा

Sport (f∘) *khel-kūd* खेल-कूद

Spot (m∘) 1. (mark) *dhabbā, dāg* धब्बा, दाग; 2. (place) *sthān* स्थान

Spring (m∘) 1. (coil) *kamānī* कमानी, 2. (flow) *jharnā* झरना, 3. (season) *vasant* वसंत

Spring (v∘) *uchhalnā* उछलना

Sprinkle (v∘) *chhiḍaknā* छिडकना*

Sprout (m∘) *aṅkur* अंकुर

Spurious (adj∘) *naklī, jālī* नकली, जाली

Spurn (v∘) *ṭhukrānā* ठुकराना*

Spurt (m∘) *fuhārā* फुहारा

Spy (m∘) *jāsūs* जासूस

Squabble (f∘) *tū-tū maĩ-maĩ* तू-तू मैं-मैं

Squad (f∘) *ṭukḍī* टुकड़ी

Squalor (f∘) *gandagī* गंदगी

Square (adj∘) *vargākār, chauras* वर्गाकार, चौरस

Square (m∘) *chaturbhuj* चतुर्भुज

Squash (v∘) *kuchalnā* कुचलना*

Squat (adj∘) *thignā* ठिगना

Squatted (adj∘) *ukḍū̃* उकडूँ

Squawk (m∘) *kal-rav* कलरव

Squeak (v∘) *charamarānā* चरमराना

Squeal (f∘) *charamarāhaṭ* चरमराहट

Squeeze (m◦) *nichoḍ, dabāv* निचोड़, दबाव

Squeeze (v◦) *nichoḍnā* निचोड़ना*

Squirm (v◦) *chhaṭpaṭānā* छटपटाना

Squirrel (f◦) *gilharī* गिलहरी

Squirt (m◦) *fuhārā* फुहारा

Squirt (v◦) *fuhārā chhoḍnā* फुहारा छोड़ना*

Sstick (v◦) *chipaknā, chipakānā** चिपकना, चिपकाना*

Ssuperintendent (m◦) *sañchālak* संचालक

Stab (v◦) *bhoṅknā* भोंकना

Stable (adj◦) *sthir* स्थिर

Stable (m◦) *astabal* अस्तबल

Stack (m◦) *ḍher* ढेर

Stag (m◦) *hiran* हिरन

Stage, condition (f◦) *avasthā* अवस्था

Stage, podium (m◦) *mañch* मंच

Stagger (v◦) *laḍkhaḍānā* लड़खड़ाना

Stagnet (v◦) *ṭharnā* ठहरना

Staid (adj◦) *nīras* नीरस

Stain (m◦) *dhabbā, dāg* धब्बा, दाग

Stair (f◦) *sīḍhī, jīnā* सीढ़ी, जीना

Stake, peg (m◦) *khūṅṭā* खूँटा

Stale (adj◦) *bāsā* बासा

Stallion (m◦) *ghoḍā* घोड़ा

Stalwart (adj◦) *pakkā* पक्का

Stamina (m◦) *dam* दम

Stammer (v◦) *halkānā, tutlānā* हलकाना, तुतलाना

Stamp (f◦) *ṭikaṭ* टिकट; (m◦) *chhāpā* छापा

Stamp (v◦) *chhāpā lagānā* छापा लगाना*

Stampede (f◦) *bhagdaḍ* भगदड़

Stance (m◦) *drishṭikoṇ* दृष्टिकोण

Stand (v◦) *khaḍā honā* खड़ा होना

Standard (adj◦) *sāmānya* सामान्य

Star (m◦) *tārā* तारा

Starch (m◦) *kalaf* कलफ़

Stare (v◦) *ghūrnā* घूरना

Stark (adj◦) *kaḍā* कड़ा

Start (m◦) *ārambha* आरंभ

Start (v◦) *ārambha karnā* आरंभ करना*

Starvation (f◦) *bhūkhmarī* भूखमरी

Starve (v◦) *bhūkhoṅ marnā* भूखों मरना

State 1. (m◦ province) *prānt* प्रांत; 2. (condition) *avasthā* अवस्था

Statement (m◦) *kathan* कथन

Static (adj◦) *thamā huā* थमा हुआ

Station (m◦) *aḍḍā,* (f◦) *chaukī* अड्डा, चौकी

Stationary (adj◦) *sthir* स्थिर

Statue (f◦) *mūrtī* मूर्ति

Stature (m◦) *kad* कद

Status (m◦) *darjā, pad* दर्जा, पद

Staunch (adj◦) *pakkā* पक्का

Stay (v◦) *rahnā, ṭhaharnā* रहना, ठहरना

Steadfast (adj◦) *pakkā, aṭal* पक्का, अटल

Steady (adj◦) *sthir* स्थिर

Steak (m◦) *ṭikkā* टिक्का

Steal (v◦) *churānā* चुराना*

Stealth (adj◦) *gupt* गुप्त

Steam (f◦) *bhāp* भाप

Steel (m◦) *faulād, ispāt* फ़ौलाद, इस्पात

Steep (adj◦) *chaḍhāī vālā* चढाई वाला

Steeple (m◦) *minār* मिनार

Stem (m∘) *ḍanṭhal, tanā* डंठल, तना

Stench (f∘) *badbū* बदबू

Step (m∘) *kadam* कदम

Step (v∘) *kadam rakhnā* कदम रखना*

Sterile (adj∘) *bajnar* बंजर

Stern (adj∘) *gambhīr* गंभीर

Stick (f∘) *chhaḍī* छड़ी

Sticky (adj∘) *chipchipā* चिपचिपा

Stiff (adj∘) *sakht* सख़्त

Stigma (m∘) *kalaṅk, lāñchhan* कलंक, लांछन

Still (adj∘) *sthir* स्थिर

Still (av∘) *ab tak, to bhī* अब तक, तो भी

Stimulant (adj∘) *prerak, uttejak* प्रेरक, उत्तेजक

Stimulate (v∘) *uksānā* उकसाना*

Stimulus (m∘) *uttejan* (f∘) *prerṇā* उत्तेजन, प्रेरणा

Sting (m∘) *ḍaṅk* डंक

Sting (v∘) *ḍaṅk mārnā* डंक मारना*

Stingy (adj∘) *kañjūs* कंजूस

Stink (f∘) *badbū* बदबू

Stir (v∘) *viloḍnā* विलोड़ना*

Stitch (m∘) *ṭā̃kā* टाँका

Stitch (v∘) *silnā, sīnā* सिलना, सीना*

Stock (m∘) *māl* माल

Stock (v∘) *māl rakhnā* माल रखना*

Stolid (adj∘) *bhāva-śhūnya* भावशून्य

Stomach (m∘) *peṭ* पेट

Stomp (v∘) *raundnā* रौंदना*

Stone (m∘) *patthar* पत्थर

Stony (adj∘) *pathrīlā* पथरीला

Stool (f∘) *chārpaī, tipāī* चारपाई, तिपाई

Stoop (v∘) *jhuknā* झुकना

Stop (f∘) *rukāvaṭ* रुकावट

Stop (v∘) *ruknā* रुकना

Stopper (m∘) *kāg, ḍāṭ* काग, डाट

Storage (m∘) *godām* गोदाम

Store (f∘) *dukān, bhanḍār* दुकान, भंडार

Store (v∘) *bharnā, jamā karnā* भरना, जमा करना*

Storey (m∘) *tallā,* (f∘) *manzil* तल्ला, मंज़िल

Stork (m∘) *sāras* सारस

Storm (m∘) *tūfān* तूफ़ान

Stormy (adj∘) *tūfānī* तूफ़ानी

Story (f∘) *kathā, kahānī* कथा, कहानी

Stout (adj∘) *pakkā, mazbūt* पक्का, मज़बूत

Stove (m∘) *chūlhā* चूल्हा

Straight (adj∘) *saral* सरल

Straightforward (adj∘) *sīdhā* सीधा

Strain (m∘) *tanāv, dabāv* तनाव, दबाव

Stress (m∘) *tanāv, dabāv* तनाव, दबाव

Stress (v∘) *jor lagānā* जोर लगाना*

Str etc.h (m∘) *tanāv, khĩchāv* तनाव, खींचाव

Str etc.h (v∘) *tānanā. khĩchanā* तानना, खींचना*

Strew (m∘) *bikhernā, chhitarnā* बिखेरना, छितरना

Strict (m∘) *kaḍā, sakht* कड़ा, सख़्त

Stride (v∘) *lāṅghnā* लाँघना*

Strife (m∘) *saṅgharṣh* संघर्ष

Strike (m∘) *haḍtāl* हड़ताल

Strike (v∘) *mārnā* मारना*

String (f∘) *ḍorī, mālā* डोरी, माला

String (v∘) *pironā* पिरोना*

Stringent (m∘) *kaḍā, sakht* कड़ा, सख़्त

Strip (m∘) *naṅgā karnā* नंगा करना

Strip (m∘) *paṭṭī* पट्टी

Stripe (f∘) *dhār, paṭṭī* धार, पट्टी

Strive (v∘) *prayās karnā* प्रयास करना*

Stroke (m∘) *āghāt* आघात

Stroke (v∘) *thapthapānā* थपथपाना*

Stroll (v∘) *ṭahalnā* टहलना

Strong (adj∘) *balavān* बलवान्

Structure (m∘) 1. (makeup) *banāvaṭ* बनावट; 2. (building) *bhavan* भवन

Struggle (m∘) *saṅgharṣh* संघर्ष

Struggle (v∘) *khaṭnā* खटना

Stubborn (m∘) *aḍiyal, ziddī* अड़ियल, ज़िद्दी

Stud (f∘) *kīl* कील

Student (m∘) *chhātra* छात्र

Studious (adj∘) *mehnatī* मेहनती

Study (f∘) *paḍhāī* पढ़ाई

Study (v∘) *paḍhanā* पढ़ना*

Stuff (m∘) *sāmān,* (f∘) *sāmagrī* सामान, सामग्री

Stumble (v∘) *ṭhokar khānā* ठोकर खाना

Stun (v∘) *hakkā-bakkā honā* हक्का बक्का होना

Stunt (m∘) *kartab* करतब

Stupendous (adj∘) *mahān* महान

Stupis (adj∘) *mūrkh* मूर्ख

Sturdy (adj∘) *mazbūt, ṭhos* मज़बूत, ठोस

Stutter (v∘) *haklānā, tutlānā* हकलाना, तुतलाना

Style (f∘) *śhailī, banāvaṭ* शैली, बनावट

Subdue (m∘) *kābū karnā* काबू करना

Subject (m∘) *viṣhay* विषय

Sublime (adj∘) *udātta* उदात्त

Submarine (f∘) *panḍubbī* पनडुब्बी

Submission (m∘) *samarpaṇ* समर्पण

Subsequent (adj∘) *bād kā* बाद का

Subside (v∘) *ghaṭnā* घटना

Substance (m∘) *padārtha* पदार्थ

Subtle (m∘) *sūkṣhma, mahīn* सूक्ष्म, महीन

Suburb (m∘) *upnagar* उपनगर

Subway (m∘) *suraṅg-path* सुरंग-पथ

Succed (v∘) *uttara!dhikārī honā* उत्तराधिकारी होना

Succeptible (adj∘) *grahaṇśhīl* ग्रहणशील

Success (m∘) *yaśha* यश

Succession (m∘) *uttarādhikār* उत्तराधिकार

Successive (adj∘) *kramik* क्रमिक

Successor (m∘) *uttarādhikārī* उत्तराधिकारी

Such (adj∘) *aisā* ऐसा

Suck (v∘) *chūsnā* चूसना*

Suction (m∘) *chūṣhaṇ* चूषण

Sudden (adj∘) *achānak* अचानक

Suddenly (av∘) *ekdam* एकदम

Sue (v∘) *mukadmā karnā* मुकदमा करना*

Suffer (v∘) *bhugatnā* भुगतना

Suffering (f∘) *pīḍā* पीड़ा

Suffice (v∘) *bas honā* बस होना

Sufficient (adj∘) *kāfī* काफ़ी

Sufficiently (av∘) *paryāpta* पर्याप्त

Suffix (m∘) *pratyay* प्रत्यय

Suffocate (v∘) *dam ghuṭnā* दम घुटना

Sugar (f∘) *chīnī, śhakkar* चीनी, शक्कर

Sugarcane (m∘) *īkh* ईख, *gannā* गन्ना

Suggest (v∘) *sujhāv denā* सुझाव देना*

Suggestion (m∘) *sujhāv* सुझाव

Suicide (f∘) *ātmahtyā* आत्महत्या

Suit (m∘) *mukadmā* मुकदमा

Suit (v∘) *ṭhīk honā* ठीक होना

Suitable (adj∘) *ṭhīk, uchit* ठीक, उचित

Sulk (v∘) *rūṭhnā* रूठना

Sullen (adj∘) *chiḍchiḍā* चिड़चिड़ा

Sulphur (m∘) *gandhak* गंधक

Sum (m∘) *yog* योग

Sum (v∘) *milānā* मिलाना*

Summary (m∘) *sārāṁśh* सारांश

Summer (m∘) *grīṣhma* ग्रीष्म

Summit (f∘) *choṭī* चोटी

Summon (v∘) *bulānā* बुलाना*

Summons (m∘) *bulāvā* बुलावा

Sun (m∘) *sūraj, sūrya* सूरज, सूर्य

Sunday (m∘) *ravivār, itwār* रविवार, इतवार

Sundry (adj∘) *fuṭkar, vividh* फुटकर, विविध

Sunflower (f∘) *sūrajmukhī* सूरजमुखी

Super- (pref∘) *atyadhik, asāmānya, asādhāraṇ* अत्यधिक, असामान्य, असाधारण

Superb (adj∘) *baḍhiyā, śhreṣhṭha* बढ़िया, श्रेष्ठ

Supercilious (adj∘) *magrūr, dambhī* मग़रूर, दंभी

Superficial (adj∘) *ūparī, bāharī, bāhya, chhichhlā* ऊपरी, बाहरी, बाह्य, छिछला

Superfluous (adj∘) *fazūl, fāltū* फ़ज़ूल, फ़ालतू

Superior (adj∘) *behtar, śhreṣhṭha, uccha* बेहतर, श्रेष्ठ, उच्च

Superiority (f∘) *śhreṣhṭhatā, ucchatā* श्रेष्ठता, उच्चता

Superlative (m∘) *sarvaśhreṣhṭha, ucchatama* सर्वश्रेष्ठ, उच्चतम

Supernatural (adj∘) *alaukik* अलौकिक

Supersede (m∘) *kā sthān lenā* का स्थान लेना

Superstition (m∘) *andhaviśhvās* अंधविश्वास

Supervise (v∘) *nigrānī karnā* निगरानी करना*

Supervision (f∘) *nigrānī* निगरानी

Supervisor (m∘) *nirīkṣhak* निरीक्षक

Supple (adj∘) *lachīlā* लचीला

Supplement (m∘) *pūrak,* (f∘) *pūrti* पूरक, पूर्ति

Supplementary (adj∘) *pūrak, pariśhiṣhṭ* पूरक, परिशिष्ट

Suppliment (v∘) *pūrti karnā* पूर्ति करना*

Supply (m∘) *pūrti, āpūrti* पूर्ति, आपूर्ति

Supply (v∘) *pūrti karnā* पूर्ति करना*

Support (f∘) *sahāyatā, madad* सहायता, मदद

Supporting Actor (m∘) *upanāyak* उपनायक

Supportive (adj∘) *sahayak* सहायक

Suppose (v∘) *mānanā* मानना*

Supposing (av∘) *agar, yadi* अगर, यदि

Supreme (m∘) *sarvaśhreṣhṭha, ucchatam* सर्वश्रेष्ठ, उच्चतम

Supress (v∘) *dabānā* दबाना*

Supression (m∘) *dabāv* दबाव

Sure (adj∘) *nischit, pakkā* निश्चित, पक्का

Surely (av∘) *niśhchit, avaśhya* निश्चित, अवश्य

Surface (f∘) *satah, priṣhṭha* सतह, पृष्ठ

Surge (m∘) *baḍhāvā,* (f∘) *baḍhatī* बढ़ावा, बढ़ती

Surge (v∘) *laharnā, baḍhnā* लहरना, बढ़ना

Surgeon (m∘) *śhalya chikitsak* शल्य चिकित्सक

Surgery (f∘) *śhalya chikitsā* शल्य चिकित्सा

Surmise (m∘) *andāz, anumān* अंदाज़, अनुमान

Surmount (v∘) *pār karnā* पार करना*

Surname (m∘) *kulanām* कुलनाम

Surpass (v∘) *se āge baḍhnā* से आगे बढ़ना

Surplus (f∘) *bachat* बचत

Surprise (m∘) *āscharya, achambhā* आश्चर्य, अचंभा

Surrender (m∘) *ātmasamarpaṇ,* (f∘) *śharaṇ* आत्मसमर्पण, शरण

Surreptitious (adj∘) *pracchhanna* प्रच्छन्न

Surround (v∘) *ghernā* घेरना*

Surveillance (f∘) *nigrānī* निगरानी

Survey (f∘) *jā̃ch, nirīkṣhaṇ, paimāiśh* जाँच, निरीक्षण, पैमाइश

Survey (v∘) *nihārnā, jā̃chnā* निहारना, जाँचना*

Survival (m∘) *bachnā* बचना

Survive (v∘) *bachnā* बचना

Survivor (m∘) *bachā huā* बचा हुआ

Suspect (v∘) *sandeha karnā* संदेह करना*

Suspend (v∘) *laṭknā, jaṭkānā,* ṭāṅgnā* लटकना, लटकाना*, टाँगना*

Suspense (f∘) *duvidhā* (m∘) *saṁśhay* दुविधा, संशय

Suspension (m∘) *laṭaknā* लटकना

Suspicion (m∘) *sandeha, śhak* संदेह, शक

Suspicious (adj∘) *śhaṅkāyukta* शंकायुक्त

Sustain (v∘) *sahanā* सहना

Sustenance (m∘) *sahārā* सहारा

Susurration (m∘) *fusfusānā* फुसफुसाना

Suzerain (m∘) *adhipati, rājā* अधिपति, राजा

Svelte (adj∘) *komal* कोमल

Swab (f∘) *kū̃chī* कूँची

Swainish (adj∘) *dehātī* देहाती

Swallow (v∘) *nigalnā* निगलना*

Swallower (adj∘) *bhukkhaḍ* भुक्खड़

Swamp (f∘) *daldal* दलदल

Swan (m∘) *haṁsa* हंस

Swap (f∘) *adal-badal* अदल-बदल

Swap (v∘) *adal-badal karnā* अदल-बदल करना*

Swash (m∘) *kolāhal, śhor* कोलाहल, शोर

Sway (m∘) *jhuknā, jhukānā** झुकना, झुकाना*

Swear (f∘) 1. (vow) *śhapath, kasam* शपथ, कसम 2. (rebuke) *gālī* गाली

Swear (v∘) 1. (vow) *śhapath khānā* शपथ खाना 2. (rebuke) *gālī baknā* गाली बकना

Sweat (m∘) *pasīnā* पसीना

Sweep (v∘) *jhāḍnā* झाड़ना*

Sweeper, broom (m∘) *jhāḍū* झाड़ू

Sweet (adj∘) *mīṭhā* मीठा

Sweets (f∘) *miṭhāī* मिठाई

Swell (m∘) *fūlnā, sūjnā* फूलना, सूजना

Swelling (f∘) *sūjan* सूजन

Swerve (v∘) *bhaṭaknā* भटकना

Swift (adj∘) *tez* तेज़

Swim (v∘) *tairnā* तैरना

Swindle (v∘) *ṭhagnā* ठगना*

Swindler (adj∘) *ṭhag* ठग

Swine (m∘) *sūar* सूअर

Swing (m∘) *jhūlā* झूला

Swing (v∘) *jhūlnā* झूलना

Swipe (m∘) *āghāt* आघात

Swirl (m∘) *chakkar, bhā̃var* चक्कर, भँवर

Swirl (v∘) *ghūmnā, ghumānā** घूमना, घुमाना*

Swish (f∘) *sarsarāhaṭ* सरसराहट

Switch (v∘) *badalnā* बदलना*

Swivel (v∘) *chakrākār ghūmnā* चक्राकार घूमना

Swoon (f∘) *mūrchhā* मूर्छा

Swoon (v∘) *mūrchhit honā* मूर्छित होना

Swoop (m∘) *jhapaṭṭā* झपट्टा

Sword (f∘) *talvār* तलवार

Sycophant (adj∘) *chāplūs, chāṭū* चापलूस, चाटू

Syllabus (m∘) *pāṭhyakram* पाठ्यक्रम

Symbol (m∘) *chihna, pratīk* चिह्न, प्रतीक

Symmetrical (adj∘) *sama-mit* सममित

Symmetry (f∘) *samānatā* समानता

Sympathetic (adj∘) *hamdard* हमदर्द

Sympathy (f∘) *sahānubhūti, hamdardī* सहानुभूति, हमदर्दी

Symphony (m∘) *svarsaṅgīt* स्वरसंगीत

Symposium (m∘) *sammelan* सम्मेलन

Symptom (m∘) *lakṣhaṇ* लक्षण

Syndicate (m∘) *jvyāpār saṅgh* व्यापार संघ

Synonym (m∘) *paryāyvāchī śhabd* पर्यायवाची शब्द

Synopsis (m∘) *sārāṁśh* सारांश

Syntax (f∘) *vākya rachanā* वाक्य रचना

Synthesis (m∘) *saṁyog* संयोग

Synthetic (adj∘) *kritrim* कृत्रिम

Syring (f∘) *pichkārī* पिचकारी

Syrup (f∘) *chāṣhnī* चाशनी

System (m∘) *tantra,* (f∘) *vyavasthā* तंत्र, व्यवस्था

Systematic (adj∘) *vyavasthit* व्यवस्थित

T

Table, chart (f∘) *tālikā, sāraṇī* तालिका, सारणी

Table, desk (m∘) *mez* मेज़

Tablet (f∘) *golī* गोली

Tack (f∘) *birañjī* बिरंजी

Tact (m∘) *kauśhalya* कौशल्य

Tactic(f∘) *chāl* चाल

Tadpole (f∘) *beṅgchī* बेंगची

Tag (f∘) *parachī* परची

Tail (f∘) *dum, pūँchh* दुम, पूँछ

Tailor (m∘) *arjī* दर्जी

Take (v∘) *lenā* लेना*

Tale (f∘) *kathā, kahānī* कथा, कहानी

Talent (f∘) *pratibhā* (m∘) *guṇ* प्रतिभा, गुण

Talisman (m∘) *tāviz* ताविज़

Talk (f∘ v∘) *bolanā* बोलना

Tall (adj∘) *lambā* लंबा

Tallow (f∘) *charbī* चरबी

Tally (m∘) *mel, hisāb* मेल, हिसाब

Talon (m∘) *pañjā, chaṅgul* पंजा, चंगुल

Tamarind (f∘) *imlī* इमली

Tamper (v∘) *chheḍnā* छेड़ना*

Tangible (adj∘) *sparśhanīya* स्पर्शनीय

Tangle (m∘) *gutthā, uljhan* गुत्था, उलझन

Tank, container (f∘) *ṭaṅkī* टंकी

Tank, reservoir (m∘) *tālāb* तालाब

Tanslation (m∘) *bhāṣhāntar, anuvād* भाषांतर, अनुवाद

Tantalize (v∘) *tarasnā, lalchānā* तरसना, ललचाना

Tantamount (adj∘) *barābar* बराबर

Tap, faucet (m∘) *nal, ṭoँṭī* नल, टोंटी

Tap, knock (v∘) *khaṭkhaṭānā* खटखटाना*

Tap, pat (f∘) *thapkī* थपकी

Tapia (m∘) *galīchā* गलीचा

Tar (m∘) *tārkol* तारकोल

Tarantula (f∘) *makḍī* मकड़ी

Tardiness (f∘) *susti* सुस्ति

Tardy (adj∘) *sust, dīrghasūtrī* सुस्त, दीर्घसूत्री

Target (m∘) *dhyeya, lakṣhya, nis̕hānā* ध्येय, लक्ष्य, निशाना

Tarnish (v∘) *kalaṅk lagānā* कलंक लगाना*

Tarpaulin (m∘) *tirpāl* तिरपाल

Tart (adj∘) *khaṭās* खटास

Task (m∘) *kārya* कार्य

Taste (m∘) *svād, zāykā* स्वाद, ज़ायका

Taste (v∘) *chakhanā* चखना*

Tattoo (v∘) *godnā* गोदना*

Taught (adj∘) *kasī, tanī* कसी, तनी

Taunt (m∘) *tānā* ताना

Taunt (v∘) *tānā mārnā* ताना मारना*

Taurus (f∘) *vriṣhabh rās̕hi* वृषभ राशि

Tavern (m∘) *s̕harāb khānā* शराबखाना

Tax (m∘) *kar* कर

Tea (f∘) *chāy* चाय

Teacher (m∘) *gurujī, s̕hikṣhak* (f∘)*s̕hikṣhikā* गुरुजी, शिक्षक, शिक्षिका

Teak, wood (m∘) *sāgaun* सागौन

Team (m∘) *dal* दल

Tear (f∘) *ā̃sū* आँसू

Tear (v∘) *fāḍnā* फ़ाड़ना*

Tease (v∘) *chiḍhānā* चिढ़ाना*

Technical (adj∘) *tāntrīk, taknaīkī* तांत्रिक, तकनीकी

Technique (m∘) *tantra, taknīk* तंत्र, तकनीक

Teciturn (adj∘) *maunī* मौनी

Tedious (adj∘) *thakāū* थकाऊ

Teenage (f∘) *kis̕horāvasthā* किशोरावस्था

Teenager (m∘) *kis̕hor* किशोर

Teeth (m∘) *dānt* दांत

Telegram (f∘) *tār* तार

Telepathy (m∘) *dūrbodh* दूरबोध

Telephone (m∘) *dūrbhāṣh* दूरभाष

Telescopr (f∘) *dūrbīn* दूरबीन

Television (m∘) *dūrdars̕han* दूरदर्शन

Tell (v∘) *batānā, batalānā* बताना, बतलाना*

Temper (f∘) *mizāj, tabīyat* मिज़ाज, तबीयत

Temperament (m∘) (f∘) *mizāj, tabīyat* मिज़ाज, तबीयत

Temperamental (adj∘) *saṅkī* सनकी

Temperance (m∘) *saṁyam* संयम

Temperature (m∘) *tāpmān* तापमान

Tempest (m∘) *tūfān* तूफ़ान

Temple (m∘) *mandir* मंदिर

Tempo (f∘) *gati* गति

Temporal (adj∘) *saṅsārik* सांसारिक

Temporary (adj∘) *asthāyī* अस्थायी

Tempt (v∘) *bahkānā* बहकाना*

Temptation (m∘) *bahkāvā,* (f∘) *pralobhanā* प्रलोभना

Ten (adj∘) *das* दस

Tenacious (adj∘) *pakkā, haṭhī* पक्का, हठी

Tenant (m∘) *kirāedār* किराएदार

Tender, bid (m∘) *ṭhekā* ठेका

Tender, delicate (adj∘) *nazuk* नाज़ुक

Tendon (m∘) *kaṇḍarā* कंडरा

Tendril (f∘) *pratān* प्रतान

Tenet (m∘) *mat* मत

Tenous (adj∘) *nāzuk* नाज़ुक

Tense (adj∘) *bechain* बेचैन

Tension (m∘) *tanāv, dabāv* तनाव, दबाव

Tent (m∘) *tambū* तंबू

Tentatively (adj∘) *dekhane ke lite* देखने के लिये

Tenure (f∘) *avadhi* अवधि

Term 1. period (f∘) *avadhi* अवधि; 2. expression (f∘) *abhivyakti* अभिव्यक्ति; 3. (relationship) *sambandha* संबंध

Term, name (v∘) *kahnā* कहना*

Terminal (adj∘) *ākharī, lāilāj* आखरी, लाइलाज

Terminate (v∘) *samāpta karnā* समाप्त करना*

Termination (f∘) *samāpti* समाप्ति

Terminology (f∘) *paribhāṣhā* परिभाषा

Terminus (m∘) *aḍḍā* अड्डा

Termite (f∘) *dīmak* दीमक

Terresterial (adj∘) *bhū-jīvī* भूजीवी

Terrible (adj∘) *bhayānak* भयानक

Terrific (adj∘) *mahān* महान

Terrify (v∘) *darnā, rānā** डरना, डराना*

Territory (m∘) *kṣhetra* क्षेत्र

Terror (m∘) *bhay, dar* भय, डर

Terrorism (m∘) *ātaṅkvād* आतंकवाद

Terrorist (m∘) *ātaṅkvādī* आतंकवादी

Tertiary (adj∘) *tīsrā* तीसरा

Test (f∘) *parīkṣhā* परीक्षा

Test (v∘) *jā̃chanā* जाँचना*

Testament, legal (m∘) *vasīyatnāmā* वसीयतनामा

Testify (v∘) *gavāhī denā, bayān denā* गवाही देना, बयान देना*

Testimonial (m∘) *pramāṇpatra* प्रमाणपत्र

Testimony (m∘) *bayān,* (f∘) *gavāhī* बयान, गवाही

Text (m∘) *lekhā* लेखा

Textbook (f∘) *pāṭhya-pustak* पाठ्यपुस्तक

Textile (m∘) *vastra* वस्त्र

Texture (m∘) *banāvaṭ* बनावट

Than (av∘) *se* से

Thank (v∘) *dhanyavād denā* धन्यवाद देना*

Thankful (adj∘) *kritagya* कृतज्ञ

Thanks (m∘) *dhanyavād, śhukriyā* धन्यवाद, शुक्रिया

That (pron∘) *vah* वह

Thaw (v∘) *pighalnā* पिघलना

Theatre (f∘) *raṅgśhālā* रंगशाला

Theft (f∘) *chorī* चोरी

Their (pron∘) u*nakā* उनका

Them (pron∘) *uṅko* उनको

Theme (m∘) *viṣhay* विषय

Then (av∘) *tab, fir* तब, फिर

Thence (av∘) *us kāraṇa se* उस कारण से, *vahā̃ se* वहाँ से

Thenceforward (av∘) *us ke bād* उसके बाद

Theology (m∘) *āstikvād* आस्तिकवाद

Theorem (m∘) *siddhānt* सिद्धांत

Theoritical (adj∘) *saiddhāntik* सैद्धांतिक

Theory (m∘) *siddhānt* सिद्धांत

Therby (av∘) *us se, us tarah se* उससे, उस तरह से

There (av∘) *vahā̃, udhar* वहाँ, उधर

Thereafter (av∘) *tab se, usake bād* तब से, उसके बाद

Therefore (av∘) *ataḥ, isaliye* अत:, इसलिए

Thereupon (av∘) *tatkāl, to fir* तत्काल, ते फिर

Thermal (adj∘) *garmaī kā* गरमी का

Thermometer (m∘) *tāpmāpak* तापमापक

Thesaurus (m∘) *paryāy-kośh* पर्यायकोश

These (pron∘) *ye* ये

Thesis (m∘) *prabandh* प्रबंध

Thick (adj∘) 1. (slice) *moṭā,* 2. (dense) *ghanā,* 3. (liquid) *gaḍhā* मोटा, घना, गाढ़ा

Thicket (f∘) *jhāḍī* झाड़ी

Thickness (f∘) *moṭāī, ghanatva, gāḍhāpan* 1. मोटाई, 2. घनत्व, 3. गाढ़ापन

Thief (m∘) *chor* चोर

Thigh (f∘) *jāṅgh, jaṅghā* जाँघ, जंघा

Thin (adj∘) *patalā, bārīk* पतला, बारीक

Thing (f∘) *bāt, chīj* बात, चीज

Think (v∘) *sochanā* सोचना*

Thinker (adj∘) *manīṣhī* मनीषी

Thinking (m∘) *vichār* विचार

Third (adj∘) *tīsrā* तीसरा

Third-class (adj∘) *ghatiya* घटिया

Thirteen (adj∘) *terah* तेरह

Thirty (adj∘) *tīs* तीस

This (pron∘) *yah* यह

Thistle (m∘) *bhaṭ-kaṭaiyā* भटकटैया

Thorax (m∘) *chhātī, sīnā* छाती, सीना

Thorn (m∘) *kā̃ṭā* काँटा

Thorney (adj∘) *kā̃ṭedār* काँटेदार

Thorough (adj∘) *pakkā, parioūrṇa* पक्का, परिपूर्ण

Those (pron∘) *ve* वे, वह

Though (av∘) *yadyapi, hālāki, bhale hī* यद्यपि, हालाँकि, भले ही

Thought (m∘) *vichār* विचार

Thousand (m∘) *hazār, sahasra* हज़ार, सहस्र

Thrash (v∘) *pīṭnā* पीटना*

Thrashing (f∘) *piṭāī* पिटाई

Thread (m∘) *dhāgā* धागा

Thread (m∘) *dhāgā, tāgā, sūt, tantu* धागा, तागा, सूत, तंतु

Threat (m∘) 1. (danger) *musībat, saṅkaṭ, khatrā* मुसीबत, संकट, खतरा 2. (challenge) *dhamkī, dhaũs* धमकी, धौंस

Threaten (v∘) *dhamkānā* धमकाना*

Three (adj∘) *tīn* तीन

Thresh (v∘) *kūṭnā, pīṭnā* कूटना, पीटना*

Threshold (m∘) *dahlīz* दहलीज़

Thrice (av∘) *tīn bār* तीन बार

Thrill (m∘) *romāñch* रोमांच

Thrilling (adj∘) *romāñchkārī* रोमांचकारी

Throat (m∘) *galā* गला

Throat (m∘) *galā, kaṇṭh* गला, कंठ

Throb (f∘) *dhaḍkan,* (m∘) *spandan* धड़कन, स्पंदन

Throb (v∘) *dhaḍaknā* धड़कना

Throne (m∘) *siṁhāsan* सिंहासन

Throng (f∘) *bhīḍ* भीड़

Throttle (v∘) *galā ghõṭnā* गला घोंटना*

Through (prep∘) *ār-pār, bīch sae* आरपार, बीच से

Throughfare (m∘) *ām rastā* आम रस्ता

Throught (av∘) *sarvatra* सर्वत्र

Throw (v∘) *fẽknā* फेंकना*

Throw up (v∘) *ulṭī karnā* उल्टी करना*

Thrust (m∘) *prahār* प्रहार

Thug (m∘) *ṭhag* ठग

Thumb (m∘) *aṅgūṭhā* अंगुठा

Thump (m∘) *āghāt, dhamākā* आघात, धमाका

Thump (v∘) *ṭhoknā* ठोकना*

Thunder (f∘) *garjan, garjanā* गरजन, गर्जना

Thunder (v∘) *garajnā* गरजना

Thunderstruck (adj∘) *hakkā-bakkā* हक्काबक्का

Thursday (m∘) *guruvār, brihaspativār* गुरुवार, बृहस्पतिवार

Thus (av∘) *is prakār se* इस प्रकार से

Tide (f∘) *bāḍh* बाढ़

Tidy (adj∘) *ṭhik-ṭhāk* ठीक-ठाक

Tie (m∘) *fītā* फीता

Tie (v∘) *bāndhanā* बाँधना*

Tiger (m∘) *bāgh, śher* बाघ, शेर

Tight (adj∘) *kasā, taṅg* कसा, तंग

Tighten (v∘) *kasnā, jakaḍnā* कसना, जकड़ना*

Tigings (f∘) *khabar* खबर

Tigress (f∘) *bāghin, śhernī* बाघिन, शेरनी

Till, farming (v∘) *jotnā* जोतना*

Tilt (m∘) *jhukāv* झुकाव

Tilt (v∘) *jhuknā, jhukānā** झुकना, झुकाना*

Timber (f∘) *imārtī lakḍī* इमारती लकड़ी

Time (m∘) *samay, kāl* समय, काल

Timely (adj∘) *samayovhit* समयोचित

Timid (adj∘) *kāyar* कायर

Tin, can (m∘) *ḍibba* डिब्बा

Tingle (f∘) *jhuñjhunī* झुनझुनी

Tinkle (f∘) *ṭin-ṭin* टिन-टिन

Tint (f∘) *jhalak* झलक

Tiny (adj∘) *sūkṣhma, nanhā* सूक्ष्म, नन्हा

Tip (f∘) *nok̐* नोंक

Tip (v∘) *ulṭānā* उलटाना*

Tire (v∘) *thaknā* थकना

Tit (m∘) *stanāgra* स्तनाग्र

Tit for tat (adj∘) *jaise ko taisā* जैसे को तैसा

Title (m∘) *śhīrśhak, upādhi, khitāb, padvī* शीर्शक, उपाधि, ख़िताब, पदवी

To (suff∘) *ko* को

Toad (m∘) *meṇḍhak* मेंढ़क

Toadstool (m∘) *kukurmuttā* कुकुरमुत्ता

Toast (v∘) *sek̐nā* सेंकना*

Tobacco (m∘) *tambākū* तंबाकू

Today (av∘) *āj* आज

Toe (f∘) *pair kī aṅgulī* पैर की अँगुली

Together (av∘) *ekatra, ek sāth* एकत्र, एक साथ

Together (av∘) *sāth me̐* साथ में

Token (adj∘) *pratīk* प्रतीक

Tolerate (v∘) *sahnā* सहना

Toll (m∘) *mahasūl, kar* महसूल, कर

Tomato (m∘) *ṭamāṭar* टमाटर

Tomb (m∘) *makbarā, samādhi* मकबरा, समाधि

Tomorrow (av∘) *kal* कल

Tone (m∘) *sūr, lahajā* सूर, लहजा

Tongs (m∘) *chimṭā* चिमटा

Tongue (f∘) *jībh* जीभ

Tonight (f∘) *āj rāt* आज रात

Tonsil (m∘) *galsuā* गलसुआ

Tonsure (m∘) *muṇḍan* मुंडन

Tool (m∘) *auzār* औज़ार

Toot (m∘) *bho̐pū,* (f∘) *sīṭī)* भोंपू, सीटी

Toot (v∘) *bho̐pū bajānā* भोंपू बजाना*

Tooth (m∘) *dāṅt* दाँत

Top (m∘) 1. (tip) *śhikhar,* (f∘) *choṭī* शिखर, चोटी; 2. (lid) *ḍhakkan* ढक्कन; 3. (toy) *laṭṭū* लट्टू

Topaz (m∘) *pukhrāj* पुखराज

Topic (m◦) *viṣhay* विषय

Topple (v◦) *luḍhaknā, luḍhakānā** लुढ़कना, लुढ़काना*

Topsy-turvey (adj◦) *ulṭā-pulṭā* उलटा-पुलटा

Torch (f◦) *mas'hāl* मशाल

Torch (v◦) *jalānā, āg lagānā* जलाना, आग लगाना*

Torential (adj◦) *vegvān, muslādhār* वेगवान, मुसलाधार

Torment (v◦) *satānā* सताना*

Torn (adj◦) *phaṭā* फटा

Tornado (m◦) *tūfān* तूफ़ान

Torso (m◦) *dhaḍ* धड़

Tortoise (m◦) *kachhuā* कछुआ

Tortuous (adj◦) *chakkardār, ṭeḍhā-meḍhā* चक्करदार, टेढ़ा-मेढ़ा

Torture (f◦) *pīḍā* पीड़ा

Torture (v◦) *pīḍā denā* पीड़ देना*

Toss (v◦) *uchhālnā* उछालना

Total (adj◦) *kul, pūrṇa* कुल, पूर्ण

Totalitarian (adj◦) *ekādhikārī* एकाधिकारी

Totter (v◦) *laḍkhaḍānā* लड़खड़ाना

Touch (m◦) *spars'ha* स्पर्श

Touch (v◦) *chhūnā* छूना*

Touchy (adj◦) *tunak mizāj* तुनक मिज़ाज

Tough (adj◦) *sakht, kaḍā* सख़्त, कड़ा

Tour (m◦) *daurā,* (f◦) *yātrā* दौरा, यात्रा

Tourism (m◦) *paryaṭan* पर्यटन

Tourist (m◦) *yātrī, musāfir* यात्री, मुसाफिर

Tournament (f◦) *pratiyogitā* प्रतियोगिता

Tow (v◦) *khĩchnā* खिंचना*

Towards (av◦) *kī or, kī taraf* की ओर, की तरफ

Towel (m◦) *tauliyā* तौलिया

Tower (m◦) *minār* मिनार

Town (m◦) *gā̃v, kasbā* गाँव, कसबा

Toxic (adj◦) *zaharīlā* ज़हरीला

Toxin (m◦) *zahar, viṣh* ज़हर, विष

Toy (m◦) *khilaunā* खिलोना

Trace (m◦) *avas'heṣh* अवशेष

Trace (v◦) *ckhojnā* खोजना*

Track (f◦) *paṭrī* पटरी

Tract (m◦) *ilākā, bhūbhāg* इलाका, भूभाग

Traction (m◦) *khĩchāv* खिंचाव

Trade (m◦) *vyāpār, pes'hā* व्यापार, पेशा

Trade (v◦) *vyāpār karnā, denā-lenā* व्यापार करना, देना-लेना*

Trader (m◦) *vyāpārī, saudāgar* व्यापारी, सौदागर

Tradition (f◦) *paramparā* परंपरा

Traffic (m◦) *yātāyāt* यातायात

Tragedy (adj◦) *dukhad* दुखद

Tragery (f◦) *durghaṭnā* दुर्घटना

Trail (m◦) *nis'hān, chihna* निशान, चिह्न

Trail (v◦) *ghasīṭnā* घसीटना*

Train (f◦) *gāḍī* गाड़ी

Train (v◦) *sikhānā* सिखाना*

Trait (f◦) *vis'heṣhtā* विशेषता

Traitor (m◦) *dorhī, ghatak* द्रोही, घातक

Traitorous (adj◦) *ghātakī* घातकी

Tramp (adj◦) *āvārā, ghumakkaḍ* आवारा, घुमक्कड़

Trample (v◦) *kuchalnā, raundnā* कुचलना, रौंदना*

Trance (f◦) *behos'hī, supti* बेहोशी, सुप्ति

Tranquil (adj◦) *stabdha, s'hānt* स्तब्ध, शांत

Transaction (m◦) *kārobār, saudā* कारोबार, सौदा

Transcend (v◦) *pār jānā* पार जाना

Transcribe (v◦) *likhanā* लिखना*

Transcript (m◦) *pratilekh* प्रतिलेख

Transfer (f◦) *badlī* बदली

Transfix (v◦) *hakkā-bakkā honā* हक्का-बक्का होना

Transform (v◦) *badalnā* बदलना

Transformation (m◦) *badal* बदल

Transgression (m◦) *ullaṅghan* उल्लंघन

Transient (adj◦) *kṣhaṇik* क्षणिक

Transition (m◦) *saṅkramaṇ* संक्रमण

Transitive (adj◦) *sakarmak* सकर्मक

Translucent (adj◦) *pārabhāsī* पारभासी

Transmission (m◦) *bhejnā* भेजना

Transmit (v◦) *bhejnā* भेजना*

Transperant (m◦) *pārdarśhī* पारदर्शी

Transplant (m◦) *pratiropaṇ* प्रतिरोपण

Transport (m◦) *vahna, parivahan* वहन, परिवहन

Transport (v◦) *ḍhonā* ढोना*

Transverse (adj◦) *āḍā, tirchhā* आड़ा, तिरछा

Trap (m◦) *fandā* फंदा

Trap (v◦) *pakaḍnā* पकड़ना*

Trash (m◦) *kūḍā,* (f◦) *raddī* कूड़ा, रद्दी

Trauma (m◦) *sadmā* सदमा

Travel (m◦) *safar,* (f◦) *yātrā* सफर, यात्रा

Travel (v◦) *safar karanā* सफर करना*

Traveler (m◦) *yātrī, musāfir* यात्री, मुसाफिर

Traversity (m◦) *tamāśhā* तमाशा

Tray (f◦) *thālī, tastarī* थाली, तस्तरी

Treacherous (adj◦) *khatarnāk, viśhvāsghātī* ख़तरनाक, विश्वासघाती

Treason (m◦) *deśh-droha* देशद्रोह

Treasure (m◦) *javāhrāt* जवाहरात

Treasurer (m◦) *khajāñchī* ख़ज़ांची

Treasury (m◦) *khazānā, kośh* ख़ज़ाना, कोष

Treatment (m◦) 1. (behavior) *bartāv* बरताव; 2. (remedy) *ilāj* इलाज

Treaty (f◦) *sulah, sandhi* सुलह, संधि

Treble (adj◦) *tīn gunā* तीन गुना

Trechery (m◦) *droha, ghāt, dhokhā, khatrā* द्रोह, घात, धोखा, ख़तरा

Tree (m◦) *peḍ* पेड़

Tremble (v◦) *laḍkhaḍānā, thartharānā* लड़खड़ाना, थरथराना

Tremendous (adj◦) *bahut acchhā* बहुत अच्छा

Tremor (m◦) *kamp,* (f◦) *kam̐pkam̐pī* कंप, कँपकँपी

Trench (f◦) *khāī* खाई

Trend (f◦) *pravritti* प्रवृत्ति

Trepidation (f◦) *ghabrāhaṭ* घबराहट

Trespass (m◦) *atikramaṇ* अतिक्रमण

Tresses, hair (f◦) *laṭ* लट

Trial, court (m◦) *mukadmā* मुक़दमा

Trial, test (m◦) *oarīkṣhaṇ* परीक्षण

Triamphant (adj◦) *vijayī, kāmayāb, safal* विजयी, कामयाब, सफल

Triangle (m◦) *trikoṇa* त्रिकोण

Tribe (f◦) *jāti* जाति

Tribularion (m◦) *musībat* मुसीबत

Tributary (adj◦) *sahāyak* सहायक

Tribute (m◦) *upahār, bheṭ̐* उपहार, भेंट

Trick (f◦) *chāl,* (m◦) *dā̐v* चाल, दाँव

Trickle (v◦) *ṭapaknā* टपकना

Tricky (adj∘) *kaptī* कपटी

Trident (m∘) *triśhūl* त्रिशूल

Trifle (adj∘) *naganya, tucchha* नगण्य, तुच्छ

Trigger (m∘) *ghoḍā* घोड़ा

Trigonometry (f∘) *trikoṇamiti* त्रिकोणमिती

Trillion (adj∘) *ek lākh karoḍ* एक लाख करोड

Trim (f∘) *sajāvaṭ* सजावट

Trim (v∘) *kutarnā* कुतरना*

Trinity (f∘) *trimūrti* त्रिमूर्ति

Trio (m∘) *tigaḍḍā* त्रिगड्डा

Trip (f∘) *sair* सैर

Trip (v∘) *laḍkhaḍānā* लड़खड़ाना

Tripmph (f∘) *vijay, kāmyābī, safaltā,* विजय, कामयाबी, सफलता

Tripod (f∘) *tipāī* तिपाई

Tripple (adj∘) *tigunā* तिगुना

Trivial (adj∘) *naganya* नगण्य

Trombone (f∘) *turahī* तुरही

Trophy (m∘) *padak* पदक

Trouble (m∘) *kaṣhṭa, pareṣhānī* कष्ट, परेशानी

Trowel (f∘) *karnī, khurpī* करनी, खुरपी

Truce (m∘) *virām* विराम

Truck (m∘) *ṭhelā* ठेला

True (adj∘) *sachchā* सच्चा

Truly (adj∘) *sach-sach* सच-सच

Truly (av∘) *sachmuch* सचमुच

Trumpet (f∘) *turahī* तुरही

Truth (m∘) *satya, sacha* सत्य, सच

Try (m∘) *prayatna, prayās* प्रयत्न, प्रयास

Try (v∘) 1. (make effort) *kośhiśh karnā* कोशीश करना*,
2. (test) *āzmānā, parakhnā* आज़माना, परखना*

Tube (f∘) *nalī* नली

Tuber (m∘) *kand* कंद

Tuberculosis (m∘) *kṣhay* क्षय

Tuck (f∘) *chunaṭ, tah* चुनट, तह

Tuck (v∘) *chunaṭ ḍālnā* चुनट डालना*

Tuesday (m∘) *maṅgalvār* मंगलवार

Tuft (m∘) *guchhā* गुच्छा

Tune (f∘) *dhun* धुन

Tunnel (m∘) *suraṅg* सुरंग

Turban (f∘) *pagaḍī, sāfā* पगड़ी, साफ़ा

Turbulence (m∘) *gaḍbaḍī* गड़बड़ी

Turbulent (adj∘) *ugra* उग्र

Turmoil (f∘) *khalbalī* खलबली

Turn (f∘) *moḍ* मोड़

Turn (v∘) *muḍnā, moḍnā** मुड़ना, मोड़ना*

Turnip (m∘) *śhalgam* शलगम

Turquoise (adj∘) *firozī* फ़िरोज़ी

Turquoise (m∘) *firozā* फ़िरोज़ा

Turret (m∘) *kaṅhūrā* कँगूरा

Turtle (m∘) *kachhuā* कछुआ

Tusk, elephant (m∘) *dā̃t* दाँत

Tussel (f∘) *hāthāpāī* हाथापाई

Tutor (m∘) *śhikṣhak* शिक्षक

TV (m∘) *dūradarśhan* दूरदर्शन

Tweak (v∘) *umeṭhnā* उमेठना*

Tweezers (m∘) *chimṭā* चिमटा

Twelve (adj∘) *bārah* बारह

Twenty (adj∘) *bīs* बीस

Twice (av∘) *dobārā* दोबारा

Twiddle (v◦) *ghumānā* घुमाना*

Twig (f◦) *ṭahnī* टहनी

Twilight (m◦) *jhuṭpuṭā* झुटपुटा; *antakāl* अंतकाल

Twin (adj◦) *juḍvā̃* जुड़वाँ

Twine (f◦) *dorī, sutlī* डोरी, सुतली

Twinge (f◦) *ṭīs* टीस

Twinkle (v◦) *ṭimṭmānā* टिमटिमाना

Twirl (v◦) *ghūmnā, ghumānā** घूमना, घुमाना*

Twist (f◦) *maroḍ* मरोड

Twist (v◦) *lapeṭnā, maroḍnā* लपेटना*

Twitch (f◦) *faḍfaḍ* फड़फड़

Twitter (f◦) *chahachahānā* चहचहाना

Two (adj◦) *do* दो

Tycoon (m◦) *pū̃jīpati* पूँजीपति

Type, kind (m◦) *prakār,* (f◦) *jāti* प्रकार, जाति

Type, printing (m◦) *mudraṇ* मुद्रण

Typhoon (m◦) *tūfān* तूफ़ान

Typical (adj◦) *lākṣhaṇik* लाक्षणिक

Tyranny (f◦) *tānāśhāhī,* (m◦) *atyāchār* तानाशाही, अत्याचार

Tyrant (m◦) *atyāchārī* अत्याचारी

U

Ugly (adj◦) *badsūrat* बदसूरत

Ulcer (m◦) *foḍā* फोड़ा

Ultimate (adj◦) *antim* अंतिम

Ultimatum (f◦) *dhamkī* धमकी

Umbrella (f◦) *chhatrī,* (m◦) *chhātā* छत्री, छता

Unable (adj◦) *asamartha* असमर्थ

Unacceptable (adj◦) *agrāhya* अग्राह्य

Unanimity (m◦) *ekmat, mataikya* एकमत, मतैक्य

Unanimous (adj◦) *ekmat* एकमत

Unarmed (adj◦) *nihatthā* निहत्था

Unauthorised (adj◦) *avaidh* अवैध

Unaware (adj◦) *añjān* अंजान

Unbalanced (adj◦) *asantulit* असंतुलित

Unbearable (adj◦) *asahnīya* असहनीय

Unbelievable (adj◦) *aviśhvasanīya* अविश्वसनीय

Unborn (adj◦) *ajanmā* अजन्मा

Unbroken (adj◦) *aṭūṭ* अटूट

Uncertain (adj◦) *anischit* अनिश्चित

Uncle (m◦) *chāchā, tāyā, māmā, mausā, fūfā* चाचा, ताया, मामा, मौसा, फूफा

Unclear (adj◦) *aspaṣhṭa* अस्पष्ट

Uncomfortable (adj◦) *bechain* बेचैन

Uncommon (adj◦) *asāmānyā* असामान्य

Uncompromising (adj◦) *haṭhī* हठी

Unconcerned (adj◦) *chintāhīn* चिंताहीन

Unconscious (adj◦) *behośh* बेहोश

Uncountable (adj◦) *asaṅkhya* असंख्य

Uncouth (adj◦) *asabhya* असभ्य

Uncover (v◦) *ughāḍnā* उघाड़ना*

Under (prep◦) *nīche* नीचे

Undercover (adj◦) *jāsūsī* जासूसी

Underdone (adj◦) *adhpakā* अधपका

Undergo (v◦) *bhugatnā, sahnā* भुगतना, सहना

Underground (adj◦) *bhūmigat* भूमिगत

Underhanced (adj◦) *beīmān* बेईमान

Underneath (prep◦) *tale, nīche* तले, नीचे

Understand (v◦) *samajhanā* समझना*

Unemployed (adj◦) *bekār* बेकार

Unending (adj∘) *anant* अनंत

Unequal (adj∘) *asamāna* असमान

Unequivocal (adj∘) *sāf-sāf* साफ़-साफ़

Unerring (adj∘) *achūk* अचूक

Unethical (adj∘) *anaitik* अनैतिक

Uneven (adj∘) 1. (rough) *khurdarā* खुरदरा; 2. (level) *asamatal* असमतल

Unexpected (adj∘) *apratyāśhit* अप्रत्याशित

Unexplained (adj∘) *aspaṣhṭa* अस्पष्ट

Unfair (adj∘) *anyāypūrṇa* अन्यायपूर्ण

Unfaithful (adj∘) *bewafā, namak harām* बेवफ़ा, नमक हराम

Unfamiliar (adj∘) *aparichit* अपरिचित

Unfashionable (adj∘) *aprachalit* अप्रचलित

Unfasten (v∘) *kholnā* खोलना*

Unfavourable (adj∘) *apratikūl* अप्रतिकूल

Unfit (adj∘) *ayogya, bekār* अयोग्य, बेकार

Unfold (v∘) *khulnā, kholnā** खुलना, खोलना*

Unforeseen (adj∘) *apratyāśhit* अप्रत्याशित

Unforgettable (adj∘) *avismaraṇīya* अविस्मरणीय

Unfortunate (adj∘) *abhāgā* अभागा

Unfounded (adj∘) *nirādhār* निराधार

Ungrateful (adj∘) *kritaghna* कृतघ्न

Unhappy (adj∘) *dukhī* दुखी

Unhealthy (adj∘) *asvastha* अस्वस्थ

Unheard (adj∘) *abhūtapūrva* अभूतपूर्व

Unification (m∘) *ekīkaraṇ* एकीकरण

Uniform (adj∘) *sama, ekrūp* सम, एकरूप

Uniform, dress (m∘) *pośhak,* (f∘) *vardī* पोशाक, वरदी

Unify (v∘) *joḍnā* जोड़ना*

Unike (adj∘) *asamān, bhinna* असमान, भिन्न

Union (f∘) *sandhi,* (m∘) *saṅgha* संधि, संघ

Unique (adj∘) *ananya, advitīya* अनन्य, अद्वितीय

Unit (adj∘) *ikāī* इकाई

Unite (v∘) *joḍnā* जोड़ना*

Unity (f∘) *ektā* एकता

Universal (adj∘) *sārvabhaumaik* सार्वभौमिक

Universally (av∘) *viśhvataḥ* विश्वत:

Universe (adj∘) *brahmāṇḍ* ब्रह्मांड

Unjust (adj∘) *anyāyī* अन्यायी

Unkind (adj∘) *krūr, nirdayī* क्रुर, निर्दयी

Unknown (adj∘) *agyāt* अज्ञात

Unlawful (adj∘) *avaidh* अवैध

Unlikely (adj∘) *asambhavanīya* असंभवनीय

Unlimited (adj∘) *asīmit* असीमित

Unlucky (adj∘) *abhāgā* अभागा

Unmarried (adj∘) *avivāhit, chhaḍā* अविवाहित, छड़ा

Unmistakable (adj∘) *sāf, spaṣhṭa* साफ़, स्पष्ट

Unnecessary (adj∘) *anāvaśhyak* अनावश्यक

Unnoticed (adj∘) *alakṣhit* अलक्षित

Unpleasant (adj∘) *apriya* अप्रिय

Unpopular (adj∘) *apriya* अप्रिय

Unprecedented (adj∘) *abhūtpūrva* अभूतपूर्व

Unpreparedness (f∘) *gaflat* गफ़लत

Unpretentious (adj∘) *vinit* विनित

Unqualified (adj∘) *ayogya* अयोग्य

Unquestionable (adj∘) *nischit* निश्चित

Unravel (v∘) *suljhānā* सुलझाना*

Unreal (adj∘) *kritrim* कृत्रिम

Unreal (adj∘) *naklī, banāvaṭī* नकली, बनावटी

Unreasonable (adj∘) *anuchit* अनुचित

Unreliable (adj∘) *avis'havsanīya* अविश्वसनीय

Unrest (adj∘) *as'hānti* अशांति

Unrivalled (adj∘) *nishkanṭak* निष्कंटक

Unsafe (adj∘) *asurakṣhit, khatarnāk* असुरक्षित, ख़तरनाक

Unsavory (adj∘) *apriya* अप्रिय

Unscrupulous (adj∘) *kapṭī* कपटी

Unsightly (adj∘) *kurūp* कुरूप

Unspeakable (adj∘) *akathanīya* अकथनीय

Unstable (adj∘) *asthir* अस्थिर

Unsteady (adj∘) *asthir* अस्थिर

Unsuccessful (adj∘) *asafal* असफल

Unsuitable (adj∘) *anupayukta* अनुपयुक्त

Unsure (adj∘) *sandigdha* संदिग्ध

Untamed (adj∘) *jaṅglī* जंगली

Untangle (v∘) *suljhānā* सुलझाना*

Unthinkable (adj∘) *lakpanātīt* कल्पनातीत

Untidy (adj∘) *avyavasthit* अव्यवस्थित

Untie (v∘) *kholnā* खोलना*

Until (prep∘) *tak* तक

Untimely (adj∘) *asāmayik* असामयिक

Unto (prep∘) *tab tak* तब तक

Untold (adj∘) *asaṅkhya* असंख्य

Untouchable (adj∘) *achhūt* अछूत

Untrue (adj∘) *jhūṭhā* झूठा

Untruth (m∘) *jhūṭh* झूठ

Unuguarded (adj∘) *arakṣhit* अरक्षित

Unuruly (adj∘) *bekābū* बेक़ाबू

Unused (adj∘) *korā* कोरा

Unusual (adj∘) *anūṭhā* अनूठा

Unveil (v∘) *dikhānā* दिखाना*

Unwanted (adj∘) *anāvas'hyak* अनावश्यक

Unwelcome (adj∘) *anchāhā* अनचाहा

Unwell (adj∘) *bīmār* बीमार

Unwilling (adj∘) *anicchhuk* अनिच्छुक

Unwitting (adj∘) *anabhigya* अनभिज्ञ

Unwrap (v∘) *kholnā* खोलना*

Uoroar (m∘) *haṅgāmā* हंगामा

Up (av∘) *ūpar* ऊपर

Upheaval (f∘) *ulath-pulath* उलथ-पुलथ

Uphil (adj∘) *kaṭhin* कठिन

Uphold (v∘) *samarthan karnā* समर्थन करना*

Upkeep (adj∘) *rakh-rakhāv* रख-रखाव

Upper (adj∘) *ūparī* ऊपरी

Uppermost (adj∘) *sarvoccha* सर्वोच्च

Upright (adj∘) *sīdhā* सीधा

Uprising (m∘) *vidroha, bagāvat* विद्रोह, बग़ावत

Uproot (v∘) *ukhāḍnā* उखाड़ना*

Upset (v∘) *gaḍbaḍānā* गड़बड़ाना

Upshot (m∘) *pariṇām* परिणाम

Upside-down (adj∘) *ulṭā-pulṭā* उल्टा-पुल्टा

Uptight (adj∘) *bhay-bhīt* भयभीत

Upward (av∘) *ūpar* ऊपर

Urban (adj∘) *s'haharī* शहरी

Urbane (adj∘) *sabhya* सभ्य

Urge (f∘) *lalak* ललक

Urge (v∘) *sujhānā* सुझाना*

Urgency (m∘) *s'hīghratā* शीघ्रता

Urgent (adj∘) *s'hīghra* शीघ्र

Urine (m∘) *mūtra,* (f∘) *pes'hab* मूत्र, पेशाब

Urn (m◦) *asthikalaśh* अस्थिकलश

Use (m◦) *istemāl, prayog* इस्तेमाल, प्रयोग

Use (v◦) *istemal karanā* इस्तेमाल करना*

Used to (v◦) *tā thā, tī thī, te the* ता था, ती थी, ते थे

Useful (adj◦) *upayogī* उपयोगी

Useless (adj◦) *bekār* बेकार

Uselessly (av◦) *vrithā, vyartha* वृथा, व्यर्थ

User (m◦) *upabhoktā* उपभोक्ता

Usual (adj◦) *sāmānya* सामान्य

Utensil (m◦) *bartan* बरतन

Utility (f◦) *upayogitā* उपयोगिता

Utilization (m◦) *prayog, upayog* प्रयोग, उपयोग

V

Vacant (adj◦) *khālī* खाली

Vacate (v◦) *khālī karnā* खाली करना*

Vacation (f◦) *chhuṭṭī* छुट्टी

Vaccination (m◦) *ṭīkā* टीका

Vacuum (m◦) *nirvāt* निर्वात

Vagabond (adj◦) *āvārā* आवारा

Vague (adj◦) *aspaṣhṭa* अस्पष्ट

Vainly (av◦) *bekār, fāltū* बेकार, फालतू

Valiant (adj◦) *śhūr, vīr* शूर, वीर

Valid (adj◦) *vaidh* वैध

Valour (adj◦) *bahādurī* बहादुरी

Valuable (adj◦) *kīmtī* कीमती

Valuation (m◦) *mūlyāṅkan* मूल्यांकन

Value (f◦) *kīmat* कीमत

Vanished (adj◦) *farār* फरार

Vanity (m◦) *dambh* दंभ

Variety (f◦) *bhinnatā* भिन्नता

Various (adj◦) *vividh* विविध

Variously (av◦) *nānāvidh* नानाविध

Vassal (m◦) *jāgīrdār* जागीरदार

Vast (adj◦) *viśhal* विशाल

Vegetable (f◦) *sabzī, tarkārī* सब्ज़ी, तरकारी

Vegetarian (m◦) *śhākāhārī* शाकाहारी

Vegetation (f◦) *vanaspati* वनस्पति

Vehicle (m◦) *vāhan* वाहन

Veil (m◦) *pardā* परदा

Vein (f◦) *nas* नस

Velocity (f◦) *gati,* (m◦) *veg* गति, वेग

Velvel (f◦) *makhmal* मख़मल

Vendetta (m◦) *bair* बैर

Venerable (adj◦) *pūjya* पूज्य

Vengeance (m◦) *badlā* बदला

Venom (m◦) *zahar, viṣh* ज़हर, विष

Vent (m◦) *nikās* निकास

Venturesome (m◦) *niḍar, sāhsī* निडर, साहसी

Venus (m◦) *śhukra* शुक्र

Veracity (f◦) *sacchāī* सच्चाई

Veranda (m◦) *dālān, barāmdā* दालान, बरामदा

Verb (m◦) *kriyāpad* क्रियापद

Verbal (adj◦) *śhābdik* शाब्दिक

Verdict (m◦) *nirṇay* निर्णय

Verification (f◦) *jā̃ch* जाँच

Verily (av◦) *sachmuch* सचमुच

Vermilion (adj◦) *sindūrī* सिंदूरी

Vermilion (m◦) *sindūr* सिंदूर

Verse (m◦) *padya* पद्य

Versed (adj∘) *anubhavī* अनुभवी

Versus (prep∘) *viruddha* विरुद्ध

Vertical (adj∘) *sīdhā* सीधा

Very (av∘) *ati, bahut* अति, बहुत

Vessel, boat (m∘) *jahāz* जहाज़

Vessel, pot (m∘) *pātra* पात्र

Vestige (m∘) *avas'heṣh* अवशेष

Vet (m∘) *pas'huchikitsak* पशुचिकित्सक

Vex (v∘) *chiḍhānā* चिढ़ाना*

Vibrant (adj∘) *chamkīlā* चमकीला

Vibrate (v∘) *kā̃pnā* काँपना

Vicar (m∘) *pādrī* पादरी

Vice (m∘) *vyasan* व्यसन

Vice, clamp (m∘) *s'hikañjā* शिकंजा

Vicinity (f∘) *samīptā* समीपता

Vicious (adj∘) *kaṭu* कटु

Victim (m∘) *s'hikār* शिकार

Victor (adj∘) *vijetā* विजेता

Victory (m∘) *vijay* विजय

View (f∘) *nazar, driṣhṭi* नज़र, दृष्टि

Vigil (f∘) *nigrānī* निगरानी

Vigilant (adj∘) *satark* सतर्क

Vigor (m∘) *utsāh* उत्साह

Vile (adj∘) *ghaṭiyā* घटिया

Villa (m∘) *mahal* महल

Village (m∘) *gā̃v* गाँव

Villian (m∘) *khalanāyak* खलनायक

Vine (f∘) *latā* लता

Vinegar (m∘) *sirkā* सिरका

Violation (m∘) *ullaṅghan* उल्लंघन

Violence (f∘) *hiṁsā* हिंसा

Violent (m∘) *ugra, zabardast* उग्र, ज़बरदस्त

Violet (adj∘) *baiṅganī* बैंगनी

Violin (f∘) *belā* बेला

Virgin (adj∘) *kumārī* कुमारी

Virgo (f∘) *kanyā rās'hi* कन्या राशि

Virtue (m∘) *sadguṇ* सद्गुण

Virtuous (adj∘) *sadguṇī* सद्गुणी

Virulent (adj∘) *ugra* उग्र

Virus (m∘) *viṣhāṇu* विषाणु

Visible (m∘) *driṣhṭi-gochar* दृष्टिगोचर

Vision (f∘) *driṣhṭi* दृष्टि, *nazar* नजर

Visitor (m∘) *paryaṭak* पर्यटक

Vivid (adj∘) *chaṭkīlā* चटकीला

Vocabulary (f∘) *s'habdabhaṇḍār* शब्दभंडार

Vocal (adj∘) *maukhik* मौखिक

Vocation (m∘) *pes'hā* पेशा

Voice (m∘) *āvāz,* (f∘) *vāṇī* आवाज़, वाणी

Void (adj∘) *khālī* खाली

Volatile (adj∘) *chañchal* चंचल

Volcano (m∘) *jwālāmukhī* ज्वालामुखी

Volume (m∘) *āyātan* आयातन

Volunteer (m∘) *svayaṁsevak* स्वयंसेवक

Vomit (f∘) *ulṭī* उल्टी

Voracious (adj∘) *khāū* खाऊ

Vote (m∘) *mata* मत

Vote (v∘) *mata denā* मत देना*

Vow (f∘) *pratigyā, kasam* प्रतिज्ञा, कसम

Voyage (f∘) *yātrā,* (m∘) *safar* यात्रा, सफर

Vulgar (adj∘) *asabhya* असभ्य

Vulnarable (adj∘) *asurakṣhit* असुरक्षित

Vulture (m∘) *gidda* गिद्द

W

Wage (f∘) *mazdūrī* मज़दूरी

Wager (f∘) *śhart* शर्त

Waist (f∘) *kamar* कमर

Wait (v∘) *rāh dekhanā* राह देखना*

Waiter (m∘) *bairā* बैरा

Wake (v∘) *jagnā, jāgānā** जगना, जगाना*

Walk (m∘) *chalanā* चलना

Wall (f∘) *dīwār* दीवार

Wallet (m∘) *baṭuā* बटुआ

Walnut (m∘) *akhroṭ* अखरोट

Wander (v∘) *bhaṭaknā* भटकना

Want (f∘) *chāh* चाह

Want (v∘) *chāhanā* चाहना*

Wanton (adj∘) *chañchal* चंचल

War (m∘) *yuddha,* (f∘) *laḍāī* युद्ध, लड़ाई

Warble (v∘) *kūjanā, chahchahānā* कुजना, चहचहाना

Ward (m∘) *vibhāg* विभाग

Warm (adj∘) *garam* गरम

Warm (v∘) *garam karnā* गरम करना

Warn (v∘) *chetāvanī denā* चेतावनी देना*

Warning (f∘) *chetāvanī* चेतावनी

Warrior (m∘) *yoddhā, sainik* योद्धा, सैनिक

Wart (m∘) *massā* मस्सा

Wary (adj∘) *sāvadhān* सावधान

Was (v∘) *thā, thī, thī* था, थी, थे

Wash (f∘) *dhulāī* धुलाई

Wash (v∘) *dhonā* धोना*

Washerman (m∘) *dhobī* धोबी

Wasp (f∘) *tataiyā* ततैया

Waste (f∘) *barbādī, kharābī* बरबादी, खराबी

Waste (f∘) *kharābī* खराबी

Waste (v∘) *kharāb karanā* खराब करना*

Watch, Clock (f∘) *ghaḍī* घड़ी

Water (m∘) *pānī, jal* पानी, जल

Watermelon (m∘) *tarbūja* तरबूज

Watery (adj∘) *patlā* पतला

Wave (f∘) *lahar, taraṅg* लहर, तरंग

Wave (v∘) *laharānā* लहराना

Waver (v∘) *ḍagmagānā* डगमगाना

Wax (m∘) *mom* मोम

Way (m∘) *rastā, mārg* मार्ग, रस्ता

We (pron∘) *ham* हम

Weak (adj∘) *kamazor* कमज़ोर

Wear (v∘) *pahananā* पहनना*

Weather (m∘) *mausam, ritu* मौसम, ऋतु

Weave (f∘) *bunāī* बुनाई

Weave (v∘) *bunanā* बुनना*

Weaver (m∘) *julāhā* जुलाहा

Web (m∘) *jālā* जाला

Wed (v∘) *śhādī karnā* शादी करना*

Wedding (m∘) *vivāh,* (f∘) *śhadī* विवाह, शादी

Wedge (f∘) *pachchar* पच्चर

Wednesday (m∘) *budhvār* बुधवार

Week (m∘) *haftā, saptāh* हफ़्ता, सप्ताह

Weekly (adj∘) *sāptāhik* साप्ताहिक

Weep (v∘) *ronā* रोना

Weigh (v∘) *taulnā* तौलना*

Weight (m∘) *vajan, bhār* वजन, भार

Weird (adj∘) *ajībogarīb* अजीबोग़रीब

Welcome (m∘) *svāgatam* स्वागतम्

Welfare (m∘) *kalyāṇ* कल्याण

Well (adj∘) *acchhā* अच्छा

Well (m∘) *kuā̐* कुआँ

Were (pron∘) *the, thī̐* थे, थीं

West (f∘) *paschim* पश्चिम

Western (adj∘) *pāschātyā* पाश्चात्य

Wet (adj∘) *gīlā* गीला

Wharf (m∘) *ghaṭ* घाट

What (pron∘) *kyā, kaun* क्या? कौन?

What else (av∘) *aur kyā* और क्या

Whatever (pron∘) *jo kuchh bhī* जो कुछ भी

Whatsoever (adj∘) *kuchh bhī* कुछ भी

Wheat (m∘) *gehū̐* गेहूँ

Wheel (m∘) *pahiyā, chakkā* पहिया, चक्का

When (av∘) *jab* जब

When? (av∘) *kab* कब?

Whence (av∘) *jahā̐ se* जहाँ से

Whenever (av∘) *jab-jab, jab bhī* जब-जब, जब भी

Where (av∘) *jahā̐* जहाँ

Where? (av∘) *kahā̐, kidhar* कहाँ, किधर

Whereas (conj∘) *jabki, kyo̐ki* जबकि, क्योंकि

Wherefore (m∘) *jisliye* जिसलिये

Whereto (av∘) *jahā̐ tak* जहाँ तक

Wherever (av∘) *jahā̐ kahī̐, jahā̐-jahā̐* जहाँ कहीं, जहाँ-जहाँ

Whether (conj∘) *ki* कि

Which (pron∘) *kaunsā* कौनसा

Whichever (pron∘) *jo koī, jo bhī* जो कोई, जो भी

While (conj∘) *jab* जब

Whim (f∘) *sanak* सनक

Whimper (v∘) *ṭhunaknā, pinpinānā* ठुनकना, पिनपिनाना

Whimsical (adj∘) *sankī, jhakkī* सनकी, झक्की

Whine (v∘) *karāhnā* कराहना

Whip (m∘) *koḍā, chābuk* कोड़ा, चाबुक

Whip (v∘) *chābuk mārnā* चाबुक मारना*

Whirl (v∘) *ghūmnā, ghumānā** घूमना, घुमान*

Whistle (f∘) *sīṭī* सीटी

Whistle (v∘) *sīṭī mārnā* सीटी मारना*

White (adj∘) *safed* सफेद

Whizz (v∘) *sansanānā* सनसनाना

Who (pron∘) *kaun* कौन

Whoever (pron∘) *jo koī* जो कोई

Whole (adj∘) *pūrā, pūrṇa* पूरा, पूर्ण

Wholesale (adj∘) *thok* थोक

Wholly (av∘) *sarvaśhaḥ* सर्वशः

Why (av∘) *kyo̐* क्यों

Wicked (adj∘) *duṣhṭa* दुष्ट

Wide (adj∘) *chauḍā, viśhāl* चौड़ा, विशाल

Widely (av∘) *dūr tak* दूर तक

Widow (f∘) *vidhvā* विधवा

Widower (m∘) *vidhur* विधुर

Width (adj∘) *chauḍāī* चौड़ाई

Wife (f∘) *patnī* पत्नी

Wild (adj∘) *jaṅglī* जंगली

Wilily (av∘) *kapaṭ se* कपट से

Will (f∘) *icchhā* इच्छा

Willfully (av∘) *apane āp* अपने आप

Willingly (av∘) *svecchhā se, apane āp* स्वेच्छा से, अपने आप

Willy (adj∘) *chālāk* चालाक

Wilt (v∘) *murjhānā* मुरझाना

Win (v∘) *jītanā* जीतना

Wind (f∘) *havā* हवा

Window (f∘) *khiḍakī* खिड़की

Windy (adj∘) *hvāī* हवाई

Wine (f∘) *madirā* मदिरा; *śharāb* शराब

Wing (m∘) *paṅkh* पंख

Wink (f∘) *palak* पलक

Wink (v∘) *ā̃kh mārnā* आँख मारना*

Winner (adj∘) *vijetā* विजेता

Winning (f∘) *jīt* जीत

Winnow (v∘) *osānā* ओसाना*

Winter (m∘) *śhītkāl* शीतकाल

Wintery (adj∘) *ṭhaṇḍā* ठंडा

Wipe (v∘) *pōchhnā* पोंछना*

Wire (f∘) *tār* तार

Wireless (adj∘) *betār* बेतार

Wisdom (m∘) *gyān* ज्ञान

Wise (adj∘) *gyānī* ज्ञानी

Wise man (m∘) *gyānī* ज्ञानी

Wish (f∘) *icchhā, chāh* इच्छा, चाह

Wish (f∘) *ichchhā* इच्छा

Wish (v∘) *chāhanā* चाहना*

Wisper (v∘) *fusfusānā* फुसफुसाना

Witch (f∘) *chuḍail, ḍāin* चुडैल, डाइन

With (prep∘) *se, saha, sāth* से, सह, साथ

Withdraw (v∘) *nikālnā* निकालना*

Wither (v∘) *murjhānā, kumhalānā* मुरझाना, कुम्हलाना

Within (av∘) *bīch, ke andar* बीच, के अंदर

Withold (v∘) *roknā* रोकना*

Without (av∘) *binā, sivāy* बिना, सिवाय

Withstand (v∘) *sahanā* सहना

Witness (f∘) *gavāh* गवाह

Wittingly (av∘) *jānbūjhkar* जानबूझकर

Wizard (m∘) *ustād* उस्ताद

Wobble (v∘) *ḍhulmulānā* डुलमुलाना

Woe (f∘) *pīḍā* पीड़ा

Wok (f∘) *kaḍāhī* कड़ाही

Wolf (m∘) *bheḍiyā* भेड़ीया

Woman (f∘) *strī, nārī, aurat* स्त्री, नारी, औरत

Womb (f∘) *kokh* कोख

Wonder (m∘) *āśhcharya* आश्चर्य

Wont (adj∘) *ādī* आदी

Wood (f∘) *lakaḍī* लकड़ी

Woodcutter (m∘) *lakaḍhārā* लकड़हारा

Woodpecker (m∘) *kaṭhphoḍvā* कठफोड़वा

Wool (f∘) *ūn* ऊन

Work (m∘) *kām* काम

Work (v∘) *kām karanā* काम करना*

Worker (m∘) *śhramik, majdūr* श्रमिक, मजदूर

World (m∘) *duniyā, jagat* दुनिया, जगत

Worm (m∘) *kīḍā* कीड़ा

Worry (f∘) *chintā, pareśhānī* चिंता, परेशानी

Worry (v∘) *chintā karnā* चिंता करना*

Worse (adj∘) *badtar* बदतर

Worship (f∘) *pūjā* पूजा

Worship (v∘) *pūjā karanā* पूजा करना*

Worst (adj∘) *sabase burā* सबसे बुरा

Worthy (adj∘) *yogya* योग्य

Wound (f∘) *jakhm,* (m∘) *ghāv* ज़ख़्म, घाव

Wrangle (m∘) *jhagḍā,* (f∘) *takrār* झगड़ा, तकरार

Wrap (v∘) *lapeṭnā* लपेटना*

Wrath, anger (m∘) *roṣh* रोष

Wreath (m∘) *hār* हार

Wrench (m∘) *pānā* पाना

Wrest (v∘) *chhīnanā* छीनना*

Wrestle (v∘) *laḍnā* लड़ना

Wrestler (m∘) *pahalwān* पहलवान

Wrestling (f∘) *kuśhti* कुश्ति

Wr etc.h (adj∘) *abhāgā* अभागा

Wr etc.hed (adj∘) *badnasīb* बदनसीब

Wriggle (v∘) *chhaṭpaṭānā* छटपटाना

Wring (v∘) *nichoḍnā* निचोड़ना*

Wrinkle (f∘) *śhikan, jhurrī* शिकन, झुर्री

Wrist (f∘) *kalāī* कलाई

Write (v∘) *likhanā* लिखना*

Writer (m∘) *lekhak* लेखक

Writhe (v∘) *chhaṭpaṭānā* छटपटाना

Writing (m∘) *lekh* लेख

Wrong (adj∘) *agalat* ग़लत

Wrongdoing (m∘) *anyāy* अन्याय

Wrought (adj∘) *krit, ghaṭit* कृत, घटित

Y

Yam (m∘) *ratālū* रतालू

Yard, 3ft. (m∘) *gaz* गज़

Yard, court (m∘) *āṅgan* आंगन

Yarn (m∘) *dhāgā, sūt* धागा, सूत

Yawn (f∘) *jambhāī* जँभाई

Year (m∘) *sāl, varṣh* साल, वर्ष

Yearn (v∘) *lalaknā* ललकना

Yeast (f∘) *khamīr* खमीर

Yellow (adj∘) *pīlā* पीला

Yelp (v∘) *chīkhanā, chillānā* चीखना, चिल्लाना

Yesterday (m∘) *kal* कल

Yet (av∘) *ab tak* अब तक

Yogurt (m∘) *dahī* दही

Yoke (m∘) *jūā* जूआ

Yolk (f∘) *zardī* ज़रदी

Yonder (av∘) *udhar* उधर

You (pron∘) *tū, tum, āp* तू, तुम, आप

Young (adj∘) *jawān* जवान

Your (pron∘) *terā, tumhārā, āpkā* तेरा, तुम्हारा, आपका

Your honour (m∘) *śhrīmān,* (f∘) *śhrīmatī* श्रीमान्, श्रीमती

Yourself (pron∘) *āp hī* आप ही

Youth (m∘) *yuvak,* (f∘) *yuvatī* युवक, युवती

Z

Zebra (m∘) *gorkhar* गोरखर

Zero (adj∘) *śhūnya* शून्य

Zest (m∘) *ras* रस

Zigzag (adj∘) *ṭeḍhā-meḍhā* टेढ़ा–मेढ़ा

Zink (m∘) *jastā* जस्ता

Zone (m∘) *vibhāg* विभाग

Zoo (m∘) *chiḍiyāghar* चिड़ियाघर

Zoology (m∘) *prāṇīśhāstra* प्राणीशास्त्र

Zucchini (f∘) *laukī* लौकी

HNIDI
PARTS OF SPEECH
वाणी के अष्टांग

When we speak about any thing (वस्तु) or about any topic (विषय), we use signifying words (वाचक शब्द) that are related to each other to make a meaningful sentence (वाक्य). The sentences in our speech (वाणी) or writing (लेखन) are of four types.

Types of Sentences
वाक्य के प्रकार

1. Statement or Assertion (*kathan* or *adhikathan* कथन, अधिकथन) : e.g. 1. Today Sun did not arise. आज सूरज नहीं निकला. 2. Sun rises in the East. सूरज पूरब में निकलता है.
2. Question (*praśhna* प्रश्न) : e.g. What is your name? आपका नाम क्या है?
3. Command or Request (*agya or vinati* आज्ञा, विनती) : 1. Be quiet! 2. Please stay quiet.
4. Exclamation (*udgār* उद्गार) : e.g. What a wonder! क्या आश्चर्य है.

Subject and Predicate
कर्ता और विधेय

When we make a sentence we name some thing or some person and we speak about that thing or person. The part that names the thing or that person is called the **Subject** (*kartā* कर्ता) of that sentence. The part of that sentence which tells something about that thing oe person is the **Predicate** (*vidheya* विधेय) of that sentence. e.g. Nature is the best doctor : Nature is the Subject and "is the best doctor" is the Predicate of this sentence.

In Hindi as well as in English, the Subject of a statement comes first and then the Predicate. Hindi is SOV (Subject-Object-Verb) lenguage, whie English is SVO (Subject-Verb-Object) language. e.g. Hindi :

Eight Parts of Speech
वाणी के आठ अंग

Grammatically, words that make up a sentence in general are classified into eight types.

1. **Noun** (संज्ञा) : Names of things (वस्तु) or persons (व्यक्ति). They are also called **Nāma** (नाम) e.g. राम, गाय, पानी, आकाश.
2. **Pronoun** (सर्वनाम) : Word used in place of nouns (नाम). e.g. मैं, आप, वह, वे, सब.
3. **Adjective** (विशेषण) : Word used to add something to the meaning of a noun or pronoun. e.g. बहुत, अच्छा, पतला, नीला, थोड़ा, तीन.
4. **Verb** (क्रिया) : Word used to describe an action. e.g. खाना, पीना, चलना, रोना.
5. **Adverb** (क्रियाविशेषण) : Word used to add something to the meaning of a verb, an adjective or another adverb. e.g. बहुत, तेज, धीरे, आहिस्ता.
6. **Preposition** (संबंध सूचक) : Word used with noun or pronoun to indicate how it stands in relation to something else in the sentence. e.g. में in, पर on, का of, से with. Please note that : the pre-positions or the prefixes of English language are all post-positions or suffixes in Hindi language.
7. **Conjunction** (समुच्चय सूचक) : Word used for joining words two or more words of a sentence. e.g. औरं and, अथवा or, अत: therehore, इसलिए thus.
8. **Interjection** (विस्मय सूचक) : Word or words used for expression of some sudden feeling (मनोविकार). e.g. हे! अरे! हे! आहा! हरे राम!

NOTE : From the above eight Parts of Speech, the Nouns, Pronouns, Adjectives and Verbs are called **Declinable** (विकारी), because they change according to their Gender, Number and Case (विभक्ति). The Adverbs, Prepositions, Conjunctions and Interjections are called Indeclinable (अविकारी), because do not change in their Gender, Number or Case.

CHAPTER 6

THE NOUN

संज्ञा, नाम.

Sangya (संज्ञा) is not the thing (*vastu* वस्तु) itself, but it is the name (*nām* नाम) of that thing. The word thing (वस्तु) could be anything tangible or intangibla.

1a. Five types of Nouns
नाम-संज्ञा के पाँच प्रकार

1. **Common Noun** (*sāmānya nām* सामान्य नाम) : The names of the things in general. e.g. King, Yoga. Rāma was a king राम राजा था. Karma-Yoga is superior Yoga कर्मयोग श्रेष्ठ योग है.
2. **Generic Noun** (*jāti vāchak nām* जातिवाचक नाम) : The name applied to a common group of beings or things. e.g. Eskimo एस्किमो, horse घोड़े, tree वृक्ष, mountain पर्वत, river नदी, etc.
3. **Proper Noun** (*vis'heṣh nām* विशेष नाम) : The name applied to a particular person, thing or place. e.g. Sītā सीता, Gangā गंगा, Toronto टोरंटो, etc.
4. **Collective Noun** (*samuday vāchak nām* समुदायवाचक नाम) : The name applied to a number of persons or things taken as a whole. e.g. Army सेना, Crowd भीड़, Alphabet वर्णमाला, etc.
5. **Abstract Noun** (*bhāva vāchak nām* भाववाचक नाम) : The name applied to a quality (*bhāva* भाव), possessed by an object. There are five bases that create Abstract Nouns.

5a. **Quality** (*yogyatā, guṇa or dharma* योग्यता, गुण, धर्म) : e.g. Kindness (*karuṇā* करुणा), Brightness (*dīpti* दीप्ति), Wisdom (*aklamandī* अक्लमंदी), Skill (*nipuṇatā* निपुणता), etc.

5b. **Action** (*kriyā* क्रिया) : to Sit (*baiṭhanā* बैठना) → Seat (*baiṭhak* बैठक), to Decorate (*sajānā* सजाना) → Decoration (*sajāvaṭ* सजावट), to Confuse (*ghabarāna* घबराना) → (*ghabarāhaṭ* घबराहट), etc.

5c. **Pronoun** (*sarvanām* सर्वनाम) : e.g. You *āp* आप → Your self *āpā* आपा, Mine *mama* मम → Myness *mamatā* ममता, Our *apnā* अपना → Kinship *apnāpan* अपनापन, etc.

5d. **Adjective** (*visheṣhaṇ* विशेषण) : e.g. Kind *kripālu* कृपालु → Kindness, Hot *rarm* गर्म → Heat *garmī* गर्मी, Sweet *mīṭhā* मीठा → Sweetness *miṭhās* मिठास, Honest *bhalā* भला → Honesty *bhalāī* भलाई, Good *acchā* अच्छा → Goodness *achhāī* अच्छाई, etc.

5e. **State** (*sthiti* स्थिति) : e.g. Child *bachchā* बच्चा → Childhood *bachchpan* बचपन, Slave *ghulām* ग़ुलाम → Slavary *ghulāmī* ग़ुलामी, Sick *bīmār* बीमार → Sickness *bīmārī* बीमारी, Poor *garīb* ग़रीब → Poverty *garībī* ग़रीबी, etc.

1b. Two types of Genders
लिंग के दो प्रकार

1. Gender is **<u>the single most important</u>**, delicate and tricky aspect of the Hindi language.
2. There are only two Genders in Hindi, Masculine Noun and Feminine Noun. The Neuter Gender of the Sanskrit language is dropped in Hindi language.
3. All Nouns and Pronouns are tagged Masculine or Feminine.
4. A Masculine Noun can be converted into its Feminine form.
5. A Feminine Noun can be converted into its Masculine form.
6. The Adjectives and Verbs do not have Gender of their own.
7. The Adjectives take Gender from the Noun or Pronoun they qualify.
8. The Verbs take Gender from either the Subject or the Object, depending on the Tense of the sentence.
9. Adverbs do not take any Gender.
10. If a living being exists in the nature as a male-female pair, then the male is given a Masculine name and the female as feminine name. e.g. नर-मादी, पुरुष-स्त्री, घोड़ा-घोड़ी, तोता-तोती, etc.

10. If it is difficult or unnecessary to ascertain a gender to any thing, the Masculine Gender is default.
11. Even if several rules are formulated to give masculine and feminine genders to things in Hindi, there are exceptions (अपवाद) to falsify every rule.

Hindi is an Inflected language. All nouns, Pronouns and Adjectives inflect into Cases affected by Genders and Numbers.

Even though the **Gender is one Single most important aspect of the Hindi Language**, there are no logical rules for determining whether a noun is Masculine or Feminine. In addition, a noun may have some masculine words and some feminine words, arbitrarily. e.g. Book = M. *granth* ग्रंथ; F. *kitaab* किताब, F. *pustak* पुस्तक.

In general, the object that is looked up on as having more strength or size is given masculine name and the thing that is considered delicate, beautiful or loving is attributes a feminine word. e.g. A small glass is *pyalī* (प्याला) and a bigger glass is *pyālā* (प्याला), a small box is *ḍabbī* (डब्बी) and a bigger box is *ḍabbā* (डब्बा), etc. **NOTE:** for more nouns and their genders, see the ***Transliterated Dictionary*** given in the section above.

GENDER CONVERTION FROM MASCULINE TO FEMININE

(1) If a noun, pronoun or adjective ends in अ or आ → it is changed to ई

देव (*dev*) → देवी (*devī*)	दास (*dās*) → दासी (*dāsī*)	पुत्र (*putra*) → पुत्री (*putrī*)
साला (*sālā*) → साली (*sālī*)	नाना (*nānī*) → नानी (*nānī*)	काला (*kālā*) → काली (*kālī*)
खड़ा → खड़ी	बैठा → बैठी	नीला → नीली

(2) If a word ends in आ → it is changed to ई as shown above, or it is changed to इया

बूढ़ा → बुढ़िया	चूहा → चुहिया	डिब्बा → डिबिया
मुन्ना → मुनिया	गुड्डा → गुडिया	कुत्ता → कुतिया

(3) If a word (relating to an occupation or profession) ends in अ, आ, इ or ई → it is sometimes changed to इन

लुहार	→ लुहारिन,	ग्वाला	→ ग्वालिन,	धोबी	→ धोबिन

(4) The words (relating to a status) are sometimes suffixed with आइन at the end

पंडित	→ पंडिताइन,	ठाकुर	→ ठकुराइन,	चौबे	→ चौबाइन

(5) To several words ending in अ → नी or आनी is aded

सिंह	→ सिंहनी,	ऊँट	→ ऊँटनी,	शेर	→ शेरनी
नौकर	→ नौकरानी,	देवर	→ देवरानी,	सेठ	→ सेठानी

(6) Some word ending in ई are changed to → इनी

योगी	→ योगिनी,	स्वामी	→ स्वामिनी,	तपस्वी	→ तपस्विनी

(7) If a word ends in आन् → आन् is changed to अती

भगवान्	→ भगवती,	श्रीमान्	→ श्रीमती,	गुणवान्	→ गुणवती

(8) If a word ends in अक → it is changed to इका

लेखक	→ लेखिका,	अध्यापक	→ अध्यापिका,	सेवक	→ सेविका

(9) Original Sanskrit words ending in अ → change अ to आ

चंचल	→ चंचला,	मूर्ख	→ मूर्खा,	सुत	→ सुता

(10) Some original Sanskrit words are changed to त्री

कवि	→ कवयित्री,	कर्ता	→ कर्त्री,	सविता	→ सवित्री

(11) Many masculine words take an unspecific form when changed to feminine gender.

राजा	→ रानी,	वर	→ वधू,	बैल	→ गाय,
पुरुष	→ स्त्री,	पिता	→ माता	मर्द	→ औरत,
देव	→ देवता,	ससुर	→ सास,	विधुर	→ विधवा

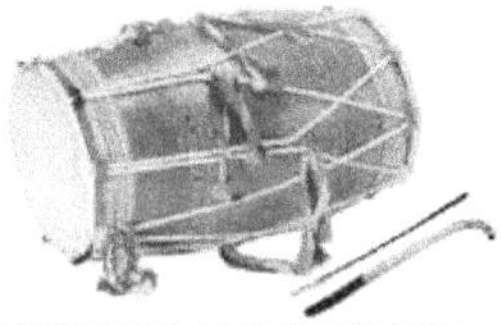

1c. Two types of Number
वचन के दो प्रकार

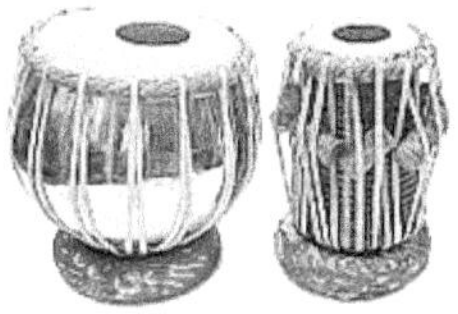

HINDI NUMBER :

1. Number is another tricky property of the Hindi words.
2. There are Two Numbers in Hindi language, Singular Number and Plural Number. The Dual Number of Sanskrit language is omitted in the Hindi language.
3. A Singular word can be converted into its Plural Form.
4. A Plural Word can be converted into its Singular Form.
5. The Nouns of the Subject and Object, the Pronouns, the Adjectives and the Verb terminations take Number.
6. The Singular Masculine Noun that ends in long *'aa, ā आ,'* the *'ā आ'* is changed to *'e' ए* in plural.
7. The Singular Feminine Noun that ends in long *'ā आ,' 'ẽ एँ'* is added to it in plural.
8. The Singular Feminine Noun that ends in a consonant, *'ẽ एँ'* is added to it in plural.
9. The Singular Feminine Noun that ends in long *'ī ई,'* the *'ī ई'* is changed to *'iyā̃ इयाँ'* in plural.
10. For most other nouns, the Singular form does not change when pluralized.

NUMBER CONVERSION

NUMBER CONVERTION : FROM SINGULAR TO PLURAL

(1) If a Masculine word ends in अ, इ, ई, उ or ऊ → it remains unchanged in plural numbers.

एक घर	→ चार घर	मकान	→ मकान	साँप	→ साँप
बाल	→ बाल	दृढ़	→ दृढ़	दूषित	→ दूषित
लाल	→ लाल	मुनि	→ मुनि	हाथी	→ हाथी
योगी	→ योगी	साधु	→ साधु	लघु	→ लघु
कुरु	→ कुरु	रघु	→ रघु	बाबू	→ बाबू

(2) If a Masculine word ends in आ → आ changes to ए

लड़का	→ लड़के	गधा	→ गधे	बड़ा	→ बड़े,

अच्छा	→ अच्छे	काला	→ काले	दूल्हा	→ दूल्हे,
खाता है	→ खाते हैं	जाता है	→ जाते हैं	कुत्ता	→ कुत्ते,

(3) If a Feminine word ends in अ or आ → एँ is added

रात	→ रातें	बात	→ बातें,	पुस्तक	→ पुस्तकें,
दुकान	→ दुकानें	माता	→ माताएँ	बाला	→ बालाएँ,
लता	→ लताएँ	शाखा	→ शाखाएँ	राह	→ राहें.

(4) If a Feminine word ends in या → या changes to याँ

चिड़िया	→ चिड़ियाँ	कुटिया	→ कुटियाँ	गुड़िया	→ गुड़ियाँ

(5) If a Feminine word ends in इ or ई → that इ or ई is changed to इयाँ

गति	→ गतियाँ	रीति	→ रीतियाँ	तिथि	→ तिथियाँ
नदी	→ नदियाँ	चींटी	→ चींटियाँ	घंटी	→ घंटियाँ
थाली	→ थालियाँ	बिल्ली	→ बिल्लियाँ	विदुषी	→ विदुषियाँ
गाड़ी	→ गाड़ियाँ	चाबी	→ चाबियाँ	रानी	→ रानियाँ

(6) If a Feminine word ends in उ, ऊ or औ → एँ is added to the word

वस्तु	→ वस्तुएँ	धेनु	→ धेनुएँ	ऋतु	→ ऋतुएँ
जूँ	→ जुँएँ	बहू	→ बहुएँ	गौ	→ गौएँ

NOTES : 1. Names of relationships should be kept unchanged in plural, e.g.

मामा	→ मामा,	चाचा	→ चाचा	नाना	→ नाना
ताया	→ ताया	चाची	→ चाची	दादा	→ दादा

2. Names of titles from Persian, Arabic, Urdu should should be made by attaching आन or इयान or आत suffix. e.g.

साहब	→ साहबान	मालिक	→ मालिकान	पटवारी	→ पटवारियान
कागज़	→ काग़जात	ख्याल	→ ख्यालात	मकान	→ मकानात

DICTIONARY OF COMMON HINDI NOUNS

सामान्य हिंदी शब्दों का वर्गीकृत कोश

INDEX

5.1 ANIMALS, Domastic पालतु प्राणी pāltu prāṇī

Bitch	कुकुरी, कुतिया *f◦ kukurī, kutiyā*
Buffalo	भैंसा, भैंस *m◦ Bhaĩsā, f◦ bhaĩs*
Bull, Bullock	ऋषभ, बलीवर्द, बैल, वृषभ *m◦ riṣhabh, balīvard, bail, vriṣhabha*
Calf	बछड़ा, वत्स *m◦ bachhaḍā, vatsa*
Camel	ऊँट, स्त्री◦ उँटनी, *m◦ ũṭ; f◦ ũṭanī*
Cat	बिल्ला, (स्त्री◦) बिल्ली; *m◦ billā; f◦ billī*
Colt	बछेड़ा *m◦ bachheḍā*
Cow	गाय, गौ, धेनु *f◦ gāy, gau, dhenu*
Dog	कुक्कुर, कुत्ता *m◦ kukkura, kuttā (f◦) see* bitch ↑
Donkey	खर, गधा, गर्दभ, रासभ *m◦ khar, gadhā, gardabha, rāsabha*
Ewe	एडका, मेषी *f◦ eḍakā, meṣhī*
Foal	बछड़ा, वत्स *m◦ bachhaḍā, vatsa*
Goat	अज, बकरा; (स्त्री◦) अजा, बकरी; *aja, bakrā, f◦ ajā, bakrī*
Hare	खरगोश, शशक *m◦ khargosh́, śhaśhak*
Horse	अश्व, घोड़ा *m◦ śhva, ghoḍā* (f◦ See Mare↓)
Kitten	बिलौटा; *m◦ bilauṭā*
Lamb	मेमना *m◦ memnā*
Lizard	छिपकली *f◦ chhipkalī*
Mare	अश्वा, घोड़ी; *f◦ aśhvā, ghoḍī*
Mouse	चूहा, मूषक *m◦ chhūhā*
Mule	खच्चर, बेसर *m◦ khachchar, besar*
Ox	बैल *m◦ bail*
Pig	वराह, सूअर *m◦ varāha, śuar*

Puppy पिल्ला *m∘ pillā*

Rabbit खरगोश, शशक *m∘ khargosh́, śhaśhak*

Ram एडका, मेष *m∘ eḍakā, meṣha*

Rat चूहा, मूषक *m∘ chhūhā, mūd́hak*

5.2 ANIMALS, Wild वन्य पशु vanya pashu

Alligator घड़ियाल, मगरमच्छ, नक्र *m∘ ghaḍiyāl, magarmachchha, nakra*

Bat चमगादड़ *m∘ chamgādaḍ*

Bear भालू *m∘ bhālū*

Beast पशु, मृग *m∘ paśhu, mriga*

Boa अजगर *m∘ ajagar*

Boar वराह, सूअर *m∘ varāha, sūar*

Cobra नाग, फणी *m∘ nāga, faṇī*

Crocodile घड़ियाल, मगरमच्छ, नक्र *m∘ ghaḍiyāi, magarmachchha, nakra*

Deer कुरंग, हरिण *m∘ kurańga, hariṇ*

Elephant हस्ती, हाथी *m∘ hastī, hāthī*

Fawn हिरनौटा *m∘ hirnauṭā*

Fish झष, मछली, मत्स्य, मीन, *m∘ jhaṣh, machhalī, matsya, mīn*

Fox शृगाल, लोमड़ी *m∘ śhrigāl; f. lomḍī*

Frog दर्दूर, भेक, मंडूक, मेंढक *dardūr, bhek, maṇḍūk, meṇḍhak*

Hippo करियाद *m∘ kariyād*

Jackal शृगाल, लोमड़ी *m∘ śhrigāl; f. lomḍī*

Leopard चित्रक, चीता *m∘ chitraka, chīttā*

Lion केसरी, सिंह *m∘ kesarī, sim̊ha*

Mongoose अंगुष, नकुल *m∘ ańguṣh, nakul*

Monkey	कपि, प्लवंग, वानर	*m◦ kapi, plavanga, vānar*
Mosquito	मशक, मच्छर	*mas̍hak, machhar*
Panther	तेंदुआ	*m◦ tenduā*
Porcupine	शल्य, साही	*m◦ s̍halya, sāhī*
Rhino	गंडक, गेंडा	*m◦ gaṇḍak, geṇḍā*
Snake	अहि, नाग, भुजग, सर्प, साँप	*m◦ ahi, nāg, hujaga, sarpa; sāmp*
Squirrel	गिलहरी	*f◦ gilharī*
Stag	हरिण	*m◦ hariṇ*
Tiger	व्याघ्र, शार्दूल, शेर	*m◦ vyāgra, s̍hārdūla, s̍her*
Turtle (m◦)	कछुआ, कच्छप, कूर्म	*m◦ kachhuā, kachchhap, kūrma*
Turtle (f◦)	कछूई, कूर्मी	*f◦ kachhūī, kūrmī*
Wolf	वृक, भेड़िया	*m◦ vrik, bheḍiyā*
Zebra	रासभ, गोरखर	*m◦ rāsabh, gorkhar*

5.3 INSECTS कीड़े kīḍe

Ant	चींटी, पिपीलिका; दीमक	*f◦ chīṇṭī, pipīlikā; dīmak* (Anthill वल्मीक *valmīk)*
Bedbug	मत्कुण, खटमल	*m◦ matkuṇ, khaṭmal*
Bee	मधुमक्खी, भृंग, भ्रमर	*m◦ madhu-makkhī, bhring, bhramar*
Bookworm	पुस्तकी-कीड़ा	*m◦ pustakī-kīḍā*
Bug	कीड़ा	*m◦ kīḍā*
Butterfly	तितली	*m◦ titlī*
Centipede	शतपदी	*f◦ s̍hatapadī*
Cockroach	तिलचटा	*f◦ tilchaṭā*
Crab	कर्कट, केकड़ा	*m◦ karkaṭ, kekḍā*
Cricket	झिंगुर, झिल्ली	*f◦ jhingur, jhillī*

Earthworm केंचुआ *m◦ keñchuā*

Flea पिस्सू *f◦ pissū*

Fly मक्खी, मक्षिका *f◦ makkhī, makṣhikā*

Glow worm खद्योत, जुगनु *m◦ khadyot, juganu*

Grasshopper शरभ, टिड्डा *m◦ śharabh, ṭiḍḍā*

Honey bee मधुकर; (स्त्री◦) मधुमक्खी *m◦ madhukar, f◦ madhumakkhī*

Hornet हाड़ा m◦ *hāḍā*

Insect कीड़ा, कृमि *m◦ kīḍā, krimi*

Locust टिड्डी *f◦ ṭiḍḍī*

Millipede सहस्रपदी *f◦ sahasrapadī*

Moth शलभ, पतंगा *m◦ śhalabh, pataṅgā*

Oyster कस्तुरा, शुक्ति *m. kstaurā; f. śhukti*

Scorpion बिच्छू, वृश्चिक *m◦ bichchhū, vriśhchik*

Silkworm कोशकार, रेशमकीट *m◦ kośhakār, tesham-kīṭ*

Snail शंबूक, घोंघा *m◦ śhambūk, ghoṅghā*

Spider मकड़ी, लूता (स्त्री◦) *makḍī, lūtā*

Termite दीमक *f◦ dīmak*

Worm कीड़ा, कृमि *m◦ kīḍā, krimi*

5.4 BIRDS पक्षी pakṣhī

Black bird कोकिला, पिका *f◦ kokilā, pikā*

Blue bird नीलकंठ *m◦ nīlakaṇṭha*

Chicken चूज़ा चिंगना *m◦ chūjā, chingnā*

Cock कुक्कुट, मुरगा (मुरगी) *m◦ kukkuṭ, murgā; f. murgī*

Crane बलाक, सारस *m◦ balāk, sāras*

Crow	काक, कौआ, वायस	*m◦ kāka, kauā, vāyas*
Dove	कपोत, कबूतर, कलरव, पारावत	*m◦ kapota, kabūtar, kalarav, pārāvat*
Duck	कलहंस, कदंब, बत्तख	*m◦ kalahaṁsa, kadamb, battakh*
Eagle	गरुड़	*m◦ garuḍ*
Flamingo	मराल, हंसावर	*m◦ marāl, haṁsāvar*
Goose	कलहंस, चक्रवाक	*m◦ kalahaṁsa, chakravāk*
Hawk	श्येन, बाज़, शिकरा	*m◦ śhyen, bāz, śhikrā*
Hen	कुक्कुटी, मुरगी	*f◦ kukkuṭī, maurgaī*
Heron	क्रौंच, सारस, बगुला, बक	*m◦ krauncha, sāras, bagulā, bak*
Kite	(स्त्री◦) आतापी, चील	*f◦ ātāpī, chīl*
Nightangle	बुलबुल	*m◦ bulbul*
Owl	उल्लू, मुआ	*m◦ ullū, muā*
Parrot	कीर, शुक, तोता	*m◦ kīra, śhuka, totā*
Partridge	चकोर, तीत्तर	*m◦ chakor, tītar*
Pigeon	कपोत, कबूतर, कलरव, पारावत	*m◦ kapot, kabūtar, kalarav, pārāvat*
Peacock	केकी, मयूर, मोर, शिखंडी, शिखी	*m◦ kekī, mayūr, mor, śhikhaṇḍī, śhikhī*
Quail	वर्तक, बटेर	*m◦ vartak, baṭer*
Raven	काकोल, काला-कौआ	*m◦ kākol, kālā-kauā*
Rooster	कुक्कुट, ताम्रचूड़, मुरगा	*m◦ kukkuṭa, tāmrachuḍ, murgā*
Sparrow	चिड़िया, चटका, गौरया,	*m◦ chiḍiyā, chaṭakā, gauraiyā*
Swan	राजहंस, हंस	*m◦ rājhaṁsa, haṁsa*
Vulture	गृध्र, गीध,. गिद्ध	*m◦ gridhra, gīdh, giddha*
Woodpecker	काष्ठकूट, कठफोड़वा:	*m◦ kāṣhṭhakūṭ, kaṭhafoḍvā*

5.5 THE BODY PARTS शरीर के अंग śharīra ke aṅg

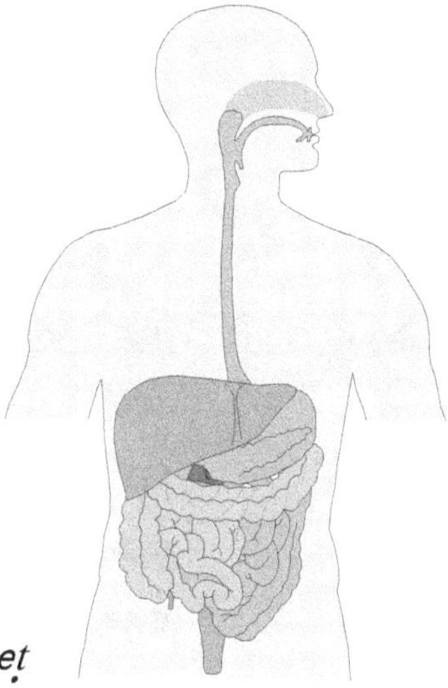

Abdomen उदर, पेट *m∘ udar, peṭ*

Ankle गुल्फ, टखना *m∘ gulfa, ṭakhanā*

Anus अपान, गुदा *m∘ apān, gudā*

Arm बाहु, भुजा, बाँह *f∘ bāhu, bhujā, bā̐h*

Armpit काँख, बगल *m∘ kā̐kh, bagal*

Artery धमनी *f∘ dhamanī*

Back पृष्ठ, पीठ *f∘ prishṭha, pīṭh*

Bald गंज *f∘ gañj*

Beard कूर्च, दाढ़ी *f∘ kūrcha, dāḍhī*

Belly उदर, जठर, तुन्द, पेट *m∘ udar, jaṭhar, tunda, peṭ*

Bellybutton नाभि *f∘ nābhi*

Blood रक्त, रुधिर, लोहित, शोणित, खून, लहू
m∘ rakta, rudhir, lohit, shoṇit, khūn, lahū

Bloodvessel नाड़ी, रक्तवाहिका, शिरा *f∘ nāḍī, raktavāhikā, śhirā*

Bosom क्रोड, वक्ष, छाती *m∘ kroḍam, vakṣha; f∘ chhātī*

Body अङ्ग, कलेवर, गात्र, तन, देह, वपु, विग्रह, शरीर; काया
m∘ ang, kalevar, gātra, tan, deha, vapu; vigraha, śharīra; f∘ kāyā,

Brain मस्तिष्क, भेजा, दिमाग *m∘ gordam, bhejā, dimāg*

Breath श्वास *m∘ śhvāsa*
(i) in-breath श्वास *m∘ śhvāsa; (ii) out-breath* उच्छ्वास *m∘ uchchhvāsa*

Breast क्रोड, वक्ष, छाती; स्तन *m∘ kroḍa, vakṣha; f∘ chhātī; (for female) m∘ stana*

Bun नितम्ब *m∘ nitamba*

Cadaver शव; लाश *m∘ śhava; f∘ lāśh*

Calf पिण्डिका, पिण्डली *f∘ pinḍikā , pinḍalī*

Cartilage	उपास्थि, कुरकुरी *f◦ upāsthi, kurkurī*
Cheek	कपोल, गाल *m◦ kapol, gāl*
Chest	क्रोड, वक्ष, छाती *f◦ kroḍa, vakṣha, chhātī*
Chin	चिबुक, हनु, ठुड्डी *f◦ chibuk, hanu, ṭhuḍḍī*
Corpse	शव; लाश *m◦ śhava, f◦ lāśh*
Ear	कर्ण, कान *m◦ karṇa, kān*
Elbow	कोहनी *f◦ kohanī*
Eye	अक्षि, आँख; चक्षु, नयन, नेत्र, लोचन *f◦ akṣhi, ā̃kh, nayana, netra, lochan*
Eyebro	भ्रू, भौंह, भृकुटी *f◦ bhrū, bhō̃ha, bhrikuṭī*
Eyelash	पक्ष्म, बरौनी *f◦ paksma, baraunī*
Eyelid	पलक *f◦ palak*
Face	आनन, मुख, वदन, मुँह, चेहरा; *m◦ ānana, mukh, vadan, mũh, cheharā*
Far-sight	दूरदृष्टि *f◦ dūradriṣhṭi*
Feather	पंख *m◦ paṅkh*
Finger	अंगुलि, उँगली *f◦ anguli, uṅgalī*
Fist	मुष्टि, मुठ *f◦ muṣhṭi; muṭh*
Foetus	गर्भ, पिण्ड, भ्रूण *m◦ garbha, piṇda, bhrūṇa*
Foot	चरण, पद, पाद, पाँव *m◦ charaṇa, pad, pād, pā̃v*
Fore-finger	तर्जनी *f◦ tarjanī*
Forehead	ललाट, मस्तक, माथा *m◦ lalāṭa, mastak, māthā*
Gum	दन्तमांस *m◦ dantamāṁsa*
Hair	कुन्तल, केश, बाल *m◦ kuntal, keśha, bāl*
Hand	कर, पाणि, हस्त, हाथ *m◦ kar, pāṇi, hast, hāth*
Head	मूर्धा, शिर, सिर, शीर्ष *m◦ mūrdhā, śhira, sir, śhīrṣha*
Heart	हृदय, दिल *m◦ hridaya, dil*

Heel	एड़ी *f∘ edī*
Hide	अजिन, चर्म; खाल *m∘ ajin, charma; f∘ khāl*
Hip	नितंब, कूल्हा, पुट्ठा; कटी, श्रोणी *m∘ nitamb, kūlhā, puṭṭhā; f∘ kaṭī, śhroṇī*
Horn	शृङ्ग, सिंग *m∘ śhriaṅga, siṅg*
Index-finger	तर्जनी *f∘ tarjanī*
Intestine	अन्त्र; अँतड़ी, आँत *m∘ antra; f∘ antaḍī, ā̃t*
Jaw	हनु *f∘ hanu*
Jaw, lower	हनु; चिबुक, जबड़ा *f∘ hanu; f∘ chbuk, jabḍā*
Jaw-tooth	दंष्ट्रा *f∘ daṁṣhtrā*
Joint	सन्धि *m∘ sandhi*
Kidney	गुरदा, वृक्क *m∘ guradā, vrikka*
Knee	जानु; घुटना *f∘ jānu; m∘ ghuṭnā*
Knot	ग्रन्थि; गाँठ *f∘ granthi; m∘ gā̃ṭh*
Knuckle	अङ्गुलपर्व; पोर *m∘ aṅguliparva; f∘ por*
Lap	अङ्क; क्रोड, गोद *m∘ aṅka, f∘ kroḍa; god*
Life	चैतन्य, जीवन, प्राण *m∘ chaitanya, jīvan, prāṇ*
Limb	अङ्ग, अवयव, गात्र *m∘ aṅga, m∘ avayav, m∘ gātra*
Lip	ओष्ठ, ओंठ, होंठ *upper-lip m∘ oṣhṭha; lower-lip* अधर *m∘ adhara*
Little-finger	कनिष्ठा, कनिष्ठिका, कनीका *f∘ kaniṣhṭhā, kaniṣhṭhikā, kanīkā*
Liver	यकृत *m∘ yakrita*
Lower-lip	अधर *m∘ adhar*
Lungs	फुप्फुस *m∘ fuffus*
Marrow	मज्जा, मेदा *f∘ majjā, m∘ medā*
Meat	माँस *m∘ māṁsa*
Menses	रज *m∘ raja*

Middle-finger	मध्यमा	*f∘ madhyamā*
Moustaches	श्मश्रु, मूँछ	*f∘ śhmaśhru, mūँchh*
Mouth	आनन, मुख, वदन, मुँह, चेहरा;	*m∘ ānana, mukh, vadan, muँh, cheharā*
Muscle	पेशी, शिरा, स्नायु	*f∘ peśhī, śhirā, snāyu*
Nail	नख, नाखून	*m∘ nakh, nākhūn*
Navel	नाभि, नाभी,	*f∘ nābhi, nābhī*
Neck	ग्रीवा, गरदन	*f∘ grīvā, gardan*
Nerve	मज्जा, शिरा, स्नायु, नस	*f∘ majjā, śhirā, snāyu, nas*
Nipple	चूचुक; चूची, ढिपनी	*m∘ chūchuka; f∘ chūchī, ḍhipnī*
Nose	घ्राण; नासिका, नाक	*m∘ ghrāṇa; f∘ nāsikā, nāk*
Nostril	नासारन्ध्र, नथना	*m∘ nāsārandhra, nathanā*
Palm	करतल, चपेट; हथेली	*m∘ kartal, chapeṭ, f∘ hathelī*
Penis	लिङ्ग, शिश्न	*m∘ liṅga, śhiśhna*
Ponytail	शिखा, चोटी	*f∘ śhikhā, choṭī*
Poop	पुरीष, मल, विष्टा	*f∘ puriṣha, mala, f∘ viṣhṭā*
Pore	रन्ध्र	*m∘ randhra*
Pulse	स्पन्द, नब्ज़	*m∘ spanda, nabja*
Rib	पसली	*f∘ paslī*
Ring-finger	ऊर्मिका	*f∘ ūrmikā*
Rump	चूतड़, पुट्ठा, नितंब	*m∘ chutaḍ, puṭṭhā, nitamb*
Saliva	लाला, लार	*f∘ lālā, lār*
Semen	रेत, वीर्य, शुक्र	*m∘ reta, vīrya, śhukra*
Shoulder	स्कन्ध, कन्धा	*m∘ skandha, kandhā*
Sight	दृष्टि	*f∘ driṣhṭi*
Skeleton	कङ्काल, पञ्जर	*m∘ kaṅkāl, pañjar*

Skin	त्वचा, चमड़ी *f◦ tvachā, chamḍī*
Skull	कपाल, खोपड़ी *m◦ kapāl, f◦ khopadī*
Snout	सुंड, थूथनी *f◦ suṇd, thūthanī*
Sole	पादतल, तलवा *m◦ pādatal, talvā*
Soul	आत्मा *f◦ ātmā*
Spit	थूक *f◦ thūk*
Stomach	अन्नाशय, उदर, पेट *m◦ annāśhaya, udara, peṭ*
Tail	पुच्छ, लाङ्गुल, पूँछ, दुम *f◦ puchchha, lāṅgul, pũchh, dum*
Tear	अश्रु, आँसु *m◦ aśhru, ā̃su*
Testicle	अण्डकोष, वृषण *m◦ aṇḍkoṣh, vriṣhaṇ*
Thigh	ऊरु, जंघा *f◦ ūru, jaṅghā*
Throat	कण्ठ, गला *m◦ kaṇṭha, galā*
Thumb	अङ्गुष्ठ, अँगूठा *m◦ aṅguṣhṭha, angūṭhā*
Tongue	जिह्वा, रसना, जीभ *f◦ jihvā, rasanā, jībh*
Tooth	दन्त, दाँत *m◦ dant, dā̃t*
Trunk	शुण्ड, सूँड़ *f◦ śhuṇḍ, sūṇḍ*
Udder	स्तन *m◦ stana*
Uterus	गर्भाशय, योनि *m◦ garbhāśhay, f◦ yoni*
Vagina	भग, योनि *m◦ bhag, f◦ yoni*
Vein	रक्तवाहिनी, रग, नस *f◦ raktavāhinī, rag, nas*
Vision	दृष्टि *f◦ driṣhṭi*
Waist	कटि, कटी, कमर *f◦ kaṭi, kaṭī, kamar*
Whiskers	गुम्फ *m◦ gumph*
Womb	गर्भ, गर्भाशय *m◦ garbha, garbhāśhay*
Wrist	मणिबंध; कलाई, *m◦ maṇibandh; f◦ kalāī*

5.6 AILMENTS and BODY CONDITIONS रोग विकार rog-vikār

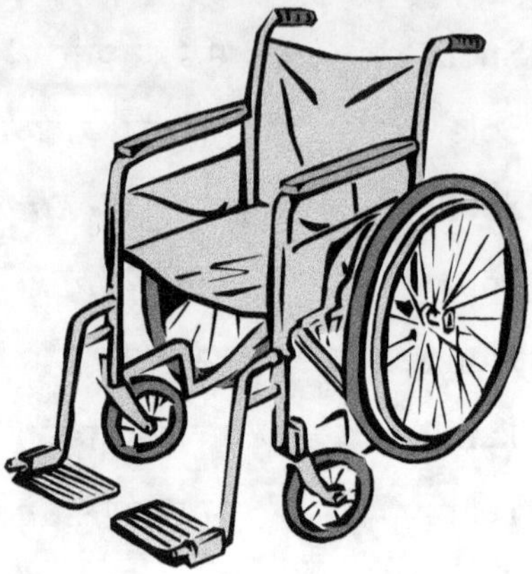

Abortion	गर्भपात *m∘ garbhapāt*
Acidity	अम्लता, शुक्तता *f∘ amlatā, śhuktatā*
Asthma	श्वास रोग *m∘ śhvās rog*
Bald	मुण्ड, खल्वाट *m∘ muṇḍa, khalvāṭ*
Belching	उद्गिरण; डकार *m∘ udgiraṇ, f∘ ḍakār*
Bleeding	रक्तस्राव *m∘ raktasrāv*
Blindness	अन्धता *f∘ andhatā*
Boil	फोड़ा, व्रण *m∘ foḍā, vraṇ*
Bone	अस्थि, हड्डी *f∘ asthi, haḍḍī*
Cancer	कर्करोग, कर्कट रोग *m∘ karkarog, karkaṭa rog*
Chill	कँपकँपी, झुरझुरी, ठिठुरन, सिहरन *m∘ kãpkãpī, jhurjhurī, ṭhiṭhuran, siharan*
Constipation	बद्धकोष्ठ, कब्ज़ *m∘ baddhakoṣhṭha, kabza*
Cough	कास, खाँसी *m∘ kās, f∘ khā̃sī*
Craze	भ्रांतचित्त, सनक, पागलपन *m∘ bhrāntchitta, sanak, pāgalpan*
Diabetes	मधुमेह *m∘ madhumeha*
Diarrhoea	अतिसार *m∘ atisār*
Disease	अस्वास्थ्य, रोग, विकार, व्याधि *m∘ asvāsthya, rog, vikār, vyādhi*
Dwarf	खर्व, वामन, बौना, गिट्ठा *m∘ kharva, vāman, baunā, giṭṭhā*
Dysentry	अतिसार, पेचिश *m∘ atisār; f∘ pechiśh*
Eczema	पामा, छाजन *m∘ pāmā; f∘ chhājan*
Eyesore	अक्षिशूल *m∘ akṣhisūl*
Frail	क्षयी, भङ्गुर *m∘ kṣhayī, bhaṅgur*
Giddiness	घुमड़ी; घुमटा, सिरचक्कर *f∘ ghumḍī, m∘ ghumṭā, sirchakkar*
Headache	शिरोवेदना; सरदर्द *f∘ śhirovedanā; m∘ sardard*

Health	आरोग्य, स्वास्थ्य, सेहत, तन्दुरुस्ती	*m◦ ārogya, svāsthya; f◦ sehat, tandurustī*
Hiccup	हिक्का, हिचकी	*f◦ hikkā, hichakī*
Hunchback	कुब्ज	*m◦ kubja*
Hurt	अपकार, क्षति, दुख	*m◦ apkār, f◦ kṣhati, m◦ dukh*
Indigestion	अजीर्ण, अपच; बदहज़मी	*m◦ ajīrṇa, apach; f◦ badhazmī*
Jaundice	पाण्डुरोग	*m◦ pāṇḍurog*
Leprosy	कुष्ठ, कोढ़, महारोग	*m◦ kuṣhṭha, koḍh, mahārog*
Lunacy	उन्माद, पागलपन, विक्षिप्तता	*m◦ unmād, pāgalpan; f◦ vikṣhiptatā*
Madness	पागलपन, विक्षेप; दीवानगी	*m◦ pāgalpan, vikṣhep; f◦ dīwānagī*
Obese	पीन, मोटा, स्थूल	*m◦ pīna, moṭā, sthūla*
Pain	उद्वेग, कष्ट, क्लेश, ताप, दुख; पीडा, वेदना, व्यथा	*m◦ udvega, kaṣhṭa, kleśh, tāp, dukh, f◦ pīḍā, vednā, vyathā*
Phlegem	कफ, श्लेष्म	*m◦ kaf, m◦ śhleṣhma*
Pimple	पिटिका, फुंसी	*f◦ piṭikā, fuṁsī*
Piles	अर्श, बवासीर	*m◦ arśha; f◦ bavāsīr*
Plague	महामारी, ताऊन	*f◦ mahāmārī; m◦ tāūn*
Pus	पीप, मवाद, पूय	*f◦ pīp; m◦ mavād, pūya*
Saliva	लाला, लार	*f◦ lālā, lār*
Sick	अस्वस्थ, पीडित, रुग्ण, रोगी	*m◦ asvastha, pīḍit, rugṇa, rogī*
Sleeplessness	उन्निद्रता	*f◦ unnidratā*
Sleepy	उनिंदा, निद्रालु, शयालु	*m◦ unindā, nidrālu, śhayālu*
Sneeze	क्षव, छींक	*m◦ kṣhava, f◦ chhīk̐*
Sore	क्षत, व्रण	*m◦ kṣhat, m◦ vraṇ*
Sprain	मोच	*m◦ moch*
Stool	मल, विष्टा, गू, पाखाना	*m◦ mal, f◦ viṣhṭā; m◦ gū, pākhānā*

Sweat	घर्म, स्वेद, पसीना *m◦ gharma, sveda, pasīnā*
Swelling	सूजन *m◦ suījan*
Tears	अश्रु, आँसु *m◦ aśhru, ā̃sū*
Thirst	तृषा, तृष्णा, पिपासा, प्यास *f◦ trishā, trishṇā, pipāsā, pyās*
Tuberculosis	क्षयरोग *m◦ kṣhayarog*
Urine	मुत्र, मेह, मूत, पेशाब *m◦ mutra, meha, mūt, peśhāb*
Vomit	वमन, उलटी, कै, *m◦ vamanam; f◦ ulṭī, kai*
Wart	मस्सा *m◦ massā*
Wound	क्षति, व्रण, घाव; जखम, चोट *m◦ kṣhati, vraṇa, ghāv, f◦ jakham, choṭ*
Yawn	जृंभा *f◦ jrimbhā*

5.7 CLOTHING, DRESS etc. परिधान paridhān

Belt	मेखला, पेटी, कमरबंद *mekhalā, peṭī, kmarband*
Blanket	कम्बल, आवरण *m◦ kambal, āvaraṇ*
Button	घुण्डी *m◦ ghuṇḍī*
Cap	टोपी; ढक्कन *f◦ ṭopī, m◦ ḍhakkan*
Cloth	कपड़ा; वस्त्र *m◦ kapḍā; vastra*
Coat	अँगरखा; कुरता *m◦ aṅgarkhā; kurtā*
Colour	रङ्ग *m◦ rang*
Cotton	कपांस, तूल, रुई, रूई *m◦ karpāṁs, tūl, ruī, rūī*
Glove	दस्ताना *m◦ dastānā*
Gown	कटिवस्त्र, चोगा, लबादा *m◦ kaṭivastra, chogā, labādā*
Hat	शिरस्क, शिरस्त्राण, टोपी *f◦ śhirask, śhirastrāṇ, f◦ ṭopī*
Jacket	निचोल, मिरजई *m◦ nichol, f◦ mirjaī*
Lace	तसमा, फीता *m◦ tasmā, f◦ fītā*

Measurement परिमिति, परिमाण, मान, मापन *f∘ parimiti, parimāṇ, mānm, māpan*

Needle सूई, सूची, सेवनी *f∘ sūī, sūchī, sevanī*

Pocket कोष, ज़ेब *m∘ koṣha, zeb*

Quilt रज़ाई, दुलाई *f∘ razāī, dulāī*

Satin रेशम *m∘ reśham*

Scarf दुपट्टा *m∘ dupaṭṭā*

Sheet चादर, चद्दर *f∘ chādar, chaddar*

Shirt चोला, कुरता, कमीज़ *m∘ chola, kurtā, kamīz*

Silk रेशम *m∘ resham*

Size आकार, परिमाण, मान *m∘ ākār, parimāṇ, mān*

Skirt घागरा, लहंगा *m∘ ghāgrā, lahaṅgā*

Sleeve आस्तीन, बाँह *m∘ āstīn, bā̃h*

Sock जुर्राब, मोजा *m∘ jurrāb, mojā*

Style प्रकार, ढंग, तरीका, शैली, रीति *m∘ prakār, ḍhaṅg, tarīkā, śhailī, rīti*

Thread तन्तु, सूत्र, धागा, तागा, सूत *m∘ tantu, sūtra, dhāgā, tāgā, sūt*

Towel अँगोछा, गमछा, तौलिया *m∘ aṅgochhā, gamchhā, tauliyā*

Turban पगड़ी, पाग, मुरेठा, साफ़ा *f∘ pagaḍī, pāg, mureṭhā, sāfā*

Uniform वेष, वरदी *m∘ veṣh, vardī*

Veil परदा, घूँघट, ओढ़नी, दुपट्टा *m∘ pardā, ghū̃ghaṭ, oḍhanī, dupaṭṭā*

Wool ऊर्ण, ऊन, पशम, लोम *f∘ ūrṇa, ūn, paśham, lom*

Yarn तन्तु, सूत्र, धागा, तागा, सूत *m∘ tantu, sūtra, dhāgā, tāgā, sūt*

5.8 RELATIONS नाते सम्बन्ध nāte sambandha

Adopted अङ्गीकृत, परिगृहित; दत्तक *adj∘ aṅgīkrit, parigrihit; dattak*

Adopted, daughter दत्तक पुत्री *f∘ dattak putrī*

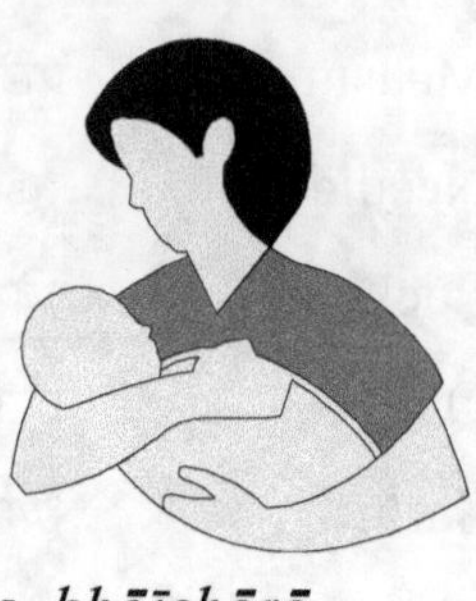

Adopted, son	कृतक पुत्र, दत्तक *m◦ kritak putra, dattak*
Aunt	चाची, बूआ, फूफी, काकी, मौसी, खाला, मामी *f◦ chāchī, būā, fūfī, kākī, mausī, khāla, māmī*
Brother	बंधु, भाई, भ्राता, सहोदर; अनुज, अग्रज *m◦ bandhu, bhāī, bhrātā, sahodar; anuj, agraj*
Brotherhood	बंधुता, बंधुत्व, भाईचारा *f◦ bandhutā, m◦ bandhutva, bhāīchārā*
Brotherly	भ्रात्रीय *a◦ bhrātrīya*
Brother' son	भतीजा *m◦ bhatījā*
Brother's daughter	भतीजी *f◦ bhatījī*
Brother's wife	भाभी *f◦ bhābhī*
Child	अपत्य, अर्भक, संतति, सन्तान *m◦ apatya, arbhak, f◦ santti, m◦ santān*
Childless	नि:संतान *adj◦ nisantān*
Country-folk	जानपद *m◦ jānapad*
Country-man	देशबंधु, स्वदेशीय *m◦ deśhabandhu, svadeśhīya*
Couple	युगल, युग्म, दम्पती *m◦ yugal, yugma; dampatī*
Daughter	अंगजा, आत्मजा, कन्या, कुमारी, तनया, तनुजा, दुहिता, नन्दिनी, पुत्री, सुता *f◦ aṅgajā, ātmajā, kanyā, kumārī, tanayā, tanujā, duhitā, nandinī, putrī, sutā*
Daughter-in-law	वधू, स्नुषा *f◦ vadhū, snuṣhā*
Family	कुटुम्ब, कुल, गोत्र, वंश *m◦ kuṭumba, kul, gotra, vaṁśha*
Father	जनक, पिता, तात, बाप *m◦ janak, pitā, tāt, bāp*
Fatherhood	पितृत्व, पितृधर्म, पितृभाव *m◦ pitritva, m◦ pitridharma, pitribhāv*
Fatherless	अनाथ, अपितृक, पितृहीन *adj◦ anāth, apitrik, pitrihīn*
Fatherly	पितृतुल्य *adv◦ pitritulya*
Father-in-law	श्वशुर *m◦ śhvaśhur*

Father's brother	चाचा, ताया *m◦ chāchā, tāyā*
Father's father	पितामह, दादा *m◦ pitamaha, dādā*
Father's mother	पितामही दादी *m◦ pitāmahī, dādī*
Father's sister	बूआ *f◦ būā*
Forefathers	पितर, पूर्वज *m◦ pitar, pūrvaj*
Friend	बंधु, मित्र, सखा, सुहृद् *m◦ bandhu, mitra, sakhā, suhrid*
Grand-child	पौत्र, पोता, नातिन *m◦ pautra, potā, natin f◦* पौत्री, पोती *pautrī, potī*
Grand-daughter	पौत्री, पोती *f◦ pautrī, potī*
Grand-father	पितामह; मातामह, दादा, नाना *m◦ pitāmaha; mātāmaha, dādā, nānā*
Grand-son	पौत्र, पोता *m◦ pautra, potā*
Grand-son, son's son	नप्ता, पुत्रसुत, पौत्र *m◦ naptā, putrasuta, pautra*
Grandee	अभिजन, कुलीनजन, महाजन, *m◦ abhijan, kulīnajan, mahājan*
Grand-son, dauther's son	पौत्र, दौहित्र *m◦ pautra, dauhitra*
Great-gand-daughter	प्रपौत्री *f◦ prapautrī*
Great-grand-son	प्रपौत्र *m◦ prapautra*
Great-great-grand-son	परप्रपौत्र *m◦ paraprapaūtra*
Great-great-gand-daughter	परप्रपौत्री *f◦ paraprapautrī*
Heair	उत्तराधिकारी, *m◦ uttarādhikārī*
Husband	कान्त, धव, नाथ, पति, भर्ता *m◦ kānt, dhav, nāth, pati, bhartā*
Husband's brother	देवर *m◦ devar*
Husband and wife	दम्पती *m◦ dampatī*
Husband's sister	ननंद साली *◦ nanānd, śālī*
Lord	ईश, ईश्वर, प्रभु, स्वामी *m◦ īśha, īśhvar, prabhu, swāmī*
Love	अनुकम्पा, अभिलाषा, प्रीति; अनुराग, प्रणय, प्रेम, राग, वात्सल्य, स्नेह *f◦ anukampā, abhilāṣhā, prīti;*

	m◦ anurāg, praṇay; prem, rāg, vātsalya, sneha
Lover	प्रेमी, प्रमिका *m◦ premī, f◦ premikā*
Mistress	दयिता, रमणी, रखेली *f◦ dayitā, ramaṇī, rakhelī*
Mother	अंबा, जननी, जनयित्री, जन्मदा, माँ, माता
	f◦ ambā, jananī, janayitrī, janmadā, mā̃, mātā
Motherhood	मातृत्व, मातृधर्म, मातृभाव *m◦ mātritva, mātridharma, mātribhāv*
Motherless	अमातृक *m◦ amātrik*
Motherly	मातृवत् *adv◦ mātrivat*
Mother-in-law	श्वश्रू, सास *f◦ śhvaśhrū, sās*
Mother's brother	मातुल, मामा *m◦ mātula, māmā*
Mother's brother's wife	मातुला, मातुलानी, मामी *f◦ mātulā, mātaulānī, māmī*
Mother's father	मातामह, नाना *m◦ mātānaha, nānā*
Mother-land	जन्मभूमि, स्वदेश *f◦ janmabhūmi, m◦ svadeśha*
Mother's mother	मातामही, नानी *f◦ mātāmahī, nānī*
Mother's sister	मातृस्वसा मौसी, मासी *f◦ mātrisvasā, mausī, māsī*
Neighbor	प्रतिवेशी, पड़ोसी *m◦ prativeśhī, paḍosī*
Neighborly	मिलनसार *m◦ milansār*
Own, my	मदीय, अपना *adj◦ madīya, apnā*
Own, one's	आत्म, आत्मीय, अपना, निज, स्व, स्वकीय, स्वीय
	adj◦ ātma, ātmīya, apnā, nija, sva, svakīya, svīya
Own, your	त्वदीय, युष्मदीय, आपका *adj◦ tvadīya, yuṣhmadīya, āpkā*
Pupil	अन्तेवासी, छात्र, शिष्य *m◦ antevāsī, chhātra, śhiṣhya*
Relation	सम्बंध, नाता *m◦ sambandha, nātā*
Relative	संबद्ध, संबंधित, रिश्तेदार *m◦ sambaddha, sambandhit, riśhtedār*
Sister	भगिनी, बहिन *f◦ bhaginī, bahin*

Sister, elder	अग्रजा *f∘ agrajā*
Sister, younger	अनुजा, अवरजा *f∘ anujā, avarajā*
Sister's daughter	भागिनेयी, स्वस्रीया, भानजी *f∘ bhāgineyī, svasrīyā, bhānajī*
Sisterhood	भगिनित्व *m∘ bhaginitva*
Sisterly	स्वस्रीय *adj∘ svasrīya*
Sister's husband	जीजा *m∘ jījā*
Sister-in-law	ननन्द, साली *f∘ nanand, śālī*
Sister's son	भागिनेय, स्वसृपुत्र, भानजा *m∘ bhāgineya, svasriputra, bhānajā*
Son	अङ्गज, आत्मज, कुमार, तनय, तनुज, पुत्र, सुत *m∘ angaj, ātmaj, kumār, tanaya, tanuj, putra, sut*
Sonless	अपुत्रक, निपुत्रिक *adj∘ aputrak, niputrik*
Son-in-law	जामाता, जमाई *m∘ jāmātā, jamāī*
Step-brother	विमातृज, वैमात्रेय *m∘ vimātrij, vaimātreya*
Step-daughter	सपत्नीसुता *f∘ sapatnīsutā*
Step-father	मातृपति *m∘ mātripati*
Step-mother	विमाता *f∘ vimātā*
Step-sister	विमातृजा, वैमात्री *f∘ vimātrijā, vaimātrī*
Step-son	सपत्नीसुत *m∘ sapatnīsut*
Stranger	अनभिज्ञ, अन्यजन, अपरिचित, आगन्तुक, पर, विदेशीय *m∘ anabhigjña, anyajan, aparichit, āgantuk, par, videśhīya*
Widow	अनाथा, विधवा, बेवा *f∘ anāthā, vidhavā, bewā*
Widower	विधुर, रँडुवा *m∘ vidhur, raṇḍuā*
Wife	कान्ता, पत्नी, भार्या, जोरू, स्त्री *f∘ kāntā, patnī, bharyā, jorū, strī*
Wife's brother	साला *m∘ śālā*
Wife's sister	साली *f∘ sālī*

5.9 HOUSEHOLD THINGS घरेलु वस्तु gharelu vastu

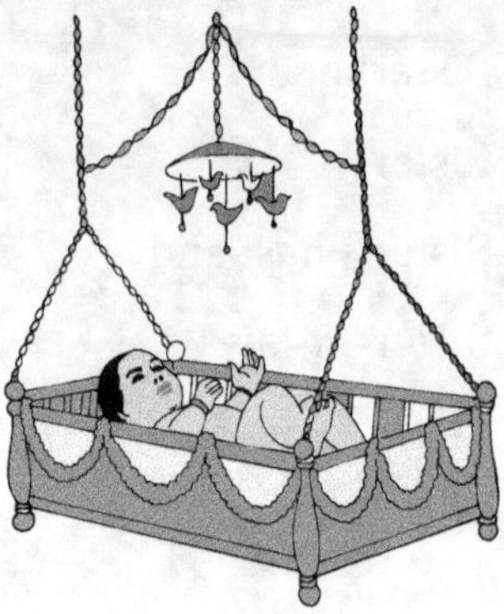

Bag	कोष, थैला, झोला, बोरा *m◦ kośh, thailā, jholā, borā*
Basket	मंजूषा, डलिया, टोकरी *f◦ mañjūṣhā, ḍaliyā, ṭokrī*
Bed	शय्या, खाट; पलंग *f◦ śhaiyyā, khāṭ, m◦ palaṅg*
Blanket	कम्बल *m◦ kambal*
Bottle	कूपी, शीशी *f◦ kūpī, śhīśhī*
Bowl	कटोरा *m◦ kaṭorā*
Box	संदूक, डिब्बा *m◦ sandūk, ḍibbā*
Broom	झाड़ू *f◦ jhāḍū*
Brush	मार्जनी, तूलिका *f◦ mārjanī, tūlikā*
Bucket	बालटी *f◦ bālṭī*
Button	घुंडी *f◦ ghuṇḍī*
Candle	दीपिका, मोमबत्ती *f◦ dīpikā, mombattī*
Chair	आसन, कुरसी *m◦ āsan, f◦ kursī*
Comb	कंघी प्रसाधनी *f◦ kaṅghī, prasādhanī*
Cot	खाट; पलंग *f◦ khāṭ, m◦ palaṅg*
Cup	चषक, प्याला *m◦ chaṣhak, pyāla*
Dictionary	अभिधान, शब्दकोष *m◦ abhidhān, śhabdakoṣh*
Dish	थाली *f◦ thālī*
Fuel	ईन्धन *m◦ īndhan*
Furniture	उपस्कर, सामान *m◦ upaskar, sāmān*
Glass	चषक, प्याला *m◦ chaṣhak, pyālā*
Glue	लेप, गोंद *m◦ lep, gond*
Hearth	चूल्हा *m◦ chūlhā*
Key	कुञ्चिका, ताली, चाबी *f◦ kuñćikā, tālī, chābī*

Knife	छुरी; चाकू	*f∘ chhurī; m∘ chākū*
Lamp	दीप, दीया	*m∘ dīp, dīyā*
Lock	ताल, ताला	*m∘ tāl, tāla*
Mat	आस्तरण, चटाई	*m∘ āstaraṇ, chaṭāī*
Mirror	आदर्श, दर्पण, मुकुर, आईना	*m∘ ādarśha, darpaṇ, mukur, āīnā*
Needle	सूचिका, सूई, सूची, सेवनी	*f∘ sūchikā, sūī, sūchī, sevanī*
Oven	चूल्हा	*m∘ chūlhā*
Paper	पत्र, कागज़	*m∘ patra, kāgaz*
Pen	कलम, लेखनी	*f∘ kalam, lekhanī*
Pillow	उपधान, बालिश, तकिया	*m∘ upadhān, takiyā*
Plate	थाली	*f∘ thālī*
Pot	कलश, कुंभ, घट, पात्र, बरतन	*m∘ kalaśh, kumbha, ghaṭ, pātra, bartan*
Rolling pin	वेलन	*m∘ vellan*
Rope	रज्जु, रस्सी	*f∘ rajju, rassī*
Sack	स्यूत, बोरा	*m∘ syūt, borā*
Soap	साबुन	*m∘ sābun*
Spoon	चमच	*m∘ chamach*
Stove	चूल्हा	*m∘ chulhā*
String	तन्तु, धागा; रज्जु, रस्सी	*m∘ tantu, dhagā; f∘rajju, rassī*
Swing	दोला, हिन्दोला, झूला	*m∘ dolā, hindolā, jhūlā*
Table	मञ्च, मेज़	*m∘ mañch, mez*
Thread	त्तन्तु, धागा; रज्जु, रस्सी	*m∘ tantu, dhagā; m∘ rajju, rassī*
Umbrella	छत्री; छाता	*f∘ chhatrī; m∘ chhātā*
Wire	तार	*m∘ tār*
Wok	कड़ाही	*f∘ kaḍāhī*

5.10 TOOLS **उपकरण, औज़ार** upakaraṇ, auzār

Anvil	अहरन, निहाई; संदान *f∘ aharan, nihāī; m∘ sandān*
Awl	आरी *f∘ ārī*
Axe	कुल्हाड़ी *m∘ kulhāḍī*
Blade	धार, पत्ती *f∘ dhār, pattī*
Chisel	छेनी *f∘ chhenī*
Clamp	शिकंजा *m∘ śhikañjā*
Compass	दिङ्निर्णययन्त्र *m∘ diṅgnirṇayayantra*
Drill	वेधनिका *f∘ vedhanikā*
File	पत्रपरशु, व्रश्चन *m∘ patraparaśhu, vraśhchan*
Gauge	मापक *m∘ māpak*
Hammer	हथौड़ा, घन, मुद्गर *m∘ hathauḍā, ghan, mudgar*
Knife	छुरी; चाकू *f∘ chhūrī, m∘ chākū*
Lever	उत्तोलक *m∘ uttolak*
Planer	तक्षणी, रंदा *f∘ takṣhaṇī; m∘ randā*
Plough	लाङ्गल, हल *m∘ lāṅgal, hal*
Razor	क्षुर, उस्तरा *m∘ kṣhur, ustarā*
Saw	आरी *f∘ ārī*
Scale, length	मापक *m∘ māpak*
Scale, weight	काँटा, पलड़ा, तराजू, तुला *m∘ kā̃ṭa, palḍā, tarāzū f∘ tulā*
Scissors	कैंची, कर्तरी, कतरनी *f∘ kaiñchī, kartarī, katarnī*
Sickle	लवित्र, हँसीया *m∘ lavitra; f∘ haṁsīyā*
Spade	खनित्र, फावड़ा; कुदाल *m∘ khanitra, fāvḍā, f∘ kudāl*
Syringe	पिचकारी सूई *f∘ pichkārī, sūī*

5.11 FLOWERS फूल–पत्ते fūl-patte

Bud कलिका, कली, मुकुल *f◦ kalikā, klī; m◦ kaul*

Flower कुसुम, पुष्प, प्रसूनं सुमन, फूल, गुल

m◦ kusum, puṣhpa, prasūna, suman, fūl, gul

Fragrance गन्ध, परिमल, वास, सुगन्ध, सुवास, सौरभ

m◦ gandha, parimal, vās, sugandh, sauvās, saurabha

Jasmine कुन्द, बकुल, मल्लिका, माधवी, मालती *m◦ kunda, bakul, f◦ mallikā, mādhavī, mālatī*

Lotus अम्बुज, अब्ज, अम्भोज, अम्भोरुह, अरविन्द, उत्पल, कमल, कुशेशय, तामरस, नलिन, पङ्कज, पंकेरुह, पद्म, पुष्कर, मरोरुह, महोत्पल, मृणालिनी, राजीव, विसप्रसून, शतपत्र, सरसिज, सरसीरुह, सहस्रपत्र, सारस

m◦ ambuj, abja, ambhoj, ambhoruha, aravinda, utpala, kamala, kuśheśhaya, tāmarasa, nalin, paṅkaj, paṅkeruh, padma, puṣhkar, maroruha, mahotpal, f◦ mriṇālinī, m◦ rājīva, viprasūna, śhatapatra, sarasija, sarasīruha, sahasrapatra, sāras

Lotus, blue कमल, कुवलय, इन्दीवर, नीलोत्पल *m◦ kamal, kuvalay, indīvar, nīlotpal*

Lotus, red कमल, कोकनद, रक्तोत्पल *m◦ kamal, kokanad, raktotpal*

Lotus, white कमल, कुमुद, पुण्डरीक, सीताभोज *m◦ kamal, kumud, puṇḍarīk, sītābhoj*

Marigold गन्धपुष्प, गेंदा *m◦ gandhapuṣhpa, gendā*

Narium कर्णिकार *m◦ karṇikar*

Nectar अमृत, पीयूष, मकरन्द, मरन्द, मधु, सुधा

m◦ amrit, pīyūṣha, makarand, marand, madhu, f◦ sudhā

Night Jasmine रजनीगन्धा *f◦ rajanīgandhā*

Petal दल, पत्र *m◦ dal, patra*

Pollen पराग, रज, रेणु *m◦ parāg, raj, reṇu*

Rose जपा, गुलाब *m∘ japā, gulāb*

Sunflower सूर्यपुष्प, सूरजमुखी *m∘ sūryapuṣhpa, sūrajmukhī*

5.12 FRUITS फल phala

Almond बादाम *m∘ bādām*

Apple आताफलं, सेब *m∘ ātāphal, seb*

Banana कदली, केला *f∘ kadalī, m∘ kelā*

Chestnut पांगर *m∘ pāṅgar*

Cocoanut नारियल, श्रीफल *m∘ nāriyal, ś́hrīfal*

Custard-apple सीताफल *m∘ sītāphala*

Date dry क्षुधाहर, खजूर, छुहारा *m∘ kṣhudhāhar, khajūr, chhuhārā*

Fig अञ्जीर *m∘ añjīr*

Grape द्राक्ष *m∘ drākṣha*

Guava अमरूद *m∘ amrūd*

Lemon जम्बीर, नींबू, मातुलङ्गक *m∘ jambīr, nimbū, mātulangak*

Mango आम्र, आम *m∘ āmra, ām*

Melon खरबूजा *m∘ kharabūjā*

Mulberry तूत *m∘ tūta*

Orange ऐरावत, नारंग, संतरा; मुसम्मी *m∘ airāvata, nāranga, santrā; f∘ musammī*

Papaya पपीता *f∘ papītā*

Peach आद्रालु, आडू, सतालू *m∘ ādrālu, āḍū, satālū*

Pineapple अनन्नास *m∘ anannās*

Plum बेर *m∘ ber*

Plum purple आलूचा, आलुबुखारा *m∘ ālūchā, alūbukhārā*

Pomegranate दाडिम, अनार *m∘ dāḍim, anār*

Tamarind अम्लिका, इमली *f∘ amlikā, imlī*

Walnut अक्षोट, अखरोट *m∘ akṣhoṭ, akharoṭ*

Watermelon कालिन्द, तरबूजा *m∘ kālind, tarbūjā*

5.13 VEGETABLES शाक-सब्ज़ी śhāk-sabzī

Beans सेम *f∘ sem*

Bittergourd करेला *m∘ karelā*

Cabbage बंदगोभी *f∘ bandgobhī*

Carrot गाजर *m∘ gājar*

Cauliflower गोभी *f∘ gobhī*

Celentro धनिया *m∘ dhāniyā*

Chilli मिरची *f∘ mirchī*

Cocoanut नारिकेल, नारियल *m∘ nārikel, nāriyal*

Coriander धनिया *m∘ dhāniyā*

Cucumber ककड़ी, खीरा *f∘ kakaḍī, khīrā*

Eggplant बैगन *m∘ baigan*

Lemon जम्बीर, नीबू *m∘ jambīra, nību*

Lotus, root भें *m∘ bhe̐*

Okra भिण्डी *f∘ bhiṇḍī*

Onion पलाण्डु, प्याज़ *m∘ palāṇḍu, pyāz*

Peas मटर *m∘ maṭar*

Potato आलु *m∘ ālu*

Pumpkin कुष्माण्ड, कुमड़ा, कद्दू, *m∘ kuṣhmāṇḍ, kumḍā, kaddū*

Raddish मूली *f∘ mūlī*

Rapini शाक *f∘ śhāk*

Salad	शद, सलाद *m∘ śhad, salād*
Spinach	पालक *f∘ pālak*
Sugarcane	इक्षु, गन्ना *m∘ ikṣhu, gannā*
Tomato	टमाटर *m∘ ṭamāṭar*
Turnip	शलगम *m∘ śhalgam*
Vegetable	शाक, सब्ज़ी *f∘ śhāk, sabzī*
Yam	अरबी, रतालू *m∘ arbī, ratālu*
Zuchini	तोरी, तुराई *f∘ torī, turāī*

5.14 PLANTS **वनस्पति** vanaspati

Bamboo	बाँस, वेणु *m∘ bā̃s, veṇu*
Banyan	अश्वत्थ, न्यग्रोध, वट *m∘ aśhvattha, nyagrodha, vaṭ*
Bark	वल्क, वल्कल, खाल *m∘ valka, valkala; f∘ khāl*
Branch	शाखा, डाल *f∘ śhākhā, ḍāl*
Bud	अङ्कुर, कुड्मल, पल्लव, मुकुल, कलिका, कली *m∘ aṅkur, kuḍmal, pallav, mukul, f∘ kalikā, kalī*
Bulb	कन्द *m∘ kand*
Chlorophyll	हरितद्रव्य *m∘ haritadravya*
Climber	वल्लरी, वल्ली, बेल *f∘ vallarī, vallī, bel*
Farm	क्षेत्र, खेत *m∘ kṣhetra, khet*
Flower	कुसुम, पुष्प, प्रसून, सुमन *m∘ kusum, puṣhpa, prasūna, suman*
Forest	अटवी, अरण्य, कानन, वन, विपिन, जंगल *f∘ aṭavī, m∘ araṇya, kānana, vana, vipin, jungle*
Grass	घास, तृण *m∘ ghās, triṇa*
Green	हरा, हरित *adj∘ harā, harit*

Guava	अमरूद *m◦ amrūd*
Gum	गोंद *m◦ gond*
Juice	रस *m◦ ras*
Leaf	पत्र, पर्ण, पत्ता *m◦ patra, parṇa, pattā*
Lemon	जम्बीर, नीबू *m◦ jambīr, nībū*
Mango	आम्रं *m◦ āmra*
Palm	ताल *m◦ tāl*
Peel	वल्क, छिलका, खाल *m◦ valka, chhilkā, khāl*
Pine	देवदार *m◦ devadār*
Pollen	पराग, रज, रेणु *m◦ parāg, raj, reṇu*
Root	मूल *m◦ mūl*
Seed	बीज *m◦ bīja*
Shade	छाया *f◦ chhāyā*
Stem	काण्ड, तना *m◦ kāṇḍ, tanā*
Stone	गुठली *f◦ guṭhalī*
Tamarind	इमली *f◦ imlī*
Teak	सागौन *m◦ sāgaun*
Thorn	कण्टक, काँटा, शल्य *m◦ kaṇṭak, kā̃ṭā, śhalya*
Tree	तरु, द्रुम, पादप, वनस्पति, विटप, वृक्ष *m◦ taru, druma, pādapa, vanaspati, viṭapa, vrikṣha*
Vine	लता, वल्लरी, वल्ली, बेल *f◦ latā, vallarī, vallī, bel*
Wood	काष्ठ, लकड़ी *m◦ kāṣhṭha, f◦ lakḍī*

5.15 FOOD STUFF **खाद्य–पेय** khādya-peya

Barley	यव, यौ *m◦ yav, yau*

Beverage	पान, पानीय, पेयं *m◦ pāna, pānīya, peya*
Bread	रोटी *m◦ roṭī*
Bread roṭi	रोटी, जीविका *f◦ roṭī, jīvikā*
Butter	नवनीत, मक्खन, माखन *m◦ navanīta, makkhan, mākhan*
Butter ghee	आज्य, घृत, घी *m◦ ājya, ghrita, ghī*
Buttermilk	तक्र, छाछ, मट्ठा *m◦ takra, chhāchh, maṭṭhā*
Black mung	उड़िद, मा *m◦ urid, mā*
Cheese	पनीर *m◦ panīr*
Chickpea	चना, छोला *m◦ chanā, chholā*
Coffee	कफघ्नी, कहवा *f◦ kafaghnī; m◦ kahavā*
Cook	पाचक, बल्लव, बावरची, रसोइया *m◦ pāchak, ballav, bāvarchi, rasoiyā*
Corn	शस्य, मक्की *m◦ śhasya; f◦ makkī*
Cream	मलाई *m◦ malāī*
Drink	पान, पानीय, पेय *m◦ pān, pānīy, peya*
Flour	आटा, पिष्ट *m◦ āṭā, pishṭa*
Food	अन्न, ओदन, भोजन *m◦ anna, odan, bhojan*
Grain	धान्य, शस्य *m◦ dhānya, śhasya*
Honey	मधु, शहद *m◦ madhu, śhahad*
Ice	हिम, बर्फ *m◦ hima, barf*
Kidney beans	राजमा *m◦ rajmā*
Kitchen	पाकशाला, रसोई *f◦ pākśhālā, rasoī*
Lentil	मसूर *m◦ masūr*
Marmalade	मुरब्बा *m◦ murabbā*
Meat	माँस *m◦ māṁs*
Milk	क्षीर, दुग्ध, दूध *m◦ kṣhīra, dugdha, dūdh*

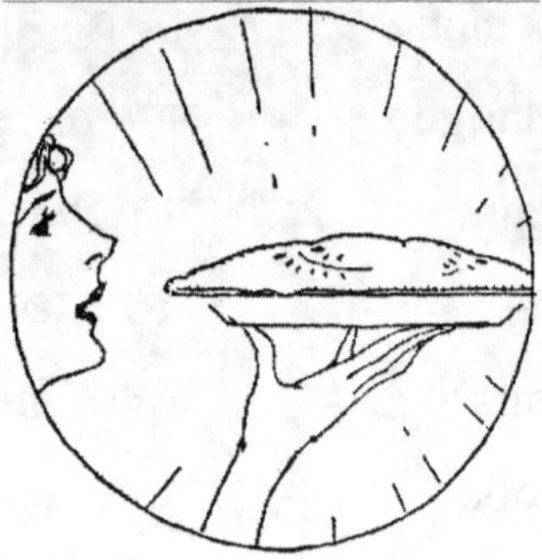

Mung green	मूँग *m◦ mūng*
Oil	तेल *m◦ tel*
Paddy	धान *m◦ dhān*
Pea	मटर *m◦ maṭar*
Pigeon-peas	रोंगी *f◦ rongī*
Pickle	अचार *m◦ achār*
Pulse	दाल *f◦ dāl*
Rice	चावल *m◦ chāval*
Rice cooked	भात, चावल *m◦ bhāt, chāval*
Salt	लवण, नमक *m◦ lavaṇa, namak*
Samosa	समोसा *m◦ samosā*
Sauce	चटनी *m◦ chaṭnī*
Seasum	तिल *m◦ til*
Sorghum	जवार *m◦ jawār*
Sugar	शर्करा, शक्कर, चीनी *f◦ śharkarā, śhakkar, chīnī*
Sweets	मिष्टान्न, मीठा, पक्वान *m◦ miṣhṭānna, mīṭhā, pakwān*
Syrup	चाशनी *m◦ chāśhanī*
Vinegar	सिरका *m◦ śirkā*
Wheat	गोधूम, गेहूँ *m◦ godhūm, gehū̃*
Water	पानी, अम्बु, अम्भ, उदक, जल, तोय, पय, पानीय, वारि, सलिल *m◦ pānī, ambu, ambha, udak, jal, toya, paya, pānīya, vāri, salil*
Wine	मदिरा, मद्य, सुरा, अंगूरी, शराब *f◦ madirā, madya, surā, aṅgūrī, śharāb*
Yougrt	दधि, दही *m◦ dadhi, dahī*

5.16 SPICES मसाले masāle

Aniseed सौंफ *f*◦ *saũf*

Asafoetida हिंगु, हींग *m*◦ *hiṅgu, hīṅg*

Basil तुलसी *f*◦ *tulsī*

Betel-nut ताम्बूल, सुपाड़ी *m*◦ *tāmbūlam, supāḍī*

Cardamom इलायची *f*◦ *ilāychī*

Cinnamon दालचीनी *m*◦ *dālchīnī*

Clove लवङ्ग *m*◦ *lavaṅg*

Coriander धनिया *m*◦ *dhāniyā*

Cumin जीरा *f*◦ *jīrā*

Garlic लशुन, लहसुन *m*◦ *laśhun, lahasun*

Ginger अदरक *m*◦ *adarak*

Ginger, dry सोंठ *f*◦ *śoṇṭh*

Hot spice सौरभ, गरम मसाला *m*◦ *saurabh, garam masālā*

Linseed अतसी, अलसी *f*◦ *atasī, alsī*

Mace जावित्री *f*◦ *jāvitrī*

Mango powder आम्रचूर्ण, आमचूर *m*◦ *āmracūrṇa, āmchūr*

Mint पुदिना *m*◦ *pudinā*

Mustard राई, सरसों *f*◦ *rājikā, sarsõ*

Nutmeg जातिफल, जायफल *m*◦ *jātifal, jāyfal*

Poppy seeds खसखस *m*◦ *khaskhas*

Pepper मिरची, मिर्च *m*◦ *mirchī, mirch*

Spice उपस्कर, मसाला *m*◦ *upaskar, masālā*

Saffron केसर *m*◦ *kesar*

Salt लवण, नमक *m*◦ *lavaṇ, namak*

Salt, rock सैन्धव नमक *m*◦ *saindhav namak*

Sugar शर्करा, शक्कर, चीनी *f∘ śharkarā, śhakkar, chīnī*

Tamarind इमली, चिञ्चा *f∘ imalī, chinchā*

Turmeric हलदी *f∘ haldī*

Walnut अक्षोट, अखरोट *m∘ akṣhoṭ, akhroṭ*

Yeast खमीर *m∘ khamīr*

5.17 MINERALS, METALS and JEWELS खनिज khanīj

Coal अंगार, कोयला *m∘ angar, koylā*

Brass पीतल्अ *m∘ pītal*

Copper ताम्र, तामा *m∘ tāmra, tāmā*

Diamond हीरा *m∘ hīrā*

Emerlad मरकत *m∘ marakat*

Gold कनक, काञ्चन, सुवर्ण, हेम, हिरण्य
m∘ kanak, kāñchan, suvarṇa, hem, hiraṇya

Iron अयस, लोह, लोहा *ayas, loha, lohā*

Jade अश्वक *m∘ aśhvak*

Jewel मणि, रत्न *m∘ maṇi, ratna*

Lead सीसा *m∘ sīsā*

Marble मर्मर, संगमरमर *m∘ marmar, saṅgmarmar*

Mercury पारद, पारा *m∘ pārada, pārā*

Mica अभ्रक *m∘ abhrak*

Mine खान, खदान *m∘ khān, khadān*

Mineral खनिज, धातु *m∘ khanij, f∘ dhātu*

Opal पुलक, विमलक *m∘ pulak, vimalak*

Pearl मुक्ता, मुक्ताफल, मौक्तिक, मोती *f∘ muktā, muktāfal, mauktik, motī*

Ruby	पद्मराग, माणिक्य, लोहितक	*m∘ padmarāg, māṇikya, lohitak*
Sapphire	इन्द्रनील, नील,	*m∘ indranīl, nīl*
Silver	रजत, रूप्य, चाँदी	*m∘ rajat, rūpya, chāndī*
Soil	मृद्, मृत्तिका, मिट्टी	*f∘ mrid, mrittikā, miṭṭī*
Sulphur	गन्धक	*m∘ gandhak*
Tin	रांगा	*m∘ rāṅgā*
Topaz	पीताश्म	*m∘ pītāśhma*
Turquoise	हरिताश्म	*m∘ haritāśhma*
Zinc	जस्त, जस्ता	*f∘ jast, jastā*

5.18 MUSIC सङ्गीत Sangīta

Ascending आरोह *m∘ āroha*

Bell घण्टा *f∘ ghanṭā*

Bugle शृङ्ग, सिंग *m∘ śhriṅga, sīng*

Conch कम्बु, शंख *m∘ kambu, śhankha*

Cymbal झाँझ, करताल, मजीरा, छेना *m∘ jhāñjh, kartāl, majīrā, chhenā*

Descending अवरोह *m∘ avaroha*

Devotional song भजन *m∘ bhajan*

Drum डिण्डिम, ढोल भेरी, दुन्दुभि, *m∘ ḍinḍim, ḍhol; f∘ bherī dundubhī*

Flute मुरली, बंसी, वेणु *f∘ muralī, bansī, veṇu*

Guitar Indian पिनाकी, वल्लकी, विपञ्ची, वीणा, सारंगी
f∘ pinākī, vallakī, vipanchī, vīnā, sārangī

Harp पिनाकी, वल्लकी, विपंची, सारंगी *f∘ pinākī, vallakī, vipanchī, sārangī*

Kettledrum डिण्डिमा, दुन्दुभि, भेरी *f∘ ḍinḍimā, dundubhi, bherī*

Melody राग *m∘ rāg*

Note स्वर *m∘ svar*

Notation स्वरलिपी *f∘ svaralipī*

Prayer आरती *m∘ ārtī*

Octave सप्तक *m∘ saptak*

Rhythm ताल *m∘ tāl*

Song गान, गीत *m∘ gān, gīt*

Tabor मृदङ्ग *m∘ mridang*

Tambourine कर्णदुन्दुभि *f∘ karṇadundubhi*

Tempo लय *m∘ laya*

Tomtom पटह, भेरी *m∘ paṭaha, f∘ bherī*

Violin पिनाकी, सारङ्गी *m∘ pinākī, sāraṅgī*

Whistle सीटी *f∘ sīṭī*

5.19 PROFESSIONS व्यवसाय vyavasāya

Actor अभिनेता, नट *m∘ abhinetā, naṭ*

Actress अभिनेत्री, नटी *f∘ abhinetrī, naṭī*

Advocate पक्ष-समर्थक, वक्ता *m∘ pakṣha-samarthaka, vaktā*

Agent प्रतिनिधि *m∘ pratinidhi*

Artizan कलाकार, चित्रकर, शिल्पी *m∘ kalākār, chitrakar, śhilpī*

Artist कलाकार, चित्रकर, शिल्पी *m∘ kalākār, chitrakar, śhilpī*

Assassin घातक, हन्ता, वधिक, हत्यारा *m∘ ghātaka, hantā, vadhik, hatyārā*

Barber नापित, नाई *m∘ nāpit, nāī*

Blacksmith लोहकार, लोहार *m∘ lohakār, lohār*

Boatman नाविक, केवट, खेवैया, मल्लाह, धीवर, माँझी

m∘ nāvika, kavaṭ, khevaiyā, mallāh, dhīvar, māñjhī

Broker	आढ़तिया, दलाल	*m◦ āḍhtiyā, dalāl*
Butcher	कसाई	*m◦ kasāī*
Butler	भण्डारी	*m◦ bhaṇḍārī*
Carpenter	काष्ठकार, बढ़ई, सुतार, खाती	*m◦ kāṣṭhakār, baḍhaī, sutār, khātī*
Carrier	वाहक	*m◦ vāhak*
Cashier	खजानची	*m◦ khajāñchī*
Chemist	रसज्ञ, रसायनी	*m◦ rasagya, rasāyanī*
Clerk	लिपिक, मुंशी	*m◦ lipik, muṁshī*
Conductor	अग्रणी, मार्गदर्शक	*m◦ agraṇī, mārgadarśhak*
Confectioner	हलवाई	*m◦ halwāī*
Constable	सिपाही	*m◦ sipāhī*
Contractor	ठेकेदार	*m◦ ṭhekedār*
Cook	बावरची, रसोइया	*m◦ bāvarchī, rasoiyā*
Dancer	नर्तक *m◦ nartak;* नर्तकी	*f◦ nartakī*
Dentist	दन्त वैद्य	*m◦ danta vaidya*
Doctor	वैद्य	*m◦ vaidya*
Dramist	नाटककार	*m◦ nāṭakakār*
Editor	संपादकः	*m◦ sampādak*
Engineer	अभियन्ता, यन्त्रकार	*m◦ abhiyantā, yantrakār*
Examiner	परीक्षक	*m◦ parīkṣhak*
Farmer	कृषक, किसान	*m◦ kriṣhak, kisān*
Fisherman	धीवर, मछुआ	*m◦ dhīvar, machhuā*
Florist	मालाकार	*m◦ mālākār*
Gardener	माली, बागवान	*m◦ mālī, bāgvān*
Goldsmith	सुनार, स्वर्णकार	*m◦ sunār, svarṇakār*

Guard	रक्षक, पहरेदार, रक्षी *m∘ rakṣhak, paharedār, rakṣhī*
Inspector	निरीक्षक *m∘ nirīkṣhak*
Jeweler	जौहरी, मणिकार *m∘ jauharī, maṇikār*
Landlord	भू स्वामी *m∘ bhū svāmī*
Lawyer	विधिज्ञ, वकील *m∘ vidhigya, vakīl*
Magician	इन्द्रजालिक, जादूगर *m∘ indrajālik, jādūgar*
Manager	प्रबंधक, व्यवस्थापक *m∘ prabandhak, vyavasthāpak*
Mason	राज, राजगीर, थबई *m∘ rāj, rājgīr, thabaī*
Merchant	वणिक, दुकानदार, सौदागर, व्यापारी *m∘ vaṇik, dukāndār, saudāgar, vyāpārī*
Messenger	दूत *m∘ dūt*
Midwife	सूतिका *f∘ sūtikā*
Milkman	आभीर, गोप, दोहक *m∘ ābhīra, gop, dohak*
Milkmaid	आभीरी, गोपिका, गोपी *f∘ ābhīrī, gopikā, gopī*
Novelist	उपन्यासकार *m∘ upanyāskār*
Nurse	परिचारिका; धाय, दाई *f∘ parichārikā, dhāy, dāī*
Operator	कारक, कर्ता *m∘ kārka, kartā*
Painter	रंगवाला *m∘ raṅgvālā*
Peon	चपरासी *m∘ chaprāsī*
Photographer	छायाचित्रकार *m∘ chhāyāchitrakār*
Physician	वैद्य *m∘ vaidya*
Poet	कवि *m∘ kavi*
Police	रक्षक, रक्षी, आरक्षक *m∘ rakṣhak, rakṣhī, ārakṣhak*
Politician	राजनीतिज्ञ *m∘ rājanītigya*
Postman	पत्रवाह, डाकीया *m∘ patravāha, ḍākīyā*
Priest	पण्डित, पुरोधस, पुरोहित *m∘ paṇḍit, purodhas, purohit*

Printer मुद्रक *m◦ mudrak*

Publisher प्रकाशक *m◦ prakāśhak*

Retailer परचूनिया *m◦ parchūniyā*

Sailor नाविक, नौवाहक, पोतवाह, मल्लाह *m◦ nāvik, nauvāhak, potavāha, mallāh*

Sculptor तक्षक, मूर्तिकार *m◦ takṣhak, mūrtikār*

Shoe-maker चर्मकार, मोची *m◦ charmakār, mochī*

Shopkeeper दुकानदार *m◦ dukāndār*

Sorcerer मान्त्रिक *m◦ māntrik*

Surgeon चिकित्सक, शल्यकार *m◦ chikitsak, śhalyakār*

Tailor सूचिक, दरजी *m◦ sūchika, darjī*

Teacher अध्यापक, गुरु, शिक्षक *m◦ adhyapaka, guru, śhikṣhak*

Treasurer कोषाध्यक्ष *m◦ koṣhādhyakṣh*

Waiter परिवेषक, परिवेष्टा, सेवक, बैरा *m◦ pariveṣhaka, pariveṣhṭā, sevaka, bairā*

Washerman रजक, धोबी *m◦ rajak, dhobī*

Washerwoman रजकी, धोबिन *f◦ rajakī, dhobin*

Watchman रक्षक, चौकीदार, पहरेदार *m◦ rakṣhak, chaukīdār, paharedār*

Weaver जुलाहा *m◦ julāhā*

5.20 BUSINESS व्यापार vyāpār

Account गणना, हिसाब, लेखा, खाता *f◦ gaṇanā, m◦ hisāb, lekhā, khātā*

Accountant गणक, लेखाकार *m◦ gaṇak, lekhākār*

Advance पेशगी, उपनिधि, अग्रिम-धन *f◦ peśhagī, upanidhi, agrimdhan*

Advancement उत्कर्ष, उन्नति, वर्धन *m◦ utkarṣha, f◦ unnati, m◦ vardhan*

Advantage लाभ, हित, फ़ायदा, नफ़ा *m◦ lābh, hit, fāydā, nafā*

Adventure साहस, जोखिम *m◦ sāhas, jokhim*

Adverse	प्रतिकूल, विरुद्ध *adj◦ pratikūl, viruddha*
Advertise	विज्ञापन. *m◦ vijñāpan*
Annual	वार्षिक, सालाना *adj◦ vārṣhik, sālānā*
Annuity	वार्षिक वेतन *m◦ vārṣhik vetan*
Annulment	लोप *m◦ lop*
Application	याचना पत्र *m◦ yāchanā patra*
Arrears	ऋणशेष *m◦ riṇaśheṣh*
Assistant	सहायक, सहयोगी, मददगार *m◦ sahāyak, sahayogī, madadgār*
Average	स्थूल प्रमाण, औसत *m◦ sthūl pramāṇ, ausat*
Balance	अवशेष, शेष, बकाया *m◦ avaśheṣha, śheṣha, bakāyā*
Balance scale	तुला, काँटा, तराजू *f◦ tulā; ◦ kāṇṭā, tarājū*
Bank	धनागार, अधिकोष *m◦ dhanāgār, adhikoṣh*
Bankruptcy	दिवाला *m◦ diwālā*
Broker	आढ़तिया, दलाला *m◦ āḍhatiyā, dalāl*
Brokerage	दलाली *f◦ dalālī*
Business	नियोग, यवहार, व्यवसाय, व्यापार *m◦ niyog, yavahār, vyavasāy, vyāpār*
Businessman	नियोगी, व्यवसायी, व्यापारी *m◦ niyogī, vyavasāyī, vyāpārī*
Buyer	क्रेता, खरीददार *m◦ kretā, khariddār*
Capital	मूलद्रव्य *m◦ mūla-dravya*
Cash	नगदी, रोकड *f◦ nagdī, rokaḍ*
Cell phone	जङ्गम दूरवाणी *f◦ jaṅgam dūravāṇī*
Charges	मूल्य, दाम *m◦ mūlya, dām*
Clerk	लिपीकार, मुंशी *m◦ lipīkār, muṁśhī*
Coin	टंक, मुद्रा, सिक्का *m◦ ṭaṅk, f◦ mudrā; m◦ sikkā*
Commerce	क्रयविक्रय, निगम, वाणिज्य, व्यापार *m◦ krayavikray, nigam, vāṇijya, vyāpār*

Company	परिषद् *f∘ parișhad*
Courier	दूत, वार्ताहर *m∘ dūta, vārtāhar*
Court	न्यायालय, अदालत, कचहरी *m∘ nyāyālay, m∘ adālat, kachaharī*
Consumer	विनियोजक, उपभोक्ता *m∘ viniyojak, upabhoktā*
Customer	क्रेता, ग्राहक *m∘ kretā, grāhak*
Credit	प्रतिष्ठा, विश्वास, भरोसा *f∘ pratișhțhā, m∘ viśhvās, bharosā*
Creditor	ऋणदाता, धनिक *m∘ riņadātā, dhanik*
Current	प्रचलित, वर्तमान, विद्यमान *adj∘ prachalit, vartamān, vidyamān*
Currency	प्रचलन, प्रचलित मुद्रा *m∘ prachalan, f∘ prachalit mudrā*
Daily	दैनिक *adj∘ dainik*
Debt	ऋण *m∘ riņa*
Demand	अभियोग, याचना *m∘ abhiyoga, f∘ yāchnā*
Deposit	निक्षेप *m∘ nikșhep* (ii) a deposit as an advance उपनिधि *m∘ upanidhi*
Depreciation	अपकर्ष, अवमानता *m∘ apakarșha, f∘ avamānatā*
Discount	उद्धृतभाग *m∘ uddhritabhāg*
Document	पत्र, लेख *m∘ patra, lekh*
Draft	आलेख्य *m∘ ālekhya*
Duty	कर, शुल्क *m∘ kar, śhulka*
Earnings	वेतन *m∘ vetan*
Economy	अर्थशास्त्र, वित्तशास्त्र *m∘ arthaśhāstra, vittaśhāstra*
Electricity	विद्युत् *f∘ vidyut*
Employee	कर्मचारी, नौकर *m∘ karmachārī, naukar*
Employer	नियोजक, मालिक *m∘ niyojak, mālik*
Endowment	वृत्ति *f∘ vritti*
Exchange	परिवर्तन, विनिमय *m∘ parivartan, vinimay*

Expense	व्यय, खर्च *m॰ vyay, kharch*
Export	निर्यात *m॰ niryāt*
Factory	कारखाना *f॰ kārkhānā,*
Finance	धन, वित्त, अर्थ *m॰ dhan, vitta, artha*
Financier	कोशाध्यक्ष, धनाधिकारी *m॰ kośhādhyakṣha, dhanādhikārī*
Fixed	निश्चित *adj॰ niśhchit*
Foreign	विदेशीय *adj॰ videśhīya*
Fraud	धोखा, *m॰ dhokhā*
Freight	भाड़ा *m॰ bhāḍā*
Fund	पुंजी, निधि, कोष, *m॰ puñjī, nidhi; m॰ koṣh*
Goods	द्रव्य, माल, सौदा; सामग्री, *m॰ dravya, māl, saudā; f॰ sāmagrī*
Gross	स्थूल, मोटा *adj॰ sthūl, moṭā*
Import	आयात *m॰ āyāt*
Income	आय, आमदनी; वेतन *m॰ āya, āmadanī; m॰ vetana*
Industry	उद्योग, व्यवसाय *m॰ udyoga, vyavasāy*
Inflation	स्फीति, बढ़त *m॰ sfīti, baḍhat*
Insurance	बीमा *m॰ bimā*
Job	काम, नौकरी *m॰ karma; f॰ naukrī*
Joint	जोड़., संयुक्त *adj॰ joḍ, saṁyukta*
Labour	उद्यम, श्रम *m॰ udyam, śhram*
Labourer	मजदूर *m॰ mazdūr*
Land	भूमि, जमीन *f॰ bhūmi; zamīn*
Ledger	खाता, पंजी *m॰ khātā; f॰ pañjī*
Legal	वैध, कानूनी *adj॰ vaidh, kānūnī*
Letter	पत्र, खत *m॰ patra, khat*

Loan	ऋण, कर्ज, उधार	*m◦ ṛṇa, karj, udhār*
Lock	ताला	*m◦ tālā*
Locker	कोष्ठ, संदूक	*m◦ koṣhṭha, sandūk*
Loss	अपचय, हानि, नुक़सान	*m◦ apachay, f◦ hāni; m◦ nuksān*
Management	शासन, प्रबंध, इंतजाम, व्यवस्था	*m◦ śhāsan, prabandha, intajām; f◦ vyavasthā*
Market	बाजार,	*m◦ bāzār*
Merchandise	माल, सामान	*m◦ māl, sāmān*
Merchant	वाणिक, व्यापारी, सौदागर, दुकानदार	*m◦ vāṇik, vyāpārī, saudāgar, dukāndār*
Mint	टकसाल	*f◦ ṭaksāl*
Mobile phone	जङ्गमदूरवाणी	*f◦ jaṅgama-dūravāṇī*
Money	अर्थ, धन, द्रव्य, वित्त, पैसा	*m◦ artha, dhana, dravya, vitta, paisā*
Moneyless	धनहीन, निर्धन	*adj◦ dhanahīn, nirdhan*
Monthly	मासिक	*adj◦ māsik*
Net	अशेष; शुद्ध, खालिस, असली	*adj◦ aśheṣha; śhuddha, khālis, aslī*
Notice	निर्देश, सूचना	*m◦ nirdeśh, f◦ sūchanā*
Occupation	व्यवसाय, धंधा, पेशा	*m◦ vyavasāu, dhandhā, peśhā*
Office	कार्यालय, दफ्तर	*m◦ kāryālay, daftar*
Officer	अधिकारी	*m◦ adhikārī*
Owner	स्वामी, मालिक	*m◦ swāmī, mālik*
Partner	सहभागी, साथी, संगी, साझेदार	*m◦ sahabhāgī, sāthī, saṅgī, sāzedār*
Phone	दूरवाणी	*f◦ dūravāṇī*
Price	मूल्य, कीमत, दाम	*m◦ mūlya, kīmat, dām*
Private	स्व, व्यक्तिगत, खास	*adj◦ sva, vyaktigat, khās*
Profit	आय, लाभ, हित, फायदा	*m◦ āy, lābh, hit, fāydā*
Public	जन, लोग	*adj◦ jan, log*

Publication	प्रकाशन *m◦ prakāśhan*
Rate	गति, मान *f◦ gati, m◦ mān*
Receipt	स्वीकारपत्र *m◦ svīkār-patra*
Rent	कर, भाड़ा *m◦ kar, bhāḍā*
Sale	विक्रय, विक्री *m◦ vikraya, f◦ vikrī*
Saving	सञ्चय, संग्रह, बचत *m◦ sañchay, saṁgraha; f◦ bachat*
Seal	मुद्रा, मुहर *f◦ mudrā, muhar*
Secretary	सचिव *m◦ sachiv*
Servant	कर्मकरी, सेवक *m◦ karmakar, sevak*
Shop	दुकान *f◦ dukān*
Signature	हस्ताक्षर *m◦ hastākṣhar*
Stamp	मुद्रा, ठप्पा *f◦ mudrā; m◦ ṭhappā*
Stock	सञ्चय, माल, सामान *m◦ sañchay, māl, sāmān*
Store, shop	दुकान *f◦ dukān*
Store, warehouse	भंडार *m◦ bhaṇḍār*
Trade	वाणिज्य, व्यवसाय, व्यापार *m◦ vāṇijya, vyavasāy, vyāpār*
Telephone	दूरवाणी *f◦ dūravāṇī*
Treasury	कोष, कोषागार *m◦ koṣha, koṣhāgār*
Warehouse	कोष, कोषागार, भाण्डार *m◦ koṣh, koṣhāgār, bhāṇḍār*
Wholesale	थोक *m◦ thok*

5.21 WARFARE युद्ध yuddha

Aggression	अतिक्रमण, आक्रमण *m◦ atikramaṇ, ākramaṇ*
Aggressor	अतिक्रमक, आक्रमक *m◦ atikramak, ākramak*
Airforce	वायुसेना *f◦ vāyusenā*

Arm	अस्त्र, आयुध, शस्त्र, शस्त्रास्त्र	*m◦ astra, āyudh, ś́hastr, ś́hastrāstr*
Armless	नि:शस्त्र	*adj◦ nihś́hastra*
Army	दल, वाहिनी, सेना, सैन्य	*m◦ dal, f◦ vāhinī, senā, m◦ sainya*
Armament	युद्धोपकरण	*m◦ yuddhopakaraṇ*
Armour	कवच	*m◦ kavach*
Armour, head	शिरस्त्राण	*m◦ ś́hirastrāṇ*
Armoury	शस्त्रागार	*m◦ ś́hastrāgār*
Arrow	इषु, बाण, शर	*m◦ iṣhu, bāṇ, ś́har*
Atom bomb	अण्वास्त्र	*m◦ aṇvāstra*
Attack	आक्रमण	*m◦ ākramaṇ*
Battle	युद्ध, रण, समर, संग्राम, लड़ाई	*m◦ yuddha, raṇ, samar, sangrām, laḍāī*
Battle array	व्यूह	*m◦ vyūha*
Battle cry	नारा	*m◦ nārā*
Battle field	रण, रणभूमि, रणाङ्गण, समर, मैदान	*m◦ raṇa, f◦ raṇabhūmi, m◦ raṇāṅgaṇa, m◦ samar, maidāna*
Blockade	अवरोध, रोक	*m◦ avarodh, f◦ rok*
Bomb	अग्न्यस्त्र, बम	*m◦ agnyastra, bam*
Bloodshed	नृहत्या, रक्तपात	*f◦ nrihatyā, m◦ raktapāt*
Blow	आघात, प्रहार	*m◦ āghāt, prahār*
Blunder	अनवधान	*m◦ anavadhān*
Bow	कोदण्ड, चाप, धनु, धनुष	*m◦ kodaṇḍa, chāp, dhanu, dhanuṣh*
Bow-man	धनुर्धर, धन्वी	*m◦ dhanurdhar, dhanvī*
Bow string	गुण, ज्या, डोरी	*m◦ guṇa, f◦ jyā, ḍorī*
Brave	धीर, पराक्रमी, वीर, शूर, साहसी	*adj◦ dhīr, parākramī, vīr, ś́hūr, sāhasī*
Bull's eye	लक्ष्य	*m◦ lakṣhya*

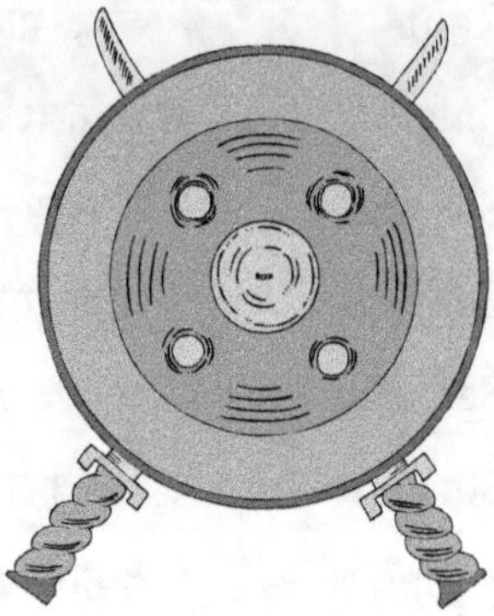

Bullet	गोली *f◦ golī*
Campaign	युद्धप्रवृत्ति *f◦ yuddhapravritti*
Cannon	तोप *f◦ top*
Cartridge	गोली *f◦ golī*
Cavalry	अश्व दल *m◦ aśhva dal*
Chariot	रथ *m◦ rath*
Civil-war	जन प्रकोप *m◦ jana prakop*
Cold war	शीत युद्ध *m◦ śhīta yuddha*
Colonel	सेनाध्यक्ष *m◦ senādhyakṣha*
Combat	द्वन्द्व, युद्ध, समर *m◦ dvandva, yuddha, samar*
Combatant	भट, योद्धा, वीर *m◦ bhaṭ, yoddhā, vīr*
Command	अधिकार, अधिपत्य, प्रभुत्व *m◦ adhikār, adhipatya, prabhutva*
Commander	चमूपति, सेनाध्यक्ष, सेनानायक, सेनानी *m◦ chamūpati, senādhyakṣha, senānāyak, senānī*
Death	निधन, मरण *m◦ nidhan, maraṇ*
Defeat	अभिभव, पराजय, पराभव *m◦ abhibhav, parājay, parābhav*
Defence	त्राण, रक्षण, रक्षा, संरक्षण *m◦ trāṇ, rakṣhaṇ, f◦ rakṣhā, m◦ saṁrakṣhaṇ*
Democracy	प्रजातन्त्र, लोकतन्त्र *n. prajātantra, loktantra*
Destroyer	ध्वंसक, नाशक *m◦ dhvaṁsak, nāśhak*
Dictator	एकाधिपति, तानाशाह *m◦ ekādhipati, tānāśhāh*
Enemy	अरि, रिपु, वैरी, शत्रु *m◦ ari, ripu, vairī, śhatru*
Fight	द्वन्द्व, युद्ध, रण, समर, संग्राम *m◦ dvandva, yuddha, raṇ, samar, sangrām*
Fighter plane	युद्धविमान *m◦ yuddhavimān*
Fist fight	मुष्टियुद्ध *m◦ muṣhṭiyuddha*
Foot soldier	पदाति, पैदल *m◦ padāti, paidal*

Fort कोट, कीला, दुर्ग *m∘ koṭ, kilā, durga*

Fortification कोट, परिखा *m∘ koṭ, f∘ parikhā*

Freedom स्वातन्त्र्य *m∘ svātantrya*

Gun बंदूक *f∘ bandūk*

Gunpowder बारूद *f∘ bārūd*

Hand-to-hand fight बाहुयुद्ध *m∘ bāhuyuddha*

Helmet शिरस्त्राण, टोप *m∘ śhirastrāṇ, ṭop*

Hostage ओल, बंधक *m∘ ol, bandhak*

Human shield मनुष्याश्रय *m∘ manuṣhyāśhray*

Indemnity प्रतिफल, हानिपूरण *m∘ pratiphal, hānipūraṇ*

Marine fight नौयुद्ध *m∘ nauyuddha*

Mariner नाविक, पोतवाह *m∘ nāvik, potvāh*

Maritime समुद्रीय *adj∘ samudrīya*

Medal पदक, मुद्रा *m∘ padak, f∘ mudrā*

Mutiny द्रोह, संक्षोभः *m∘ droha, saṅkṣhobha*

Navy जलसेना, नौसेना *f∘ jalasenā, nausenā*

Non-violence अहिंसा, शान्ति *f∘ ahimsā, śhānṭi*

Occupation कब्ज़ा *m∘ kabjā*

Peace शांति *f∘ śhānti*

Plan of action प्रयुक्ति *f∘ prayukti*

Prisoner of war युद्धबन्दी *m∘ yuddhabandī*

Recruit नव सैनिक *m∘ nava sainik*

Sacrifice त्याग *m∘ tyāg*

Secret गुह्य, गौप्य, रहस्य *m∘ guhya, gaupya, rahasya*

Service सेवा *f∘ sevā*

Ship	जलयान, पोत, नाव	*m◦ jalayān, pot; f◦ nāv*
Signal	सङ्केत	*m◦ sanket*
Shot	क्षेप	*m◦ kṣhep*
Siege	घेरा, घेराबंदी	*m◦ gherā; f◦ gherābandī*
Slaughter	संहार	*m◦ saṁhāhār*
Strategy	युद्धकौशल	*m◦ yuddhakauśhal*
Spear	कुन्त, भाला, बरछा	*m◦ kunt, bhālā, barchhā*
Spy	गुप्तचर, चर	*m◦ guptachar, char*
Sword	असि, कृपाण, खड्ग, तलवार,	*f◦ asi, m◦ kripāṇ, khaḍga, talwār*
Traitor	राजद्रोही, देशद्रोही	*m◦ rājdrohī, deśhdrohī*
Treaty	सन्धान, सन्धि	*m◦ sandhān, f◦ sandhi*
Trechery	द्रोह	*m◦ droha*
Trench	खंदक, खाई	*m◦ khandak, f◦ khāī*
Troops	सैनिक, सैन्यं	*m◦ sainik, m◦ sainya*
Victor	जिष्णु, जेता, विजेता	*m◦ jiṣhṇu, jetā, vijetā*
Victory	जय, विजय	*m◦ jaya, vijaya*
War	युद्ध, रण, समर, संग्राम, लड़ाई	*m◦ yuddha, raṇ, samar, sangrām, laḍāī*
Warfare	वैर	*m◦ vair*
War time	युद्धकाल	*m◦ yuddhakāl*
World war	महायुद्ध, विश्वयुद्ध	*m◦ mahāyuddha, viśhvayuddha*

5. 22 TIME

समय samay

COUNTING THE TIME ELEMENTS

Time समय, काल, वेला *m◦ samay, kāl, velā*

Second	क्षण, निमिष *m◦ kṣhaṇ, nimiṣh*
Minute	पल, कला *m◦ pal, f◦ kalā*
Hour	घण्टा *f◦ ghaṇṭā*
Day	दिन, दिवस, वार, तिथि *m◦ din, divas, vār, f◦ tithi*
Night	रात्रि, निशा *f◦ rātri, niśhā*
Dawn	उषा, प्रभात *f◦ uṣhā, m◦ prabhāt*
Noon	मध्यदिन, मध्याह्न *m◦ madhya-din, madhyanha*
Afternoon	अपराह्न, पराह्न, दोपहर *m◦ aparānha, parānha, f◦ dopahar*
Midnight	मध्यरात्रि, अर्धरात्रि *f◦ madhyarātri, ardharātri*
Week	सप्ताह, हफ्ता *m◦ saptāha, haftā*
Year	वर्ष, वत्सर, अब्द, समा।*m◦ varṣha, vatsara, abda, f◦ samā*
Age	कल्प, युग *m◦ kalpa, yuga*
Day-before-yesterday	परसों *adv◦ arsŏ̐*
Yesterday	कल *adv◦ kal*
Today	अद्य, आज *adv◦ adya, āj*
Now	अब, अभी, सम्प्रति *adv◦ ab, abhī, samprati*
Tomorrow	कल *adv◦ kal*
Day-after-tomorrow	परसों *adv◦ parsŏ̐*
Always	सदा, सर्वदा, सतत, निरन्तर *adv◦ sadā, sarvadā, satat, nirantar*
Periodically	समयतः, कभी-कभी *adv◦ samayatah, kabhī-kabhī*
Sometime	एकदा, कभी *adv◦ ekadā, kabhī*
Sometimes	क्वचित्, कदाचित् *adv◦ kvachit, kadāchit*
Maybe	कदाचित् *adv◦ kadāchit*
Never	न कदापि, कभी नहीं *adv◦ na kadāpi, kabhī nahī̐*
Eever	कभी भी *adv◦ kabhī bhī*

(2) DECLENSIONS AND CASES

कारक और विभक्ति

The form of a Noun, Pronoun or Adjective (substantive) by which it connects or relates with the other words in a sentence, that form is called the declension (*kārak* कारक) of that substantive. And, the suffix (*pratyay* प्रत्यय) that is attached to the substantive to connect it to the other words of the sentence is called the Case Suffix (विभक्ति प्रत्यय). There are eight such case suffixes in Hindi Grammar. The process of forming the Declensions (कारक) of a substantive is called Inflection (विभक्ति रूपांतरण) of that Noun, Pronoun or Adjective.

TABLE 1 : The Case Suffixes

Form रूप	*Kārak*	कारक	Name of Case	विभक्ति का नाम	Suffix	प्रत्यय
Subject	*karttā*	कर्ता	**Nominative**	प्रथमा	*ne**	ने*
Object	*karma*	कर्म	**Accusative**	द्वितीया	*ko*	को
Instrument	*karaṇ*	करण	**Instrumental**	तृतीया	*sae*	से
For whom	*sampradān*	संप्रदान	**Dative**	चतुर्थी	*ke liye*	के लिए
From where	*Apādān*	अपादान	**Ablative**	पंचमी	*se*	से
Relation	*sambamdh*	संबंध	**Possessive**	षष्ठी	*kā*	का
To where	*adhikaraṇ*	अधिकरण	**Locative**	सप्तमी	*maẽ par*	में, पर
Address	*sambodhan*	संबोधन	**Vocative**	संबोधन	*he! are! aho!*	हे! अरे! अहो!

* Normally, the Subject takes no suffix, but when the action is Transitive in Perfect Tense then only in that case the subject takes *ne* (ने) suffix. Now the Verb changes according to the Gender and Number of the Object and the Subject has no effect on the Verb.

CHARACTERISTICS OF THE DECLENSIONS AND CASES

कारक और विभक्ति के गुण स्वभाव

(1) Kartā Kārak, Nominative Case (कर्त्ता कारक, प्रथमा-विभक्ति)

The subject of the verb, i.e. the doer of the action. The form of the noun used for indicating the doer (*kartā* कर्ता) of the action (*kriyā* क्रिया) in a sentence is the *kartā kārak* (कर्त्ता कारक) of that sentence. The suffix (pratyay प्रत्यय) attached to the noun to form the *kartā Kārak* is the Nominative Case Suffix (प्रथमा विभक्ति प्रत्यय).

Scope : In Active Voice, this noun (संज्ञा) is the doer or subject of the sentence. In Passive voice, it is the object. Normally, in Nominative Case, the Subject takes no suffix, but if the action is a Transitive Verb in any Perfect Tense then, only in that case, the subject takes *ne* (ने) suffix. As a result, now the Verb changes according to the Gender and Number of the Object the Subject has no effect on the Verb. e.g. **(1)** राम केला खाता है, राम रोटी खाता है, सीता केला खाती है, सीता रोटी खाती है, राम केले खाता है, सीता केले खाती है, etc. **(2)** राम ने केला खाया है, राम ने रोटी खायी है, सीता ने केला खाया है, सीता ने रोटी खायी है, राम ने केले खाये हैं, सीता ने केले खाये हैं, etc.

(2) Karma Kārak, Accusative Case (कर्म कारक, द्वितीया विभक्ति)

On whom the action is performed.

The object (*karma* कर्म) on which the subject performs the verb (क्रिया) is the *karma kārak* (कर्म कारक) of that sentence. The suffix attached to the object to form the *karma kārak* is Accusative Case Suffix (द्वितीया विभक्ति प्रत्यय).

Scope : Secondary Suffixes (उपपद प्रत्यय) of the Accusative Case are - to what, to who (को); to where (को), below (अध:, अधोऽध:, अध्यधि), above (ऊर्ध्व), between (अन्तर, बीच), after (अनु), along (अनु), towards (प्रति), in front of (अग्रे, अग्रत:, पुर:, पुरत:, समक्ष), around (अभित:), on all sides of (परित:), on both sides of (उभयत:), verrywhere (सर्वत:), to fie on (धिक्), without (विना, ऋते, अन्तरेण), without concerning (बिना), to go to (गति – गमन चलन,

वहन), to become, the time period (वर्ष, दिन); to sleep upon, to lie down (अधि√शी), to resort to, to reside, to dwell, to occupy (अधि√स्थ, अधि√आस्, अधि√वस्, आ√वस्, अनु√वस्, उप√वस्), following (अनु, अभि–नि√विश्).. etc.

(3) Karaṇ Kārak, Instrumental Case (करण–कारक, तृतीया–विभक्ति)

The instrument or vehicle (साधन) with or by whch the (active or passive) action is performed.

The medium used for performing action on the object (कर्म) is the *karaṇ kārak* (करण कारक) of the sentence. The suffix attached to the object to form the *karaṇ kārak* is Instrumental Case Suffix (तृतीया विभक्ति प्रत्यय).

Scope : by, with, without (के बिना), because (के द्वारा), along with (सह, के साथ), owing to, on account of, out of-, for the reason of (प्रयोजनार्थ), by nature (स्वभाव -जिससे), enough, enough of (बस), through (के माध्येम से, जरिए, द्वारा), simile (के समान, सदृश), etc.

NOTE : Normally, the Present Tense is indicated by such Verbs as: am, is, are, has, have. However, in order to denote **POSSESION**, in English we say I have one brother, I have 100 Rupees (Active Construction), etc. but in Hindi you have to speak about material possession in Passive construction, 100 Repees are with me मेरे पास 100 रुपये हैं. Because, the Hindi philosophy says you don't have 100 Rupees, like you have a brother, but 100 Rupees are with you temporarily, which may not be with you later.

(4) Sampradān Kārak, Dative Case (सम्प्रदान कारक, चतुर्थी विभक्ति)

To whom or for whom the action is directed through something.

When the verb is performed for (*ke liye* के लिए) or to (*ko* को) someone or something, that person or thing assumes *sampradān kārak* (संप्रदान कारक). The suffix attached to the noun to form the *sampradān kārak* is Dative Case Suffix (चतुर्थी विभक्ति प्रत्यय).

Scope : for, to, to give to (को देना), to owe to (धारण करना), to send for (के वास्ते, निमित्त, हेतु,

के अर्थ), to promise to, to show to, to be angry with (√कृध्, √कुप्, √द्रुह्, √असू), to do for the purpose of (के निमित्त), to desire, to long for, liking (रुचि, स्पृहा), for some one, to go to, to be (√क्लृप्), be able (समर्थ), salutation, hail to (नमः, स्वस्ति), in the meaning of the के लिए (तुमुन्) infinitive, etc.

(5) Apādān Kārak, Ablative Case (अपादान कारक, पंचमी विभक्ति)

From where the subject is moved, or a comparison between TWO things, but not more than two things.

When the subject moves from (से) any location to (को) other location, the location from where the subject moves is in *apādān kārak* (अपादान कारक). The suffix attached to the name of that location is Dative Case Suffix (पंचमी विभक्ति प्रत्यय).

Scope : from, than (अपेक्षा), without, except (बिना), far or away (दूर), outside, since, until, after, before (पूर्व), to the direction of (प्रति), to desist from (वि√रम्, नि√वृत्), to protect (√रक्ष्, त्रै), with or without motivation (अकस्मात्), in the meanings of away (अलग, पृथक्), fear (भय), break (विराम), accept (√ग्रह), other (अन्य), with expressions प्रभृति, etc.

(6) Sambandh Kārak, Genitive Case (सम्बन्ध कारक, षष्ठी विभक्ति)

Also called Possessive Case is the **relation** between two things; or a comparison between more than two things i.e. superlative degree, but not comparative.

When a noun (भेदक) has a relationship *sambandh kārak* (संबंध कारक) with the subject (भेद्य) of the sentence, this relationship (भेदक) forms *sambandh kārak*. The suffix attached to the noun (भेदक) is called Genetive Case Suffix (षष्ठी विभक्ति प्रत्यय). e.g. कुत्ते का पाँव टूटा, कुत्ते की दुम टूटी, बिल्ली का पाँव टूटा, बिल्ली की दुम टूटी, etc. Here, the suffixes (का. की, etc.) in the *bhedak* phrases कुत्ते का, कुत्ते की, बिल्ली का, बिल्ली की change according to the Gender and Number of the words पाँव, दुम, etc. which are the subjects (भेद्य) of the sentence.

Scope : of (का, की, के, रा, री, रे), above (के ऊपर), below (के नीचे), in front of (के आगे), behind (के पीछे), beyond (के पार), away (के परे), in the presence of (के समक्ष), for the sake of (के के कारण), with the subject of participles (क्त = प्रतिष्ठा का पतन), words with suffix अत:, with the object of participles (पय पान), in the use of word हेतु, in the meaning of remembering with verb √स्मृ etc.

(7) Adhikaraṇ Kārak, Locative Case (अधिकरण कारक, सप्तमी विभक्ति)

Shows a locative relationship between two things, or a quality within a group of things.

The word that says about the location in (में) or on (पर) of the subject, that location is *adhikaraṇ kaErak* (अधिकरण कारक). The suffix attached to the name of that place or object is Locative Case Suffix (सप्तमी विभक्ति प्रत्यय). e.g. गिलास में पानी है, पुस्तक मेज़ पर थी, etc.

Scope : in, on, at (में, पर, ऊपर), in side (मध्ये, भीतर), under (तले), upon (पर), among (में, में से), concerning (विषय में), in the matter of (के बारे में), to express feelings for, to enter, to place, to fall, to send, to indicate time (दिने में, प्रतःकाल में, मध्याह्न में, सायङ्काल में), in occurance of the first event after which some other event takes place, with the use of expressions मध्ये, कृते, समक्ष, अन्त:, etc.

When the object is First Person, Singuler or Plural, all suffixes which begin with letter क (का, की, के, के साथ, के पास, के लिए, के...), other than kae, change to words beginning with letter र (रा, री, रे, रे साथ, रे पास, रे लिए, रे...).

(8) Sambodhan Kārak, Vocative Case (सम्बोधन)

To call or address someone.

The words used for calling, addressing ot expressing surprise are sambandh kārak (संबंध कारक). It probably is not a separate or independent *kārak* (विभक्ति), but a modified form of the karttā *kārak* (कर्त्ता कारक)

Scope : अरे! हे! अहो! भो:! हाय! हे राम! .. etc.

TABLE 2 - CHART OF CASE SUFFIXES FOR MASCULINE NOUNS

THE Hindī Chart (The English Chart is on the Next Page)

NOTES : **(i)** ए *(e)* is added to m∘ singular nouns ending in आ *(ā)* and

(ii) ओं *(ō̃)* is added to all **plural** nouns m∘ and f∘, before attaching any suffix.

		m. (i) child,	m. (ii) boy,	m. (iii) saint,	m. (iv) saint
Words ending in →		(i) अ (बालक)	(ii) आ (लड़का)	(iii) इ (योगी)	(iv) उ (साधु)
with suffix ने	singular→	बालक ने	लड़के ने	योगी ने	साधु ने
1N∘ (Perfect, transitive)	plural→	बालकों ने	लड़कों ने	यागियों ने	साधुओं ने
2 A∘ to को	singular→	बालक को	लड़के को	योगी को	साधु को
	plural→	बालकों को	लड़कों को	योगियों को	साधुओं को
3 I∘ with, by से	singular→	बालक से	लड़के से	योगी से	साधु से
	plural→	बालकों से	लड़कों से	योगियों से	साधुओं से
4 D∘ for के लिये	singular→	बालक के लिये	लड़के के लिये	योगी के लिये	साधु के लिये
	plural→	बालकों के लिये	लड़कों के लिये	योगियों के लिये	साधुओं के लिये
5 A∘ from से	singular→	बालक से	लड़के से	योगी से	साधु से
	plural→	बालकों से	लड़कों से	योगियों से	साधुओं से
6 P∘ of का	singular→	बालक का	लड़के का	योगी का	साधु का
	plural→	बालकों का	लड़कों का	योगियों का	साधुओं का
7 L∘ in में	singular→	बालक में	लड़के में	योगी में	साधु में
	plural→	बालकों में	लड़कों में	योगियों में	साधुओं में
on, at पर	singular→	बालक पर	लड़के पर	योगी पर	साधु पर
	plural→	बालकों पर	लड़कों पर	योगियों पर	साधुओं पर

TABLE 3 - CHART OF CASES, MASCULINE NOUNS

The English Chart (The Hindī Chart is on the Previous Page)

NOTES : **(i)** ए *(e)* is added to m◦ singular nouns ending in आ *(ā)* and

(ii) ओं *(o̐)* is added to all **plural** nouns m◦ and f◦, before attaching any suffix.

			m◦ a child,	m◦ a boy,	m◦ a saint,	m◦ a saint
Word ending in →			(i) *a (bālak)*	(ii) *ā (laḍkā)*	(iii) *ī (yogī)*	(iv) *u (sādhu)*
with suffix *ne*		singular→	*bālak ne*	*laḍke ne*	*yogī ne*	*sādhu ne*
1N◦ (Perfect, transitive)		plural→	*bālako̐ ne*	*laḍko̐ ne*	*yogiyo̐ ne*	*sādhuo̐ ne*
2 A◦	to *ko*	singular→	*bālak ko*	*laḍke ko*	*yogī ko*	*sādhu ko*
		plural→	*bālako̐ ko*	*laḍko̐ ko*	*yogiyo̐ ko*	*sādhuo̐ ko*
3 I◦	with, by *se*	singular→	*bālak se*	*laḍke se*	*yogī se*	*sādhu se*
		plural→	*bālako̐ se*	*laḍko̐ se*	*yogiyo̐ se*	*sādhuo̐ se*
4 D◦	for *ke liye*	singular→	*bālak ke liye*	*laḍke ke liye*	*yogī ke liye*	*sādhu ke liye*
		plural→	*bālako̐ ke liye*	*laḍko̐ ke liye*	*yogiyo̐ ke liye*	*sādhuo̐ ke liye*
5 A◦	from *se*	singular→	*bālak se*	*laḍke se*	*yogī se*	*sādhu se*
		plural→	*bālako̐ se*	*laḍko̐ se*	*yogiyo̐ se*	*sādhuo̐ se*
6 P◦	of *kā*	singular→	*bālak kā*	*laḍke kā*	*yogī kā*	*sādhu kā*
		plural→	*bālako̐ kā*	*laḍko̐ kā*	*yogiyo̐ kā*	*sādhuo̐ kā*
7 L◦	in *me̐*	singular→	*bālak me̐*	*laḍke me̐*	*yogī me̐*	*sādhu me̐*
		plural→	*bālako̐ me̐*	*laḍko̐ me̐*	*yogiyo̐ me̐*	*sādhuo̐ me̐*
	on, at *par*	singular→	*bālak par*	*laḍke par*	*yogī par*	*sādhu par*
		plural→	*bālako̐ par*	*laḍko̐ par*	*yogiyo̐ par*	*sādhuo̐ par*

TABLE 4 - CHART OF CASES : FEMININE NOUNS

The Hindī Chart (The English Chart is on the Next Page)

NOTES : **(i)** To make plural of a femimine noun ending in a consonant, add एं *(ẽ)* to it.

(ii) ओं *(õ)* is added to all **plural** nouns (m◦ and f◦), before attaching any suffix.

		f◦ a book,	f◦ a girl,	f◦ a girl,	f◦ a thing
Words ending in →		(i) अ (किताब)	(ii) आ (बालिका)	(iii) ई (लड़की)	(iv) उ (वस्तु)
with suffix ने	singular→	किताब ने	बालिका ने	लड़की ने	वस्तु ने
1N◦ (Perfect, transitive)	plural→	किताबों ने	बालिकाओं ने	लड़कियों ने	वस्तुओं ने
2 A◦ to को	singular→	किताब को	बालिका को	लड़की को	वस्तु को
	plural→	किताबों को	बालिकाओं को	लड़कियों को	वस्तुओं को
3 I◦ with, by से	singular→	किताब से	बालिका से	लड़की से	वस्तु से
	plural→	किताबों से	बालिकाओं से	लड़कियों से	वस्तुओं से
4 D◦ for के लिये	singular→	किताब के लिये	बालिका के लिये	लड़की के लिये	वस्तु के लिये
	plural→	किताबों के लिये	बालिकाओं के लिये	लड़कियों के लिये	वस्तुओं के लिये
5 A◦ from से	singular→	किताब से	बालिका से	लड़की से	वस्तु से
	plural→	किताबों से	बालिकाओं से	लड़कियों से	वस्तुओं से
6 P◦ of का	singular→	किताब का	बालिका का	लड़की का	वस्तु का
	plural→	किताबों का	बालिकाओं का	लड़कियों का	वस्तुओं का
7 L◦ in में	singular→	किताब में	बालिका में	लड़की में	वस्तु में
	plural→	किताबों में	बालिकाओं में	लड़कियों में	वस्तुओं में
on, at पर	singular→	किताब पर	बालिका पर	लड़की पर	वस्तु पर
	plural→	किताबों पर	बालिकाओं पर	लड़कियों पर	वस्तुओं पर

TABLE 5 - CHART OF CASES : FEMININE NOUNS

The English Chart (Hindī Chart is on the Previous Page)

NOTES : (i) To make plural of a femimine noun ending in a consonant, add एँ *(e̐)* to it.

(ii) ओँ *(o̐)* is added to all **plural** nouns m∘ and f∘, before attaching any suffix.

		f∘ a book,	f∘ a girl,	f∘ a girl,	f∘ a thing
Word ending in →		(i) *a (kitāb)*	(ii) *ā (bālikā)*	*ī (laḍkī)*	*u (vastu)*
with suffix *ne*	singular→	*kitāb ne*	*bālikā ne*	*laḍkī ne*	*vastu ne*
1N∘ (Perfect, transitive)	plural→	*kitābo̐ ne*	*bālikao̐ ne*	*laḍkiyo̐ ne*	*vastuo̐ ne*
2 A∘ to *ko*	singular→	*kitāb ko*	*bālikā ko*	*laḍkī ko*	*vastu ko*
	plural→	*kitābo̐ ko*	*bālikāo̐ ko*	*laḍkiyo̐ ko*	*vastuo̐ ko*
3 I∘ with, by *se*	singular→	*kitāb se*	*bālikā se*	*laḍkī se*	*vastu se*
	plural→	*kitābo̐ se*	*bālikāo̐ se*	*laḍkiyo̐ se*	*vastuo̐ se*
4 D∘ for *ke liye*	singular→	*kitāb ke liye*	*bālikā ke liye*	*laḍkī ke liye*	*vastu ke liye*
	plural→	*kitābo̐ ke liye*	*bālikāo̐ ke liye*	*laḍkiyo̐ ke liye*	*vastuo̐ ke liye*
5 A∘ from *se*	singular→	*kitāb se*	*bālikā se*	*laḍkī se*	*vastu se*
	plural→	*kitābo̐ se*	*bālikāo̐ se*	*laḍkiyo̐ se*	*vastuo̐ se*
6 P∘ of *kā*	singular→	*kitāb kā*	*bālikā kā*	*laḍkī kā*	*vastu kā*
	plural→	*kitābo̐ kā*	*bālikāo̐ kā*	*laḍkiyo̐ kā*	*vastuo̐ kā*
7 L∘ in *me̐*	singular→	*kitāb me̐*	*bālikā me̐*	*laḍkī me̐*	*vastu me̐*
	plural→	*kitābo̐ me̐*	*bālikāo̐ me̐*	*laḍkiyo̐ me̐*	*vastuo̐ me̐*
on, at *par*	singular→	*kitāb par*	*bālikā par*	*laḍkī par*	*vastu par*
	plural→	*kitābo̐ par*	*bālikāo̐ par*	*laḍkiyo̐ par*	*vastuo̐ par*

CHAPTER 7

THE PRONOUN

सर्वनाम

DEFINITION :

Words such as I, we, you, he, she, they, that etc. are used in place of the names of those persons, therefore, they are Personal Pronouns. Pronouns such as who, which, whom -are called Relative Pronouns because they always relate or refer to some noun. The word that is used in place of a noun (*nāma* नाम) is a PRONOUN (*sarvanāma* सर्वनाम).

In Hindi there are 12 basic singular pronouns. namely, मैं, तू, तुम, आप, यह, वह, जो, सो, कुछ, कोई, कौन, क्या, etc. The most commonly used pronoun forms are : I (*maĩ* मैं); We (*ham* हम); You (*tū, tum* तू, तुम); You plural (*tum* तुम), Your honour (*āp* आप), Your honour Sir! / Madam! (m. *śhrīmān* श्रीमन्! *mahoday!* महोदय! / f. *śhrīmāatī* श्रमिती! *mahodayā!* महोदया!); He, She, That (*vah, vo, so* वह, वो, सो), They, Those (*ve* वे); It, this (यह, ये यह, ये), These (*ye* ये); What? (*kyā?* क्या?), Which? (*kaunsā?* कौनसा?), Who (*kaun?* कौन?); What, Which (*jo* जो); Who (*kaun* कौन), Whom? (*kise?* किसे?), Whom (*jise* जिसे), Whose? (*kiskā?* किसका?), Whose (*jiskā* जिसका), etc.

DEFINITIONS :

(1) The word used in place of a noun (in order to avoid its repetition) is called a *Pronoun.*

(2) If a pronoun qualifies a noun, then the pronoun is called a *Pronominal or Possessive Adjective.*

EXPLANATION :

(i) <u>See this sentence</u> :

Rām is going to Rām's school to see Rām's teacher and to return Rām's teacher Rām's

teacher's books.
राम राम के शिक्षक को मिलने और राम के शिक्षक की पुस्तकें राम के गुरुजी को लौटाने राम के विद्यालय को जा रहा है। It sounds improper and confusing.

(ii) Now see this one

(Same sentence can be re-written properly with the use of pronouns) :

Rām is going to his school to see his teacher and to return him his books. *(Rām apane gurujī ko milane aur un kī pustakẽ un ko lauṭāne apane vidyālay jā rahā hai)*
राम अपने शिक्षक को मिलने और उनकी पुस्तकें उनको लौटाने अपने विद्यालय जा रहा है। Now it looks improper.

Dictionary of Hindi Pronouns
हिंदी के सर्वनाम

another (*dūsrā* दूसरा)
any (*koī, kuch* कोई, कुछ)
anybody (*koī bhī* कोई भी)
anyone (*koī bhī* कोई भी)
anything (*kuchh bhī* कुछ भी)
both (*ubhay, donõ* उभय, दोनों)
each (*ek-ek, pratyek, har, harek* एक-एक, प्रत्येक, हर, हरएक)
either (*koī ek, donõ* कोई एक, दोनों)
enough (*kafī* काफी)
everybody (*pratyek, har, harek* प्रत्येक, हर, हरएक)
everyone (*sab* सब)
everything (*sab-kuchh* सब-कुछ)
half (*ardha, apūrṇa, ādhā* अर्ध, अपूर्ण, आधा)
he (*vah* वह)
her (*uskā* उसका)
herself (*vah-svayam* वह-स्वयं)
him (*usko* उसको)
himself (*vah-svayam* वह-स्वयं)
his (*uskā* उसका)
I (*maĩ* मैं)
it (*yah* यह)
itself (*yah-svayam* यह-स्वयं)

less (*kam* कम)

little (*kuchh hī* कुछ ही)

many (*kaī* कई)

me (*mujhe* मुझे)

mine (*merā* मेरा)

more (*adhik, aur* अधिक, और)

most (*adhikāṁśh* अधिकांश)

much (*adhiktar* अधिकतर)

myself (*maĩ-svayam* मैं-स्वयं)

no (*koī bhī nahī̃* कोई भी नहीं)

no one (*koī nahī̃* कोई नहीं)

nobody (*koī nahī̃* कोई नहीं)

none (*koī nahī̃, kuchh nahī̃* कोई नहीं, कुछ नहीं)

nothing (*kuchh nahī̃* कुछ नहीं)

one (*ek, koī* एक, कोई)

other (*Anya* अन्य)

ours (*hmārā* हमारा)

ourselves (*ham-svayam* हम-स्वयं)

own (*apnā* अपना)

plenty (*prachur* प्रचुर)

same (*vahī* वही)

several (*kaī* कई)

she (*vah* वह)

some (*kuchh* कुछ)

somebody (*koī* कोई)

someone (*koī* कोई)

something (*kuchh* कुछ)

that (*vah* वह)

themselves (*vae-svaya* वे-स्वयं)

these (*ye* ये)

they (*ve* वे)

this (*yah* यह)

those (*ve* वे)

us (*hma* हम)

we (*ham* हम)

what (*kyā* क्या)

whatever (*kuchh bhī* कुछ भी)

which (*jo* जो)

who (*jo* जो)

whose (*jis kā* जिसका)

you (*āp, tum, tū* आप, तुम, तू)

yours (*āpkā, tumhārā, terā* आपका, तुम्हारा, तेरा)

yourself (*āp-svayam* आप-स्वयं)

Seven types of Pronouns
सर्वनाम के सात प्रकार

1. **Personal Pronouns** (पुरुषवाचक सर्वनाम) :

NOTE : A word used in place of the name of a person is a Personal Pronoun (a thing, is Impersonal Pronoun वस्तुवाचक सर्वनाम) both categories come in this group.

Similar to the Nouns, Personal Pronouns also have forms according to their Gender (*liṅg* लिंग), Number (*vachan* वचन) and Cases (*kārak* कारक). These changes are visible in some forms while change in few other forms are not apperent. e.g.

I, we (*maĩ, ham* मैं, हम)

You, you (*tū, tum. āp* तू, तुम आप)

He, she (*vah, vah* वह, वह)

This, these (*yah, ye* यह, ये)

That, those (*vah, ve* वह, वे)

1a. **First Person** (*uttam puruṣh* उत्तम पुरुष) :

I (*maĩ* मैं), we (*ham* हम) etc. and their case inflections.

1b. **Second Person** (*madhyam puruṣh* मध्यम पुरुष) :

You (*tū, tum, āp* तू, तुम, आप), etc. and their case inflections.

1c. **Third Person** (*anya puruṣh* अन्य पुरुष) :

He, she, that (*vah,* वह), it, this (*yah* यह), those (*ve* वे), t

hese (*ye* ये), etc. and their case inflections.

TABLE 6 :

Declensions of Personal Pronouns (पुरुषवाचक सर्वनाम)										
Case / Declension	Rirst Person		Second Person 1		Second Person 2		Second Person 3 Honor		Third Person	
	Sg.	Pl.	Sg.	Pl.	Sg.	Pl.	Sg.	Pl.	Sg.	Pl.
Nominative ने	I मैं	we हम	you तू	you तुम	you तुम	you तुम	you आप	you आप	he-she, It-This वह, यह	they- those these वे, ये
Accusative (to) को	me मुझे	us हमें	you तुझे	you तुम्हें	you तुम्हें	you तुम्हें	you आपको	you आपको	him-her उसे, इसे	them उन्हें, इन्हें
Instrumental (with, by) से	me मुझसे	us हमसे	you तुझसे	you तुमसे	you तुमसे	you तुमसे	you आपसे	you आपसे	him-her उससे, इससे	them उनसे इनसें
Dative (for, to) के लिए, को	me मुझको मुझे	us हमको हमें	you तुझको तुझे	you तुमको तुम्हें	you तुमको तुम्हें	you तुमको तुम्हें	you आपको	you आपको	him-her उसको, इसको उसे, इसे	them उनको इनकों उन्हें इन्हें
Ablative (from) से	me मुझसे	us हमसे	you तुझसे	you तुमसे	you तुमसे	you तुमसे	you आपसे	you आपसे	him-her उससे, इससे	them उनसे इनसें
Possessive (of) का, की, के रा, री, रे	my मेरा मेरी मेरे	our हमारा हमारी हमारे	your तेरा तेरी तेरे	your तुम्हारा तुम्हारी तुम्हारे	your तुम्हारा तुम्हारी तुम्हारे	your तुम्हारा तुम्हारी तुम्हारे	your आपका आपकी आपके	your आपका आपकी आपके	his-her उसका, इसका	thir उनका इनका
Locative (in, on-at) में, पर	me मुझमें	us हममें	you तुझमें	you तुममें	you तुममें	you तुममें	you आपमें	you आपमें	him-her उसमें, इसमें	them उनमें इनमें

TABLE 7 : CHART FOR THE PRONOUNS

The Hindī Chart (English Chart is on the Next Page)

		I, we, us	You	He, she, him, her, that, It, these, they, them, those
1st., 2nd., 3rd. Person →		मैं, हम	आप	वह, वे, यह, ये
with suffix ने	singular→	मैंने	आपने	उसने, इसने
1N◦ (Perfect, transitive)	plural→	हमने	आपने	उन्हों ने, इन्हों ने
2 A◦ to को	singular→	मुझको, मुझे	आपको	उसको, उसे, इसको, इसे
to	plural→	हमको, हमें	आपको	उनको , उन्हें, इनको, इन्हें
3 I◦ with, by से	singular→	मुझसे	आपसे	उससे, इससे
	plural→	हमसे	आपसे	उनसे, इनसे
4 D◦ for के लिये	singular→	मेरे लिये	आपके लिये,	उसके लिये, इसके लिये
	plural→	हमारे लिये	आपके लिये,	उनके लिये, इनके लिये
5 A◦ from से	singular→	मुझसे, मेरेसे	आपसे,	उससे, इससे
	plural→	हमसे	आपसे,	उनसे, इनसे
6 P◦ of का, रा-	singular→	मेरा–मेरी	आपका–की,	उसका–की, इसका–की
	plural→	हमारा–री	आपका–की,	उनका–की, इनका–की
7 L◦ in में	singular→	मुझमें	आपमें,	उसमें, इसमें
	plural→	हममें	आपमें,	उनमें, इनमें
in पर	singular→	मुझ पर	आप पर,	उस पर, इस पर
	plural→	हम पर	आप पर,	उन पर, इन पर

TABLE 8 : CHART FOR THE PRONOUNS

The English Chart   (Hindī Chart is on the Previous Page)

NOTE : When any suffix is attached to these pronouns : *maĭ* changes to *muz; vah* changes to *us; yah* changes to *is; ve* changes to *un; ye* changes to *in.*

		I, we, us	**You**	**He, she, him, her, that, It, these they, them, those**
1st., 2nd., 3rd. Person →		*maĭ, ham*	*āp*	*vah, ve, yah, ye*
with suffix *ne* singular→		*maĭ ne*	*āp ne*	*us ne, is ne*
1N◦ (Perfect, transitive) plural→		*ham ne*	*āp ne*	*unhŏ ne, inhŏ ne*
2 A◦ to*ko* singular→		*mujh ko, mujhe*	*āp ko*	*us ko, use, isko, ise*
plural→		*hamĕ*	*āp ko*	*un ko, unhĕ, inko, inhĕ*
3 I◦ with, by*se* singular→		*mujh se*	*āp se*	*us se, is se*
plural→		*ham se*	*āp se*	*un se, in se*
4 D◦ for *ke liye* singular→		*mere liye*	*āpke liye*	*us ke liye, is ke liye*
plural→		*hamāre liye*	*āpke liye*	*un ke liye, in ke liye*
5 A◦ from *se* singular→		*mujh se*	*āp se*	*us se, is se*
plural→		*ham se*	*āp se*	*un se, in se*
6 P◦ of *kā, rā* singular→		*merā-meri*	*āpkā-kī*	*uskā-kī, iskā-kī*
plural→		*hamārā-rī*	*āpkā-kī*	*unkā-kī, inkā-kī*
7 L◦ in *mĕ* singular→		*mujh mĕ*	*āp mĕ*	*us mĕ, un mĕ*
plural→		*ham mĕ*	*āp mĕ*	*un mĕ, in mĕ*
on, at *par* singular→		*mujh par*	*āp par*	*us par, is par*
plural→		*ham par*	*āp par*	*un par, in par*

2. Reflexive Pronoun (निजीवाचक सर्वनाम) :

When the suffix 'self' (*svayam, svatah, khud* स्वयं, स्वत:, खुद), is added to a Personal Pronoun, it forms Reflexive Pronoun (*niji-vāchak sarvanām* निजीवाचक सर्वनाम).

TABLE 9 : Reflexive Pronouns

Reflexive Pronouns						
Subject	कर्त्ता	Personal Pronoun	पुरुषवाचक सर्वनाम	Reflexive Pronoun	निजीवाचक सर्वनाम	Eamples उदाहरण
I	मैं	I	मैं, मैंने	myself	मैं स्वयं, मैं स्वत:	मैंने स्वयं देखा
We	हम	We	हम, हम ने	ourselves	हम स्वयं	हम स्वयं लड़ते हैं
You	तू	You	तू, तूने	yourself	तू स्वयं	तू स्वत: देख
You	तुम	You	तुम, तुम ने	yourself	तुम वयं	तुम स्वयं चुप थे
You	आप	You	आप, आपने	yourself	आप स्वयं	आप स्वत: आए
He	वह	He	वह, उसने	himself	वह स्वयं	वह स्वत: जाएगा
She	वह	She	वह, उसने	herself	वह स्वयं	वह स्वयं योग्य है
It	यह	It	यह, इसने	itself	यह स्वयं	यह स्वयं अक्षम है
That	वह	That	वह, उसने	itself	वह स्वयं	वह स्वयं खड़ा है
These	ये	These	ये, इन्हों ने	thmemselves	ये स्वयं	ये स्वयं चल रहे
They	वे	They	वे, उन्हों ने	themselves	वे स्वयं	वे स्वयं शांत हैं

3. Emphatic Pronoun (निश्चयवाचक सर्वनाम) :

Sometimes Compound Personal Pronouns are used for the purpose of emphasis on a particular word and, therefore, these Personal Pronouns are called Emphatic Pronouns (निश्चयवाचक सर्वनाम). These pronouns say something emphatic about something near or away from the speaker of the sentence.

TABLE 10 : Emphatic Pronouns

Eamples	उदाहरण
This is not any new thing.	यह कोई नई बात नहीं है.
Only we know this thing.	यह बात हम ही जानते हैं.

We also know this thing.	यह हम भी जानते हैं
We saw it with our own eyes.	यह हमने अपनी आखों से देखा है.
Now I am leaving	मैं अब जा रहा हूँ.

4. Indefinite Pronoun (अनिश्चयवाचक सर्वनाम) :

The pronouns that refer to a person or thing in a general way, but do not refer to any particular person or thing, are called Indefinite Pronouns (अनिश्चयवाचक सर्वनाम). Such pronouns are mainly of two types, 1. Referring to someone (*koī* कोई) and 2. Referring to something (*kuchh* कुछ). e.g.

1. Someone :

Someone is sitting there. कोई वहाँ बैठा है.

Please call **someone**. कृपया किसी को बुलाइये.

Anybody can understand this. कोई भी यह समझ सकता है.

Everybody know this. यह सभी जानते हैं.

Everyone is not helpful. सारे ही मददगार नहीं होते हैं.

I don't know **anyone** here. मैं यहाँ किसी को नहीं जानता.

Each person has his opinion. प्रत्येक को अपने मत का हक है.

2. Something :

Quantitative :

Please give me some **money**. कृपया मुझे कुछ पैसे दीजिये.

Few people know **this**. यह कुछ ही लोग जानते हैं.

Nothing was present there. वहाँ कुभ भी विद्यमान नहीं था..

I know **it** all. मैं यह सब कुछ जानता हूँ.

Qualitative:

I want to tell you **something**. मैं आपको कुछ बताना चाहता हूँ.

Something is wrong with me. मुझे कुछ हुआ है.

Special Usage :

I am not talking in any foreigh language. मैं कुछ पश्तो तो नहीं बोल रहा हूँ.

Don't ask anything about this place. यहाँ का हाल कुछ मत पूछो.

We will get something to eat there. हमें वहाँ कुछ तो खाने को मिलेगा ही.

He says something else and does something else. वह बोलता कुछ और और करता कुछ और.

You are yapping something elas. आप कुछ के कुछ बके जारहे हो.

Till now a lot has happened. अभी तक यहाँ बहुत कुछ होगया है.

You sing something and we play something. आप कुछ गाइये हम कुछ बजाते हैं

5. Distributive Pronoun (व्यष्टिवाचक सर्वनाम) :

The pronouns such as each (प्रत्येक), either (यह या वह, इस या उस), neither (न यह न वह), etc. are Distributive Pronouns (व्यष्टिवाचक सर्वनाम) because they refer to persons or things one at a time. Thus, they are always singular and they are always connected to a singular verb. e.g.

1. Each of the students knows his own password. प्रत्येक विद्यार्थी उसका संकेत जानता है.
2. Either of the ways is solution to the problem. यह या वह रीति इस समस्या का समाधान है.
3. Either of the ways will solve the problem. इस या उस विधि से समस्या हल हो सकेगी.
4. Neither of the statements is true. न यह न वह बात सच है.

6. Relative Pronoun (संबंधवाचक सर्वनाम) :

The connecting words who (), or which (), in their Nominative, Accusative and Genetive forms in Singular and Plural numbers form Relative Pronouns (संबंधवाचक सर्वनाम).

TABLE 11 : **Relative Pronoun** (संबंधवाचक सर्वनाम)

Case	Singular		Plural	
Nominative	who, which	जो, जिसने	who, which	जो, जिन्हों ने
Accusative	whom	जिसको, जिसे	whom	जिन को, जिन्हें
Genetive	whose	जिसका	whose	जिन का
Nominative	whoever	जो भी, जिसने भी	who, which	जो भी, जिन्हों ने भी
Accusative	whom	जिसको भी, जिसे भी	whom	जिन को भी, जिन्हें भी
Genetive	whose	जिसका भी	whose	जिन का भी

EXAMPLES :

1. यह वही लड़का है जो सम्मानित है. He is the boy who received honor.
2. ये वही लड़कियाँ हैं जो सम्मानित हैं. These are the girls who are honored.
3. यह वही पुस्तक है जिसको (जिसे) सभी जानते हैं. This is the book which everyone knows.
4. यह वही कुत्ता है जिसका चित्र वहाँ लगा है. This is the dog of which picture is there.
5. यह वही बिल्ली है जिसकी आँखें नीली हैं. This is the cat of which eyes are blue.
6. यह वही समोसे हैं जो मैंने कल बनाए थे. These are the Samosās which I made yesterday.
7. ये वही चोर हैं जिनको (जिन्हें) पकड़ा गया था.These are the thieves who got caught.
8. जो भी बोलेगा वही कुण्डी खोलेगा. He who speakes will open the door.
9. जो भी खिड़की खुली है वह बंद कर दो. Whichever window is open, please close it.
10. जो भी कहोगे हम मानेंगे. Whatever you say, we will agree.

7. Interrogative Pronoun (प्रश्नवाचक सर्वनाम) :

Interrogative Pronouns (प्रश्नवाचक सर्वनाम) are similar to the Relative Personal Pronouns, but they serve the function of asking indirect questions about persons or things. In Hindi, they have Masculine, Feminine, Singular and Plural forms in Nominative, Accusative and Genitive Cases. e.g.

1. Who? (Person, Masculine, Feminine, Singular, Plural)
2. Whose? (Person, Masculine, Feminine, Singular, Plural)
3. Whom? (Person, Masculine, Feminine, Singular, Plural)
4. What? (Thing, Masculine, Feminine, Singular, Plural)
5. Which? (Person or thing, Masculine, Feminine, Singular, Plural)

TABLE 12 : **Interrogative Pronoun** (प्रश्नवाचक सर्वनाम)

Case	Pronoun	Masculine Singular	Masculine Plural	Feminine Singular	Feminine Plural
Nominative	who?	कौन? किसने?	कौन? किन्हों ने?	कौन? किसने?	कौन? किन्हों ने?
Accusative	whom?	किसको?	किनको? किन्हें?	किसको?	किन को? किन्हें?
Genitive	whose?	किसका?	किसके?	किसकी?	किसकीं?

EXAMPLES :

1. Who told you this? (person). Who ate the mango? (person)
2. Whose book is it? (person). Whose books are these? (person)
3. To whom it may concern. (person). Whom will you take in the bus? (persons)
4. What do you want? (thing). What names do you remember? (things)
5. Which one is your friend? (person). Which ones are your friends? (people) Which one is your car? (thing). Which cars are damaged in the accident?

(1) कौन (*kaun?* who) : Who sleeps here? *(yahā̃ kaun sotā hai?)* यहाँ कौन सोता है?

(2) क्यों (*kyõ?* why) : Why do you sleep here? आप यहाँ सोते क्यों हैं?

(3) क्या (*kyā?* what) : What are you doing here now? *(āp ab yahā̃ kyā kar rahe haĩ?).* आप अब यहाँ क्या कर रहे हैं? What is your name? *āpkā nām kyā hai?* आप का नाम क्या है?

(4) कब (*kab?* When) : When will you come? *(āp kab āyeṅge?)* आप कब आयेंगे?

(5) कहाँ (*kahā̃?* where) : Where does he live? *(vah kahā̃ rahatā hai?)* वह कहाँ रहता है?

TABLE 13 : SIMILARITY BETWEEN VARIOUS PRONOUNS

He	*vah*	वह
She	*vah*	वह
That	*vah*	वह
This	*yah*	यह
This	*yah*	यह
That	*vah*	वह
Who?	*kaun*	कौन?
Who	*jo*	जो
Here	*yahā̐*	यहाँ
There	*vahā̐*	वहाँ
Where?	*kahā̐*	कहाँ?
Where	*jahā̐*	जहाँ
On this side	*idhar*	इधर
On that side	*udhar*	उधर
On which side?	*kidhar*	किधर?
On which side	*jidhar*	जिधर
Now	*ab*	अब
Then	*tab*	तब
When?	*kab*	कब?
When	*jab*	जब
Like this	*aisā*	ऐसा
Like that	*vaisā*	वैसा
Like what, how?	*kaisā*	कैसा?
Like which, as	*jaisā*	जैसा
Like this	*is tarah*	इस तरह
Like that	*us tarah*	उस तरह
Like what?	*kis tarah*	किस तरह?
Like which	*jis tarah*	जिस तरह
Like these	*aise*	ऐसे
Like those	*vaise*	वैसे
Like what, how?	*kaise*	कैसे?
Like which	*jaise*	जैसे
This much	*itnā*	इतना
That much	*utanā*	उतना
How much?	*kitnā*	कितना
As much	*jitnā*	जितना
This much (f∘)	*itnī*	इतनी
That much	*utnī*	उतनी
How much?	*kitnī*	कितनी
As much	*jitnī*	जितनी
These many	*itne*	इतने
That many	*utne*	उतने
How many?	*kitne*	कितने?
As many	*jitne*	जितने
This person (did)	*is ne*	इसने
He, she (did)	*us ne*	उसने

Who (did ?)	*kis ne*	किसने	Of what?	*kis kā*	किसका?
Who (did)	*jis ne*	जिसने	Of which	*jis kā*	जिसका
To this	*is ko*	इसको	Of this	*is kī*	इसकी
To that	*us ko*	उसको	Of that	*us kī*	उसकी
To him	*us ko*	उसको	Of what?	*kis kī*	किसकी?
To her	*us ko*	उसको	Of which	*jis kī*	जिसकी
To these	*in ko*	इनको	Of this	*is ke*	इसके
To those	*un ko*	उनको	Of that	*us ke*	उसके
To them	*un ko*	उनको	Of what?	*kis ke*	किसके?
To whom?	*kis ko*	किसको	Of which	*jis ke*	जिसके
With this	*is se*	इससे	In this	*is mẽ*	इसमें
With that	*us se*	उससे	In that	*us mẽ*	उसमें
With what?	*kis se*	किससे?	In what?	*kis mẽ*	किसमें?
With which	*jis se*	जिससे	In which	*jis mẽ*	जिसमें
For this	*is liye*	इस लिये	On this	*is par*	इस पर
For that	*us liye*	उस लिये	On that	*us par*	उस पर
For what?	*kis liye*	किस लिये?	On what?	*kis par*	किस पर
For which	*jis liye*	जिस लिये	On which	*jis par*	जिस पर
From this	*is se*	इससे	Why?	*kyõ*	क्यों?
From that	*us se*	उससे	*so*	*yõ*	यों
From what?	*kis se*	किससे	*thus*	*tyõ*	त्यों
From which	*jis se*	जिससे	*as*	*jyõ*	ज्यों
Of this	*is kā*	इसका			
Of that	*us kā*	उसका			

CHAPTER 8

THE ADJECTIVES

विशेषण

DEFINITION :

The declinable word that is used to describe, point out, qualify or limits the span (*vyāpti* व्याप्ति) of a Noun or Pronoun is called an Adjective (*viśheṣhaṇ* विशेषण) and the word (noun or pronoun) the adjective qualifies is called *viśheṣhya* (विशेष्य).

1a. Three types of Adjectives
विशेषण के तीन प्रकार

1. **Qualitative Adjectives** (*guṇa vāchak* गुणवाचक विशेषण) :

These adjectives are based on their properties of colour, shape, condition, smell, taste, touch, attributes, time, direction and place.

1a. Colour (*raṅg* रंग) : e.g. Orange नारंगी, pink (गुलाबी), yellow (पीला), green (हरा), blue (नीला), sky (आसमानी), purple (जामनी), red (लाल), white (सफेद), black (काला), shiny (चमकीला), gold (सुनहरा), silver (रजत), brown (भूरा), grey (धूसर), smokey (धुँधला), etc.

1b. Shape (*ākār* आकार) : e.g. triangular (तिकोना), square (चौकोर); round (गोल), Long (लंबा), pointed (नुकीला), crooked (वक्र), wide (चौड़ा), straight (सीधा), etc.

1c. State (*sthiti* स्थिति) : e.g. good (स्वस्थ), bad (अस्वस्थ), wet (गीला), dry (सूखा), fresh (ताजा), wilted (बासी), putrified (सड़ा), weak (दुबला), strong (पुष्ट), soft (नरम), soiled (मैला), clean (साफ), pure (शुद्ध), etc.

1d. Smell (*gandh* गंध) : e.g. fragrent (सुवासित), stench (दुर्गंधित), scented (महकता), rotten (सड़ा), etc.

1e. Taste (*swād* स्वाद) : e.g. sweet (मीठा), bitter (कड़वा), salty (नमकीन), pungent (तीखा, कसैला, तिक्त), mild (फीका), sour (खट्टा, अम्ल), alchoholic (मादक), etc.

1f. Touch (*sparśha* स्पर्श) : e.g. soft (मुलायम, मृदु, कोमल), rough (खुरदरा), smooth (चिकना), stickey (चिपका), hard (कड़ा), hot (गरम), cold (ठंडा, ठंढा), etc.

1g. Attribute (*guṇa* गुण) : e.g. good (अच्छा), bad (बुरा), righteous (सात्त्विक), thief (चोर), liar (झूठा), wicked (दुष्ट), peaceful (शाँत), fighter (झगड़ालु), truthful (सच्चा), fake (मिथ्या), charitable (उदार), miser (कंजूस), etc.

1h. Time (*kāl* काल) : e.g. new (नया, नवीन, नूतन), old (पुरातन, पुराना), contemporary (वर्तमान), past (भूत), future (भविष्यत्), ancient (प्राचीन), coming (आगामी), past (गुजरा), etc.

1i. Direction (*diśhā* दिशा) : e.g. western (पाश्चात्य), eastern (पौर्वात्य, पूर्वी), southern (दक्षिणी), northern (उत्तरीय), etc.

1j. Place (*asthānr* स्थान) : e.g. from Konkan (कोंकनी), from China (चीनी), from mountain (पहाड़ी), from forest (जंगली), flooded (जलमय), desert (रेगिस्तानी), heavenly (स्वर्गीय), etc.

For Example : नारंगी संतरा, गुलाबी गाल, पीला केला, हरा तोता, नीला आसमान, आसमानी समुद्र, जामनी बैंगन, लाल टमाटर, सफेद खरगोश, काला कौआ, चमकीला हीरा, सुनहरा मुकुट, रजत सिक्का, भूरा कुत्ता, धूसर बादल, धुँधला कोहरा, तिकोना समोसा, चौकोर मैदान, गोल गेंद, लंबा रास्ता, नुकीला भाला, वक्र चाप, चौड़ा आंगन, सपाट खेत, सीधी रेखा, स्वस्थ सेहत, अस्वस्थ मन, गीला कपड़ा, सूखा चारा, ताजा सब्ज़ी, बासी खाना, सड़ा अंडा, दुबला लड़का, पुष्ट भैसा, नरम बिछौना, मैला कुरता, साफ कमरा, शुद्ध दूध, सुवासित पुष्प, दुर्गंधित नाला, महकता गुलाब, सड़ा माँस, मीठा पकवान, कड़वा नीम, नमकीन परोंठा, तीखा मसाला, कसैला पकौड़ा, तिक्त मिरची, फीकी चाय, खट्टा नीबू, अम्ल आम, मादक पेय, मुलायम बाल, मृदु चर्म, कोमल पंखुड़ी, खुरदरा बोरा, चिकना शीशा, चिपका गोंद, कड़ा चमड़ा, गरम चूल्हा, ठंडा बरफ, अच्छा सुझाव, बुरा आदमी, सात्त्विक स्वभाव, चोर आदमी, झूठा कहना, दुष्ट मनुष्य, शाँत प्रकृति, झगड़ालु स्त्री, सच्चा इनसान, मिथ्या सपना, उदार दिल, कंजूस व्यक्ति, नया खिलौना, नवीन कल्पना, नूतन वर्ष, पुरातन खंडहर, पुराना किला, वर्तमान खबर, भूत इतिहास, भविष्यत् काल, प्राचीन मंदिर, आगामी कार्यक्रम, गुजरा जमाना, पाश्चात्य लोग, पौर्वात्य संस्कृति, दक्षिणी देश, उत्तरीय प्रदेश, कोंकनी भाषा, चीनी औषधि, पहाड़ी इलाका, जंगली भाग, जलमय भूमि,

रेगिस्तानी प्रांत, स्वर्गीय सुख, etc.

2. **Quantitative Adjectives** (*sankhyā-pariman vāchak* संख्या-परिमाणवाचक विशेषण) :

These adjectives are divided in two groups - (2a) Numerical Adjectives (गिनती सूचक) and (2b) Dimentional Adjectives (नाप-तौल सूचक).

2a. Numbers based Adjectives (संख्या सूचक) :

i. Specific amount based (निश्चित् मात्रा सूचक) :

ia. Counting based Adjectives (गणना सूचक) :

a. Whole Numbers based (पुर्णांक सूचक) : दस

b. Fractions based (अपुर्णांक सूचक) : आधा

ib. Sequence based Adjectives (क्रम सूचक) : पहला

ic. Recurrence based Adjectives (आवृत्ति सूचक) : रोज का

id. Grouping based Adjectives (समुदाय सूचक) : हजारों लोग

ie. Individual based Adjectives (प्रत्येक सूचक) : हर लड़का

ii. Non-specific amount based (अनिश्चित् मात्रा सूचक) :

2b. Dimension based Adjectives (नाप-तौल सूचक) :

i. Width based Adjectives (नाप सूचक) : दस मिल

ii. Weight based Afjectives (तौल सूचक) : दो सेर

3. **Demonstrative Pronominal Adjectives** (*sārvanāmic* सार्वनामिक विशेषण) :

The adjectives formed from the pronouns are Pronominal adjectives (सार्वनामिक विशेषण). All pronouns other than the Personal Pronouns (पुरुषवाचक सर्वनाम) and Reflexive Pronoun (निजीवाचक सर्वनाम) can be used as adjectives. Main two groups of Pronominal Adjectives are (1) Original (मूल) and (2) Compound (यौगिक) Pronominal Adjectives.

The original pronoun is when a pronoun without any suffix or modification acts as an adjective. The compound pronoun is derived from an original pronoun by adding a suffix and modifying it in a new form.

The Interrogative Pronouns, Emphatic Pronouns and Exclamatory Pronouns are included in this group.

3a. Pronominal Adjectives :

TABLE 14 : **Demonstrative Pronominal Adjectives** (*sārvanāmic* सार्वनामिक विशेषण)

Original Pronouns मूल विशेषण		Compound Pronouns यौगिक विशेषण	
I (* feminine) (* Plural)	मैं	मुझसा, मुझ जैसा (Masculine singular) (* मुझ जैसी) (Feminine singular, plural) (* मुझ जैसे) (Masculine plural)	like me
We	हम	हमसा, हमारे जैसा	like us
You	तू	तुझसा, तुझ जैसा	like you
You	तुम	तुमसा, तम्हारे जैसा	like you
You	आप	आपसा, आपके जैसा	like you
He, She, That	वह	वैसा, उस जैसा, उतना	like him, like her, like that, that much
This, It	यह	ऐसा, इस जैसा, इतना	like this, this much
Who, Which	जो	जैसा, जितना, जौनसा, जो भी	as, as much, whichever
Who? What? Which?	कौन?	कैसा? किस जैसा? कितना? कौनसा?	like what? how much? which one?

DEGREE OF COMPARISON
तुलनात्मक विशेषण

The change adjectives undergo in their form to show comparison (*tulnā* तुलना) betwee two or more objects is called Degree of Comparison and the new form the adjective assumes is called Adjective of Comparison (तुलनात्मक विशेषण).

There are three states of Degrees of Comparison.

1. Original State (मूल अवस्था) : **No suffix** is attached to the adjective
2. Comparative State (उत्तर अवस्था) : **Comparitive Suffix** तर is attached to adjective
3. Superlative State (उत्तम अवस्था) : **Superlative Suffix** तम is attached to the adjective

Thus,

1. Original State (मूल अवस्था) : **GOOD, BAD**

It is the form in which an adjective **does not** indicate any comparison with any person or thing. e.g. Water is dear to me. मुझे पानी **प्रिय** है. Here the object water is not compared with any other thing.

2. Comparitive State (उत्तर अवस्था) : **BETTER, WORSE**

It is the form in which an adjective shows a comparison **between two** persons or things. e.g. Juice is dearer to me than water. मुझे पानी से रस **प्रियतर** है. Here the object water is compared with another object juice.

3. Superlative State (उत्तम अवस्था) : **BEST, WORST**

It is the form in which an adjective shows a comparison **between more than two** persons or things. e.g. Milk is dearest to me (most* dear than any other drink). मुझे दूध **प्रियतम** है. Here the object milk is compared with all other drinkable objects.

* It could be : i. Most (mximun अधिकतम) or ii. Least (minimun न्यूनतम, लघुतम, अल्पतम).

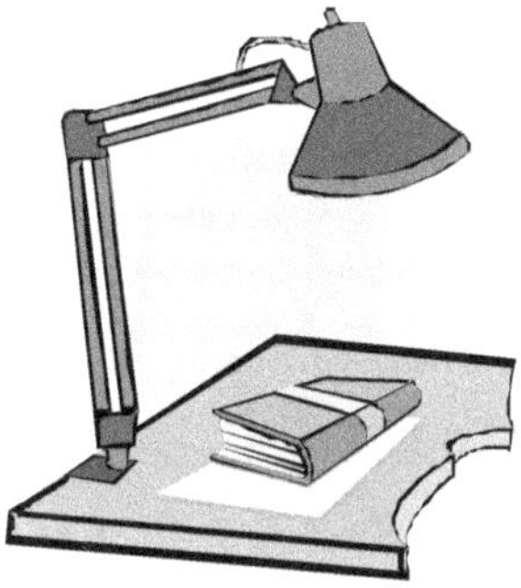

CHAPTER 9

THE PARTICIPLES

dhātusādhit or kridant

धातुसाधित अथवा कृदंत

यल्लिङ्गं यद्वचनं या च विभक्तिर्विशेष्यस्य । तल्लिङ्गं तद्वचनं सा च विशेषणस्यापि ।।

The adjective that comes straight from a root verb (मूल धातु) is a PARTICIPLE (*kridant/ dhātusādhit vis'heṣhaṇ* कृदन्त अर्थात् धातुसाधित विशेषण).

Even though the participles appear like verbs, they are not verbs. Therefore, **they do not have Tenses; rather they have Gender, Number and Cases**. e.g.

TABLE 15 : Passive Participle **(कृदन्त अर्थात् धातुसाधित विशेषण)**

Root verb	Past Perfect	Participle Present Past Future	Nominative for Example	Gender Number m. f. sing. plu.	Tense Present Past Future use
to (go)	went	**gone***	He who has gone		है,
√gam (√गम्)	*agachchhat* अगच्छत्	*gata* गत	*gataḥ* गत:		हैं था,
जाना (जा)	गया	गया हुआ	वह जो गया	m.	थी,
जाना (जा)	गई	गई हुई	वह जो गई	f.	थे होगा
जाना (जा)	गए	गए हुए	वह जो गए	plural	होगी
NOTE : Gone* (गत = गया) **Present** use : He who has gone, **Past** use : He who had gone, **Future** use : He who will have gone. जो गया है, जो गया था, जो गया होगा, etc.					होंगे

HOW TO MAKE PARTICIPLES ?

PARTICIPLES (धातुसाधित / कृदन्त) are derived directly from verb roots (√) by attaching any of the primary *krit* suffixes (कृत् प्रत्यय)

NOTE : Even though the words with primary suffixes indicate a meaning of some action, they are not verbs. Therefore, they do not have tenses. They are adjectives or indeclinables. And thus, as adjectives they have gender, number and cases.

1. ~~PAST~~ PERFECT PASSIVE PARTICIPLE (ppp∘)

kta-viśeṣaṇ क्त-विशेषण

NOTE : The term ppp∘ actually stands for PERFECT Passive Participle. As seen in the above table, the ppp∘ does not necessarily mean only the PAST (tense) action, but necessarily means a PERFECT action, an action that is completed.

For Example : There are four Perfect Tenses with the ppp∘ ate or eaten खाया *khāyā* .

PLEASE REMEMBER : गया *gayā* is neither a Verb nor a Past Tense. It is Passive Participle Adjective (from the verbal noun जाना *jānā*.). All Participles are Adjectives, not verbs or Tenses.

1. Simple (indefinite) Perfect Tense use : I ate a Samosā = मेरे द्वारा समोसा खाया गया = मेरे द्वारा (passive) समोसा (object) खाया गया (perfect participle). मैंने समोसा खाया.
2. Present Perfect Tense use : Samosā is eaten by me. = मेरे द्वारा समोसा खाया गया है = मेरे द्वारा (passive) समोसा (object) खाया गया (perfect participle) है (Present Tense verb 'is').
3. Past Perfect Tense use : = Samosā **was** eaten by me. = मेरे द्वारा समोसा खाया गया था = मेरे द्वारा (passive) समोसा (object) खाया गया (perfect participle) था (Past Tense verb 'was')..
4. Future Perfect Tense : Samosā **will be** eaten by me. = मेरे द्वारा समोसा खाया गया होगा = मेरे द्वारा (passive) समोसा (object) खाया गया (perfect participle) होगा (Future Tense verb 'will be').

As seen above ALL are Perfect actions. They are not PAST Tenses. They include

Indefinite, Present and Future tenses too. Even though all are using a ppp◦ खाया.

THEREFORE, ppp◦ more correctly stands for PERFECT Passivce Participles, rarther than Past Passive Participle (a misnomer).

HOW TO MAKE ~~PAST~~ PERFECT PASSIVE PARTICIPLES?

The *kta* (क्त) suffix is added to verb roots (in Passive and Abstract voices in perfect tense) to make a ppp◦. As a result, while adding a *kta* क्त suffix, the *k* क is dropped and only *ta* त is attached to the root verb.

NOTE : With the roots such as √री, ली, ब्ली, प्ली, धू, पू, लू, ॠ, कॄ, गॄ, जॄ, नॄ, पॄ, भॄ, वॄ, शॄ, स्तॄ and हा, the suffix *ta* (त) becomes suffix *na* (न).

Use of this *kta* (क्त) suffix produces Adjectives of the Perfect Tense.

√gam + kta (ta) = gata (gone) √गम् + क्त (त) = गत।

1. PAST ACTIVE PARTICIPLE (Past-AP)

ktavatu-viśeṣaṇam क्तवतु–विशेषणम्।

A Past Active Participle is formed by attaching वत् *vat* suffix to a Past passive participle (ppp◦). e.g. गत + वत् → गतवत्।

The Past-AP गतवत् becomes गतवान् in Nominative case.

Singular - (m◦) अहं गतवान्। त्वं गतवान्। स: गतवान्। अश्व: गतवान्। (f◦) चटिका गतवती।

Plural - (m◦) वयं गतवन्त:। यूयं गतवन्त:। ते गतवन्त:। अश्वा: गतवन्त:। (f◦) चटिका: गतवन्त्य:।

√गत् to go, PAST ACTIVE PARTICIPLE

Verb	Singular		Plural	
1. I ate (m◦)	अहं गतवान्	मैं गया	वयं गतवन्त:	हम गए
2. You ate (m◦)	त्वं गतवान्	तू गया	यूयं गतवन्त:	तुम गए
3. He ate (m◦)	स: गतवान्	वह गया	ते गतवन्त:	वे गया
4. She ate (f◦)	सा गतवती	वह गयी	ता: गतवत्य:	वे गयीं

5. It ate (n◦) तत् खादितवत् *tat khāditavat* तानि खादितवन्ति *tāni khāditavanti*

2. PRESENT ACTIVE PARTICIPLES

śatri-śānach-viśeṣaṇāni शतृ-शानच्-विशेषण

There are two types of Present Active Participles pap (शतृ-शानच् विशेषण).

(i) The *Parasmaipadī* परस्मैपदी Participle (पर हेतु शतृ विशेषण)

(ii) The *Ātmanepadī* आत्मनेपदी Participle (आत्म हेतु शानच् विशेषण).

(i) The Parasmaipadī Present Active Participle (PPAP)

śatri viśeṣaṇam **पर हेतु शतृ कर्तरी विशेषण**

The *śatri* (शतृ) suffix *at* अत् is added to a *parasmaipadī* root verb to form an adjective of Present Continuous tense. e.g.

(ii) *√kri + śatri (at) = kurvat* (while doing) √कृ + शतृ (अत्) = कुर्वत् (करते हुए)

HOW TO MAKE A शतृ PPAP ADJAVTIVE FROM A VERB?

(1) first, take the desired *parasmaipadī* verb (e.g. √कृ);

(2) determine the third-person, plural, present tense of that verb (e.g. कुर्वन्ति);

(3) remove the last suffix (e.g. कुर्वन्ति – अन्ति = कुर्व्); and then to this modified word,

(4) attach the अत् suffix (e.g. कुर्व् + अत्), then you get PPAP कुर्वत्

The शतृ adjectives give a (gerund like) meaning with 'ing' attached to the verb. e.g.

कुर्वत् = doing, while doing; गच्छत् = going, while going; कथयत् = while saying .. etc.

In the Nominative (1st) case :

The Masculine forms of these words will be कुर्वन्, कुर्वन्तौ, कुर्वन्तः। गच्छन्, गच्छन्तौ, गच्छन्तः। कथयन्, कथयन्तौ, कथयन्तः। .. etc.

The Feminine forms will be कुर्वन्ती, कुर्वन्त्यौ, कुर्वन्त्यः। गच्छन्ती, गच्छन्त्यौ, गच्छन्त्यः। कथयन्ती, कथयन्त्यौ, कथयन्त्यः। and

The Neuter gender forms will be कुर्वत्, कुर्वती, कुर्वन्ति। गच्छत्, गच्छती, गच्छन्ति। कथयत्, कथयती, कथयन्ति। etc.

The Ātmanepadī Present <u>Active</u> Participles (ĀPAP)

***śānach-kartari-viśeṣaṇāni* आत्म हेतु शानच् कर्तरि विशेषण**

Either *śānach* (शानच्) suffix *āna* (आन) or *māna* (मान) is added to the *ātmanepadī* root verbs to form adjectives of Present Continuous Tense. e.g.

(i) **आन शानच्** - *√bhuj + śānach (āna) = bhuñjāna* (enjoying, eater) √भुज् + शानच् (आन) = भुञ्जान while enjoying, enjoyer उपभोग करता हुआ, उपभोग करने वाला.

(ii) **मान शानच्** - *√yudh + śānach (māna) = yotsyamāna* (fighting, fighter लड़ता हुआ, लड़ने वाला) √युध् + शानच् (मान)= योत्स्यमान while fighting, fighter लड़ता हुआ, लड़ने वाला.

Ātmanepadī Present Active Participle शानच् is formed by attaching आन or मान suffix to a verb.

(a) If the verb belongs to the FIRST GROUP of Conjugations (1st, 4th, 6th or 10th conjugation गण), then it takes the मान (*māna*) suffix.

(b) But, if the verb belongs to the SECOND GROUP of conjugations (2nd, 3rd, 5th, 7th, 8th or 9th conjugation), then it takes the आन (*āna*) suffix.

The शानच् adjectives give a (gerund like) meaning with 'ing' or 'er' attached to the verb.
e.g. √लभ्→ लभमान = attaining; attainer. √कृ→ कुर्वाण = working(man) = worker.

1. ĀPAP of the FIRST GROUP

mān śānach-kartari-viśeṣaṇ

आत्म हेतु <u>मान</u> शानच् कर्तरी विशेषण

HOW TO KAKE A मान-शानच् ADJECTIVE?

(1) first take the desired *ātmanepadī* verb (e.g. 1√लभ् to obtain प्राप्त करना);

(2) determine the third-person, plural, present tense of that verb (e.g. लभन्ते, प्राप्त करते हैं);

(3) remove the ending न्ते-ते suffix (e.g. लभन्ते - न्ते = लभ); and then to that word,

(4) attach the मान suffix (लभ + मान → लभमान = obtaining, obtainer प्राप्त करते हुए, प्राप्त करने वाला).

The verbs belonging to the FIRST GROUP i.e. 1st, 4th, 6th or 10th conjugation गण, take the मान suffix. e.g.

1√लभ्→ लभन्ते→ लभमान = obtaining; 4√मन्→ मन्यते→ मन्यमान = thinking मानने वाला; 6√दिश्→ दिश्यते→ दिश्यमान = showing देखने वाला; 10√गण्→ गण्यते→ गण्यमान = counting, गिनने वाला, etc.

2. ĀPAP of the SECOND GROUP

ān śānach-kartari-viśeṣaṇ

आत्म हेतु आन शानच् कर्तरी विशेषण

HOW TO MAKE AN आन-शानच् ADJECTIVE?

(1) Take the desired *ātmanepadī* verb (e.g. 9√ज्ञा to know, जानना);

(2) determine the third-person, plural, present tense (जानते, जानते हैं);

(3) remove the ending न्ते-ते suffix (e.g. जानन्ते - न्ते = जान); and then to that word,

(4) add the *ān* आन suffix (जान + आन → जानान = knowing, knower जानते हुए, जानने वाला)

The verbs belonging to the SECOND GROUP (2nd, 3rd, 5th, 7th, 8th or 9th conjugation गण), take आन् suffix. e.g. 2√ब्रू→ ब्रुवते→ ब्रुवाण = speaking बोलने वाला; 3√दा→ ददते→ ददान = giving देने वाला; 5√वृ→ वृण्वन्ते→ वृण्वान = choosing वरण करने वाला; 7√भुज्→ भुञ्जन्ते→ भुञ्जान = enjoying, उपभोग करने बाला; 8√कृ→ कुर्वन्ते→ कुर्वाण doing करने वाला; 9√ज्ञा→ जानन्ते→ जानान knowing, जानने वाला .. etc.

Examples :

(1) Men doing sacrifice are rare. त्यागं कुर्वाणा: जना: दुर्लभा:। त्याग करने वाले लोग दुर्लभ हैं.

(2) Many are men who talk too much. अतीव ब्रुवाणा: जना: सुलभा:। बहुत बोलने वाले लोग सुलभ हैं.

3. The Ātmanepadī Present Passive Participles (ĀPPP)

yamān śānach karmaṇi viśeṣaṇ

आत्म हेतु यमान शानच् कर्मणि विशेषण

Thse ĀPPP adjectives are formed from *ātmanepadī* root verbs only, and therefore, they take मान (यमान) suffix only.

HOW TO MAKE A कर्मणि यमान शानच् ADJECTIVE?

(i) first take the desired *ātmanepadī* verb (e.g. 8√कृ to do करना) from any group (1st or 2nd group);

(ii) take the first part of the third person plural present tense and remove the tense suffix.

(iii) then attach the यमान suffix to it (e.g. कृ (क्रि) + यमान → क्रियमाण = is being done किए जाते हुए). e.g.

प्रकृते: क्रियमाणानि गुणै: कर्माणि सर्वश:। (Gītā 3.27)

(1)	1√लभ् →	लभ्	+ यमान	=	लभ्यमान	being obtained प्राप्त कए जाते हुए
(2)	2√ब्रू →	उच्	+ यमान	=	उच्यमान	being said कहे जाते हुए
(3)	5√श्रु →	श्रू	+ यमान	=	श्रूयमाण	being heard सुने जाते हुए
(4)	7√छिद् →	छिद्	+ यमान	=	छिद्यमान	being cut काटे जाते हुए
(5)	4√नश् →	नश्	+ यमान	=	नश्यमान	being destroyed नष्ट कए जाते हुए
(6)	6√दिश् →	दिश्	+ यमान	=	दिश्यमान	being shown देखे जाते हुए
(7)	9√मन्थ् →	मन्थ्	+ यमान	=	मन्थ्यमान	being chruned मंथन किए जाते हुए
(8)	3√धा →	धी	+ यमान	=	धीयमान	being borne धारण किए जाते हुए
(9)	10√वर्ण् →	वर्ण्	+ वर्ण्यमान	=	वर्ण्यमान	being described वर्णन किए जाते हुए, etc.

4. THE POTENTIAL PARTICIPLES (pp◦)

vidyarthī viśeṣaṇ

विध्यर्थि विशेषण

To form these potential participle adjectives we can optionally attach either तव्य, अनीय or य suffix to the verb roots. In all three cases their meaning remains same.

एकस्य धातोः एव प्रत्ययत्रयम् अपि योजयितुं शक्नुमः एतेषां प्रत्ययानाम् अर्थः समानः एव।

However, use of one suffix is more popular for some roots, while the other is used for some other roots.

Use of these adjectives is quite frequent and should be understood properly.

Thus, please remember that :

(1) These participles are passive (कर्मणि) and never active (कर्तरि).

(2) These can be formed from almost any verb root, transitive or intransitive.

(3) Here, the subject is always in Instrumental (3rd) case (करण कारक) and the object in Nominative (1st) case (कर्त्ता कारक).

(4) The gender and number of the adjective follows those of the object.

(5) Sometimes, these adjectives are used as regular non-potential adjectives or as nouns also.

(6) These are adjectives, not verbs.

Six affixes are included in this pp◦ category of *kritya* (कृत्य प्रत्यय) suffixes, namely : *tavyat* (तव्यत्), *tavya* (तव्य), *anīyar* (अनीयर्), *yat* (यत्), *kyap* (क्यप्) and *ṇyat* (ण्यत्).

These *kritya* suffixes are attached to:

(i) the transitive verbs (सकर्मक-धातु) in the Passive voice (कर्मवाच्य), and

(ii) the intransitive verbs (अकर्मक-धातु) in the Abstract voice (भाववाच्य).

5. The Future Passive (Potential) Participles

tavyat (तव्यत्), *anīyar* (अनीयर्) and *tavya* (तव्य) suffixes

(A) The ***tavyat*** (तव्यत्) and ***tavya*** (तव्य) suffixes :

The *tavyat* (तव्यत्) and *tavya* (तव्य) suffixes of Future passive participles produce Potential Adjectives (विध्यर्थि-विशेषण). e.g.

(i) √śru + tavyat (tavya) = śrotavya (fit to be heard) √श्रु + तव्यत् (तव्य) = श्रोतव्य, सुनने योग्य

(ii) √śru + anīyar (anīya) = śrvaṇīya (fit to be heard) √श्रु + अनीयर (अनीय) = श्रवणीय, सुनने योग्य

(B) The ***yat*** (यत्), ***kyap*** (क्यप्) and ***ṇyat*** (ण्यत्) suffixes :

The *yat* (यत्), *kyap* (क्यप्) and *ṇyat* (ण्यत्) suffixes produce adjectives with a sense of 'fit for' or 'ought to be' by adding y (य) to the final root.

(i) √jñā + yat (y) = jñeya (to be known) √ज्ञा + यत् (य) = ज्ञेय, जानने लायक

(ii) √kri + kyap (y) = kritya (to be done) √कृ+ क्यप् (य) = कृत्य, करने लायक

(iii) a-vi√kri+ ṇyat (y) = avikāraya (indistructible) अ-वि√कृ + ण्यत् (य) = अविकार्य, अविनाशी

√kri (to do) → pp◦ karaṇīya, kartavya, kārya = Ought to be done, fit to be done, must be done, good to be done, should be done, worth doing (करने लायक, करने योग्य, करना चाहिए, करना अच्छा है, करें, करना उचित है).

SOME COMMON EXAMPLES OF POTENTIAL PARTICIPLES

P◦ = parasmaipadī, A◦ ātmamepadī, U◦ ubhaypadī

1A◦√ईक्ष् → ईक्षितव्य, ईक्षणीय, ईक्ष्य । 1P◦√गै → गातव्य, गानीय, गेय । 1P◦√त्यज् → त्यक्तव्य, त्यजनीय, त्याज्य । 1P◦√दह् → दग्धव्य, दहनीय, दाह्य । 1P◦√दा → दातव्य, दानीय, देय । 1P◦√दा → दातव्य, दानीय, देय (देने योग्य) । 1P◦√निन्द् → निन्दितव्य, निन्दनीय, निन्द्य (निंदा करने योग्य) । 1P◦√भू → भवितव्य, भवनीय, भाव्य (होने योग्य) । 1A◦√रम् → रन्तव्य, रमणीय, रम्य (रममाण होने योग्य) । 1A◦√वृत् → वर्तितव्य, वर्तनीय, वृत्य (वर्तन करने योग्य) । 1A◦√वृध् → वर्धितव्य, वर्धनीय, वृध्य । 1A◦√वन्द् → वन्दितव्य, वन्दनीय, वन्द्य (वंदन करने योग्य) । प्र1P◦√शंस् → प्रशंसितव्य, प्रशंसनीय, प्रशंस्य (प्रश्ंसा करने योग्य) । 1A◦√श्लाघ्

→ श्लाघितव्य, श्लाघनीय, श्लाघ्य (सराहना करने योग्य)। 1P॰√स्था → स्थातव्य, स्थानीय, स्थेय (रहने योग्य)। 1P॰√स्मृ → स्मर्तव्य, स्मरणीय, स्मार्य (स्मरण करने योग्य)। 1A॰√स्वाद् → स्वादितव्य, स्वादनीय, स्वाद्य (खाने योग्य)। 1P॰√हृ → हर्तव्य, हरणीय, हार्य (हरण करने योग्य)।

2P॰√अस् → भवितव्य, भवनीय, भाव्य (होने योग्य)। अधि2A॰√इ → अध्येतव्य, अध्ययनीय, अध्येय (अभ्यास करने योग्य)। 2U॰√दुह् → दोग्धव्य, दोहनीय, दोह्य (दुहने योग्य)। 2U॰√ब्रू → वक्तव्य, वचनीय, वाच्य (बोलने योग्य)। 2P॰√रुद् → रोदितव्य, रोदनीय, रोद्य (शोक करने योग्य)। 2P॰√शांस् → शासितव्य, शासनीय, शिष्य (शासन करने योग्य)। 2P॰√श्वस् → श्वसितव्य, श्वसनीय, श्वास्य (जीने योग्य)। 2P॰√स्तु → स्तोतव्य, स्तवनीय, स्तुत्य (स्तुति करने योग्य)। 2P॰√हन् → हन्तव्य, हननीय, वध्य (मारने योग्य)।

3U॰√दा → दातव्य, दानीय, देय (देने योग्य)। अभि3U॰√धा → अभिधातव्य, अभिधानीय, अभिधेय (कहलाने योग्य)। 3P॰√भी → भेतव्य, भयनीय, भेय (डरने योग्य)। 3U॰√भृ → भर्तव्य, भरणीय, भृत्य (पोषण करने योग्य)।

4P॰√क्षम् → क्षमितव्य-क्षन्तव्य, क्षमणीय, क्षम्य (क्षमा करने योग्य)। 4A॰√जन् → जनितव्य, जननीय, जन्य (जानने योग्य)। 4P॰√नृत् → नर्तितव्य, नर्तनीय, नृत्य (नाच करने योग्य)। 4P॰√पुष् → पोष्टव्य, पोषणीय, पोष्य (पालन-पोषण करने योग्य)। प्र4P॰√मद् → प्रमदितव्य, प्रमदनीय, प्रमाद्य (प्रमाद करने योग्य)। 4A॰√मन् → मन्तव्य, मननीय, मान्य (मानने योग्य)। 4P॰√शम् → शमितव्य, शमनीय, शम्य (शमन करने योग्य)।

प्र 5P॰√आप् → प्राप्तव्य, प्रापणीय, प्राप्य (प्राप्त करने योग्य)। 5U॰√चि → चेतव्य, चयनीय, चेय (चयन करने योग्य)। 5P॰√शक् → शक्तव्य, शकनीय, शक्य (शक्य होने योग्य)। 5P॰√श्रु → श्रोतव्य, श्रवणीय, श्राव्य (सुनने योग्य)।

6U॰√क्षिप् → क्षेप्तव्य, क्षेपणीय, क्षेप्य (फेंकने योग्य)। 6P॰√पैच्छ् → प्रष्टव्य, प्रच्छनीय, प्रच्छ्य (पूछने योग्य)। 6U॰√मुच् → मोक्तव्य, मोचनीय, मोच्य (मुक्ति करने योग्य)। 6A॰√मृ → मर्तव्य, मरणीय, मार्य-मर्त्य । मरने योग्य)। प्र6P॰√विश् → प्रवेष्टव्य, प्रवेशनीय, प्रवेश्य (प्रवेश करने योग्य)। 6P॰√सृज् → स्त्रष्टव्य, सजनीय, सृज्य (सृजन करने योग्य)। 6U॰√सिंच् → सेक्तव्य, सेचनीय, सेच्य (सिंचन करने योग्य)।

7U॰√छिद् → छेत्तव्य, छेदनीय, छेद्य (छेदन करने योग्य)। 7U॰√भिद् → भत्तव्य, भेदनीय, भेद्य (भेदन करने योग्य)। 7U॰√भुज् → भेक्तव्य, भोजनीय, भोज्य (उपभोग करने योग्य)। 7U॰√रुध् → रोद्धव्य, रोधनीय, रोध्य (विरोध करने योग्य)।

8U∘√कृ → कर्तव्य, करणीय, कार्य (करने योग्य)। 8U∘√तन् → तनितव्य, तननीय, तान्य (ढकने योग्य)। 8A∘√मन् → मनितव्य, माननीय, मान्य (मनन करने योग्य)।

9U∘√क्री → क्रेतव्य, क्रयणीय, क्रय (खरीदने योग्य)। 9P∘√ग्रन्थ् → ग्रन्थितव्य, ग्रन्थनीय, ग्रन्थ्य (लिखने योग्य)। 9U∘√ग्रह् → ग्रहीतव्य, ग्रहणीय, ग्राह्य (लेने योग्य)। 9P∘√बन्ध् → बन्द्धव्य, बन्धनीय, बन्द्धय (बांधने योग्य)। 9P∘√मुष् → मोषितव्य, मोषणीय, मोष्य (छिपाने योग्य)। 9A∘√वृ → वरितव्य, वरणीय, वार्य (विवाह करने योग्य)।

प्र10A∘√अर्थ् → प्रार्थयितव्य, प्रार्थनीय, प्रार्थ्य (प्रार्थना करने योग्य)। 10U∘√क्षल् → क्षलितव्य, क्षालनीय, क्षाल्य (धोने करने योग्य)। 10U∘√पूज् → पूजयितव्य, पूजनीय, पूज्य (पूजने योग्य)। 10U∘√भक्ष् → भक्षयितव्य, भक्षणीय, भक्ष्य (खाने योग्य)। 10U∘√भूष् → भूषयितव्य, भूषणीय, भूष्य (सजाने योग्य)। 10U∘√रच् → रचयितव्य, रचनीय, रच्य । (रचना करने योग्य), etc.

6. INDECLINABLE PARTICIPLES

kridanta avyay

कृदन्त अव्यय

The word that is not affected by Gender, Number, Person, Tense nor Case is an INDECLINABLE word (अव्यय).

सदृशं त्रिषु लिङ्गेषु सर्वासु च विभक्तिषु ।
वचनेषु च सर्वेषु यन्न व्येति तदव्ययम् ।।

If same subject does two actions, one after other, then in that case : In order to indicate completion of a subordinate (first) action, prior to the commencement of the main (second) action, an Indeclinable Past Participle (क्त्वा or ल्यप् = having done करके) is used, in stead of joining two clauses with the phrase 'and then' ततः च (करने के बाद फिर)।

These single-word participles (क्त्वा and ल्यप्) imply completion of the specific preceding subordinate action ('having done, or doing' पूर्वकालिक), before the following main action begins. **These participles are widely used.**

6a. Indeclinable Past Participle (ktvā-ipp◦) with *ktvā* (क्त्वा) suffix

RULE 1 : The *tvā* त्वा of the Indeclinable Past Participle *ktvā* क्त्वा may be added only to those verb-root to which any prefix, other than अ, is NOT attached.

The त्वा participle has same nature as the त in the Past Passive Participles (ppp◦) we studied in Chapter 28.3.

√दा (*dā*, to give देना), दत्त (ppp◦ - *datta,* given दिया), दत्त्वा (ipp◦ - *dattvā,* having given, giving देकर)

The *ktvā* suffix is used for forming a Gerund ending in suffix 'ing' that are dependent on some previous event (पूर्वकालिक–क्रिया)

√driś+ktvā (tvā) = driṣṭvā (having seen, seeing) √दृश्+ क्त्वा (त्वा) = दृष्ट्वा, देख कर.

RULE 2 : The *lyp* (ल्यप्) suffix is attached only to those verb-roots that have any prefix, other than *a* (अ), is attached. The meaning and the nature of a *lyp*-participle remains same as of a *ktvā*-participle.

6b. Indeclinable Past Participle (lyp-ipp◦) with *lyp* (ल्यप्) Suffix, ल्यबंत

As said earlier, the suffix य or त्य of the Indeclinable Past Participle (ल्यप् lyp-ipp◦) may be added only to that verb-root to which a prefix (other than अ *a*) is already attached.

(i) आ√दा give, आदत्त ppp◦ taken, आदाय ipp◦ having taken लेकर.

(ii) *upa-sam√gam + lyp (ya) = upa-saṅgmya* (having approached) √गम् + क्त्वा (त्वा) = गत्वा having gone, जाकर. उप–सम्√गम् + ल्यप् (य) = उपसङ्गम्य having approached पास जाकर.

7. THE INFINITIVE PARTICIPLE

tumun kridant avyay तुमुन् कृदंत अव्यय (के लिए)

Another important Indeclinable Participle, the INFINITIVE *tumun* (तुमुन्), is formed by adding the *tum* तुम् suffix directly to any verb-root.

An infinitive gives the meaning of 'for doing or to do' the action indicated by the attached verb. e.g. √दा (to give) → दा + तुम् = दातुम् (for giving, to give देने के लिए).

USE OF TUMUN in place of POTENTIAL PARTICIPLE ipp◦

A *tumun* infinitive could be used in place of any of the three ipp◦ Indeclinable Potential Participles of अनीयर्, तव्यत्, य।

e.g. You should not lament. (i) tumun◦ न त्वं शोचितुम् अर्हसि। तुम शोक करने के लिए योग्य नहीं हो.. = (ii) ipp◦ त्वया शोकः न करणीयः, तुम्हें शोक नहीं करना चाहिए। त्वया शोकः न कर्तव्यः आपके द्वारा शोक नहीं होना चाहिए। त्वया शोकः न कार्यः तुम्हारे द्वारा शोक उचित नहीं है।

The Primary Derivatives of the Participles

कृदन्त के प्रमुख स्वरूप

EXAMPLE : Root Verb √भू (होना)

TABLE 16 : **Derivatives of Participlae कृदन्त के प्रमुख स्वरूप**

	PPP◦	PAP◦	PPAP◦	APPP◦	FPPP◦	FPPP◦	FPPP◦	IPP◦	IPP◦	INF◦
	क्त	क्तवतु	शतृ	शानच्	अनीयर्	तव्यत्	तव्य	क्त्वा	ल्यप्	तुमुन्
1. Regular Actions	भूत	भूतवत्	भवत्	भूयमान	भवनीय	भवितव्य	भव्य	भूत्वा	संभूय	भवितुम्
2. Causatives	भावित	भावयितवत्	भावयत्	भावयमान	भावनीय	भावयितव्य	भाव्य	भावयित्वा	संभाव्य	बुभूषितुम्
3. Desideratives	बुभूषित	बुभूषितवत्	बुभूषत्	बुभूषमान	बुभीषणीय	बुभूषितव्य	बुभूतव्य	बुभूषित्वा	संबुभूष्य	बोभवितुम्
4. Frequentative										
(i) यङन्त	बोभूयित	बोभूयितवत्	बोभूयत्	बोभूयमान	बोभूयनीय	बोभूयितव्य	बोभूय्य	बोभूयित्वा	संबोभूय्य	बोभोयितुम्
(ii) यङ्लुगन्त	बोभुवित	बोभुषितवत्	बोभुवत्	बोभुवमान	बोभवनीय	बोभवितव्य	बोभव्य	बोभूत्वा	संबोभूय	बोभवितुम्

The Derivatives of √भू : भव, भवदीय, भवन, भवानी, भवित्र, भविष्णु, भविष्य, भाव, भावक, भावना, भाविक, भावुक, भुवन, भूति, भूमि, भूष्णू, प्रभव, प्रभाव, प्रभु, प्रभुत्व, प्रभू, विभु, विभुति, .. etc.

CHART OF PARTICIPLES

ADJECTIVES AND INDECLINABLES

(1) ADJECTIVE PARTICIPLES

	Participle	Suffix		Example - root verbs √कृ √लभ्	
1.	**Past Passive Participle**	**त**	**(क्त)**	**कृत**	**(done, has been done)**
2.	**Past Active Participle**	**तवत्**	**(क्तवतु)**	**कृतवत्**	**(has done)**
3.	**Present Active Participle**	**अत्**	**(शतृ)**	**कुर्वत्**	**(doing, while doing, doer)**
4.	**Present Active Participle**	**आन**	**(शानच्)**	**कुर्वाण**	**(doing)**
5.	**Present Active Participle**	**मान**	**(शानच्)**	**लभमान**	**(getting)**
6.	**Present Passive Participle**	**यमान**	**(शानच्)**	**क्रियमाण**	**(being done)**
7.	**Potential Passive Participle**	**तव्य**	**(तव्यत्)**	**कर्तव्य**	**(ought, fit to be done)**
		अनीय	**(अनीयर्)**	**करणीय**	**(ought, fit to be done)**
		य	**(यत्)**	**कार्य**	**(ought, fit to be done)**

(2) INDECLINABLE PARTICIPLES

Participle	Suffix		Example - root verbs √कृ √लभ्
8. Indeclinable Past Participle (without a prefix, Gerund)	**त्वा**	**(क्त्वा)**	**कृत्वा (having done)** करके
9. Indeclinable Past Participle (with a prefix)	**य**	**(ल्यप्)**	**अनुकृत्य (having done accordingly)** के अनुसार
10. Infinitive of Purpose	**तुम्**	**(तुमुन्)**	**कर्तुम् (for doing)** करने के लिए

CHAPTER 10

THE VERBS

क्रिया

1. √ROOT VERB

√धातु

The verb (*kriyā* क्रिया) is a word used for saying or asserting something about an action or function performed by a person or a thing. It is the heart of a sentence. The verb tells us what a person or thing is, what a person or thing does or what is done to a person or thing. e.g.

(i) What a person is or thing : राम राजा था, सीता लड़की है, फल ताज़ा हैं.

(ii) What a person ot thing does : बाबा खेती करते हैं, पत्ते गिर रहे हैं.

(iii) What is done to a person or thing : ताला बंद किया, मैं सब्ज़ी काट चुका हूँ.

According to the Sanskrit grammer, Nouns, Pronouns, Adjectives, Verbs, Adverbs, Prepositions, Conjunctions, Interjections, Articles, Infinitives, Gerunds, et. all originates from some kind of action visible or invisible. Therefore, root action words or the root verbs (मूल धातु) are the building-bricks for every construction aspect of Sanskrit grammer. The symbol √ is attached before each verb word to indicate the word as a Root Verb (धातु). e.g. The verb do would be √कृ in Sanskrit and √कर in Hindi.

Many people think that "to do करना" is Root Verb. Where as, "Do कर" is the Root Verb (धातु) and "to do" करना is an Infinitive, Verbal Noun or a Gerund.

1. **An Infinitive** (*sāmānya-kriyā-rūp* सामान्य क्रियारूप) is a verb in the Infinitive Mood (*tumunnatapad* तुमुन्नतपद or *bhāva-vachan* भाववचन). e.g. Infinitives : to do करना, to take लेना, to give देना, to walk चलना, to shine चमकना, to write लिखना, to read, पढ़ना, etc.
2. **A Verbal Noun** (*kriyā-vāchak-nām* क्रियावाचक नाम or *dhātu-sādhit-nām* धातुसाधित नाम) is a Verb in its Infinitive form used as a Noun (नाम). e.g. Verbal Nouns : to do - अच्छा काम करना चाहिए, to take - हरि नाम लेना चाहिए, to give - सुख देना चाहिए, to walk - सत्य मार्ग पर चलना चाहिए, to shine- चमकना सोने का गुण है, to write - मैं पत्र लिखना चाहता हूँ, to read - गीता पढ़नी चाहिए, etc.
3. **A Gerund** is that form of a verb to be done or being done (*dhātu-sādhit-kridant* धातुसाधित कृदन्त). e.g. Gerund : to do = for doing, I come here to do study = I come here for studying. मैं यहाँ पढ़ने आता हूँ = मैं यहाँ पढ़ने के लिए आता हूँ, etc.
4. **The Root Verb** (मूल धातु) : The original Verb is without any prefix (upasarg उपसर्ग) or suffix (pratyay प्रत्यय) from which other words originate. e.g. Root Verbs : do √कर, take √ले, give √दे, walk √चल, shine √चमक, write √लिख, read √पढ़, etc.

2. DENOMINATIVE VERBS

नामधातु

As we have seen earlier, words are made by attaching a prefix or suffix to the Root Verbs (मूल धातु). Then, a secondary word in the form of Verbal Noun (*kriyā-vāchak-nām* क्रियावाचक नाम or *dhātu-sādhit-nām* धातुसाधित नाम) can also be formed by adding prefix and/or suffix to a Root Verb. Such words which are formed from nouns (नाम) using them as Root Words (धातु), are called Demonstrative Nouns (नामधातु). e.g.

Root Verb √कृ (Hindi, √कर) : स्वी√कृ + ल्युट् = स्वीकार (नाम noun, acceptance)

स्वीकार + ना = स्वीकारना (नामधातु to accept / accepting)

Root Verb √कृ (Hindi, √कर) : धिक् + कृ = धिक्कार (नाम noun, rejection)

धिक्कार + ना = धिक्कारना (नामधातु to reject / rejecting)

Root Verb √कृ (Hindi, √कर) : न√कृ + ल्युट् = नकार (नाम noun, refusal)

नकार + ना = नकारना (नामधातु to refuse / refusing)

Root Verb √कृ (Hindi, √कर) : स्वी√कृ + ल्युट् = स्वीकार (नाम noun, acceptance)

स्वीकार + ना = स्वीकारना (नामधातु to accept / accepting)

Root Verb √धृ (Hindi, √धारण) : सु√धृ + णिच् + ल्युट् = सुधार (नाम noun, improvement)

सुधार + ना = सुधारना (नामधातु to improve / improving)

Similarly, दुतकारना, उतारना, कुचलना, पुकारना, निकालना, उबालना, उछालना, सँभालना, etc.

3. COMPOUND VERBS

संयुक्त क्रिया

Verbs such as सक (can), आ (be able), चाह (want), कर (having done), जा (be possible), पड़ (be compelled), लग (start), हो (become), चुक (be finished), etc. can be joined with other verbs to form new compound verbs (संयुक्त क्रिया). e.g.

सक (can) : बोल (speak) + सक (can) = मैं संस्कृत बोल सकता हूँ
I can speak Sansskrit (Active Voice)

आ (be able) : बोल (speak) + आ (be able) = मुझे संस्कृत बोलना आता है.
I am able to speak Sansskrit (Passive Voice)

चाह (want) : पी (drink) + चाह (want) = वह चाय पीना चाहती है
She wants to drink tea.

कर (do) : खा (eat) + कर (having done) = वह नाश्ता खा कर आया है.
He came having eaten breakfast..

जा (be possible) : तोड़ (break) + जा (be possible) = वादा तोड़ा जाता है.
It is possible to break a promise.

पड़ (be compelled) : आ (come) + पड़ (be compelled) = उसे यहाँ आना पड़ा.
He was compelled to come here.

लग (start) : चल (move) + लग (start) = गाड़ी चलने लगी.
Train started to move.

हो (become) : उग (rise) + हो (become) = सूरज उगा हुआ है.
Sun rise has become.

चुक (be finished) : गिर (fall) + चुक (be already done) = दाम गिर चुके हैं.
Prices have already fallen.

0

HINDI INTENSIVE COMPOUND VERBS
यङ्गंत संयुक्त हिंदी क्रिया

Some Verbs such as उठना, बैठना, लेना, देना, आना, जाना, डालना, पड़ना, लगना, चुकना, etc. when attached as a suffix to other Verbs, they form Intensive Compound Verbs. Also, by repeating some words, an effect of intensiveness is given to the compound word (यङ्गंत संयुक्त क्रिया). e.g.

1. **उठना :** वह बोला He spoke. वह अचानक बोल उठा He suddenly spoke out. मैं जागा हूँ. I am awake. मैं जाग उठा हूँ. I have become aware of the facts.
2. **बैठना :** उसने गलती की. She made a mistake. वह गलती कर बैठी. Mistake occured by her. मैंने दो घर खरीदे. I bought two houses. मैं दो घर खरीद बैठा हूँ. I am stuck with two houses.
3. **लेना :** उसने पैसे नहीं लिए. He did not take money. उसने रिश्वत ले ली. He eccepted the bribe. मैंने काम किया है. I have finished the job. मैंने काम कर लिया है. I have already finished the work, now I am free. .
4. **देना :** उसने काम नहीं किया. He did not do the job. उसने काम कर दिया. He unwillingly finished the job. उसने घड़ी खोई. He lost his watch. उसने घड़ी खो दी है. He carelessly lost his watch.
5. **आना :** वह पैसे लाया. He brought money. वह पैसे ले आया. He eventually brought the money. वह पढ़ता है. He reads. उसने किताब पढ़ ली. He read the book by himself. मैं गाड़ी चलाता हूँ.

I drive car. मुझे गाड़ी चलाना आता है. I know how to drive a car.

6. **जाना :** वह गई. She went. वह चली गई. Shee left. जाइये. Please go. चले जाओ! Get uot!

7. डालना : आईना टूटा. The mirror broke. उसने आईना तोड़ डाला. He knowingly broke the mirror. मैंने काम किया. I did the job. मैंने काम कर डाला. I unwillingly finished the job.

8. **पड़ना :** टीवी चल नहीं रहा.The TV is not working. टीवी चल पड़ा. TV automatically or all of a sudden started working. बच्चा गिरा. The child fell. बच्चा मेरे हाथ से गिर पड़ा. The child slipped and fell down from hand. मैंने मूर्ति खरीदी. I bought a statue. दूकान में मेरे हाथ से मूर्ति टूट गई अत: मुझे वह खरीदनी पड़ी. The statue accidently broke with my hands, therefore I had to buy it.

9. **लगना :** बच्चा हँसा. The child laughs. बच्चा हँसने लगा. The child started laughing. वह सच बोल रहा था. He was telling truth. वह झूठ बोलने लगा. He was telling truth and then some how started telling lies.

10. **चुकना :** मैंने काम किया है. I have done the work. मैं काम कर चुका हूँ. I have already completed the whole job. वह आया. He came. वह आ चुका है. He has already arrived.

1. वहाँ बच्चा रो रहा है. A child is crying there. वहाँ बच्चा-बच्चा रो रहा है. Every child is crying there.

2.पके फल लाइये. Bring ripe fruits. पके-पके फल लाइये. Bring only the ripe fruits.

3. मैं बाजार से क्या लाऊँ. What should I bring from the market? मैं बाजार से क्या-क्या लाऊँ? Give me the list of all items I should bring from the market.

4. बचा जोर से रो रहा था. The child was crying loudly. बच्च जोर-जोर से रो रहा था. The child was crying his heart out.

5. वहाँ एक काला साँप था. There was a black snake there. वहाँ एक काला-काला साँप था. There was a completely dark black snake there.

6. मैं चल कर थका हूँ. I am tired walking. मैं चल-चल कर थक गया हूँ. I am completely tired with constant walking.

7. लड़की गोरी है. The girl has fair colour. लड़की गोरी-गोरी है. The girl is attractive and beautiful.

8. आलू खराब है. The potato is not good. आलू पड़े-पड़े खराब हो गए. The potatoes got spoild lying there for a very long time.

9. मैंने उनको दो सो रुपये दिये. I give them two hundred Rupees. मैंने उनको दो-दो सौ रुपये दिए. I gave them two hundred Rupees each.

10. घर में टीवी है. There is a TV in the house. घर-घर में टीवी है. Every house has TV.

4. INTRANSITIVE, TRANSITIVE, DUAL VERBS

अकर्मक, सकर्मक, उभयविध क्रिया

There are various ways to define or determine if a verb is (1) **Intransitive** Verb (*akarmak kriyā* अकर्मक क्रिया) or (2) **Transitive** Verb (*sakarmak kriyā* सकर्मक क्रिया) oris it a (3) **Dual Function** Verb.(*Ubhay vidh kriyā* उभयविध क्रिया).

Definition i. A Transitive Verb denotes an action of which the effect, fruit or result PASSES OVER from the doer of the action or the subject of the sentence to the object of the sentence. e.g.

लड़की आम खा रही है. Here, the verb is eat (खा) and the effect of the verb eat is transferred to the object mango (आम). Therefore, the verb (खा) is Transitice.

An Intransitive Verb denotes an action of which the effect, fruit or result DOES NOT pass over from the doer of the action or the subject of the sentence to an object of the sentence. e.g.

बालक सो रहा है. Here, subject child is performing the verb sleep (सो) and the effect (परिणाम) of the action is not transferred to any object but it stays with the subject. Therefore, the verb (सो) is Intransitice.

Definition ii. A Transitive Verb denotes that an object is required to perform that verb, but an Intransitive Verb denotes that any object is NOT required to perform that verb. e.g.

लड़की आम खा रही है. Here, the verb is eat (खा) requires an object (आम) to perform the action of the Verb. Therefore the Verb eat (खा) is a Transitive Verb.

बालक सो रहा है. Here, subject child is performing the verb sleep (सो) requires no object. Therefore, the verb (सो) is Intransitive.

Definition iii. If you ask question "what?" about the action and if you get a proper reply, then the verb is considered Transitive, otherwise the verb is Intransitive. e.g.

लड़की आम खा रही है. Here, the verb is eat (खा). If you ask question "What is she eating? There is a proper reply, Mango (आम). Therefore the Verb eat (खा) is a Transitive Verb.

बालक सो रहा है. Here, if you ask a question "What is he sleeping? There is no proper reply because the question is not proper. Therefore, the verb (सो) is Intransitive.

THE THREE TYPES OF VERBS

Intransitive, Transitive and Causative Verbs

अकर्मक, सकर्मक और प्रयोजक क्रिया

(1) **Intransitive** Verb (*akarmak kriyā* अकर्मक क्रिया) :

As seen in the definitions given above, the Intransitive Verbs do not need an object to transfer the effect of the action and the effect of the action stays in the subject itself.

TABLE 17 : Intransitive Verb, Masculine Subject, come (आ)

No.	PERSON	Number	Pronoun	Hindi	Present Tense	Past Tense	Future Tense
	Masculine Subject, Intransitive Verb, come (आ)						
1	1st Person	Singular	I	मैं	मैं आता हूँ	मैं आया	मैं आऊँगा
2	1 st Person	Plural	We	हम	हम आते हैं	हम आए	हम आएँगे
3	2nd Person	Singular	You	तू	तू आता है	तू आया	तू आएगा
4	2nd Person	Plural	You	तुम	तुम आते हो	तुम आए	तुम आओगे
5	2nd Person	Singular	You	तुम	तुम आते हो	तुम आए	तुम आओगे
6	2nd Person	Plural	You	तुम	तुम आते हो	तुम आए	तुम आओगे
7	2nd Person	Singular	You	आप	आप आते हो	आप आए	आप आओगे
8	2nd Person	Plural	You	आप	आप आते हो	आप आए	आप आओगे
9	3rd Person	Singular	He	वह	वह आता है	वह आया	वह आएगा

10	3ed Person	Plural	They	वे	वे आते हैं	वे आए	वे आएँगे
11	3rd Person	Singular	It	यह	यह आता है	यह आया	यह आएगा
12	3ed Person	Plural	These	ये	ये आते हैं	ये आए	ये आएँगे

(2) **Transitive** Verb (*sakarmak kriyā* सकर्मक क्रिया) :

As said in the definitions given above, the Transitive Verbs need an object to transfer the effect of the action and the effect of the action transfers to the object.

TABLE 18 : Ttransitive Verb, Masculine Subject, eat (खा)

No.	PERSON	Number	Pronoun	Hindi	Present Tense	Past Tense	Future Tense
Masculine Subject, Intransitive Verb, eat (खा)							
1	1st Person	Singular	I	मैं	मैं खाता हूँ	मैंने खया	मैं खाऊँगा
2	1 st Person	Plural	We	हम	हम खाते हैं	हमने खाया	हम खाएँगे
3	2nd Person	Singular	You	तू	तू खाता है	तूने खाया	तू खाएगा
4	2nd Person	Plural	You	तुम	तुम खाते हो	तुमने खाया	तुम खाओगे
5	2nd Person	Singular	You	तुम	तुम खाते हो	तुमने खाया	तुम खाओगे
6	2nd Person	Plural	You	तुम	तुम खाते हो	तुमने खाया	तुम खाओगे
7	2nd Person	Singular	You	आप	आप खाते हो	आपने खाया	आप खाओगे
8	2nd Person	Plural	You	आप	आप खाते हो	आपने खाया	आप खाओगे
9	3rd Person	Singular	He	वह	वह खाता है	उसने खाया	वह खाएगा
10	3ed Person	Plural	They	वे	वे खाते हैं	उन्हों ने खाया	वे खाएँगे
11	3rd Person	Singular	It	यह	यह खाता है	इसने खाया	यह खाएगा
12	3ed Person	Plural	These	ये	ये खाते हैं	इन्हों ने खाया	ये खाएँगे

NOTE : The above Table shows that, when the action is completed or perfected (Perfect Tense) on a Transitive Verb, suffix **ने** is added to the Subject. Now, this suffix **ने** detaches the Subject from the Verb and thus as a result, the Gender and Number of the Subject has no effect on the Verb. Now, the Verb changes according to the Gender and Number of the Object.

(3) **Dual Function** Verb.(*Ubhay vidh kriyā* उभयविध क्रिया) :

As the name indicates, a Dual Function Verb can act as an Intransitive Verb as well can act as a Transitive Verb, depends on the construction of the sentence. e.g.

i. पानी से घड़ा भरा The pot got filled with wter. Verb भरना (to fill) used intransitively.

सीता ने पानी से घड़ा भरा. Sita filled the pot with water. Verb भरना (to fill) used transitively.

ii. परिश्रम से मैं घिस गया हूँ I am worn out with hard work.Verb घिसना (to wear out) used intransitively.

मैं फर्श घिस रहा हूँ. I am polishing the floor. Verb घिसना (to burnish) used transitively.

ALSO :

Dual Karma Verbs (द्विकर्मक) : In Hindi Grammer, there is another class of Verbs called Dual Karma Verbs (द्विकर्मक) in which the verb is related to two objects (कर्म) in that sentence. e.g.

The teacher teaches Math to the students. गुरुजी छात्रों को गणित पढ़ाते हैं.

Here,

i the Teacher is doing the act of teaching, thus the teacher is the subject (कर्ता).

ii. The the Verb "teach" is related to two Objects, Math and the Students.

Therefore, the verb पढ़ाना is a Dual Karma Verbs (द्विकर्मक क्रियापद).

iii. In this case, the Generic Noun (वस्तुवाचक नाम) is the Direct Object (प्रत्यक्ष कर्म) and the Personal Noun (व्यक्तिवाचक नाम) is the Indirect Objects (अप्रत्यक्ष कर्म) of the sentence.

iv. Other examples of Dual Karma Verbs are मिलाना, देखना, देना, प्रणाम करना, etc.

4. CAUSATIVE VERBS

प्रेरणार्थक क्रिया

If the verb is Intransitive (e.g. मरना to die), it can be converted to Transitive form (e.g.

मारना to kill) and from Transitive form (e.g. मरवाना to get killed) to give a causative (*preraṇārthak* प्रेरणार्थक) meaning.

Causative forms can be prepared by adding suffix वा to the Root form of the verb. e.g.

Intransitive	Transitive	+ Suffix	=	Causative
चलना (to move)	चलाना (to drive)	चल + वा	=	चलवाना (to get driven by someone)
होना (to happen)	करना (to do)	कर + वा	=	करवाना (to get done, cause to happen)

Sometimes same causative verb having different meanings could be produced from different transitive verbs with different meanings. e.g.

1. Transitive verb खाना (to eat) - Causative verb खिलाना (to feed)
2. Transitive verb खेलना (to play) - Causative verb खिलाना (to cause to play)
3. Transitive verb खिलना (to bloom) - Causative verb खिलाना (to cause to bloom)

DICTIONARY OF INTRANSITIVE-TRANSITIVE-CAUSATIVE VERBS

अकर्मक, सकर्मक, प्रयोजक क्रिया

English Meaning,	Intransitive अकर्मक	Transitive सकर्मक	Causative प्रयोजक
to abandon		तजना	तजाना
to agree	मानना	मनाना	मानवाना
to alter	बदलना	बदलाना	बदलवाना
to anger	तिनकना	तिनकाना	तिनकवाना
to appear	दिखना	देखना	दिखाना
to arrange		रचना	रचवाना
to arrive	पधारना		
to ask		पूछना	पुछवाना
to babble	बर्राना		

to be adorned	सजना	सजाना	सजवाना
to be agitated	अकुलाना		
to be amused	बहलना	बहलाना	बहलवाना
to be ashamed	लजना	लजाना	लजवाना
to be be stiff	ऐंठना		
to be bored	अकना	अकाना	अकवाना
to be bored	ऊबना	ऊबाना	ऊबवाना
to be born	उपजना	उपजाना	उपजवाना
to be brought up	पलना	पालना	पलवाना
to be chewed	चबना	चबाना	चबवाना
to be coloured	रँगना	रँगाना	रँगवाना
to be completed	सधना	सधाना	सधवाना
to be confused	चकराना	चकराना	चकरवाना
to be confused	हड़बड़ाना	हड़बड़ाना	हड़बड़वाना
to be connected	गठना	गाँठना	गठवाना
to be corrected	सँवरना	सँवारना	सँवरवाना
to be cut off	कटना	काटना	कटवाना
to be damp	सिलना	सीलना	सिलवाना
to be dealt with	निपटना	निपटाना	निपटवाना
to be defeated	हारना	हराना	हरवाना
to be deluded	बहकना	बहकाना	बहकवाना
to be digested	पचना	पचाना	पचवाना
to be dissolved	घुलना	घुलाना	घुलवाना
to be distressed	कलपना	कलपाना	कलपवाना

to be done	चुकना	चुकाना	चुकवाना
to be engrossed	रमना	रमाना	रमवाना
to be exposed	उघड़ना	उघाड़ना	उघड़वाना
to be filled	डबडबना	डबडबाना	डबडबवाना
to be flayed	उधड़ना	उधेड़ना	उधड़वाना
to be flirtatious	मटकना	मटकाना	मटकवाना
to be fulfilled	निभना	निभाना	निभवाना
to be ground	पिसना	पीसना	पिसलाना
to be hanged	लटकना	लटकाना	लटकवाना
to be infatuated	पगना	पगाना	पगवाना
to be irritable	चिड़चिड़ना	चिड़चिड़ाना	चिड़चिड़वाना
to be kindled	सुलगना	सुलगाना	सुलगवाना
to be loaded	लदना	लादना	लदवाना
to be misled	भरमना	भरमाना	भरमवाना
to be moveed	सरकना	सरकाना	सरकवाना
to be noisy	खड़बड़ना	खड़बड़ाना	खड़बड़वाना
to be parched	झुलसना	झुलसाना	झुलसवाना
to be peeled	छिलना	छीलना	छिलवाना
to be picked out	छँटना	छाँटना	छँटवाना
to be pierced	बिंधना	बिंधना	बिंधवाना
to be placed	डलना	डालना	डलवाना
to be pleased	रिझना	रिझाना	रिझवाना
to be provoked	चिढ़ना	चिढ़ाना	चिढ़वाना
to be razed	उजड़ना	उजाड़ना	उजड़वाना

to be restive	मचलना	मचलाना	मचलवाना
to be restless	तड़पना	तड़पाना	तड़पवाना
to be restless	सिटपिटना	सिटपिटाना	सिटपिटवाना
to be roasted	भुनना	भूनना	भुनवाना
to be satisfied	अघना	अघाना	अघवाना
to be saved	बचना	बचाना	बचवाना
to be scared	बिदकना	बिदकाना	बिदकवाना
to be scattered	बिखरना	बिखेरना	बिखरवाना
to be seived	छनना	छानना	छनवाना
to be separated	बिछुड़ना	बिछुड़ाना	बिछुड़वाना
to be snatch	छिनना	छीनना	छिनवाना
to be sold	बिकना	बेचना	बिकवाना
to be sprinkled	छिटकना	छिटकाना	छिटकवाना
to be squeezed	दबना	दबाना	दबवाना
to be squeezed	पिचकना	पिचकाना	पिचकवाना
to be starteled	बिचकना	बिचकाना	बिचकवाना
to be sticky	चिपचिपाना	चिपचिपाना	चिपचिपवाना
to be streched	तनना	तानना	तनवाना
to be surprised	चकपकना	चकपकाना	चकपकवाना
to be surprised	चौंकना	चौंकाना	चौंकवाना
to be surrounded	घिरना	घेरना	घिरवाना
to be tangled	उलझना	उलझाना	उलझवाना
to be tearful	गिड़गिड़ना	गिड़गिड़ाना	गिड़गिड़वाना
to be tired	थकना	थकाना	थकवाना

to be touched	लगना	लगाना	लगवाना
to be twisted	कचकना	कचकाना	कचकवाना
to be uprooted	उखड़ना	उखाड़ना	उखड़वाना
to be used up	खपना	खपाना	खपवाना
to be vexed	कुढ़ना	कुढ़ाना	कुढ़वाना
to be vexed	खिजना	खिजाना	खिजवाना
to be warm	तपना	तपाना	तपवाना
to be worn out	घिसना	घिसना	घिसवाना
to be yoked	जुतना	जुताना	जुतवाना
to bear		झेलना	झिलवाना
to bear fruit	फलना	फलाना	फलवाना
to become	बनना	बनाना	बनवाना
to become free	छुटना	छोड़ना	छुड़वाना
to befit	फबना	फबाना	फबवाना
to beg		माँगना	मँगवाना
to belch	डकारना		
to bellow	रेंकना		रेंकवाना
to bend	लचकना	लचकाना	लचकवाना
to bite		डसना	डसवाना
to bloom	खिलना	खिलाना	खिलवाना
to blossom	डहकना	डहकाना	डहकवाना
to blow		फूँकना	फूँकवाना
to blow up	फूलना	फूलाना	फूलवाना
to blush	तमकना	तमकाना	तमकवाना

to boil	उबलना	उबालना	उबलवाना
to boil	खौलना	खौलाना	खौलवाना
to boil	भभकना	भभकाना	भभकवाना
to boil over	उफनना	उफनाना	उफनवाना
to brand		दागना	दागवाना
to break	टूटना	तोड़ना	तुड़वाना
to break out	छिड़ना	छेड़ना	छिड़वाना
to break up	फूटना	फोड़ना	फुड़वाना
to bring		लाना	लिबाना
to bubble	गुड़गुड़ना	गुड़गुड़ाना	गुड़गुड़वाना
to bubble	बुदबुदना	बुदबुदाना	बुदबुदना
to burn	जलना	जलाना	जलवाना
to bury		दफनाना	दफनवाना
to buy		खरीदना	खरीदवाना
to buzz	भिनकना	भिनकाना	भिनकवाना
to call		पुकारना	बुलवाना
to call (bird)	कूकना	कूकना	कूकवाना
to call (bird)	कूजना		कूजवाना
to carry		ढोना	ढोआना
to catch		पकड़ना	पकड़वाना
to caugh	खाँसना		खाँसवाना
to challenge		टोकना	टोकवाना
to challenge		ललकारना	
to chatter	बकना	बकाना	बकवाना

to cheat	ठगना	ठगाना	ठगवाना
to chirp	चहकना	चहकाना	चहकवाना
to choose		चुनना	चुनवाना
to cleanse		माँजना	मँजवाना
to clench teeth	किटकिटना	किटकिटाना	किटकिटवाना
to climb	चढ़ना	चढ़ाना	चढ़वाना
to close		मुँदना	मुँदवाना
to collide	टकराना	टकराना	टकरवाना
to confuse	गड़बड़ाना	गड़बड़ाना	गड़बड़वाना
to count	गिनना	गिनाना	गिनवाना
to count beads		जपना	जपवाना
to cover		ओढ़ना	ओढ़वाना
to cover		ढाँपना	ढपवाना
to crack		ढँकना	ढँकवाना
to crackle	तड़कना	तड़काना	तड़कवाना
to croak	टरटरना	टरटराना	टरटरवाना
to cross		लाँघना	लँघवाना
to crush		कुचलना	कुचलवाना
to cry	रोना	रुलाना	
to droop	झुकना	झुकाना	झुकवाना
to dry	सूखना	सुखाना	सूखवाना
to earn		कमाना	कमवाना
to earn		कमाना	कमवाना
to extinguish	बुझना	बुझाना	बुझवाना

to exude	टपकना	टपकाना	टपकवाना
to fade	कुम्हलाना	कुम्हलाना	कुम्हलवाना
to fall	डिगना	डिगाना	डिगवाना
to fall behind	पिछड़ना	पिछड़ाना	पिछड़वाना
to fear	घबराना		घबरवाना
to feel shame	शरमना	शरमना	शरमवाना
to fight	झगड़ना	झगड़ाना	झगड़वाना
to flutter	फहरना	फहराना	फहरवाना
to flare	धधकना	धधकाना	धधकवाना
to flare up	भड़कना	भड़काना	भड़कवाना
to float	तरना	तरना	तरवाना
to flutter	फड़फड़ाना	फड़फड़ना	फड़फड़वाना
to fly	उड़ना	उड़ाना	उड़वाना
to fondle		दुलारना	दुलारवाना
to forget	भूलना	भूलना	भुलवाना
to fry		तलना	तलवाना
to gather		बटोरना	बटोरवाना
to gaze		ताकना	ताकवाना
to get		पाना	पवाना
to get down	उतरना	उतारना	उतरवाना
to get out	निकलना	निकालना	निकलवाना
to get printed	छपना	छापना	छपवाना
to get spoiled	बिगड़ना	बिगड़ाना	बिगड़वाना
to get spread	बिछना	बिछाना	बिछवाना

to get stuck	अटकना	अटकाना	अटकवाना
to get stuck	फँसना	फँसाना	फँसवाना
to get tied	बँधना	बाँधना	बँधवाना
to get washed	धुलना	धोना	धुलवाना
to get wet	भीगना	भीगना	भीगवाना
to give		देना	दिलाना
to glitter	लहकना	लहकाना	लहकवाना
to go	जाना	भेजना	जिलाना
to go around	घूमना	घूमाना	घुमवाना
to go away	टरकना	टरकाना	टरकवाना
to go back	मुकरना	मुकराना	मुकरवाना
to go for walk	टहलना	टहलाना	टहलवाना
to go well	पटना	पटाना	पटवाना
to graze	चरना	चराना	चरवाना
to grow	बढ़ना	बढ़ाना	बढ़वाना
to growl	गुर्राना		
to guess	खटकना	खटकाना	खटकवाना
to hammer		भाँपना	भाँपवाना
to hang		ठोंकना	ठुकवाना
to have access	टँगना	टाँगना	टँगवाना
to hear	फटकना	फटकाना	फटकवाना
to hem		सुनना	सुनवाना
to hesitate		तुरपना	तुरपवाना
to hesitate	झिझकना	झिझकाना	झिझकवाना

to hesite	हिचकिचाना	हिचकिचाना	हिचकिचवाना
to hide	छिपना	छिपाना	छिपवाना
to hold fast	खटना	खटाना	खटवाना
to hover	मँडराना		मँडरवाना
to hum	गुनगुनना		गुनगुनवाना
to improve	सुधरना	सुधारना	सुधरवाना
to inform	कहना	बताना	कहलवाना
to insult		लताड़ना	लताड़वाना
to investigate		टटोलना	टटोलवाना
to irritate	अखरना	अखराना	अखरवाना
to jingle	खनकना	खनकाना	खनकवाना
to join		जोड़ना	जुड़वाना
to jump	कूदना		कुदवाना
to kick		लतियाना	
to kiss		चूमना	चूमवाना
to know	जानना		
to laugh	हँसना	हँसाना	हँसवाना
to learn	सीखना	सिखाना	सिखलाना
to lick	चटना	चाटना	चटवाना
to limp	लँगड़ना	लँगड़ाना	लँगड़वाना
to measure		नापना	नपवाना
to melt, dissolve	गलना	गलाना	गलवाना
to melt, swet	पिघलना	पिघलाना	पिघलवाना
to move away	हटना	हटाना	हटवाना

to nurture		पोसना	पोसवाना
to observe		निरखना	निरखवाना
to offer	ललचाना	ललचाना	ललचवाना
to open		मापना	मपवाना
to overpower	भिड़ना	भिड़ाना	भिड़वाना
to palpitate	पसीजना		पसीजवाना
to pee	मूतना		मूतवाना
to penetrate	घुसना	घुसाना	घुसवाना
to penetrate	धँसना	धँसाना	धँसवाना
to pierce		भेदना	भिदवाना
to plant		रोपना	रोपवाना
to poop	हगना	हगाना	हगवाना
to reach	पहुँचना		पहुँचवाना
to read		पढ़ना	पढ़वाना
to recognize		पहचानना	पहचानवाना
to recover	सँभलना	सँभलाना	सँभलवाना
to reduce	कमना	कमाना	कमवाना
to regret	पछताना		
to reject		ठुकराना	ठुकरवाना
to return	लौटना	लौटाना	लौटवाना
to rip	फटना	फाड़ना	फटवाना
to ripen	पकना	पकाना	पकवाना
to ripple	लहराना	लहराना	लहरवाना
to rise	उठना	उठाना	उठवाना

to roar	गरजना		गरजवाना
to roar	दहाड़ना		दहाड़वाना
to roll	लुढ़कना	लुढ़काना	लुढ़कवाना
to rot	सड़ना	सड़ाना	सड़वाना
to rub		मलना	मलवाना
to rub		रगड़ना	रगड़वाना
to run	दौड़ना	दौड़ाना	दौड़वाना
to run	भागना		भागवाना
to scold		प्रताड़ना	
to search		खोजना	खोजवाना
to scratch	उलटना	उलटाना	उलटवाना
to roast	भूनना	भुनाना	भुनवाना
to seize		दबोचना	दबोचवाना
to send		भेजना	भिजवाना
to serve food		परोसना	परोसवाना
to shake	कँपना	कँपाना	कँपवाना
to shake		घोंटना	घुंटवाना
to shape	गढ़ना	गढ़ाना	गढ़वाना
to shape	घड़ना	घड़ाना	घड़वाना
to shine	चमकना	चमकाना	चमकवाना
to shiver	सिहरना	सिहराना	सिहरवाना
to shout	चिल्लाना		
to shrink	सकुचना	सकुचाना	सकुचवाना
to sing		गाना	गवाना

to sink	डूबना	डूबाना	डूबवाना
to sit	बैठना	बिठाना	बिठलाना
to slip	फिसलना		फिसलवाना
to smear		पोतना	पुतवाना
to smell		सूँघना	सूँघवाना
to smile	मुसकराना		मुसकरवाना
to sneeze	छिंकना		छिंकवाना
to sob	काँपना	काँपना	काँपवाना
to sob	ठिठुरना		ठिठुरवाना
to sob	सिसकना		सिसकवाना
to sound	किलकारना		किलकारवाना
to speak	बोलना	बुलाना	बुलवाना
to spill	छलकना	छलकाना	छलकवाना
to spit		थूकना	थूकवाना
to spread	फैलना	फैलाना	फैलवाना
to sprout	उगना	उगाना	उगवाना
to squeeze		निचोड़ना	निचोड़वाना
to stay awake		थोपना	थोपवाना
to stop	रुकना	रुकाना	रुकवाना
to str etc.h	फैलना	फैलाना	फैलवाना
to stumble	लड़खड़ाना	लड़खड़ाना	लड़खड़वाना
to swallow		निगलना	निगलवाना
to tell		बताना	कहलवाना
to think	सोचना		

to tremble	थर्राना		
to understand	समझना	समझाना	समझवाना
to vex		कचोटना	कचोटवाना
to vomit	ओकना		ओकवाना
to wake up	जगना	जगाना	जगवाना
to walk	चलना	चलाना	चलवाना
to wander	भटकना	भटकाना	भटकवाना
to warm up	गरमना	गरमाना	गरमवाना
to wear		पहनना	पहनवाना
to weather	झड़ना	झड़ाना	झड़वाना
to weave		बीनना	बीनवाना
to weave		बुनना	बुनवाना
to weigh		तोलना	तोलवाना
to win	जीतना	जीताना	जीतवाना
to wipe		पोंछना	पोंछवाना
to withdraw		फेंकना	फिकवाना
to wither	घौँपना		घौँपवाना
to worship		पूजना	पूजवाना

5. REPETATIVE COMPOUND VERBS

पुनरुक्त संयुक्त क्रिया

When two verbs of similar class and similar rhyme are linked together, they form a Repetative Compound Verb (पुनरुक्त संयुक्त क्रिया), such as :

लिखना-पढ़ना (reading and writing), खाना-पीना (eating and drinking),
रोना-धोना (crying and whining), आना-जाना (coming and going),
खेलना-कूदना (playing and rejoicing), लेना-देना (taking and giving), etc.

REPETATIVE COMPOUND NOUNS

पुनरुक्त संयुक्त नाम

As a product of the Repetative Compound Verb (पुनरुक्त संयुक्त क्रिया), Repetative Nouns (पुनरुक्त संयुक्त नाम) can be formed by joining two nouns, verbal nouns or adjectives of similar class. e.g.

खेल-कूद (playing and rejoicing), दिन-रात (day and night),
जीना-मरना (living and dying), सुबह-शाम (morning and evening),
थोड़ा-बहुत (more or less), खरा-खोटा (Truth and false), etc.

CHAPTER 11

THE TENSES AND MOODS

क्रिया के काल और अर्थ

TENSE :

Tense is the transformation of a Verb to tall its period or time of operation and state of completion. This time is divided in to three main periods, namely : (1) Present (*vartmān* वर्तमान), the event that is curren, (2) Past (*bhūt* भूत), the event that has passed, and (3) Future (*bhaviṣhya* भविष्य), the event that will happen. e.g.

1. Present : मैं चाय पी रहा हूँ (पी रही हूँ). I am drinking tea.
2. Past : मैं चाय पी रहा था (पी रही थी). I was drinking tea.
3. Future : मैं चाय पीऊँगा (पीऊँगी). I will drink tea.

MOOD :

Mood (अर्थ) is the Mode or Manner (रीति) in which the Verb (क्रिया) is utilized in the sentence. The completion and incompletion of a Verb in these three Tenses is further divided in to three main Mode, namely : (1) Habitual Mode (सामान्य रीति), (2) Continuous Mode (अपूर्ण रीति), (3) Perfect Mode (पूर्ण रीति).

TABLE 19 : The Three Main States of the Three Main Tenses

Tense काल	1. Habitual State सामान्य अवस्था	2. Continuous State अपूर्ण अवस्था	3. Completed or Perfect State पूर्ण अवस्था
1. Present Tense	He plays	He is playing	He has played
वर्तमान काल	वह खेलता है	वह खेल रहा है	वह खेला है
2. Past Tense	He used to play	He was playning	He had played
भूत काल	वह खेलता था	वह खेल रहा था	वह खेला था
3. Future Tense	He will play	He will be playing	He will have played
भविष्यत् काल	वह खेलेगा	वह खेलता रहेगा	वह खेला होगा

TABLE 20 : The Three Main Tenses, Three Persons, Singular-Plural, Habitual Mode

No.	PER0SON	Number	Pronoun	Hindi	Present Tense	Past Tense	Future Tense
	Masculine Gender						
1	1st Person	Singular	I	मैं	मैं खेलता हूँ	मैं खेला	मैं खेलूँगा
2	1 st Person	Plural	We	हम	हम खेलते हैं	हम खेले	हम खेलेंगे
3	2nd Person	Singular	You	तू	तू खेलता है	तू खेला	तू खेलेगा
4	2nd Person	Plural	You	तुम	तुम खेलते हो	तुम खेले	तुम खेलोगे
5	2nd Person	Singular	You	तुम	तुम खेलते हो	तुम खेले	तुम खेलोगे
6	2nd Person	Plural	You	तुम	तुम खेलते हो	तुम खेले	तुम खेलोगे
7	2nd Person	Singular	You	आप	आप खेलते हो	आप खेले	आप खेलोगे
8	2nd Person	Plural	You	आप	आप खेलते हो	आप खेले	आप खेलेंगे
9	3rd Person	Singular	He	वह	वह खेलता है	वह खेला	वह खेलेगा
10	3ed Person	Plural	They	वे	वे खेलते हैं	वे खेले	वे खेलेंगे
11	3rd Person	Singular	It	यह	यह खेलता है	यह खेला	यह खेलेगा
12	3rd Person	Plural	These	ये	ये खेलते हैं	ये खेले	ये खेलेंगे
	Feminine Gender						
13	1st Person	Singular	I	मैं	मैं खेलती हूँ	मैं खेली	मैं खेलूँगी
14	1 st Person	Plural	We	हम	हम खेलती हैं	हम खेले	हम खेलेंगे
15	2nd Person	Singular	You	तू	तू खेलती है	तू खेली	तू खेलेगी
16	2nd Person	Plural	You	तुम	तुम खेलती हो	तुम खेलीं	तुम खेलोगी
17	2nd Person	Singular	You	तुम	तुम खेलती हो	तुम खेली	तुम खेलोगी
18	2nd Person	Plural	You	तुम	तुम खेलती हो	तुम खेलीं	तुम खेलोगी
19	2nd Person	Singular	You	आप	आप खेलती हो	आप खेली	आप खेलोगी
20	2nd Person	Plural	You	आप	आप खेलती हो	आप खेलीं	आप खेलेंगी
21	3rd Person	Singular	She	वह	वह खेलती है	वह खेली	वह खेलेगी
22	3ed Person	Plural	They	वे	वे खेलती हैं	वे खेलीं	वे खेलेंगी
23	3rd Person	Singular	This	यह	यह खेलती है	यह खेली	यह खेलेगी
24	3rd Person	Plural	These	ये	ये खेलती हैं	ये खेलीं	ये खेलेंगी

1. THE PRESENT TENSE
वर्तमान काल

The Present Tense covers the events of the current time. Present Tense is optionally expressed in four Modes, namely :

1. **Habitual Present** Tense (नित्य वर्तमान काल), in which the Subject currently performs the Verb normally as his or her habit or tendency or its nature, e.g. राम चाय पीता है. Rām drinks tea.

2. **Present Continuous** Tense (अपूर्ण वर्तमान काल), in which the Subject has started the action but has not yet finished it. e.g. राम किताब पढ़ रहा है. Rām is reading a book.

3. **Perfect Present** Tense (पूर्ण वर्तमान काल), in which the Subject has completed the action, e.g. राम ने किताब पढ़ी ह, राम किताब पढ़ चुका है. Rām has read the book.

4. **Presumptive Present** Tense (संदिग्ध वर्तमान काल), in which the Subject may be or may not be currently performing the action. e.g. राम (शायद) किताबे पढ़ रहा होगा. Rām may be reading the book.

TABLE 21 : Four Modes of Present Tense : **1. Present Habitual Tense** Mode (नित्य वर्तमान काल)

No.	Subject	कर्ता	उदाहरण, अकर्मक	उदाहरण, सकर्मक	Example, Intransitive	Example, Transitive
1	I	मैं	मैं चलता हूँ	मैं लिखता हूँ	I walk	I write
2	We	हम	हम चलते हैं	हम लिखते हैं	We walk	We write
3	You	तू	तू चलता है	तू लिखता है	You walk	You write

4	You	तुम	तुम चलते हो	तुम लिखते हो	You walk	You write
5	You	आप	आप चलते हैं	आप लिखते हैं	You walk	You write
6	He	वह	वह चलता है	वह लिखता है	He walks	He writes
7	She	वह	वह चलती है	वह लिखती है	She walks	She writes
8	It	यह	यह चलता है	यह लिखता है	It walks	It writes
9	They	वे	वे चलते हैं	वे लिखते हैं	They walk	They write
10	These	ये	ये चलते हैं	ये लिखते हैं	These walk	These write

TABLE 22 : Four Modes of Present Tense : **2. Present Continuous Tense** Mode
(अपूर्ण वर्तमान काल)

No.	Subject	कर्ता	उदाहरण, अकर्मक	उदाहरण, सकर्मक	Example, Intransitive	Example, Transitive
1	I	मैं	मैं चल रहा हूँ	मैं लिख रहा हूँ	I am walking	I am writing
2	We	हम	हम चल रहे हैं	हम लिख रहे हैं	We are walking	We are writing
3	You	तू	तू चल रहा है	तू लिख रहा है	You are walking	You are writing
4	You	तुम	तुम चल रहे हो	तुम लिख रहे हो	You walking	You writing
5	You	आप	आप चल रहे हैं	आप लिख रहे हैं	You walking	You writing
6	He	वह	वह चल रहाा है	वह लिख रहा है	He walking	He writing
7	She	वह	वह चल रहीी है	वह लिख रही है	She walking	She writing
8	It	यह	यह चल रहा है	यह लिख रहा है	It walking	It writing
9	They	वे	वे चल रहो हैं	वे लिख रहे हैं	They walking	They writing
10	These	ये	ये चल रहे हैं	ये लिख रहे हैं	These walking	These writing

TABLE 23 : Four Modes of Present Tense : **3. Present Perfect Tense** Mode
(पूर्ण वर्तमान काल)

	Subject	कर्ता	उदाहरण, अकर्मक	उदाहरण, सकर्मक	Example, Intransitive	Example, Transitive
1	I	मैं	मैं चला हूँ	मैंने लिखा है	I have walked	I have written
2	We	हम	हम चले हैं	हमने लिखा है	We have walked	We have written

3	You	तू	तू चला है	तूने लिखा है	You have walked	You have written
4	You	तुम	तुम चले हो	तुमने लिखा है	You have walked	You have written
5	You	आप	आप चले हैं	आपने लिखा है	You have walked	You have written
6	He	वह	वह चला है	उसने लिखा है	He has walked	He has written
7	She	वह	वह चली है	उसने लिखा है	She has walked	She has written
8	It	यह	यह चला है	इसने लिखा है	It has walked	It has written
9	They	वे	वे चले हैं	उन्हों ने लिखा है	They have walked	They have written
10	These	ये	ये चले हैं	इन्हों ने लिखा है	These have walked	These have written

TABLE 24 : Four Modes of Present Tense : **4. Presumptive Present** Tense (संदिग्ध वर्तमान काल)

	Subject	कर्ता	उदाहरण, अकर्मक	उदाहरण, सकर्मक	Example, Intransitive	Example, Transitive
1	I	मैं	मैं चला हूँगा	मैंने लिखा होगा	I may have walked	I may have written
2	We	हम	हम चले होंगे	हमने लिखा होगा	We may have walked	We may have written
3	You	तू	तू चला होगा	तूने लिखा होगा	You may have walked	You may have written
4	You	तुम	तुम चले होगे	तुमने लिखा होगा	You may have walked	You may have written
5	You	आप	आप चले होंगे	आपने लिखा होगा	You may have walked	You may have written
6	He	वह	वह चला होगा	उसने लिखा होगा	He may have walked	He may have written
7	She	वह	वह चली होगी	उसने लिखा होगा	She may have walked	She may have written
8	It	यह	यह चला होगा	इसने लिखा होगा	It may have walked	It may have written
9	They	वे	वे चले होंगे	उन्हों ने लिखा होगा	They may have walked	They may have written
10	These	ये	ये चले होंगे	इन्हों ने लिखा होगा	These may have walked	These may have written

2. THE PAST TENSE

भूतकाल

The Past Tense covers the events of the time that has passed. Past Tense is optionally expressed in five Modes or Moods (अर्थ), namely :

1. **Habitual Past** Tense (नित्य भूतकाल) : The action that used to take place in the past, but does not happen at the present. e.g. (Intransitive) Rām used to walk 5 miles. राम 5 मिल चलता था. (Transitive) Rām used write poem. राम कविता लिखता था.
2. **Simple Past** Tense (सामान्य भूतकाल) : The action that had taken place some time before the present moment. e.g. (Intransitive) Rām walked 5 miles. राम 5 मिल चला. (Transitive) Rām wrote poem. राम ने कविता लिखी.
3. **Past Continuous** Tense (अपूर्ण भूतकाल) : The action that had begun but not yet completed and it was going on. e.g. (Intransitive) Rām was walking. राम चल रहा था. (Transitive) Rām was writing. राम लिख रहा था.
4. **Past Perfect** Tense (पूर्ण भूतकाल) : The action that had begun and had completed quite a while ago. e.g. (Intransitive) Rām had walked 5 miles. राम 5 मिल चला था. (Transitive) Rām had written a poem. राम ने कविता लिखी थी.
5. **Adjacent Past** Tense (आसन्न or निकटवर्ती भूतकाल) : The action that had just taken place. e.g. (Intransitive) Rām just now walked 5 miles. राम अभी–अभी 5 मिल चला. (Transitive) Rām wrote a poem just now. राम ने अभी कविता लिखी.
6. **Presumptive Past** Tense (संदिग्ध भूतकाल) : The action that may have happened but there is a doubt. e.g. (Intransitive) Rām may have written. राम कदाचित् आया होगा. (Transitive) Rām may have written. राम ने शायद लिखा होगा.
7. **Conditional Past** Tense (हेतु–हेतुमद् भूतकाल) : The action that was conditional. e.g. (Intransitive) If Rām had said then I would have come. यदि राम कहता तो मैं आता. (Transitive) If Rām had said the I would have written. यदि राम कहता तो मैं लिखता.

TABLE 25 : Four Modes of Present Tense : **1. Past Habitual** Mode

(नित्य भूत काल)

No.	Subject	कर्ता	उदाहरण, अकर्मक	उदाहरण, सकर्मक	Example, Intransitive	Example, Transitive
1	I	मैं	मैं चलता था	मैं लिखता था	I used to walk	I used to write
2	We	हम	हम चलते थे	हम लिखते थे	We used to walk	We used to write
3	You	तू	तू चलता था	तू लिखता था	You used to walk	You used to write
4	You	तुम	तुम चलते थे	तुम लिखते थे	You used to walk	You used to write
5	You	आप	आप चलते थे	आप लिखते थे	You used to walk	You used to write
6	He	वह	वह चलता था	वह लिखता था	He used to walk	He used to write
7	She	वह	वह चलती थी	वह लिखती थी	She used to walk	She used to write
8	It	यह	यह चलता था	यह लिखता था	It used to walk	It used to write
9	They	वे	वे चलते थे	वे लिखते थे	They used to walk	They used to write
10	These	ये	ये चलते थे	ये लिखते थे	These used to walk	These used to write

TABLE 26 : Four Modes of Present Tense : **2. Simple Past** Mode

(सामान्य भूत काल)

No.	Subject	कर्ता	उदाहरण, अकर्मक	उदाहरण, सकर्मक	Example, Intransitive	Example, Transitive
1	I	मैं	मैं चला	मैंने लिखा	I walked	I wrote
2	We	हम	हम चले	हमने लिखा	We walked	We wrote
3	You	तू	तू चला	तूने लिखा	You walked	You wrote
4	You	तुम	तुम चले	तुमने लिखा	You walked	You wrote
5	You	आप	आप चले	आपने लिखा	You walked	You wrote
6	He	वह	वह चला	उसने लिखा	He walked	He wrote
7	She	वह	वह चली	उसने लिखा	She walked	She wrote
8	It	यह	यह चला	इसने लिखा	It walked	It wrote
9	They	वे	वे चले	उन्हों ने लिखा	They walked	They wrote
10	These	ये	ये चले	इन्हों ने लिखा	These walked	These wrote

TABLE 27 : Four Modes of Present Tense : **3. Past Continuous** Mode

(अपूर्ण भूत काल)

No.	Subject	कर्ता	उदाहरण, अकर्मक	उदाहरण, सकर्मक	Example, Intransitive	Example, Transitive
1	I	मैं	मैं चल रहा था	मैं लिख रहा था	I was walking	I was writing
2	We	हम	हम चल रहे थे	हम लिख रहे थे	We were walking	We were writing
3	You	तू	तू चल रहा था	तू लिख रहा था	You were walking	You were writing
4	You	तुम	तुम चल रहे थे	तुम लिख रहे थे	You were walking	You were writing
5	You	आप	आप चल रहे थे	आप लिख रहे थे	You were walking	You were writing
6	He	वह	वह चल रहा था	वह लिख रहा था	He was walking	He was writing
7	She	वह	वह चल रही थी	वह लिख रही थी	She was walking	She was writing
8	It	यह	यह चल रहा था	यह लिख रहा था	It was walking	It was writing
9	They	वे	वे चल रहे थे	वे लिख रहे थे	They were walking	They were writing
10	These	ये	ये चल रहे थे	ये लिख रहे थे	These were walking	These were writing

TABLE 28 : Four Modes of Present Tense : **4. Past Perfect** Mode

(पूर्ण भूत काल)

No.	Subject	कर्ता	उदाहरण, अकर्मक	उदाहरण, सकर्मक	Example, Intransitive	Example, Transitive
1	I	मैं	मैं चला था	मैंने लिखा था	I had walked	I had written
2	We	हम	हम चले थे	हमने लिखा था	We had walked	We had written
3	You	तू	तू चला था	तूने लिखा था	You had walked	You had written
4	You	तुम	तुम चले थे	तुमने लिखा था	You had walked	You had written
5	You	आप	आप चले थे	आपने लिखा था	You had walked	You had written
6	He	वह	वह चला था	उसने लिखा था	He had walked	He had written
7	She	वह	वह चली थी	उसने लिखा था	She had walked	She had written
8	It	यह	यह चला था	इसने लिखा था	It had walked	It had written
9	They	वे	वे चले थे	उन्हों ने लिखा था	They had walked	They had written
10	These	ये	ये चले थे	इन्हों ने लिखा था	These had walked	These had written

TABLE 29 : Four Modes of Present Tense : 5. **Adjacent Past** Mode

(आसन्न or निकटवर्ती भूतकाल)

No.	Subject	कर्ता	उदाहरण, अकर्मक	उदाहरण, सकर्मक	Example, Intransitive	Example, Transitive
1	I	मैं	मैं अभी चला	मैंने अभी लिखा	Ijust walked	I just wrote
2	We	हम	हम अभी चले	हमने अभी लिखा	We just walked	We just wrote
3	You	तू	तू अभी चला	तूने अभी लिखा	You just walked	You just wrote
4	You	तुम	तुम अभी चले	तुमने अभी लिखा	You just walked	You just wrote
5	You	आप	आप अभी चले	आपने अभी लिखा	You just walked	You just wrote
6	He	वह	वह अभी चला	उसने अभी लिखा	He just walked	He just wrote
7	She	वह	वह अभी चली	उसने अभी लिखा	She just walked	She just wrote
8	It	यह	यह अभी चला	इसने अभी लिखा	It just walked	It just wrote
9	They	वे	वे अभी चले	उन्हां ने अभी लिखा	They just walked	They just wrote
10	These	ये	ये अभी चले	इन्हों ने अभी लिखा	These just walked	These just wrote

TABLE 30 : Four Modes of Present Tense : 6. **Presumptive Past** Mode

(संदिग्ध भूतकाल)

No.	Subject	कर्ता	उदाहरण, अकर्मक	उदाहरण, सकर्मक	Example, Intransitive	Example, Transitive
1	I	मैं	मैं चला हूँगा	मैंने लिखा होगा	I may have walked	I may have written
2	We	हम	हम चले होंगे	हमने लिखा होगा	We may have walked	We may have written
3	You	तू	तू चला होगा	तूने लिखा होगा	You may have walked	You may have written
4	You	तुम	तुम चले होंगे	तुमने लिखा होगा	You may have walked	You may have written
5	You	आप	आप चले होंगे	आपने लिखा होगा	You may have walked	You may have written
6	He	वह	वह चला होगा	उसने लिखा होगा	He may have walked	He may have written
7	She	वह	वह चली होगी	उसने लिखा होगा	She may have walked	She may have written
8	It	यह	यह चला होगा	इसने लिखा होगा	It may have walked	It may have written
9	They	वे	वे चले होंगे	उन्हों ने लिखा होगा	They may have walked	They may have written
10	These	ये	ये चले होंगे	इन्हों ने लिखा होगा	These may have walked	These may have written

3. THE FUTURE TENSE

भविष्य काल

The Future Tense covers spectrum of events of the future time. Future Tense is optionally expressed in seven Modes or Moods (अर्थ), namely :

1. **Simple Future** Tense (सामान्य भविष्य काल) : The action that will begin, but has not begun yet. e.g. (Intransitive) Rām will walk 5 miles. राम 5 मिल चलेगा. (Transitive) Rām will wrote poem. राम कविता लिखेगा.
2. **Future Continuous** Tense (अपूर्ण भविष्य काल, सातत्य भविष्य काल) : The action that will take place and will continue in the future time. e.g. (Intransitive) Rām will be walking. राम चलता रहेगा. (Transitive) Rām will be writing. राम लिखता रहेगा.
3. **Future Perfect** Tense (पूर्ण भविष्य काल) : The action that will take place and will be completed at a specific time in the future. e.g. (Intransitive) Rām will have walked 5 miles in two hours. राम दो घंटों में 5 मिल चला होगा. (Transitive) Rām will have written poem by Saturday. राम ने शनिचर तक कविता लिखी होगी.
4. **Potential Future** Tense (संभाव्य भविष्य काल) : The action that will possibly be finished in the future is Potential Mood of the Future Tense. e.g. (Intransitive) Rām may be able to walk 20 miles. राम कदाचित् 20 मिल चल सकेगा. (Transitive) Rām may be able to write it in Sanskrit. राम शायद यह संस्कृत में लिख सकेगा.
5. **Imperative Future** Mood (आज्ञार्थ भविष्य काल) : The action that will be performed as an Order or a Request to a second Person Subject. e.g. (Intransitive) Please keep quiet! कृपया चुप रहिए! (Transitive) Please do not make noise! कृपया शोर मत मचाइये!
6. **Demonstrative Future** Mood (संकेतार्थ भविष्य काल) : The action that will possibly be finished in the future is Potential Mood of the Future Tense. e.g. (Intransitive) Rām may be able to walk 20 miles. राम कदाचित् 20 मिल चल सकेगा. (Transitive) Rām may be able

to write it in Sanskrit. राम शायद यह संस्कृत में लिख सकेगा.

7. **Benedictory Future** Mood (आशीर्वचनार्थ भविष्य काल) : The action that will possibly be finished in the future is Potential Mood of the Future Tense. e.g. (Intransitive) May Rām be able to walk 20 miles. राम कदाचित् 20 मिल चल सके. (Transitive) Rām may be able to write it in Sanskrit. राम यह संस्कृत में लिख सके.

TABLE 31 : Four Modes of Present Tense : **1. Simple Future** Mode (सामान्य भविष्य काल)

No.	Subject	कर्ता	उदाहरण, अकर्मक	उदाहरण, सकर्मक	Example, Intransitive	Example, Transitive
1	I	मैं	मैं चलूँगा	मैं लिखूँगा	I will walk	I will write
2	We	हम	हम चलेंगे	हम लिखेंगे	We will walk	We will write
3	You	तू	तू चलेगा	तू लिखेगा	You will walk	You will write
4	You	तुम	तुम चलोगे	तुम लिखोगे	You will walk	You will write
5	You	आप	आप चलोगे	आप लिखेंगे	You will walk	You will write
6	He	वह	वह चलेगा	वह लिखेगा	He will walk	He will writes
7	She	वह	वह चलेगी	वह लिखेगी	She will walk	She will writes
8	It	यह	यह चलता है	यह लिखेगा	It will walk	It will writes
9	They	वे	वे चलेंगे	वे लिखेंगे	They will walk	They will write
10	These	ये	ये चलेंगे	ये लिखेंगे	These will walk	These will write

TABLE 32 : Four Modes of Present Tense : **2. Future Continuous** Mode (अपूर्ण, सातत्यबोधक भविष्य काल)

No.	Subject	कर्ता	उदाहरण, अकर्मक	उदाहरण, सकर्मक	Example, Intransitive	Example, Transitive
1	I	मैं	मैं चलता रहूँगा	मैं लिखता रहूँगा	I will be walking	I will be writing
2	We	हम	हम चलते रहेंगे	हम लिखते रहेंगे	We will be walking	We will be writing
3	You	तू	तू चलता रहेगा	तू लिखता रहेगा	You will be walking	You will be writing

4	You	तुम	तुम चलते रहोगे	तुम लिखते रहोगे	You will be walking	You will be writing
5	You	आप	आप चलते रहोगे	आप लिखते रहोगे	You will be walking	You will be writing
6	He	वह	वह चलता रहेगा	वह लिखता रहेगा	He will be walking	He will be writing
7	She	वह	वह चलती रहेगी	वह लिखती रहेगी	She will be walking	She will be writing
8	It	यह	यह चलता रहेगा	वह लिखता रहेगा	It will be walking	It will be writing
9	They	वे	वे चलते रहेंगे	वे लिखते रहेंगे	They will be walking	They will be writing
10	These	ये	ये चलते रहेंगे	ये लिखते रहेंगे	These will be walking	These will be writing

OTHER FOUR MOODS OF THE VERBS
क्रिया के अन्य चार भावार्थ

1. **Indicative Mood** (विधानार्थ) : A Verb which makes a Statement (विधान) indicating a fact, asking a question or expressing an assumption which is accepted as a fact, is the Indicative Mood (विधानार्थ). e.g.

Fact :

i. He does exercise everyday. वह रोज व्यायाम करता है.

ii. Shivaji was a Maraṭhā King. शिवाजी एक मराठा राजा था.

iii. English is spoken widely in the world. अंग्रेज़ी जग में बहुत बोली जाती है.

iv. The milk is white. दूध सफेद होता है.

v. She learns Hindi at Home. वह घर पर हिंदी पढ़ती है.

Question :

i. How are you? आप कैसे हैं?

ii. Where do you live? आप कहाँ रहते हैं?

iii. Are you vegeterian? क्या आप शाकाहारी हैं?

iv. Is your brother well now? क्या आपका भाई अब सुस्थ है?

v. Do you know her phone nomber? आप उसका फोन नंबर जानते हैं क्या?

Supposed fact :

i. A he is poor does not mean he is dishonest. गरीब का मतलब यह नहीं की वह बेईमान है.

ii. If it snows, the roads will be empty. यदि बरफ गिरी तो रस्ते खाली होंगे.

iii. If you want, I will lend him money. यदि आप कहें, तो मैं उसे पैसे उधार दूँगा.

iv. If you drink milk, you will be healthy. अगर आप दूध पीएँगे तो आप तनदुरुस्त रहेंगे.

v. The necklace glitters because it is made of gold. हार सोने का है इस लिए चमकता है.

2. Subjuntive Mood (संभाव्यार्थ) :

The traditional phrases or the statements expressing a desire, intension, resolution, wish etc. belong to the Subjuntive Mood (संभाव्य अर्थ). e.g.

i. God bless you! भगवान आपको आशीर्वाद दे.

ii. He desires to be the President. वह अध्यक्ष बनना चाहता है.

iii. I intend to earn a million Rupees. मैं लखपति बनना चाहता हूँ.

iv. I shall never eat meat! मैं कभी भी माँस नहीं खाऊँगा!

v. I wish I was rich. काश कि मैं अमीर होता!

3. Inperative Mood (आज्ञार्थ) :

The sentence in which the Verb expresses a command, request, exhoration, entreaty or prayer, etc. is the Imperative Mood (आज्ञार्थ). Imperative Mood can strictly be used in Second Person, as it is made to the person being spoken to. e.g.

i. Be Quiet! चुप रहो!

ii. Sit down! नीचे बैठो!

iii Please stop here! कृपया यहाँ रुकिए!

iv. Be careful! सावधान रहिए!

v. Try to be cool! शाँत रहो.

vi. Let us go. चलिए!

vii. Please give me time. मुझे समय दीजिए!

viii. Take care! ध्यान रखिए!

4. **Desiderative or Benedictive Mood** (इच्छार्थ, विध्यर्थ) : A Verb which expresses a wish or blessing is the Indicative Mood (इच्छार्थ). e.g.

1.Have mercy on the poor. गरीबों पर दया करो!

2. O God! Please help us! हे भगवन्! हमारी मदद करो!

3.. May you live long. आप लंबी उमर जीएँ. etc.

THE HINDI IRREGULR VERBS

Take, Give, Do, Drink, Become and Go

अनियमित क्रिया

ले, दे, कर, पी, हो, जा

The following four tables show that, six verbs namely "**Take, Give, Do, Drink, Become** and **Go**" have irregular inflections in the :

(i) Perfect Tense, **(ii) Imperative Mood,**

(iii) Future Tenas and **(iv) Potential Mood.**

(i). **PERFECT TENSE :** Prefect Simple, Perfect Present, Perfect Past and Perfect future

Irregular verbs : "Take, Give, Do, Become, Go"

TABLE 33 : Irreguar verbs in the Perfect Ternse

	Verb	becomes	Suffix		Perfect Tense	Example
			m◦	f◦		m◦ f◦
1	Take : ले le	**लि li** or **ली lī**	या yā	यी yī	लिया liyā लियी/ली liyi or lī	पानी लिया pānī liyā चाय ली chāy lī
2	Give : दे de	**दि di** or **दी dī**	या yā	यी yī	दिया diyā दियी/दी diyi or dī	पानी दिया pānī diyā चाय दी chāy dī
3	Do : कर kar	**कि ki** or5r **की kī**	या yā	यी yī	किया kiyā कियी/की liyi or lī	काम किया kām kiyā शादी की shadī kī
4	Be, Become : हो ho	**हु hu**	आ yā	ई ī	हुआ huā हुई hulī	काम हुआ kām huā शादी हुई shadī huī
5	Go : जा ja	**ग ga**	या yā	यी yi	गया gayā गयी/गई gayi	राम गया Rām gayā सीता गयी Sītā gaylī

(ii). **IMPERATIVE MOOD :**

Irregular verbs : "Take, Give, Do, Drink"

TABLE 34 : Irreguar verbs in the Imperative Mood

	Verb	**becomes**	Suffix	Imperative	Example
					m◦ f◦
1	Take : ले le	**ली lī**	जिये jiye	लीजिये lījiye	पानी लीजिये pānī lījiye
2	Give : दे de	**दी dī**	जिये jiye	दीजिये dījiye	पानी दीजिये pānī dījiye
3	Drink : पी pī	**पी pī**	**जिये jiye**	पीजिये lījiye	पानी पीजिये pānī pijiye
4	Do : कर kar	**की kī**	जिये jiye	कीजिये kījiye	काम कीजिये kām kījiye

(iii). **FUTURE TENSE : First Person, Singular only : I Will xxx**

Irregular verbs : "Take, Give, Become"

TABLE 35 : Irreguar verbs in the Future Tense (First Person, Singular - I मैं)

	Verb	**becomes**	Suffix	Future Tense	Example
					m◦ f◦
1	Take : ले le	**लू lū**	ऊँगा ūngā ऊँगी ūngī	लूँगा lūngā लूँगी lūngī	पानी लूँगा pānī lūngā पानी लूँगी pānī lūngī
2	Give : दे de	**दू dū**	ऊँगा ūngā ऊँगी ūngī	दूँगा dūngā दूँगी dūngī	पानी दूँगा pānī dūngā पानी दूँगी pānī dūngī
3	Become : हो ho	**हू hū**	ऊँगा ūngā ऊँगी ūngī	हूँगा hūngā हूँगी hūngī	सफल हूँगा safal hūngā सफल हूँगी safal hūngī

(iv). **POTENTIAL MOOD : First Person, Singular only : I should xxx**

Irregular verbs : "Take, Give, Become"

TABLE 36 : Irreguar verbs in the Potential Mood (First Person, Singular - I मैं)

	Verb	**becomes**	Suffix	Future Tense	Example : m◦ f◦ both
1	Take : ले le	**लू lū**	ऊँ ū̐	लूँ lū̐	पानी लूँ pānī lū̐
2	Give : दे de	**दू dū**	ऊँ ū̐	दूँ dū̐	पानी दूँ pānī dū̐
3	Become : हो ho	**हू hū**	ऊँ ū̐	हूँ hū̐	सफल हूँगा safal hū̐

CHAPTER 12

MAKING YOUR OWN SENTENCES IN THE THREE TENSES

तीनों काल का स्वयं रचित प्रयोग

1. MAKING SIMPLE SENTENCES about a 'Present' event, with 'is' (*hai* है)

Key words : I = मैं *(maĩ),* am = हूँ *(hũ),* is = है *(hai),* are = हैं *(haĩ),* name = *nām* नाम।

my = मेरा *(merā),* your = आपका *(āp-kā),* his/her = उसका *(us-kā),* their = उनका *(un-kā)*

I	मैं *(maĩ)*	am	हूँ *(hũ)*	I am	मैं हूँ	*maĩ hũ*
You	आप *(āp)*	are	हैं *(haĩ)*	You are	आप हैं	*āp haĩ*
He, she, that	वह *(vah)*	is	है *(hai)*	He, she, that is	वह है	*vah hai*
This, it	यह *(yah)*	is	है *(hai)*	This, it is	यह है	*yah hai*

NOTE: The ँ sign is just a slight nasal tone added to the syllable below that ँ sign

TABLE 37 : Speaking a Present Event ◦ = Singular * = Plural

	Subject (colloquial)	am	is	are (colloquial)
	I मैं *(maĩ)*	हूँ *(hũ)*		
◦	He, that वह *(vah)* वो *(vo)*		है *(hai)*	
◦	She, that वह *(vah)* वो *(vo)*		है *(hai)*	
*	We हम *(ham)*			हैं *(haĩ)*
*	Youआप *(āp)* Respect, formal			हैं *(haĩ)* हो *(ho)*
◦	Youतुम *(tum)* Equal			हो *(ho)*
◦	Youतू *(tū)* Informal, low			है *(hai)*
*	They वे *(ve)* वो *(vo)*			हैं *(haĩ)*
*	Theseये *(ye)*			हैं *(haĩ)*

NOTE : **The above table shows that :**

(i) A Present Event is shown by suffix hū̃, hai, ho or haĩ (हूँ, है, हैं) = *h* + ū̃, *h* + ai, *h* + aĩ

(ii) In the suffixes hū̃, hai, ho, haĩ (हूँ, है, हो, हैं), the letter *'h'* (ह) stands for a 'Present' tense

(iii) letter *'ū̃'* (ऊँ) stands for 'first' person ◦singular subject 'I' (*h + ū̃ = hū̃* ह + ऊँ = हूँ)

(iv) letter *'ai'* (ऐ) shows a second or third person ◦singular subject (you, he, she)

(*h + ai = hai* ह + ऐ = है)

(v) letter *'aĩ'* (ऐं) stands for all 'plural' *subjects. (*h + aĩ = haĩ* ह + ऐं = हैं)

TABLE 38 : Present Tense Suffixes SUMMARY

	Subject	Suffix
Singular	I	हूँ *(hū̃)*
Singular	He/she	है *(hai)*
Plural	We	हैं *(haĩ)*
Plural	You *(āp)*	हैं *(haĩ)*
Plural	They	हैं *(haĩ)*

तुम हो *tum ho;* तू है *tū haĩ*

Masuline			Feminine		
I am a boy	मैं लड़का हूँ	*maĩ laḍkā hū̃*	I am a girl	मैं लड़की हूँ	*maĩ laḍkī hū̃*
You are a boy	आप लड़का हैं	*āp laḍkā haĩ*	You are a girl	आप लड़की हैं	*āp laḍkī haĩ*
He, that is a boy	वह लड़का है	*vah laḍkā hai*	She, that is a girl	वह लड़की है	*vah laḍkī hai*
This is a boy	यह लड़का है	*yah laḍkā hai*	This is a girl	यह लड़की है	*yah laḍkī hai*

2. USING HINDI PLURAL WORDS

RATNAKAR'S FIRST THREE NOBLE TRUTHS : (Singular to Plural)

FIRST : If the word is Masculine ending in ā (आ), the ā (आ) changes to e (ए) in plural.

e.g. singular m◦ Boy लड़का *laḍkā* → plural m◦ Boys लड़के *laḍke*

SECOND: If the word is Feminine and ends in a consonant or vowel ā (आ), then *ẽ* (एँ) is added to make it plural. e.g. singular f∘ Book किताब *kitāb* → plural f∘ Books किताबें *kitābẽ.* f∘ Necklace माला *mālā* → plural f∘ Necklaces मालाएँ *mālāẽ*

THIRD : If the word is Feminine ending in ī (ई), the ī (ई) changes to iyā̃ (इयाँ) in plural.

e.g. singular f∘ Girl लड़की *laḍkī* → plural f∘ Girls लड़कियाँ *laḍkiyā̃*

Dog (m∘) कुत्ता *(kuttā)* → Dogs कुत्ते *(kutte),* Cat (f∘) बिल्ली (billī) → Cats बिल्लियाँ *(billiyā̃),*
Car (f∘) गाड़ी *(gāḍī)* → Cars गाड़ियाँ *(gāḍiyā̃),* *House (m∘) घर (ghar) → Houses घर *(ghar),*
Thing (f∘) चीज *(chīz)* → Things चीजें *(chīzẽ),* Cow (f∘) गाय (gāy) → Cows गाएँ *(gāẽ).*

SINGULAR				PLURAL			
I	**मैं *(maĩ)***	**am**	**हूँ *(hū̃)***	**We**	**हम *(ham)***	**are**	**हैं *(haĩ)***
You	**आप *(āp)***	**are**	**हैं *(haĩ)***	**You**	**आप *(āp)***	**are**	**हैं *(haĩ)***
He, she, that	**वह *(vah)***	**is**	**है *(hai)***	**They**	**वे *(ve)***	**are**	**हैं *(haĩ)***
This, it	**यह *(yah)***	**are**	**है *(hai)***	**These**	**ये *(ye)***	**are**	**हैं *(haĩ)***

I am	मैं हूँ	*maĩ hū̃*	We are	हम हैं	*ham haĩ*
You are	आप हैं	*āp haĩ*	You are	आप हैं	*āp haĩ*
He, she, that is	वह है	*vah hai*	They are	वे हैं	*ve haĩ*
This, it is	यह है	*yah hai*	These are	ये हैं	*ye haĩ*

I am a boy	मैं लड़का हूँ	*maĩ laḍkā hū̃*	We are boys	हम लड़के हैं	*ham laḍke haĩ*
You are a boy	आप लड़का हैं	*āp laḍkā haĩ*	You are boys	आप लड़के हैं	*āp laḍke haĩ*
He is a boy	वह लड़का है	*vah laḍkā hai*	They are boys	वे लड़के हैं	*ve laḍke haĩ*
This is a boy	यह लड़का है	*yah laḍkā hai*	These are boys	ये लड़के हैं	*ye laḍke haĩ*
I am a girl	मैं लड़की हूँ	*maĩ laḍkī hū̃*	We are girls	हम लड़कियाँ हैं	*ham laḍkiyā̃ haĩ*
You are a girl	आप लड़की हैं	*āp laḍkī haĩ*	You are girls	आप लड़कियाँ हैं	*āp laḍkiyā̃ haĩ*
She is a girl	वह लड़की है	*vah laḍkī hai*	They are girls	वे लड़कियाँ हैं	*ve laḍkiyā̃ haĩ*
This is a girl	यह लड़की है	*yah laḍkī hai*	These are girls	ये लड़कियाँ हैं	*ye laḍkiyā̃ haĩ*

3. SPEAKING A PAST EVENT - WITH 'WAS' (था)

Key words : Here = *yahā̐* यहाँ। There = *vahā̐* वहाँ। Where? = *kahā̐?* कहाँ?

Rich = *amīr* अमीर। Poor = *garīb* गरीब। Do not = मत। Up to = *tak* तक ।

TABLE 39 : Speaking a Past Event

	Subject	was m∘	was f∘	were m∘	were f∘
	I मैं *(maĩ)*	था *(thā)*	थी (thī)		
∘	He वह *(vah)*	था *(thā)*			
∘	She वह *(vah)*	थी *(thī)*			
*	We हम *(ham)*			थे *(the)*	थीं *(thī̐)*
*	You आप *(āp)*			थे *(the)*	थीं *(thī̐)*
∘	You तुम *(tum)*			थे *(the)*	थी *(thī)*
∘	You तू *(tū)*			था *(thā)*	थी (thī)
*	They वे *(ve)*			थे *(the)*	थीं *(thī̐)*

NOTE : The above table shoes that :

(i) A Past Event is shown by a suffixs *thā, thī, the* or *thī̐* (था थी थे थीं) = *th*+ā, *th*+e, *th*+ī, th+ī̐

(ii) In these suffixes the letter *'th'* (थ) stands for a 'Past' tense

(iii) letter *'ā'* (आ) stands for masculine gender, singular subject (I, you, he)

(iv) letter *'ī'* (ई) shows a feminine singular subject (I, she)

(v) letter *'e'* (एं) stands for masculine plural subject (we, you, they)

(vi) letter *'ī̐'* (ईं) stands for feminine plural subject (we, you, they)

Masculine subject :

I was	मैं था	*maĩ thā*	We were	हम थे	*ham the*
You were	आप थे	*āp the*	You were	आप थे	*āp the*
He, that was	वह था	*vah thā*	They were	वे थे	*ve the*
This, it was	यह था	*yah thā*	These were	ये थे	*ye the*

I was here	मैं यहाँ था	*maĩ yahā̐ thā*	We werehere	हम यहाँ थे	*ham yahā̐ the*
You were here	आप यहाँ थे	*āp yahā̐ the*	You were here	आप यहाँ थे	*āp yahā̐ the*
He was here	वह यहाँ था	*vah yahā̐ thā*	They were here	वे यहाँ थे	*ve yahā̐ the*
It was here	यह यहाँ था	*yah yahā̐ thā*	These were here	ये यहाँ थे	*ye yahā̐ the*
I was rich	मैं अमीर था	*maĩ amīr thā*	We wererich	हम अमीर थे	*ham amīr the*
You were rich	आप अमीर थे	*āp amīr the*	You were rich	आप अमीर थे	*āp amīr the*
He was rich	वह अमीर था	*vah amīr thā*	They were rich	वे अमीर थे	*ve amīr the*

Feminine subject :

I was	मैं थी	*maĩ thī*	We were	हम थीं	*ham thī̐*
You were	आप थीं	*āp thī̐*	You were	आप थीं	*āp thī̐*
She was	वह थी	*vah thī*	They were	वे थीं	*ve thī̐*
I was here	मैं यहाँ थी	*maĩ yahā̐ thī*	We were here	हम यहाँ थीं	*ham yahā̐ thī̐*
You were here	आप यहाँ थीं	*āp yahā̐ thī̐*	You were here	आप यहाँ थीं	*āp yahā̐ thī̐*
She was here	वह यहाँ थी	*vah yahā̐ thī*	They were here	वे यहाँ थीं	*yahā̐ thī̐*
I was rich	मैं अमीर थी	*maĩ amīr thī*	We were rich	हम अमीर थीं	*ham amīr thī̐*
You were rich	आप अमीर थीं	*āp amīr thī̐*	You were rich	आप अमीर थीं	*āp amīr thī̐*
She was rich	वह अमीर थी	*vah amīr thī*	They were rich	वे अमीर थीं	*ve amīr thī̐*

TABLE 40 : Past Tense Suffixes SUMMARY

	Subject	Suffix M∘	Suffix F∘
Singular	I	था *(thā)*	थी *(thī)*
Singular	He/she	था *(thā)*	थी *(thī)*
Plural	We	थे *(the)*	थी *(thī),* थीं *(thī̐)*
Plural	You *(āp)*	थे *(the)*	थी *(thī),* थीं *(thī̐)*
Plural	They	थे *(the)*	थी *(thī),* थीं *(thī̐)*

TABLE 41 : SUMMARY : What we learned so far, the 'cumulative review'

Subject	am	is	are	was m◦	was f◦	were m◦	were f◦
I मैं *(maĩ)*	हूँ *(hũ)*			था *(thā)*	थी (thī)		
He वह *(vah)*		है *(hai)*		था *(thā)*			
She वह *(vah)*		है *(hai)*			थी *(thī)*		
We हम *(ham)*			हैं *(haĩ)*			थे *(the)*	थीं *(thī̃)*
You आप *(āp)*			हैं *(haĩ)*			थे *(the)*	थीं *(thī̃)*
You तुम *(tum)*			हो *(ho)*			थे *(the)*	थी *(thi)*
You तू *(tū)*			हैं *(haĩ)*			था *(thā)*	थी *(thi)*
They वे *(ve)*			हैं *(haĩ)*			थे *(the)*	थीं *(thī̃)*

REVIEW : The above table shows that :

(i) A Present Event is shown by suffix hũ, hai, ho or haĩ (हूँ, है, हो, हैं) = *h* + ũ, *h* + ai, *h* + aĩ

(ii) In the suffixes hũ, hai, ho, haĩ (हूँ, है, हो, हैं), the letter *'h'* (ह) stands for a 'Present' tense

(iii) letter *'ũ'* (ऊँ) stands for 'first' person singular subject 'I'

(iv) letter *'ai'* (ऐ) shows a second or third person singular subject (you, he, she)

(v) letter *'aĩ'* (ऐं) stands for the 'plural' subjects.

(vi) Past Event is shown by a suffixs *thā, thī, the* or *thī̃* (था थी थे थीं) = *th*+ā, *th*+e, *th*+ī, th+ī̃

(vii) In these suffixes the letter *'th'* (थ) stands for a 'Past' tense

(viii) letter *'ā'* (आ) stands for masculine gender, singular subject (I, you, he)

(ix) letter *'ī'* (ई) shows a feminine singular subject (I, she)

(x) letter *'e'* (ए) stands for masculine plural subject (we, you, they)

(xi) letter *'ī̃'* (ईं) stands for feminine plural subject (we, you, they)

4. MAKING SENTENCES FOR FUTURE EVENTS

The future events are generally of three kinds, viz◦ :

1. I will do (you will do; he, she, it will do; we, they will do) see - Table 13
2. I should do, I may do (you should do; he, she do; we, we should do, they should do)
3. Should I do? May I do? (should you do? should he do? she should do? should they do?)

TABLE 42 : Future and Subjunctive actions : I will do, I should-may do.. etc.

Subject	verb	I will m∘	I will f∘	Suffix m∘ f∘	Should I? m∘ f∘
I मैं *maĩ*	पी *pī*	ऊँगा *ūṅgā*	ऊँगी *ūṅgī*	ऊँ *ū̃*	ऊँ क्या? *ū̃ kyā?*
He वह *vah*	पी *pī*	एगा *egā*	--	ए *e*	ए क्या? *e kyā?*
She वह *vah*	पी *pī*	--	एगी *egī*	ए *e*	ए क्या? *e kyā?*
We हम *ham*	पी *pī*	एँगे *eṅge*	एँगी *eṅgī*	एँ *ẽ*	एँ क्या? *ẽ kyā?*
You आप *āp*	पी *pī*	एँगे *eṅge*	एँगी *eṅgī*	एँ *ẽ*	एँ क्या? *ẽ kyā?*
They वे *ve*	पी *pī*	एँगे *eṅge*	एँगी *eṅgī*	एँ *ẽ*	एँ क्या? *ẽ kyā?*

NOTE : **The above table shows that :**

(i) A Future Event (will) is shown in Hindī with letter *'g'* (ग) to which :

(ii) add the 'person' operative *ū̃, e, ẽ* (ऊँ, ए, एँ), as described earlier, and then

(iii) add the 'gender' operative ā, e, ī, ī̃ (आ ए ई ईं), as said earlier in Table 6:

NOTE : (a) suffix 'ā' (आ) means masculine singular subject

(b) suffix 'e' (ए) means masculine plural subject

(c) suffix 'ī' (ई) means feminine singular subject

(d) suffix 'ī̃' (ईं) means feminine plural subject

TABLE 43 : Future Tense Suffixes SUMMARY

	Subject	Suffix M∘	Suffix F∘
Singular	I (मैं)	ऊँगा *(ungā)*	ऊँगी *(ungī)*
Singular	He/she (वह)	एगा *(egā)*	एगी *(egī)*
Plural	We (हम)	एँगे *(enge)*	एँगे *(enge)* / एँगी *(engī)*
Plural	You (आप)		
Plural	They (वे)		

NOTE : **masculine plural** एँगे *(enge)* is commonly used for **feminine plural** also.

5. MAKING SENTENCES FOR COMPLETED ACTIONS

A perfected or completed action indicates what you did, have done or had done.

(i) suffix (m◦) *ā* (आ) or (f◦) *ī* (ई) is attached to the verb that ends in a consonant or a short vowel. e.g. verb *chal* चल (to walk) →

(1) walked *chal + ā = chalā;*

(2) I walked m◦ *maĩ chalā,* f◦ *maĩ chalī.* चल + आ = चला, (m◦) मैं चला, (f◦) मैं चली।

TABLE 44 : The **Perfect** Action Suffix for verbs ending in short vowels

	Verb	SUFFIX	
		Singular	Plural
1	Masculine	आ *ā*	ए *e*
2	Feminine	ई *ī*	ईं *ī̃* (or यी *yī*)

(ii) suffix *yā (y + ā)* या or *yī (y + ī)* यी is attached to the verb that ends in a long vowel such as *ā, ī* or *o* (आ, ई, ओ). e.g. verb *so* सो (sleep) → (slept) m◦ *so + y + ā = soyā,* I slept m◦ *maĩ soyā,* f◦ *maĩ soyī.* सो + या = सोया, (m◦) मैं सोया, (f◦) मैं सोयी।

TABLE 45 : The **Perfect** Action Suffix for verbs ending in long vowels

	Verb	SUFFIX	
		Singular	Plural
1	Masculine	या *yā*	ये *ye*
2	Feminine	यी *yī*	यीं *yī̃* (or यी *yī*)

(iii) If a completed action is Transitive, the suffix *ne* (ने) is attached to the subject. e.g. verb *khā* खा (eat) → (ate) *khā + yā = khāyā,* (I ate) *maĩne khāyā.* खा + या = खाया, मैंने खाया। *pī* पी (drink) → (drank) *pī + yā = pīyā,* (I drank) *maĩne pīyā.* पी + या = पीया, मैंने पीया।

(iv) When suffix *ne* (ने) is attached to a subject, the verb changes according to the Object (the thing on which the action is done). Now the Subject has no effect on the verb. e.g. m∘ and f∘ subject → I ate a banana. *maĩ ne kelā khāyā* मैंने केला खाया। I ate bananas. *maĩ ne kele khāye* मैंने केले खाये। I ate a roṭī *maĩ ne roṭī khāyī* मैंने रोटी खायी। I ate roṭīs *maĩ ne roṭiyā̃ khāyī̃* मैंने रोटियाँ खायीं।

TABLE 46 : The **Perfect** Tense, **Transitive** suffix ने *ne*

Subject	Singular	Plural
I /we	मैंने *maĩ-ne*	हमने *ham-ne*
He/she/they	उसने *us-ne*	उन्हों ने *unhõ ne*
You आप *(āp)*	आपने *āp-ne*	आपने *āp-ne*
You तुम *(tum)*	तुमने *tum-ne*	तुमने *tum-ne*
You तू *(tū)*	तूने *tū-ne*	तुमने *tum-ne*
Rām	राम ने *Rām ne*	
Sītā	सीता ने *Sītā ne*	

RATNAKAR'S SIXTH NOBLE TRUTH : (Perfect tense)

If an action is completed on a transitive verb, suffix *ne* (ने) is attached to the subject.

(a) Completed or perfected action = I did, I have done, I had done .. etc.

(b) Transitive action is where the action is performed on an object, not on the subject. e.g. I (the subject) ate (the verb) a mango (the object), I drank tea, I wrote a book .. etc.

(c) Intransitive action is where the action is performed by the doer (subject) on him himself, i.e. the action is not transferred to any external object. e.g. I (the subject) went, Bob slept, John walked, dog ran, cat died, they stayed, we came, you lived, baby cried, water leaked, house burnt, Sonia won, she swam, he sat, monkey jumped, sun rose, rain fell, etc.

The perfect (completed) actions are mainly of three kinds, such as :

1. I did (you did; he, she, it did; we did; they did)
2. I have done (you have done; he, she has done; we have done; they have done)
3. I had done (you had done; he, she had done; we had done; they had done)

TABLE 47 : I did; you did; he, she, it did; we did; they did .. etc.

Doer of the action Intransitive actions Transitive actions

Subject	intransitive action	suffix	transitive action suffix	verb type 1 consonant end	suffix	verb type 2 Long vowel	suffix
I मैं *maĩ*	*chal* चल	*ā* आ	*maĩ ne* मैंने	*kah* कह	*ā* आ	पी *pī*	*yā* या
He वह *vah*	*chal* चल	*ā* आ	*usne* उसने	*kah* कह	*ā* आ	पी *pī*	*yā* या
She वह *vah*	*chal* चल	*ī* ई	*usne* उसने	*kah* कह	*ā* आ	पी *pī*	*yā* या
We हम *ham*	*chal* चल	*e* ए	*hamne* हमने	*kah* कह	*ā* आ	पी *pī*	*yā* या
You आप *āp*	*chal* चल	*e* ए	*āpne* आपने	*kah* कह	*ā* आ	पी *pī*	*yā* या
They वे *ve*	*chal* चल	*e* ए	*unhõne* उन्होंने	*kah* कह	*ā* आ	पी *pī*	*yā* या

NOTE : Many people use masculine plural tenses for feminine plural tenses also.

(a). **Intransitive** actions, such as I came, I went, I fell, I walked :

I walked *maĩ chalā (chalī)* मैं चला (चली)। You fell *āp gire* आप गिरे। He came *vah āyā.* वह आया। She went *vah gayaī* वह गयी। We slept *ham soye* हम सोये। They stayed *ve rahe.* वे रहे।

(b). Intransitive actions, such as I have come, I have gone, I have fallen, I have walked

I have walked. *maĩ chalā (chalī) hū̃.* मैं चला (चली) हूँ। You have fallen. *āp gire haĩ.* आप गिरे हैं। He has come. *vah āyā hai.* वह आया है। She has gone. *vah gayaī hai.* वह गयी है। We have slept. *ham soye haĩ.* हम सोये हैं। They have stayed. *ve rahe haĩ.* वे रहे हैं।

(c). Intransitive actions, such as I had come, I had gone, I had fallen, I had walked :

I had walked. *maiँ chalā thā (chalī thī).* मैं चला था (चली थी)। You had fallen. *āp gire the.* आप गिरे थे। He had come. *vah āyā thā.* वह आया था। She had gone. *vah gayaī thī.* वह गयी थी। We had slept. *ham soye the.* हम सोये थे। They had stayed. *ve rahe the.* वे रहे थे।

(d). **Transitive** actions, such as I did, I wrote, I drank, I saw :

I ate. *maiँ ne khāyā.* मैंने खाया। I ate a mango. *maiँ ne ām khāyā.* मैंने आम खाया। I ate one banana. *maiँ ne ek kelā khāyā.* मैंने एक केला खाया। I ate two bananas. *maiँ ne do kele khāye.* मैंने दो केले खाये। I ate one Roṭī. *maiँ ne ek Roṭī khāyī.* मैंने एक रोटी खायी। I ate two Roṭīs. *maiँ ne do Roṭiyāँ khāyīँ.* मैंने दो रोटियाँ खायीं।

You drank tea. *āp ne chāy pī.* आपने चाय पी (पीयी)। Jack washed hands. *Jack ne hāth dhoye.* जैक ने हाथ धोये। Sunitā touched TV. *Sunita ne TV chhūā.* सुनीता ने टीवी छूआ। We peeled bananas. *hamne kele chhīle.* हमने केले छीले। Rām and Shyām did the work. *Rām aur Shyām ne kām kiyā.* राम और श्याम ने काम किया।

(e). Transitive actions, such as - I have done, I have written, I have drunk, I have seen :

I have eaten. *maiँ ne khāyā hai.* मैंने खाया है। I have eaten a mango. *maiँ ne ām khāyā hai.* मैंने आम खाया है। I have eaten one banana. *maiँ ne ek kelā khāyā hai.* मैंने एक केला खाया है। I have eaten two bananas. *maiँ ne do kele khāye hai.* मैंने दो केले खाये है। I have eaten one roṭī. *maiँ ne ek roṭī khāyī hai.* मैंने एक रोटी खायी है। I have eaten two roṭīs. *maiँ ne do roṭiyāँ khāyīँ haiँ.* मैंने दो रोटियाँ खायीं हैं।

You have drunk tea. *āp ne chāy pī hai.* आपने चाय पी है। Jack has washed hands. *Jack ne hāth dhoye haiँ.* जैक ने हाथ धोये हैं। Sunitā has touched TV. *Sunita ne TV chhūā hai.* सुनीता ने टीवी छूआ है। We have peeled bananas. *hamne kele chhīle haiँ.* हमने केले छीले हैं। Rām and Shyām have done the work. *Rām aur Shyām ne kām kiyā hai.* राम और श्याम ने काम किया है।

(f). Transitive actions, such as - I had done, I had written, I had drunk, I had seen :

I had eaten. *maiँ ne khāyā thā.* मैंने खाया था। I had eaten a mango. *maiँ ne ām khāyā thā.* मैंने आम खाया था। I had eaten one banana. *maiँ ne ek kelā khāyā thā.* मैंने एक केला खाया था। I had eaten two bananas. *maiँ ne do kele khāye the.* मैंने दो केले खाये थे। I had eaten one roṭī. *maiँ ne ek roṭī khāyī thī.* मैंने एक रोटी खायी थी। I had eaten two roṭīs. *maiँ ne do roṭiyāँ khāyī thīँ.* मैंने दो रोटियाँ खायी थीं।

You had drunk tea. *āp ne chāy pī thī.* आपने चाय पी थी। Jack had washed hands. *Jack ne hāth dhoye the.* जैक ने हाथ धोये थे। Sunitā had touched TV. *Sunita ne TV chhūā thā.* सुनीता ने टीवी छूआ था। We had peeled bananas. *hamne kele chhīle the.* हमने केले छीले थे। Rām and Shyām had done the work. *Rām aur Shyām ne kām kiyā thā.* राम और शाम ने काम किया था।

RATNAKAR'S SEVENTH NOBLE TRUTH : (The Suffixes) **The 18 SUFFIXES :** **(1) Present tense = 'h' (ह); (2) Past tense = 'th' (थ); (3) Future tense = 'g' (ग); (4) Habitual 'do' mode = 't' (त); (5) Continuous (imperfect) '-ing' mode = 'rah' (रह); (6) Already 'done' mode = 'chuk' (चुक); (7) Masculine singular= 'ā ' (आ); (8) Masculine plural = 'e' (ए); (9) Feminine singular = 'ī ' (ई); (10) Feminine plural = 'iyāँ' (इयाँ); (11) First person singular (I) = 'ūँ ' (ऊँ); (12) Third person singular (he, she) = 'ai' (ऐ); (13) Any Third person plural (we, you, they) = 'aiँ ' (एँ) ; (14) Any Perfect action = 'ā ' (आ); (15) Transitive Perfect action = 'ne' (ने). ALSO : (16) am = 'hūँ ' (हूँ); (17) is, has, have = 'hai' (है); (18) was, had = 'thā ' (था).**

IN DEPTH VIEW OF THE PERFECT (COMPLETED) ACTIONS

TABLE 48 : (completed Intransitive actions) I walked, I have walked, I had walked

Doer of the action Intransitive actions

Subject	action type 1 end in consonant	suffix		action type 2 Long vowel	suffix		HAVE		HAD

I मैं *maĩ*	*chal* चल	*ā* आ	सो *so*	*yā* या	हूँ *hũ*		*thā* था
He वह *vah*	*chal* चल	*ā* आ	सो *so*	*yā* या	है *hai*		*thā* था
She वह *vah*	*chal* चल	*ī* ई	सो *so*	*yī* यी	है *hai*		*thī* थी
We हम *ham*	*chal* चल	*e* ए	सो *so*	*ye* ये	हैं *haĩ*		*the* थे
You आप *āp*	*chal* चल	*e* ए	सो *so*	*ye* ये	हैं *haĩ*		*the* थे
They वे *ve*	*chal* चल	*e* ए	सो *so*	*ye* ये	हैं *haĩ*		*the* थे

TABLE 49 : (Presently completed actions) I have written, I have eaten .. etc.

*** for m◦ object**

Doer of the action Transitive actions

Subject	transitive action suffix	verb type 1 consonant end	suffix	present action (have) suffix	verb type 2 Long vowel	suffix	present action (have) suffix
I मैं *maĩ*	*ne* ने	*likh* लिख	*ā* आ*	है *hai*	*khā* खा	*yā* या*	है *hai*
He *उस *us*	*ne* ने	*likh* लिख	*ā* आ*	है *hai*	*khā* खा	*yā* या*	है *hai*
She *उस *us*	*ne* ने	*likh* लिख	*ā* आ*	है *hai*	*khā* खा	*yā* या*	है *hai*
We हम *ham*	*ne* ने	*likh* लिख	*ā* आ*	है *hai*	*khā* खा	*yā* या*	है *hai*
You आप *āp*	*ne* ने	*likh* लिख	*ā* आ*	है *hai*	*khā* खा	*yā* या*	है *hai*
They *उन्हों *unhõ*	*ne* ने	*likh* लिख	*ā* आ*	है *hai*	*khā* खा	*yā* या*	है *hai*

TABLE 50 : (Previously completed actions) I had written, I had eaten .. etc.

Doer of the action Transitive actions * Masculine

Subject	transitive action suffix	verb type 1 consonant end	suffix	past action (had) suffix	verb type 2 Long vowel	suffix	past action (had) suffix
I मैं *maĩ*	*ne* ने	*likh* लिख	*ā* आ*	*thā* था*	*khā* खा	*yā* या*	*thā* था*

He *उस *us*	*ne* ने	*likh* लिख	*ā* आ*	*thā* था*	*khā* खा	*yā* या*	*thā* था*
She *उस *us*	*ne* ने	*likh* लिख	*ā* आ*	*thā* था*	*khā* खा	*yā* या*	*thā* था*
We हम *ham*	*ne* ने	*likh* लिख	*ā* आ*	*thā* था*	*khā* खा	*yā* या*	*thā* था*
You आप *āp*	*ne* ने	*likh* लिख	*ā* आ*	*thā* था*	*khā* खा	*yā* या*	*thā* था*
They *उन्हों *unhõ*	*ne* ने	*likh* लिख	*ā* आ*	*thā* था*	*khā* खा	*yā* या*	*thā* था*

NOTES : (i) For the changes from *vah* वह to *us* उस and *ve* वे to *un* उन

Intransitive actions, I did xxx

1. I did walk or I walked. *maĩ chalā.* मैं चला। He did walk or he walked. *vah chalā.* वह चला। She did walk or she walked. *vah chalī.* वह चली। We did walk or we walked. *ham chale.* हम चले। You did walk or You walked. *āp chale.* आप चले। They did walk or They walked. *ve chale.* वे चले। * I did sleep or I slept. *maĩ soyā.* मैं सोया। He did sleep or he slept. *vah soyā.* वह सोया। She did sleep or she slept. *vah soyī.* वह सोयी। We did sleep or we slept. *ham soye.* हम सोये। You did sleep or You slept. *āp soye.* आप सोये। They did sleep or They slept. *ve soye.* वे सोये।

2. I **have** walked. *maĩ chalā hũ.* मैं चला हूँ। He has walked. *vah chalā hai.* वह चला है। She has walked. *vah chalī hai.* वह चली है। We have walked. *ham chale haĩ.* हम चले हैं। You have walked. *āp chale haĩ.* आप चले हैं। They have walked. *ve chale haĩ.* वे चले हैं। * I have slept. *maĩ soyā hũ.* मैं सोया हूँ। He has slept. *vah soyā hai.* वह सोया है। She has slept. *vah soyī hai.* वह सोयी है। We have slept. *ham soye haĩ.* हम सोये हैं। You have slept. *āp soye haĩ.* आप सोये हैं। They have slept. *ve soye haĩ.* वे सोये हैं। They have slept now. *ve ab soye haĩ.* वे अब सोये हैं। They have slept right now. *ve abhi soye jaĩ.* वे अभी सोये हैं।

3. I **had** walked. *maĩ chalā thā.* मैं चला था। He had walked. *vah chalā thā.* वह चला था। She had walked. *vah chalī thī.* वह चली थी। We had walked. *ham chale the.* हम चले थे। You had walked. *āp chale the.* आप चले थे। They had walked. *ve chale the.* वे चले थे। * I had slept. *maĩ soyā thā.* मैं सोया था। He had slept. *vah soyā thā.* वह सोया था। She had slept.

vah soyī thī. वह सोयी थी। We had slept. *ham soye the.* हम सोये थे। You had slept. *āp soye the.* आप सोये थे। They had slept. *ve soye the.* वे सोये थे।

Transitive actions, I have done xxx

4. I **did** write or I wrote. *maĩ-ne likhā.* मैंने लिखा। He did write or he wrote. *us-ne likhā.* उसने लिखा। She did write or she wrote. *us-ne likhā.* उसने लिखा। We did write or we wrote. *ham-ne likhā.* हमने लिखा। You did write or You wrote. *āp-ne likhā.* आपने लिखा। They did write or They wrote. *unhõ-ne likhā.* उन्होंने लिखा। * I did eat or I ate. *maĩ-ne khāyā.* मैंने खाया। He did eat or he ate. *us-ne khāyā.* उसने खाया। She did eat or she ate. *us-ne khāyā.* उसने खाया। We did eat or we ate. *ham-ne khāyā.* हमने खाया। You did eat or You ate. *āp-ne khāyā.* आपने खाया। They did eat or They ate. *unhõ -ne khāyā.* उन्होंने खाया।

5. I **have** written. *maĩ-ne likhā hai.* मैंने लिखा है। He has written. *us-ne likhā hai.* उसने लिखा है। She has written. *us-ne likhā hai.* उसने लिखा है। We have written. *ham-ne likhā hai.* हमने लिखा है। You have written. *āp-ne likhā hai.* आपने लिखा है। They have written. *unhõ-ne likhā hai.* उन्होंने लिखा है। * I have eaten. *maĩ-ne khāyā hai.* मैंने खाया है। He has eaten. *us-ne khāyā hai.* उसने खाया है। She has eaten. *us-ne khāyā hai.* उसने खाया है। We have eaten. *ham-ne khāyā hai.* हमने खाया है। You have eaten. *āp-ne khāyā hai.* आपने खाया है। They have eaten. *unhõne khāyā hai.* उन्होंने खाया है।

Transitive actions, I had done xxx

6. I **had** written. *maĩ-ne likhā thā.* मैंने लिखा था। He had written. *us-ne likhā thā.* उसने लिखा था। She had written. *us-ne likhā thā.* उसने लिखा था। We had written. *ham-ne likhā thā.* हमने लिखा था। You had written. *āp-ne likhā thā.* आपने लिखा था। They had written. *unhõ-ne likhā thā.* उन्होंने लिखा था। * I had eaten. *maĩ-ne khāyā thā.* मैंने खाया था। He had eaten. *us-ne khāyā thā.* उसने खाया था। She had eaten. *us-ne khāyā thā.* उसने खाया था। We had eaten. *ham-ne khāyā thā.* हमने खाया था। You had eaten. *āp-ne khāyā thā.*

आपने खाया था। They had eaten. *unhõ-ne khāyā thā.* उन्होंने खाया था।

7. I **did** walk or I walked ten k.m. *maĩ das k.m. chalā.* मैं दस कि.मि. चला। He walked up to temple. *vah mandir tak chalā.* वह मंदिर तक चला। She walked yesterday. *vah kal chalī.* वह कल चली। We walked slowly. *ham dhīre chale.* हम धीरे चले। You walked fast. *āp tej chale.* आप तेज चले। They walked more. *ve jyādā chale.* वे ज्यादा चले। * I slept less. *maĩ kam soyā.* मैं कम सोया। He did not sleep. *vah nahĩ soyā.* वह नहीं सोया। She did sleep. *vah soyī.* वह सोयी। We slept enough. *ham kāfī soye.* हम काफी सोये। You slept a lot. *āp bahut soye.* आप बहुत सोये। They slept a little bit. *ve jarā (thoḍā) soye.* वे जरा (थोड़ा) सोये।

8. I **have** always walked. *maĩ hameshā chalā hũ.* मैं हमेशा चला हूँ। He has never walked. *vah kabhī nahĩ chalā hai.* वह कभी नहीं चला है। She has walked sometimes. *vah kabhī kabhī chalī hai.* वह कभी कभी चली है। We have walked ahead. *ham āge chale haĩ.* हम आगे चले हैं। You have walked behind. *āp pīchhe chale haĩ.* आप पीछे चले हैं। They have walked together. *ve sāth sāth chale haĩ.* वे साथ साथ चले हैं।

9. I **had** walked outside. *maĩ bāhar chalā thā.* मैं बाहर चला था। He had walked inside. *vah andar chalā thā.* वह अंदर चला था। She had walked in front. *vah sāmane chalī thī.* वह सामने चली थी। We had walked today. *ham āj chale the.* हम आज चले थे।

Transitive actions, I have done xxx

10. I **did** write or I wrote a letter. *maĩ-ne patra likhā.* मैंने पत्र लिखा। I wrote one letter. *maĩ-ne patra likhā.* मैंने एक पत्र लिखा।He wrote letters. *us-ne patra likhe.* उसने पत्र लिखे। She wrote a letter. *us-ne patra likhā.* उसने पत्र लिखा। We wrote a letter. *ham-ne chiṭṭhī likhī.* हमने चिट्ठी लिखी (*patra likhā.* हमने पत्र लिखा)। You wrote letters. *āp-ne chiṭṭhiyā̃ likhī.* आपने चिट्ठियाँ लिखी (*maĩne patra likhe.* मैंने पत्र लिखे)। They wrote books. *unhõ-ne kitābẽ likhī.* उन्होंने किताबें लिखी। * I ate a banana. *maĩ-ne kelā khāyā.* मैंने केला खाया। He ate bananas. *us-ne kele khāyā.* उसने केले खाया। She ate a roṭī. *us-ne roṭī khāyī.* उसने

रोटी खायी। We ate roṭīs. *ham-ne roṭiyā̃ khāyī.* हमने रोटियाँ खायी। You ate a mango. *āp-ne ām khāyā.* आपने आम खाया। They ate mangos. *unho̐-ne ām khāye.* उन्होंने आम खाये।

11. I **have** written a book. *maĩ-ne kitāb likhī hai.* मैंने किताब लिखी है। He has written a book. *us-ne kitāb likhī hai.* उसने किताब लिखी है। She has written a letter. *us-ne khat likhā hai.* उसने खत लिखा है (*maĩne patra likhā hai.* मैंने पत्र लिखा है)। We have written letters. *ham-ne khat likhe haĩ.* हमने खत लिखे हैं (*patra likhe haĩ.* मैंने पत्र लिखे हैं)। You have written Hindī. *āp-ne hindī likhā hai.* आपने हिंदी लिखा है। They have written Hindī letter. *unho̐-ne hindī khat likhā hai.* उन्होंने हिंदी लिखा है। * I have eaten two apples. *maĩ-ne do seb khāye haĩ.* मैंने दो सेब खाये हैं। He has eaten three Samosas. *us-ne tīn samose khāye haĩ.* उसने तीन समोसे खाये हैं। She has eaten four Paraṭhās. *us-ne chār parāṭhe khāye haĩ.* उसने चार पराठे खाये हैं। We have eaten five grapes. *ham-ne pāñch angūr khāye haĩ.* हमने पाँच अंगूर खाये हैं। You have eaten six chillies. *āp-ne chhah mirchiyā̃ khāyī haĩ.* आपने छह मिरचियाँ खायी हैं। They have eaten seven tomatos. *unho̐ne sāt ṭamāṭar khāye haĩ.* उन्होंने सात टमाटर खाये हैं।

Transitive actions, I had done xxx (Table 17)

12. I **had** eaten sugarcane. *maĩ-ne īkh khāyā thā.* मैंने ईख खाया था। He had eaten eight pomegranates. *us-ne āṭh anār khāye the.* उसने आठ अनार खाये थे। She had eaten nine lemons. *us-ne nau nīmbū khāye the.* उसने नौ नींबू खाये थे। We had eaten ten dates. *ham-ne das chhuāre khāye the.* हमने दस छूआरे खाये थे। You had not eaten garlic. *āp-ne lahsun nahĩ khāyā thā.* आपने लहसुन नहीं खाया था। They had eaten a little. *unho̐-ne thoḍā khāyā thā.* उन्होंने थोड़ा खाया था।

13. **PRESENT HABITUAL, 'do' mode** (suffixes ता, ती, ते *tā, tī, te*): I walk or I do walk. (m∘) *maĩ chaltā hū̃.* मैं चलता हूँ। (f∘) *maĩ chaltī hū̃.* मैं चलती हूँ। He walks, he does walk. *vah chaltā hai.* वह चलता है। She walks, she does walk. *vah chaltī hai.* वह चलती है। We

walk, we do walk. *ham chalte haĩ.* हम चलते हैं। You walk, you do walk. *āp chalte haĩ.* आप चलते हैं। They walk, they do walk. *ve chalte haĩ.* वे चलते हैं।

14. **CONTINUOUS, 'doing' mode** (suffixes रहा, रही, रहे *rahā, rahī, rahe*): I **am** walking. (m∘) *maĩ chal rahā hū̃.* मैं चल रहा हूँ। (f∘) *maĩ chal rahī hū̃.* मैं चल रही हूँ। He is walking. *vah chal rahā hai.* वह चल रहा है। She is walking. *vah chal rahī hai.* वह चल रही है। We are walking. *ham chal rahe haĩ.* हम चल रहे हैं। You are walking. *āp chal rahe haĩ.* आप चल रहे हैं। They are walking. *ve chal rahe haĩ.* वे चल रहे हैं। * I **was** walking. (m∘) *maĩ chal rahā thā.* मैं चल रहा था। (f∘) *maĩ chal rahī thī.* मैं चल रही थी। He was walking. *vah chal rahā thā.* वह चल रहा था। She was walking. *vah chal rahī thī.* वह चल रही थी। We were walking. (m∘) *ham chal rahe the.* हम चल रहे थे। (f∘) *ham chal rahī thī̃.* हम चल रही थीं। You were walking. (m∘) *āp chal rahe the.* आप चल रहे थे। (f∘) *āp chal rahī thī̃.* आप चल रही थीं। They were walking. (m∘) *ve chal rahe the.* वे चल रहे थे। (f∘) *ve chal rahī thī̃.* वे चल रहीं थीं।

15. **ALREADY COMPLETED, 'already done' mode** (suffixes चुका, चुकी, चुके *chukā, chukī, chuke*): I **have** already walked. (m∘) *maĩ chal chukā hū̃.* मैं चल चुका हूँ। (f∘) *maĩ chal chukī hū̃.* मैं चल चुकी हूँ। He has already walked. *vah chal chukā hai.* वह चल चुका है। She has already walked. *vah chal chukī hai.* वह चल चुकी है। We have already walked. *ham chal chuke haĩ.* हम चल चुके हैं। You have already walked. *āp chal chuke haĩ.* आप चल चुके हैं। They have already walked. *ve chal chuke haĩ.* वे चल चुके हैं। * I **had** already walked. (m∘) *maĩ chal chukā thā.* मैं चल चुका था। (f∘) *maĩ chal chukī thī.* मैं चल चुकी थी। He had already walked. *vah chal chukā thā.* वह चल चुका था। She had already walked. *vah chal chukī thī.* वह चल चुकी थी। We had already walked. *ham chal chuke the.* हम चल चुके थे। You had already walked. *āp chal chuke the.* आप चल चुके थे। They had already walked. *ve chal chuke the.* वे चल चुके थे।

16. PAST HABITUAL : 'used to do' mode (suffixes ता था, ती थी, ते थे *tā thā, tī thī, te the*): I used to walk. (m॰) *maĩ chal tā thā.* मैं चल<u>ता</u> था। (f॰) *maĩ chal tī thī.* मैं चल<u>ती</u> थी। He used to walk. *vah chal tā thā.* वह चलता था। She used to walk. *vah chal tī thī.* वह चलती थी। We used to walk. *ham chal te the.* हम चलते थे। You used to walk. *āp chal te the.* आप चलते थे। They used to walk. *ve chal te the.* वे चलते थे।

17. FUTURE, 'will' mode (suffixes ऊँगा, ऊँगी, एगा, एगी, एंगे *ū̃gā, ū̃gī, egā, egī, enge*): I will walk. (m॰) *maĩ chalū̃gā.* मैं चलूँगा। (f॰) *maĩ chalū̃gā.* मैं चलूँगी। He will walk. *vah chalegā.* वह चलेगा। She will walk. *vah chalegī.* वह चलेगी। We will walk. *ham chalenge.* हम चलेंगे। You will walk. *āp chalenge.* आप चलेंगे। They will walk. *ve chalenge.* वे चलेंगे।

18. POTENTIAL, 'should or may' mode (suffixes ऊँ, ए, एं *ū̃, e, ẽ, enge*): I (m॰ and f॰) should walk. *maĩ chalū̃.* मैं चलूँ। He or she should walk. *vah chale.* वह चले। We should walk. *ham chalẽ.* हम चलें। You should walk. *āp chalẽ.* आप चलें। They should walk. *ve chalẽ.* वे चलें।

19. INTERROGATIVE, 'should I? or may I?' mode (suffixes ऊँ? ए? एं? *ū̃? e? ẽ? enge?*): Should I walk. (m॰ and f॰) *maĩ chalū̃?* मैं चलूँ? *maĩ chalū̃ kyā?* मैं चलूँ क्या? Should he or she walk. *vah chale?* वह चले? *vah chale kyā?* वह चले क्या? Should we walk. *ham chalẽ?* हम चलें? *ham chalẽ kyā?* हम चलें क्या? Will you walk. *āp chalenge?.* आप चलेंगे? *āp chalenge kyā?.* Will they walk? *ve chalenge?* वे चलेंगे? * *ve chalenge kyā?* वे चलेंगे क्या?

20. SIMPLE PERFECT, 'did' mode (suffixes आ, या, ई, यी *ā. yā, ī, yī*): I <u>did</u> walk or I walked. (m॰) *maĩ chalā.* मैं चल<u>ा</u>। (f॰) *maĩ chalī.* मैं चल<u>ी</u>। He did walk or he walked. *vah chalā.* वह चला। She did walk or she walked. *vah chalī.* वह चली। We did walk or we walked. *ham chale.* हम चले। You did walk or you walked. *āp chale.* आप चले। They did walk or they walked. *ve chale.* वे चले।

21. Transitive Actions

I (m∘ and f∘) did eat or I ate a banana. *maĩne kelā khāyā.* मैंने केला खाया। I ate two bananas. *maĩne do kele khāye.* मैंने दो केले खाये। I ate a roṭī. *maĩne roṭī khāyī.* मैंने रोटी खायी। I ate two roṭīs. *maĩne do roṭiyā̃ khāyī̃.* मैंने दो रोटियाँ खायीं। * He or she ate a banana. *usne kelā khāyā.* उसने केला खाया। He or she ate two bananas. *usne do kele khāye.* उसने दो केले खाये। He ate a roṭī. *usne roṭī khāyī.* उसने रोटी खायी। He ate two roṭīs *usne do roṭiyā̃ khāyī̃.* उसने दो रोटियाँ खायीं। * We ate a banana. *hamne kelā khāyā.* हमने केला खाया। We ate two bananas. *hamne do kele khāye.* हमने दो केले खाये। We ate a roṭī. *hamne roṭī khāyī.* हमने रोटी खायी। We ate two roṭīs *hamne do roṭiyā̃ khāyī̃.* हमने दो रोटियाँ खायीं। * You (m∘ and f∘) ate a banana. *āpne kelā khāyā.* आपने केला खाया। You ate two bananas. *āpne do kele khāye.* आपने दो केले खाये। You ate a roṭī. *āpne roṭī khāyī.* आपने रोटी खायी। You ate two roṭīs *āpne do roṭiyā̃ khāyī̃.* आपने दो रोटियाँ खायीं। * They (m∘ and f∘) ate a banana. *unhõne kelā khāyā.* उन्होंने केला खाया। They ate two bananas. *unhõne do kele khāye.* उन्होंने दो केले खाये। They ate a roṭī. *unhõne roṭī khāyī.* उन्होंने रोटी खायी। They ate two roṭīs *unhõne do roṭiyā̃ khāyī̃.* उन्होंने दो रोटियाँ खायीं।

22. PRESENT PERFECT, 'have done' mode (sucffixes आ है, ई है, ए हैं *ā hai, ī hai, e haĩ*):

I have walked. (m∘) *maĩ chalā hū̃.* मैं चला हूँ। (f∘) *maĩ chalī hū̃.* मैं चली हूँ। He has walked. *vah chalā hai.* वह चला है। She has walked. *vah chalī hai.* वह चली है। We have walked. *ham chale haĩ.* हम चले हैं। You have walked. *āp chale haĩ.* आप चले हैं। They have walked. *ve chale haĩ.* वे चले हैं।

23. Transitive Actions:

I (m∘ and f∘) have eaten a banana. *maĩne kelā khāyā hai.* मैंने केला खाया है। I have eaten two bananas. *maĩne do kele khāye haĩ.* मैंने दो केले खाये हैं। I have eaten a roṭī. *maĩne roṭī khāyī hai.* मैंने रोटी खायी है। I have eaten two roṭīs. *maĩne do roṭiyā̃ khāyī haĩ.* मैंने

दो रोटियाँ खायी हैं। * He or she has eaten a banana. *usne kelā khāyā hai.* उसने केला खाया है। He or she has eaten two bananas. *usne do kele khāye haĩ.* उसने दो केले खाये हैं। He or she has eaten a roṭī. *usne roṭī khāyī hai.* उसने रोटी खायी है। He or she has eaten two roṭīs *usne do roṭiyā̃ khāyī haĩ.* उसने दो रोटियाँ खायी हैं। * We, you or they have eaten a banana. *hamne, āpne, unhõne kelā khāyā hai.* हमने, आपने, उन्होंने केला खाया है। We, you or they have eaten two bananas. *hamne, āpne, unhõne do kele khāye haĩ.* हमने आपने, उन्होंने दो केले खाये हैं। We, you or they have eaten a roṭī. *hamne, āpne, unhõne roṭī khāyī hai.* हमने आपने, उन्होंने रोटी खायी है। We, you or they have eaten two roṭīs *hamne, āpne, unhõne do roṭiyā̃ khāyi haĩ.* हमने आपने, उन्होंने दो रोटियाँ खायी हैं।

24. **PAST PERFECT, 'had done' mode** (suffixes आ था, ई थी, ए थे *ā thā, ī thī, e the*): I had walked. (m◦) *maĩ chalā thā.* मैं चला था। (f◦) *maĩ chalī thī.* मैं चली थी। He had walked. *vah chalā thā.* वह चला था। She had walked. *vah chalī thī.* वह चली थी। We had walked. *ham chale the.* हम चले थे। You had walked. *āp chale the.* आप चले थे। They had walked. *ve chale the.* वे चले थे।

25. **Transitive Actions (As said before, refer Tables 23-24 for changes to pronouns *vah* वह and *ve* वे)**

I (m◦ and f◦) had eaten a banana. *maĩne kelā khāyā thā.* मैंने केला खाया था। I had eaten two bananas. *maĩne do kele khāye the.* मैंने दो केले खाये थे। I had eaten a roṭī. *maĩne roṭī khāyī thī.* मैंने रोटी खायी थी। I had eaten two roṭīs. *maĩne do roṭiyā̃ khāyī thĩ.* मैंने दो रोटियाँ खायी थीं। * He or she had eaten a banana. *usne kelā khāyā the.* उसने केला खाया थे। He or she had eaten two bananas. *usne do kele khāye the.* उसने दो केले खाये थे। He or she had eaten a roṭī. *usne roṭī khāyī hai.* उसने रोटी खायी थी। He or she had eaten two roṭīs *usne do roṭiyā̃ khāyī thĩ.* उसने दो रोटियाँ खायी थीं। * We, had eaten a banana. *hamne kelā khāyā thā.* हमने केला खाया था। You had eaten two bananas. *āpne do kele khāye the.* आपने दो केले खाये थे। They had eaten a roṭī. *unhõne roṭī khāyī thī.* उन्होंने रोटी खायी थी। They had eaten two roṭīs *unhõne do roṭiyā̃ khāyi thĩ.* उन्होंने दो रोटियाँ खायी थीं।

TABLE 18 : SUMMARY OF SUFFIXES FOR ALL TEN ACTIONS WE LEARNED SO FAR in Tables 1-17

TABLE 18-A : FOR MASCULINE SUBJECTS

REMEMBER : For Transitive Perfect Actions you have to add *ne* (ने) to the subject, and change the verb according to the gender and number of the object.

Doer of the action------		to Drink	Habitual	Imperfect	Already done	Present•	Past•	Future•	Request	Question	Completed Intransitive Actions -------------		
Masc-uline	subject	verb	do	-doing	done	am, is	was, had	will do	I should	should I?	did	have done	had done
I (m•)	मैं *mai̐*	पी *pī*	ता *tā*	रहा *rahā*	चुका *chukā*	हूँ *hū̐*	था *thā*	ऊँगा *ū̐gā*	ऊँ *ū̐*	ऊँ *ū̐?*	आ *ā*	आ हूँ *ā hū̐*	आ था *ā thā*
He	वह *vah*	पी *pī*	ता *tā*	रहा *rahā*	चुका *chukā*	है *hai*	था *thā*	एगा *egā*	ए *e*	ए *e?*	आ *ā*	आ है *ā hai*	आ था *ā thā*
We	हम *ham*	पी *pī*	ते *te*	रहे *rahe*	चुके *chuke*	हैं *hai̐*	थे *the*	एंगे *ẽge*	एं *ẽ*	एं *ẽ?*	ए *e*	ए हैं *e hai̐*	ए थे *e the*
You	आप *āp*	पी *pī*	ते *te*	रहे *rahe*	चुके *chuke*	हैं *hai̐*	थे *the*	एंगे *ẽge*	एं *ẽ*	एं *ẽ?*	ए *e*	ए हैं *e hai̐*	ए थे *e the*
They	वे *ve*	पी *pī*	ते *te*	रहे *rahe*	चुके *chuke*	हैं *hai̐*	थे *the*	एंगे *ẽge*	एं *ẽ*	एं *ẽ?*	ए *e*	ए हैं *e hai̐*	ए थे *e the*
			1	2	3		4	5	6	7	8	9	10

Remember : In Transitive Completed actions, suffix ने (*ne*) is added to the Subject; NOW the verb is controlled by theGender and Number of the Object.
The suffixes for : (i) m• singular = आ *ā* (ii) f• sing• = ई *ī* (iii) plural• = ए *e*. Shown above are the suffixes only for actions with m• singular Object.

TABLE 18-B : FOR FEMININE SUBJECTS

REMEMBER : For Transitive Perfect Actions you have to add *ne* (ने) to the subject, and change the verb according to the gender and number of the object.

Doer of the action------		to Drink	Habitual	Imperfect	Already done	Present•	Past•	Future•	Request	Question	Completed Intransitive Actions -------------		
Femin-ine	subject	verb	do	-doing	done	am, is	was, had	will do	I should	should I?	did	have done	had done
I (f•)	मैं *mai̐*	पी *pī*	ती *tī*	रही *rahī*	चुकी *chukī*	हूँ *hū̐*	थी *thī*	ऊँगी *ū̐gī*	ऊँ *ū̐*	ऊँ *ū̐?*	ई *ī*	ई हूँ *ī hū̐*	ई थी *ī thī*
She	वह *vah*	पी *pī*	ती *tī*	रही *rahī*	चुकी *chukī*	है *hai*	थी *thī*	एगी *egī*	ए *e*	ए *e?*	ई *ī*	ई है *ī hai*	ई थी *ī thī*
We	हम *ham*	पी *pī*	तीं *tī̐*	रहीं *rahī̐*	चुकीं *chukī̐*	हैं *hai̐*	थीं *thī̐*	एंगे *ẽge*	एं *ẽ*	एं *ẽ?*	ईं *ī̐*	ईं हैं *ī̐ hai̐*	ईं थीं *ī̐ thī̐*
You	आप *āp*	पी *pī*	तीं *tī̐*	रहीं *rahī̐*	चुकीं *chukī̐*	हैं *hai̐*	थीं *thī̐*	एंगे *ẽge*	एं *ẽ*	एं *ẽ?*	ईं *ī̐*	ईं हैं *ī̐ hai̐*	ईं थीं *ī̐ thī̐*
They	वे *ve*	पी *pī*	तीं *tī̐*	रहीं *rahī̐*	चुकीं *chukī̐*	हैं *hai̐*	थीं *thī̐*	एंगे *ẽge*	एं *ẽ*	एं *ẽ?*	ईं *ī̐*	ईं हैं *ī̐ hai̐*	ईं थीं *ī̐ thī̐*
			1	2	3		4	5	6	7	8	9	10

Remember : In Transitive Completed actions, suffix ने (*ne*) is added to the Subject; NOW the verb is controlled by the Gender and Number of the Object.
The suffixes for : (i) m• singular = आ *ā* (ii) f• sing• = ई *ī* (iii) plural• = ए *e*. Shown above are the suffixes only for actions with m• singular Object.

NOTES : (i) He, she, that = वह, *वो (*vah,* vo*); (ii) Those = वे, *वो (*ve, *vah* vo*); (iii) It, this, these = यह, *ये (*yah, *ye*); *colloquial

For detailed expansion and extended variations of these pronouns, see Table 25

CHAPTER 13

THE THREE VOICES OF THE VERBS

क्रिया के तीन वाच्य अथवा तीन प्रयोग

A Sentence (वाक्य) is the group uf words stating our thought. The most important word or the heart of the sentence is the Verb (क्रिया or क्रियापद). The Subject (उद्देश्य), a person or the thing, indicated by this Verb as the Performer of that action, is the Doer (कर्ता) in that sentence. This action may not only be limited to the Doer of the verb but it may also have an effect on the Object (कर्म) in that sentence. Therefore, the Doer (कर्ता), Object (कर्म) and the Verb (क्रियापद) are the three important building blocks of the sentence.

Also, in a sentence, as we change the focus or importance of the sentence from the Doer (कर्ता) to the Object (कर्म), the form of the Verb (क्रिया) also changes accordingly. This mutual relationship of connection, concord and construction between Doer-Object-Verb (कर्ता-कर्म-क्रिया) is called Voice (वाच्य or प्रयोग).

The transformation of the verbs that reveals us whether the sentence is talking about or focused on the Subject (उद्देश्य) or the Object (कर्म) or about an abstract form (भाव) in the sentence, determines the type of the Voice (वाच्य or प्रयोग) of the sentence.

In Hindi Grammer, there are three types of Voices namely, Active Voice (कर्तरि प्रयोग), Passive Voice (कर्मणि प्रयोग) and Abstract Voice (भावे प्रयोग). The English Grammer has only Active and Passive Voices.

1. The Active Voice (कर्तरि प्रयोग or कर्तृवाच्य) :

The sentence in which the person or thing denoted by Subject (उद्देश्य) is the Doer (कर्ता) of the Verb of sentence, such construction is called **Active Voice** (कर्तरि प्रयोग or कर्तृवाच्य). क्रिया का कर्ता के अनुसार प्रयोग कर्तरि प्रयोग अथवा कर्तृवाच्य है. e.g.

i. राम रावण को मारता है. (Rāma kills Rāvaṇ). Here, the form of the Verb (मारता है) shows that the person (राम) denoted by the Subject (उद्देश्य) is the doer of the action (मारना).

ii. चाबी ताले को खोलती है. (the key opens the lock). Here, the form of the Verb (खोलती है है) shows that the thing (चाबी) denoted by the Subject (उद्देश्य) is the doer of the action (खोलना).

iii. 1. राम समोसा खाता है, 2. राम समोसे खाता है, 3. सीता समोसा खाती है, 4. सीता समोसे खाती है, 5. वे सामोसा खाते हैं, 6. वे सामोसे खाते हैं, 7. मैं सामोसा खाता हूँ. 8. मैं सामोसे खाता हूँ. 9. राम रोटी खाता है, 10. राम रोटियाँ खाता है, 11. सीता रोटी खाती है, 12. सीता रोटियाँ खाती है, 13. वे रोटी खाते हैं, 14. वे रोटियाँ खाते हैं, 15. मैं रोटी खाता हूँ. 16. मैं रोटियाँ खाता हूँ.

From the above examples we can see that, the Gender, Number and Person of the Verb changes only according the the Gender, Number and Person of the Doer (कर्ता) of the sentences. Therefore, and only therefore, this Voice is called **Active Voice** (कर्तरि प्रयोग or कर्तृवाच्य). Thus we can conclude that, in Active Voice, the Subject or the Doer is the controller of the Verb. The object has no effect on the verb. In other words, in Acrive Voice, the Verb changes only according to the Subject of the sentence.

NOTE : The Active Voice can be recognized from the fact that that the Subject (कर्ता) is alway in Nominative Case (कर्ता कारक) and the Object (कर्म) is in Accusative Case (कर्म कारक).

2. The Passive Voice (कर्मणि प्रयोग or कर्मवाच्य) :

The construction in which the form of the Verb (क्रिया) shows that something is done to the person or thing denoted by Subject (उद्देश्य, कर्ता) in the sentence. Such construction in which Object (कर्म) chas control over the Verb, is called **Passive Voice** (कर्मणि प्रयोग or कर्मवाच्य). क्रिया का कर्म के अनुसार प्रयोग कर्मणि प्रयोग अथवा कर्मवाच्य है.e.g.

i. राम के द्वारा रावण मरता है. (Rāvaṇ gets killed by Rāma). Here, the form of the Verb (मरता है) shows that the person (रावण) denoted by the Subject (उद्देश्य) is the doer (कर्ता) of the action (मरना). The कर्ता of the Passive voice is the कर्म of the Active Voice. Therefore, this counsruction is called कर्मवाच्य.

ii. चाबी के द्वारा ताला खुलता है. (the lock opens by the key). Here, the form of the Verb (खुलता है) shows that the thing (ताला) denoted by the Object (कर्म) is the doer of the action (खुलना).

iii. 1. राम के द्वारा समोसा खाया जाता है, 2. सीता के द्वारा समोसा खाया जाता है, 3. राम के द्वारा समोसे खाए जाते हैं, 4. सीता के द्वारा समोसे खाए जाते हैं, 5. उनके द्वारा समोसा खाया जाता है, 6. उनके द्वारा समोसे खाए जाते हैं, 7. मेरे द्वारा समोसा खाया जाता है, 8. मेरे द्वारा सामोसे खाए जाते हैं, 9. राम के द्वारा रोटी खायी जाती है, 10. सीता के द्वारा रोटी खायी जाती है, 11. राम के द्वारा रोटियाँ खायी जाती हैं, 12. सीता के द्वारा रोटियाँ खायी जाती हैं, 13.उनके द्वारा रोटी खायी जाती है, 14. उनके द्वारा रोटियाँ खायी जाती हैं, 15. मेरे द्वारा रोटी खायी जाती है, 16. मेरे द्वारा रोटियाँ खायी जाती हैं.

From the above examples we can see that, the Gender, Number and Person of the Verb changes only according the the Gender, Number and Person of the Object (कर्म) of the sentences. Therefore, and only therefore, this Voice is called **Passive Voice** (कर्मणि प्रयोग or कर्मवाच्य). Thus we can conclude that, in Passive Voice, the Object (कर्म) is the controller of the Verb. The subject has no effect on the verb. In other words, in Passive Voice, the Verb changes only according to the Obbject of the sentence.

The Passive Voice can be recognized from the fact that that the Verb is "done to" the person denoted by Subject (कर्ता) which is not active but it is passive because it receives or suffers the action.

NOTE : In Passive Voice the कर्ता is never in in Nominative Case (कर्ता कारक). कर्ता is usually in the Instrumental Case (करण कारक). The कर्म is in Nominative Case (कर्ता कारक).

3. The Abstract Voice (भावे प्रयोग or भाववाच्य) :-

English Grammer does not have Bhave Voice. In Hindi Grammer, The construction in which the form of Verb neither changes with the Gender or Number of the Subject (कर्ता) nor with the Gender and Number of the Object (कर्म), is called **Abstract Voice** (भावे प्रयोग or भाववाच्य). It is also called Impersonal Voice. The verb stays independent of the Subject and Object. It is usually in the Instrumental Case (करण कारक) or sometimes it is in the Dative Case (संप्रदान कारक). If the Verb is Intransitive, the verb will be Benedictive (विध्यर्थ). If the Verb is in Potential Mood (शक्यार्थ) then it will always be Abstract Voice (भावे प्रयोग, भाव वाच्य). e.g.

1. राम ने रावण को मारा.
2. बिल्ली ने चूहों को खाया.
3. नानी ने पोतियों को बुलाया.
4. लड़कों ने चित्रों को रंगाया.
5. शिक्षक ने छात्रों को पढ़ाया
6. उससे अकेले नहीं जाया जाता.
7. सबका मालिक एक! .
8. जीते रहो!
9. सबको यश मिले!
10. हे भगवन्! सबका भला हो!
11. "घास पर चलना मना है."
12. यहाँ पर गाड़ी मत रखिए!

In above sentences, if you try to change the Gender and Number of the Subject and Object, the Verb does not change. Therefore, these are the statements in Abstract Voice (भावे प्रयोग or भाववाच्य). There is no Abstract Voice in English Grammer.

SUMMARY :

1. If the Verb of the sentence changes according to the Gender and Number of the Subject, it is **Active Voice** (कर्तरि प्रयोग or कर्तृवाच्य).
2. If the Verb of the sentence changes according to the Gender and Number of the Object, it is **Passive Voice** (कर्मणि प्रयोग or कर्मवाच्य).
3. If the Verb of the sentence does not chasnge according to the Gender and Number of the Subject or Object, it is **Abstract Voice** (भावे प्रयोग or भाववाच्य)

CHAPTER 14

THE INDECLINABLE WORDS

अविकारी शब्द

The Parts of Speech which do not change with the change in their Gender, Number or Case are called **Indeclinable Words** (अविकारी शब्द). Indeclinable words are of four types, namely (1) Adverbs (क्रियाविशेषण), (2) Relational Indeclinables (संबंध सूचक अव्यय), (3) Conjunctions (समुच्चय सूचक) and (4) Interjections (विस्मय सूचक) words (शब्द).

1. THE ADVERBS

क्रियाविशेषण

The word that qualifies a Verb or an Adjective ai called an Adverb (क्रियाविशेषण). An adverb may also qualify another Adverb. Depending of the manner or meaning (अर्थ), the adverbs are divided into four main types, namely (1) Adverbs of Place or Direction (स्थान और दिशा), (2) Adverbs of Time and Duration (समय और अवधि), (3) Adverbs of Degree or Quantity (परिमाण और संख्या), and (4) Adverbs of Manner or Mode (रीति, परिपाटी).

NOTE : Few examples of each type are giver here for reference, but for a detailed list please see the Dictionary of Adverbs given below.

NOTE : Please note that several adverbs may be classified in more than one type.

(1) the **Adverbs of Place or Direction** (स्थान और दिशा)

The adverbs of this type are further divided in two sub classes, namely :

(i) the **Adverbs of Place** (स्थान) : अन्यत्र (elsewhere), आगे (in front), सामने (facing), ऊपर (above), कहाँ (where?), जहाँ (where), तहाँ (there), दूर (far), नीचे (below), पीछे (behind),

बाहर (outside), भीतर (inside), वहाँ (there), यहाँ (here), सर्वत्र (everywhere), सामने (in front), etc.

(ii) the **Adverbs of Direction** (दिशा) : इधर (this side), उधर (that side), किधर? (which side?), जिधर (which side), दाँए (on the right), बाँए (on the left), एक तरफ (on one side), आर पार (through), इस ओर (on this side), उस ओर (on that side), किस ओर? (on which side?), जिस ओर (on which side), etc.

(2) the **Adverbs of Time and Duration** (समय और अवधि)

The adverbs of this type are further divided in two sub classes, namely :

(i) the **Adverbs of Time** (समय) : अब (now), कब? (when?), जब (when), तब (then), अभी (right now), कभी (ever), जभी (whenever), तभी (at thet time), फिर (again), आज (today), कल (tomorrow), कल (yesterday), परसों (day after tomorrow or day before tomorrow), तरसों (after or before two days), नरसों (before or after three days), तुरंत (right away), सवेरे (in the morning), शाम को (in the evening), पहले (at first), के बाद (after), बाद में (later), आखिर (at the end), निदान (at least), etc.

(ii) the **Adverbs of Duration** (अवधि) : सदा (always), रोज (every day), हमेशा (always), अब तक (till now), आजकल (now a days), कब का (form long time), कभी न कभी (some day), अब भी (still now), इतनी देर (so long), कभीकभी (sometimes), निरंतर (ever), अनवरत (non stop), लगातार (continuously), दिन भर (all day), रात भर (all night), etc.

(3) **Adverbs of Degree or Quantity** (परिमाण और संख्या)

The adverbs of this type are further divided in two sub classes, namely :

i. **Adverbs of Degree** (परिमाण सूचक) : This category occurs in five different ways, namely,

1. **Adverbs of Excess** (अधिकता सूचक) : अधिक (extra), अतिशय (plenty), अत्यंत (extremely), सर्वथा (completely), बहुत (very much), भारी (great), खूब (great deal), पूर्णत:

(fully), etc.

2. **Adverbs of Shortfall** (न्यूनता सूचक) : थोड़ा कम (little less), मामूली (less that normal), तनिक (a bit), लेश (fraction), रंचमात्र (a bit), कम (less), जरा (few), टुक (a bit), किंचित् (slightly), थोड़ा बहुत (partly) etc.

3. **Adverbs of Adequateness** (पर्याप्तता सूचक) : बस (enough), प्रचुर (plenty), भरपूर (plenty), विपुल (plenty), सिर्फ (only), केवल (only), मात्र (only), काफी (quite), पर्याप्त (enough), यथेष्ट (as much wanted), ठीक (proper), etc.

4. **Adverbs of Comparison** (तुलनात्मक) : जितना (as much), उतना (so much), और (more), बढ़कर (ahead), etc.

5. **Adverbs of Series** (क्रम सूचक) : क्रम से (sequencially), यथाक्रम (in order), तिल-तिल (little by little), एक-एक (one after other), एक-एक करके (one by one), etc.

ii. **Adverbs of Quantity** (परिमाण सूचक) : कितना? (how much?), जितना (as much), उतना (that much, so much), अमर्याद (infinitely, indefinitely) etc.

(4) **Adverbs of Manner or Mode** (रीति, परिपाटी)

The adverbs of this type are further divided in five sub classes, namely :

i. **Adverbs of Certainty** (निश्चय सूचक) : बिलकुल (absloutely), बेशक (no doubt), दरअसल (in fact), सचमुच (really), निस्संदेह (certainly), वस्तुत: (as a matter of fact), etc.

ii. **Adverbs of Uncertainty** (अनिश्चय सूचक) : कदाचित् (probably), शायद (may be), यथासंभव (possibly), etc.

iii. **Adverbs of Acceptance** (स्वीकार सूचक) : हाँ (affirmative), ठीक (alright), जी (yes), सच (right), etc.

iv. **Adverbs of Reasoning** (कारण सूचक) : क्यों कि (because), इसलिए (therefore), अत: (thus), अतएव (that's why), etc.

v. **Adverbs of Limit** (अवधारणा सूचक) : भर (fully), तक (up to), भी (also), पर्यंत (till).

2. THE RELATIONAL INDECLINABLES
संबंध सूचक अव्यय

The Indeclinable words which form relationship with other words of the sentence by coming before or after nouns are the Relational Indeclinables (संबंध सूचक अव्यय). The Relational Indeclinables can be grouped under at least ten categories, namely Adverbs of - (1) Time (काल), (2) Place and Direction (स्थान और दिशा), (3) Means (साधन), (4) Cause (हेतु), (5) Choice (विकल्प), (6) Similarity (सादृश्य), (7) Opposition (विरोध), (8) Association (सहयोग), (9) Limit (मर्यादा) and (10) Comparison (तुलना). Note that many of these Relational Words have already been classified under several other categories.

(1) **Adverbs of Time** (काल सूचक अव्यय) : के पहले (before), के बाद (after), के पश्चात् (after), के अनंतर (after), के उपरांत (after), के आगे (after), के पीछे (before), बाद में (later), etc.

(2) **Adverbs of Place and Direction** (स्थान और दिशा सूचक) : के पास (near), के निकट (near), के आसपास (near about), के प्रति (towards), के करीब (near), के नज़दीक (near), के पड़ोस में (next to), के सन्निकट (close), के समीप (near), के ऊपर (above), की तरफ (towards), की ओर (towards), के पार (beyond), etc.

(3) **Adverbs of Means** (साधन सूचक) : के बल (with the aid of), के द्वारा (through), के मारफत (by), के सहारे (with help of), के माध्यम से (through), के जरिए (by), etc.

(4) **Adverbs of Cause** (हेतु सूचक) : के कारण (for the reason), के लिए (for), की वजह से (reason), के निमित्त (motive), के वास्ते (for), के खातिर (with consideration), etc.

(5) **Adverbs of Choice** (विकल्प सूचक) : के बदले (in stead), के सिवाय (without), के अलावा (without), के एवज (in stead of), के बिना (without), के पलटे (on the other hand), के अतिरिक्त (besides), के बगैर (without), की जगह (in place of), etc.

(6) **Adverbs of Similarity** (सादृश्य सूचक) : के समान (similarly), के तुल्य (equal), की तरह

(like), के सदृश्य (similar to), के अनुरूप (in the form of), के बराबर (equal to), की भाँति (like), के अनुसार (accordingly), के सरीखा (like), के जैसा (like), के मुताबिक (like), के लायक (similar), के साम्य (similarity), etc.

(7) **Adverbs of Opposition** (विरोध सूचक) : के विरुद्ध (in opposition), के उल्टा (reverse to), के विपरीत (opposite to), के खिलाफ (against), के प्रतिकूल (in contrary), के विमुख (in opposition), के प्रतिमुख (oppositely), etc.

(8) **Adverbs of Association** (सहयोग सूचक) : के सहित (with), के साथ (in company of), के संग (with), के बरोबर (with), के समेत (including), के पूर्वक (in accordance), के सोहबत (with), etc.

(9) **Adverbs of Limit** (मर्यादा सूचक) : के पर्यंत (up to), के तलक (up to), के परे (beyond), के बाहर (beyond), के भीतर (in), से दूर (far), से अलग (separate), आमरण (un to death), आजन्म (life-long), तड़के (by daybreak), etc.

(10) **Adverbs of Comparison** (तुलना सूचक) : की अपेक्षा (than), की तुलना में (compared to), के तुल्य (in comparison), की नाईं (similar to), etc.

3. THE CONJUGATIONS

समुच्चय सूचक अव्यय

The Indeclinable words which connect two clauses of a sentence without qualifying the verbs therein are the Conjugational Indeclinables (समुच्चय सूचक अव्यय). The conjugations are divided in eight types.

(1) **Linking Adverbs** (संयोजक अव्यय) : और (and), तथा (similarly), एवं (also), व (as well as), etc.

(2) **Optional Adverbs** (विभाजक अव्यय) : या (or), अथवा (or), वा (or), किंवा (or), या–या (either-or), etc.

(3) **Alternative Adverbs** (पर्याय अव्यय) : तथापि (however), मगर (but), फिर भी (even then), परंतु (but rather), लेकिन (but even so), मगर (but), अपितु (nonetheless), etc.

(4) **Result indicaing Adverbs** (परिणाम सूचक अव्यय) : अत: (therefore), इसलिए (thus), अतएव (hence), सो (that's why), क्यों कि (because of), चूँकि (as), etc.

(6) **Purpose indicating Adverbs** (उद्देश्य सूचक अव्यय) : ताकि (so that), इसलिए कि (for the purpose), जिससे कि (for intention of), etc.

(7) **Signal indicating Adverbs** (संकेत सूचक अव्यय) : चाहे (even if), तथापि (similarly), तदपि (even if), तदैव (as well as), etc.

(8) **Form indicating Adverbs** (स्वरूप सूचक अव्यय) : अर्थात् (of course), मानो (imaginey), etc.

4. THE EXCLAMATORY WODRS

विस्मय सूचक अव्यय

The Indeclinable words which express a feeling of astonishment, dismay, surprise, amazement, agreement, rejection or vocation are the Exclamatory Indeclinables (विस्मय सूचक अव्यय). The Exclamatory are divided in seven types.

(1) **Adverbs of Joy** (हर्ष सूचक अव्यय) : आहा! क्या कहने! क्या खूब! धन्य-धन्य! वह-वाह! शाबास! etc.

(2) **Adverbs of Sorrow** (शोक सूचक अव्यय) : अरे-अरे! हाय-हाय! हे राम! बाप रे! तोबा-तोबा! दैया-दैया! etc.

(3) **Adverbs of Surprise** (आश्चर्य सूचक अव्यय) : ओहो! क्या बात! etc.

(4) **Adverbs of Agreement** (अनुमोदन सूचक अव्यय) : ठीक! अच्छा! हाँ, etc.

(5) **Adverbs of Acceptance** (स्वीकार सूचक अव्यय) : ठीक है! जी हाँ! अच्छा जी! etc.

(6) **Adverbs of Rejection** (तिरस्कार सूचक अव्यय) : अरे! छि:-छि:!, धत्तेरे! etc.

(7) **Adverbs of Address** (संबोधन सूचक अव्यय) : अजी! अहो! हे! अरे! etc.

5. THE AFFIRMATIVE and NEGATIVE WODRS
सकारात्मक और नकारात्मक अव्यय

The Indeclinable words which express a feeling of agreement or disagreement are the Affirmative and Negative Indeclinables (सकारात्मक और नकारात्मक अव्यय).

(1) **Affirmative Indeclinables** (सकारात्मक अव्यय) : हाँ! ठीक है! जी! etc.

(2) **Negative Indeclinables** (नकारात्मक अव्यय) : न! ना! नहीं! मत! etc.

A positive statement can be converted into a negative statements using the negative adverbs such as न (not, neither), ना (no), नहीं (no, not), मत (don't), etc.

NOTE : A **Positive starement** can be converted to a negative sentence. with the help of the **Negative Indeclinables** (नकारात्मक अव्यय) : न! ना! नहीं! मत! etc. as shown below.

Positive Sentences :

i. Today it is cold, yesterday it was warm. आज ठंढ है, कल गरमी थी.

ii. He said, yes! उसने हाँ! कहा.

iii. A seat is empty there. वहाँ एक कुर्सी खाली है.

iv. You may discuss here. आप यहाँ आलाप कर सकते हैं.

Negative sentences:

i. Today it is neither cold nor hot. आज न ठंढ है न गरमी.

ii. He said, no!. उसने ना कहा.

iii. Not a single seat is empty there. वहाँ एक भी कुर्सी खाली नहीं है.

iv. Din't make noise! शोर मत मचाइये!

DICTIONARY Of ADVERBS
क्रियाविशेषण कोश

Englidh to Hindi

Above (ūrdhva, ūpar ऊर्ध्व, ऊपर)

Abruptly (सहसा sahasā, अकस्मात् akasmāt)

Absolutely (सर्वथा sarvathā, सर्वशः sarvaśhah, केवल keval)

Absurdly (अविचार से avichār se)

After (अनन्तर anantar, पश्चात् paśhchāt)

Afterwards (फिर, बाद में fir, bād mẽ)

Again (पुनः punah, पुनर् punar)

Again and again (बारबार bārbār, बारंबार bārambār)

Against (ke viruddha के विरुद्ध)

All (akhil, sarva अखिल, सर्व)

All around (अभित abhita, परित parita)

Almost (प्रायः prāyah, लगभग lagbhag)

Already (पहले ही pahale hī, प्राक् prāk)

Also (पुनश्च punaśhcha)

Alternately (पर्याय से paryāye se)

Always (सदा sadā, सर्वदा sarvadā)

All around (सर्वतः sarvatah)

All at once (एकदम ekdam)

Among (में से, mẽ se)

A little (किंचित् kiñchit, मनाक् manāk)

Anyhow (किसी प्रकार kisī prakār, किसी हालत में kisī hālat mẽ)

Anything (कुछ भी kuchh bhī)

Anywhere (कहीं भी kahī̃ bhī)

Apart (अलग, पृथक् alag, prithak)

Around (सर्वतः, ईर्दगीर्द sarvatah, īrdgīrd)

As (यथा yathā, यद्वत् yadvat; जैसे jaise)

As far as (जहाँ तक jahā̃ tak)

As much as (लगभग lagbhag)

As if (मानो māno)

At all (बिलकुल bilkul)

At any time (कभी भी kbhī bhī)

At once (एकदम ekdam)

At one time (एकदा ekadā, सहसा sahasā)

At present (अब, आज ab, āj)

At random (अकस्मात् akasmāt, सहसा sahasā)

At the same time (साथ-साथ sāth-sāth)

At this time (सम्प्रति, अब samprati, ab)

At what time (कब kab)

Away (दूर dūr)

Backwards (उलटे, पृष्ठतः ulṭe, prishṭhata)

Badly (बुरी तरह से burī tarah se)

Because (kuoँ ki, isliye ki, ke kāraṇ क्यों कि, इसलिए कि, के कारण)

Before, in front (सम्मुख, समक्ष, आगे, सामने, साक्षात् sammukh, samakṣha, āge, sāmane, sākṣhāt)

Before, time-place (पहले, पूर्व; आगे, सामने pahale, pūrva; āge, sāmne)

Behind (pīcche पीछे)

Below (नीचे nīche)

Besides (के अतिरिक्त, के अलावा, को छोड़ कर ke atirikta, ke alāvā, ko chhoḍ kar)

Between (के बीच में ke bīch meँ)

Beyond (ke pare, ke pār के परे, के पार)

But (परन्तु, मगर, लेकिन parantu, magar, lekin)

Ceaselessly (सतत, निरंतर satat, nirantar)

Certainly (असंशय, निश्चित् asaṁśhaya, niṣchit)

Clearly (स्पष्टतया, साफ-साफ spaṣhṭatayā, sāf-sāf)

Close by (पास pād)

Consequently (ततः, अतः, फलतः, फलस्वरूप tatah, atah, falatah, falasvarūp)

Constantly (सदा, बराबर, निरंतर, एकतार sadā, barābar, nirantar, ektār)

Conversely (उलटे, विलोमत: ulṭe, vilomatah)

Daily (प्रतिदिन, रोज pratidina, roz)

Day after tomorrow (परसों parasoँ)

Day before yesterday (परसों parsoँ)

Deeply (दूर तक, गहराई से dūr tak, gaharāī se)

Don't (मत mat)

Downwards (नीचे की ओर nīche kī or)

Elsewhere (अन्यत्र anyatra)

Enough (बस, काफी bas, kāfī)

Entirely (संपूर्णत: sampūrṇatah)

Equally (तुल्य tulya)

Eternally (नित्य nitya, सदा sadā, निरन्तर nirantar)

Ever (कदापि, कभी, सदा, सदैव, हमेशा kadāpi, kabhī, sadā. sadaiva. hameṣhā)

Every day (प्रतिदिन, रोज़ pratidin, roz)

Every time (जब भी, हर बार jab bhī, har bār)

Everywhere (सर्वत्र, सब ओर sarvatra, sab or)

Evidently (स्पष्टतया spaṣhṭatayā)

Except (को छोड़ कर, के सिवा, के अतिरिक्त ko chhoḍ kar, ke sivā, ke atirikta)

Extensively (भीषणता से bhīṣhaṇtā se)

Falsely (मिथ्या mithyā, मृषा mriṣhā)

Far (दूर dūr)

Forcibly (बल से, ज़बरदस्ती से bal se,

zabardastī se)

Forthwith (तुरंत, अविलंब, फौरन, तत्काल, तत्क्षण turant, avilamb, fauran, tatkṣhaṇ)

Fortunately (सौभाग्य से saubhāgya se)

Forward (आगे, सामने āge, sāmne)

Frequently (पुनः पुनः, punahpunah, मुहुर्मुहु muhurmuhu, बारंबार bārambār)

Fully (पूर्णतः pūrṇatah)

Further (और आगे aur āge)

Gladly (खुशी से khushī se)

Happily (सुख से sukh se)

Hastily (सहसा sahasā, झट से jhaṭ se)

Hence (इस लिए is liye)

Here (यहाँ yahā̃, इह iha)

Here after (अतः atah, अब से ab se)

Here before (इसके पहले iske pahale)

Here and there (इधर-उधर, यहाँ-वहाँ idhar-udhar, yahā̃-vahā̃)

Highly (अत्यंत atyanta)

How (कैसे kaise)

How else (और कैसे aur kaise)

However (तथापि, फिर भी tathapi, fir bhī)

However (कंतु kintu, अपि तु api tu, तथापि tathāpi, परन्तु parantu)

Idly (वृथा, व्यर्थ, बेकार vrithā, vyartha, bekār)

If (यदि yadi, अगर agar)

If not (नहीं तो nahĩ to, अन्यथा anyathā)

If-then (यदि-तो yadi-to)

Ignorantly (अज्ञानतः ajñānatah)

Immediately (तुरंत, तत्काल, अविलंब, फौरन turant, tatkāl, avilamb, fauran)

Improperly (अनुचित anuchit)

In (madhye मध्ये)

In a short time (तुरंत, तत्काल, अविलंब, फौरन turant, tatkāl, avilamb, fauran)

In detail (vistār se विस्तार से)

In front of (आगे, सामने āge, sāmane)

In order (क्रमशः kramaśhah)

In heaven (अमुत्र, उधर amutra, उधर)

In short (alpaśhah, sārāṁśh se अल्पशः, सारांश से)

In the evening (शाम कों shām ko)

In the morning (सवेरे, तड़के savere, taḍke)

In the noon (दोपहर में do pahar mẽ)

In the afterworld (मर कर mar kar)

In this world (इह iha, यहाँ aratra, yahā̃)

Indeed (सचमुच, बेशक वस्तुतः sachmuch, beśhak, vastutah)

Incessantly (अविरत avirata)

Into (मध्ये madhye)

Lately (हाल में hāl mẽ)

Later (पश्चात्, बाद में paśhchāt, bād meँ)
Like this (ऐसे aise)
Like that (वैसे vaise)
Like what? (कैसे? kaise?)
Loudly (जोर से zor se)
Luckily (सौभाग्य से saubhāgya se)
Manifestly (साक्षात् sākṣhāt)
Many times (कई बार kaī bār)
Moreover (इसके- अलावा, -अतिरिक्त, -सिवाय is ke- alāvā, -atirikta, -sivāy)
Mostly (बहुधा bahudhā)
Most probably (संभवत: sambhavatah)
Much (अत्यन्त atyanta)
Mutually (परस्पर paraspara)
Near (समीप, निकट, पास samip, nikaṭ, pās)
No, not (न na, नहीं nahīँ, ना nā)
Not at all (बिलकुल नहीं bilkul nahīँ)
Now (अभी, अब abhī, ab)
Now a days (आज-कल āj-kal)
Nowhere (कहीं भी नहीं kahīँ bhī nahīँ)
Often (बहुधा bahudhā, बारंबार bārambār)
On, Over (ūpar ऊपर)
On both sides (उभयत: ubhayatah)
Once (एकदा ekadā)
Only (केवल kevala, मात्र mātra)
Openly (सुस्पष्ट suspaṣhṭa, व्यक्त vyakta)
Or (अथवा athavā, वा vā, अन्यथा anyathā)
Or else (अन्यथा anyathā)
Out (bāhar बाहर)
Outwardly (बाह्यत: bāhyatah)
Perhaps (कदाचित् kadāchit)
Possibly (कदाचित् kadāchit)
Privately (अकेले में akele meँ)
Probably (संभवत: sambhavatah)
Properly (उचित uchita, सम्यक् samyak)
Quickly (झट से, जल्दी, तुरंत jhaṭ se, jaldī, turant)
Quietly (शान्ती पूर्वक śhāntī pūrvak)
Rarely (क्वचित् kvachit)
Repeatedly (बारंबार bārambārपुन:पुन: punapunah)
Rightly (यथातथा yathātathā, सम्यक् samyak)
Separately (पृथक्, अलग prithak, alag)
Shortly (झट jhaṭ, शीघ्र śhīghra)
Silently (चुपचाप chupchāp)
Similarly (तद्वत्, वैसे ही tadvat, vaise hī)
Simultaneously (साथ-साथ, एकसाथ sāth-sāth, eksāth)
Slightly (जरा zarā)
Slowly (श्धीरे-धीरे dhīre-dhīre)

So (तथा tathā, तद्वत् tadvat, ऐसे aise)
So that (जिससे कि jisse ki)
Somehow (किसी तरह kisi tarah)
Sometimes (कदाचित् kadāchit, क्वचित् kvachit, कभी-कभी kabhī-kabhī)
Somewhat (किंचित् kiñchit)
Somewhere (कहीं kahī̐)
Somewhere else (अन्यत्र anyatra)
Spontaneously (स्वयम् svayam)
Suddenly (अकस्मात् akasmāt)
Sufficiently (पर्याप्त paryāpta)
Surely (निश्चित् niśhchit, अवश्य avaśhya)
Then (फिर, बाद में fir, bād mē̐)
Thence (तत: tatah, वहाँ से vahā̐ se)
There (तत्र, वहाँ tatra, vahā̐)
Therefore (अत: atah, इस लिए is liye)
Thus (इस लिए, ऐसे, वैसे is liye, aise. vaise)
Today (आज āj)
Together (एकत्र, एक साथ ekatra, ek sāth)
Tomorrow (कल kal)
Truly (वस्तुत: vastutah, तत्त्वत: tattvatah)
Under (नीचे nīche)
Universally (सर्वत: sarvatah, विश्वत: viśhvatah)
Uselessly (वृथा vriyhā, व्यर्थ vyartha)
Vainly (वृथा vrithā)
Variously (नानाविध nānāvidha)
Verily (सत्य satya)
Very (अतीव, बहुत atīva, bahut)
Well (सम्यक् samyak, अस्तु astu)
What? (क्या kyā?)
What else (और क्या aur kyā)
What more (किंबहुना kimbahunā)
When (यदा, जब yadā, jab)
When? (कब kab?)
Whence (कहाँ से kahā̐ se)
Where (जहाँ jahā̐)
Where? (कहाँ, kahā̐?)
Wherever (जहाँ कहीं jahā̐ kahī̐)
Whether (baharhāl बहरहाल)
Which (jo जो)
Wholly (पूर्णतया, समग्र pūrṇatayā, samagra)
Why? (क्यों? kyō̐)
Widely (दूर तक dūr tak)
With (सह saha, सहित sahita, साथ sāth)
Willingly (स्वेच्छा से svechchhā se)
Within (अन्दर, भीतर andar, bhītar)
Without (बिना ninā)
Yes (हाँ hā̐)
Yesterday (कल kal)

CHAPTER 15

SYNTAX

वाक्य विन्यास

Syntax : Syntax is the technical branch of Grammar which deals with the relationship between the words of the sentence.

1. Subject and Predicate
कर्ता और विधेय

As we have seen earlier, a sentence normally has two main parts, 1. the Subject (कर्ता) and (2) the Predicate (विधेय). e.g. She writes a book :- 'She' is the Subject and 'writes a book' is Predicate.

2. Order of Words
शब्दों का क्रम

As also said earlier, Hindi is a SOV (Subject-Object-Verb) language, while the English is SVO (Subject-Verb-Object) Language. e.g. (SOV) मैं पानी पीता हूँ. (SVO) I drink water. In Hindi as well as English, normally the Adjective come before the Noun or Pronouns which it qualifies and the Adverb come before the Verb, Adjective or another Adverb which it qualifies. e.g. मैं **गरम** चाय **धीरे से** पी रहा हूँ. I am **slowly** drinking the **hot** tea.

Even though the Hindi sentences normally begin with the Subject, the Interjections (विस्मय सूचक अव्यय), Vocatives (संबोधन) and the time elements (समय सूचक शब्द) may be placed before the Subject. e.g. हाय राम! यह क्या हुआ! O Rāma! what happened here! हे श्याम तू कहा जा रहा है? O Shyām where are you going? कल मैं नहीं आऊँगा. I will not come tomorrow etc.

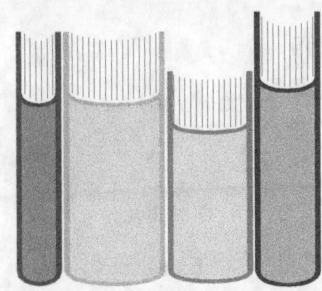

3. Concord of Words
शब्दों का मेल

As we have also seen, in Active Voice, the Subject is in Nominative Case (कर्ता कारक) and it agrees with its Subject in Gender and Number.

In passive Voice, when Transitive (सकर्मक) Verb is used, the ने suffix is added to the Subject and now the Gender and Number of the Object (कर्म) controls the Gender and Number of the Verb.

For the purpose of respect, a Pulral Verb should be used for a singular Noun. e.g. बालक सो रहा है. The child is sleeping. पिताजी सो रहे हैं. Father is sleeping. At the same time, when we add a fiffix to a Masculine, Singular Noun ending in आ (लड़का), if the noun is respectable (पिता) or private (श्री भल्ला), the end vowel आ should not be changed to ए. e.g. लड़के ने कहा. The boy said. पिता ने कहा. Fther said. हमारी माता आई. Our mother came. हमारे माता जी आए. Our mother came etc.

Some Singular Nouns are always used in their Plural form. e.g. प्राण : उसके प्राण निकले. Life : He lost his life (singular). आँसू टपके. A tear fell.

When one Verb has two or more Subjects of different Gender and Number, then the Verb agrees with the Gender and Number of the last Subject. e.g. दो कुत्ते, तीन लड़के और एक लड़की इधर आ रही है. Tow doge, three boys and one boy is coming this way.

NOTE: While translating an English sentence in to Hindi, simple and easy trick is to Keep the Subject at the beginning and then translate the English sentence backwards into Hindi. However keep the Adjective-Noun and the Adverb-Verb pairs as they are, without switching them around. See the following diagram of Brain Surgery of Hindi Grammar.

RATNAKAR'S BRAIN SURGERY OF THE HINDI GRAMMAR

From the charts of tenses we studied in previous lessons, **following facts can be discovered :**

(1) I drink hot tea = *maĩ garam chāy pītā hũ* = maĩ garam chāy pī t ā h ũ

subject | verb and its mode | tense & person | #1 verb stem | #2 mode

subject | verb | adjective | object | adjective | object | #3 gender and number | #4 present tense | #5 person

Note: #2 *'t'* = habitual mode (do), *rah* = incomplete mode (-ing), *chuk* = 'already done' mode.

#3 *ā* = m◦ singular; *ī* = f◦ singular, *e* = m◦ plural; *ĩ* = f◦ plural.

#5 *ũ* = 1st person singular; *ai, e* = second and third person singular; *aĩ, ẽ* = plural.

(2) I was drinking tea = *maĩ chāy pī rahā thā* = maĩ chāy pī rah ā th ā

#2 mode | #3 gender, number | #6 past tense | #3 gender, number

Note : #6 '*th*' = was, had, *used to

* used to = #2 + #3 and #6 + #3 (*t + ā, th + ā*)

Therefore, m◦ (i) Was = *thā* था, (ii) Had = *thā* था, (iii) Used to = *tā thā* ता था।

(3) I will drink tea = *maĩ chāy pīũgā* = maĩ chāy pī ũ g ā

Note : #7 for future tense, logically the Tense operative '*g*' goes after #5 Person indicator.

#5 person | #7 future tense | #3 gender and number

(4) I should drink tea (the Potential mood) = *maĩ chāy pīũ* = maĩ chāy pī ũ

#5 person

Note : Potential mood needs only #5. It does not need any tense operative such as, *h* for present, *th* for past or *g* for future tense.

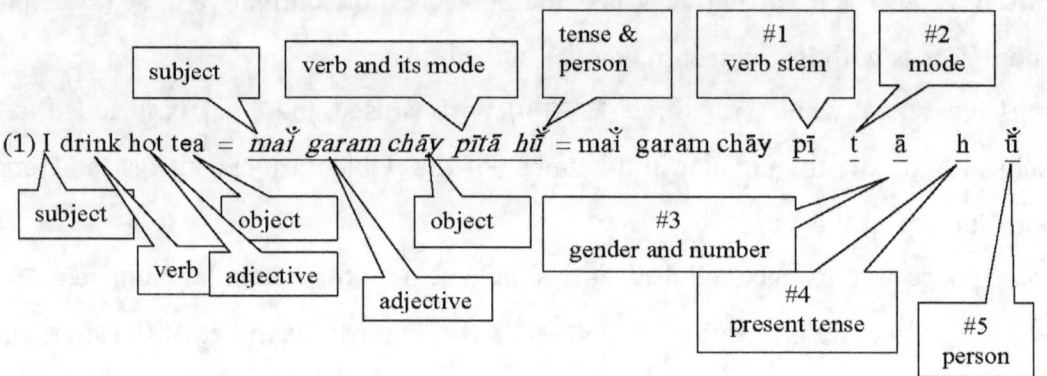

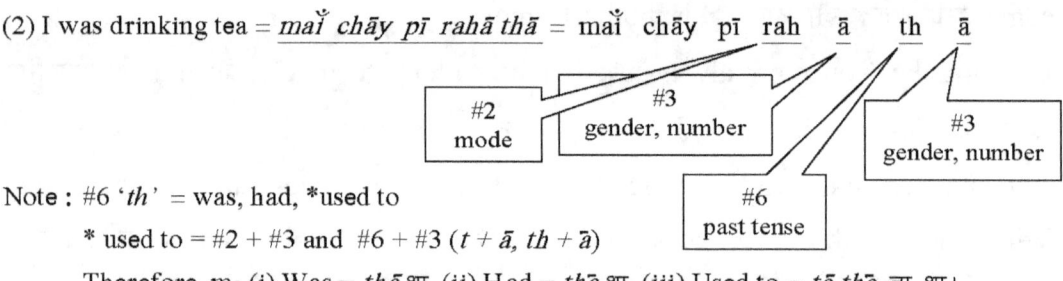

(5) I walked = I did walk = *maĩ chalā* = maĩ chal ā

perfect, intransitive verb | indefinite, perfect action | subject | intransitive verb | #3 perfect tense suffix, gender and number See the Note below

Note : #3 The perfect tense suffix ***ā* (आ)** changes with gender (m◦ ā आ, f◦ ī ई) and number (pl◦ e ए, ī̃ ईं). Also, when the verb ends with a long vowel, (such as *ā, ī, o* आ, ई, ओ) letter *y* य is prefixed to the perfect tense suffix ***ā* (आ)** e.g. (1) 'chal' *ā* = chalā. (2) 'so' y + ā = soyā

(6) I have walked slowly = *maĩ dhīre chalā hũ* = maĩ dhīre chal ā h ũ

present | perfect action | adverb | subject | adverb | intransitive verb | #3 perfect tense suffix, *yā* for a long vowel | #4 present tense | #5 person

Note : The first-person Present-perfect-tense indicator 'have' translates into Hindī as *'hũ'* हूँ

(7) I had walked = *maĩ chalā thā* = maĩ chal ā th ā

past | perfect action | subject | intransitive verb | #3 perfect tense suffix, *yā* for a long vowel | #6 past | #3 gender and number

Note : **#6** Past tense suffix '*th*' थ is added is added to the verb ONLY when there is 'was,' 'had' or 'used to' in the sentence.

(8) I saw (have seen, had seen) = *maĩ ne dekhā (hai, thā)* = maĩ ne dekh ā (hai, thā)

perfect, transitive action | present tense | past tense | #8 transitive perfect action suffix | #3 perfect tense suffix, *yā* for a long vowel | #4 present tense | #6 past

Note : #8 When the action is transitive and perfected (present, past or future), suffix '*ne*' (ने) is attached to the verb. With suffix *ne* (ने), the Subject has no effect on the verb. Now, the Object affects the verb. e.g. (1) m◦ *Rām chāy pītā hai,* f◦ *Sītā chāy pītī hai.* (2) perfect actions (object f◦ *chāy* , m◦ *ām*) *Rām ne chāy pī, Sītā ne chāy pī, Rām ne ām khāyā, Sītā ne ām khāyā.*

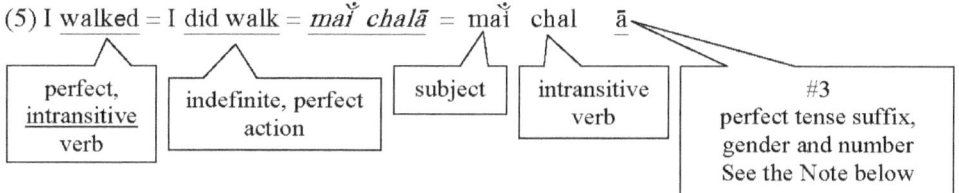

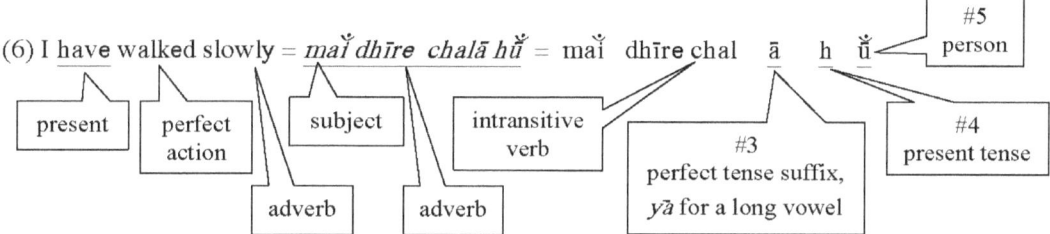

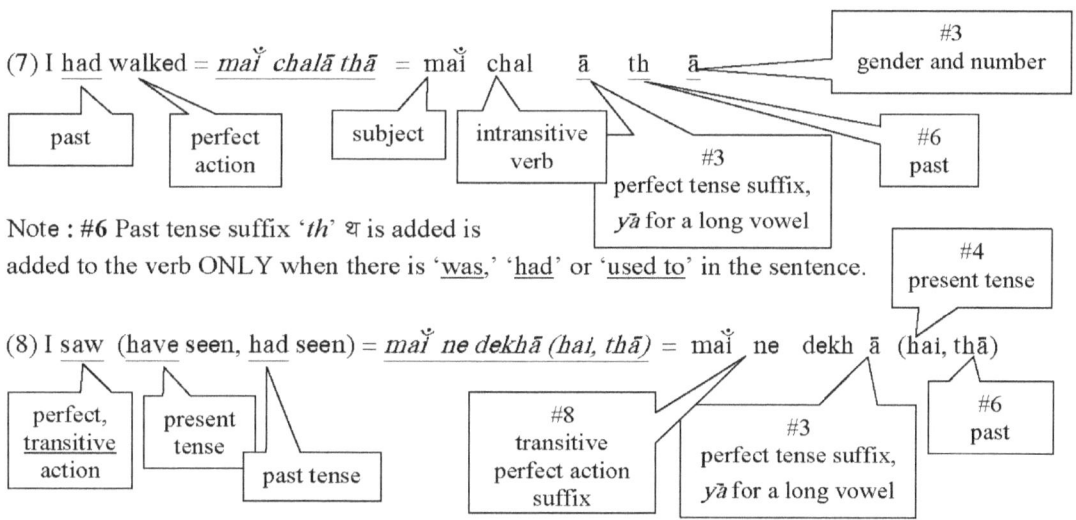

THE X-Ray VISION, SEEING THROUGH THE HINDI SYNTAX

From the charts given on previous two pages following structural skeleton can be seen through the Hindī Syntax :

eg. I drink hot tea slowly, I eat a sweet banana, I eat sweet bananas, I eat sweet roṭī, I eat sweet rotīs ...etc

English syntax: I (subject) drink (verb + tense) hot (adjective) tea (object) slowly (adverb)

Hindī syntax: *maĩ* (subject) *garam* (adj∘) *chāy* (object) *dhīre* (adverb) *pītā hũ* (verb + tense, gender, number, person)

main *mīṭhā (mīṭhī) kelā (roṭī)* *khātā-khatī hũ*

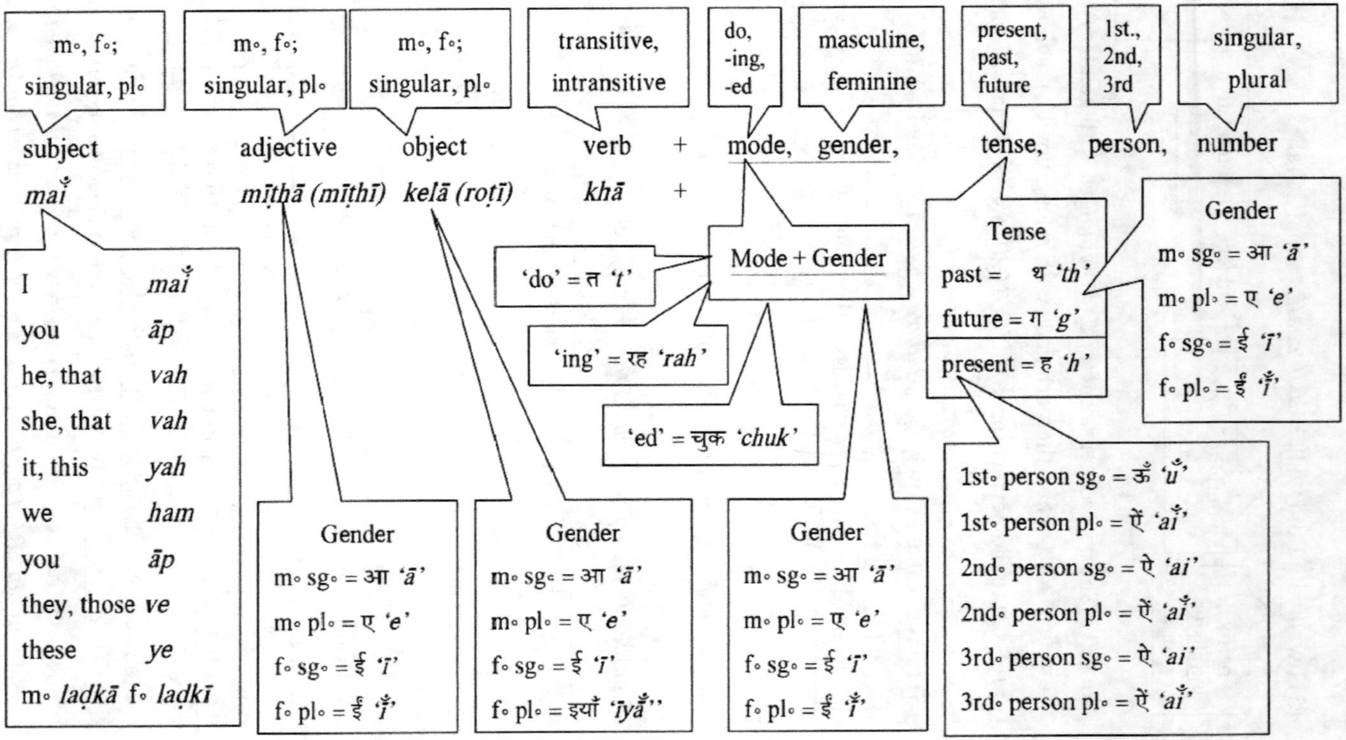

CHAPTER 16

THE PREPOSITIONS

aupasargika-s̒habdā औपसर्गिकशब्द

The preposition (उपसर्ग *upasarga*) is an indeclinable word (*avyayam* अव्यय), prefixed to a verb (*kriyāpad* क्रियापद) or its derivative (*sādhita-s̒habda* साधित-शब्द:). The 22 prepositional prefixes listed by Pāṇini and Varadāchārya do intensify, modify, alter, change or make no change in the sense of the root verb.

उपसर्गेण धात्वर्थो बलादन्यत्र नीयते। प्रहाराहारसंहारविहारपरिहारवत्।।

धात्वर्थं बाधते कश्चित्कश्चित्तमनुवर्तते। तमेव विशिनष्ट्यन्य: उपसर्गगतिस्त्रिधा।।

(1) *ati* (अति) over, beyond. (i) क्रम a step, pace → अतिक्रम aransgression. (ii) रिक्त empty → अतिरिक्त remaining; supreme.

(2) *adhi* (अधि) power, right. (i) कार causer → अधिकार the right, power. (ii) क्षिप casting away → अधिक्षेप censure.

(3) *anu* (अनु) along, after, behind; each, every. (i) कम्प shaking, a tremor → अनुकम्पा compassion. (ii) √कृ to do → अनुकृति imitation.

(4) *antar* (अन्तर्) with interval, within, inner. (i) याम restraint, control → अन्तर्याम inner control. (ii) धान a seat → अन्तर्धान disappearance.

(5) *apa* (अप) away, away from. (i) शकुन a good omen → अपशकुन a bad omen. (ii) कार doer, causer → अपकार Harm.

(6) *api* (अपि) also; over, near, near to; indeed, also. (i) अयन entrance → अप्ययन junction, union. (ii) हित benefit → अपिहित openly, visibly.

(7) *abhi* (अभि) towards, near. (i) मुखम् mouth, face → अभिमुख In front of. (ii) मान pride → अभिमान ego, self-pride.

(8) *ava* (अव) away, off, down. (i) √स्था to stay → अवस्था condition, state. (ii) गुण quality, character → अवगुण a bad quality

(9) *ā* (आ) up to, towards, from, around; a little. (i) गमन going → आगमन coming. (ii) जन्म birth → आजन्म from the birth जनम से.

(10) prefixes *ut, ud* (उत्, उद्) over, superior, higher; facing. (i) √स्था to stay → उत्थान Getting up, rising. (ii) भव Existence → उद्भव Birth.

(11) *upa* (उप) secondary; towards, near to, by the side of. (i) √विश् to enter → उपविश to sit. (ii) √स्था to stay → उपस्थ the middle part.

(12) *dur, dus,* (दुर्, दुस्) hard to do, difficult. (i) √लभ् to get, obtain → दुर्लभ difficult to attain. (ii) बुद्धि mind → दुर्बुद्धि malignity, evil mind.

(13) *ni* (नि) in, into; great; opposed to, without. (i) बन्ध A bond, tie → निबन्ध an essay. (ii) दान a gift, giving → निदान a cause, diagnosis.

(14) *nir* (निर्) out of, away from, without, ◦less, un◦ (i) मल dirt → निर्मल a clean thing.

(15) *nis* (निस्) out of, away from, without, ◦less, un◦ (ii) √चल् to move → निश्चल steady.

(16) *parā* (परा) away, back, opposed to. (i) क्रमः a step, pace → पराक्रम bravery. (ii) भव existence → पराभव Defeat.

(17) *pari* (परि) about. (i) भाषा language → परिभाषा definition. (ii) नाम name → परिणाम result.

(18) *pra* (प्र) good, opposite, excess, progress. (i) कृति action, doing → प्रकृति nature. (ii) वदन mouth → प्रवदन announcement.

(19) *prati* (प्रति) towards, back, in return, in opposition; each. (i) √ज्ञा to know → प्रतिज्ञा vow. (ii) दिन day → प्रतिदिन every day.

(20) *vi* (वि) reverse of, apart, separate from. (i) कृति action, doing → विकृति disorder. (ii) क्रम a step, pace → विक्रम bravery.

(21) *sam* (सम्) together with, full, excellent. (i) बन्ध A bond, tie → सम्बन्ध relationship. (ii) योग union → संयोग bondage.

(22) *su* (सु) very, good, well; thorough. (i) रूप Form → सुरूप beauty. (ii) कृत done → सुकृत done well.

These Prefixes are for the use with Verbs

PREFIXES (PREPOSITIONS)
उपसर्ग

(A) SANSKRIT PREFIXES
संस्कृत के उपसर्ग

Prefix (उपसर्ग) is the word attached to a root verb (√धातु) or a Noun (संज्ञा), Pronoun (सर्वनाम) or Adjective (विशेषण) formed from root verb. The same prefix may impart a little or no effect, a negetive effect or a positive effect to different words.

The prefixes are attached before the root verbs and their derivatives, as prepositions, the suffixes are the words attached after the Nouns, Pronouns and Adjectives, as postpositions. For suffixes that are attached to the verb roots and words, see the next chapter on Postpositions.

In Sanskrit (as well as in Hindi), the primary suffixes (कृत्-प्रत्यय) are attached only to the root verbs. Secondary suffixex (तद्धित-प्रत्यय) are attached to words or their derivatives.

The same prefix attached to different words can either (i) cause little or no effect on the attached word, or (ii) can cause a negative effect, or (iii) can cause a positive effect. e.g.

(i) No effect :	भाग = Part	वि√भाग	= Part.
(ii) Negative effect :	फल = Fruit.	वि√फल	= Fruitless.
(iii) Positive effect :	वाद = Argument.	वि√वाद	= Conversation.

The 22 SANSKRIT PREFIXES
संस्कृत के २२ उपसर्ग

There are 22 common prefixes in Sanskrit as listed below:

1. अति	*ati*	beyond, over, across, past, surpassing, to excess.
2. अधि	*adhi*	over, above, upon, on, onto.
3. अनु	*anu*	after, along, like, towards, following.
4. अप	*apa*	away, off, from, forth.
5. अपि	*api*	over, on, close, proximate.
6. अभि	*abhi*	to, towards, into, against, near, opposite.
7. अव	*ava*	down, off, away, from.
8. आ	*ā*	towards, near, to, into, at, from, back, return (reversing).
9. उद्	*ud*	up, upwards, out, above.
10. उप .	*upa*	towards, near, to, next to, less, down, under.
11. दुर्	*dur*	bad, difficult, hard.
12. दुश्-दुस्	*duśh, dus*	bad, difficult, hard.
13. नि	*ni*	down, in, on, under, into.
14. निर्	*nir*	away, out, forth.
15. निश्-निस्	*niśh, nis*	away, out, forth.
16. परा	*parā*	back, backwards, away, forth, to a distance.
17. परि	*pari*	around, about.
18. प्र	*pra*	before, forward, forth, onward, fore or more.
19. प्रति	*prati*	against, towards, to, at, near, back, again, return, reverse.
20. वि	*vi*	apart, asunder, away, out, implying separation or dispersion.
21. सम्	*sam*	with, together, along with, cojoined with.
22. सु	*su*	good, excellent, well.

(B) HINDI PREFIXES
हिंदी के उपसर्ग

While the prefixes are attached **before** the Root Verbs (धातु) and their derivatives (व्युत्पन्न शब्द) as Prepositions, the suffixes are attached **after** the verbs and their derivatives, as Postpositions. For suffixes that are attached to the verb roots and words, see the next chapter on Postpositions.

In Sanskrit as well as in Hindi, the primary suffixes (कृत्-प्रत्यय) are attached only to the root verbs. Secondary suffixex (तद्धित-प्रत्यय) are attached to words or their derivatives.

The same prefix attached to different words can either (i) cause little or no effect on the attached word, or (ii) can cause a negative effect, or (iii) can cause a positive effect. e.g.

(i)	No effect :	सक्ति	= attachment	आ√सक्ति	= Attachment
(ii)	Negative effect :	सुर	= God	आ√सुर	= Demon
(iii)	Positive effect :	जन्म	= birth	आ√जन्म	= Whole life from birth

THE 38 HINDI PREFIXES WITH EXAMPLES :

1a. अंत: (भीतर inside) – अंत:करण (soul), अंत:कक्ष, अंत:पुर (inner chamber), अंत:कालीन (provisional), अंत:क्रिया (hidden process), अंत:प्रकृति (inner nature), अंत:स्थित (medial), अंतस्वर (inner voice), etc.

1b. अंतर् (भीतर inside) – अंतरंग (heart), अंतराल (interval), अंतर्गत (included), अंतर्गति (mental state), अंतर्ग्रस्त (involved), अंतर्ज्ञान (intuition), अंतर्ज्वाला (grief), अंतर्दृष्टि (perceptive vision), अंतर्देशीय, अंतर्राष्ट्रीय (international), अंतर्द्वंद्व (inner conflict), अंतर्द्वार (private door), अंतर्धान (disappearance), अंतर्ध्यान (sunk in thinking), अंतर्निहित (hidden), अंतर्भुक्त (included), अंतर्मनन (cognition), अंतर्मुख (introspective), अंतर्यामी (Supreme being), अंतर्वर्ती (inner), अंतर्वासित (interned), अंतर्वेदना (inward suffering), अंतर्हित (secret), etc.

1c. अंतस् (भीतर inside) – अंतस्तप्त (agitated), अंतस्तल (soul), अंतस्ताप (mental torment),

अंतस्स्ता (heart), अंतश्चक्षु (inner vision), etc.

2. **अ** (विपरीत opposite) – अकण्टक (unimpeded), अकम्पित (unshaken), अकथ, अकथ्य (indescribable), अकर (difficult), अकर्म (vice), अकलंक (pure), अकल्पनीय (unimaginable), अकाज (harm), अकारण (senseless), अकाल (drought), अकिंचन (poor), अकीर्ति (infamy), अकृत्य (wrongful), अक्रूर (gentle), अक्षत (unbroken), अक्षय (imperishable), अक्षर (eternel), अक्षुण्ण (continuing), असंड (uninterrupted), अखाद्य (inedible), अगण्य (innumerable), अगति (helpless), अगम्य (inaccessible), अगाध (profound), अगुण (vice), अगोचर (unseen), अघोर (terrible), अचंड (gentle), अचक्षु (blind), अचपल (calm), अचला (earth), अचिंत्य (inconceivable), अचिर (quickly), अचूक (unerring), अचेत (unconscious), अचेष्ट (inert), अछूत (untouchable), अछेद (indivisible), अज (unborn), अजरामर (immortal), अजान (ignorant), अज्ञात (unknown), अज्ञान (ignorance), अटल (permanent), अटूट (unbroken), अतर्क्य (illogical), अतिथि (guest), अतुल (immeasurable), अतृप्त (unsatisfied), अदय (cruel), अथक (vigilant), अथाह (bottomless), अदय (cruel), अदृष्ट (invisible), अद्वितीय (unique), अद्वेष (good will), अधम (vile), अधर्म (immorality), अपात्र (unfit), अपार (infinite), अपूर्ण (incomplete), अपूर्व (new), अभेद्य (invincible), अमनुष्य (inhuman), अमर (immortal), अमल (clean), अप्रशतम (unique), अप्रत्यक्ष (invisible), अप्रसन्न (dissatisfied), अप्राप्त (unattained), अप्रिय (unpleasant), अबोध (stupid), अभद्र (indecent), अभाग (misfortune), अभय (fearless), अमर्त्य (immortal), अमिट (immutable), अमूल्य (priceless), अमोघ (unfailing), अयश (failure), अयोग्य (unfit), अलख (invisible), अलभ्य (rare), अलोक (invisible), अविकार (unchanging), अविचल (steady), अविनाश (everlasting), अविरल (dense), अविलंब (prompt), अशिष्ट (crude), अशुचि (impure), अशुद्ध (corrupt), अशुभ (sinister), असंख्य (innumerable), असंगत (abssurd), असंपूर्ण (imperfect), असंबद्ध (incoherent), असंभव (impossible), असंशय (undoubting), असज्जन (coarse), असमर्थ (incapable), असमान (unequal), असुख (suffering), अस्थिर (unstable), अहिंसा (non-violence), अहेतु (vain), etc.

3. **अति** (बहुत very) – अतिकाय (huge), अतिक्रमण (aggression), अतिचार (tresspass), अतिरिक्त (extra), अतिरेक (excess), अतिवाद (extremism), अतिशय (very much), अतिसार (dysentery), अतीत (past), अतीव (extreme), अत्यंत (endledd), अत्यधिक (excessive), अत्याचार (atrocity), अत्युत्तम (best), etc.

4. **अध:** (नीचे below) – अध:पतन, अध:पात (downfall), अधोगति (decline), अधोभूमि, अधोलोक (hell), अधोमुख (facedown), अधोरेखा (underline), अधोलिखित (underwritten), अधोवस्त्र (undergarment), etc.

5. **अध** (अर्ध half) – अधकचरा (raw), अधकट (half worn-out), अधकहा (half-told), अधखिला (half-bloomed), अधखुला (ajaj), अधगला (half-cooked), अधच्क्कर (semicircle), अधचंद्र (crescent), अधजला (half-burnt), अधपका, अधपक्का (half-ripe), अधपेट (half-fed), अधबना (half-made), अधमरा, अधमुआ (half-dead), etc.

6. **अधि** (अधिक more) – अधिकरण (Locative case), अधिकाई (excess), अधिकार (authority), अधिकृत (authorized), अधिगत (acquired), अध्यादेश (mandate), अधिनियम (act), अधिपति (Lord), अधिभार (surcharge), अधियाना (to divide), अधिराज (monarch), अधिरोपण (imposition), अधिवक्ता (advocate), अधिवासी (resident), अधिष्ठाता (ruler), अधिष्ठान (abode), अधिसूचित (notified), अधिक्षक (superintendent), अधित (studied), अधीन (dependent), अधीर (restless), अधीश (master), अधुना (now), अधूरा (incomplete), अधेड़ (middle-aged), अध्यक्ष (president), अध्ययन (study), अध्यात्म (spirituality), अध्यापक (instructor), अध्याय (chapter), अध्यास (error), अध्येता (student), अध्रुव (uncertain), etc.

7. **अन** (नहीं not) – अनदेखा (unseen), अनंग (Cupid), अनंत (endless), अनंतर (continuous), अनक्षर (illiterate), अनगिनत (countless), अनघ (sinless), अनजान (ignorant), अनदेखा (unseen), अनन्य (unique), अनपढ़ (illiterate), अनपेक्ष (indifferent), अनबन (quarrel), अनभीज्ञ (unaware), अनमना (distracted), अनमोल (priceless), अनर्थ (wrong), अनल (fire), अनवधान (inattentive), अनवधि (limitless), अनवरत (non-stop), अनशन (hunger strike), अनश्वर (eternal), अनसुना (unheadr), अनहंकार (humility), अनहित (disadvantage), अनहोनी (disaster), अनाचार (dishonesty), अनाड़ी (ignorant), अनाथ (orphan), अनादर (disrespect), अनादि (eternal), अनामय (healthy), अनायस (automatic), अनावृत (unveiled), अनाहत (unhurt), अनिच्छ (reluctance), अनित्य (temporary), अनिपुण (unskilled), अनिर्णित (undecided), अनिवार्य (unavoidable), अनिश्चित (uncertain), अनिष्ट (undesirable), अनीत (immortality), अनीह (apathetic), etc.

8. **अनु** (पीछे after) – अनुकम्पा (compassion), अनुकरण (following), अनुकूल (favorable), अनुकृति (imitation), अनुक्रम (order), अनुक्रमणिका (index), अनुगामी (follower), अनुग्रह (patronage), अनुचर (follower), अनुच्छेद (paragraph), अनुज (younger), अनुज्ञा (command), अनुताप (remorse), अनुदान (grant), अनुदेश (command), अनुनय (courtsey), अनुनासिक (nasal), अनुपकार (harm), अनुपम (excellent), अनुपात (incidence), अनुबंध (agreement), अनुभव (experience), अनुभूत (perceived), अनुमति (permission), अनुमान (estimate), अनुमोदन (approval), अनुयायी (follower), अनुरक्ति, अनुराग (attachment), अनुरूप (similar), अनुरोध

(request), अनुवाद (translation), अनुशासन (rule), अनुष्ठान (rite), अनुसंधान (research), अनुसार (according), अनुहार (imitation), अनूदित (translated), अनूप (best), etc.

9. **अप** (बुरा bad) – अपकर्म (bad deed), अपकर्ष (fall), अपकार (harm), अपकीर्ति (disgrace), अपचय (loss), अपभ्रंश (degeneration), अपभ्रष्ट (corrupt), अपमान (insult), अपयश (failure), अपराजित (invincible), अपराध (fault), अपरिचित (atrange), अपरिहार्य (obligatory), अपवाद (exception), अपवित्र (unholy), अपशब्द (abuse), अपहरण (kidnapping), अपेक्षा (expectation), etc.

10. **अभि** (आगे ahead) – अभिकथन (allegation), अभिजित (conquerred), अभिज्ञान (recognition), अभिधान (designation), अभिनय (acting), अभिनव (new), अभिप्रेत (implied), अभिमान (pride), अभियंता (engineer), अभियान (campaign), अभिलाषा (desire), अभिवादन (greeting), अभिव्यक्ति (manifestation), अभ्यस्त (accustomed), अभ्यास (study), etc.

11. **अव** (बुरा bad) – अवगत (known), अवगुण (vice), अवच्छेद (part), अवज्ञा (disregard), अवतरण (descending), अवधान (attention), अवयव (limb), अवरोध (obstacle), अवलंब (delay), अवलोकन (scrutiny), अवशेष (remainder), अवसान (end), अवस्थान (situation), etc.

12. **आ** (तक up to) – आकलन (evaluation), आजन्म,आजीवन (lifelong), आमरण (unto death), आकर्षण (attraction), आकांक्ष (desire), आकाश (sky), आकृति (form), आक्रमण (attack), आक्रांत (overpowered), आक्रोश (scolding), आक्षेप (accusation), आख्यान (narrative), आगत (present), आगम, आगमन (entry), आगामी (impending), आग्रह (insistence), आचरण (conduct), आतिथ्य (hospitality), आधार (support), आनंद (joy), आभार (obligation), आमंत्रण (invitation), आमर्ष (envy), आमोद (pleasure), आयाम (extent), आरंभ (brginning), आरक्षण (reservation), आराधना (worship), आराम (rest), आरूढ़ (mounted), आरोग्य (health), आरोप (allegation), आरोह (ascend), आलंब (aupport), आलिंगन (embracing), आलोकन (scrutiny), आलोचना (critism), आवरण (cover), आवास (abode), आवृत (covered), आशंका (doubt), आश्रम (abode), आसंग (association), आसक्ति (attachment), आसुरी (evil), आस्थान (place), आस्वाद (taste), आहार (food), आहलाद (joy), आह्वान (challaenge), etc.

13. **उत्** (उभरना arise) – उतार (slope), उतरना (get down), त्कर्ष (progress), उत्कृष्ट (excellent), उत्तम (best), उत्तर (reply), उत्तुंग (high), उत्तेजित (excited), उत्पत्ति (birth), उत्पाटन (uprooting), उत्पात (turmoil), उत्पादन (production), उत्पीड़ित (oppressed), उत्सर्ग (let loose), उत्साह (enthusiasm), उत्सुक (eager), उद्दयन (flying), उदित (arose), उद्गम (origin), उद्गार (exclamation), उद्घाटन (opening), उद्धरण (quotation), उद्भव (birth), उद्यम (effort), उद्यान

(garden), उद्योग (endavour), उद्वेग (agitation), etc.

14. उन (कम less) – उनचास (forty-nine), उन्मन (disturbed), उन्मुद्र (unsealed), etc.

15. उप (छोटा sub.) – उपकथा (an episode), उपग्रह (satellite), उपद्रव (turmoil), उपनगर (suburb), उपनाम (nickname), उपनिवेश (colony), ापनिषद् (session), उपपत्नी (concubine), उपभाषा (dialect), उपराष्ट्रपति (vice-president), उपवास (fast), उपविष्ट (seated), उपसर्ग (prefix), उपहास (ridicule), उपाख्यान (legend), उपल्अंभ (reproach), उपेक्षा (neglect), etc.

16. औ, अव (नीचे down) – अवनति (decline), अवज्ञात (disregarded), औंधा (face down), औकल (restless), अवकर्षण (boycott), अवकीर्ण (scattered), अवक्रय (rent), अवगमन (approach), अवगीत (badly sung), अवगुण (vice), अवज्ञान (insult), अवदीर्ण (broken), अवनति (regress), अवमान (insult), अवरूढ (dismount, got down), अवरूप (ugly), अवरोह (discend), अवशिष्ट (remainder), अवसन्न (dejected), अवहेलना (hate), etc.

17. क, कु (बुरा bad) – कपूत, कुपुत्र (brat), कुचक्र (plot), कुचाल (misconduct), कुढंग (ill-manner), कुपथ (immoral), कुपथ्य (unwholesome), कुबुद्धि (wickedness), कुमंत्रणा (intrigue), कुरूप (ugly), कुलक्षण (bad omen), कुसंगति (bad compny), etc.

18. चिर (देर तक long-lasting) – चिरंजीवी, चिरायु (long living), चिरकाल (long time), चिरकालीन, चिरातन (ancient), चिरपरिचय (long acquaintance), चिरस्थायी (stable), चिरस्मरणीय (unforgatable), etc.

19. तत्, तद्, तन् (उसी– that, same) – तत्काल, तत्क्षण (immedialety), तत्पर (ready), तदनंतर (next), तदनुकूल (corresponding), तदनुरूप (similar), तदनुसार (accordingly), तदुत्तर (thereafter), तद्भव (of same nature), तद्रूप, तद्वत (like that), तन्मय (engrossed), etc.

20. दुः, दुर्, दुश्, दुष्, दुस् (कठिन hard) – दुःशासन (maladministration), दुःशील (wicked), दुःसह (intolerable), दुःसाध्य (ardous), दुःसाहस (rashness), दुःस्वप्न (bad dream), दुःस्वभाव (wicked), दुराग्रह (prejudice), दुराचरण, दुराचार (crime), दुरात्मा (rascal), दुराशा (vain hope), दुरूह (hard to understand), दुर्गंध (stench), दुर्गम (profound), दुर्घट (unattainable), दुर्घटना (accident), दुर्जन (scoundrel), दुर्जय (invincible), दुर्दर्श (incorrigible), दुर्दशा (misery), दुर्दैव (misfortune), दुर्बल (weak), दुर्बुद्धि (foolish), दुर्भाग्य (misfortune), दुर्भाव (ill-will), दुर्मद (crazy), दुर्मिल, दुर्लभ (rere), दुर्वचन (abuse), दुर्ग (inaccessible), दुर्दम्य (indomitable); दश्चक्र (vicious circle), दुश्चर (unattainable), दुश्चरित, दुश्चरित्र (wicked), दुश्चलन (bad conduct); दुष्कर (ardous), दुष्कृत, दुष्कृत्य (sin), दुष्प्राप्य (unattainable), दुष्प्रेक्ष्य (fearsome), दुस्साहस (rashness), etc.

21. नि, निः, निर्, निश्, निष्, निस् (बिना withut) – निकम्मा (useless), निडर (fearless), निबद्ध (bound), निपूत (childless), नि:शंक, निश्शंक (doubtless), नि:शक्त, निश्शक्त (weak), नि:शब्द, निश्शब्द (silent), नि:शस्त्र, निश्शस्त्र (unarmed), नि:शुल्क, निश्शुल्क (free), नि:शेष, निश्शेष (entire), नि:संकोच, निस्संकोच, नि:संदेह, निस्संदेह (unhesitated), नि:सरण, निस्सरण (death), नि:सीम, निस्सीम (limitless), नि:स्पृह, निस्स्पृह (indifferent), नि:स्वार्थ, निस्स्वार्थ (selfless); निरंकार, निराकार (formless), निरंकुश (unrestrained), निरंजन (pure), निरंतर (continuous), निरपेक्ष (impartial), निरभ्र (cloudless), निरर्थक (pointless), निरादर (disrespect), निराधार (helpless), निराशा (despair), निराहार (starvation), निरीक्षित (inspected), निरुत्तर (speechless), निरुत्साह (discourage), निरुद्यमी (inactive), निरुपाय (helpless), निर्गमन (exit), निर्घृण (sensless), निर्जन (barren), निर्जल (dry), निर्जीव (lefeless), निर्दोष (innocent), निर्धन (poor), निर्बंध (free), निर्भय (fearless), निर्मम (selfless), निर्मल (clean), निर्मूलन (uprooting), निर्यात (export), निर्वस्त्र (bare), निर्वात (vacuum), निर्वासित (banished), निर्विकार (changeless), निर्विघ्न (secure), निर्विवाद (indisputable), निर्व्याज (candid), etc.

22. पर (छोटा sub.) – परजन्म (subsequent birth), परतंत्र (dependence), परदेश (foreigh), परधर्म (other's religion), परस्त्री (other's wife), परपक्ष (apposition), परपुरुष (lover), परराष्ट्र (foreign), परलोक (paradise), परवश (subject), परहित (other's well-being), पराधीन (dependent), पराह्न (afternoon), परोपकार (beneficence), प्रोपजीवी (parasite),

23. परा (परे beyond.) – पराकाष्ठा (climax), पराजय, पराभव (defeat), परामर्श (discussion), परावर्तन (reflection), etc.

24. परि (पूरा full) – परिधि (circle), परिभाषा (definition), परिकथा (tale), पेंकिल्पना (imagination), परिक्रमा (orbit), परिक्रय (redemption), परिग्रहण (accepting), परिचय (introduction), परिचर्या (nursing), परिच्छेद (section), परिजन (family), परिणय (marriage), परिणाम (effect), परितोष (satisfaction), परित्याग (renunciation), परित्राण (pritection), परिपक्व (matured), परिपाटी (order), परिपूर्ण (brimful), परिमाण (measure), परिवर्तन (transformation), परिवार (family), परिश्रम (diligence), परिष्कृत (purified), परिसर (proximity), परिस्थिति (state), परिहास (ridicule), परीक्षा (examination), etc.

25. पुनः, पुनर्, पुनश् (फिर से again) – पुन:-पुन: (again and again), पुन:संगठन (reorganization), पुन:स्थापना (restoration), पुनरपि (even so), पनरागमन (return), पुनरावर्तन (recurrence), पुनरीक्षण (review), पुनरुत्थान, पुनरुद्धार (revival), पुनर्जीवन (rebirth), पुनर्वास (resettlement), पुनविचार (rethinking), पुनर्विवाह (remarriage); पुनश्च (and further),

26. पुरो (आगे ahead) – पुरोगमन (advance), पुरोगामी (orogressive), पुरोहित (priest), etc.

27. पूर्व (पहले का pre.) – पूर्वकालिक, पूर्वकालीन (ancient), पूर्वगत (former), पूर्वगामी (predecessor), पूर्वज (ancestor), पूर्ववत् (as before), पूर्ववर्ती (preceeding), पूर्वग्रह (bias), पूर्वाभास (premonition), पूर्वाभ्यास (rehearsal), पूर्वाह्न (morning), पूर्वोत्तर (north-east), पूर्वोपाय (precaution), etc.

28. प्र (अधिक more) – प्रकट (evident), प्रकरण (exposition), प्रकांड (superlative), प्रकार (type), प्रकाश (light), प्रकाशन (publication), प्रकृति (nature), प्रकोप (wrath), प्रक्रिया (process), प्रक्षेप (flight), प्रखर (sharp), प्रख्यात (famous), प्रगति (progress), प्रगाढ़ (vast), प्रचंड (vehment), प्रचलित (current), प्रचार (publicity), प्रचुर (abundant), प्रच्छन्न (covered), प्रजनन (procreation), प्रजा (subjects), प्रज्ञा (intelligence), प्रणत (bowing), प्रणय (love), प्रणिधान (regard), प्रणेता (composer), प्रताप (valour), प्रदर्शन (exhibition), प्रदान (grant), प्रदीप (radiance), प्रदूषण (pollution), प्रदेश (region), प्रधान (chief), प्रफुल्ल (joyful), प्रबंध (arrangement), प्रबल (strong), प्रबुद्ध (enlightened), प्रबोध (vigilance), प्रभव (birth), प्रभा (splendour), प्रभात (dawn), प्रभाव (influence), प्रभु (lord), प्रभूति (birth), प्रमत्त (intoxicated), प्रमाण (measure), प्रमाणित (proven), प्रमाद (intoxication), प्रमुख (chief), प्रमेय (theorem), प्रमोद (joy), प्रयत्न (effort), प्रयाण (death), प्रयोग (experiment), प्रयोजन (need), प्रलय (disaster), प्रलोभन (tempting), प्रवंचना (deceit), प्रवर्तक (founder), प्रवास (journey), प्रवाह (flow), प्रविधि (technique), प्रवीण (expert), प्रवृत्ति (tendency), प्रवेश (entry), प्रशंसा (praise), प्रशस्त (excellent), प्रशांत (calm), प्रशासन (government), प्रशिक्षण (training), प्रसन्न (pleased), प्रसाधन (attire), प्रसार (spread), प्रसिद्धि (fame), प्रस्थान (departure), प्रस्थापित (installed), प्रहार (blow), प्रहास (ridicule), प्रहेलिका (riddle), etc.

29. प्रति 1. (हर एक each) – प्रतिदिन (everyday), प्रतिशत (percent), प्रतिलिपि (copy);

2. (विपरीत counter) – प्रतिकर्म (retaliation), प्रतिकार (retaliation), प्रतिकूल (contrary), प्रतिक्रिया (reaction), प्रतिज्ञा (vow), प्रतिद्वंद्व (rivalry), प्रतिपक्ष (opposition), प्रतिबंध (ban), प्रतिबद्ध (restricted), प्रतिबिंब (reflection), प्रतिभा (brilliance), प्रतिभास (illusion), प्रतिमा (image), प्रतियोगिता (competition), प्रतिरोध (opposition), प्रतिवादी (defendant), प्रतिशत (percent), प्रतिशोध (revenge), प्रतिष्ठा (prestige), प्रतिष्ठान (installation), प्रतीक (symbol), प्रतीक्षा (wait), प्रतीत (evident), प्रत्यक्ष (vivid), प्रत्यादेश (order), प्रत्याशी (candidate), प्रत्युत्तर (reply), प्रत्यूह (obstacle), प्रत्येक (each), etc.

30. बहु (अनेक many) – बहुगुणी (talented), बहुजन (community), बहुज्ञ (erudite), बहुदर्शी (far knowing), बहुभाषी (polyglot), बहुमत (majority), वहुमूल्य (precious), बहुरूप (diverse), बहुविध (variously), बहुशः (greatly), बहुसंख्य (majority), etc.

31. वि 1. (अविकारी not much effect) - कंप-विकंप (trembling), कराल-विकराल (fearsome), कल्प-विकल्प (option), ज्ञापन-विज्ञापन (advertisement), गत-विगत (departed), घ्न-विघ्न (obstacle), चरण-विचरण (wandering), चल-विचल (mobile), छिन्न-विछिन्न (broken), जनन-विजनन (giving birth), जय-विजय (victory), दग्ध-विदग्ध (inflamed), द्रोह-विद्रोह (revolt), ध्वंस-विध्वंस (destruction), नाश-विनाश (ruin), भाजन-विभाजन (division), भूषण-विभूषण (decoration), भेद-विभेद (division), भ्रांत-विभ्रांत (confused), मुक्ति-विमुक्ति (freedom), मुग्ध-विमुग्ध (charmed), मूढ़-विमूढ़ (foolish), मोचन-विमोचन (release), राज-विराज (to reign), रुद्ध-विरुद्ध (opposition), आलंब-विलंब (delay), लय-विलय (dissolution), वर्जन-विवर्जन (shunning), वश-विवश (helpless), श्रांति-विश्रांति (rest), etc.

वि 2. (नकारात्मक negative effect) - विकृति (disorder), विकाल (dusk), विक्षिप्त (insane), विग्रह (deparation), विघटन (decomposition), विजाति (other tribe), वितर्क (argument), विदेश (foreign), विपक्ष (opposition), विपत्ति (distress), विपथ (wrong way), विपरीत (contrary), विपर्याय (reversal), विमुख (opposed), वियुक्त (separated), विरंग (faded), विरक्ति (alienation), विराग (unattachment), विवाद (dispute), etc.

वि 3. (सकारात्मक positive effect) - विकास (progress), विक्रम (valour), विक्रय (sale), विख्यात (famous), विचित्र (peculiar), विज्ञ (well-versed), विपुल (abundent), विभास (splendour), विभिन्न (diverse), विभु (eternal), विभूति (grandeur), विमर्श (debate), विराट् (ruler), विलक्षण (extra ordinary), विशारद (well-versed), विशिष्ट (distinct), etc.

32. स (साथ with) - सकाम (desirous), सक्रिय (active), सक्षम (able), सगुण (qualified), सधन (rich), सचित्र (pictorial), सचेत (mindful), सजग (vigilant), सजात (same), सजीव (living), सटीक (with criticism), सतर्क (alert), सत्वर (swift), सदेह (incarnate), सदोष (guilty), सनाथ (married), सपिंड (bodied), सफल (fruitful), सबल (strong), सलग (joined), etc.

33. सं, सङ्, सञ् (साथ with) - संकाय (university), संकेत (sign), संक्षिप्त (abridged), संक्षोभ (agitation), संग (company), संगठन (group), संगम (union), संगीत (music), संग्रह (collection), संघ (society), संघर्ष (friction), संचय (collection), दसंचार (circulation), संचेतना (mindfulness), संजीवन (making alive), संज्ञा (sense), संयम (restraint), संयोग (union), संरक्षण (protection),संलग्न (associated), संबेदना (sympathy), संशय (doubt), संस्कार (instinct), संस्कृत (civilized), संसर्ग (cohabitation), संसार (world), संहार (carnage), संहित (codified), etc.

34. सत्, सद्, सन् (अच्छा good) – सत्कर्म, सत्कार्य, सत्कृत (virtuous deed), सत्पुरुष (gentleman), सत्संग (good company), सद्गुण (virtue), सद्भाव, सद्भावना (good will), सदाचार (righteousness), सद्धर्म (righteousness), सन्निकट (adjacent), सान्निध (vicinity), सन्निपात (collision), सन्निवेश (assembly), सन्निहित (near), संताप (anguish), संतुष्ट (satisfied), संदर्भ (context), संदिग्ध (doubtful), संदेश (message), संदेह (doubt), संधित (united), संन्यास (abandonment), etc.

35. सम् (सकारात्मक positive) – संपर्क (contact), संपात (coincidence), संपादक (editor), संपूर्ण (whole), संपडरान (gift), संबंध (relation), संबद्ध (affiliated), संभव (origin), संभावना (probability), संभाषण (lecture), संभोग (intercourse), संभ्रांत (confused), संमति (good will), संमान (respect), etc.

36. सह (साथ with) – सहकार (colleague), सहकारी (associate), सहज (innate), सहभागी (partner), सहमति (agreement), सहयोग (collaboration), सहानुभूति (sympathy), सहायता (help), etc.

37. सु (अच्छा good) – सुकर्म, सुकृत (good deed), सुकाल (good time), सुकीर्ति (repute), सुगंध (fragrance), सुगम (easy), सुचारु (lovely), सुचेत (aware), सुजन (gentleman), सुजान (wise), सुडौल (graceful), सुढंग (attractive), सुधीर (steadfast), सुनाम (good name), सुनीति (prudence), सुफल (fertile), सुभग (blessed), सुभाषित (aphorism), सुमन (flower), सुरक्षा (security), सुरूप (beauty), सुलभ (convenient), सुवर्ण (gold), सुवासित (scented), सुविख्यात (renowned), सुविचार (good thinking), सुशील (good character), सुस्थ (happy), सुहृद (warm hearted person), etc.

38. स्व (निजी own) – स्वचलित (automatic), स्वकार्य, स्वकर्म (duty), स्वतंत्र (free), स्वदेश (native land), स्वभाव (inborn nature), स्वराज्य (independence), स्वरूप (appearence), स्वाधीन (independent), स्वार्थ (selfishness), etc.

(B) URDU PREFIXES

उर्दू के उपसर्ग اردو کے سابقے

1. कम (हीन without) – कमअक्ल, कमसमझ (foolish), कमउम्र (young), कमखर्च (cheap), कमज़ोर (weak), कमबख़्त (wicked), कमसीन (young), etc.

2. ग़ैर (नहीं without) – ग़ैरआबाद (unsettled), ग़ैरकानूनी (illegal), ग़ैरजिम्मेदार (irresponsible), ग़ैरमामूली (special), ग़ैरज़रूरी (unnecessary), ग़ैरमुकम्मल (incomplete), ग़ैरमुल्की (foreign),

ग़ैरवाजिब (wrong), ग़ैरसरकारी (private), ग़ैरहाज़िर (absent), etc.

3. ना (नहीं not) – नाइनसाफ़ (unjust), नाउम्मीद (hopeless), नाकाबिल (unfit), नाकाम, नाकामयाब (unsuccessful), नाखुश (sad), नाचीज़ (worthless), नाज़यज़ (unlawful), नादान (ignorant), नापसंद (disliked), नापाक (impure), नाबालिग़ (minor), नामंज़ूर (disapproved), नामर्द (unmanly), नामालूम (unknown), नामुमकिन (impossible), नामुलायम (hard), नाराज़ (sad), नालायक (unfit), नावक़्त (premature), नावाक़िफ़ (ignorant), नाशाद (dejected), नाहक (improper), etc.

4. बद (बुरा bad) – बदचलन (ill-behaved), बदक़िस्मत, बदनसीब (unfortunate), बदज़बान (abusive), बदतमीज़ (uncivil), बदतर (worse), बददुआ (curse), बदनाम (disgraced), बदबू (stink), बदमाश (wicked), बदमिज़ाज (ill-tempered), बदशकल, बदसूरत (ugly), बदहाल (bad state), etc.

5. बा (सहित with) – बाअसर (effective), बाइज़्ज़त (honourably), बाक़ायदा (lawful), बाख़बर (informed), बामज़ा (delicious), बाशऊर (wise), etc.

6. बिला, ला, बे (बिना without – बिलाब्थाहा (unmarried), बिलापैसा (bankrupt), बेअक़्ल (stupid), बेअसर (ineffective), बेइनसाफ़ (unjust), बेइज़्ज़त (disgraced), बेक़ायदा (unlawful), बेकार (useless), बक़ीमत (priceless), बेकुसूर, बेगुनाह, बेजुर्म (innocent), बेख़बर (uninformed), बेखुदी (without oneself), बेघर (homeless), बेचैन (restless), बेज़बान (dumb), बेज़मीन (landless), बेजा (irrelevant), बेजान (lifeless), बेजोड़ (incomparable), बेडौल (ugly), बेढंग (disorderly), बेताब (impatient), बेतुका (pointless), बेदम (breathless), बेदर्द (mercyless), बेधड़क (fearless), बेनसीब (unfortunate), बेपता, लापता (absconded), बेपरवाह (heedless), बेफ़ायदा (useless), बेफ़िकज (careless), बबस (helpless), बेबुनियाद (groundless), बेमज़ा (boring), बेमतलब (senseless), बेमिसाल (incomparable), बेमुरौवत, बेरहम (unkind), बेमौक़ा (untimely), बेरुखग़ी (disfavour), बेरोज़गार (unemployed), बेलगाम (uncontrolled), बेलिहाज़ (unmindful), बेवकूफ़ (fool), बेवफ़ा (ungrateful), बेशक (certainly), बेशरम (shameless), बेशुमार (countless), बेसमझ (stupid), बेसुध (unconscious), बेसुरा (harsh), बेहद (limitless), बेहाल (wretched), बेहिसाब (countless), बेहूदा (rude), बेहोश (unconscious), etc.

7 हर (प्रत्येक each) – हर एक (every), हर तरह (everywhichway), हर कोई (everyone), हरदम, हरघड़ी (constantly), हर बार (every time), हरदिन, हररोज़ (everyday), हरबंद (although), हर–हमेशा (everytime), etc.

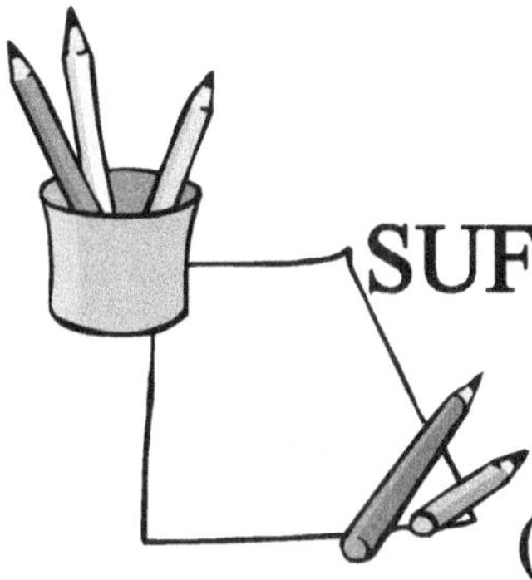

CHAPTER 17

SUFFIXES (POSTPOSITIOS)

प्रत्यय

(A) SANSKRIT SUFFIXES

संस्कृत के प्रत्यय

In Sanskrit (as well as in Hindi), the primary suffixes (कृत्-प्रत्यय) are attached only to the root verbs. Secondary suffixes (तद्धित-प्रत्यय) are attached to words or their derivatives.

While the prefixes are attached before the root verbs and their derivatives, as prepositions, the suffixes are added after the verbs, as postpositions or suffixes.

THE PRIMARY SUFFIXES (कृत्-प्रत्यय)

(A) *kvin, kañ* and *ksa* क्विन्, कञ् and क्स suffixes : When the pronouns such as त्यद्, तद्, यद्, एतद्, इदम्, युष्मद्, अस्मद्, भवत्, किम्, समान, अन्य are prefixed to the √roots, attachment of the क्विन्, कञ् and क्स suffixes give adjectives indicating similitude (समानताउ).

Prefix+√root	+ *kvin* क्विन्	+ *kañ* कञ्	+ *ksa* क्स	meaning	Hindi
त्यद् √दृश्	त्यादृक्	त्यादृश:	त्यादृक्ष	like that	वैसा
तद् √दृश्	तादृक्	तादृश:	तादृक्ष	like that	वैसा
यद् √दृश्	यादृक्	यादृश:	यादृक्ष	as	जैसा
एतद् √दृश्	एतादृक्	एतादृश:	एतादृक्ष	like this	ऐसा
इदम् √दृश्	ईदृक्	ईदृश:	ईदृक्ष	like this	ऐसा
युष्मद् √दृश्	युष्मादृक्	युष्मादृश:	युष्मादृक्ष	like you	आपके जैसा
भवत् √दृश्	भवादृक्	भवादृश:	भवादृक्ष	like you	आपके जैसा

अस्मद् √दृश्	अस्मादृक्	अस्मादृशः	अस्मादृक्ष	like me	मुझ जैसा
किम् √दृश्	कीदृक्	कीदृशः	कीदृक्ष	like what	कैसा
समान √दृश्	सदृक्	सदृशः	सदृक्ष	similar	समान
अन्य √दृश्	अन्यादृक्	अन्यादृशः	अन्यादृक्ष	like other	दूसरे जैसा

* These adjectives decline in seven cases, in three genders and in three numbers, similar to other regular adjectives.

(B) *lyuṭ* ल्युट् : *lyuṭ* ल्युट् suffix अन (*an*) is added to a √root to form a neuter abstract noun.

to read	√पठ्	+	ल्युट् (अन)	=	पठनम्	reading	पढ़ना, सीखना
to sleep	√शी	+	ल्युट् (अन)	=	शयनम्	sleep	सोना
to become	√भू	+	ल्युट् (अन)	=	भवनम्	becoming	होना

(C) *ṇini* णिनि (इन्) suffix : If there is a substantive prefixed to the √root verb, *ṇini* णिनि (इन्) suffix is attached to produce an adjective suggesting one's nature. e.g.

noun +	√root +	णिनि	=	adjective	m◦	f◦
ब्रह्मन् +	√चर् +	णिनि	=	ब्रह्मचारिन्	ब्रह्मचारी	ब्रह्मचारिणी
सुख +	√दा +	णिनि	=	सुखदायिन्	सुखदायी	सुखदायिनी
चिर +	√स्था +	णिनि	=	चिरस्थायिन्	चिरस्थायी	चिरस्थयिनी

(D) *dhiṇun* धिणुन् (इन्) suffix : If a substantive is NOT prefixed to the √root verb, then by attaching the *dhiṇun* धिणुन् (इन्) suffix, an adjective suggesting one's nature is produced.

√root	+	इन्	=	adjective	m◦	f◦
√युज्	+	इन्	=	योगिन्	योगी,	योगिनी,
√श्रम्	+	इन्	=	श्रमिन्	श्रमी,	श्रमिनी,
√भज्	+	इन्	=	भागिन्	भागी,	भागिनी,

(E) *ṇamul* णमुल् suffix : When a subject performs two actions, then to indicate completion of the first (subordinate) action prior to the last (main) action, an Indeclinable Past Participle ipp◦ (क्त्वा) is used instead of a verb. This participle (क्त्वा) implies completion of the preceding action ('having done, or doing' पूर्वकालिक) before the following action begins.

If the action indicated by ipp◦ is repeatitive, then णमुल् suffix indicates the repitition or excess of that action.

√श्रु	+ क्त्वा	=	श्रुत्वा श्रुत्वा	having heard over and over	बारंबार सुन कर, सुनने के बाद
√श्रु	+ णमुल्	=	श्रावं श्रावम्	having heard over and over	बारबार सुन कर, सुनने के बाद

(F) ***trin*** **and** ***trich*** **तृण् and तृच्** suffixes

When *triṇ* or *trich* तृण् or तृच् suffix is attached to a verb √root, it produces an adjective meaning 'having the habit that is indicated by the verb' or 'one performing the verb in the best manner.'

√भू + तृण् (तृ)	= भवितृ	*bhavitri*	One who becomes	वह, जो होता है
√भू + तृच् (तृ)	= भवितृ	*bhavitṛ*	One who becomes	वह, जो होता है

Both these suffixes produce same word, but they are different in sound. In Vedic Sanskrit, where the pronunciation is an important factor, use of each of these two suffixes makes a significant difference. However, in the Classical Sanskrit, this difference is not measurable.

√हन् + (तृ)	= हन्तृ	One who kills,	killer	हत्यारा
√जि + (तृ)	= जेतृ	One who wins,	winner	विजेता

NOTE : The adjective produced by तृ suffix in the Nominative case is same as the verb produced by लृट् (indefinite future) tense, third person, singular.

(G) *ṇvul* ण्वुल् (वु) suffix : When attached to a verb, it produces an adjective meaning 'doer' of that verb.

√कृ	+ ण्वुल् (अक)	=	कारक, कारिका, कारकम्	the doer	कर्ता, करने वाला
√सेव्	+ ण्वुल् (अक)	=	सेवक, सेविका, सेवकम्	the server	सेवक, सेवा करने वाला
√गै	+ ण्वुल् (अक)	=	गायक, गायिका, गायकम्	the singer	गायक, गाने वाला

Krit Suffixes and their Substitutes

कृत्-प्रत्यया: तेषां च आदेशा:।

The oroginal Krit Suffix	= Ramainder of the Krit Suffix
क्विन्, क्विप्, ण्वि, विच्	= the whole suffix disappears
अच्, अण्, अप्, क, खच्, खञ्, खल्, खश्, घञ्, ट, टक्, ड, ण, श	= अ
क्वुन्, ण्वुच्, ण्वुल्, वुञ्, वुन्, ष्वुन्	= अक
युच्, ल्यु, ल्युट्	= अन
झच्, झिच्	= अन्त्
णमुल्	= अम्
टाप्, डाप्, चाप्	= आ
षानक्	= आक्
क्तिञ्, फक्, ष्फ	= आयन्
णिच्, णिङ्	= इ
ठक्, ठञ्, ठन्	= इक
इनि, णिनि, घिनुण्	= इन्
घ	= इय्
इष्णुच्, खिष्णुच्	= इष्णु
ङीप्, ङीष्, ङीन्	= ई
ख	= ईन्
छ	= ईय्
उण्, डु	= उ
उकञ्	= उक
ऊङ्	= ऊ
ढक्, ढञ्	= एय्
कन्, कप्	= क
क्त	= त
क्तवतु	= तवत्
क्तिच्, क्तिन्	= ति
क्त्वा	= त्वा
नङ्, नन्	= न
क्वनिप्	= वन्
क्वरप्	= वर
क्यप्, यक्, यञ्, यत्, ण्य, ण्यत्, ल्यप्, ष्यञ्	= य

(A) SANSKRIT SECONDARY SUFFIXES
संस्कृत तद्धित प्रत्यय

Nouns or adjectives can be derived from primitive nouns, pronouns, adjectives and Indeclinables, to imply a particular relation to a thing, action or notion that belongs (*tat-dhit* तत्-हित् = तद्धित्) to that primitive subject itself.

The secondary suffix, that forms such a noun or adjective from a primitive subject, is called a derivative affix (तद्धित-प्रत्यय).

Remember, that *thddhita* suffixes are never atteched to verb roots. They are only attached to subtantives (प्रातिपादिक) to form derivative nouns, pronouns, adjectives and indeclinable words.

For convenience, the *Taddhit* suffixes can be grouped into three sections :

(A) Suffixes showing relationship of possession,

(B) Suffixes forming adverbs, and

(C) Miscellaneous secondary suffixes.

(A) Taddhit suffixes showing possession (मत्वर्थीय-आदेश)

When attached, these affixes form adjectives possessing the sense or the quality that is possessed by the noun to which they are attached. e.g.

NOTE : The words in the brackets show actual substitutes.

(1) Taddhit suffix *itach* (इतच्)

n◦ puṣhpa + *itach (it)* = adj◦ puṣhpita (Gītā 2.42)

* पुष्प + इतच् (इत) = पुष्पित। पुष्प = n◦ flower, पुष्पित = adj◦ flowery, decorated, ornamented, embellished, showey.

(2) Taddhit suffixes *ini* (इनि), *ṭhañ* (ठञ्) and *ṭhak* (ठक्)

* *jñāna + ini (in) = adj◦ jnānin* (Gītā 7.16)

ज्ञान + इनि (इन्) = ज्ञानिन्। ज्ञान = n◦ knowledge; ज्ञानिन् (ज्ञानी) = adj◦ One who possesses knowledge, wise, learned, experienced.

* *sattva + ṭhañ (ika) = sāttvika* (Gītā 1.14) सत्त्व + ठञ् (इक) = सात्त्विक (righteous),

* *ātman + ṭhak (ika) = ātmika* (Gītā 2.41) आत्मन् + ठक् (इक) = आत्मिक (own)

(3) Taddhit suffix *yap* (यप्)

* *triguṇa + yap (ya) = traiguṇya* (Gītā 2.45) त्रिगुण + यप् (य) = त्रैगुण्य (belonging to the three *gunas*); त्रिगुण = Collective noun∘ Three Guṇas; त्रैगुण्य = adj∘ that which possesses the three guṇas.

(4) Taddhit suffix *vin* (विन्)

* *medhā + vin (vin) = medhāvin* (Gītā 18.10)

मेधा + विन् (विन्) = मेधाविन्। मेधा = n∘ Intellect, intelligence; मेधाविन् (मेधावी) adj∘ Intelligent, brilliant, clever, smart, wise, astute

(B) Taddhit suffixes yield Adverbs (क्रियाविशेषणकारकाः)

These suffixes produce adverbs when they are attached attached to adjectives.

(1) Taddhit suffix *ena* (एन)

* *achira + ena (ena) = achireṇa* (Gītā 4.39) अचिर + एन (एन) = अचिरेण। अचिर = adj∘ short, quick; अचिरेण = adv∘ shortly, quickly, fast, soon (तुरंत, जल्दी).

* *nachira + ena (ena) = nachireṇa* (Gītā 5.6) नचिर + एन (एन) = नचिरेण adv∘ shortly, quickly.

(2) Taddhit suffix *tas* (तस्)

* *parmukha + ta = pramukhata* (Gītā 1.25)

प्रमुख + तस् (तः) = प्रमुखतः। प्रमुख = adj∘ facing; प्रमुखतः = प्रमुखे = adv∘ In front of, before, opposite to.

(3) Taddhit suffix *nā* (ना)

* *nā + nā (nā) = nānā* (various) (Gītā 1.9) ना + ना (ना) = नाना

ना = adj∘ Not that; नाना = adv∘ ind∘ in different ways, differently, variously.

* *vi + nā (nā) = vinā* (without) (Gītā 10.39) वि + ना = विना, बिना

(4) Taddhit suffix *vatup* (वतुप्)

Similitude of a noun or verb with another object.

* *āśhcharya + vatup (vat) = āśhcharyavat* (Gītā 2.29) आश्चर्य + वतुप् (वत्) = आश्चर्यवत्। आश्चर्य = n∘ Wonder; आश्चर्यवत् = adv∘ like a wonder, wondrously, wonderingly (आश्चर्य से).

(5) Taddhit suffix *śhas* (शस्)

* *sarva + śhas (śha) = sarvaśha* (Gītā 1.18) सर्व + शस् (शः) = सर्वशः। सर्व = pron∘ all; सर्वशः = adv∘ ind∘ all together (सब मिल कर).

(C) Miscellaneous Taddhit suffixes (सङ्कीर्ण-प्रत्ययाः)

(1) Suffixes *a, i, eya, ya* (अ, इ, एय, य) = offspring of

Usually letter *a* (अ) is added to the first chararcter of the word and then the Taddhit suffix is added. e.g.

* *pāṇḍu + a = a + pāṇḍu + a = pāṇḍava* (Gītā 1.1) पाण्डु + अ = पाण्डव, पाण्डोः अपत्यम्। पाण्डु = n∘ King Pāṇḍu; पाण्डव = n∘ King Pāṇḍu's son (पांडु का पुत्र).
* *somadatta + i = saumadatti* (Gītā 1.8) सोमदत्त + इ = सौमदत्ति, सोमदत्तस्य अपत्यम्।
* *kunti + eya = kaunteya* (Gītā 1.8) कुन्ती + एय = कौन्तेय, कुन्त्याः अपत्यम् (अर्जुन, आदि)
* *diti + ya = daitya* (Gītā 10.30) दिति + य = दैत्य, दितेः अपत्यम् (दिति का पुत्र)

(2) Taddhit suffixes *aṇ* (अण्), *tva* (त्व), *ṇyañ* (ण्यञ्), *yak* (यक्), *tal* (तल्), and *imanich* (इमनिच्)

: All these suffixes form abstract nouns.

(i) The suffixes *aṇ* (अण्), *tva* (त्व), *ṇyañ* (ण्यञ्), *yak* (यक्) form neuter nouns,

(ii) *tal* (तल्) forms feminine nouns, and

(iii) *imanich* (इमनिच्) forms masculine nouns.

* *muni + aṇ (a) = mauna* (Gītā 10.38) मुनि + अण् (अ) = मौन = मुनेः भावः (मुनि का भाव)
* मुनि = adj∘ The person who is holy, ascetic, saintly; मौन (मौनम्) = n∘. The attitude of silence, silence, taciturnity
* *śhatru + tva (tva) = śhatrutva* (Gītā 6.6) शत्रु + त्व (त्व) = शत्रुत्व
* *durbala + ṇyañ (ya) = daurbalya* (Gītā 2.3) दुर्बल + ण्यञ् (य) = दौर्बल्य, दुर्बलता

* *rājan + yak (ya) = rājya* (Gītā 1.32) राजन् + यक् (य) = राज्य

* *deva + tal (tā) = devatā* (Gītā 4.12) देव + तल् (ता) = देवता

* *mahat + imanich (iman) = mahiman* (Gītā 11.41) महत् + इमनिच् (इमन्) = महिमन्, महान

(3) Taddhit suffixes of comparison *īyasun* (ईयसुन्), *tarap* (तरप्), *tamap* (तमप्), *iṣhṭhan* (इष्ठन्)

(a) Suffix *tarap* (तरप्) is comparison between two objects, *īyasun* (ईयसुन्) is comparison between two qualities;

(b) *tamap* (तमप्) suggests comparison between more than two objects, and

(c) *iṣhṭhan* (इष्ठन्) is used optionally in place of *tamap*.

* *guru + īyasun (īyas) = garīyas* (Gītā 1.32) गुरु + ईयसुन् (ईयस्) = गरीयस्। गुरु = adj॰ big, good, great; गुरु + ईयस्, गरीयस् = comparative adj॰ better, greater (बड़ा).

* *kṣhema + tarap (tara) = kṣhematara* (Gītā 1.46) क्षेम + तरप् (तर) = क्षेमतर (अधिक भला)

* *dvija + ud + tamap (tama) = dvijottama* (Gītā 1.7) द्विज + उद् + तमप् (तम) = द्विजोत्तम

* *śhrī + iṣhṭhan (iṣhṭha) = śhreṣhṭha* (Gītā 3.21) श्री + इष्ठन् (इष्ठ) = श्रेष्ठ

* गुरु + इष्ठन् (इष्ठ) = गरिष्ठ = biggest, best, greatest (सब से श्रेष्ठ).

(4) Taddhit suffixes *matup* (मतुप्) and *maya* (मय)

Suffixes *matup* (मतुप्) and *mayad* (मयद्) suggest inclusion of one thing into another. e.g.

* *dhī + matup (mat) = dhīmat* (Gītā 1.3) धी + मतुप् (मत्) = धीमत्। धी = Intellect, intelligence; धीमत् (धीमान्) = adj॰ Intelliogent, having intelligence (बुद्धिमान).

* *mat + mayad (maya) = manmaya* (Gītā 4.10) मत् + मयद् (मय) = मन्मय (मुझमें समाया हुआ)

NOTE: Sometimes the *matup* (मत्) suffix undergoes a change (वत्व) and becomes a *vat* (वत्) suffix, and declines like the word भगवत्। e.g.

* *Bhaga + matup (vat) =* bhagavat (divine) (Gītā 10.14)
भग + (मतुप्) वत् = भगवत्

(5) Taddhit suffixes *gha* (घ) and *chh* (छ) indicating relationship

* *kṣatra + gha (iya) = kṣhatriya* (Gītā 3.31) क्षत्र + घ (इय) = क्षत्रिय

* *asmad + chh (īya) = asmadīya* (Gītā 11.26) अस्मद् + छ (ईय) = अस्मदीय (अपना)

* अस्मद् = pron◦ I, we; अस्मदीय = pronominal◦ Our

(6) Other suffixes- *āmaha* (आमह), *tyul* (ट्युल्), *tal* (तल्), *tyap* (त्यप्), and *śhālach* (शालच्)

* *pitri + āmaha (āmaha) = pitāmaha* (Gītā 1.12) पितृ + आमह (आमह) = पितामह

* *sadā + ṭyul (tana) = sanātana* (Gītā 1.40) सदा + ट्युल् (तन) = सनातन

* *sama + tal (tā) = samatā* (Gītā 10.5) सम + तल् (ता) = समता

* *ni + tyap (tya) = nitya* (Gītā 2.15) नि + त्यप् (त्य) = नित्य

* *vi + śhālach (śhāla) = viśhāla* (Gītā 9.29) वि + शालच् (शाल) = विशाल

NOTE : The *Taddhit* words may also be prepared from other Taddhit words. e.g. भरत → भारत → भारतीय; पण्डा → पण्डित → पाण्डित्य। पण्डा → पाण्डु → पाण्डुपुत्र, पाण्डव → पाण्डवीय

The Feminine Suffixes (स्त्री प्रत्यय)

In Hindi some words are feminine by nature (e.g. yudh, sam̐jñā, bheri, prithivī, chamū), however, the masculine words can also be converted into femine words using such suffixes as, *ā* (आ), *ī* (ई), ū (ऊ) and ti (ति).

e.g.

(i) m◦ dhīmat + *ṭāp*	(ā)	=	*dhīmatā*	धीमत्	+ टाप् (आ) धीमता	(बुद्धिमान स्त्री)
(ii) m◦ brahman + *ñIp*	(ī)	=	*brahmī*	ब्रह्मन्	+ ङीप् (ई) ब्राह्मी	(ब्रह्मभूत स्त्री)
(iii) m◦ bandh + *ūṅ*	(ū)	=	*vadhū*	बन्ध्	+ ऊङ् (ऊ) वधूः	(वधू)
(iv) m◦ sanga + *ktin*	(ti)	=	*saṅgati*	सङ्ग	+ क्तिन् (ति) सङ्गतिः	(पत्नी)

(A) HINDI SUFFIXES
हिंदी के प्रत्यय

The suffixes (प्रत्यय) are of two types.

(A1) The suffixes which are attached only to the Root Verbs (धातु) are called the Primary Suffixes (कृत्-प्रत्यय). The word formed by attaching a *krit* (कृत्) suffix at the end (अंत) of a word is called a *kridant* (कृत्+अंत, कृदंत).

(A2) The suffixes that are attached to words or their derivatives are called Secondary Suffixex (तद्धित-प्रत्यय).

HINDI PRIMARY SUFFIXES
हिंदी के कृत् प्रत्यय

The Hindi Primary Krit suffixes are broadly divided into five types, namely

(1) Nominative Krit Suffixes (कर्तृवाचक कृत्-प्रत्यय) :

The suffixes that impart a meaning of the Doer of a Verb (as a Subject), are called the Nominative Krit Suffixes (कर्तृवाचक कृत्-प्रत्यय). In order to make Accusative words following 17 types of suffixes are attached to the Varbs. Their few examples are as follows:

1. **अक** *(ak)*: चलाना-चालक (driver), पालना-पालक (guardian), तारना-तारक (savior), पठन करना-पाठक (reader), धारण करना-धारक (bearer), सधन होना-साधक (achiever), गणना करना-गणक (counter), नियोजन करना-नियोजक (organizer), मोद देना-मोदक (joy giver) हिंसा करना-हिंसक (killer), गायन करना-गायक (singer), etc.
2. **अक्कड़** *(ākkaḍ)*: पीना-पिअक्कड़ (drunkerd), बुझना-बुझक्कड़ (cold hearted), घूमना-घुमक्कड़ (wandering), भूलना-भुलक्कड (forgetful), etc.
3. **आऊ** *(āū)*: टिकना-टिकाऊ (long lasting), बिकना-बिकाऊ (for sale), उपजना-उपजाऊ (fertile), उड़ना-उड़ाऊ (flying), कमाना-कमाऊ (earning), चलना-चलाऊ (useful), etc.

4. **आक** *(āk)*: तैरना-तैराक (swimmer), लड़ना-लड़ाक (fighter), तपना-तपाक (ardour), चाल चलना-चालाक (cunning), etc.

5. **आकू, आलु, आलू** *(ākū, ālu, ālū)*: लड़ना-लड़ाकू (fighter), कृपा करना-कृपालु (kind), दया करना-दयालु (kind), शक करना-शंकालु (suspicious), लज्जा करना-लज्जालु (shy), श्रद्धा रखना-श्रद्धालु (faithful), निद्रा लेना-निद्रालु (sleepy), ईर्ष्या करना-ईर्ष्यालु (jealous), चाल चलना-चालू (cunning), झगड़ना-झगड़ालू (quarrelsome), etc.

6. **आड़ी** *(āḍī)*: खेलना-खिलाड़ी (player), पान बेचना-पनवाड़ी (beetle leaf seller), etc.

7. **इयल** *(iyal)*: अड़ना-अड़ियल (stubborn), मरना-मरियल (weak), सड़ना-सड़ियल (rotten), etc.

8. **इया** *(iyā)*: बढ़ना-बढ़िया (better), छल करना-छलिया (cheat), बहलाना-बहेलिया (hunter), रस रखना-रसिया (passionate), etc.

9. **ऐत** *(ait)*: डाका डालना-डकैत (robber), द्विभाव न रखना-अद्वैत (non-duality), etc.

10. **ऐया** *(aiyā)*: बचना (save) बचैया, शी-सोना (sleep) शैया, (चलना walk) चलैया, (मढ़ना to set) मढ़ैया, etc.

11. **ओड़** *(oḍ)*: हँसना-हँसोड़ (clown), गप लड़ाना-गपोड़ (talkative), etc.

12. **ओड़ा** *(oḍā)*: भागना-भगोड़ा (fugitive), हथियाना-हथौड़ा (hammer), गप लड़ाना-गपौड़ा (talketive), etc.

13. **औना** *(aunā)*: खेलना-खिलौना (toy), बेलना-बिलौना (churner), बिछना-बिछौना (bed), etc.

14. **वन** *(van)*: सुहाना-सुहावन (pleasing), चितवना-चितवन (glance), etc.

15. **वाला** *(vālā)*: आना-आनेवाला (coming), जाना-जानेवाला (going), गाना-गानेवाला (singer), ढोना-ढोनेवाला (carrier), धोना-धोनेवाला (washerman), रोना-रोनेवाला (crying), होना-होनेवाला (happening), etc.

16. **वैया** *(gavaiyā)*: **गाना-**गवैया (singer), खेवना-खेवैया (boatman), etc.

17. **सार , दार, हार** *(sār, dār, hār)*: मिलना-मिलनसार (sociable), समझना-समझदार (wise), भाग लेना-भागीदार (partner), साझा करना-साझेदार (partner), ईमान रखना-ईमानदार (honest), दम रखना-दमदार (strong), खेवना-खेवनहार (boatman), राखना-राखनहार (protector), etc.

(2) Accusative Krit Suffixes (कर्म वाचक कृत्-प्रत्यय) :

The suffixes that impart a meaning of an Object to the Verb are called the Accusative Krit

Suffixes (कर्म वाचक कृत्-प्रत्यय). In order to make Accusative words following 4 types of suffixes are attached to the Verbs. Their few examples are as follows:

1. **औना** *(aunā)*: बिछ-बिछौना (bed), खेल-खिलौना (toy), रिझ -रिझौना (charmer), बिल-बिलौना (churnerd), etc.
2. **ना** *(nā)*: ओढ़-ओढ़ना (a cove), ढक-ढकना (covering), पढ़-पढ़ना (reading), बक-बकना (yapping), भोंक-भोंकना (barking), रोक-रोकना (stopping), लिख-लिखना (writing), सीख-सीखना (learning), थक-थकना (tiring), पक-पकना (ripening), दुख-दुखना (hurting), सूख-सूखना (drying), चुग-चुगना (picking), जग-जगना (waking), ठग-ठगना (cheating), भीग-भीगना (soaking), माँग-माँगना (asking), सोच-सोचना (thinking), पोंछ-पोंछना (wiping), छू-छूना (touching), खोज-खोजना (searching), गूँज-गूँजना (buzzing), बज-बजना (ringing), टूट-टूटना (breaking), भेंट-भेंटना (meeting), लेट-लेटना (lying down), फूट-फेटना (breaking), लूट-लूटना (plundering), लौट-लौटना (returning), छेड़-छेड़ना (interfering), छोड़-छोड़ना (leaving), तोड़-तोड़ना (breaking), फोड़-फोड़ना (breaking), मोड़-मोड़ना (bending), लड़-लड़ना (fighting), बढ़-बढ़ना (advancing), जीत-जीतना (winning), खोद-खोदना (digging), बाँध-बाँधना (tying), गिन-गिनना (counting), भुन-भुनना (roasting), छाप-छापना (printing), छिप-छिपना (hiding), माप-मापना (measuring), रोप-रोपना (planting), पी-पीना (drinking), चूम-चूमना (kissing), गिर-गिरना (falling), चर-चरना (grazing), तर-तरना (floating), भर-भरना (filling), डर-डरना (being afraid), गल-गलना (melting), चल-चलना (walking), छील-छीलना (peeling), मिल-मिलना (meeting), हिल-हिलना (moving), etc.
3. **नी** *(nī)*: ओढ़-ओढ़नी (a scarf), छल-छलनी (a strainer), ढक-ढकनी (a cover), जन-जननी (mother), मथ-मथनी (a beater), हो-होनी (future), etc.
4. **हुआ, हुई** *(huā,huī)*: लिख-लिखा हुआ, लिखी हुई (written thing), पढ़-पढ़ा हुआ, पढ़ी हुई (the thing that is read), etc.

(3) Instrumental Krit Suffixes (करण वाचक कृत्-प्रत्यय) :

The suffixes that gives a Verb the meaning of an instrument or a vehicle, are called the Instrumental Krit Suffixes (करण वाचक कृत्-प्रत्यय) . In order to make Instrumental words following 8 types of suffixes are attached to the Verbs. Their few examples are as follows:

1. **आ** *(ā)*: रक्ष-रक्षा (protection), लोटना-लोटा (tumbling pot), छापना-छापा (stamp), घेरना-घेरा (circling), फेरना-फेरा (circuit), रेलना-रेला (push), झूलना-झूला (a swing), दोहना-दोहा (milk), etc.

(4) Abstract Krit Suffixes (भाव वाचक कृत्-प्रत्यय) :

The suffixes that gives a Verb the meaning of an Abstract Noun (भाववाचक संज्ञा), are called the Abstract Krit Suffixes (भाव वाचक कृत्-प्रत्यय). Again remember, the Abstract (भाव वाचक) worde do not change with the change in Gender or Number of eithr the Subject or the Object. In order to make Abstract words following 17 types of suffixes are attached to the Verbs. Their few examples are as follows:

1. **अ** *(a)*: जि-जय (winning), लिख्-लेख (writing), तुल्-तोल (balancing), मृ-मार (killing), वि√चर्-विचार (thinking), etc.
2. **अन्** *(an)*: गम्-गमन (going), लिख्-लेखन (writing), पठ्-पठन (reading), गम्-गमन (going), जन्-जनन (giving birth), ताड्-ताडन (beating), भेद्-भेदन (going), मन्-मनन (meditating); पूज्-पूजन (worshipping), भुज्-भोजन (eating, enjoying), पत्-पतन (downfall), कथ्-कथन (saying), क्रन्द्-क्रन्दन (crying), रुद्-रुदन (crying), मिल्-मिलन (meeting), लंघ्-लंघन (crosssing), हन्-हनन (killing), ज्ञाप्-ज्ञापन (knowing), शि-शयन (sleeping), दृश्-दर्शन (seeing), चल्-चलन (behaviour), जल्-जलन (burning), पाल्-पालन (raising), प्लव्-प्लवन (flying), वस्-वसन (residing), शास्-शासन (governing), सह्-सहन (bearing), etc.
3. **अंत** *(an)*: गढ्-गढंत (a fiction), कृत्-कृदंत (a participle), भद्-भदंत (a scripture), हल्-हलंत (a consonant), etc.
4. **आई** *(āī)*: एक-इकाई (unit), रंग-रंगाई (painting), बँट-बँटाई (distribution), लड़-लड़ाई (fighting), चढ़-चढ़ाई (aggression), पढ़-पढ़ाई (study), छप-छपाई (printing), धुल-धुलाई (washing), सिल-सिलाई (stitching), घिस-घिसाई (grinding), हँस-हँसाई (laughter), etc.
5. **आन** *(ān)*: उड़-उड़ान (flight), चढ़-चढ़ान (ascent), थक-थकान (fatigue), उठ-उठान (rise), रुझ-रुझान (inclination), etc.
6. **आप** *(āp)*: मिल-मिलाप (union), सर-सराप (curse), etc.
7. **आव** *(āv)*: झुक-झुकाव (inclination), खिंच-खिंचाव (attraction), अटक-अटकाव (obstruction), लग-लगाव (attachment), बच-बचाव (protection), सूझ-सुझाव (suggestion), प्रभ-प्रभाव (effect), जम-जमाव (gathering), घुम-घुमाव (complication), दुर-दुराव (concealment), घिर-घिराव

(encirclement), बदल-बदलाव (change), बह-बहाव (flow), etc.

8. **आवा** *(āvā)*: चढ़ाना-चढ़ावा (offering), छलना-छलावा (deceit), दिखाना-दिखावा (show), बढ़ना-बढ़ावा (encouragement), पछताना-पछतावा (repenting), पहनना-पहनावा (dress), बहकना-बहकावा (misleading), बढ़ना-बढ़ावा (encouragement), बोलना-बुलावा (call), भूल-भुलावा (deception), etc.

9. **आवट** *(āvāṭ)*: थकना-थकावट (fatigue), रुकना-रुकावट (stoppage), लिखना-लिखावट (script), बनना-बनावट (style), बुनना-बुनावट (weave), गिरना-गिरावट (diminish), मिलाना-मिलावट (adultration), etc.

10. **आहट** *(āhāṭ)*: जगमगाना-जगमगहट (glitter), छटपटाना-छटपटाहट (agitation), खड़खड़ाना-खड़खड़ाहट (rambling), गड़गड़ाना-गड़गड़ाहट (rumbling), गड़बड़ाना-गड़बड़ाहट (confusion), घड़घड़ाना-घड़घड़ाहट (rumbling), चिड़चिड़ाना-चिड़चिड़हट (irritation), गुनगुनाना-गुनगुनाहट (humming), फिसलना-फिसलाहट (slipping), etc.

11. **ई** *(ī)*: झिड़कना-झिड़की (scolding), झपकना-झपकी (dozing), सिसकना-सिसकी (sobbing), उलटना-उलटी (vomiting), गड़बड़ाना-गड़बड़ी (confusion), कमना-कमी (lessening), गरमना-गरमी (warmth), चुराना-चोरी (theft), बोलना-बोली (speech), etc.

12. **औता** *(autā)*: समझना-समझौता (understanding), etc.

13. **औती** *(autī)*: काटना-कटौती (reduction), छुड़ाना-छुड़ौती (freedom), चुनना-चुनौती (choice), मानना-मनौती (agreement), फिराना-फिरौती (ransome), etc.

14. **क** *(ka)*: बैठना-बैठक (seat), etc.

15. **ती** *(tī)*: चढ़ना-चढ़ती (increase), बढ़ना-बढ़ती (progress), बोलना-बोलती (speech), भरना-भरती (filling), etc.

16. **न** *(na)*: कुढ़ना-कुढ़न (vexation), भेदना-भेदन (penetretion), मढ़ना-मढ़न (lining), मथना-मथन (churning), जनना-जनन (giving birth), देना-देन (gift), हनना-हनन (murder), etc.

17. **नी** *(nī)*: चाटना-चटनी (sauce), छाँटना-छँटनी (retrenchment), etc.

(5) Participle Krit Suffixes (कृदंत अथवा क्रिया द्योतक कृत्-प्रत्यय) :

The suffixes that gives a Verb the meaning of a Participle Adjective (धातुसाधित विशेषण), are called the Participle forming Krit Suffixes (क्रिया द्योतक कृत्-प्रत्यय). There are two types of such suffixes (1) PAP Present Active Participles (वर्तमान-कालिक विशेषण) and (2) PPP

Past Passive Participles (भूत कालिक विशेषण). Their few examples are as follows:

1. PAP Present Active Participles (वर्तमानकालिक विशेषण) :

The PAP krit suffix is ता (*tā*) which denotes an active continuous (ता हुआ, ती हुई) verb action. e.g.

Verb	+ ता suffix	=	PAP			
आ	+ ता (हुआ)	=	आता (हुआ),	आती (हुई),	आते (हुए)	while coming.
जा	+ ता (हुआ)	=	जाता (हुआ),	जाती (हुई),	जाते (हुए)	while going.
खा	+ ता (हुआ)	=	खाता (हुआ)	खाती (हुई),	खाते (हुए)	while eating.
बह	+ ता (हुआ)	=	बहता (हुआ)	बहती (हुई),	बहते (हुए)	while flowing.
गा	+ ता (हुआ)	=	गाता (हुआ)	गाती (हुई),	गाते (हुए)	while coming, etc.

2. PPP Past Passive Participles (भूतकालिक विशेषण) :

The PPP krit suffix is आ (ā) or ई (ī) which denotes a Passive Perfect (आ हुआ, ई हुई, ए हुए) Verb Action.

The suffix आ becomes suffix या or यी or ये if it comes after a verb ending in a long vowel such as आ, ई, ओ of the verbs आ, जा, गा, खा, पी, धो, etc. The Verbs जा, ले, दे and कर are irregular verbs in Perfect Tense, they change to ग, ली, दी and की respectively.

Verb	+ आ suffix	=	PPP (Perfect Participle, Adjectives)			
आ	+ या (हुआ)	=	आया (हुआ),	आयी (हुई),	आए (हुए)	came.
जा	+ या (हुआ)	=	गया (हुआ),	गई (हुई),	गए (हुए)	gone.
ले	+ या (हुआ)	=	लिया (हुआ),	लियी (हुई),	लिये (हुए)	taken.
दे	+ या (हुआ)	=	दिया (हुआ),	दियी (हुई),	दिये (हुए)	given.
कर	+ या (हुआ)	=	किया (हुआ),	कियी (हुई),	किये (हुए)	done.
खा	+ या (हुआ)	=	खाया (हुआ),	खायी (हुई),	खाये (हुए)	eaten.
बह	+ आ (हुआ)	=	बहा (हुआ),	बही (हुई),	बहे (हुए)	flown.
गा	+ या (हुआ)	=	गाया (हुआ),	गायी (हुई),	गाए (हुए)	sung.
पी	+ या (हुआ)	=	पीया (हुआ),	पीयी (हुई),	पीये (हुए)	drunk.
धो	+ या (हुआ)	=	धोया (हुआ),	धोयी (हुई),	धोये (हुए)	washed.
सो	+ या (हुआ)	=	सोया (हुआ),	सोयी (हुई),	सोये (हुए)	slept, etc.

HINDI SECONDARY SUFFIXES
हिंदी के तद्धित् प्रत्यय

As said earlier, the suffixes (प्रत्यय) are of two types.

1. The suffixes which are attached only to the Root Verbs (धातु) are called the Primary Suffixes (कृत्-प्रत्यय). The word formed by attaching a *krit* (कृत्) suffix at the end (अंत) of a word is called a *kridant* (कृदंत).

2. The suffixes that are attached to words or their derivatives are called Secondary Suffixex (तद्धित-प्रत्यय).

The Hindi Secondary Taddhit Suffixes are broadly divided into 12 types, namely :

(1) Nominative Taddhit Suffixes (कर्तृवाचक तद्धित्-प्रत्यय),

(2) Abstract Taddhit Suffixes (भाववाचक तद्धित्-प्रत्यय),

(3) Genitive Taddhit Suffixes (संबंधवाचक तद्धित्-प्रत्यय),

(4) Numeral Taddhit Suffixes (गणना वाचक तद्धित्-प्रत्यय),

(5) Qualitative Taddhit Suffixes (गुणवाचक तद्धित्-प्रत्यय),

(6) Locative Taddhit Suffixes (स्थानवाचक तद्धित्-प्रत्यय),

(7) Diminution Taddhit Suffixes (ऊनवाचक तद्धित्-प्रत्यय),

(8) Similitude Taddhit Suffixes (अनेक वचन सूचक तद्धित्-प्रत्यय),

(9) Gender Changer Taddhit Suffixes (लिंग परिवर्तक तद्धित्-प्रत्यय),

(10) Pluralization Taddhit Suffixes (सादृश्यवाचक तद्धित्-प्रत्यय),

(11) Sanskrit Oriented Taddhit Suffixes (संस्कृत रूप तद्धित्-प्रत्यय),

(12) Foreigh Taddhit Suffixes (विदेशी तद्धित्-प्रत्यय) : (غیر ملکی تادیت لاحقہ) etc.

(1) Nominative Taddhit Suffixes (कर्तृवाचक तद्धित्-प्रत्यय) :

The suffixes that impart a meaning of the Doer of a Verb <u>**to a word**</u> (संज्ञा), are called the Nominative Taddhit Suffixes (कर्तृ-वाचक तद्धित्-प्रत्यय). In order to make Nominative words following 8 types of suffixes are attached to the words. Their few examples are as follows:

1. **आर** *(ār)*: सोना-सुनार, सोनार (a goldsmith), लोहा-लुहार, लोहार (ironsmith), कुम्भ-कुम्हार (potter), चर्म-चम्हार (cobbler), etc.
2. **आरी** *(ārī)*: जुआ-जुआरी (a gambler), पूजा-पुजारी (priest), भीख-भिखारी (begger), कोठा-कोठारी (store keeper), etc.
3. **इया** *(iyā)*: मुख-मुखिया (a chieftain), भेद-भेदिया (spy), गाड़र-गड़रिया (sheppard), छल-छलिया (cheat), रस-रसिया (pleasure-seeker), etc.
4. **ई** *(ī)*: तंबोल-तंबोली, तमोली (a beetle-leaf seller), सत्संग-सत्संगी (a virtuous company keeper), त्रिपाठ-त्रिपाठी (a Vedic tutor), आढ़त-आढ़ती (a broker), तेल-तेली (an oil-miller), बरात-बराती (a marriage party member), प्रतिवाद-प्रतिवादी (a defendent), शराब-शराबी (a drunkerd), अत्याचार-अत्याचारी (a tyrant), भ्रष्टाचार-भ्रष्टाचारी (a corrupt person), कोठार-कोठारी (a warehouseman), भंडार-भंडारी (a storage keepre), जौहर-जौहरी (a jeweller), etc.
5. **एरा** *(erā)*: चित्र-चितेरा (a painter), लूट-लुटेरा (a robber), ठाठ-ठठेरा (a tinsmith), साँप-सपेरा (a snakecharmer), etc.
6. **कार** *(kār)*: कला-कलाकार (an actor), काश्त-काश्तकार (a farmer), कुम्भ-कुम्भकार (a potter), चर्म-चर्मकार (a cobbler), चित्र-चित्रकार (an artist), पत्र-पत्रकार (a journalist), ग्रंथ-ग्रंथकार (an author), भाष्य-भाष्यकार (a critique), लिपि-लिपिकार (a writer), वार्ता-वार्ताकार (a hagiographer), शिल्प-शिल्पकार, मूर्तिकार (a sculptor), साहू-साहूकार (a money-lender), सुवर्ण-सुवर्णकार (a goldsmith), etc.
7. **वाला** *(vālā)*: गाँव-गाँववाला (a villager), गौ-ग्वाला (a cowherd), घर-घरवाला (a husband, landlord), ताँगा-ताँगेवाला (a horse buggy driver), फल-फलवाला (a fruit seller), फेरी-फेरीवाला (a hawker), पैसा-पैसेवाला (a rich person), रंग-रंगवाला (a painter), etc.
8. **हार, हारा** *(hār, hārā)*: पालन-पालनहार (a guardian), भूमि-भूमिहार (a cultivator), सिरजन-सिरजनहार (the Creator), लकड़ी-लकड़हारा (a wood-cutter), सृजन-सृजनहारा (the Creator), etc.

(2) Abstract Taddhit Suffixes (भाववाचक तद्धित्-प्रत्यय) :

The suffixes that impart an Abstract meaning to a noun or an adjective, are called the

Abstract Taddhit Suffixes (भाव-वाचक तद्धित-प्रत्यय). In order to make Abstract words which do not change their Gender or Number according to the change in the Gender and Number of the Subject or Object in the sentence, following 17 types of suffixes are attached to the words. Their few examples are as follows:

1. **आ** *(ā)*: छलाव-छलावा (deceit), जायज़-जायज़ा (scrutiny, धारण-धारणा (conception), दैवत-देवता (deity), निर्मित, निर्मिति-निर्माता (procucer), पछताव-पछतावा (regret), पतिव्रत-पतिव्रता (dedicated wife), बढ़ाव-बढ़ावा (instigation), बहकाव-बहकावा, बहलाव-बहलावा (misguidence), भुलाव, भुलावट-भुलावा (deception), मध्यम-मध्यमा (middle finger), एकतार-एकतारा (one stringed guitar), etc.
2. **आई** *(āī)*: अच्छा-अच्छाई (goodness), इक-इकाई (unit), गहरा-गहराई (depth), चतुर-चतुराई (dexterity), चौड़ा-चौड़ाई (beradth), जुदा-जुदाई, विदाई (separation), छोटा-छोटाई (smallness), ठंडा-ठंडाई, ठंढाई (mint, cooler), ढीठ-ढीठाई (courage), बुरा-बुराई (vice), भला-भलाई (goodness), मीठा-मिठाई (sweet), सच्चा-सच्चाई (truth), साफ-सफाई (cleaning), हँसा-हँसाई (laughter), हवा-हवाई (aerial), हलवा-हलवाई (sweets-makes), etc.
3. **आत्** *(āt)*: अर्थ-अर्थात् (of course), बल-बलात् (forcibly), हठ-हठात् (at once), etc.
4. **आन** *(ān)*: आख्या-आख्यान, उपाख्यान, व्याख्यान (speech), चौड़ा-चौड़ान (width), थक-थकान (fatigue), बाग-बागान (gardning), प्रज्ञा-प्रज्ञान (cognisance), संज्ञा-संज्ञान (advice), विधा-विधान (statement), अज्ञ-अज्ञान (ignorance), विद्या-विज्ञान (science), etc.
5. **आपा** *(āpā)*: बूढ़ा-बूढ़पा (old age), मोटा-मुटापा, मोटापा (fatness), बहन-बहनापा (sisterhood), etc.
6. **आयत** *(āyat)*: बहुत-बहुतायत (abundance), पंच-पंचायत (court), रिआ-रिआयत (abatement), etc.
7. **आरा** *(ārā)*: छूट-छुटकारा (freedom), निपट-निपटारा, निबटारा (settlement), etc.
8. **आस** *(ās)*: खट्टा-खटास (bitterness), मीठा-मिठास (sweetness), etc.
9. **आहट** *(āhat)*: कड़वा-कड़वाहट (bitterness), जगमग-जगमगहट (glitter), खड़खड़-खड़खड़ाहट (noise), गड़गड़-गड़गड़ाहट, घड़घड़ाहट, घरघराहट (roaring), गुनगुन-गुनगुनाहट, भनभनाहट, घनघनाहट (humming), थरथर-थरथराहट (shaking), मरमर-मरमराहट (fatigue), सरसर-सरसराहट, सुरसुराहट (rustling), घिसघिस-घिसघिसाहट (rubbing), etc.
10. **इमा** *(imā)*: काला-कालिमा (disgrace), गरीयस्-गरिमा (greatness), नीला-नीलिमा (blue shade,

darkness), महिमन्-महिमा (prestige), मधुर-मधुरिमा (sweetness), पूर्ण-पूर्णिमा (full moon), लाल-लालिमा (blushing), etc.

11. **ई** *(ī)*: खेत-खेती (farming), झपक-झपकी (doze), पंख-पंखी (bird), ढोंग-ढोंगी (hypocrite), त्याग-त्यागी (auster), पाप-पापी (sinner), भोग-भोगी (enjoyer), शीशा-शीशी (bottle), रोज-रोजी (pay), दाढ़-दाढ़ी (beard), रथ-रथी (charioteer), सफेद-सफेदी (whitewash), etc.

12. **एरा** *(erā)*: घेर-घेरा (perimeter), लूट-लुटेरा (plunderer), बास-बसेरा (abode), बहुत-बहुतेरा (most), अंध-अँधेरा (invisibility), etc.

13. **औती** *(autī)*: कट-कटौती (discount), कठ-कठौती (wooden bowl), चुन-चुनौती (selection), मान-मनौती (persuation), छुड़ाव-छुड़ौती (ransom), etc.

14. **कारा** *(kārā)*: चट-चटटकारा (snapping), छुट-छुटकारा (release), etc.

15. **त** *(ta)*: रंग-रंगत (pleasure), संग-संगत (good company), कुसंग-कुसंगत (bad company), बहु-बहुत (plenty), etc.

16. **त्व** *(tva)*: अंध-अंधत्व (blindness), अस्ति-अस्तित्व (existance), एक-एकत्व (uniformity), ओछा-ओछापन (baseness), कटु-कटुत्व (bitterness), कवि-कवित्व (poetics), गुरु-गुरुत्व (weight), घन-घनत्व (density), देव-देवत्व (godliness), नेतृ-नेतृत्व (leadership), पर-परत्व (difference), पुरुष-पुरुषत्व (manliness), पूर्ण-पूर्णत्व (perfection), प्रभु-प्रभुत्व (power), प्रज्ञा-प्रज्ञापन (erudition), भ्रातृ-भ्रातृत्व (brotherhood), मम-ममत्व (mineness), मातृ-मातृत्व (motherhood), व्यक्ति-व्यक्तित्व (personality), लघु-लघुत्व (inferiority), वक्तृ-वक्तृ (eloquence), सत्-सत्त्व (reality), सम-समत्व (equality), स्त्री-स्त्रत्वि, नारीत्व (womanness), स्वामी-स्वामित्व (lordship), हिंदु-हिंदु (Hinduism), etc.

17. **पन** *(pan)*: अंधा-अंधापन (blindness), अपना-अपनापन (kinship), अच्छा-अच्छापन (goodness), अल्हड़-अल्हड़पन (childishness), आवारा-आवारापन (vagarance), उजला-उजलापन (brightness), कड़ा-कड़ापन (hardness), कमीना-कमीनापन (meanness), काला-कालापन (darkness), गीला-गीलापन (wetness), दीवानाना-दीवानापन (craze), दुबला-दुबलापन (weakness), धुँधला-धुँधलापन (foggyness), सूना-सूनापन (emptyness), etc.

(3) Genitive Taddhit Suffixes (संबंधवाचक तद्धित्-प्रत्यय) :

The suffixes that impart indicates a meaning of relationshio of one word of the sentence with other word or words is Genitive Taddhit Suffixes (संबंध-वाचक तद्धित-प्रत्यय). In order to make Genitive words following 9 types of suffixes are attached to the words. Their few examples are as follows:

1. **आल** *(āl)*: कृपा-कृपाल (merciful), गोप-गोपाल (cowherd), चंड-चंडाल (violent), अंतर-अंतराल (space), ससुर-ससुराल (father-in-law's home), etc.
2. **इक** *(ik)*: अंतर-आंतरिक (internal), अधुना-आधुनिक (modern), अध्यात्म-आध्यामिक (spiritual), उद्योग-औद्योगि (industrial), कल्पना-काल्पनिक (imaginary), चिरकाल-चिरकालिक (permanent), दर्शन-दार्शनिक (philosophical), दिन-दैनिक (daily), नगर-नागरिक (resident), पक्ष-पाक्षिक (bi-weekly), परिवार-पारिवारिक (family-), पुराण-पौराणिक (ancient), प्रथम-प्राथमिक (primary), प्रदेश-प्रादेशिक (local), प्रमाण-प्रामाणिक (honest), प्रयोग-प्रायोगि (experimental), प्रसंग-प्रासंगिक (relevant), बुद्धि-बौद्धिक (intellectual), मध्यम-माध्यमिक (intermediate), मास-मासिक (monthly), मुख-मौखिक (oral), योग-यौगिक (disciplinary), लक्षण-लाक्षणिक (characteristic), लिंग-लैंगिक (sexual), लोकतंत्र-लोकतांत्रिक (democratic), विज्ञान-वैज्ञानिक (scientific), वेद-वैदिक (re Veda), शरीर-शारीरिक (bodily), शिक्षण-शैक्षणिक (educational), श्रम-श्रमिक (labourer), संविधान-संवैधानिक (constitutional), संसार-सांसारिक (worldly), समय-सामयिक (timely), समाज-सामाजिक (social), सप्ताह-साप्ताहिक (weekly), सर्वकाल-सर्वकालिक (universal), सर्वत्र-सार्वत्रिक (universal), सैन्य-सैनिक (soldier), etc.
3. **ई** *(ī)*: आसाम-आसामी (of Assam), कर्नाटक-कर्नाटकी (of Karnatak), चोर-चोरी (theft), मराठा-मराठी (of Maharashtra), पंजाब-पंजाबी (of Punjab), पहाड़-पहाड़ी (of mountain), बंगाल-बंगाली (of Bengal), बिहार-बिहारी (of Bihar), राजस्थान-राजस्थानी (of Rajastan), रेगिस्तान-रेगिस्तानी (of desert), मद्रास-मद्रासी (of Madras), समुद्र-समुद्री (of ocean), साथ-साथी (companion), सिलोन-सिलोनी (of Shri Lanka), हवा-हवाई (aerial), etc.
4. **एरा** *(erā)*: चाचा-चचेरा (paternal), फुफा-फुफेरा (cousin), मामा-ममेरा (maternal), लाख-लखेरा (lacquer worker), etc.
5. **ऊ** *(ū)*: उतार-उतारू (stooping), गँवार-गँवारू (boorish), बाजार-बाजारू (crude, vulgar), etc.
6. **एल, ऐल** *(el, ail)*: नाक-नकेल (nasal), राख-रखेल (concubine), चुड़-चुड़ैला (evil woman), etc.
7. **औती** *(autī)*: बाप-बपौति (inheritance), etc.
8. **जा** *(jā)*: बहन-भानजा (nephew), भाई-भतीजा (nephew), etc.
9. **हाल** *(hāl)*: ननिया-ननिहाल (maternal grandfather's home), etc.

(4) Numeral Taddhit Suffixes (गणना वाचक तद्धित्-प्रत्यय) :

The suffixes that show numerical relationship of a word are called the Numeral Taddhit Suffixes (गणना वाचक तद्धित्-प्रत्यय). Besides the sequence indicating adjectives (क्रम वाचक विशेषण) like प्रथम, प्रथमा, द्वितीय, द्वितीया, तृतीय, तृतीया, चतुर्थ, चतुर्थी, पंचम, पंचमी, षष्ठ, षष्ठी..., एकादशी, द्वादशी, त्रयोदशी, etc. following 7 types of suffixes are attached to the words. Their few examples are as follows:

1. **गुना** *(tgunā)*: चार-चौगुना (quadruple), तीन-तिगुना (triple), दो-दुगुना (double), दस-दसगुना, सौगुना... (ten times, hundred times, ...), etc.
2. **ठा** *(ṭhā)*: छह-छठा (sixth)
3. **था** *(thā)*: चार-चौथा (fourth)
4. **रा** *(rā)*: दो-दूसरा (second), तीन-तीसरा (third), etc.
5. **ला** *(lā)*: प्रथम-पहला (first)
6. **वाँ** *(vā̃)*: पाँच-पाँचवाँ (fifth), सात-सातवाँ (seventh), आठ-आठवाँ (eighth), नौ-नवाँ (nineth), दस-दसवाँ (tenth), सौ-सौवाँ (hundredth), हजार-हजारवाँ (thousandth), .. etc.
7. **हरा** *(harā)*: तीन-तिहरा (triplicate), दो-दुहरा (duplicate), etc.

(5) Qualitative Taddhit Suffixes (गुणवाचक तद्धित्-प्रत्यय) :

The suffixes that show qualitative attributes of the words are called the Qualitative Taddhit Suffixes (गुणवाचक तद्धित्-प्रत्यय). Following 6 types of suffixes are attached to the words. Their few examples are as follows:

1. **आ** *(ā)*: ठंड-ठंडा (cold), प्यास-प्यासा (thirsty), भूख-भूखा (hungry), आड़-आड़ा (shield), सादगी-दास (simple), अर्ध-आधा (half), छिप-छिपा (hidden), गौर-गोरा (white), नील-नीला (blue), पूर्ण-पूरा (whole), मिठास-मीठा (sweet), क्षार-खारा (salty), हरित-हरा (green) etc.
2. **इत** *(it)*: अर्चन-अर्चित (offered), अर्जन-अर्जित (earned), अर्पण-अर्पित (surrendered), च्चरण-उच्चारित (uttered), विसर्जन-विसर्जित (concluded), आनंद-आनंदित (joyful), कलंक-कलंकित (blemished), चर्चा-चर्चित (discussed), निर्णय-निर्णित (decided), पुष्प-पुष्पित (flowerycold), प्रेरणा-प्रेरित (inspired), सुगंध-सुगंधित (fragrant), etc.

3. **ई** *(ī)*: अनुभव-अनुभवी (experienced), आखिर-आखिरी (last), आभार-आभारी (greatful), उद्यम-उद्यमी (industrious), ऊन-ऊनी (woolen), ऊपर-ऊपरी (upper), काम-कामी (lustful), क्रोध-क्रोधी (angry), खून-खूनी (bloody), जंगल-जंगली (wild), ज्ञान-ज्ञानी (wise), देश-देशी, विदेशी, परदेशी (foreign), नाम-नामी (famous), द्रोह-द्रोही (hostile), नीच-निचाई (lowness), नेक-नेकी (honesty), पाप-पापी (sinful), भार-भारी (heavy), भीख-भिखारी (begger), रघुवंश-रघुवंशी, यदुवंशी, सूर्यवंशी, चंद्रवंशी... (belonging to -), राक्षस-राक्षसी (demonic), राजस-राजसी, तामसी (royal), लहर-लहरी (whimsical), लालच-लालची (greedy), विकार-विकारी (changeable), विलास-विलासी (sensous), संयम-संयमी (self controlled), साहस-साहसी (courageous), सूत-सूती (fibric), etc.

4. **ईय** *(īya)*: अनुकरण-अनुकरणीय, अनुचरणीय, आचरणीय (to be follower), अवलोकन-अवलोकनीय, दर्शनीय (to be seen), आदर-आदरणीय (respectable), उपेक्षा-उपेक्षणीय (negligible), उल्लेख-उल्लेखनीय (mentionable), कथन-कथनीय, वर्णनीय (to be told), करण-करणीय (to be done), गोपन-गोपनीय (secret), ग्रहण-ग्रहणीय (acceptable), चिंतन-चिंतनीय, मननीय (to be contempleted), तुलना-तुलनीय (comparable), पर्वत-पर्वतीय (mountenous), पठन-पठनीय (to be read), पूजन-पूजनीय (to be worshipped), भारत-भारतीय (Indian), मान-माननीय (respectable), रमण-रमणीय (pleasing), वंदन-वंदनीय (to be revered), वर्ष-वर्षीय (yearly), शंसन-शंसनीय, प्रशंसनीय (praiseworthy), स्पर्श-स्पर्शनीय (to be touched), स्मरण-स्मरणीय (to be remembered), etc.

5. **ईला, ऐला** *(īlā, elā)*: कँकड़-कँकड़ीला, खर्च-खर्चीला (expensive), जहर-जहरीला (poisonous), पथरीला (stony), गाँठ-गठीला (knotty), चमक-चमकीला (shiny), ढील-ढीला (loose), नोक-नुकीला (pointy), फुर्ती-फुर्तीला (energetic), बरफ-बरफीला (icy), भडक-भडकीला (flashy), रस-रसीला (juicy), लाज-लजीला (ashamed), हठ-हठीला (stubborn), सुर-सुरीला (melodious); कस-कसैला (astringent), etc.

6. **वान, वान्, मान, मान्**: *(vān, mān)* There is a class of Roots which prefer वान् suffix while the other class of Root Verbs take मान् suffix, though not necessarily. **:** आस्था-आस्थावान, श्रद्धावान, निष्ठावान, भक्तिवान (faithful), कीर्ति-कीर्तिमान (famous), गति-गतिमान (fast)गुण-गुणवान (virtuous), धन-धनवान (rich), पुण्य-पुण्यवान (auspicious), बल-बलवान (strong), बुद्धि-बुद्धिमान (intelligent), भाग्य-भाग्यवान (lucky), मूल्य-मूल्यवान (precious), रूप-रूपवान (beautiful), शक्ति-शक्तिमान (powerful), etc.

(6) Locative Taddhit Suffixes (स्थानवाचक तद्धित्-प्रत्यय) :

The suffixes that indicate name of some place are called the Locative Taddhit Suffixes (स्थानवाचक तद्धित्-प्रत्यय). Following 3 types of suffixes are attached to the words. Their few examples are as follows:

1. **इया, ई** *(iyā, ī)*: आसाम-आसामिया, आसामी (of Assam), ओरीसा-ओरिया (of Orissa), नागपुर-नागपुरिया, नागपुरी (from Nagpur), परदेस-परदेसिया, परदेसी (foreigner), दोआब-दोआबिया, दोआबी (from confluence), सूरत-सूरतिया, सूरती, (of Gujrat), कलकत्ता-कलकतिया (of Calcutta), मस्कत-मस्कतिया (of Muskat), etc.
2. **ई** *(ī)*: काश्मिर-काश्मिरी (of Kashmir), गुजरात-गुजराती (of Gujrat), छत्तीसगड़-छत्तीसगड़ी (of Chhattisgadh), बंगाल-बंगाली (of Bengal), बीहार-बिहारी (of Bihar), राजस्थान-राजस्थानी, अफगाणीस्तानी, युनानी, जपानी, चीनी, ईराणी, तैवानी, भूतानी, नेपाली, इराकी, सिंगापुरी, सीलोनी, रेगिस्तानी... (of Rajastan, ...), मद्रास-मद्रासी (of Madras), पंजाब-पंजाबी (of Punjab), सिंध-सिंधी (of Sindh), etc.
3. **वाला** *(vālā)*: आकाश-आकाशवाला (of sky), काश्मिर-काश्मिरवाला (of Kashmir), दिल्ली-दिल्लीवाला (of Dehli), वैकुण्ठ-वैकुण्ठवाला (of Heaven), etc.

(7) Diminutive Taddhit Suffixes (ऊनवाचक तद्धित्-प्रत्यय) :

The suffixes that impart a sense of absenty, some smallness, lowness, beauty or dearness are called the Diminution Taddhit Suffixes (ऊनवाचक तद्धित्-प्रत्यय). Following 10 types of suffixes are attached to the words. Their few examples are as follows:

1. **आ** *(ā)*: पागल-पगला (crazy), बिच्छू-बिछुआ (small scorpion), etc.
2. **इया** *(iyā)*: कुटि-कुटिया (small hut), खाट-खटिया (cot), चाँद-चँदिय (bald), चोटी-चुटिया (pigtail), टिक्की-टिकिया (pastille), डाली-डलिया (basket), पीढ़ी-पिढ़िया (stool), डिब्बा-डिबिया (box), नींद-निंदिया (nap), बाग-बगिया (garden), बेटी-बिटिया (daughter), लोटा-लुटिया (pitcher), etc.
3. **ई** *(ī)*: कड़ा-कड़ी (small ring), कण्ठा-कण्ठी (delicate necklace), थैला-थैली (small bag), दंड-डंडी (stem), ढोलक-ढोलकी (small drum), मच्छ-मच्छी (fish), रोड़ा-रोड़ी (pebble), टोकरा-टोकरी (basket), रस्सा-रस्सी (string), etc.
4. **ओला** *(olā)*: खाट-खटोला (cot), फाँप-फफोला (blister), साँप-सपोला (baby snake), etc.

5. **क** *(ak)*: ढोल-ढोलक (drum), बाल-बालक (child), पत्र-पत्रक (bulletin), हीरा-हीरक (gem), दीप-दीपक (small beautiful lamp), etc.

6. **की** *(kī)*: कण-कनकी (small fragment), चूसन-चुसकी (sip), ढोल-ढोलकी (small drum), etc.

7. **टा** *(ṭā)*: काला-कलूटा (wretched), चपत-चपेटा (slap), चोर-चोट्टा (petty thief), नाक-नकटा (disgraced), मुख-मुखौटा (disguise), रोम-रोंगटा (goose bump), etc.

8. **टी** *(ṭī)*: गोट-गोटी (counter piece), बहू-बहुटी (bride), लकुट-लकुटी (small club), etc.

9. **ड़ा** *(ḍā)*: बाछा-बछाड़ा (calf), टुक-टुकड़ा (piece), दुख-दुखड़ा (pain), पीछा-पिछड़ा (backward), मुख-मुखड़ा (face), भाग-भगोड़ा (fugitive), लोथ-लोथड़ा (lump of flesh), हाथ-हथौड़ा (hammaer), etc.

8. **ड़ी** *(ḍī)*: टाँग-टँगड़ी (leg), टुक-टुकड़ी (fragment), पीछे-पिछाड़ी (hind quarter), बाछा-बछेड़ी (calf), दंड-डंडी (stem), आँत-अंतड़ी (guts), etc.

9. **री** *(rī)*: कोठा-कोठरी (cell), गट्ठा-गठरी (bundle), पट्टा-पटरी (rail), etc.

9. **ली** *(lī)*: टिक्का-टिकली (spangle), पोट-पोटली (packet), हाथ-हथेली (palm), माछ-मछली (small fish), उखल-ओखली (wooden mortar), etc.

10. **वा** *(vā)*: बच्चा-बचवा (kid), मन-मनवा (mind), जिगर-जिगरवा (heart), लड़का-लड़कवा (boy), साजन-सजनवा (darling), etc.

(8) Similitude Taddhit Suffixes (सादृश्यवाचक तद्धित्-प्रत्यय) :

The suffixes that impart a sense of similarity with some other external object are called the Similitude Taddhit Suffixes (सादृश्यवाचक तद्धित्-प्रत्यय) Their few examples are as follows:

1. **सा** *(sā)*: थोड़ा-थोड़ासा (a little bit), जरा-जरासा (a few), सुंदर-सुंदरसा (pretty), सड़ा-सड़ासा (a bit spoiled), पागल-पागलसा (foolish), नीला-नीलासा, लाल-सा, काला-सा, पीला-सा, सफेद-सा, भूरा-सा, हरा-सा, गंदा-सा, ताजा-सा (bluish...), etc.

2. **हरा** *(harā)*: सोना-सुनहरा (golden), एक-इकहरा (single), दस-दशहरा (the 10th day), etc.

(9) Gender Changer Taddhit Suffixes (लिंग परिवर्तक तद्धित्-प्रत्यय) :

The suffixes that change the gender of a Noun, Pronoun or Adjective from Male to

Female or from Female to Male Gender are called the Gender Changer Taddhit Suffixes (लिंग परिवर्तक तद्धित्-प्रत्यय). Their few examples are as follows:

1. **अ** *(a)*: सिंहनी-सिंह (lioness-lion), देवरानी-देवर (sister-in-law - brother-in-law.), बाला-बाल (girl-boy), मादा-नर (female-male), लेखिका-लेखक (poetess-poet), औरतें-पुरुष (women-men), श्रीमती-श्रीमान (Mrs-Mr), सर्पिणी-साँप (snake f◦-m◦), etc.
2. **आ** *(ā)*: लड़की-लड़का (girl-boy), बिटिया-बेटा (daughter-son), बाल-बाला (boy-girl), रानी-राजा (queen-king), etc.
3. **आइन** *(āin)*: गुरु-गुरुआइन (teacher m◦-f◦), पंडित-पंडिताइन (priest), etc.
4. **इन** *(in)*: मालक-मालकिन (master m◦-f◦), तेली-तेलिन (oilman m◦-f◦), etc.
5. **ई** *(e)*: धोबिन-धोबी (washerwoman-washerman), बहन-भाई (sister-brother), दास-दासी बहन-भाई (sister-brother), श्रीमान-श्रीमती (Mr-Mrs), राजा-रानी (king-queen), साधु-साध्वी (saint m◦-f◦), औरतें-आदमी (women-men), etc.
6. **एँ** *(e)*: बाप-माँएँ (fathers-mothers), बैल-गाएँ (oxen-cows), आदमी-औरतें (men-women), भालु-भालुएँ (bears m◦-f◦), etc.
7. **ए** *(e)*: लड़कियाँ-लड़के (girls-boys).
8. **याँ** *(yā̃)*: पुरुष-स्त्रीयाँ (men-women), कुत्ते-कुत्तियाँ (dogs-bitches), etc.

(10) Pluralization Taddhit Suffixes (अनेक वचन सूचक तद्धित्-प्रत्यय) :

The suffixes that change a singular number to plural number of the objects are called the Pluralization Taddhit Suffixes (सादृश्यवाचक तद्धित्-प्रत्यय). Their few examples are as follows:

1. **इयाँ** *(iyā̃)*: लड़की-लड़कियाँ (girl-girls), etc.
2. **एँ** *(ẽ)*: किताब-किताबें (book-books), माला-मालाएँ (necklace-necklaces), माँ-माएँ (mother-mothers), etc.
3. **ए** *(e)*: कुत्ता-कुत्ते (dog-dogs), etc.

(11) Sanskrit Oriented Taddhit Suffixes (संस्कृत रूप तद्धित्-प्रत्यय) :

1. **अ** *(a)*: वसुदेव-वासुदेव (Vasudeva-Shri Krishna), शिव-शैव (Shiva-Shaivaite), etc.

2. **आ** *(ā)*: प्रिय-प्रिया (dear-darling), सुत-सुता (son-daughter), etc.

3. **आनी** *(ānī)*: भव-भवानी (world-Goddess), देवर-देवरानी (brother-in-law sister-in-law), etc.

4. **आयन, आयण** *(āyan, āyaṇ)*: राम-रामायण (Rama-Ramayan), पल-पलायन (run-escape),

5. **आलु** *(ālu)*: कृपा-कृपालु (mercy-merciful), श्रद्धा-श्रद्धालु (faith-faithful), etc.

6. **इत** *(it)*: पुष्प-पुष्पित (flower-flowery), फल-फलित (fruit-successful), etc.

7. **इक** *(ālu)*: दिन-दैनिक (day-daily), विज्ञान-वैज्ञानिक (science-scientific), etc.

8. **इन** *(īn)*: कुल-कुलीन (family-noble), मल-मलीन (dirt-dirty), etc.

9. **इम** *(im)*: अंत-अंतिम (end-last), अग्र-अग्रिम (tip-first), etc.

10. **इमा** *(imā)*: महिमन्-महिमा (great-greatness), गरीयस्-गरिमा (great-greatness), etc.

11. **इष्ठ** *(iṣhṭha)*: बल-बलिष्ट (strength-strong), गरीयस्-गरिष्ठ (big-bigger), etc.

12. **ई** *(ī)*: पक्ष-पक्षी (wing-bird), गुण-गुणी (virtue-virtuous), etc.

13. **क** *(k)*: शत-शतक (hundred-century), वाद्य-वादक (Music instrument-musician), etc.

14. **एय** *(eya)*: कुन्ती-कौन्तेय (Kunti-Arjun), राधा-राधेय (Kunti-Karna), etc.

15. **कार** *(kār)*: पत्र-पत्रकार (journal-journalist), ज्ञान-जानकार (knowledge-knowledgable), etc.

16. **ज** *(ja)*: पंक-पंकज (mud-lotus), देश-देशज (region-regional), etc.

17. **जीवी** *(jīvī)*: दीर्घ-दीर्घजीवी (long-long living), बुद्धि-बुद्धिजीवी (intelligence-intelligent),

18. **ज्ञ** *(gya)*: सर्व-सर्वज्ञ (all-omniscient), अ-अक्ष (nil-ignorant), etc.

19. **तः, तया** *(tah, tayā)*: स्व-स्वतः (own-ownself), मुख्य-मुख्यतः, मुख्यतया (main-mainly), etc.

20. **तन** *(tan)*: अद्य-अद्यतन (today-of today), पुरा-पुरातन (anciently-ancient), etc.

21. **ता** *(tā)*: सुंदर-सुंदरता (beautiful-beauty), गुरु-गुरुता (heavy-weight), etc.

22. **तम** *(tama)*: सुंदर-सुंदरतम (beautiful-most beautiful), गुरु-गुरुतर (heavy-haviest), etc.

23. **तर** *(tar)*: सुंदर-सुंदरतर (beautiful-more beautiful), गुरु-गुरुतर (heavy-havier), etc.

24. **त्य** *(tya)*: पश्चिम-पाश्चात्य (West-Western), पूर्व-पौर्वात्य (East-Eastern), etc.

25. **त्व** *(tva)*: मम-ममत्व (mine-mineness), गुरु-गुरुत्व (heavy-weight), etc.

26. **त्र** *(tra)*: अन्य-अन्यत्र (other-elsewhere), सर्व-सर्वत्र (all-all over), etc.

27. **था** *(thā)*: अन्य-अन्यथा (other-otherwise), सर्व-सर्वथा (all-everywhichway), etc.

28. **दा** *(dā)*: सर्व-सर्वदा (all-ever), एक-एकदा (one-once up on a time), etc.

29. **धा** *(dhā)*: शत-शतधा (hundred-hundred ways), बहु-बहुधा (many-many ways), etc.

30. **निष्ठ** *(nishtha)*: स्वामी-स्वामीनिष्ठ (master-loyal), देश-देशनिष्ठ (country-patriot), etc.

31. **म** *(ma)*: मध्य-मध्यम (middle-medium), नील-नीलम (blue-sapphire), etc.

32. **मय** *(maya)*: जल-जलमय (water-flooded), सुख-सुखमय (happiness-happy), etc.

33. **य** *(ya)*: मधुर-माधुर्य (sweet-sweetness), चतुर-चातुर्य (clever-shrewdness), etc.

34. **र** *(ra)*: मधु-मधुर (honey-sweet), शिखा-शिखर (head-tip), etc.

35. **ल** *(la)*: वत्स-वत्सल (child-tender), एक-एकल (one-lone), etc.

36. **वी** *(vī)*: माया-मायावी (magic-magical), देव-दैवी (God-divine), etc.

37 **सात्** *(sāt)*: भस्म-भस्मसात् (ash-turned to ashes), etc.

(12) Foreign Taddhit Suffixes (विदेशी तद्धित्-प्रत्यय) : (غیر ملکی تادیت لاحقہ)

There are at least 23 suffixes which are imported from foreigh languages such as Arabic, Persian and Urdu. They are called the Videshī Taddhit Suffixes (विदेशी तद्धित्-प्रत्यय). Their few examples are as follows:

1. **आ** *(ā)*: तख़्त-तख़्ता (تختہ-تختا) (seat-bench), etc.

2. **आना** *(ā)*: जुर्म-जुर्माना (جرم-جرمانا) (crime-punishment), etc.

3. **आनी** *(ā)*: जिस्म-जिस्मानी (جسم-جسمانی) (body-bodily), etc.

4. **इश** *(ish)*: फरमान-फरमाइश (فرمان-درخواست) (edict-order), etc.

5. **इयत** *(iyat)*: इंसान-इंसानियत (انسان-انسانیت) (hunam-humanity), etc.

6. **ई** *(ī)*: आसमान-आसमानी (آسمان-آسانی) (sky-sky blue), सफेद-सफेदी (سفیدی-سفید) (whitewashg), खराब-खराबी (خرابی - خراب) (defect) etc.

7. **ईचा** *(īchā)*: बाग-बागीचा (باغ باغیچہ) (garden-plantation), etc.

8. **ईन, ईना** *(īn, īnā)*: कम-कमीन, काम-कमीना (کم کمین) (کام-کمینا) (use-base), etc.

9. **इन्दा** *(indā)*: शर्म-शर्मिन्दा (شرم-شرمندا) (shame-shameful), etc.

10. **कार** *(kār)*: काश्त-काश्तकार (کاشت-کاشتکار) (farm-farmer), etc.

11. **खोर** *(khor)*: हराम-हरामखोर (ہرام-ہرام خور) (dishonesty-dishonest), etc.

12. **गर** *(gar)*: जादू-जादूगर (جادو - جادوگر) (magic-majician), etc.

13. **गार** *(gār)*: मदद-मददगार (مدد - مددگار) (help-helper), etc.

14. **गाह** *(gāha)*: बंदर-बंगरगाह (بندر بندرگاہ) (harbour-naval base), etc.

15. **गी** *(chī)*: गंदा-गंदगी (گند گندگی) (dirty-dirt), etc.

16 **गीर** *(gīr)*: उठाई-उठागीर (اٹھایا اٹھا گیا) (picking-thief), etc.

17. **ची** *(ā)*: बंदूक-बंदूकची (بندوچی بندوق) (gun-artilleryman), etc.

18. **जादा** *(zādā)*: हराम-हरामजादा (حرامزادہ-حرام) (ill - ill-begotten), etc.

19. **दान** *(dān)*: रोशनी-रोशनदान (روشندان-لائٹس) (light-lighter), etc.

20. **दार** *(dār)*: ईमान-ईमानदार (ایماندار-ایمان) (honesty-honest), etc.

21. **नाक** *(nāk)*: दर्द-दर्दनक (دردناک - دردناک) (pain-painful), etc.

22. **बान** *(bān)*: बाग-बागबान (باغبان-باغ) (garden-gardner), etc.

23. **मंद** *(mand)*: ज़रूरत-ज़रूरतमंद (ضرورت مند-ضرورت) (need-needy), etc.

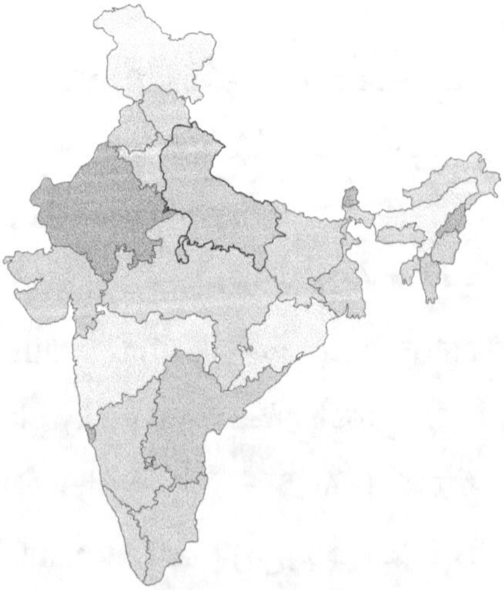

CHAPTER 18
PUNCTUATION
विरामादि विधान

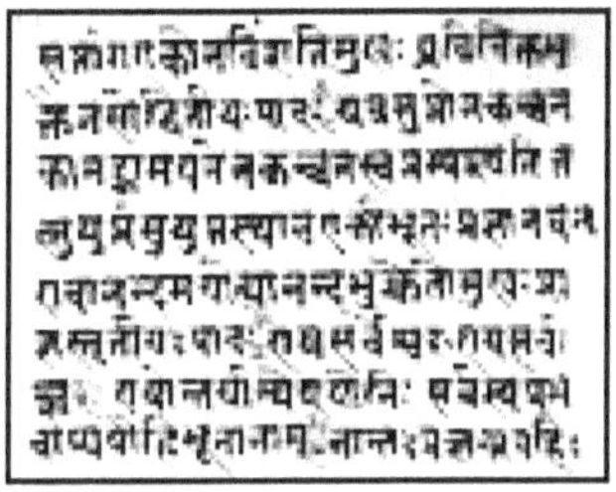

In ancient Devenagari writing wrods of a sentence were written without inserting Punctuation Marks (विरामदि विधान), other than use of Full or Half Stop signs in poetry. At the present times a dozen of Punctuation Marks borrowed from English are utilized in the prose and poetic writings to make them more intelligible and look systematic.

TABLE 51 : Hindi Punctuation Marks (विरामदि विधान)

No.	Punctuation Mark	विरामादि चिह्न	Usage
1	Comma	अल्प विराम चिह्न	Short pause, less than half unit time
2	Semicolon	अर्ध विराम चिह्न	Half pause, half unit time
3	Period mark or Full Stop sign	पूर्ण विराम चिह्न	Full pause, one unit time
4	Dash	निर्देशन चिह्न	Pairing of words
5	Hyphen	संयोजन चिह्न	Pairing of clauses
6	Question mark	प्रश्नार्थक चिह्न	Interrogation sign
7	Exclmation mark	उद्गारवाचक चिह्न	Exclamation sign
8	Parentheses	कोष्ठक चिह्न	Pair of round brackets
9	Caret sign	त्रुटि चिह्न	Insertion editing sign
10	Quotation marks Single	अवतरण चिह्न	Fact quotation sign
11	Quotation marks Double	उद्धरण चिह्न	Direct speech quotation sign
12	Abbreviation mark	लाघव चिह्न	Short form for the understood text.

THE PUNCTUATION MARKS
विरामदि चिह्न

1 Comma (अल्प विराम चिह्न) : ,

When a group of words or clauses are written, each one of them is separated with a Comma (अल्प विराम) sign (,), except the last word or clause is separated by a conjunction such as And (और) or Or (अथवा). If such group ends with etc. (आदि), then there is a Comma between the last word and this etc.

e.g. i. राम, श्याम, सीता, माला और राधा.

ii. राम, श्याम, सीता, माला, राधा, आदि.

iii. 1, 3, 5, 7, 9, etc.

Each Comma equals less than half of the unit time given to a Full Stop.

2 Semicolon (अर्ध विराम चिह्न) : ;

In a sentence if more than one groups of words or clauses come in a row, each word or clause is separated with a Comma Sign (अल्प विराम) and each group of the words or clauses is separated with a Semi Colon Mark (अर्ध विराम).

e.g. आम, केला, अमरूद; आलू, मूली; चावल, बाजरी, गेहूँ, मटर, आदि रसोईघर में हैं.

A Semicolon is a bigger pause than the Comma and smaller than the Full Stop.

3 Period mark or Full Stop sign (पूर्ण विराम चिह्न) : . or |

At the end of a sentence or a sequence of words, a Full Stop sign (पूर्ण विराम) is placed. Full Stop is a pause of one unit of time. In Hindi where it is shown as | , it is called a खड़ी पाई. In Huindi poetry, one खड़ी पाई sign | is placed after each quarter and two signs || are used after four quarters of a stanza.

4 **Dash (निर्देशन चिह्न) : —**

In Grammer, the Dash is similar to the Comma or Semicolon. Dash is used between clauses of the sentence.

e.g. राम–अयोध्या के राजा–आज वनवास को जा रहे हैं.

The Dash (निर्देशन चिह्न) is slightly longer in length than the Hyphen (संयोजन चिह्न)

5 **Hyphen (संयोजन चिह्न) : -**

Hyphen (संयोजन चिह्न) is placed between a pair of words.

e.g.. दिन-रात, सुख-दुख, माता-पिता, तन-मन-धन, etc.

6 **Question mark (प्रश्नार्थक चिह्न) : ?**

The mark is placed at the end of a sentence asking a question.

e.g. राम कहाँ है?

7 Exclmation mark (उद्गारवाचक चिह्न) : **!**

Exclamation mark is placed at the end of an expression such as surprize (आश्चर्य), fear (भय), sorrow (शोक), joy (हर्ष), disgust (जुगुप्सा), address (संबोधन), etc. For putting extra emphasis. two Expression marks are placed.

e.g. जुगुप्सा! महाजुगुप्सा!!

8 Parentheses (कोष्ठक चिह्न) : **( )**

Parentheses marks are placed around the letters or numbers indicating a sequence of the different parts of a paragraph. They are also used for separating a specific word within a sentence.

e.g. (अ) क्रिया के तीन भेद : (1) अकर्मक, (2) सकर्मक और (3) प्रयोजक

(आ) भरत ने (स्वगत) माता से कहा, तुम पापिनी हो!

9 Caret sign (त्रुटि चिह्न) : ^

In order to add a missing word between two words in a sentence while proofreading the printed copy of text, a small Caret (त्रुटि) sign is placec at the bottom of the space between those two words and the edited text is written above that space.

e.g. आपसे मेरा नाता नहीं है. → आपसे मेरा ^कोई नाता नहीं है.

10 Single Quotation marks (अवतरण चिह्न) : ' – '

The Single Quotation marks (अवतरण चिह्न) are placed on both sides of the word or phrase to indicate an Universal truth (त्रिकालाबाधित सत्य), Name of famous book, title, caption or a Specific letter.

e.g. i. 'श्रीमद्भगवद्गीता' हमारा संविधान है.

ii. 'Times of India' लोकप्रिय पत्रिका है.

iii संगत का सप्तक 'सा' से आरंभ और 'नि' से समाप्त होता है.

11 Double Quotation marks (उद्धरण चिह्न) : " – "

The Double Quotation makrs (उद्धरण चिह्न) are placed on both sides of someone's famous saying or a proverb.

e.g. i. "अहिंसा परमो धर्मः।।"

ii. उसने कहा, "अभी देख लो दूध का दूध और पानी का पानी हो जाएगा."

iii. तब राम ने कहा, "हाँ!"

NOTE : While using the Single or Double Quotation marks, make sure the punctuation maks, if any do not come after the closing Quotation maark, rather they must come before placing the closing Quotation mark.

e.g. Incorrect : तुम खून दो, मैं तुम्हें आजादी दूँगा', इस बात को ...

Correct : तुम खून दो, मैं तुम्हें आजादी दूँगा,' इस बात को ...

12 Abbreviation mark (लाघव चिह्न) : ०

For saving time as well as for avoiding repetation of same text or the understood text over and over an Abbreviation mark (लाघव चिह्न) sign os placed after the abbreviated word.

e.g. i. In place of उदाहरणार्थ, only उदा० is considered enough.

ii स० क्रि० सकर्मक क्रियापद, ए० एक वचन, दे० देखिए ...

NOTE: The लाघव mark is not same as the Full Stop period dots used in the Acronyms (परिवणई शब्द) such as, I.I.T (Indian Institute of Technology), बी.जे.पी (भारतीय जनता पार्टी.

CHAPTER 19
CHHAND RATNAKAR
छन्द-रत्नाकर

The earliest of the Hindi Prosody is the chhandaśhāstra of sage Piṅgal. Many works are then written by great authors. My present work is based on the chhandas (meters) given in chhandaśhastra, śhrutabodh, vrittaratnākara, chhandomañjarī, vrittadīpikā, chhandasārasaṅgraha, chhandorṇava, and chhandaprabhakar.

Important things to remember about the chhanda-śhāstra are : (i) chhanda (meter) is also called vritta. (ii) chhanda or vritta is the poetic expression of a thought. (iii) a chhanda could be based on the number of syllables (gaṇa vritta) or the number of short or long vowels, respectively called a short (*laghu*) mātrā or a long (*guru*) mātrā, (mātrā vritta). (iv) The laghu mātrā, that is followed by a compound csyllable, is counted as a guru mātrā. (v) The laghu matra is represented with a symbol of । and the guru mātra with the symbol of ऽ (vi) In gaṇa vritta, based on the laghu and guru syllables in a line of a poetry, each group of three syllables counted as one gaṇa. (vi) there are eight such gaṇas, namely :the । । । न-गण, । । ऽ स-गण, । ऽ । ज-गण, । ऽ ऽ य-गण, ऽ । । भ-गण, ऽ । ऽ र-गण, ऽ ऽ । त-गण, ऽ ऽ ऽ म-गण (I based this arrangement of *gaṇas* on progressive binary counting for logical and easy remembering). The common system is य, र, त, भ, ज, स, म, न (vii) Within a line where a word must end is called a *yati.* (viii) the # sign indicates the line number(s) and the @ sign says for how many lines.

Please Remamber : In the following chhanda chart, (i) Different authors have given different names to the same chhanda string (sūtra सूत्र). e.g. 120. । । । । । । ऽ । ऽ ऽ । ऽ : 12 (7:5) mandākinī मंदाकिनी, chanchalākṣhī चंचलाक्षी, prabhā प्रभा । and (ii) Didderent chhanda sūtras are presented by different authors for the same chhanda name. e.g.

1. । । । । । । । ऽ । ऽ । ऽ । ऽ । ऽ । ऽ । : 19 panchachāmar-1 पंचचामर-1

2. I I I I I IS IS IS IS IS IS IS : 19 pañchachāmara-2 पंचचामर-2

3. IS IS IS IS IS IS IS IS : (8:8, 4:4:4:4)16 pañchachāmar-3 पंचचामर-3

HOW TO READ THE FOLLOWING CHHANDA SUTRAS

Example : S S I S S I S S I S S I S S I S S I S S I S : 22 (4:6:6:6) mandāramālā मन्दारमाला

(i) S S I S S I S S I S S I S S I S S I S S I S shows that there are seven (S S I) त-गण + one guru (S) matrā in this chhanda. (ii) :22 s hows that there are 22 syllables, (iii) (4:6:6:6) shows that in these 22 syllables, there are 4 *yati* breathing pauses, at 4th-6th-6th and 6th syllable. Where the yati pause is not indicated, the yati is at the end of the line. (iv) mandāramālā मन्दारमाला shows that theis chhanda is called Mandāramāla. An example of Mandāramāla chhanda from my *Sangeet-Shri-Krishna-Ramayaṇa* is given below.

THE CHHAND SŪTRAS

Chhandas and Chhanda Sutras (छंद और छंद के सूत्र)

No.	Sūtra	No. of Varṇa	Name/Names of the Chhanda
1.	I I :	2	pushpa, madhu पुष्प, मधु
2.	I I I :	3	drik, kamal दृक्, कमल
3.	I I I I :	4	dayi दयि
4.	I I I I I :	5	yamak यमक
5.	I I I I I I :	6	damanak दमनक
6.	I I I I I I I I I I I I :	12	taralanayanā तरलनयना
7.	I I I I I I I I I I I I I I I I :	16	gītyāryā, achaladhriti गीत्यार्या, अचलधृति
8.	I I I I I I I I I I I I I I I I I I I I I I I I S S :	26 (8:8:10)	vanalatikā वनलतिका
9.	I I I I I I I I I I I I I I I I I I I I I I I I S		alakā अलका :25
10.	I I I I I I I I I I I I I I I I I I I I I I I S		atulapulaka अतुलपुलक :24
11.	I I I I I I I I I I I I I I I I I I I I I I S		amarachamarī अमरचमरी :23
12.	I I I I I I I I I I I I I I I I I I I I I S		achalavirati अचलविरतिः :22

13. | | | | | | | | | | | | | | | | | | | S : 20 kanakalatā कनकलता

14. | | | | | | | | | | | | | | | | | | S dhavala धवल :19

15. | | | | | | | | | | | | | | | | | | tumulaka तुमुलक :18

16. | | | | | | | | | | | | | | | | | achalanayana अचलनयन :17

17. | | | | | | | | | | | | | | | | achaladhriti अचलधृतिः :16

18. | | | | | | | | | | | | | | | S : 16 ch́apaladhriti चपलधृति

19. | | | | | | | | | | | | | | | S S : 17 (5:12) vasudharā वसुधारा

20. | | | | | | | | | | | | | | | śharahati शरहृतिः :15

21. | | | | | | | | | | | | | | S : 15 (4:1:4:6) ruchhirā रुचिरा,

22. | | | | | | | | | | | | | | S : 15 (6:9) srak स्रक्, śharabha शरभ

23. | | | | | | | | | | | | | | S : 15 (7:8) chandravartma चंद्रवर्त्म

24. | | | | | | | | | | | | | | S : 15 (8:7) maṇiguṇakara मणिगुणनिकर

25. | | | | | | | | | | | | | | S S | | S | | S | | S : 25 (8:7:10) haṁsalaya हंसलय

26. | | | | | | | | | | | | | | S S śhiśhubharaṇa शिशुभरण :16

27. | | | | | | | | | | | | | | S śhaśhikalā शशिकला :15

28. | | | | | | | | | | | | | | akahari अकहरि :16

29. | | | | | | | | | | | | | aḍamaru अडमरुः :13

30. | | | | | | | | | | | | S : 13 chapalā चपला, tvaritagati त्वरितगति

31. | | | | | | | | | | | | S | | | | | S | | | | | | | S : 27 (13:6:8) tridalita त्रिपदलित

32. | | | | | | | | | | | | S | | S kalahakara कलहकर : 16

33. | | | | | | | | | | | | S S : 14 (8:6) supavitra सुपवित्र, upachitra उपचित्र

34. | | | | | | | | | | | | S S | | | | S : 19 kanakalatā कनकलता

35. | | | | | | | | | | | | S S S S | S | S S S drutamukha द्रुतमुख :22

36. | | | | | | | | | | | | S S S S kalpāhārī कल्पाहारी :16

37. | | | | | | | | | | | | S haravanitā हरवनिता :13

38. | | | | | | | | | | | | taralanayana तरलनयन :12

39. | | | | | | | | | | | S S : 13 gaurī गौरी

40. | | | | | | | | | | | S kritakatikā कृतकतिका :12

41. I I I I I I I I I I I agarim अगरि :11

42. I I I I I I I I I I I S : 11 damanaka दमनक

43. I I I I I I I I I I I S I I I I I I I I I : 19 chandramālā चंद्रमाला

44. I I I I I I I I I I S I I I S S : 16 kamaladala कमलदल

45. I I I I I I I I I I S S S S S I I I I S I I S S vigāhitageha विगाहितगेह :24

46. I I I I I I I I I I S S S S S S mālyopastha माल्योपस्थ :16

47. I I I I I I I I I I S damanaka दमनक :11

48. I I I I I I I I I I kritakavali कृतकवलि :10

49. I I I I I I I I I S : 10 nilayā निलया

50. I I I I I I I I I S I S I S vitānitā वितानिता :14

51. I I I I I I I I I S S : 11 damanak दमनक

52. I I I I I I I I I S makaramukhī मकरमुखी :10

53. I I I I I I I I I chulaka चुलक :9

54. I I I I I I I I S : 9 laghumaṇiguṇanikara लघुमणिगुणनिकर

55. I I I I I I I I S I I I I S S śharakalpā शरकल्पा :15

56. I I I I I I I S I I S S - I I I I I I S I I I I S S ruchimukhī रुचिमुखी :13-13

57. I I I I I I I S I I S S - S S I I I I I I I I I I S surahitā सुरहिता :13-13

58. I I I I I I I S I I S S : 13 kamalalochanā कमललोचना

59. I I I I I I I S I I S S I I S S I I I I I I I S S rasikarasālā रसिकरसाला :25

60. I I I I I I I S I I S S S : 14 vibhramā विभ्रमा

61. I I I I I I I S I I S S S I I S S : 18 (4:9:5) paṅkajamuktā पंकजमुक्ता

62. I I I I I I I S I I S S chaṇḍī चण्डी :13

63. I I I I I I I S I S I S S anantadāmā अनन्तदामा :14

64. I I I I I I I I S I rita ऋत :10

65. I I I I I I I S S I S S : 13 gaurī गौरी

66. I I I I I I I S S S : 11 vrintā वृंता, vrittangī वृत्तांगी

67. I I I I I I I I S S S I S S S I S I S - I I I I I I S S I S S S I S aparaprīṇitā अपरप्रीणिता :16-13

68. I I I I I I I S S S S I I I I S I S I S I S I S I S S chārugati चारुगतिः :26

69. । । । । । । । । । । ऽ ऽ ऽ ऽ ś́huddhānta शुद्धान्त :12

70. । । । । । । । । । । ऽ ऽ ऽ rathapada रथपद :11

71. । । । । । । । । । । ऽ ऽ tanimā तनिमा :10

72. । । । । । । । । । ऽ madanaka मदनक :9

73. । । । । । । । । kritayu कृतयुः :8x4 = 32

74. । । । । । । । । ऽ : 8 suvikasitakusuma सुविकसितकुसुम

75. । । । । । । । । ऽ । । । ऽ : 12 kamalalochanā कमललोचना

76. । । । । । । । । ऽ । ऽ । ऽ । ऽ । ऽ । ऽ । : 19 panchachāmar-1 पंचचामर-1

77. । । । । । । । । ऽ । ऽ chitibhrita चितिभृत :10

78. । । । । । । । । ऽ ऽ । । । । । viśhambhari विशम्भरि :14

79. । । । । । । । । ऽ ऽ । ऽ gallaka गल्लक :11

80. । । । । । । । । ऽ ऽ ऽ ऽ ऽ vasanaviśhālā वसनविशाला :12

81. । । । । । । । ऽ haripada हरिपद :8

82. । । । । । । । achaṭu अचटु :7

83. । । । । । । ऽ : 7 madhumati मधुमति

84. । । । । । । ऽ । । । । । । ऽ : 14 (7:7) praharaṇakalikā प्रहरणकलिका

85. । । । । । । ऽ । । । । । । ऽ । । । । । । । । । । ऽ । : 26 kamalā कमला

86. । । । । । । ऽ । । । । । । ऽ । । । । । । । । ऽ ऽ : 24 (7:7:10) lalitalatā ललितलता

87. । । । । । । ऽ । । । । ऽ ऽ - । । । । । । । । । ऽ । । ऽ ऽ vimukhī विमुखी :13-13

88. । । । । । । ऽ । । । । ऽ ऽ । ऽ । ऽ : 17 (7:6:4) ghanamayūra घनमयूर

89. । । । । । । ऽ । । । । ऽ ऽ vidhuravitāna विधुरवितान :13

90. । । । । । । ऽ । । । ऽ dāmaghaṭitā दामघटिता :11

91. । । । । । । ऽ । । ऽ । । ऽ । ऽ : 15 gau गौ

92. । । । । । । ऽ । । ऽ । ऽ : 12 ujjavalā उज्ज्वला, chalanetrikā चलनेत्रिका

93. । । । । । । ऽ । । ऽ ऽ । । ऽ । । ऽ ऽ । । ऽ ऽ ऽ paridhānīya परिधानीय :23

94. । । । । । । ऽ । । ऽ ऽ ऽ dhavalakarī धवलकरी :12

95. । । । । । । ऽ । । ऽ phaladhara फलधर :10

96. । । । । । । ऽ । ऽ : 9 upachyuta उपच्युत

97. । । । । । । ऽ । ऽ । । । ऽ । । । ऽ । ऽ nirgalitamekhalā निर्गलितमेखला :19

98. । । । । । । ऽ । ऽ । । । ऽ । ऽ ऽ । ऽ parviṇī पर्विणी :18

99. । । । । । । ऽ । ऽ । । । ऽ । ऽ ऽ ऽ vīravis̒hrāma वीरविश्रामः :17

100. । । । । । । ऽ । ऽ । । । ऽ । ऽ chamarīchara चमरीचर :15

101. । । । । । । ऽ । ऽ । । ऽ । ऽ : 14 (7:7) aparājitā अपराजिता

102. । । । । । । ऽ । ऽ । ऽ - । । । । ऽ । । ऽ । ऽ । ऽ aparipakva अपरवक्त्र, s̒his̒hikhā शिशिरशिखा :11-12

103. । । । । । । ऽ । ऽ । ऽ - ऽ ऽ ऽ । । ऽ । ऽ । ऽ vaiyālī वैयाली :11-10

104. । । । । । । ऽ । ऽ । ऽ : 11 subhadrikā सुभद्रिका, aparavaktra अपरवक्त्र

105. । । । । । । ऽ । ऽ । ऽ । ऽ । ऽ । ऽ । ऽ : 19 pañchachāmara-2 पंचचामर-2

106. । । । । । । ऽ । ऽ । ऽ । ऽ । ऽ । ऽ । ऽ prapañchachāmara प्रपञ्चचामर :19

107. । । । । । । ऽ । ऽ । ऽ । ऽ ऽ - । । । । ऽ । । ऽ । ऽ । । । ऽ ऽ pramodapariṇītā प्रमोदपरिणीता :14-15

108. । । । । । । ऽ । ऽ । ऽ । ऽ as̒hokapuṣhpa अशोकपुष्प :13

109. । । । । । । ऽ । ऽ । ऽ ऽ - । । । । ऽ । । ऽ । ऽ । ऽ ऽ puṣhpitāgrā पुष्पिताग्रा :12-13

110. । । । । । । ऽ । ऽ । ऽ ऽ - । । ऽ ऽ । । । । । । ऽ । ऽ । ऽ s̒harāvatī शरावती :12-15

111. । । । । । । ऽ । ऽ । ऽ ऽ - ऽ ऽ ऽ । । ऽ । ऽ । ऽ ऽ surāḍhyā सुराढ्या :12-11

112. । । । । । । ऽ । ऽ । ऽ ऽ : 12 (5:7) kāmadattā कामदत्ता

113. । । । । । । ऽ । ऽ । ऽ ऽ । ऽ ऽ : 15 bhoginī भोगिनी

114. । । । । । । ऽ । ऽ । ऽ ऽ ऽ : 13 chandrikā चंद्रिका

115. । । । । । । ऽ । ऽ । ऽ ऽ parimitavijayā परिमितविजया :12

116. । । । । । । ऽ । ऽ । ऽ subhadrikā सुभद्रिका :11

117. । । । । । । ऽ । ऽ ऽ । । ऽ । ऽ । । ऽ : 18 (10:8) gajendralatā गजेंद्रलता, latā लता

118. । । । । । । ऽ । ऽ ऽ । ऽ : 12 (7:5) mandākinī मंदाकिनी, chanchalākṣhī चंचलाक्षी, prabhā प्रभा

119. । । । । । । ऽ । ऽ ऽ । ऽ ऽ । ऽ ऽ । ऽ : 18 (10:8) nārācha नाराच, nis̒hā निशा, varadā वरदा

120. । । । । । । ऽ । ऽ ऽ । ऽ ऽ । ऽ ऽ । ऽ : 18 (13:5) tārakā तारका, priyā प्रिया

121. । । । । । । ऽ । ऽ ऽ । ऽ ऽ । ऽ ऽ । ऽ ऽ । ऽ ऽ । ऽ : 24 meghalatā मेघमाला

122. । । । । । । ऽ । ऽ ऽ । ऽ ऽ । ऽ ऽ । ऽ ऽ । ऽ ऽ । ऽ ऽ । kumbhaka कुम्भक :26

123. । । । । । । ऽ । ऽ ऽ । ऽ ऽ । ऽ ऽ । ऽ nārācha **नाराच** :18

124. । । । । । । ऽ । ऽ ऽ । ऽ ऽ pramoda **प्रमोदः** :13

125. । । । । । । ऽ । ऽ ऽ । ऽ prabhā **प्रभा** :12

126. । । । । । । ऽ । ऽ ऽ ऽ : 11 kupuruṣhajanitā कुपुरुषजनिता

127. । । । । । । । ऽ ऽ : 8 ratimālā रतिमाला, tuṅga तुंग

128. । । । । । । । ऽ ऽ । । । । । aśhani **अशनिः** :13

129. । । । । । । ऽ ऽ । । । ऽ ऽ : 13 gaurī गौरी

130. । । । । । । ऽ ऽ । । ऽ । ऽ ऽ : 14 (7:7) nadī नदी

131. । । । । । । ऽ ऽ । । ऽ ऽ vijayaparichayā **विजयपरिचया** :12

132. । । । । । । ऽ ऽ । । ऽ madanayā **मदनया** :11

133. । । । । । । ऽ ऽ । ऽ । । ऽ । ऽ : 15 upamālinī उपमालिनी

134. । । । । । । ऽ ऽ । ऽ । ऽ ऽ : 13 (4:9) kṣhamā क्षमा

135. । । । । । । ऽ ऽ । ऽ ऽ । ऽ - । । । । । । । । । ऽ ऽ ऽ । ऽ ऽ । ऽ paraprīṇitā परप्रीणिता :13-16

136. । । । । । । ऽ ऽ । ऽ ऽ । ऽ : 13 (7:6) gati गति, chandrikā चंद्रिका, vidyut विद्युत्

137. । । । । । । ऽ ऽ । ऽ ऽ । ऽ ऽ : 14 vasanta वसंत, nāndīmukhī नांदीमुखी

138. । । । । । । ऽ ऽ । ऽ ऽ । ऽ chandrikā **चन्द्रिका** :13

139. । । । । । । ऽ ऽ । ऽ ऽ । vikalavakulavallī **विकलवकुलवल्ली** :12

140. । । । । । । ऽ ऽ । ऽ ऽ parimalalalita **परिमलललित** :11

141. । । । । । । । ऽ ऽ । masriṇa **मसृण** :9

142. । । । । । । ऽ ऽ ऽ : 9 madhukarikā मधुकरिका, bhujagaśhiśhubhritā भुजगशिशुभृता

143. । । । । । । ऽ ऽ ऽ । । । । । । । ऽ ऽ ऽ vilulitavanamālā **विलुलितवनमाला** :18

144. । । । । । । ऽ ऽ ऽ । । । । । । । ऽ ऽ salekhā **सलेखा** :17

145. । । । । । । ऽ ऽ ऽ । ऽ ऽ : 12 (8:4) puṭa पुट

146. । । । । । । ऽ ऽ ऽ । ऽ ऽ । । । । । । ऽ ऽ ऽ । ऽ ऽ । ऽ kuhakakuhara **कुहककुहर** :26

147. । । । । । । ऽ ऽ ऽ । ऽ ऽ । ऽ : 14 (7:7) karimakarabhujā करिमकरभुजा

148. । । । । । । ऽ ऽ ऽ । ऽ ऽ । ऽ ऽ : 15 (8:7) mālinī मालिनी

149. । । । । । । ऽ ऽ ऽ । ऽ ऽ । ऽ ऽ । ऽ ऽ nīlaśhārdūla **नीलशार्दूल** :18

150. । । । । । । ऽ ऽ ऽ । ऽ ऽ । ऽ ऽ mālinī **मालिनी** :15

151. । । । । । । ऽ ऽ ऽ । ऽ ऽ । ऽ kāmalā कामला :14

152. । । । । । । ऽ ऽ ऽ । ऽ ऽ puṭa पुटः :12

153. । । । । । । ऽ ऽ ऽ ऽ । ऽ : 12 tata तत, lalita ललित

154. । । । । । । ऽ ऽ ऽ ऽ । ऽ । । ऽ । ऽ : 17 (6:4:7) hari हरि

155. । । । । । । ऽ ऽ ऽ ऽ । ऽ ऽ : 13 (7:6) kṣhamā क्षमा

156. । । । । । । ऽ ऽ ऽ ऽ । ऽ ऽ । ऽ : 15 chandrajyota चंद्रोद्योत

157. । । । । । । ऽ ऽ ऽ ऽ । ऽ ऽ । ऽ ऽ vakrāvaloka वक्रावलोकः :16

158. । । । । । । ऽ ऽ ऽ ऽ । ऽ lalita ललित :12

159. । । । । । । ऽ ऽ ऽ ऽ ऽ । ऽ । । ऽ । ऽ : 18 (7:4:7) lalita ललित

160. । । । । । । ऽ ऽ ऽ ऽ ऽ ऽ । ऽ । । ऽ । । ऽ । । । । ऽ vis'heṣhakabalita विशेषकबलित :25

161. । । । । । । ऽ ऽ ऽ ऽ ऽ ऽ । ऽ । ऽ । ऽ ऽ ऽ ऽ mandākṣhamandara मन्दाक्षमन्दर :21

162. । । । । । । ऽ ऽ ऽ ऽ ऽ ऽ । ऽ ऽ । ऽ ऽ : 18 (7:4:7) chandramālā चंद्रमाला

163. । । । । । । ऽ ऽ ऽ ऽ ऽ ऽ mithunamālī मिथुनमाली :12

164. । । । । । । ऽ ऽ ऽ ऽ ऽ kalitakamalavilāsa कलितकमलविलासः :11

165. । । । । । । ऽ ऽ ऽ bhujagas'his'hubhritā भुजगशिशुभृता :9

166. । । । । । । ऽ ऽ tuṅgā तुङ्गा :8

167. । । । । । । ऽ madhumatī मधुमती :7

168. । । । । । । upavali उपवलि :6

169. । । । । । ऽ । : 7 karahañchī करहंची

170. । । । । । ऽ । । । । । ऽ udayanamukhī उदयनमुखी :12

171. । । । । । ऽ । । । ऽ । ऽ ऽ । ऽ vipinatilaka विपिनतिलक :15

172. । । । । । ऽ । । । ऽ ऽ : 11 as'hokā अशोका, gatavos'hokā गतविशोका

173. । । । । । ऽ । । । ऽ । ऽ ऽ । । : 15 vipinatilak विपिनतिलक

174. । । । । । ऽ । ऽ । ऽ । । ऽ । ऽ taravārikā तरवारिका :16

175. । । । । । ऽ । । ऽ । ऽ । । ऽ । mitasakthi मितसक्थि :15

176. । । । । । ऽ । । ऽ । ऽ sammadamālikā सम्मदमालिका :11

177. । । । । । ऽ । ऽ : 8 mahī मही, kamala कमल

178. । । । । । ऽ । ऽ । । । ऽ । ऽ ऽ । ऽ mālādhara मालाधरः :17

179. । । । । । ऽ । ऽ । । ऽ । ऽ : 13 laya लय

180. । । । । । ऽ । ऽ । । ऽ । ऽ upagatas'hikhā उपगतशिखा :13

181. । । । । । ऽ । ऽ । ऽ । । । ऽ । ऽ ऽ s'hāyinī शायिनी :17

182. । । । । । ऽ । ऽ । ऽ । ऽ prasrimaramarālikā प्रसृमरमरालिका :12

183. । । । । । ऽ । ऽ । ऽ ऽ - ऽ । । ऽ । । ऽ । ऽ । ऽ ऽ upāḍhya उपाढ्य :11-12

184. । । । । । ऽ । ऽ । ऽ ऽ । ऽ kaṭhinī कठिनी :13

185. । । । । । ऽ । ऽ । ऽ ऽ pañchas'hākhī पञ्चशाखी :11

186. । । । । । ऽ । ऽ । ऽ anuchāyitā अनुचायिता :10

187. । । । । । ऽ । ऽ ऽ : 9 bimba बिंब, vis'halā विशाला, s'halabhavichalitā शलभविचलिता

188. । । । । । ऽ । ऽ ऽ । ऽ ऽ । ऽ jaladarasitā जलदरसिता :14

189. । । । । । ऽ । ऽ ऽ । ऽ ऽ ऽ ऽ lalitapatākā ललितपताका :14

190. । । । । । ऽ । ऽ ऽ । ऽ ऽ mihirā मिहिरा :12

191. । । । । । ऽ । ऽ ऽ । ऽ prasrimarakarā प्रसृमरकरा :11

192. । । । । । ऽ । ऽ ऽ bimba बिम्ब :9

193. । । । । । ऽ । ऽ lasadasu लसदसु :8

194. । । । । । ऽ । ahari अहरि :7

195. । । । । । ऽ ऽ । । । । । ऽ ऽ । । ऽ । ऽ ऽ । । । ऽ । ऽ ऽ : 27 (7:7:13) tribhangī त्रिभंगी

196. । । । । । ऽ ऽ । । । ऽ niravadhigati निरवधिगतिः :11

197. । । । । । ऽ ऽ । ऽ ऽ । ऽ ऽ : 13 (6:7) chandralekhā चंद्रलेखा

198. । । । । । ऽ ऽ । harit हरित :8

199. । । । । । ऽ ऽ ऽ : 8 guṇalayanī गुणलयनी

200. । । । । । ऽ ऽ ऽ । । ऽ bhujalatā भुजलता :11

201. । । । । । ऽ ऽ ऽ । । visraṁsi विस्रंसि :10

202. । । । । । ऽ ऽ ऽ । ऽ । । ऽ vidalā विदला :13

203. । । । । । ऽ ऽ ऽ । ऽ ऽ । ऽ : 13 (6:7) vidyut विद्युत्

204. । । । । । ऽ ऽ ऽ । ऽ ऽ । ऽ : 13 vidyunmālā विद्युन्मालिका

205. । । । । । ऽ ऽ ऽ ऽ ऽ । ऽ । । ऽ । ऽ : 17 (6:4:7) hariṇī हरिणी, vriṣhabhacharita वृषभचरित

206. । । । । । ऽ ऽ ऽ ऽ ऽ ऽ । ऽ । । ऽ । ऽ : 18 (6:4:8) hariṇīpada हरिणीपद

207. । । । । । ऽ ऽ ऽ ऽ ऽ ऽ । ऽ ऽ । ऽ ऽ : 17 (6:4:7) padma पद्म

208. । । । । । ऽ ऽ ऽ ऽ ऽ ऽ ऽ । ऽ ऽ । ऽ : 17 (6:4:7) rohiṇī रोहिणी

209. । । । । । ऽ ऽ ऽ ऽ ऽ ऽ ऽ । ऽ ऽ । ऽ ऽ : 18 (6:5:7) anaṅgalekhā अनंगलेखा

210. । । । । । ऽ ऽ ऽ ऽ ऽ ऽ ऽ viṣhamavyālī विषमव्याली :12

211. । । । । । ऽ ऽ ऽ rudrālī रुद्राली :8

212. । । । । । ऽ ऽ driti दृतिः :7

213. । । । । । ऽ sari सरि :6

214. । । । । । hali हलि :5

215. । । । । ऽ । । : 7 suvāsa सुवास

216. । । । । ऽ । । । । । । ऽ ऽ : 13 madakalitā मदकलिता

217. । । । । ऽ । । । । । । ऽ ऽ । । । । । । । । । । । । ऽ : 26 vegavatī वेगवती

218. । । । । ऽ । । । । ऽ : 10 (5:5) amritagati अमृतगति

219. । । । । ऽ । । । । ऽ । । । । ऽ । । । । ऽ : 20 madakalanī मदकलनी

220. । । । । ऽ । । । । ऽ amritagati अमृतगतिः :10

221. । । । । ऽ । । । ऽ । ऽ । ऽ : 13 mañjubhāṣhiṇī मंजुभाषिणी

222. । । । । ऽ । । । ऽ । ऽ vīvadha वीवधः :11

223. । । । । ऽ । । ऽ : 8 lalitagati ललितगति

224. । । । । ऽ । । ऽ । । ऽ : 11 (5:6) sumukhī सुमुखी, drutapādagati द्रुतपादगति

225. । । । । ऽ । । ऽ । । ऽ । । ऽ । । ऽ । । ऽ । । ऽ : 23 sudhālaharī सुधालहरी, haṁsagati हंसगति

226. । । । । ऽ । । ऽ । । ऽ । । ऽ । । ऽ । । ऽ । । ऽ ऽ samāhita समाहित :24

227. । । । । ऽ । । ऽ । । ऽ । । ऽ । । ऽ । । ऽ । । ऽ ś́hravaṇābharaṇa श्रवणाभरण :23

228. । । । । ऽ । । ऽ । । ऽ । । ऽ । ऽ । । ऽ । ऽ : 21 vanamañjarī वनमंजरी

229. । । । । ऽ । । ऽ । । ऽ ऽ - ऽ । । ऽ । । ऽ । । ऽ ऽ īhā ईहा :12-11

230. । । । । ऽ । । ऽ । । ऽ ऽ : 12 (8:4) tāmarasa तामरस, kamalavilāsinī कमलविलासिनी

231. । । । । ऽ । । ऽ । । ऽ ऽ । । । । । । । । । । । । ऽ : 25 chapala चपल

232. । । । । ऽ । । ऽ । । ऽ ऽ । । । । ऽ : 17 ruchiramukhī रुचिरमुखी

233. । । । । ऽ । । ऽ । । ऽ ऽ tāmarasa तामरस :12

234. । । । । ऽ । । ऽ । । ऽ sumukhī सुमुखी :11

235. । । । । ऽ । । ऽ । ऽ । । । ऽ ऽ pramodapada **प्रमोदपद** :14-15

236. । । । । ऽ । । ऽ । ऽ । । ऽ । ऽ : 15 aravindaka अरविंदक, kalabhāṣhiṇī कलभाषिणी

237. । । । । ऽ । । ऽ । ऽ । । ऽ । heti **हेतिः** :14

238. । । । । ऽ । । ऽ । ऽ । ऽ - । । । । । । ऽ । ऽ । ऽ mridulamālati **मृदुमालती**, paravaktra **परवक्त्र** :12-11

239. । । । । ऽ । । ऽ । ऽ । ऽ - । । ऽ । । ऽ । ऽ । ऽ anūpaka **अनूपक** :12-10

240. । । । । ऽ । । ऽ । ऽ । ऽ : 12 (6:6) (5:7) mālatī मालती, tati तति, yamunā यमुना

241. । । । । ऽ । । ऽ । ऽ । ऽ ऽ - । । । । । । ऽ । ऽ । ऽ ऽ añchitāgrā **अञ्चिताग्रा** :13-12

242. । । । । ऽ । । ऽ । ऽ । ऽ ऽ - । । ऽ ऽ । । ऽ । ऽ । ऽ ऽ pramāthinī **प्रमाथिनी** :13-12

243. । । । । ऽ । । ऽ । ऽ । ऽ ऽ : 13 achala अचल, suvaktrā सुवक्त्रा, mrigendramukha मृगेंद्रमुख

244. । । । । ऽ । । ऽ । ऽ । ऽ mālatī **मालती** :12

245. । । । । ऽ । । ऽ ऽ : 9 s̍has̍hilekhā शशिलेखा

246. । । । । ऽ । । ऽ ऽ ऽ : 10 vipulabhujā विपुलभुजा

247. । । । । ऽ । । ऽ ऽ ऽ ऽ vārttāhārī **वार्त्ताहारी** :11

248. । । । । ऽ । । ऽ ऽ s̍haralīḍhā **शरलीडा** :9

249. । । । । ऽ । । ऽ akhani **अखनिः** :8

250. । । । । ऽ । । vāsaki **वासकि** :7

251. । । । । ऽ । ऽ । । । ऽ । । । ऽ । ऽ । । । । । ऽ : 23 (11:12) as̍hvalalita अश्वललित

252. । । । । ऽ । ऽ । । । ऽ । । ऽ : 14 dhriti धृति, pramadā प्रमदा, maṇikaṇṭak मणिकंटक

253. । । । । ऽ । ऽ । । । ऽ । । ऽ । । ऽ : 17 (7:10) nardaṭaka नर्दटक, kokilaka कोकिलक

254. । । । । ऽ । ऽ । । । ऽ । । ऽ । । ऽ । ऽ । । । ऽ । । ऽ : 26 (14:12) sudhākalas̍ha सुधाकलश

255. । । । । ऽ । ऽ । । । ऽ । । ऽ । । ऽ । ऽ । ऽ : 21 (11:10) pañchakāvalī पंचकावली, siddhi सिद्धि

256. । । । । ऽ । ऽ । । । ऽ । । ऽ । ऽ - ऽ ऽ । । ऽ । ऽ । । । ऽ । । ऽ । ऽ vāsavavāsinī **वासववासिनी**:16-16

257. । । । । ऽ । ऽ । । । ऽ । । ऽ । ऽ । ऽ vasupadamañjarī **वसुपदमञ्जरी** :18

258. । । । । ऽ । ऽ । । । ऽ । । ऽ । ऽ ऽ : 17 (7:10) nakurṭak नर्कुटक

259. । । । । ऽ । ऽ । । । ऽ । । ऽ kurarīrutā कुररीरुता :14

260. । । । । ऽ । ऽ । । । ऽ । ऽ । । । ऽ : 17 (12:5) samadavilāsinī समदविलासिनी

261. । । । । ऽ । ऽ । । । ऽ । ऽ । । । ऽ । । ऽ । । ऽ : 23 (11:12) adritanayā अद्रितनया

262. । । । । ऽ । ऽ । । । ऽ । ऽ । । । ऽ । ऽ । । ऽ : 22 aśhvalalita अश्वललित

263. । । । । ऽ । ऽ । । । ऽ । ऽ । ऽ : 15 sulekhaka सुलेखक, sukesara सुकेसर, prabhadraka प्रभद्रक

264. । । । । ऽ । ऽ । । । ऽ । ऽ । ऽ ऽ : 16 (7:9) vāṇinī वाणिनी

265. । । । । ऽ । ऽ । । । ऽ । ऽ । ऽ ऽ । ऽ nandana नन्दन :18

266. । । । । ऽ । ऽ । । । ऽ । ऽ । ऽ prabhadraka प्रभद्रक :15

267. । । । । ऽ । ऽ । । । ऽ । ऽ ऽ : 14 (8:6) kumārī कुमारी

268. । । । । ऽ । ऽ । । । ऽ । ऽ ऽ । ऽ : 16 garuḍaruta गरुडरुत

269. । । । । ऽ । ऽ । । । ऽ ऽ : 12 (8:4) (7:5) vanamālinī वनमालिनी, vanamālikā नवमालिका

270. । । । । ऽ । ऽ । । । ऽ ऽ । । ऽ । ऽ । ऽ : 19 (11:8) (7:12) rachanā रचना

271. । । । । ऽ । ऽ । । । ऽ ऽ nayamālinī नयमालिनी :12

272. । । । । ऽ । ऽ । ऽ : 9 budbud बुद्बुद्

273. । । । । ऽ । ऽ । ऽ । । ऽ । । । । ऽ । ऽ । ऽ । । । । ऽ virāmavāṭikā विरामवाटिका :26

274. । । । । ऽ । ऽ । ऽ । ऽ ऽ balorjitā बलोर्जिता :12

275. । । । । ऽ । ऽ । ऽ ऽ । । ऽ । । ऽ : 16 chintāmaṇi चिंतामणि, मणिकल्पिता, त्रोटक

276. । । । । ऽ । ऽ । ऽ ऽ । ऽ viśhikhalatā विशिखलता :12

277. । । । । ऽ । ऽ । ऽ halodgatā हलोद्गता :9

278. । । । । ऽ । ऽ ऽ : 8 chttavilasita चित्तविलासित

279. । । । । ऽ । ऽ ऽ । ऽ ऽ । ऽ : 13 (7:6) kuṭajagati कुटजगति

280. । । । । ऽ । ऽ ऽ । ऽ ऽ । ऽ ऽ । ऽ ऽ । । । ऽ lalitalalāma ललितललाम :21

281. । । । । ऽ । ऽ ऽ । ऽ ऽ । ऽ kirāta किरातः :13

282. । । । । ऽ । ऽ ऽ ऽ ऽ ऽ vilulitamañjarī विलुलितमञ्जरी :11

283. । । । । ऽ । ऽ puraṭi पुरटि :7

284. । । । । ऽ । puṭamardi पुटमर्दि :6

285. । । । । ऽ ऽ : 6 mukulitā मुकुलिता

286. । । । । ऽ ऽ । । । । । । ऽ madanajavanikā मदनजवनिका :13

287. । । । । ऽ ऽ । । । । । kelichara केलिचर :11

288. । । । । ऽ ऽ । । । । ऽ : 11 kamaladalākṣhī कमलदलाक्षी

289. । । । । ऽ ऽ । । । । ऽ । । ऽ ऽ parimala परिमल :15

290. । । । । ऽ ऽ । । । । ऽ ऽ - ऽ । । ऽ । । ऽ । । ऽ ऽ pāṭalikā पाटलिका :12-11

291. । । । । ऽ ऽ । । । । ऽ ऽ : 12 kusumavichitrā कुसुमविचित्रा, gajalalitā गजललित

292. । । । । ऽ ऽ । । । । ऽ ऽ । । । । । । । । । । । । । ऽ ऽ : 25 makaranda मकरंद

293. । । । । ऽ ऽ । । । । ऽ ऽ । । । । ऽ ऽ । । । । ऽ ऽ ऽ ऽ vinayavilāsa विनयविलासः :26

294. । । । । ऽ ऽ । । । । ऽ ऽ । । ऽ ऽ : 16 (12:4) kānta कांत

295. । । । । ऽ ऽ । । । । ऽ ऽ ऽ । । ऽ kamalapara कमलपर :16

296. । । । । ऽ ऽ । । । । ऽ ऽ ऽ rasadhārā रसधारा :13

297. । । । । ऽ ऽ । । । । ऽ ऽ kusumavichitrā कुसुमविचित्रा :12

298. । । । । ऽ ऽ । । । । ऽ samit समित :11

299. । । । । ऽ ऽ । । । sphuṭaghaṭitā स्फुटघटिता :9

300. । । । । ऽ ऽ । । ऽ : 9 sāraṅgikā सारंगिका

301. । । । । ऽ ऽ । । ऽ । ऽ saurabhavarddhinī सौरभवर्द्धिनी :11

302. । । । । ऽ ऽ । । ऽ ऽ ऽ : 11 māṇikyamālā माणिक्यमाला, patitā पतिता, anavasitā अनवसिता

303. । । । । ऽ ऽ । । ऽ ऽ ऽ ऽ । । ऽ jananidhivelā जननिधिवेला :15

304. । । । । ऽ ऽ । । ऽ ऽ naragā नरगा :10

305. । । । । ऽ ऽ । । ऽ mukhalā मुखला :9

306. । । । । ऽ ऽ । ऽ । ऽ । ऽ ऽ - । । ऽ ऽ । । ऽ । ऽ । । । ऽ ऽ prativinītā प्रतिविनीता :13-14

307. । । । । ऽ ऽ । ऽ । līlā लीला :9

308. । । । । ऽ ऽ । ऽ ऽ ऽ ऽ vikasitapadmāvalī विकसितपद्मावली :11

309. । । । । ऽ ऽ । ऽ ऽ ऽ surākṣhī सुराक्षी :10

310. । । । । ऽ ऽ । anu अनु :7

311. । । । । ऽ ऽ ऽ : 7 kusumavatī कुसुमवती

312. । । । । ऽ ऽ ऽ । । ऽ ऽ - ऽ ऽ । । । । ऽ । । । । ऽ sāchīkritavadanā साचीकृतवदना

:11-12

313. I I I I S S S I I S S I I I I I I I I I I I I I I S : 24 saṁbhrāntā संभ्रांता

314. I I I I S S S I I S S ś́hrutakīrtti श्रुतकीर्त्तिः :11

315. I I I I S S S I I S phalinī फलिनी :10

316. I I I I S S S I I vikachavatī विकचवती : 9

317. I I I I S S S I S I S S : 12 (6:6) kumudanibhā कुमुदनिभा

318. I I I I S S S S I I I I S S S S I karṇasphoṭa कर्णस्फोट :17

319. I I I I S S S S I I S S S vibhā विभा :13

320. I I I I S S S S I I S S vidrumadolā विद्रुमदोला :12

321. I I I I S S S S I I khaurali खौरलि :40

322. I I I I S S S S I S I S S S anindagurvindu अनिन्दगुर्विन्दुः :14

323. I I I I S S S S S S I I I I S I I S I I S kamalaśhikhā कमलशिखा :21

324. I I I I S S S S S S I I I I S S valivadana वलिवदन :16

325. I I I I S S S S S S S S I S I S S S S jhillīlīlā झिल्लीलीला :19

326. I I I I S S S S S S S S S S S sphoṭakriīḍa स्फोटकृईड :15

327. I I I I S S S S S māyāsārī मायासारी :9

328. I I I I S S S S pāñchālaṅghri पाञ्चालाङ्घ्रिः :8

329. I I I I S S S suri सुरि :7

330. I I I I S S śhaśhivadanā शशिवदना :6

331. I I I I S sulū सुलूः :5

332. I I I I paṭu पटु :4

333. I I I S : 4 satī सती, mrigavadhu मृगवधु

334. I I I S I I I I I I I S S : 12 dritapada दृतपद

335. I I I S I I I I I S S I S S : 14 (4:6:4) śharabhā शरभा

336. I I I S I I I I I S S I S S : 14 śharabhalalitā शरभललिता

337. I I I S I I I I S I S I S - I I I S I I I S I I S I S aniraya अनिरया :13-13

338. I I I S I I I I S I S I S S vilambanīyā विलम्बनीया :14

339. I I I S I I I I S I S I S virodhinī विरोधिनी :13

340. I I I S I I I S : 8 gajagati गजगति

341. I I I S I I I S I I I S I I I S : 16 (4:4:4:4) sulalitā सुललिता, naraśhikhī नरशिखी

342. I I I S I I I S I I S I I S I S : 16 (4:12) maṅgalamaṅganā मंगलमंगना

343. I I I S I I I S I I S I I S vipākavatī विपाकवती :14

344. I I I S I I I S I I S I S - I I I S I I I I I S I S I S śhiśhumukhī शिशुमुखी :13-13

345. I I I S I I I S I I S I S sārasanāvali सारसनावलिः :13

346. I I I S I I I S I I S S : 12 kalahaṁsā कलहंसा, drutapada द्रुतपद :12

347. I I I S I I I S I S I I I S I S I I I S I S : 22 madanasāyaka मदनसायक

348. I I I S I I I S I S I I I S I S I I I S I S I S : 24 mahāmadanasāyaka महामदनसायक

349. I I I S I I I S I S I S : 12 priyamvadā प्रियंवदा, mattakokila मत्तकोकिल

350. I I I S I I I S I S I S I S S - I I S S I I S I S I S I I I S S āsavavāsitā
आसववासिता:15-16

351. I I I S I I I S I S I S kilikitā किलिकिता :12, priyamvada प्रियंवदः

352. I I I S I I I S I S I kālavarma कालवर्म :11

353. I I I S I I I S I S vaḍiśhabhedinī वडिशभेदिनी :10

354. I I I S I I I S S I S S I S - I I I S S I S S I S S I S anālepana अनालेपन :14-13

355. I I I S I I I S gajagati गजगतिः :8

356. I I I S I I I vīravaṭu वीरवटु :7

357. I I I S I I S : 7 madhumati मधुमति

358. I I I S I I S I I S I S - I I S I I S I I S I S hariṇīplutā हरिणीप्लुता :12-11

359. I I I S I I S I I S I S : 12 hariṇaluptā हरिणलुप्ता

360. I I I S I I S I I S I S : 12 drutavilambita द्रुतविलंबित

361. I I I S I I S I I S I S I I I S I I S I I S I S śhambara शम्बर :24

362. I I I S I I S I I S I S I S - I I S I I S I S I S I I I S S avarodhavanitā
अवरोधवनिता :14-15

363. I I I S I I S I I S I S I S avarodhavanitā अवरोधवनिता :14

364. I I I S I I S I I S S S I I S I I S I S : 20 (11:9) mudrā मुद्रा

365. I I I S I I S I I S S rodhaka रोधक :11

366. I I I S I I S I I S ś́harat शरत :10

367. I I I S I I S I S I I S I S I I S I S : 19 (9:10) tarala तरल

368. I I I S I I S I S I vanitāvinodi वनिताविनोदि :10

369. I I I S I I S I S karaśhayā करशया :9

370. I I I S I I S S vritumukhī वृतुमुखी :8

371. I I I S I I S svanakarī स्वनकरी :7

372. I I I S I I ayamita अयमित :6

373. I I I S I S : 6 girā गिरा, maṇiruchi मणिरुचि

374. I I I S I S I I I I I I S I I S I I S I I S S mantharāyana मन्थरायन :23

375. I I I S I S I I I S I S : 12 (6:6) bahumatā बहुमता

376. I I I S I S I I I S I S I I I S I S S I S kalamatallikā कलमतल्लिका :21

377. I I I S I S I I I S I S I I I S I S ṣhaṭpaderita षट्पदेरित :18

378. I I I S I S I I I S I S I I I S S I S S saṁlakṣhyalīlā संलक्ष्यलीला :20

379. I I I S I S I I I S I S I S : 14 sukesara सुकेसर

380. I I I S I S I I I S I S S I S madanamālikā मदनमालिका :15

381. I I I S I S I I I S I S S kīralekhā कीरलेखा :13

382. I I I S I S I I I S S S S vipannakadana विपन्नकदन :13

383. I I I S I S I I I S S madanamālā मदनमाला :11

384. I I I S I S I I S I S bhujagahāriṇī भुजगहारिणी :11

385. I I I S I S I I S I krikapādi कृकपादि :10

386. I I I S I S I I pākali पाकलि :8

387. I I I S I S I S : 8 sumālatī सुमालती

388. I I I S I S I S I S : 10 (6:4) manoramā मनोरमा

389. I I I S I S I S I S I S S sukarṇapūra सुकर्णपूर :13

390. I I I S I S I S I S manoramā मनोरमा :10

391. I I I S I S I S upalinī उपलिनी :8

392. I I I S I S I maṇimukhī मणिमुखी :7

393. I I I S I S S : 7 manojñā मनोज्ञा

394. I I I S I S S I S : 9 kusumitā कुसुमिता

395. I I I S I S S I S : brihatikā बृहतिका

396. I I I S I S S I S I I I S aniloddhatamukhī अनिलोद्धतमुखी :13

397. I I I S I S S I S I S : 11 (6:5) rājahaṁsī राजहंसी, vibhūśhitā विभूषिता

398. I I I S I S S I S I S aupagava औपगव :11, kanakamañjarī कनकमञ्जरी

399. I I I S I S S I S S I S : 12 vasantā वसंता, meghāvalī मेघावली

400. I I I S I S S I nakhapadā नखपदा :8

401. I I I S I S S S kurarikā कुररिका :8

402. I I I S I S S kharakarā खरकरा :7

403. I I I S I S nirasikā निरसिका :6

404. I I I S I pāṁśhu पांशु :5

405. I I I S S I I I I I S : 11 asuvilāsa असुविलास

406. I I I S S I I I I I nīranidhi नीरनिधिः :10

407. I I I S S I I I S S I I I S S I I I S S I I I S S kumudamālā कुमुदमाला :25

408. I I I S S I I S I I I I I I I I S S I S S bhārāvatāra भारावतारः :20

409. I I I S S I I S māṇḍavaka माण्डवक :8

410. I I I S S I I murajikā मुरजिका :7

411. I I I S S I S I I S chalitaka छलितक :10

412. I I I S S I S S I S I S S : 13 (7:6) urvaśhī उर्वशी

413. I I I S S I S S I S S I S - I I I S I I I S S I S S I S ālepana आलेपन :13-14

414. I I I S S I S S I S S I S : 13 kaumudī कौमुदी

415. I I I S S I S S I S S I S S parīvāha परीवाहः :14

416. I I I S S I S S I S charapada चरपद :10, jāriṇī जारिणी

417. I I I S S I S S S S nirmedhā निर्मेधा :10

418. I I I S S I S S vāntabhāra वान्तभारः :8

419. I I I S S I S parabhrita परभृत :7

420. I I I S S I anibhrita अनिभृत :6

421. I I I S S S I I aprītā अप्रीता, śhākhoṭaki शाखोटकि :8

422. । । । S S S । kiśhalaya किशलय :7

423. । । । S S S S । S । । S । S : 14 (7:7) siṁha सिंह

424. । । । S S S S S gopāvedī गोपावेदी :8

425. । । । S S S S holā होला :7

426. । । । S S S guṇavatī गुणवती :6

427. । । । S S kalali कललि :5

428. । । । S satī सती :4

429. । । । haraṇi हरणि :3

430. । । S : 3 rajanī रजनी, ramaṇa रमण

431. । । S । : 4 kadalī कदली

432. । । S । । । । । । । । S jvalitā ज्वलिता :12

433. । । S । । । । । । S S suvritti सुवृत्तिः :11

434. । । S । । । । । S । । । S S - S S S । । । । S । । । । । । । । । । S S mārdaṅgī मार्दङ्गी :14-18

435. । । S । । । । । S S S । S : 13 budbudaka बुद्बुदक

436. । । S । । । । । S S asitadhārā असितधारा :10

437. । । S । । । । । niruda निरुद :8

438. । । S । । । । S : 8 vimalajalā विमलजला

439. । । S । । । । S । । । । S । । । । S : 18 (3:5:5:5) surabhī सुरभी, śhubha शुभ

440. । । S । । । । S । । । । S upasarasī उपसरसी :13

441. । । S । । । । S । । S S paritoṣhā परितोषा :12

442. । । S । । । । S । S । S S chamūru चमूरुः :13

443. । । S । । । । S । S । S viralā विरला :12

444. । । S । । । । S S S S uditadineśha उदितदिनेशः :11

445. । । S । । । । S S sugandhi सुगन्धिः :9

446. । । S । । । । dhanadhari धनधरि :7

447. । । S । । । S । S । S - S । । S S । S । S । S śhālabhañjikā शालभञ्जिका :11-11

448. । । S । । । S । S । S pratāritā प्रतारिता :11

449. । । S । । । S S । śhaśhikarī शशिकरी :9

450. । । ऽ । । । ऽ ऽ ऽ । ऽ ऽ - ऽ ऽ । ऽ ऽ ऽ ऽ । ऽ ऽ pātaśhīlā पातशीला :12-10

451. । । ऽ । । । ऽ yamanaka यमनक :7

452. । । ऽ । । । visasi विससि :6

453. । । ऽ । । ऽ : 6 kumuda कुमुद, tilaka तिलक, nalinī नलिनी

454. । । ऽ । । ऽ । । । । । । ऽ - ऽ ऽ ऽ ऽ । । । । । । ऽ kāmākṣhī कामाक्षी :13-11

455. । । ऽ । । ऽ । । । । । । ऽ ऽ ऽ ऽ : 16 vellitā वेल्लिता

456. । । ऽ । । ऽ । । । । । । ऽ varivaśhitā वरिवशिता :13

457. । । ऽ । । ऽ । । । ऽ ऽ ऽ lumbākṣhī लुम्बाक्षी :12

458. । । ऽ । । ऽ । । ऽ । । ऽ - ऽ ऽ । । ऽ । । ऽ । । ऽ naṭaka नटकः :12-11

459. । । ऽ । । ऽ । । ऽ । । ऽ : 12 nandinī नंदिनी, bhramarāvalī भ्रमरावली

460. । । ऽ । । ऽ । । ऽ । । ऽ । । । । ऽ । । ऽ ऽ । । ऽ । saudāmanadāma सौदामनदाम :25

461. । । ऽ । । ऽ । । ऽ । । ऽ । । । । ऽ ऽ ऽ । । ऽ svarṇābharaṇa स्वर्णाभरण :22

462. । । ऽ । । ऽ । । ऽ । । ऽ । । ऽ : 15 nalinī नलिनी

463. । । ऽ । । ऽ । । ऽ । । ऽ । । ऽ । । ऽ । । ऽ । । ऽ : 24 (8:8:8) durmila दुर्मिल, ghoṭaka घोटक

464. । । ऽ । । ऽ । । ऽ । । ऽ । । ऽ । । ऽ । । ऽ । । ऽ । । vaśhaṁvada वशंवदः :26

465. । । ऽ । । ऽ । । ऽ । । ऽ । । ऽ । । ऽ । । ऽ । । ऽ ऽ mudira मुदिर :25

466. । । ऽ । । ऽ । । ऽ । । ऽ । । ऽ । । ऽ । । ऽ । । ऽ dvimilā द्विमिला :24

467. । । ऽ । । ऽ । । ऽ । । ऽ । । ऽ । । ऽ । । ऽ ऽ ayamāna अयमान :22

468. । । ऽ । । ऽ । । ऽ । । ऽ । । ऽ । । ऽ । । ऽ pratimā प्रतिमा :21

469. । । ऽ । । ऽ । । ऽ । । ऽ । । ऽ । । ऽ ऽ : 19 taruṇivadanendu तरुणीवदनेंदु

470. । । ऽ । । ऽ । । ऽ । । ऽ । । ऽ । । ऽ pariposhaka परिपोषक :18

471. । । ऽ । । ऽ । । ऽ । । ऽ । । ऽ ऽ : 16 somaḍaka सोमडक

472. । । ऽ । । ऽ । । ऽ । । ऽ । । ऽ ऽ kaladhautapada कलधौतपद :16

473. । । ऽ । । ऽ । । ऽ । । ऽ । । ऽ bhramarāvalikā भ्रमरावलिका :15

474. । । ऽ । । ऽ । । ऽ । । ऽ । । madhupāli मधुपालि :14

475. । । ऽ । । ऽ । । ऽ । । ऽ । ऽ vinandinī विनन्दिनी :14

476. । । ऽ । । ऽ । । ऽ । । ऽ ऽ - ऽ । । ऽ । । ऽ । । ऽ । । ऽ bhujaṅgabhritā भुजङ्गभृता:13-13

477. ı ı ऽ ı ı ऽ ı ı ऽ ı ı ऽ ऽ : 13 tāraka तारक

478. ı ı ऽ ı ı ऽ ı ı ऽ ı ı ऽ toṭaka तोटक :12

479. ı ı ऽ ı ı ऽ ı ı ऽ ı ı upachitrā उपचित्रा :11

480. ı ı ऽ ı ı ऽ ı ı ऽ ı ऽ - ı ı ऽ ऽ ı ı ऽ ı ı ऽ ı ऽ hariluptā हरिलुप्ता :11-12

481. ı ı ऽ ı ı ऽ ı ı ऽ ı ऽ : 11 vidushī विदुषी

482. ı ı ऽ ı ı ऽ ı ı ऽ ı ऽ ı ऽ ı ऽ ऽ abhidhātrī अभिधात्री :16

483. ı ı ऽ ı ı ऽ ı ı ऽ ı ऽ upachitra उपचित्र :11

484. ı ı ऽ ı ı ऽ ı ı ऽ ı lulita लुलित :10

485. ı ı ऽ ı ı ऽ ı ı ऽ ऽ - ऽ ı ı ऽ ı ı ऽ ı ı ऽ ऽ vegavatī वेगवती :10-11

486. ı ı ऽ ı ı ऽ ı ı ऽ ऽ : 10 meghavitāna मेघवितान, vitā विता

487. ı ı ऽ ı ı ऽ ı ı ऽ ऽ ı ı ı ı ऽ ऽ parikhāyatana परिखायतन :16

488. ı ı ऽ ı ı ऽ ı ı ऽ ऽ ऽ ı ı ऽ krīḍāyatana क्रीडायतन :14

489. ı ı ऽ ı ı ऽ ı ı ऽ ऽ ऽ vishṭambha विष्टम्भः :11

490. ı ı ऽ ı ı ऽ ı ı ऽ ऽ udita उदित :10

491. ı ı ऽ ı ı ऽ ı ı ऽ ardhakalā अर्धकला :9

492. ı ı ऽ ı ı ऽ ı ı amanā अमना :8

493. ı ı ऽ ı ı ऽ ı ऽ ı ı ı ऽ ऽ kuberakaṭikā कुबेरकटिका :13

494. ı ı ऽ ı ı ऽ ı ऽ ı ı ı ऽ udarkarachitā उदर्करचिता :12

495. ı ı ऽ ı ı ऽ ı ऽ ı ı ऽ ı ऽ drutalambinī द्रुतलम्बिनी :13

496. ı ı ऽ ı ı ऽ ı ऽ ı ऽ - ı ı ı ı ऽ ı ı ऽ ı ऽ ı ऽ aruntuda अरुन्तुदः :12-10

497. ı ı ऽ ı ı ऽ ı ऽ ı ऽ - ı ı ऽ ऽ ı ı ı ऽ ı ऽ ı ऽ navanīlatā नवनीलता :10-12

498. ı ı ऽ ı ı ऽ ı ऽ ı ऽ - ı ı ऽ ऽ ı ı ऽ ı ऽ ı ऽ sundarī सुन्दरी :10-11

499. ı ı ऽ ı ı ऽ ı ऽ ı ऽ - ऽ ऽ ऽ ı ı ऽ ı ऽ ı ऽ prabhāsitā प्रभासिता :10-10

500. ı ı ऽ ı ऽ ı ऽ ı ऽ : 10 ekrūpa एकरूप

501. ı ı ऽ ı ı ऽ ı ऽ ı ऽ ı ı ı ऽ ı ऽ ऽ : 17 (10:7) chitralekhā चित्रलेखा

502. ı ı ऽ ı ı ऽ ı ऽ ı ऽ ı ı ı ऽ ı ऽ ऽ atiśhāyinī अतिशायिनी :17

503. ı ı ऽ ı ऽ ı ऽ ı ऽ ı ı ऽ ı ऽ ı ı ı ı ı ı ऽ ı vanavāsinī वनवासिनी :22

504. ı ı ऽ ı ı ऽ ı ऽ ı ऽ ı ऽ ऽ - ऽ ऽ ऽ ı ı ऽ ı ऽ ı ऽ ı ऽ ऽ ऽ madākrāntā मदाक्रान्ता :13-14

505. । । ऽ । । ऽ । ऽ । ऽ । ऽ ऽ jagatsamānikā जगत्समानिका :13

506. । । ऽ । । ऽ । ऽ । ऽ । pichula पिचुल :11

507. । । ऽ । । ऽ । ऽ । ऽ ऽ - :12 upodgatā उपोद्गता :11-12

508. । । ऽ । । ऽ । ऽ । ऽ ऽ - । । ऽ ऽ । । ऽ । ऽ । ऽ ऽ vasantamālikā वसन्तमालिका :11-12

509. । । ऽ । । ऽ । ऽ । ऽ ऽ ऽ sākṣhī साक्षी :12

510. । । ऽ । । ऽ । ऽ । ऽ ऽ vimalā विमला :11

511. । । ऽ । । ऽ । ऽ । ऽ ālolaghaṭikā आलोलघटिका, sahajā सहजा :10

512. । । ऽ । । ऽ । ऽ ऽ । ऽ ऽ samayaprahitā समयप्रहिता :12

513. । । ऽ । । ऽ । ऽ ऽ । ऽ javanaśhālinī जवनशालिनी :11

514. । । ऽ । । ऽ । ऽ ऽ ऽ ऽ ऽ dorlīlā दोर्लीला :12

515. । । ऽ । । ऽ । ऽ ऽ ऽ ऽ lalitāgamana ललितागमन :11

516. । । ऽ । । ऽ । ऽ kalilā कलिला :8

517. । । ऽ । । ऽ । godhi गोधि :7

518. । । ऽ । । ऽ ऽ । : 8 mahī मही

519. । । ऽ । । ऽ ऽ । । । । ऽ ऽ ऽ । । ऽ । । ऽ । । ऽ : 23 sundarikā सुंदरिका

520. । । ऽ । । ऽ ऽ । । ऽ । । । । । । ऽ śhukavanitā शुकवनिता :17

521. । । ऽ । । ऽ ऽ । । ऽ । । ऽ ऽ manmatha मन्मथः :14

522. । । ऽ । । ऽ ऽ । । ऽ । ऽ । ऽ ऽ ऽ pratīpavallī प्रतीपवल्ली :16

523. । । ऽ । । ऽ ऽ । । ऽ ऽ varṇabalākā वर्णबलाका :11

524. । । ऽ । । ऽ ऽ । । ऽ surayānavatī सुरयानवती :10

525. । । ऽ । । ऽ ऽ ऽ । ऽ ऽ । ऽ ऽ saramāsaraṇi सरमासरणिः :14

526. । । ऽ । । ऽ ऽ ऽ ऽ : 9 saumyā सौम्या

527. । । ऽ । । ऽ ऽ ऽ ऽ ऽ ऽ ऽ । । ऽ bhūriśhikhā भूरिशिखा :14

528. । । ऽ । । ऽ ऽ ऽ ऽ udaraśhri उदरश्रि :9

529. । । ऽ । । ऽ ऽ ऽ pañchaśhikhā पञ्चशिखा :8

530. । । ऽ । । ऽ ऽ karabhit करभित :7

531. । । ऽ । । ऽ tilakā तिलका :6

532. । । ऽ । । jatu जतु :5

533. । । ऽ । ऽ : 5 ramā रमा

534. । । ऽ । ऽ । । । । । । । । ऽ ऽ : 15 elā एला, rekhā रेखा

535. । । ऽ । ऽ । । । । । ऽ । ऽ । । । । । ऽ । ऽ । । । ऽ : 25 (8:8:9) kalakaṇṭha कलकंठ

536. । । ऽ । ऽ । । । । ऽ । ऽ । ऽ : 14 (5:9) sudarśhanā सुदर्शना

537. । । ऽ । ऽ । । । । ऽ dhamanikā धमनिका :10

538. । । ऽ । ऽ । । । ऽ : 9 skṣhi अक्षि

539. । । ऽ । ऽ । । । ऽ । - । । । । ऽ । ऽ । ऽ - । । । । । । । । ऽ । । ऽ - । । ऽ । ऽ । । । ऽ । ऽ । ऽ lalita ललित :10-10-12-13

540. । । ऽ । ऽ । । । ऽ । - । । । । । ऽ । ऽ । ऽ udgatā उद्गता :10-11

541. । । ऽ । ऽ । । । ऽ । । ऽ : 12 pramitākṣharā प्रमिताक्षरा

542. । । ऽ । ऽ । । । ऽ । । ऽ । ऽ । ऽ : 16 udgatā उद्‌गता

543. । । ऽ । ऽ । । । ऽ । । ऽ । ऽ ऽ : 15 riṣhabha ऋषभ

544. । । ऽ । ऽ । । ऽ । । ऽ ऽ - । । ऽ । ऽ । । । ऽ । ऽ । ऽ kalanā कलना :13-13

545. । । ऽ । ऽ । । । ऽ । । ऽ ऽ - ऽ ऽ । ऽ । । । ऽ । । ऽ ऽ padmāvatī पद्मावती :13-12

546. । । ऽ । ऽ । । । ऽ । । ऽ ऽ : 13 siṁhanādaसिंहनाद, bhramarī भ्रमरी, कलहंसः

547. । । ऽ । ऽ । । । ऽ । ऽ । ऽ - ऽ ऽ । ऽ । । ऽ । ऽ । । ऽ । madhuvāri मधुवारि :13-13

548. । । ऽ । ऽ । । । ऽ । ऽ । ऽ : 13 (5:8) sumaṅgalī सुमंगली, kanakaprabhā कनकप्रभा, jayā जया,

549. । । ऽ । ऽ । । । ऽ । ऽ । ऽ ऽ । ऽ । ऽ : 18 budbud बुद्‌बुद्

550. । । ऽ । ऽ । । । ऽ । ऽ । ऽ kalanāvatī कलनावती :13, mañjubhāṣhiṇī मञ्जुभाषिणी

551. । । ऽ । ऽ । । । ऽ । ऽ ऽ । ऽ : 14 (10:4) pathyā पथ्या

552. । । ऽ । ऽ । । । ऽ । ऽ ऽ । ऽ : 14 (5:9) vasudhā वसुधा, prathitā प्रथिता

553. । । ऽ । ऽ । । । ऽ । ऽ dārikā दारिका :11

554. । । ऽ । ऽ । । । ऽ । rasabhūma रसभूम :10

555. । । ऽ । ऽ । । । ऽ । saurabhaka सौरभक :10

556. । । ऽ । ऽ । । । ऽ ऽ - ऽ । । ऽ । ऽ । । । ऽ ऽ ketumatī केतुमती :10-11

557. । । ऽ । ऽ । । । ऽ ऽ : 10 mālā माला, pramilā प्रमिला

558. । । ऽ । ऽ । । । ऽ ऽ ऽ ऽ ऽ : 13 sunandinī सुनंदिनी

559. । । ऽ । ऽ । । ऽ । : 9 tomara तोमर

560. । । ऽ । ऽ । । ऽ । ऽ : 10 (5:5) kamalā कमला, saṁyutā संयुता

561. । । ऽ । ऽ । । ऽ । ऽ । । । ऽ kalahetikā कलहेतिका :14

562. । । ऽ । ऽ । । ऽ । ऽ । । ऽ । ऽ : 15 manohaṁsa मनोहंस

563. । । ऽ । ऽ । । ऽ । ऽ । । ऽ । ऽ । । ऽ । ऽ : 20 gītā गीता, gītikā गीतिका

564. । । ऽ । ऽ । । ऽ । ऽ । । ऽ । ऽ maṇihaṁsa मणिहंसः :15

565. । । ऽ । ऽ । । ऽ । ऽ । । ऽ । upakārikā उपकारिका :14

566. । । ऽ । ऽ । । ऽ । ऽ ऽ ऽ । sukhakārikā सुखकारिका :13

567. । । ऽ । ऽ । । ऽ । ऽ ऽ ऽ svaravarṣhiṇī स्वरवर्षिणी :12

568. । । ऽ । ऽ । । ऽ । ऽ ऽ paṭupaṭṭikā पटुपट्टिका :11

569. । । ऽ । ऽ । । ऽ । ऽ saṁhatikā संहतिका :10

570. । । ऽ । ऽ । । ऽ । tomara तोमर :9

571. । । ऽ । ऽ । । ऽ ऽ । ऽ : 11 sāraṇī सारणी

572. । । ऽ । ऽ । । ऽ ऽ ऽ ऽ lalitālabāla ललितालबाल :11

573. । । ऽ । ऽ । । muhurā मुहुरा :7

574. । । ऽ । ऽ । ऽ : 7 vimalā विमला–1

575. । । ऽ । ऽ । ऽ । । ऽ pravādapadā प्रवादपदा :10

576. । । ऽ । ऽ । ऽ । ऽ ऽ sukhelā सुखेला :10

577. । । ऽ । ऽ । ऽ । ऽ bhujaṅgasaṅgatā भुजङ्गसङ्गता :9

578. । । ऽ । ऽ । ऽ ऽ । । । । । । ऽ ऽ । ऽ ऽ । ऽ ऽ : 22 (8:7:7) mahāsragdharā महास्रग्धरा

579. । । ऽ । ऽ । ऽ ऽ । ऽ ऽ vihāriṇī विहारिणी :11

580. । । ऽ । ऽ । ऽ ऽ । ऽ upasaṁkulā उपसंकुला :10

581. । । ऽ । ऽ । ऽ ऽ । kīṭamālā कीटमाला :9

582. । । ऽ । ऽ । ऽ ऽ digīśha दिगीशः :8

583. । । ऽ । ऽ । ऽ kaṭhodgatā कठोद्गता :7

584. । । ऽ । ऽ । madhumāraka मधुमारक :6

585. । । ऽ । ऽ ऽ : 6 vimalā विमला–2

586. । । ऽ । ऽ ऽ । । ऽ । । । ऽ komalakalpakalikā कोमलकल्पकलिका :13

587. । । ऽ । ऽ ऽ । । ऽ । ऽ । ऽ : 13 sudanta सुदंत, maṇikuṇḍala मणिकुंडल

588. । । ऽ । ऽ ऽ । । ऽ । ऽ । ऽ ambudāvalī अम्बुदावली :13

589. । । ऽ । ऽ ऽ । । ऽ । ऽ ऽ : 12 kekirava केकिरव, s̓hivikā शिविका, mahendravajrā महेंद्रवज्रा

590. । । ऽ । ऽ ऽ । alālāpi अलालापि :7

591. । । ऽ । ऽ ऽ ऽ । ऽ । । ऽ ativāsitā अतिवासिता :12

592. । । ऽ । ऽ ऽ ऽ । nāgāri नागारि :8

593. । । ऽ । ऽ ऽ ऽ ऽ yugadhāri युगधारि :8

594. । । ऽ । ऽ ऽ ऽ rasadhāri रसधारि :7

595. । । ऽ । ऽ ऽ kamanī कमनी :6

596. । । ऽ । ऽ priyā प्रिया :5

597. । । ऽ । kāru कारु :4

598. । । ऽ ऽ : 4 bhramarī भ्रमरी, sumati सुमति

599. । । ऽ ऽ । । : 6 gurumadhyā गुरुमध्या

600. । । ऽ ऽ । । । । । । । । ऽ vinatākṣhī विनताक्षी :13

601. । । ऽ ऽ । । । । । । । । ऽ ऽ : 13 (4:9) rati रति

602. । । ऽ ऽ । । । । । । ऽ । ऽ । ऽ - । । । । । । ऽ । ऽ । ऽ ऽ brihaccharāvatī बृहच्छरावती :15-12

603. । । ऽ ऽ । । । । । । ऽ ऽ ऽ ऽ : 14 (4:10) kuṭila कुटिल

604. । । ऽ ऽ । । । । । ऽ । ऽ upalekhā उपलेखा :12

605. । । ऽ ऽ । । । । ऽ । ऽ । ऽ । ऽ ऽ - ऽ ऽ ऽ । । । । ऽ । ऽ । ऽ hīnatālī हीनताली :19-12

606. । । ऽ ऽ । । । । ऽ । ऽ । ऽ ऽ : 14 (4:10) sunandā सुनंदा

607. । । ऽ ऽ । । । । ऽ । ऽ । ऽ ऽ vas̓hamūla वशमूल :14

608. । । ऽ ऽ । । । ऽ ऽ । । । । ऽ ऽ । phalgu फल्गुः :17

609. । । ऽ ऽ । । । । ऽ ऽ । । ऽ ऽ ऽ bahulābhra बहुलाभ्र :15

610. । । ऽ ऽ । । । । ऽ ऽ ऽ upahitachaṇḍī उपहितचण्डी :11

611. । । ऽ ऽ । । । । ऽ ऽ baladhārī बलधारी :10

612. । । ऽ ऽ । । । ऽ anavīrā अनवीरा :9

613. । । ऽ ऽ । । । । sritamadhu सृतमधु :8

614. । । ऽ ऽ । । । ऽ । । ऽ ऽ s̓harameyā शरमेया :12, upasarasīka उपसरसीक

615. । । ऽ ऽ । । । ऽ । ऽ । ऽ - । । ऽ । । ऽ । ऽ । ऽ karīritā करीरिता :12-10

616. । । ऽ ऽ । । । lolatanu लोलतनु :7

617. । । ऽ ऽ । । ऽ । । । । ऽ । । ऽ karṇalatā कर्णलता :15

618. । । ऽ ऽ । । ऽ । । । । ऽ nagamahitā नगमहिता :12

619. । । ऽ ऽ । । ऽ । । ऽ । । arilā अरिला :12

620. । । ऽ ऽ । । ऽ । । ऽ । ऽ - । । ऽ । । ऽ । । ऽ । ऽ luptā लुप्ता :12-11

621. । । ऽ ऽ । । ऽ । । ऽ । ऽ rādhikā राधिका :12

622. । । ऽ ऽ । । ऽ । । ऽ vāravatī वारवती :10

623. । । ऽ ऽ । । ऽ । ऽ । । । ऽ ऽ - । । । । ऽ ऽ । ऽ । ऽ । ऽ ऽ atiprativinītā अतिप्रतिविनीता :14-13

624. । । ऽ ऽ । । ऽ । ऽ । । । ऽ ऽ ऽ । ऽ ऽ । ऽ : 20 (13:7) mattebhavikrīḍita मत्तेभविक्रीडित

625. । । ऽ ऽ । । ऽ । ऽ । ऽ - । । ऽ । । ऽ । ऽ । ऽ sundarī सुन्दरी :11-10

626. । । ऽ ऽ । । ऽ । ऽ । ऽ - ऽ ऽ ऽ । । । । ऽ । ऽ । ऽ vimāninī विमानिनी :11-12

627. । । ऽ ऽ । । ऽ । ऽ । ऽ - ऽ ऽ ऽ । । ऽ । ऽ । ऽ asudhā असुधा :11-10

628. । । ऽ ऽ । । ऽ । ऽ । ऽ : 11 aparāntikā अपरांतिका

629. । । ऽ ऽ । । ऽ । ऽ । ऽ । । । ऽ ऽ - । । । ऽ । । । ऽ । ऽ । ऽ । ऽ ऽ anasavavāsitā अनासववासिता:16-15

630. । । ऽ ऽ । । ऽ । ऽ । ऽ । ऽ ऽ - ऽ ऽ । । ऽ । ऽ । ऽ ऽ akoṣhakriṣhṭā अकोषकृष्टा :14-10

631. । । ऽ ऽ । । ऽ । ऽ । ऽ । ऽ ऽ madāvadātā मदावदाता :14

632. । । ऽ ऽ । । ऽ । ऽ । ऽ ऽ - । । । । ऽ । । ऽ । ऽ । ऽ ऽ apramāthinī अप्रमाथिनी :12-13

633. । । ऽ ऽ । । ऽ । ऽ । ऽ ऽ - । । ऽ । । ऽ । ऽ । ऽ ऽ pramālikā प्रमालिका, upodgatā उपोद्गता :12-11

634. । । ऽ ऽ । । ऽ । ऽ । ऽ ऽ - ऽ ऽ ऽ । । ऽ । ऽ । ऽ ऽ ऽ viyadvāṇī वियद्वाणी :12-12

635. । । ऽ ऽ । । ऽ । ऽ । ऽ ऽ arbhakapaṅkti अर्भकपङ्क्तिः :12, badhirā बधिरा :12

636. । । ऽ ऽ । । ऽ । ऽ । ऽ sīdhu सीधुः :11

637. । । ऽ ऽ । । ऽ । ऽ । mahimāvasāyi महिमावसायि :10

638. । । ऽ ऽ । । ऽ । ऽ madhumallī मधुमल्ली :9

639. । । ऽ ऽ । । ऽ । anritanarma अनृतनर्म :8

640. । । ऽ ऽ । । ऽ ऽ : 8 moda मोद

641. । । ऽ ऽ । । ऽ ऽ । । । । ऽ ऽ pratibhādarśhana प्रतिभादर्शन :14

642. । । ऽ ऽ । । ऽ ऽ । । । । ऽ abhirāmā अभिरामा :13

643. । । ऽ ऽ । । ऽ ऽ । । ऽ ऽ । । ऽ ऽ anilohā अनिलोहा :16

644. । । ऽ ऽ । । ऽ ऽ । । ऽ ऽ karamālā करमाला :12

645. । । ऽ ऽ । । ऽ ऽ । । ऽ harikāntā हरिकान्ता :11

646. । । ऽ ऽ । । ऽ ऽ ऽ । । ऽ ऽ । । ऽ : 16 skhalitavikramā स्खलितविक्रमा

647. । । ऽ ऽ । । ऽ ऽ ऽ kalaha कलह :9

648. । । ऽ ऽ । । ऽ ऽ atimohā अतिमोहा :8

649. । । ऽ ऽ । । ऽ adhikārī अधिकारी :7

650. । । ऽ ऽ । । s̍haṅkhadyuti शङ्खद्युति :6

651. । । ऽ ऽ । ऽ । । । ऽ । ऽ ऽ । ऽ ऽ । ऽ ऽ । ऽ s̍harakāṇḍaprakāṇḍa शरकाण्डप्रकाण्ड :21

652. । । ऽ ऽ । ऽ । । ऽ ऽ । ऽ sutala सुतल :12

653. । । ऽ ऽ । ऽ । ऽ । । : 8 suvilāsitā सुविलासिता

654. । । ऽ ऽ । ऽ । ऽ s̍hallakapluta शल्लकप्लुत :8

655. । । ऽ ऽ । ऽ । proñchhitā प्रोञ्छिता :7

656. । । ऽ ऽ । ऽ ऽ : 7 dīptā दीप्ता

657. । । ऽ ऽ । ऽ ऽ । valīkendu वलीकेन्दु :8

658. । । ऽ ऽ । ऽ ऽ ऽ ऽ ऽ ऽ apayodhā अपयोधा :11

659. । । ऽ ऽ । ऽ ऽ ऽ ऽ ऽ nīrohā नीरोहा :10

660. । । ऽ ऽ । ऽ ऽ ऽ paridhārā परिधारा :8

661. । । ऽ ऽ । ऽ ऽ bhūridhāmā भूरिधामा :7

662. । । ऽ ऽ । ऽ mridukīlā मृदुकीला :6

663. । । ऽ ऽ । pāli पालि :5

664. । । ऽ ऽ ऽ : 5 ghanapaṅti घनपंक्ति

665. । । ऽ ऽ ऽ । । । । । । ऽ rasikaparichitā रसिकपरिचिता :12

666. । । ऽ ऽ ऽ । । । । । ऽ ऽ । ऽ ऽ । ऽ ऽ : 18 (5:6:7) mandāramālā मंदारमाला–2

667. । । ऽ ऽ ऽ । । ऽ ऽ । । ऽ ऽ । । ऽ : 16 (4:4:4:4) pramadā प्रमदा

668. । । ऽ ऽ ऽ । । ऽ ऽ ऽ : 10 (5:5) kalagīta कलगीत

669. । । ऽ ऽ ऽ । । ऽ ऽ ऽ । । । । । । ऽ vidhuravirahitā विधुरविरहिता :17

670. । । ऽ ऽ ऽ । । ऽ ऽ ऽ । । ऽ ऽ ऽ ऽ ऽ ऽ ऽ : 19 (10:9) s̍hambhu शंभु

671. । । ऽ ऽ ऽ । । ऽ ऽ ऽ ऽ saṁsritas̍hobhāsāra संसृतशोभासारः :11

672. । । ऽ ऽ ऽ । । ऽ ऽ ऽ vis̕hadacchāya विशदच्छायः :10

673. । । ऽ ऽ ऽ । । ऽ ऽ sambuddhi सम्बुद्धिः :9

674. । । ऽ ऽ ऽ । । ऽ saraghā सरघा :8

675. । । ऽ ऽ ऽ । । kāhī काही :7

676. । । ऽ ऽ ऽ । ऽ । ऽ nibhālitā निभालिता :9

677. । । ऽ ऽ ऽ । ऽ ऽ । । । । । । । ऽ ऽ । ऽ ऽ । ऽ ऽ : 22 (8:7:7) mahāsragdharā महास्रग्धरा

678. । । ऽ ऽ ऽ । ऽ ऽ kauchamāra कौचमारः :8

679. । । ऽ ऽ ऽ । ऽ māyāvinī मायाविनी :7

680. । । ऽ ऽ ऽ । ganesh गणेश :6

681. । । ऽ ऽ ऽ ऽ : 6 sūchīmukhī सूचीमुखी

682. । । ऽ ऽ ऽ ऽ । । । । ऽ : 11 vimalā विमला, ayavatī अयवती :11

683. । । ऽ ऽ ऽ ऽ । । ऽ ऽ gaṇadehā गणदेहा :10

684. । । ऽ ऽ ऽ ऽ । । vrinta वृन्त :8

685. । । ऽ ऽ ऽ ऽ । grihiṇī गृहिणी :7

686. । । ऽ ऽ ऽ ऽ ऽ s̕hambūka शम्बूकः :7

687. । । ऽ ऽ ऽ ऽ abhikhyā अभिख्या :6

688. । । ऽ ऽ ऽ praguṇa प्रगुण :5

689. । । ऽ ऽ dolā दोला :4

690. । । ऽ ramaṇa रमणः :3

691. । । madhu मधु :2

692. । ऽ : 2 sukha सुख

693. । ऽ । : 3 mrigendra मृगेन्द्र

694. । ऽ । । : 4 japā जपा

695. । ऽ । । । । । । । । । ऽ anīchaka अनीचक :12

696. । ऽ । । । । । । kṣhara क्षर :8

697. । ऽ । । । । । ऽ । । ऽ ऽ upadhāna उपधान :12

698. । ऽ । । । । । kuradi कुरदि :7

699. । ऽ । । । । ऽ । । । । ऽ । । । । ऽ । ऽ : 19 (5:5:5:4) varūthini वरूथिनी

700. I S I I I I S I I I I S kumāragati कुमारगतिः :12

701. I S I I I I S I karañji करञ्जि :8

702. I S I I I I S svidā स्विदा :7

703. I S I I I I sudāyi सुदायि :6

704. I S I I I S I I I S I I I S S : 15 mayūralalita मयूरललित

705. I S I I I S I I S I S S : 12 kola कोल

706. I S I I I S I S I I I S : 12 (6:6) jaloddhati जलोद्धति

707. I S I I I S I S I I I S I S S I S : 17 (8:9) prithvī पृथ्वी

708. I S I I I S I S I I I S I I I S I S pārthiva पार्थिव :18

709. I S I I I S I S I I I S I S I I I S I S I I S vilambalalita विलम्बललित :23

710. I S I I I S I S I I I S I S I I I S S : 19 (6:6:7) aratilīlā रतिलीला

711. I S I I I S I S I I I S I S S I S S I S S I S : 23 vrindāraka वृंदारक

712. I S I I I S I S I I I S S S I S I I S : 19 (8:4:7) samudratatā समुद्रतता

713. I S I I I S I S I I I S S ruchivarṇā रुचिवर्णा :13

714. I S I I I S I S I I I S jaloddhatagati जलोद्धतगतिः :12

715. I S I I I S I S I I S I S garudavāritā गरुदवारिता :13

716. I S I I I S I S I S S sarojavanikā सरोजवनिका :11

717. I S I I I S I S S I S : 11 sāriṇī सारिणी, saṅgatā संगता

718. I S I I I S I S S S S S vīṇādaṇḍa वीणादण्ड :12

719. I S I I I I S I virohi विरोहि :7

720. I S I I I S S : 7 (34) (2:5) kumāralalitā कुमारललिता

721. I S I I I S S I S I I I S S : 14 (7:7) sājaramaṇīyā राजरमणीय

722. I S I I I S S I S S S : 11 ś́hikhaṇḍita शिखंडित

723. I S I I I S S S I S S upasthita उपस्थित :11

724. I S I I I S S S S S S praphullakadalī प्रफुल्लकदली :11

725. I S I I I S S S S S vīrāntā वीरान्ता :10

726. I S I I I S S S S nirvindhyā निर्विन्ध्या :9

727. I S I I I S S S bhāṙngī भाङ्गी :8

728. । ऽ । । । ऽ ऽ kumāralalitā कुमारललिता :7

729. । ऽ । । । ऽ kuhī कुही :6

730. । ऽ । । । kṣhupa क्षुप :5

731. । ऽ । । ऽ : 5 abhimukhī अभिमुखी, mrigachapalā मृगचपला

732. । ऽ । । ऽ । : 6 sumālatī सुमालती

733. । ऽ । । ऽ । । । । । । ऽ viyogavatī वियोगवती :12

734. । ऽ । । ऽ । । । ऽ । । ऽ vikatthana विकत्थन :12

735. । ऽ । । ऽ । । । ऽ । ऽ nābhasa नाभस :11

736. । ऽ । । ऽ । । ऽ । । ऽ । : 12 mauktikadāma मौक्तिकदाम

737. । ऽ । । ऽ । । ऽ । । ऽ । । ऽ । । ऽ । । ऽ । । ऽ । anāmaya अनामय :24

738. । ऽ । । ऽ । । ऽ । । ऽ । । ऽ । । ऽ । । ऽ । । ऽ mānavatī मानवती :23

739. । ऽ । । ऽ । । ऽ । । ऽ । ऽ guṇasārikā गुणसारिका :13

740. । ऽ । । ऽ । । ऽ । । ऽ । mauktikadāma मौक्तिकदाम :12

741. । ऽ । । ऽ । । ऽ । । ऽ ऽ parilekha परिलेखः :12

742. । ऽ । । ऽ । । ऽ । । ऽ khaṭakā खटका :11

743. । ऽ । । ऽ । । ऽ । ऽ : 10 uṣhitā उषिता

744. । ऽ । । ऽ । । ऽ । ऽ । ऽ ऽ atiraṁha अतिरंहः :13

745. । ऽ । । ऽ । । ऽ । ऽ । ऽ vidhāritā विधारिता :12

746. । ऽ । । ऽ । । ऽ । ऽ jarā जरा :10

747. । ऽ । । ऽ । । ऽ । kuhū कुहू :9

748. । ऽ । । ऽ । । ऽ ऽ ऽ indra इन्द्रः :10

749. । ऽ । । ऽ । । ऽ arāli अरालि :8

750. । ऽ । । ऽ । । upodari उपोदरि :7

751. । ऽ । । ऽ । ऽ । । । ऽ । । ऽ kākiṇikā काकिणिका :14

752. । ऽ । । ऽ । ऽ । ऽ avanijā अवनिजा :9

753. । ऽ । । ऽ । ऽ vahirvali वहिर्वलि :7

754. । ऽ । । ऽ । mālatikā मालतिका :6

755. । ऽ । । ऽ ऽ । richā ऋचा :7

756. । ऽ । । ऽ ऽ ऽ ऽ virājikarā विराजिकरा :8

757. । ऽ । । ऽ ऽ arajaskā अरजस्का :6

758. । ऽ । । ऽ śhilā शिला :5

759. । ऽ । । riju ऋजु :4

760. । ऽ । ऽ : 4 nagānitā नगानिता

761. । ऽ । ऽ । । । । । । । । ऽ abhīrukā अभीरुका :13

762. । ऽ । ऽ । । । । । । ऽ ऽ ऽ ऽ : 14 (4:10) kuṭila कुटिल

763. । ऽ । ऽ । । । । । ऽ । ऽ bhasalavinoditā भसलविनोदिता :12

764. । ऽ । ऽ । । । । ऽ । ऽ । ऽ : 13 (4:9) kalāvati कलावती, sadāgati सदागति, prabhāvatī प्रभावती

765. । ऽ । ऽ । । । । ऽ । ऽ । ऽ ऽ kusumbhinī कुसुम्भिनी :14

766. । ऽ । ऽ । । । । ऽ । ऽ । ऽ ruchirā रुचिरा :13

767. । ऽ । ऽ । । । । ऽ । ऽ ऽ : 12 smriti स्मृति

768. । ऽ । ऽ । । । । maru मरु :8

769. । ऽ । ऽ । । । ऽ । ऽ । ऽ : 12 priyavandā प्रियंवदा

770. । ऽ । ऽ । । । ऽ ऽ ऽ । ऽ galitanālā गलितनाला :12

771. । ऽ । ऽ । । । staradhi स्तरधि :7

772. । ऽ । ऽ । । ऽ । । ऽ kāṇḍamukhī काण्डमुखी :10

773. । ऽ । ऽ । । ऽ । ऽ । nemadhāri नेमधारि :10

774. । ऽ । ऽ । । ऽ । ऽ sahelikā सहेलिका :9

775. । ऽ । ऽ । । ऽ । kulachāri कुलचारि :8

776. । ऽ । ऽ । । ऽ ऽ chaturīhā चतुरीहा :8

777. । ऽ । ऽ । । ऽ mahodhikā महोधिका :7

778. । ऽ । ऽ । । sāvaṭu सावटु :6

779. । ऽ । ऽ । ऽ । ऽ : 8 prāmāṇika प्रामाणिक

780. । ऽ । ऽ । ऽ । ऽ । ऽ । ऽ : 12 pramāṇa प्रमाण, vasantachatvāra वसंतचत्वार, vibhāvarī विभावरी

781. । ऽ । ऽ । ऽ । ऽ । ऽ । ऽ । ऽ । ऽ : (8:8, 4:4:4:4)16 pañchachāmar-3 पंचचामर-3

782. । ऽ । ऽ । ऽ । ऽ । ऽ । ऽ । ऽ । ऽ । ऽ । ऽ । ऽ । ऽ । ऽ । ऽ : 28 manojaśhekha मनोजशेख

783. । ऽ । ऽ । ऽ । ऽ । ऽ । ऽ । ऽ । ऽ narācha नराचः :16

784. । ऽ । ऽ । ऽ । ऽ । ऽ । ऽ । ऽ kuḍaṅgikā कुडङ्गिका :14

785. । ऽ । ऽ । ऽ । ऽ । ऽ । ऽ ऽ - ऽ । ऽ । ऽ । ऽ । ऽ । ऽ । amarāvatī अमरावती :13-12

786. । ऽ । ऽ । ऽ । ऽ । ऽ । ऽ lalāmalalitādharā ललामललिताधरा :12

787. । ऽ । ऽ । ऽ । ऽ । ऽ । sainika सैनिक :11

788. । ऽ । ऽ । ऽ । ऽ । ऽ ऽ : 11 vilāsinī विलासिनी

789. । ऽ । ऽ । ऽ । ऽ । ऽ sarāvikā सराविका :10

790. । ऽ । ऽ । ऽ । ऽ ऽ ऽ ऽ amoghamālikā अमोघमालिका :11

791. । ऽ । ऽ । ऽ । ऽ pramāṇikā प्रमाणिका :8

792. । ऽ । ऽ । ऽ । pratardi प्रतर्दि :7

793. । ऽ । ऽ । ऽ ऽ : 7 subhadrā सुभद्रा

794. । ऽ । ऽ । ऽ ऽ । : 8 suchandraprabhā सुचंद्रप्रभा

795. । ऽ । ऽ । ऽ ऽ । । ऽ । ऽ : 12 haṁsākhya हंसाख्य

796. । ऽ । ऽ । ऽ ऽ । ऽ । ऽ । ऽ akhaṇḍamaṇḍana अखण्डमण्डन :13

797. । ऽ । ऽ । ऽ ऽ । ऽ । ऽ ऽ asudhārā असुधारा :12

798. । ऽ । ऽ । ऽ ऽ । amānikā अमानिका :8

799. । ऽ । ऽ । ऽ ऽ ऽ yaśhaskarī यशस्करी :8

800. । ऽ । ऽ । ऽ ऽ purohitā पुरोहिता :7

801. । ऽ । ऽ । ऽ valīmukhī वलीमुखी :6

802. । ऽ । ऽ । vārddhi वार्द्धि :5

803. । ऽ । ऽ ऽ : 5 śhikhā शिखा

804. । ऽ । ऽ ऽ । । । । । । ऽ ऽ ऽ sambodhā सम्बोधा :14

805. । ऽ । ऽ ऽ । । । । । ऽ । ऽ kalanāyikā कलनायिका :13

806. । ऽ । ऽ ऽ । । । ऽ । ऽ । ऽ : 13 (5:8) mañjuṣhabhāṣhnī मंजुभाषिणी

807. । ऽ । ऽ ऽ । । । ऽ । ऽ ऽ kumudinīvikāśha कुमुदिनीविकाशः :12

808. । ऽ । ऽ ऽ । । । ऽ । ऽ kanakakāminī कनककामिनी :11

809. । ऽ । ऽ ऽ । । । ākatanu आकतनु :8

810. । ऽ । ऽ ऽ । । ऽ । । । ऽ । ऽ ऽ । ऽ kālasāroddhata कालसारोद्धतः :17

811. । ऽ । ऽ ऽ । । ऽ । । ऽ । ऽ āpaṇikā आपणिका :13

812. ।ऽ ।ऽऽ ।।ऽ ।ऽ ।ऽ-ऽऽ ।ऽऽ ।।ऽ ।ऽ ।ऽ-।ऽ ।ऽऽ ।।ऽ ।ऽ ।ऽ-ऽऽ ।ऽऽ ।।
ऽ ।ऽ ।ऽ manahāsā मनहासा :12-12-12-12

813. ।ऽ ।ऽऽ ।।ऽ ।ऽ ।ऽ : 12 (6:6) vaṁśhastha वंशस्थ, abhravaṁsā अभ्रवंशा

814. ।ऽ ।ऽऽ ।।ऽ ।ऽ ।ऽ #1,2,3 + #4 ऽऽ ।ऽऽ ।।ऽ ।ऽ ।ऽ śhīlāturā शीलातुरा :12-12-12-12

815. ।ऽ ।ऽऽ ।।ऽ ।ऽ ।ऽ #1,3,4 + #2 ऽऽ ।ऽऽ ।।ऽ ।ऽ ।ऽ ramaṇā रमणा :12

816. ।ऽ ।ऽऽ ।।ऽ ।ऽ ।ऽ + @3 ऽऽ ।ऽऽ ।।ऽ ।ऽ ।ऽ varāsikā वरासिका :12-12-12-12

817. ।ऽ ।ऽऽ ।।ऽ ।ऽ ।ऽ indumā इन्दुमा, उपमेया, वैधात्री, vaṁśhastha वंशस्थ 12

818. ।ऽ ।ऽऽ ।।ऽ ।ऽऽ-ऽऽ ।ऽऽ ।।ऽ ।ऽऽ kīrti कीर्तिः :11-11

819. ।ऽ ।ऽऽ ।।ऽ ।ऽऽ-ऽऽ ।ऽऽ ।।ऽ ।ऽऽ viparītākhyānakī विपरीताख्यानकी :11-11

820. ।ऽ ।ऽऽ ।।ऽ ।ऽऽ : 11 (5:6) upendravajrā उपेंद्रवज्रा

821. ।ऽ ।ऽऽ ।।ऽ ।ऽऽ @2 + ऽऽ ।ऽऽ ।।ऽ ।ऽऽ @2 mālā माला :11-11-11-11

822. ।ऽ ।ऽऽ ।।ऽ ।ऽऽ @3 + ऽऽ ।ऽऽ ।।ऽ ।ऽऽ māyā माया :11-11-11-11

823. ।ऽ ।ऽऽ ।।ऽ ।ऽऽ । nimagnakīlā निमग्नकीला :12

824. ।ऽ ।ऽऽ ।।ऽ ।ऽऽ ārdrā आर्द्रा, haṁsī हंसी, प्रेमा, riddhi ऋद्धिः, upendravajrā उपेन्द्रवज्रा :11

825. ।ऽ ।ऽऽ ।।ऽऽ ।ऽऽ kalavallivihaṅga कलवल्लिविहङ्गः :12

826. ।ऽ ।ऽऽ ।। kharpari खर्परि :7

827. ।ऽ ।ऽऽ ।ऽ ।।।ऽ ।ऽ udāttahāsa उदात्तहासः :13

828. ।ऽ ।ऽऽ ।ऽ ।ऽ : 9 chāruhāsinī चारुहासिनी

829. ।ऽ ।ऽऽ ।ऽऽ : 8 vitā विता। । ।

830. ।ऽ ।ऽऽ ।ऽऽ ।ऽ-ऽऽ ।ऽऽ ।ऽऽ ।ऽ ataila अतैल :10-10

831. ।ऽ ।ऽऽ ।ऽऽ ।ऽऽ ।ऽऽ ।ऽऽ । pataṅgapāda पतङ्गपादः :18

832. ।ऽ ।ऽऽ ।ऽऽ ।ऽऽ ।ऽ pravāhikā प्रवाहिका :13

833. ।ऽ ।ऽऽ ।ऽऽ ।ऽ viśhālaprabha विशालप्रभ :10

834. ।ऽ ।ऽऽ ।ऽऽ vāriśhālā वारिशाला :8

835. ।ऽ ।ऽऽ ।ऽ kuṭhārikā कुठारिका :7

836. ।ऽ ।ऽऽ । kṣhamāpāli क्षमापालि :6

837. ।ऽ ।ऽऽऽ । śhroṇī श्रोणी :7

838. ।ऽ ।ऽऽऽऽ padyā पद्या, sumohitā सुमोहिता :7

839. । ऽ । ऽ ऽ ऽ kañjā कञ्जा :6

840. । ऽ । ऽ ऽ kaṇṭhī कण्ठी :5

841. । ऽ । ऽ kalā कला :4

842. । ऽ । mrigendu मृगेन्दु :3

843. । ऽ ऽ : 3 dhritiā धृति, śhaśhi शशी

844. । ऽ ऽ । : 4 sadma सद्म

845. । ऽ ऽ । । । । । chayana चयन :8

846. । ऽ ऽ । । । । ऽ ऽ ऽ ऽ kaḍāra कडार :11

847. । ऽ ऽ । । । । ahati अहतिः :7

848. । ऽ ऽ । । । ऽ । ऽ ऽ । । । ऽ । ऽ ऽ । । । ऽ । ऽ ऽ । ऽ viṣhāṇāśhrita विषाणाश्रित :26

849. । ऽ ऽ । । । ऽ chiraruchi चिररुचिः :7

850. । ऽ ऽ । । । arti अर्ति :6

851. । ऽ ऽ । । ऽ । । ऽ । ऽ । । । । ऽ ऽ ऽ parāmoda परामोदः :18

852. । ऽ ऽ । । ऽ । ऽ । । । ऽ suvihitā सुविहिता :12

853. । ऽ ऽ । । ऽ । ऽ ऽ ऽ kalāpāntaritā कलापान्तरिता :10

854. । ऽ ऽ । । ऽ । parabhānu परभानु :7

855. । ऽ ऽ । । ऽ ऽ : 7 muditā मुदिता

856. । ऽ ऽ । । ऽ ऽ ऽ manolā मनोला :8

857. । ऽ ऽ । । ऽ ऽ mahanīyā महनीया :7

858. । ऽ ऽ । । ऽ maśhagā मशगा :6

859. । ऽ ऽ । । varīya वरीयः :5

860. । ऽ ऽ । ऽ : 5 jayā जया

861. । ऽ ऽ । ऽ । । upohā उपोहा :7

862. । ऽ ऽ । ऽ । ऽ mahoddhatā महोद्धता :7

863. । ऽ ऽ । ऽ । vrittahāri वृत्तहारि :6

864. । ऽ ऽ । ऽ ऽ : 6 somarājī सोमराजी

865. । ऽ ऽ । ऽ ऽ । । ऽ । । ऽ kuraṅgāvatāra कुरङ्गावतारः :12

866. । ऽ ऽ । ऽ ऽ । । ऽ । ऽ । ऽ karapallavodgatā करपल्लवोद्गता :13

867. I S S I S S I I vātuli वातुलि :8

868. I S S I S S I S I I I S S ś́halabhalolā शलभलोला :13

869. I S S I S S I S S : 9 brihattha बृहत्थ

870. I S S I S S I S S I S S : 12 (5:7) bhujaṅgaprayāta भुजंगप्रयात, apremeyā अप्रमेया

871. I S S I S S I S S I S S I : 13 kanda कंद

872. I S S I S S I S S I S S I S S I S S I S S I S S I S : 26 cheṭagati चेटीगति

873. I S S I S S I S S I S S I S S I S S I S S I S S I mallapallīprakāśha मल्लपल्लीप्रकाश :25

874. I S S I S S I S S I S S I S S I S S I S S I S S bhujaṅga भुजङ्गः :24

875. I S S I S S I S S I S S I S S I S S I S S vidyadālī विद्यदाली :21

876. I S S I S S I S S I S S I S S I S S I S avandhyopachāra अवन्ध्योपचारः :20

877. I S S I S S I S S I S S I S S I S S krīḍachandra क्रीडचन्द्र :18

878. I S S I S S I S S I S S I S S siṁhapuccha सिंहपुच्छ :15

879. I S S I S S I S S I S S I S prapāta प्रपातः :14

880. I S S I S S I S S I S S I kanda कन्दः :13

881. I S S I S S I S S I S S S : 13 kanduka कंदुक

882. I S S I S S I S S I S S S I S S I S S I S S vīranīrājanā वीरनीराजना :22

883. I S S I S S I S S I S S S S I S S I S S I S S I S S ābhāsamāna आभासमान :26

884. I S S I S S I S S I S bhujaṅgī भुजङ्गी :11

885. I S S I S S I S S viśhalya विशल्य :9

886. I S S I S S I S vihāvā विहावा :8

887. I S S I S S I narhi नर्हि :7

888. I S S I S S S I S I S prapātāvatāra प्रपातावतार :11

889. I S S I S S S I S S I S S darpamālā दर्पमाला :13

890. I S S I S S S I S S I S sarojāvālī सरोजावाली :11

891. I S S I S S S S S S S amālīna अमालीन :11

892. I S S I S S S S S S dhūmrālī धूम्राली :10

893. I S S I S S S S bhūmadhārī भूमधारी :8

894. I S S I S S S abhīka अभीक :7

895. । ऽ ऽ । ऽ ऽ somarājī सोमराजी :6

896. । ऽ ऽ । ऽ nārī नारी :5

897. । ऽ ऽ । vāri वारि :4

898. । ऽ ऽ ऽ । । । । । । ऽ ऽ । ऽ । । ऽ । ऽ : 19 (12:7) maṇimañjarī मणिमंजरी

899. । ऽ ऽ ऽ । । । । । ऽ । ऽ । । ऽ । ऽ : 17 (4:6:7) bhārākrāntā भाराक्रांता, krāntā क्रांता

900. । ऽ ऽ ऽ । । । bhūrivasu भूरिवसु :7

901. । ऽ ऽ ऽ । । ऽ ऽ ऽ ऽ vaṁśhāropī वंशारोपी :10

902. । ऽ ऽ ऽ । । ऽ keśhavatī केशवती :7

903. । ऽ ऽ ऽ । । somaśhruti सोमश्रुति :6

904. । ऽ ऽ ऽ । ऽ । । bhāṣhā भाषा :8

905. । ऽ ऽ ऽ । ऽ । mayūrī मयूरी :7

906. । ऽ ऽ ऽ । ऽ ऽ । : 8 suchandrābhā सुचन्द्राभा

907. । ऽ ऽ ऽ । ऽ ऽ ऽ । ऽ ऽ । ऽ ऽ driptadehā दृप्तदेहा :14

908. । ऽ ऽ ऽ । ऽ ऽ ऽ kulādhārī कुलाधारी :8

909. । ऽ ऽ ऽ । ऽ ऽ vayasya वयस्यः :7

910. । ऽ ऽ ऽ । ऽ kacchapī कच्छपी :6

911. । ऽ ऽ ऽ । bhrū भ्रूः :5

912. । ऽ ऽ ऽ ऽ । । । । । । ऽ ऽ । । । ऽ : 17 kalātantra कलातंत्र

913. । ऽ ऽ ऽ ऽ । । paddhari पद्धरि :7

914. । ऽ ऽ ऽ ऽ । ऽ ऽ pārāntachārī पारान्तचारी :8

915. । ऽ ऽ ऽ ऽ । ऽ ūpika ऊपिक :7

916. । ऽ ऽ ऽ ऽ । vindu विन्दु :6

917. । ऽ ऽ ऽ ऽ ऽ : 6 vriddhi वृद्धि, vrīḍā व्रीडा, śhikhaṇḍinī शिखंडिनी

918. । ऽ ऽ ऽ ऽ ऽ । । । । । । ऽ । ऽ ऽ । ऽ ऽ : 19 (6:7:6) mugdhaka मुग्धक

919. । ऽ ऽ ऽ ऽ ऽ । । । । । । ऽ ऽ । ऽ ऽ । ऽ ऽ : 20 (6:7:7) śhobhā शोभा

920. । ऽ ऽ ऽ ऽ ऽ । । । । । ऽ । ऽ । । ऽ । ऽ : 19 (6:6:7) makarandikā मकरंदिका

921. । ऽ ऽ ऽ ऽ ऽ । । । । । ऽ ऽ । । । ऽ : 17 (6:11) śhikhariṇī शिखरिणी

922. । ऽ ऽ ऽ ऽ ऽ । । । । । ऽ ऽ । । ऽ ऽ । ऽ : 19 (6:6:7) chhhāyā छाया

923. I S S S S S I I I I I S S I S S : 16 (6:10) jayānanda जयानंद

924. I S S S S S I I I I I S S I S S I S S : 19 (6:6:7) medhavisphurjitā मेधाविस्फूर्जिता, rambhā रंभा

925. I S S S S S I I I I I S S I S S I kāntāra कान्तार :17

926. I S S S S S I I I I I S S I S S pravaralalita प्रवरललित :16

927. I S S S S S I I I I I S S S I I I S : 18 (6:6:6) kriḍā क्रीडा, sudhā सुधा, muktamālā मुक्तमाला

928. I S S S S S I I I I I S S S I S S I S : 19 (5:7:7) chhāyā छाया

929. I S S S S S I S S I S S I S S I S S : 18 krīḍāchakra क्रीडाचक्र

930. I S S S S S I S S I S S ādhidaivī आधिदैवी :12

931. I S S S S S I S S S bodhāturā बोधातुरा :10

932. I S S S S S I kaṁsāsāri कंसासारि :7

933. I S S S S S S I S S I S S : 13 (6:7) pañcharikāvalī पंचरिकावली, chandrikā चंद्रिका

934. I S S S S S S I S S I S S chañcharīkāvalī चञ्चरीकावली :13

935. I S S S S S S S S S ś́hephālī शेफाली :10

936. I S S S S S S S S meghāloka मेघालोकः :9

937. I S S S S S S S anirbhāra अनिर्भारः :8

938. I S S S S S S prahāṇa प्रहाणः :7

939. I S S S S S panthā पन्था :6

940. I S S S S nālī नाली :5

941. I S S S krīḍā क्रीडा :4

942. I S S balākā बलाका :3

943. I S mahī मही :2

944. I snu स्नु :1

945. S : 1 uktā उक्ता

946. S I : 2 dukha दुःख, ś́hatru शत्रु

947. S I I : 3 hridya हृद्य

948. S I I I : 4 jatu जतु

949. S I I I I I I I I I I I I I S : 14 chakrapada चक्रपद, chakra चक्र

950. S | | | | | | | | | | S S | | | | S | | S | | S S nīpavanīyaka नीपवनीयक :25

951. S | | | | | | | | | | S S S S | | | | | | | | | | S : 26 (13:13) (14:12) āpiḍa आपीड

952. S | | | | | | | | | | S bhāsitasaraṇi भासितसरणिः :12

953. S | | | | | | | | S | | S S S | | | | | | | S | | S ś́hrikhalavalayita शृखलवलयित :26

954. S | | | | | | | | S kritamaṇitā कृतमणिता :10

955. S | | | | | | | S S upadhāyyā उपधाय्या :10

956. S | | | | | | | S dhaunika धौनिक :9

957. S | | | | | | | veśhi वेशि :8

958. S | | | | | | S : 8 nadī नदी

959. S | | | | | | S | | | | | | S | | | | | | S | | S S : 26 (7:7:7:5) rajana रजन

960. S | | | | | | S | | S | | : 13 paṅkāvalī पंकावली

961. S | | | | | | S | | S | | S | | | | | | | | | | S S ujjhitakadana उज्झितकदन :26

962. S | | | | | | S | | S | | alparuta अल्परुत :13, paṅkavatī पङ्कवती

963. S | | | | | | S | | S | S upachitaratikā उपचितरतिका :13

964. S | | | | | | S | | S S - S | | S | | S | | S S akusumachara अकुसुमचर :12-11

965. S | | | | | | S | | S S S | | | | | | | | | | S S bhāskara भास्कर :25

966. S | | | | | | S | | S S pathikāntā पथिकान्ता :12

967. S | | | | | | S | | S arthaśhikhā अर्थशिखा :11

968. S | | | | | | S | S | S aviralaratikā अविरलरतिका :12

969. S | | | | | | S | kaṭhināsthi कठिनास्थि :9

970. S | | | | | | S S | | | | | | S | S | S : 20 (3:6:11) dīpikāśhikhā दीपिकाशिखा

971. S | | | | | | S S | | | | | | S S titikṣhā तितिक्षा :17

972. S | | | | | | S S | | | | ardharuta अर्धरुत :13, paṅkāvali पङ्कावलिः :13

973. S | | | | | | S S | S | S S vāṭikāvikāśha वाटिकाविकाशः :14

974. S | | | | | | S S S | | | | | | S S | | S S | saṁbhritaśharadhi संभृतशरधिः :23

975. S | | | | | | S S S S S | | | | | | | | | | S S pārṣhatasaraṇa पार्षतसरण :24

976. S | | | | | | S ari अरि :8

977. S | | | | | | kośhi कोशि :7

978. S I I I I I I S : 7 chitrā चित्रा

979. S I I I I I I S I I S gahanā गहना :10

980. S I I I I I I S I S I I S I I S śhāntasurabhi शान्तसुरभिः :15

981. S I I I I I I S I S S I S I I S dhorita धोरित :15

982. S I I I I I I S S S S : 10 bandhuka बंधूक

983. S I I I I I I S ulapā उलपा :7

984. S I I I I I amati अमति :6

985. S I I I I S I I I I I I I S ardhakusumitā अर्धकुसुमिता :13

986. S I I I I S I I I I S I I I I S I S : 18 (6:5:7) hiraka हीरक

987. S I I I I S I I I I S S I I I I I I I S I I S S pulakāñchita पुलकाञ्चित :23

988. S I I I I S I I I I S S arpitamadanā अर्पितमदना :12

989. S I I I I S I I S S I I vāsaramaṇikā वासरमणिका :12

990. S I I I I S I I S S S S S S S krīḍitakaṭakā क्रीडितकटका :15

991. S I I I I S I I S S S krośhitakuśhalā क्रोशितकुशला :11

992. S I I I I S I I S rañjaka रञ्जक :9

993. S I I I S I I I S : 12 udaya उदय

994. S I I I I S I S I I I S I S S I S bālavikrīḍita बालविक्रीडित :17

995. S I I I I S I S I I I S S mayūkhasaraṇi मयूखसरणिः :13

996. S I I I I S I S I I S I S amitanagānikā अमितनगानिका :13

997. S I I I I S I S I S I I S prapātalikā प्रपातलिका :13

998. S I I I I S I S I S S I S bhasalamada भसलमद :13

999. S I I I I S I S I S S amandapāda अमन्दपादः :11

1000. S I I I I S I S I S kupya कुप्य :10

1001. S I I I I S I varajāpi वरजापि :7

1002. S I I I I S S : 7 vishuvaktrā विधुवक्त्रा

1003. S I I I I S S I I S I I I I S I S I S I I S S vilāsavāsa विलासवासः :23

1004. S I I I I S S I I S S śhramitaśhikhaṇḍī श्रमितशिखण्डी :11

1005. S I I I I S S I I S virala विरल :10

1006. S I I I I S S I S I I S arjitaphalikā अर्जितफलिका :12

1007. S I I I I S S S I S S I S S - S S I I S S S I S S I S S lāsyalīlā लास्यलीला :14-13

1008. S I I I I S S S I S S I S S : 14 rudrā रुद्रा

1009. S I I I I S S S I S S I S S puṣhpaśhakaṭikā पुष्पशकटिका :14

1010. S I I I I S S S S S S I I I I S : 16 (8:8) chakita चकित

1011. S I I I I S S S S S S I I I I S chakitā चकिता :16

1012. S I I I I S S S S S S S bhāsitabharaṇa भासितभरण :12

1013. S I I I I S S S S karmiṣhṭhā कर्मिष्ठा :9

1014. S I I I I S S ruchira रुचिर :7

1015. S I I I I S saurabhi सौरभि :6

1016. S I I I I kṣhut क्षुत :5

1017. S I I I S : 5 śharma शर्म

1018. S I I I S I I I I I I S saṅgamavatī सङ्गमवती :12

1019. S I I I S I I I S I I I I S : 14 induvadanā इंदुवदना

1020. S I I I S I I I S I I I S I S : 15 vipinatilaka विपिनतिलक, niśhipāla निशिपाल

1021. S I I I S I I I S I I I S S : 14 varasundarī वरसुंदरी, कांता, वनमयूर, इन्द्रवदना

1022. S I I I S I I I S I I S nīlagirikā नीलगिरिका :12

1023. S I I I S I I I S I S s aubhagakalā सौभगकला :11

1024. S I I I S I I S I I S S varatrā वरत्रा :12

1025. S I I I S I I S I I S śhalkaśhakala शल्कशकल :11

1026. S I I I S I I S I S I I I S añchalavatī अञ्चलवती :14

1027. S I I I S I I S I S I I S I S mayūvadanā मयूवदना :15

1028. S I I I S I I S I S I I S I hemamihikā हेममिहिका :14

1029. S I I I S I I S I S I S pikālikā पिकालिका :12

1030. S I I I S I S : 7 śhāradī शारदी

1031. S I I I S I S I I I S I I S kāraviṇī कारविणी :14

1032. S I I I S I S I S S I S viplutaśhikhā विप्लुतशिखा :12

1033. S I I I S I S I S pravahlikā प्रवह्लिका :9

1034. S I I I S I S S I S S I S vāmavadanā वामवदना :13

1035. S I I I S I S S I S khetaka खेटक :10

1036. S I I I S I S S krishnagatikā कृष्णगतिका :8

1037. S I I I S I S undari उन्दरि :7

1038. S I I I S I I jāsari जासरि :7

1039. S I I I S S : 6 kāmalatikā कामलतिका

1040. S I I I S S īti ईतिः :6

1041. S I I I S S I I S I I S I S S : 15 ketana केतन

1042. S I I I S S I nandathu नन्दथु :7

1043. S I I I S S S S I I S S siktamaṇimālā सिक्तमणिमाला :12

1044. S I I I S S S S S S S uddhatikarī उद्धतिकरी :11

1045. S I I I S S S S vātyā वात्या :8

1046. S I I I S S S kiṇapā किणपा :7

1047. S I I I S maṇḍala मण्डल :5

1048. S I I I anriju अनृजु :4

1049. S I I S : 4 sumukhī सुमुखी

1050. S I I S I I I I I I I I S kanakitā कनकिता :13

1051. S I I S I I I I I I S I I S S S ārabhaṭī आरभटी :16

1052. S I I S I I I I I S I S virataprabhā विरतप्रभा :12

1053. S I I S I I I I S I I S I I I I I I I I I S S S S dhaureya धौरेय :24

1054. S I I S I I I I S I I S S I unnarma उन्नर्म :14

1055. S I I S I I I I S I I S vanitābharaṇa वनिताभरण :12

1056. S I I S I I I I S S S śhritakamalā श्रितकमला :11

1057. S I I S I I I I S priyatilakā प्रियतिलका :9

1058. S I I S I I I S I I S S dhrishṭapada धृष्टपद :12

1059. S I I S I I I S I S S S S kalādhāma कलाधाम :13

1060. S I I S I I I S I S bhinnapada भिन्नपद :10

1061. ऽ । । ऽ । । । paurasari पौरसरि :7

1062. ऽ । । ऽ । । ऽ : 7 kalikā कलिका

1063. ऽ । । ऽ । । ऽ । । । । ऽ sammadavadanā सम्मदवदना :12

1064. ऽ । । ऽ । । ऽ ऽ ऽ ऽ : 16 dodhaka दोधक

1065. ऽ । । ऽ । । ऽ । । ऽ । । : 12 (3:3:3:3) bhāminī भामिनी, modaka मोदक

1066. ऽ । । ऽ । । ऽ । । ऽ । । । । । । ऽ ऽ : 18 (6:4:8) bhaṅgī भंगि, vichchhita विच्छित

1067. ऽ । । ऽ । । ऽ । । ऽ । । । । ऽ ऽ : 16 smaraśharamālā स्मरशरमाला

1068. ऽ । । ऽ । । ऽ । । ऽ । । ऽ - । । ऽ । । ऽ । । ऽ । । ऽ ऽ anaṅgapada अनङ्गपद :13-13

1069. ऽ । । ऽ । । ऽ । । ऽ । । ऽ : 13 aṅgaruchi अंगरुचि

1070. ऽ । । ऽ । । ऽ । । ऽ । । ऽ । । । । ऽ : 18 (11:7) maṇimālā मणिमाला, aśhvagati अश्वगति

1071. ऽ । । ऽ । । ऽ । । ऽ । । ऽ । । । ऽ । ऽ ऽ ऽ talpakatallaja तल्पकतल्लज :21

1072. ऽ । । ऽ । । ऽ । । ऽ । । ऽ । । ऽ : 16 nīla नील, khagati खगति, aśhvakāntā अश्वकांता

1073. ऽ । । ऽ । । ऽ । । ऽ । । ऽ । । ऽ । । । । । । ऽ ऽ ardita अर्दित :24

1074. ऽ । । ऽ । । ऽ । । ऽ । । ऽ । । ऽ । । ऽ । । ऽ : 22 madirā मदिरा, latākusuma लताकुसुम

1075. ऽ । । ऽ । । ऽ । । ऽ । । ऽ । । ऽ । । ऽ । । ऽ । । : 24 subhadra सुभद्र, kirīṭa किरीट

1076. ऽ । । ऽ । । ऽ । । ऽ । । ऽ । । ऽ । । ऽ । । ऽ । । ऽ ऽ priyajīvita प्रियजीवित :26

1077. ऽ । । ऽ । । ऽ । । ऽ । । ऽ । । ऽ । । ऽ । । ऽ । । ऽ śhivikā शिविका :25

1078. ऽ । । ऽ । । ऽ । । ऽ । । ऽ । । ऽ । । ऽ । । ऽ । । meduradanta मेदुरदन्त :24

1079. ऽ । । ऽ । । ऽ । । ऽ । । ऽ । । ऽ । । ऽ । । ऽ । chakora चकोरः :23

1080. ऽ । । ऽ । । ऽ । । ऽ । । ऽ । । ऽ । । ऽ । । ऽ ऽ : 23 (12:11) mayūragati मयूरगति,
mattagajendra मत्तगजेन्द्रः

1081. ऽ । । ऽ । । ऽ । । ऽ । । ऽ । । ऽ । । ऽ । । ऽ madirā मदिरा :22

1082. ऽ । । ऽ । । ऽ । । ऽ । । ऽ । । ऽ । । ऽ । । taḍidambara तडिदम्बर :21

1083. ऽ । । ऽ । । ऽ । । ऽ । । ऽ । । ऽ । । ऽ । ऽ : 21 mattavilāsinī मत्तविलासिनी

1084. ऽ । । ऽ । । ऽ । । ऽ । । ऽ । । ऽ । । ऽ ऽ vīravimāna वीरविमान :20

1085. ऽ । । ऽ । । ऽ । । ऽ । । ऽ । । ऽ । । hīrakahāradhara हीरकहारधर :18

1086. ऽ । । ऽ । । ऽ । । ऽ । । ऽ । । ऽ khagati खगतिः :16

1087. ऽ । । ऽ । । ऽ । । ऽ । । ऽ । ऽ । । ऽ । ऽ : 20 bhāsura भासुर, nandaka नंदक

1088. S I I S I I S I I S I I S S jāhamukhī जाहमुखी :14

1089. S I I S I I S I I S I I S karmaṭha कर्मठः :13

1090. S I I S I I S I I S I I modaka मोदक :12

1091. S I I S I I S I I S S - I I I I S I I S I I S S drutamadhyā द्रुतमध्या :11-12

1092. S I I S I I S I I S S - I I I I S S I I I I S S korakitā कोरकिता :11-12

1093. S I I S I I S I I S S - I I S I I S I I S S vargavatī वर्गवती :11-10

1094. S I I S I I S I I S S - S I I I I I I I S I I S S kamalākarā कमलाकरा :11-12

1095. S I I S I I S I I S S : 11 bhittaka भित्तक, avahitrā अवहित्रा

1096. S I I S I I S I I S S I I I I I I I I I I I I I I S : 24 drutalaghupadagati द्रुतलघुपदगति

1097. S I I S I I S I I S S I I S karṇiśhara कर्णिशरः :14

1098. S I I S I I S I I S S S I I S I I I I I I I I I S vellitavela वेल्लितवेल :24

1099. S I I S I I S I I S S S S vāsavilāsavatī वासविलासवती :13

1100. S I I S I I S I I S viśhvamukhī विश्वमुखी :10

1101. S I I S I I S I I dadhi दधि :9

1102. S I I S I I S I S : 9 utsuka उत्सुक

1103. S I I S I I S I S I I S I S : 14 darduraka दर्दुरक

1104. S I I S I I S I S I S S - I I I I I S I S I S S upāḍhya उपाढ्य :12-11

1105. S I I S I I S I S I S S ulapohā उलपोहा, valabhī वलभी :12

1106. S I I S I I S I S I hīralambi हीरलम्बि :10

1107. S I I S I I S I S S S : 11 rochaka रोचक

1108. S I I S I I S I S madanoddhurā मदनोद्धुरा :9

1109. S I I S I I S S : 8 chitrapadā चित्रपदा

1110. S I I S I I S S I I I I I I I S S S valvaja वल्वज :17

1111. S I I S I I S S I I S kalasvanavaṁśha कलस्वनवंशः :11

1112. S I I S I I S S I S I I S I S plavaṅgama प्लवङ्गमः :15

1113. S I I S I I S S S I I S : 12 (4:8) jalamālā जलमाला

1114. S I I S I I S S S I I S I I S : 15 saṅgataka संगतक

1115. S I I S I I S S S S : 10 bandhuka बंधूक

1116. S I I S I I S S chitrapadā चित्रपदा :8

1117. S I I S I I S mauralika मौरलिक :7

1118. S I I S I I nandi नन्दि :6

1119. S I I S I S : 6 madhumālinī मधुमालिनी

1120. S I I S I S I I I I I I I I I I I I S : 18 (9:9) bhramarapadaka भ्रमरपदक

1121. S I I S I S I I I I I I I I I I S : 16 (7:9) mattagajavilasita मत्तगजविलसित, riṣhabhagajavilasita ऋषभगजविलसित :16

1122. S I I S I S I I I I I I I I S I I S I I S S : 21 narendra नरेंद्र

1123. S I I S I S I I I I I I S I I I S I S I I I S bhadraka भद्रक :22

1124. S I I S I S I I I S I I I I I I S : 17 (10:7) vaṁśhapatrapatita वंशपत्रपतित, vaṁśhadala वंशदल

1125. S I I S I S I I I S I I S I I S : 16 (5:6:5) bhāminī भामिनी, śhailaśhikhā शैलशिखा

1126. S I I S I S I I I S I I S I I S I S I S : 20 utpalamālikā उत्पलमालिका

1127. S I I S I S I I I S I I S lavalīlatā लवलीलता :13

1128. S I I S I S I I I S I S I I I I S : 16 (10:6) dhauralalitā धौरललिता, प्रमुदिता

1129. S I I S I S I I I S I S I I I S I S I I I S : 22 (10:12) viśhuddhacharita विशुद्धचरित

1130. S I I S I S I I I S I S I I I S I S S I S : 21 (10:11) lalitavikrama ललितविक्रम

1131. S I I S I S I I I S S - I I S I S I I I S S ketu केतुः :10-11

1132. S I I S I S I I S niṣhadha निषध :9

1133. S I I S I S I S : 8 nāharaka नागरक

1134. S I I S I S I S S I I I I I I I S : 16 (10:6) varayuvatī वरयुवती

1135. S I I S I S I mīnapadī मीनपदी :7

1136. S I I S I S S I S I S aupagavīta औपगवीत :11, vārayātrika वारयात्रिक :11

1137. S I I S I S S hoḍapadā होडपदा :7

1138. S I I S I S śhunaka शुनक :6

1139. S I I S I viṭ विट् :5

1140. S I I S S : 5 paṁti पंक्ति

1141. S I I S S I I I I I I S : 12 lalanā ललना, rati रति

1142. S I I S S I I I I I I S S I I S I I I I I I I S S : 24 tanvī तन्वी

1143. S I I S S I I I I I I S vīraṇamālā वीरणमाला :12

1144. S I I S S I I I I S : 10 mrigachapalā मृगचपला, suradayitā सुरदयिता

1145. S I I S S I I I I S I : 11 sāndrapada सांद्रपद,

1146. S I I S S I I I I S S : 11 (5:6) pratyabodha प्रत्यबोध

1147. S I I S S I I I I S S I I I I S S S I I S S arbhakamālā अर्भकमाला :22

1148. S I I S S I I I I S S I I I I S sāravarohā सारवरोहा :16

1149. S I I S S I I I I S S I I S S I I I I S I I S gotragarīya गोत्रगरीयः :23

1150. S I I S S I I I I S S I I S S dīpaka दीपक :15

1151. S I I S S I I I I S S S S I I I I I I I I S S indravimāna इन्द्रविमान :23

1152. S I I S S I I I I S S anukūlā अनुकूला :11

1153. S I I S S I I S I I S I I S I I S vaṁśhala वंशलः :17

1154. S I I S S I I S I vāridhiyāna वारिधियान :9

1155. S I I S S I I S S I I S S ānanamūla आननमूल :13

1156. S I I S S I I S S śhambaradhārī शम्बरधारी :9

1157. S I I S S I I S māṇavaka माणवक :8

1158. S I I S S I I śhantanu शन्तनु :7

1159. S I I S S I S I S I S - I I S I I I S I S I S karabhoddhatā करभोद्धता :11-11

1160. S I I S S I S S I S S I S svinnaśharīra स्विन्नशरीर :13

1161. S I I S S I S S S S S lakṣhaṇalīlā लक्षणलीला :11

1162. S I I S S I S kalpamukhī कल्पमुखी :7

1163. S I I S S I rāhi राहि :6

1164. S I I S S S : 6 vikrāntā विक्रांता

1165. S I I S S S I I I S : 10 vrittasamṛddhā वृत्तसमृद्धा

1166. S I I S S S I I I S I I I I I I I I I I I I S S : 23 puṣhpasamriddhā पुष्पसमृद्धा

1167. S I I S S S I I S : 9 maṇimadhyā मणिमध्या, hiṁsakāntā सिंहकांता

1168. S I I S S S I I S I I S : 12 (5:7) lalanā ललना

1169. S I I S S S I I S S : 10 (5:5) rukmavatī रुक्मवती, champakamālā चंपकमाला

1170. S I I S S S I I S S I I I I I I I I I I I I I I S : 25 (5:5:8:7) kraunchapadā क्रौंचपदा

1171. ऽ । । ऽ ऽ ऽ । । ऽ ऽ । । । । । । । । । । । । । । । ऽ kroshapadā क्रोशपदा :25

1172. ऽ । । ऽ ऽ ऽ । । ऽ ऽ । । । । । । । । । । । । । ऽ : 23 chapalagati चपलगति

1173. ऽ । । ऽ ऽ ऽ । । ऽ ऽ । । । । । । । । । । । । । ऽ ऽ : 24 (5:5:8:6) hamsapada हंसपद

1174. ऽ । । ऽ ऽ ऽ । । ऽ ऽ । । । । । । । । । । । । ऽ ऽ kokapada कोकपद :24

1175. ऽ । । ऽ ऽ ऽ । । ऽ ऽ । । । । ऽ : 15 bhūtalatanvī भूतलतन्वी

1176. ऽ । । ऽ ऽ ऽ । । ऽ ऽ । kāmukalekhā कामुकलेखा :11

1177. ऽ । । ऽ ऽ ऽ । । ऽ ऽ ऽ । । ऽ ऽ । । ऽ ऽ । । ऽ nishkalakanthī निष्कलकण्ठी

1178. ऽ । । ऽ ऽ ऽ । । ऽ ऽ ऽ । । ऽ ऽ ऽ । । ऽ ऽ ऽ ऽ vāsakalīlā वासकलीला :22

1179. ऽ । । ऽ ऽ ऽ । । ऽ ऽ ऽ ऽ : 12 kāntotpīḍā कान्तोत्पीडा

1180. ऽ । । ऽ ऽ ऽ । । ऽ ऽ ऽ kandavinoda कन्दविनोदः :11

1181. ऽ । । ऽ ऽ ऽ । । ऽ ऽ champakamālā चम्पकमाला :10

1182. ऽ । । ऽ ऽ ऽ । । ऽ maṇimadhya मणिमध्य :9

1183. ऽ । । ऽ ऽ ऽ । । pañjari पञ्जरि :8

1184. ऽ । । ऽ ऽ ऽ । ऽ । ऽ : 10 dīpakamālā दीपकमाला

1185. ऽ । । ऽ ऽ ऽ । vyāhāri व्याहारि :7

1186. ऽ । । ऽ ऽ ऽ ऽ ऽ । । । । । । ऽ । । । । ऽ saurabhashobhāsāra सौरभशोभासारः :20

1187. ऽ । । ऽ ऽ ऽ ऽ ऽ । । kīlāla कीलाल :10

1188. ऽ । । ऽ ऽ ऽ ऽ ऽ ऽ 9 (5:4) snigdhā स्निग्धा, vaktra वक्त्र

1189. ऽ । । ऽ ऽ ऽ ऽ ऽ ऽ ऽ ऽ । । । । । । । ऽ ऽ ऽ bhekāloka भेकालोकः :20

1190. ऽ । । ऽ ऽ ऽ ऽ ऽ indraphalā इन्द्रफला :8

1191. ऽ । । ऽ ऽ ऽ ऽ adhīrā अधीरा :7

1192. ऽ । । ऽ ऽ ऽ sindhurayā सिन्धुरया :6

1193. ऽ । । ऽ ऽ pankti पङ्क्तिः :5

1194. ऽ । । ऽ valā वला :4

1195. ऽ । । mandari मन्दरि :3

1196. ऽ । ऽ : 3 mrigī मृगी, sudhī सुधी

1197. ऽ । ऽ । : 4 vartma वर्त्म

1198. ऽ । ऽ । । । : 6 kachchhapī कच्छपी

1199. S I S I I I I I I I I I I I I I S : 16 lalanā ललना

1200. S I S I I I I I I I S I S mukulitakalikāvalī मुकुलितकलिकावली :12

1201. S I S I I I I I S : 9 (3,6) halamukhī हलमुखी

1202. S I S I I I I I S I I I S paragati परगतिः :13

1203. S I S I I I I I I S I chāruchāraṇa चारुचारण :10

1204. S I S I I I I I S S S I S S S ānaddha आनद्ध :15

1205. S I S I I I I I S S achalapaṅkti अचलपङ्क्तिः :10

1206. S I S I I I I I S halamukhī हलमुखी :9

1207. S I S I I I I I kus'haka कुशक :8

1208. S I S I I I I S I I S S arditapāda अर्दितपाद :12

1209. S I S I I I I S I S I S - I I S I I I I S I S I S S chamūrubhīru चमूरुभीरुः :12-13

1210. S I S I I I I varas'has'hi वरशशि :7

1211. S I S I I I S I I I I S : 12 chandravartma चंद्रवर्त्म, vitā विता। । ।

1212. S I S I I I S I I S I I S I S : 15 (3:12) ramaṇīyaka रमणीयक, utsara उत्सर,

1213. S I S I I I S I I S I I S I S : 15 (5:10) sundara सुंदर, maṇibhūṣhaṇa मणिभूषण

1214. S I S I I I S I I S I I S I S nūtana नूतन :15

1215. S I S I I I S I I S I I S S : 14 vanalatā वनलता

1216. S I S I I I S I I S I S : 12 yuthikā युथिका

1217. S I S I I I S I I S S - S I S I I I S I S I S karṇinī कर्णिनी :11-11

1218. S I S I I I S I I S S : 11 svāgatā स्वागता, dīpak दीपक

1219. S I S I I I S I I S S svāgatā स्वागता :11

1220. S I S I I I S I S : 9 bhadrikā भद्रिका

1221. S I S I I I S I S I I I S I S I I I S I S : 21 (6:6:6:3) suranartakī सुरनर्तकी

1222. S I S I I I S I S I I I S I S I I I S I S : 21 taraṅgamālikā तरंगमालिका

1223. S I S I I I S I S I I I S I S I I I S I S I I I S bhāvinīvilasita भाविनीविलसित :25

1224. S I S I I I S I S I I I S I S I I I S I S I S : 23 urutaraṅgmālikā उरुतरंगमालिका

1225. S I S I I I S I S I I I S I S I I I S I S kanakamālikā कनकमालिका :21

1226. S I S I I I S I S I I I S I S I I I S ṭaṅkaṇa टङ्कण :19

1227. ऽ । ऽ । । । ऽ । ऽ । । । ऽ । ऽ   sāriṇī सारिणी :15

1228. ऽ । ऽ । । । ऽ । ऽ । । । ऽ   prabodhaphalitā प्रबोधफलिता :13

1229. ऽ । ऽ । । । ऽ । ऽ । । ऽ । ऽ   gaganodgatā गगनोद्गता :14

1230. ऽ । ऽ । । । ऽ । ऽ । ऽ - । । । ऽ । । । ऽ । ऽ । ऽ   kilikitā किलिकिता :11-12

1231. ऽ । ऽ । । । ऽ । ऽ । ऽ - ऽ । ऽ । । । ऽ । । ऽ ऽ   sārikā सारिका :11-11

1232. ऽ । ऽ । । । ऽ । ऽ । ऽ : 11   rathoddhatā रथोद्धता

1233. ऽ । ऽ । । । ऽ । ऽ ।   vireki विरेकि :10

1234. ऽ । ऽ । । । ऽ । ऽ   bhadrikā भद्रिका :9

1235. ऽ । ऽ । । । ऽ   bahulayā बहुलया :7

1236. ऽ । ऽ । । ।   pratari प्रतरि :6

1237. ऽ । ऽ । । ऽ । । । । ऽ । । । । ऽ । । ऽ । ऽ : 21 (11:10)   padmasadma पद्मसद्म

1238. ऽ । ऽ । । ऽ । । ऽ । । ऽ । । ऽ । । ऽ । ऽ : 20   puṭabheda पुटभेद

1239. ऽ । ऽ । । ऽ । । ऽ । ऽ : 11   achyuta अच्युत

1240. ऽ । ऽ । । ऽ । । ऽ ऽ : 10   maṇirāga मणिराग, maṇiraṅga मणिरंग

1241. ऽ । ऽ । । ऽ । । ऽ ऽ ऽ । । ऽ । । ऽ । ऽ : 19 (10:9)   śhaṅrgi शार्ंगि, ūrjita ऊर्जित

1242. ऽ । ऽ । । ऽ । ऽ । । । । । ऽ   gaganagatikā गगनगतिका :14

1243. ऽ । ऽ । । ऽ । ऽ । । ऽ । ऽ । । ऽ । ऽ : 18 (8:5:5)   vibudhapriyā विबुधप्रिया

1244. ऽ । ऽ । । ऽ । ऽ । । ऽ । ऽ । । ऽ । ऽ । । ऽ । ऽ । । ऽ kākalīkalakokila काकलीकलकोकिलः :26

1245. ऽ । ऽ । । ऽ । ऽ । । ऽ । ऽ । । ऽ । ऽ । । ऽ । ऽ ऽ ऽ   śharabhūriṇī शरभूरिणी :25

1246. ऽ । ऽ । । ऽ । ऽ । । ऽ । ऽ । । ऽ । ऽ   mattakokila मत्तकोकिल :18

1247. ऽ । ऽ । । ऽ । ऽ । । ऽ । ऽ   chandrahāsakarā चन्द्रहासकरा :13

1248. ऽ । ऽ । । ऽ । ऽ । । ऽ ऽ ऽ । । ऽ । ऽ : 18 (6:5:7)   varakrittan वरकृत्तन

1249. ऽ । ऽ । । ऽ । ऽ । ऽ : 10   lālinī लालिनी

1250. ऽ । ऽ । । ऽ । ऽ । ऽ । ऽ   paripuṅkhitā परिपुङ्खिता :12

1251. ऽ । ऽ । । ऽ । ऽ । ऽ   akṣharāvalī अक्षरावली :10

1252. ऽ । ऽ । । ऽ । ऽ ऽ । ऽ । । ऽ ।   ūhinī ऊहिनी :15

1253. ऽ । ऽ । । ऽ । ऽ ऽ ऽ ऽ ऽ   kiṁśhukāstaraṇa किंशुकास्तरण :12

1254. ऽ । ऽ । । ऽ ।   methikā मेथिका :7

1255. ऽ । ऽ । । ऽ ऽ : 7 udyatā उद्यता

1256. ऽ । ऽ । । ऽ ऽ । ऽ । । ऽ bhujaṅgajuṣhī भुजङ्गजुषी :12

1257. ऽ । ऽ । । ऽ ऽ ऽ : 8 gātha गाथ

1258. ऽ । ऽ । । ऽ ऽ s̒haragīti शरगीतिः :7

1259. ऽ । ऽ । । ऽ karmadā कर्मदा :6

1260. ऽ । ऽ । । kalki कल्कि :5

1261. ऽ । ऽ । ऽ : 5 bhāminī भामिनी

1262. ऽ । ऽ । ऽ । । । । ऽ । ऽ vipulapālikā विपुलपालिका :12

1263. ऽ । ऽ । ऽ । । । ऽ । ऽ : 11 (5:6) lalita ललित, drutā द्रुता, rajitā रजिता

1264. ऽ । ऽ । ऽ । । । ऽ । ऽ । ऽ mañjumālatī मञ्जुमालती :13

1265. ऽ । ऽ । ऽ । । । ऽ । ऽ upadārikā उपदारिका :11

1266. ऽ । ऽ । ऽ । । । ākhrṭa आरब्ट :8

1267. ऽ । ऽ । ऽ । । ऽ । ऽ varmitā वर्मिता :10

1268. ऽ । ऽ । ऽ । । ऽ s̒hraddharā श्रद्धरा :8

1269. ऽ । ऽ । ऽ । । kārpikā कार्पिका :7

1270. ऽ । ऽ । ऽ । ऽ : 7 raktā रक्ता

1271. ऽ । ऽ । ऽ । ऽ । : 8 samānikā समानिका, samānī समानी

1272. ऽ । ऽ । ऽ । ऽ । । । । ऽ । ऽ । ऽ । । । । ऽ । ऽ ऽ bhāsamānabimba भासमानबिम्ब :24

1273. ऽ । ऽ । ऽ । ऽ । ऽ : 9 bhujaṅgasaṅgatā भुजंगसंगता

1274. ऽ । ऽ । ऽ । ऽ । ऽ : 9 kāminī कामिनी, taraṅgavatī तरंगवती, bhāvinī भाविनी

1275. ऽ । ऽ । ऽ । ऽ । ऽ । ऽ : 11 s̒hreṇi श्रेणि, s̒hyenī श्येनी, senikā सेनिका

1276. ऽ । ऽ । ऽ । ऽ । ऽ । ऽ । - । ऽ । ऽ । ऽ । ऽ । ऽ । ऽ ऽ amarāvatī अमरावती :12-13

1277. ऽ । ऽ । ऽ । ऽ । ऽ । ऽ । : 12 samāna समान

1278. ऽ । ऽ । ऽ । ऽ । ऽ । ऽ । ऽ । ऽ : 15 (7:8) tūṇaka तूणक, utasava उत्सव, चामर–1

1279. ऽ । ऽ । ऽ । ऽ । ऽ । ऽ । ऽ । ऽ । : 16 chtras̒hobha चित्रशोभा

1280. ऽ । ऽ । ऽ । ऽ । ऽ । ऽ । ऽ । ऽ । ऽ । । ऽ : 20 mālava मालव

1281. ऽ । ऽ । ऽ । ऽ । ऽ । ऽ । ऽ । ऽ । ऽ । ऽ । : 20 gaṇḍaka गंडका, īdriṣha ईदृष :20

1282. ऽ । ऽ । ऽ । ऽ । ऽ । ऽ । ऽ । ऽ । ऽ । ऽ । ऽ । ऽ । ऽ ऽ vikuṇṭhakaṇṭha विकुण्ठकण्ठः :26

1283. ऽ । ऽ । ऽ । ऽ । ऽ । ऽ । ऽ । ऽ । ऽ । ऽ kalāpadīpaka कलापदीपक :19

1284. ऽ । ऽ । ऽ । ऽ । ऽ । ऽ । ऽ । ऽ ऽ chitra चित्र :16

1285. ऽ । ऽ । ऽ । ऽ । ऽ । ऽ । ऽ । ऽ ऽ : 16 chitra चित्र

1286. ऽ । ऽ । ऽ । ऽ । ऽ । ऽ । ऽ ऽ arkaśheṣhā अर्कशेषा :14

1287. ऽ । ऽ । ऽ । ऽ । ऽ । ऽ । ऽ kalāpatiprabhā कलापतिप्रभा :13

1288. ऽ । ऽ । ऽ । ऽ । ऽ ऽ : 10 mayūrasāriṇī मयूरसारिणी

1289. ऽ । ऽ । ऽ । ऽ । ऽ ऽ ऽ ऽ ऽ ऽ ऽ । ऽ । ऽ । ऽ ऽ ऽ ऽ vaṁśhalonnatā वंशलोन्नता :24

1290. ऽ । ऽ । ऽ । ऽ ऽ । । । । । । । । । । । । । ऽ : 21 chandanaprikriti चंदनप्रकृति

1291. ऽ । ऽ । ऽ । ऽ ऽ । ऽ । ऽ । ऽ sudhādhārā सुधाधारा :14

1292. ऽ । ऽ । ऽ । ऽ ऽ ऽ ऽ ऽ kūlachāriṇī कूलचारिणी :11

1293. ऽ । ऽ । ऽ । ऽ ऽ siṁhalekhā सिंहलेखा :8

1294. ऽ । ऽ । ऽ । ऽ chāmara चामर :7

1295. ऽ । ऽ । ऽ । ārbhava आर्भव :6

1296. ऽ । ऽ । ऽ ऽ । । । । ऽ ऽ : 12 kumudinī कुमुदिनी

1297. ऽ । ऽ । ऽ ऽ । । ऽ । ऽ । ऽ sārddhapadā सार्द्धपदा :13

1298. ऽ । ऽ । ऽ ऽ । ऽ : 8 haṁsinī हंसिनी

1299. ऽ । ऽ । ऽ ऽ । ऽ । ऽ : 10 (5:5) mauktika मौक्तिक, pathyā पथ्या, paṅtikā पंक्तिका

1300. ऽ । ऽ । ऽ ऽ । ऽ । ऽ karṇapālikā कर्णपालिका :10

1301. ऽ । ऽ । ऽ ऽ । ऽ ऽ ऽ ऽ vallavīvilāsa वल्लवीविलासः :11

1302. ऽ । ऽ । ऽ ऽ । anāsādi अनासादि :7

1303. ऽ । ऽ । ऽ ऽ ऽ ऽ maulimālikā मौलिमालिका :8

1304. ऽ । ऽ । ऽ ऽ ऽ ahiṁsā अहिंसा :7

1305. ऽ । ऽ । ऽ ऽ pikālī पिकाली :6

1306. ऽ । ऽ । ऽ vainasa वैनस :5

1307. ऽ । ऽ । dhāri धारि :4

1308. ऽ । ऽ ऽ : 4 riddhi ऋद्धि, samriddji समृद्धि

1309. ऽ । ऽ ऽ । । । ऽ । ऽ । ऽ : 12 dugdha दुग्ध

1310. ऽ । ऽ ऽ । । । ऽ । ऽ ऽ । ऽ ऽ । ऽ ऽ । ऽ : 19 (10:9) bhāgyavallakī भाग्यवल्लकी

1311. ऽ । ऽ ऽ । । । ऽ kurucharī कुरुचरी :8

1312. ऽ । ऽ ऽ । । । harṣhiṇī हर्षिणी :7

1313. ऽ । ऽ ऽ । । ऽ । । ऽ kerama केरम :10

1314. ऽ । ऽ ऽ । । ऽ saurakāntā सौरकान्ता :7

1315. ऽ । ऽ ऽ । । sopadhi सोपधि :6

1316. ऽ । ऽ ऽ । ऽ : 6 dviyodhā द्वियोधा

1317. ऽ । ऽ ऽ । ऽ । । । ऽ ऽ । ऽ alipada अलिपद :13

1318. ऽ । ऽ ऽ । ऽ । ऽ । । ऽ । ऽ । ऽ : 15 (7:8) chāmara चामर–2

1319. ऽ । ऽ ऽ । ऽ । ऽ । ऽ । ऽ । ऽ kalādhara कलाधरः :14

1320. ऽ । ऽ ऽ । ऽ । ऽ hemarūpa हेमरूप :8

1321. ऽ । ऽ ऽ । ऽ । sāmikā सामिका :7

1322. ऽ । ऽ ऽ । ऽ ऽ : 7 haṁsamālā हंसमाला

1323. ऽ । ऽ ऽ । ऽ ऽ । ऽ : 9 mahālakṣhamī महालक्ष्मी

1324. ऽ । ऽ ऽ । ऽ ऽ । ऽ । । । । ऽ । ऽ ऽ । ऽ ऽ । ऽ ऽ । ऽ chittachintāmaṇi चित्तचिन्तामणिः :25

1325. ऽ । ऽ ऽ । ऽ ऽ । ऽ । ऽ । ऽ । ऽ । kalpadhāri कल्पधारि :16

1326. ऽ । ऽ ऽ । ऽ ऽ । ऽ । ऽ gahvara गह्वर :11

1327. ऽ । ऽ ऽ । ऽ ऽ । ऽ ऽ : 10 trayī त्रयी

1328. ऽ । ऽ ऽ । ऽ ऽ । ऽ ऽ । । । ऽ kūrchalalita कूर्चललित :14

1329. ऽ । ऽ ऽ । ऽ ऽ । ऽ ऽ । ऽ : 12 padminī पद्मिनी, lakṣhmīdhara लक्ष्मीधर, stragviṇī स्त्रग्विणी

1330. ऽ । ऽ ऽ । ऽ ऽ । ऽ ऽ । ऽ । ऽ । ऽ । ऽ । ऽ । ऽ । ऽ । ऽ vinidrasindhura विनिद्रसिन्धुरः :26

1331. ऽ । ऽ ऽ । ऽ ऽ । ऽ ऽ । ऽ । ऽ kalpamīlitā कल्पमीलिता :14

1332. ऽ । ऽ ऽ । ऽ ऽ । ऽ ऽ । ऽ ऽ । ऽ : 15 chandralekhā चंद्रलेखा

1333. ऽ । ऽ ऽ । ऽ ऽ । ऽ ऽ । ऽ ऽ । ऽ ऽ । ऽ ऽ । ऽ ऽ । ऽ : 24 (8:8:8) svairiṇīkrīḍana स्वैरिणीक्रीडन

1334. ऽ । ऽ ऽ । ऽ ऽ । ऽ ऽ । ऽ ऽ । ऽ ऽ । ऽ ऽ । ऽ ऽ । ऽ ऽ hrīṇahaiyaṅgavīna ह्रीणहैयङ्गवीन :25

1335. ऽ । ऽ ऽ । ऽ ऽ । ऽ ऽ । ऽ ऽ । ऽ ऽ । ऽ ऽ । ऽ ऽ । ऽ gaṅgodaka गङ्गोदक :24

1336. ऽ । ऽ ऽ । ऽ ऽ । ऽ ऽ । ऽ ऽ । ऽ ऽ । ऽ ऽ । ऽ ऽ kaṅkaṇakvāṇa कङ्कणक्वाणः :22

1337. ऽ । ऽ ऽ । ऽ ऽ । ऽ ऽ । ऽ ऽ । ऽ ऽ । ऽ ऽ lolalolambalīla लोललोलम्बलील :19

1338. ऽ । ऽ ऽ । ऽ ऽ । ऽ ऽ । ऽ ऽ । ऽ ऽ । ऽ sindhusauvīra सिन्धुसौवीर :18

1339. ऽ । ऽ ऽ । ऽ ऽ । ऽ ऽ । ऽ ऽ । ऽ ऽ । pratīhāra प्रतीहारः :17

1340. ऽ । ऽ ऽ । ऽ ऽ । ऽ ऽ । ऽ ऽ । ऽ lāsyakārī लास्यकारी :15

1341. ऽ । ऽ ऽ । ऽ ऽ । ऽ ऽ । ऽ ऽ । kāmaśhālā कामशाला :14

1342. ऽ । ऽ ऽ । ऽ ऽ । ऽ ऽ । ऽ ऽ śhraddharāntā श्रद्धरान्ता :13

1343. ऽ । ऽ ऽ । ऽ ऽ । ऽ ऽ । ऽ sragviṇī स्रग्विणी :12

1344. ऽ । ऽ ऽ । ऽ ऽ । ऽ ऽ । gambhāri गम्भारि :11

1345. ऽ । ऽ ऽ । ऽ ऽ । ऽ ऽ ऽ dārudehā दारुदेहा :11

1346. ऽ । ऽ ऽ । ऽ ऽ । ऽ ऽ hemahāsa हेमहासः :10

1347. ऽ । ऽ ऽ । ऽ ऽ । ऽ bhaurika भौरिक :9

1348. ऽ । ऽ ऽ । ऽ ऽ । lakṣhmī लक्ष्मी :8

1349. ऽ । ऽ ऽ । ऽ ऽ ऽ : 8 padminī पद्मिनी, padmamālā पद्ममाला

1350. ऽ । ऽ ऽ । ऽ ऽ ऽ । ऽ ऽ । । ऽ ऽ : 15 (7:8) chandrakāntā चंद्रकांता

1351. ऽ । ऽ ऽ । ऽ ऽ ऽ । ऽ ऽ । ऽ ऽ ऽ : 15 (8:7) chandralekh चंद्रलेखा

1352. ऽ । ऽ ऽ । ऽ ऽ ऽ । ऽ ऽ । ऽ ऽ babhrulakṣhmī बभ्रुलक्ष्मीः :14

1353. ऽ । ऽ ऽ । ऽ vijohā विजोहा :6

1354. ऽ । ऽ ऽ । hrī ह्रीः :5

1355. ऽ । ऽ ऽ ऽ : 5 prīti प्रीति

1356. ऽ । ऽ ऽ ऽ । । ऽ ऽ ऽ dvāravahā द्वारवहा :10

1357. ऽ । ऽ ऽ ऽ । । gūrṇikā गूर्णिका :7

1358. ऽ । ऽ ऽ ऽ । ऽ ऽ । ऽ ऽ । ऽ ऽ kalpakāntā कल्पकान्ता :14

1359. ऽ । ऽ ऽ ऽ । ऽ mriṣhṭapādā मृष्टपादा :7

1360. ऽ । ऽ ऽ ऽ । mantrikā मन्त्रिका :6

1361. ऽ । ऽ ऽ ऽ ऽ : 6 nīlatoyā नीलतोया

1362. ऽ । ऽ ऽ ऽ ऽ । । ऽ ऽ : 10 kalikā कलिका

1363. ऽ । ऽ ऽ ऽ ऽ । kharviṇī खर्विणी :7

1364. ऽ । ऽ ऽ ऽ ऽ ऽ sairavī सैरवी :7

1365. ऽ । ऽ ऽ ऽ ऽ kareṇu करेणुः :6

1366. ऽ । ऽ ऽ ऽ sūriṇī सूरिणी :5

1367. ऽ । ऽ ऽ nanda नन्दः :4

1368. ऽ । ऽ mrigī मृगी :3

1369. ऽ । chāru चारु :2

1370. ऽ ऽ : 2 strī स्त्री, nau नौ

1371. ऽ ऽ । : 3 senā सेना

1372. ऽ ऽ । । : 4 trapu त्रपु

1373. ऽ ऽ । । । । । । । । । । । ऽ - । । । । । । । । । ऽ । । ऽ ऽ atisurahitā अतिसुरहिता :13-13

1374. ऽ ऽ । । । । । । । । । ऽ rūpāvali रूपावलिः :12

1375. ऽ ऽ । । । । । । । । ऽ : 11 abhihitā अभिहिता, mukhachapalā मुखचपला

1376. ऽ ऽ । । । । । । । । ऽ ऽ । । ऽ ऽ bhogāvali भोगावलिः :16

1377. ऽ ऽ । । । । । । । । ऽ ऽ ऽ ऽ pārāvāra पारावारः :14

1378. ऽ ऽ । । । । । । । । ऽ ऽ viratimahatī विरतिमहती :12

1379. ऽ ऽ । । । । । । ऽ । sarasamukhī सरसमुखी :10

1380. ऽ ऽ । । । । । । ऽ ऽ ऽ ऽ vivaravilasita विवरविलसित :12

1381. ऽ ऽ । । । । । । ऽ ऽ unnāla उन्नाल :10

1382. ऽ ऽ । । । । । । ऽ ākekara आकेकर :9

1383. ऽ ऽ । । । । । । sindhuk सिंधुक :8

1384. ऽ ऽ । । । । । ऽ īḍā ईडा :8

1385. ऽ ऽ । । । । । ऽ । । ऽ ऽ chalitakapada छलितकपद :12

1386. ऽ ऽ । । । । । ऽ ऽ kāmā कामा :9

1387. ऽ ऽ । । । । । muśhaki मुशकि :7

1388. ऽ ऽ । । । । ऽ : 7 vajra वज्र, madhukarikā मधुकरिका

1389. ऽ ऽ । । । । ऽ । । । । ऽ - । । । । ऽ ऽ ऽ । । ऽ ऽ avāchīkritavadanā अवाचीकृतवदना :12-11

1390. ऽ ऽ । । । । ऽ । । ऽ । । । । । । ऽ vāhāntarita वाहान्तरित :17

1391. ऽ ऽ । । । । ऽ । । ऽ ऽ । । ऽ ऽ ऽ : 16 bālā बाला

1392. ऽ ऽ । । । । ऽ । ऽ । ऽ : 11 udyatā उद्यता

1393. ऽ ऽ । । । । ऽ । ऽ । ऽ nīlā नीला :11

1394. ऽ ऽ । । । ऽ ऽ । । । । । । । ऽ ऽ ऽ krūrāśhana क्रूराशन :17

1395. ऽ ऽ । । । । ऽ ऽ । । । । ऽ ऽ । । । ऽ dandī दण्डी :18

1396. ऽ ऽ । । । । ऽ ऽ । । ऽ samayavatī समयवती :11

1397. ऽ ऽ । । । । ऽ ऽ । ऽ nīrāñjali नीराञ्जलिः :10

1398. ऽ ऽ । । । । ऽ ऽ ऽ : 9 kanakalatā कनकलता, makaralatā मकरलता

1399. ऽ ऽ । । । । ऽ ऽ ऽ । । ऽ । । । । । । । । । । । । । ऽ abhrabramaṇa अभ्रब्रमण :25

1400. ऽ ऽ । । । । ऽ ऽ ऽ ऽ । । । । ऽ । ऽ ऽ ऽ mārābhisaraṇa माराभिसरण :19

1401. ऽ ऽ । । । । ऽ ऽ ऽ ऽ ऽ ऽ ऽ s̍hampā शम्पा :12

1402. ऽ ऽ । । । । ऽ ऽ ऽ rambhā रम्भा :9

1403. ऽ ऽ । । । । ऽ ऽ sandhyā सन्ध्या :8

1404. ऽ ऽ । । । । ऽ hīra हीर :7

1405. ऽ ऽ । । । । atikali अतिकलि :6

1406. ऽ ऽ । । ऽ : 6 vasumati वसुमति

1407. ऽ ऽ । । ऽ । ऽ । । । ऽ suvanamālikā सुवनमालिका :12

1408. ऽ ऽ । । ऽ । ऽ । । ऽ । ऽ kanakaketakī कनककेतकी :13

1409. ऽ ऽ । । ऽ । ऽ । ऽ - । । ऽ । । ऽ । ऽ । ऽ ghaṭikā घटिका :10-10

1410. ऽ ऽ । । ऽ । ऽ । ऽ ahilā अहिला :10

1411. ऽ ऽ । । ऽ । ऽ ऽ ऽ ऽ ऽ vis̍hālāmbhojālī विशालाम्भोजाली :12

1412. ऽ ऽ । । ऽ । saralāṅghri सरलाङ्घ्रि :7

1413. ऽ ऽ । । ऽ ऽ : 7 vajraka वज्रक

1414. ऽ ऽ । । ऽ ऽ ऽ : 8 s̍hyāmā श्यामा

1415. ऽ ऽ । । ऽ ऽ ऽ ऽ ऽ kūla कूल :10

1416. ऽ ऽ । । ऽ ऽ ऽ ऽ vaisāru वैसारुः :9

1417. ऽ ऽ । । ऽ ऽ sthūlā स्थूला :7

1418. ऽ ऽ । । ऽ vasumatī वसुमती :6

1419. ऽ ऽ । । । chidra छिद्र :5

1420. ऽ ऽ । ऽ : 5 nandā नंदा, mandā मंदा

1421. ऽ ऽ । ऽ । । । । । । ऽ vyāyogavatī व्यायोगवती :12

1422. ऽ ऽ । ऽ । । ऽ । । ऽ । ऽ ऽ : 15 s̍his̍hu शिशु

1423. ऽ ऽ । । ऽ । । ऽ । ऽ mālavikā मालविका :11

1424. ऽ ऽ । । ऽ । । ऽ : 8 anushṭup अनुष्टुप्

1425. ऽ ऽ । । ऽ । । ऽ । । ऽ - । । ऽ । । ऽ । । ऽ । । ऽ kinnaṭaka किन्नटकः :11-12

1426. ऽ ऽ । । ऽ । । ऽ । । ऽ : 11 moṭaka मोटक

1427. ऽ ऽ । । ऽ । । ऽ । । ऽ । । ऽ । । ऽ । । ऽ । । ऽ : 23 s'haṅkha शंख

1428. ऽ ऽ । । ऽ । । ऽ । । ऽ moṭanaka मोटनक :11

1429. ऽ ऽ । । ऽ । । ऽ । ऽ : 10 upasthitā उपस्थिता

1430. ऽ ऽ । । ऽ । । ऽ । ऽ ऽ : 11 upasthitā उपस्थिता

1431. ऽ ऽ । । ऽ । । ऽ ऽ ऽ । । ऽ ऽ kritamāla कृतमाल :14

1432. ऽ ऽ । । ऽ । । ऽ vidyā विद्या :8

1433. ऽ ऽ । । ऽ । । doṣhā दोषा :7

1434. ऽ ऽ । । ऽ । ऽ । । । ऽ । । ऽ । ऽ - । । । । ऽ । ऽ । । । ऽ । । ऽ । ऽ vāsinī वासिनी :16-16

1435. ऽ ऽ । । ऽ । ऽ । ऽ । ऽ । । । । । । ऽ ऽ । ऽ ऽ । ऽ utkaṭapaṭṭikā उत्कटपट्टिका :24

1436. ऽ ऽ । । ऽ । ऽ । ऽ ऽ - ऽ ऽ ऽ । । । ऽ । ऽ । ऽ ऽ s'hukāvalī शुकावली :10-13

1437. ऽ ऽ । । ऽ । ऽ । ऽ ऽ - ऽ ऽ ऽ । । ऽ । ऽ । ऽ ऽ bhadraviraṭ भद्रविराट् : samudrakāntā समुद्रकान्ता :10-11

1438. ऽ ऽ । । ऽ । ऽ । ऽ ऽ nameru नमेरुः :10

1439. ऽ ऽ । । ऽ । ऽ । ऽ ऽ vilāsavāpī विलासवापी :10

1440. ऽ ऽ । । ऽ । ऽ । ऽ ravonmukhī रवोन्मुखी :9

1441. ऽ ऽ । । ऽ । ऽ । ऽ vaisārī वैसारी :9

1442. ऽ ऽ । । ऽ । ऽ ऽ । ऽ । । । । । । । । ऽ ऽ kiraṇakīrtti किरणकीर्त्तिः :19

1443. ऽ ऽ । । ऽ । ऽ ऽ sārāvanadā सारावनदा :8

1444. ऽ ऽ । । ऽ । ऽ pūrṇā पूर्णा :7

1445. ऽ ऽ । । ऽ । hāṭakas'hāli हाटकशालि :6

1446. ऽ ऽ । । ऽ ऽ : 6 tanumadhyā तनुमध्या

1447. ऽ ऽ । । ऽ ऽ । । ऽ ऽ : 10 madirākṣhī मदिराक्षी

1448. ऽ ऽ । । ऽ ऽ । । ऽ ऽ । । । । ऽ ऽ sūtas'hikhā सूतशिखा :16

1449. ऽ ऽ । । ऽ ऽ । । ऽ ऽ । । ऽ ऽ : 14 (6:8) kalahaṁsī कलहंसी

1450. ऽ ऽ । । ऽ ऽ । । ऽ ऽ । । ऽ ऽ śhāradachandra शारदचन्द्रः :14

1451. ऽ ऽ । । ऽ ऽ । । ऽ ऽ । । ऽ abhrabhramaśhīlā अभ्रभ्रमशीला :13

1452. ऽ ऽ । । ऽ ऽ । । ऽ ऽ ऽ ऽ ऽ ऽ vaṁśhottaṁsā वंशोत्तंसा :14

1453. ऽ ऽ । । ऽ ऽ । guñjā गुञ्जा :7

1454. ऽ ऽ । । ऽ ऽ ऽ । । ऽ : 10 suṣhamā सुषमा

1455. ऽ ऽ । । ऽ ऽ ऽ । । ऽ । । । । । । । । । । । । । । । ऽ : 25 (10:15) haṁsapadā हंसपदा

1456. ऽ ऽ । । ऽ ऽ ऽ । । ऽ । । । । ऽ śhīrśhavirahitā शीर्शविरहिता :15

1457. ऽ ऽ । । ऽ ऽ ऽ । । ऽ । । ऽ ऽ ratirekha रतिरेख :14

1458. ऽ ऽ । । ऽ ऽ ऽ । । ऽ ऽ । । ऽ nāsābharaṇa नासाभरण :14

1459. ऽ ऽ । । ऽ ऽ ऽ । । ऽ suṣhamā सुषमा :10

1460. ऽ ऽ । । ऽ ऽ ऽ । ऽ ऽ । ऽ ऽ -ऽ । । । । ऽ ऽ ऽ । ऽ ऽ । ऽ ऽ lāsyalīlālaya लास्यलीलालयः :13-14

1461. ऽ ऽ । । ऽ ऽ ऽ । ऽ ऽ । ऽ ऽ bhājanaśhīlā भाजनशीला :13

1462. ऽ ऽ । । ऽ ऽ ऽ ऽ । । ऽ ऽ : 12 (6:6) maṇimālā मणिमाला, puṣhpavichitrā पुष्पविचित्रा

1463. ऽ ऽ । । ऽ ऽ ऽ ऽ । ऽ । ऽ ऽ ऽ prapannapānīya प्रपन्नपानीय :14

1464. ऽ ऽ । । ऽ ऽ ऽ ऽ ऽ । ऽ ऽ : 12 (7:5) vāhinī वाहिनी

1465. ऽ ऽ । । ऽ ऽ ऽ ऽ ऽ ऽ ऽ ऽ ऽ ऽ ऽ vajrālī वज्राली :15

1466. ऽ ऽ । । ऽ ऽ ऽ ऽ ऽ ऽ ऽ meghadhvanipūra मेघध्वनिपूरः :11

1467. ऽ ऽ । । ऽ ऽ ऽ vedhā वेधाः :7

1468. ऽ ऽ । । ऽ ऽ tanumadhyā तनुमध्या :6

1469. ऽ ऽ । । ऽ kaṇikā कणिका :5

1470. ऽ ऽ । । tāvuri तावुरि :4

1471. ऽ ऽ । ऽ : 4 tārā तारा

1472. ऽ ऽ । ऽ । । । । । । । । ऽ narāvali नरावलिः :13

1473. ऽ ऽ । ऽ । । । । ऽ । ऽ । ऽ : 13 (4:9) lakṣhmī लक्ष्मी, ruchī रुचि

1474. ऽ ऽ । ऽ । । । । ऽ । ऽ । ऽ ऽ chalāñchala चेलाञ्चल :14

1475. ऽ ऽ । ऽ । । । । ऽ । ऽ । ऽ prabhāvatī प्रभावती :13

1476. ऽ ऽ । ऽ । । । । ऽ । ऽ ऽ : 12 (4:8) śhruti श्रुति

1477. ऽ ऽ । ऽ । । । ऽ । । । । ऽ ऽ । ऽ ऽ । ऽ ऽ viṣhvagvitāna विष्वग्वितान :20

1478. ऽ ऽ । ऽ । । । ऽ । । ऽ : 11 viśhloka विश्लोक, utthāpanī उत्थापनी

1479. ऽ ऽ । ऽ । । । ऽ । । ऽ । ऽ : 13 abhraka अभ्रक

1480. ऽ ऽ । ऽ । । । ऽ । । ऽ । ऽ । ऽ : 15 mridaṅga मृदंग

1481. ऽ ऽ । ऽ । । । ऽ । । ऽ । ऽ ऽ : 14 (8:6) vasantatilakā वसंततिलका, siṁhoddhatā सिंहोद्धता

1482. ऽ ऽ । ऽ । । । ऽ । । ऽ । ऽ pramodatilakā प्रमोदतिलका :13

1483. ऽ ऽ । ऽ । । । ऽ । । ऽ ऽ - । । ऽ । ऽ । । । ऽ । । ऽ ऽ padmāvatī पद्मावती :12-13

1484. ऽ ऽ । ऽ । । । ऽ । । ऽ ऽ nirantika निरन्तिक :12, sarasīka सरसीक :12

1485. ऽ ऽ । ऽ । । । ऽ । । ऽ jihmāśhayā जिह्माशया :11

1486. ऽ ऽ । ऽ । । । ऽ । ऽ । । । ऽ । ऽ । । । । । । । । । । ऽ karṇāṭaka कर्णाटक :26

1487. ऽ ऽ । ऽ । । । ऽ । ऽ । । । ऽ । ऽ । । । ऽ : 20 śhaśhaṅkarachita शशंकरचित

1488. ऽ ऽ । ऽ । । । ऽ । ऽ । ऽ : 12 lalitā ललिता

1489. ऽ ऽ । ऽ । । । ऽ । ऽ । ऽ lalitā ललिता :12

1490. ऽ ऽ । ऽ । । । ऽ । ऽ ऽ । ऽ marmasphura मर्मस्फुर :13

1491. ऽ ऽ । ऽ । । । ऽ ऽ : 9 ruchirā रुचिरा

1492. ऽ ऽ । ऽ । । । ऽ ऽ । ऽ । । । ऽ ऽ । ऽ । । । ऽ : 22 (7:15) mattebha मत्तेभ, sitastavaka सितस्तवकः :22

1493. ऽ ऽ । ऽ । । । ऽ ऽ ऽ । । । । ऽ । । ऽ । । ऽ । ऽ । ऽ vyākośhakośhala व्याकोशकोशल :25

1494. ऽ ऽ । ऽ । । । krodāntika क्रोडान्तिक :7

1495. ऽ ऽ । ऽ । । ऽ : 7 chūḍāmaṇī चूडामणि

1496. ऽ ऽ । ऽ । । ऽ । । ऽ । ऽ ऽ māṇavikāvikāṣha माणविकाविकाषः :13

1497. ऽ ऽ । ऽ । । ऽ । । ऽ parichāravatī परिचारवती :10

1498. ऽ ऽ । ऽ । । ऽ । ऽ । । । । । ऽ śhaṅkāvalī शङ्कावली :15

1499. ऽ ऽ । ऽ । । ऽ । ऽ । । ऽ । । । । । । । । ऽ । ऽ bhogāvalī भोगावली :22

1500. ऽ ऽ । ऽ । । ऽ । ऽ । । ऽ । ऽ alakālikā अलकालिका :14

1501. ऽ ऽ । ऽ । । ऽ । ऽ । । ऽ । aṭṭāsinī अट्टासिनी :13, nirmadhuvāri निर्मधुवारि :13

1502. ऽ ऽ । ऽ । । ऽ । ऽ । ऽ । ऽ : 13 (4:9) prabhāvatī प्रभावती

1503. ऽ ऽ । ऽ । । ऽ । ऽ । kāmachāri कामचारि :10

1504. ऽ ऽ । ऽ । । ऽ । ऽ ऽ । ऽ । । ऽ ऽ । ऽ । । । ऽ bhujaṅgoddhata भुजङ्गोद्धत :22

1505. ऽ ऽ । ऽ । । ऽ । amarandi अमरन्दि :8

1506. ऽ ऽ । ऽ । । ऽ ऽ । ऽ ऽ īhāmrigī ईहामृगी :11

1507. ऽ ऽ । ऽ । । ऽ ऽ । ऽ varhāturā वर्हातुरा :10

1508. ऽ ऽ । ऽ । । ऽ nirvādhikā निर्वाधिका :7

1509. ऽ ऽ । ऽ । । indhā इन्धा :6

1510. ऽ ऽ । ऽ । ऽ : 6 jalā जला

1511. ऽ ऽ । ऽ । ऽ । ऽ : 8 nārāchikā नाराचिका

1512. ऽ ऽ । ऽ । ऽ । ऽ । ऽ । ऽ antarvikāsavāsaka अन्तर्विकासवासकः :12

1513. ऽ ऽ । ऽ । ऽ । ऽ nārāchikā नाराचिका :8

1514. ऽ ऽ । ऽ । ऽ । vrindā वृन्दा :7

1515. ऽ ऽ । ऽ । ऽ ऽ । । । । । । ऽ । ऽ । । ऽ । ऽ : 21 (7:7:7) kathāgati कथागति

1516. ऽ ऽ । ऽ । ऽ ऽ । ऽ । ऽ । ऽ priṣhadvatī पृषद्वती :13

1517. ऽ ऽ । ऽ । ऽ ऽ ऽ : 8 vibhā विभा

1518. ऽ ऽ । ऽ । ऽ ऽ bhīmārjuna भीमार्जुन :7

1519. ऽ ऽ । ऽ । ऽ sthālī स्थाली :6

1520. ऽ ऽ । ऽ । kiñjalki किञ्जल्कि :5

1521. ऽ ऽ । ऽ ऽ : 5 hāri हारि

1522. ऽ ऽ । ऽ ऽ । : 6 manthāna मंथान

1523. ऽ ऽ । ऽ ऽ । । । । ऽ ऽ uditavijohā उदितविजोहा :11

1524. ऽ ऽ । ऽ ऽ । । । ऽ । ऽ ऽ vanitāviloka वनिताविलोकः :12

1525. ऽ ऽ । ऽ ऽ । । ऽ । ऽ । ऽ - । ऽ । ऽ ऽ । । ऽ । ऽ । ऽ kumārī कुमारी, śhiśhirā शिशिरा :12-12

1526. ऽ ऽ । ऽ ऽ । । ऽ । ऽ । ऽ : 12 indravaṁśhā इंद्रवंशा

1527. ऽ ऽ । ऽ ऽ । । ऽ । ऽ । ऽ #1,2,3 + #4 । ऽ । ऽ ऽ । । ऽ । ऽ । ऽ vāsantikā वासन्तिका :12-12-12-12

1528. ऽ ऽ । ऽ ऽ । । ऽ । ऽ । ऽ #1-3-4 + #2 । ऽ । ऽ ऽ । । ऽ । ऽ । ऽ ratākhyānakī रताख्यानकी :12-12-12-12

1529. ऽ ऽ । ऽ ऽ । । ऽ । ऽ । ऽ induvaṁśhā इन्दुवंशा :12

1530. ऽ ऽ । ऽ ऽ । । ऽ । ऽ । ऽ puṣhṭidā पुष्टिदा :12

1531. ऽ ऽ । ऽ ऽ । । ऽ । ऽ । ऽ śhaṅkhachūḍā शङ्खचूडा, saurabheyī सौरभेयी :12

1532. ऽ ऽ । ऽ ऽ । । ऽ । ऽ ऽ - । ऽ । ऽ ऽ । । ऽ । ऽ ऽ - । ऽ । ऽ ऽ । । ऽ । ऽ ऽ - ऽ ऽ । ऽ ऽ । । ऽ । ऽ ऽ

jāyā जाया :11-11

1533. ऽ ऽ । ऽ ऽ । । ऽ । ऽ ऽ - । ऽ । ऽ ऽ । । ऽ । ऽ ऽ bhadrā भद्रा :11-11

1534. ऽ ऽ । ऽ ऽ । । ऽ । ऽ ऽ : 11 indravaṁśhā इंद्रवज्रा

1535. ऽ ऽ । ऽ ऽ । । ऽ । ऽ ऽ #1,2 + #3,4 । ऽ । ऽ ऽ । । ऽ । ऽ ऽ rāmā रामा :11-11-11-11

1536. ऽ ऽ । ऽ ऽ । । ऽ । ऽ ऽ #1,2,3 + #4 ऽ ऽ । ऽ ऽ । । ऽ । ऽ ऽ śhālā शाला :11-11-11-11

1537. ऽ ऽ । ऽ ऽ । । ऽ । ऽ ऽ #1,3,4 + #2 । ऽ । ऽ ऽ । । ऽ । ऽ ऽ vāṇī वाणी :11-11-11-11

1538. ऽ ऽ । ऽ ऽ । । ऽ । ऽ ऽ @3 + । ऽ । ऽ ऽ । । ऽ । ऽ ऽ bālā बाला :11-11-11-11

1539. ऽ ऽ । ऽ ऽ । । ऽ । ऽ ऽ । ऽ vriddhavāmā वृद्धवामा :13

1540. ऽ ऽ । ऽ ऽ । । ऽ । ऽ ऽ ākhyānakī आख्यानकी :11, बुद्धिः, indravajrā इन्द्रवज्रा

1541. ऽ ऽ । ऽ ऽ । । kāmoddhatā कामोद्धता :7

1542. ऽ ऽ । ऽ ऽ । ऽ । ऽ ऽ : 10 (5:5) āndolikā आंदोलिका

1543. ऽ ऽ । ऽ ऽ । ऽ । kiṣhku किष्कु :8

1544. ऽ ऽ । ऽ ऽ । ऽ ऽ : 8 ketumālā केतुमाला

1545. ऽ ऽ । ऽ ऽ । ऽ ऽ । ऽ । saṁśhrayaśhrī संश्रयश्रीः :11

1546. ऽ ऽ । ऽ ऽ । ऽ ऽ । ऽ ऽ : 11 layagrahī लयग्रही, vidhyaṅkamālā विध्यंकमाला

1547. ऽ ऽ । ऽ ऽ । ऽ ऽ । ऽ ऽ । : 12 saEraṅgarūpaka सारंगरूपक

1548. ऽ ऽ । ऽ ऽ । ऽ ऽ । ऽ ऽ । ऽ ऽ । ऽ ऽ । ऽ ऽ । ऽ : 22 (4:6:6:6) mandāramālā मन्दारमाला

1549. ऽ ऽ । ऽ ऽ । ऽ ऽ । ऽ ऽ । ऽ ऽ । ऽ ऽ । ardhāntarālāpi अर्धान्तरालापि :18

1550. ऽ ऽ । ऽ ऽ । ऽ ऽ । ऽ ऽ । ऽ pārāvata पारावतः :13

1551. ऽ ऽ । ऽ ऽ । ऽ ऽ । ऽ ऽ । sāraṅga सारङ्गः :12

1552. ऽ ऽ । ऽ ऽ । ऽ ऽ । ऽ ऽ prākārabandha प्राकारबन्धः :11

1553. ऽ ऽ । ऽ ऽ । ऽ ऽ । ऽ viśhālāntika विशालान्तिक :10

1554. ऽ ऽ । ऽ ऽ । ऽ ऽ । ऽ viśhvapramā विश्वप्रमा :10

1555. ऽ ऽ । ऽ ऽ । ऽ ऽ । valgā वल्गा :9

1556. ऽ ऽ । ऽ ऽ । ऽ ऽ karālī कराली :8

1557. ऽ ऽ । ऽ ऽ । ऽ rājarājī राजराजी :7

1558. ऽ ऽ । ऽ ऽ । manthānaka मन्थानक :6

1559. ऽ ऽ । ऽ ऽ ऽ । ऽ ऽ ऽ । ऽ ऽ ऽ । ऽ : 16 (4:4:4:4) mandākinī मंदाकिनी

1560. ऽ ऽ । ऽ ऽ ऽ । varddhiṣhṇu वर्द्धिष्णु :7

1561. ऽ ऽ । ऽ ऽ ऽ ऽ । : 8 mrityuñjaya मृत्युंजय

1562. ऽ ऽ । ऽ ऽ ऽ ऽ । ऽ ऽ - । । ऽ । । । ऽ ऽ ऽ । ऽ ऽ saṁpātas'hīlā संपातशीला :10-12

1563. ऽ ऽ । ऽ ऽ ऽ ऽ । ऽ ऽ ऽ ऽ । ऽ ऽ । dantālikā दन्तालिका :16

1564. ऽ ऽ । ऽ ऽ ऽ ऽ । ऽ ऽ ऽ jālapāda जालपादः :11

1565. ऽ ऽ । ऽ ऽ ऽ ऽ ऽ ऽ ऽ ऽ ārādhinī आराधिनी :11

1566. ऽ ऽ । ऽ ऽ ऽ ऽ nimnās'hayā निम्नाशया :7

1567. ऽ ऽ । ऽ ऽ ऽ vabhrū वभ्रूः :6

1568. ऽ ऽ । ऽ ऽ lol लोल :5

1569. ऽ ऽ । dharā धरा :3

1570. ऽ ऽ । pāñchāli पाञ्चालि :3

1571. ऽ ऽ ऽ : 3 nārī नारी, tālī ताली

1572. ऽ ऽ ऽ । : 4 vallī वल्ली

1573. ऽ ऽ ऽ । ऽ ऽ ऽ : 26 (9:6:6:5) apavāha अपवाह

1574. ऽ ऽ ऽ । । । । । । । । ऽ । । ऽ । ऽ । ऽ kalpalatāpatākinī कल्पलतापताकिनी :19

1575. ऽ ऽ ऽ । । । । । । । ऽ । ऽ । ऽ । ऽ ऽ satketu सत्केतुः :18

1576. ऽ ऽ ऽ । । । । । । ऽ : 10 kumudinī कुमुदिनी, kusumasumuditā कुसुमसुमुदिता

1577. ऽ ऽ ऽ । । । । । । ऽ । । । । ऽ । । । । ऽ । । ऽ ऽ adhīrakarīra अधीरकरीर :24

1578. ऽ ऽ ऽ । । । । । । ऽ । ऽ । ऽ ऽ kumāralīlā कुमारलीला :15

1579. ऽ ऽ ऽ । । । । । । ऽ ऽ । । । । ऽ ऽ ऽ ऽ vidhunidhuvana विधुनिधुवन :19

1580. ऽ ऽ ऽ । । । । । ऽ ऽ । । ऽ ऽ । । । । । । । । । ऽ ऽ virahavirahasya विरहविरहस्य :25

1581. ऽ ऽ ऽ । । । । । । ऽ ऽ । ऽ ऽ । ऽ ऽ ऽ : 18 (4:7:7) chtralekhā चित्रलेखा

1582. ऽ ऽ ऽ । । । । । । । ऽ ऽ ऽ malayasurabhi मलयसुरभिः :12

1583. ऽ ऽ ऽ । । । । । । । ऽ ऽ mātrā मात्रा :11

1584. ऽ ऽ ऽ । । । । । ऽ । । । ऽ ऽ ऽ । ऽ ऽ । ऽ : 20 sadratnamālā सद्रत्नमाला

1585. ऽ ऽ ऽ । । । । । ऽ ऽ ऽ । ऽ । ऽ ऽ : 16 suratalalitā सुरतललिता

1586. ऽ ऽ ऽ । । । । ऽ । । । । । । । । । ऽ ऽ - । । ऽ । । । । । । ऽ । । । ऽ ऽ mārdaṅgī मार्दङ्गी :18-14

1587. ऽ ऽ ऽ । । । । ऽ । । ऽ kus'halakalāvatikā कुशलकलावतिका :11

1588. ऽ ऽ ऽ । । । । ऽ । ऽ : 10 paṇava पणव

1589. ऽ ऽ ऽ । । । । ऽ । ऽ । । । । । । । ऽ । ऽ । ऽ । ऽ vipulāyita विपुलायित :23

1590. ऽ ऽ ऽ । । । । ऽ । ऽ । ऽ - । । ऽ ऽ । । । । ऽ । ऽ । ऽ । ऽ ऽ ahīnatālī अहीनताली :12-16

1591. ऽ ऽ ऽ । । । । ऽ । ऽ । ऽ - । । ऽ ऽ । । ऽ । ऽ । ऽ vimāninī विमानिनी :12-11

1592. ऽ ऽ ऽ । । । । ऽ । ऽ । ऽ ऽ - ऽ ऽ । । ऽ । ऽ । ऽ ऽ kiṁśhukāvalī किंशुकावली :13-10

1593. ऽ ऽ ऽ । । । । ऽ । ऽ । ऽ ऽ : 13 (3:10) praharṣhiṇī प्रहर्षिणी, mayūrapichchha मयूरपिच्छ

1594. ऽ ऽ ऽ । । । । ऽ । ऽ ऽ । ऽ ऽ । ऽ ऽ । ऽ ऽ । ऽ ऽ । ऽ ऽ vīravikrānta वीरविक्रान्तः :26

1595. ऽ ऽ ऽ । । । । ऽ ऽ : 9 makaralatā मकरलता

1596. ऽ ऽ ऽ । । । । ऽ ऽ ऽ : 10 (3:7) kuvalayamālā कुवलयमाला

1597. ऽ ऽ ऽ । । । । ऽ ऽ ऽ hīrāṅgī हीराङ्गी :10

1598. ऽ ऽ ऽ । । । । ऽ ऽ kāṁsīka कांसीक :9

1599. ऽ ऽ ऽ । । । । ऽ śhikhilikhitā शिखिलिखिता :8

1600. ऽ ऽ ऽ । । । । amati अमतिः :7

1601. ऽ ऽ ऽ । । । ऽ । ऽ ऽ । ऽ ऽ ānatā आनता :13

1602. ऽ ऽ ऽ । । । ऽ ऽ : 8 haṁsaruta हंसरुत

1603. ऽ ऽ ऽ । । । ऽ ऽ ऽ ऽ ऽ bhūrighaṭaka भूरिघटक :11

1604. ऽ ऽ ऽ । । । ऽ ऽ ऽ ayanapatākā अयनपताका :9

1605. ऽ ऽ ऽ । । । ऽ ऽ haṁsaruta हंसरुत :8

1606. ऽ ऽ ऽ । । । ऽ navasarā नवसरा :7

1607. ऽ ऽ ऽ । । । prothā प्रोथा :6

1608. ऽ ऽ ऽ । । ऽ : 6 vīthī वीथी

1609. ऽ ऽ ऽ । । ऽ । । । । ऽ sāmapadā सामपदा :11

1610. ऽ ऽ ऽ । । ऽ । । ऽ : 9 kanaka कनक, gāthā गाथा

1611. ऽ ऽ ऽ । । ऽ । । ऽ । । ऽ ऽ lodhraśhikhā लोध्रशिखा :13

1612. ऽ ऽ ऽ । । ऽ । । ऽ ऽ : 10 uddhatā उद्धत

1613. ऽ ऽ ऽ । । ऽ । । ऽ ऽ । ऽ ऽ । ऽ ऽ । ऽ : 18 (3:6:8:1) vilāsa विलास

1614. ऽ ऽ ऽ । । ऽ । । ऽ ऽ ऽ vilambitamadhyā विलम्बितमध्या :11

1615. ऽ ऽ ऽ । । ऽ । । ऽ ऽ prasarā प्रसरा :10

1616. ऽ ऽ ऽ । । ऽ । ऽ । । । । । ऽ । ऽ ऽ । ऽ   śhilīmukhojjrimbhita **शिलीमुखोज्जृम्भित** :19

1617. ऽ ऽ ऽ । । ऽ । ऽ । । । ऽ । । । । ऽ । ऽ : 19 (12:7)   vāyuvegā वायुवेगा

1618. ऽ ऽ ऽ । । ऽ । ऽ । । । ऽ । । ऽ । । ऽ । ऽ ऽ । ऽ ऽ । ऽ   sūrasūchaka **सूरसूचकः** :26

1619. ऽ ऽ ऽ । । ऽ । ऽ । । । ऽ । ऽ । । । ऽ । ऽ । ऽ : 22 (12:10)   dīpārchi दीपार्चि

1620. ऽ ऽ ऽ । । ऽ । ऽ । । । ऽ ऽ । ऽ ऽ ऽ ऽ : 18 (12:6)   śhārdūla शार्दूल

1621. ऽ ऽ ऽ । । ऽ । ऽ । । । ऽ ऽ ऽ । । । ऽ : 18 (12:6)   śhārdūlalalita शार्दूलललित

1622. ऽ ऽ ऽ । । ऽ । ऽ । । । ऽ ऽ ऽ । ऽ ऽ । ऽ : 19 (12:7)   śhārdūlavikrīḍita शार्दूलविक्रीडित

1623. ऽ ऽ ऽ । । ऽ । ऽ । । । ऽ ऽ ऽ । ऽ ऽ । ऽ । । ऽ । ऽ : 24   vibhramagati विभ्रमगति

1624. ऽ ऽ ऽ । । ऽ । ऽ । । । ऽ ऽ   paṅkajadhāriṇī **पङ्कजधारिणी** :13

1625. ऽ ऽ ऽ । । ऽ । ऽ । । । ऽ   viraloddhatā **विरलोद्धता** :12

1626. ऽ ऽ ऽ । । ऽ । ऽ । । ऽ । ऽ । । ऽ । ऽ : 18 (8:5:5)   haranartaka हरनर्तक

1627. ऽ ऽ ऽ । । ऽ । ऽ । । ऽ ऽ ऽ । । ऽ । । । । । ऽ : 22   lālitya लालित्य

1628. ऽ ऽ ऽ । । ऽ । ऽ । ऽ - । । । । । । । ऽ । ऽ । ऽ   karadhā **करधा** :10-11

1629. ऽ ऽ ऽ । । ऽ । ऽ । ऽ - । । ऽ । । ऽ । ऽ । ऽ   prabhāsitā **प्रभासिता** :10-10

1630. ऽ ऽ ऽ । । ऽ । ऽ । ऽ - । । ऽ ऽ । । ऽ । ऽ । ऽ   sudhā **सुधा** :10-11

1631. ऽ ऽ ऽ । । ऽ । ऽ । ऽ - ऽ ऽ । । ऽ । ऽ । ऽ   vāsavavanditā **वासववन्दिता** :10-9

1632. ऽ ऽ ऽ । । ऽ । ऽ । ऽ : 10   śhuddhavirāṭ शुद्धविराट्

1633. ऽ ऽ ऽ । । ऽ । ऽ । ऽ । । ऽ ऽ - । । ऽ । । । । ऽ । ऽ । ऽ ऽ - । । । । । । । । । ऽ । । । । । । । । । ऽ - । । ।
। । । । । । । ऽ । । ऽ ऽ   varddhamāna **वर्द्धमान** :14-13-18-15

1634. ऽ ऽ ऽ । । ऽ । ऽ । ऽ । । ऽ ऽ - । । ऽ । । । । ऽ । ऽ । ऽ ऽ   upasthitaprachupita
उपस्थितप्रचुपित :14-13

1635. ऽ ऽ ऽ । । ऽ । ऽ । ऽ । ऽ ऽ ऽ   sammadākrāntā **सम्मदाक्रान्ता** :14

1636. ऽ ऽ ऽ । । ऽ । ऽ । ऽ ऽ - ऽ ऽ । । ऽ । ऽ । ऽ ऽ   yuddhavirāṭ **युद्धविराट्** :11-10

1637. ऽ ऽ ऽ । । ऽ । ऽ । ऽ ऽ : 11 (6:5)   ekrūpa एकरूप, maṇi मणि, merurūpā मेरुरूपा

1638. ऽ ऽ ऽ । । ऽ । ऽ । ऽ ऽ ऽ - । । ऽ ऽ । । ऽ । ऽ । ऽ ऽ viyadvāṇī **वियद्वाणी** :12-12

1639. ऽ ऽ ऽ । । ऽ । ऽ । ऽ ऽ   asurāḍhyā **असुराढ्या**, viśhvavirāṭ **विश्वविराट्** :11

1640. ऽ ऽ ऽ । । ऽ । ऽ । ऽ   virāṭ **विराट्** :10

1641. ऽ ऽ ऽ । । ऽ ।   maulisrak **मौलिस्रक** :7

1642. S S S I I S S : 7 madalekhā मदलेखा

1643. S S S I I S S I I I I I I S I S I S I I S S bhastrānistaraṇa भस्त्रानिस्तरण :22

1644. S S S I I S S I I vandāru वन्दारुः :9

1645. S S S I I S S I S I I S S S I I S I I I I S : 22 lālitya लालित्य

1646. S S S I I S S S I I I I S S : 14 lakṣhmī लक्ष्मी

1647. S S S I I S S S I I kāmanibhā कामनिभा :10

1648. S S S I I S S S S S I I S S : 14 (7:7) alolā अलोला

1649. S S S I I S S S S S S antarvanitā अन्तर्वनिता :11

1650. S S S I I S S S S khelāḍhya खेलाढ्य :9

1651. S S S I I S S madalekhā मदलेखा :7

1652. S S S I I S niskā निस्का :6

1653. S S S I I mālīna मालीन :5

1654. S S S I S : 5 sāvitrī सावित्री

1655. S S S I S I I S haṭhinī हठिनी :8

1656. S S S I S I I kālambī कालम्बी :7

1657. S S S I S I S mahonmukhī महोन्मुखी :7

1658. S S S I S I maṅkura मङ्कुर :6

1659. S S S I S S : 6 ramyā रम्या, sunandā सुनंदा

1660. S S S I S S I I I S S I I I I I I I S I S I I S I S : 26 (8:11:7) bhujaṅgarita भुजंगरित

1661. S S S I S S I I manthari मन्थरि :8

1662. S S S I S S I S S I S S S I S S S S S S S I S S I S S viśhvaviśhvāsa विश्वविश्वासः :26

1663. S S S I S S I devala देवल :7

1664. S S S I S S S ibhabhrāntā इभभ्रान्ता :7

1665. S S S I S S tantrī तन्त्री :6

1666. S S S I S hāsikā हासिका :5

1667. S S S I mugdha मुग्ध :4

1668. S S S S : 4 kanyā कन्या

1669. S S S S I I I I I I I I I I I I I I I I I I I I I I S : 27 (4:8:8:7) vikasitakusuma विकसितकुसुम

1670. S S S S I I I I I I I I I I I I S S bhīmāvartta भीमावर्त्तः :16

1671. S S S S I I I I I I I I I S I S S I S krodakrīda क्रोडक्रीड :18

1672. S S S S I I I I I I S - I I S I I S I I I I I I I S baddhā बद्धा :11-13

1673. S S S S I I I I I I I S : 11 (4:7) bhramaravilasita भ्रमरविलसित

1674. S S S S I I I I I I I S I S I I S I S : 18 (4:7:7) chala चल

1675. S S S S I I I I I I I S S I S : 14 chandraurasa चंद्रौरस

1676. S S S S I I I I I I I S S I S S I S S : 18 (4:7:7) chandralekhā चंद्रलेखा

1677. S S S S I I I I I I I S S I S S I S hāriṇī हारिणी :17

1678. S S S S I I I I I I I S S S prajJāmūla प्रज्ञामूल :13

1679. S S S S I I I I I I I S S S I S S I S : 18 (4:7:7) keśhara केशर

1680. S S S S I I I I I I I S S S S : 14 (4:10) haṁsasyāmā हंसश्यामा

1681. S S S S I I I I I I I S S S S : 14 (4:6:4) kuṭilaka कुटिलक

1682. S S S S I I I I I I I S S S S chūḍāpīḍa चूडापीड :14

1683. S S S S I I I I I I I S bhramaravilasitā भ्रमरविलसिता :11

1684. S S S S I I I I I S : 10 (4:6) haṁsī हंसी

1685. S S S S I I I I I S I I I I I S I S S S I S S I S S aśhokānokaha अशोकानोकह :26

1686. S S S S I I I I I S I S I I S I S : 17 (4:6:7) bhārākrāntā भाराक्रांता

1687. S S S S I I I I I S S I S S I S S : 17 (4:6:7) mandākrāmtā मंदाक्रांता, śhrīdharā श्रीधरा

1688. S S S S I I I I I S S S I I I S : 16 madanalalitā मदनललिता

1689. S S S S I I I I I S S S I S S I S : 17 (4:6:7) hāriṇī हारिणी

1690. S S S S I I I I I S S S S S : 14 (4:10) haṁsaśhyenī हंसश्येनी, madhyakṣhāmā मध्यक्षामा

1691. S S S S I I I I S : 9 siṁhakrāntā सिंहाक्रांता, pavitrā पवित्रा

1692. S S S S I I I I S I I śheṣhāpīḍa शेषापीड :11

1693. S S S S I I I I S I S S vasantahāsa वसन्तहासः :12

1694. S S S S I I I I S I S āśhāpāda आशापादः :11

1695. S S S S I I I I S S : 10 (4:6) vilāsitā विलासिता, mattā मत्ता

1696. S S S S I I I I S S I I I I S S mālāvalaya मालावलय :16

1697. S S S S I I I I S S I I I I S viśhakalitā विशकलिता :15

1698. S S S S । । । । S S । । S S । । । । S S । । S rāmābaddha रामाबद्ध :23

1699. S S S S । । । । S S । । S S । । S S S S S vāṇīvāṇa वाणीवाणः :20

1700. S S S S । । । । S S । । S S । । S virudaruta विरुदरुत :17

1701. S S S S । । । । S S । । S S S S S । । S grāvāstaraṇa ग्रावास्तरण :19

1702. S S S S । । । । S S । । S S pariṇāhī परिणाही :14

1703. S S S S । । । । S S S : 11 panis'hroṇi पनिश्रोणि

1704. S S S S । । । । S S S S : 12 (4:8) jaladharamālā जलधरमाला

1705. S S S S । । । । S S S S । । । । S S S S । । । । S S bhasalas'halākā भसलशलाका :26

1706. S S S S । । । । S S S S S dhīrāvartta धीरावर्त्तः :13, līlālola लीलालोलः :13

1707. S S S S । । । । S S S S jaladharamālā जलधरमाला :12

1708. S S S S । । । । S S mattā मत्ता :10

1709. S S S S । । । । S vīrā वीरा :9

1710. S S S S । । । । atijani अतिजनि :8

1711. S S S S । । । S । । S S kumbhodhnī कुम्भोध्नी :12

1712. S S S S । । । S S S S S । । । S । । । । । । । S : 24 (8:8:8) ves'hyāprīti वेश्याप्रीति

1713. S S S S । । । bhūrimadhu भूरिमधु :7

1714. S S S S । । S : 7 sarala सरल

1715. S S S S । । S । । S : 10 (4:6) hamsakrīḍā हंसक्रीडा

1716. S S S S । । S । । S । । S : 13 (4:9) mohapralāpa मोहप्रलाप

1717. S S S S । । S । । S S : 11 (4:7) vātormī वातोर्मी

1718. S S S S । । S । । S S S S S S chārvaṭaka चार्वटक :15

1719. S S S S । । S । S : 9 ratnākarā रत्नाकर

1720. S S S S । । S । S । S S : 12 (4:8) puṇḍarīka पुंडरीक

1721. S S S S । । S S । । S S sukhas'haila सुखशैल :12

1722. S S S S । । S S । S S : 11 (4:7) ūrmimālā ऊर्मिमाला, vātormimālā वातोर्मिमाला

1723. S S S S । । S S S S madhyādhārā मध्याधारा :10

1724. S S S S । । S S S dhritahālā धृतहाला :9

1725. S S S S । । S S pratisīrā प्रतिसीरा :8

1726. S S S S I I S varkaritā वर्करिता :7

1727. S S S S I I kaṁsari कंसरि :6

1728. S S S S I S : 6 taṭī तटी

1729. S S S S I S I S : 8 kṣhamā क्षमा

1730. S S S S I S I ammethī अम्मेथी :7

1731. S S S S I S S I I I I I I I S I I S S S : 20 (7:6:7) suvaṁśhā सुवंशा

1732. S S S S I S S I I I I I I S S I I I S : 19 (7:7:5) surasā सुरसा

1733. S S S S I S S I I I I I I S S I S S I S S : 21 (7:7:7) sragdharā स्रग्धरा

1734. S S S S I S S I I I I I I S S S I I I S : 20 (7:7:6) suvadanā सुवदना

1735. S S S S I S S I I I I I I S S S I S S I S dūrāvaloka दूरावलोकः :21

1736. S S S S I S S I I I I I I S nirmuktamālā निर्मुक्तमाला :14

1737. S S S S I S S I I I I I S I I I I I I S : 19 sumadhurā सुमधुरा

1738. S S S S I S S I I I I I S S I I I S : 18 (7:11) mahāsena महासेन

1739. S S S S I S S I I I I I S S I S S I S S : 20 (7:6:7) suprabhā सुप्रभा

1740. S S S S I S S I I I I I S S I S S kāmarūpa कामरूप :17

1741. S S S S I S S I I I I S I I S I S I S : 19 (7:12) mādhavīlatā माधवीलता

1742. S S S S I S S I I I S S S I S S I S : 18 kāñchī कांची

1743. S S S S I S S I S I I I I I I I S I S I S I S I S I S śhakuntakuntala शकुन्तकुन्तलः :26

1744. S S S S I S S I S I I S I S : 14 (7:7) jayā जया

1745. S S S S I S S I S S I S S I S S I S S I S S kaṅkaṇakvāṇavāṇī कङ्कणक्वाणवाणी :22

1746. S S S S I S S S I S S I S S : 14 (7:7) chandraśhālā चंद्रशाला

1747. S S S S I S S S I S S I S S bimbālakṣhya बिम्बालक्ष्य :14

1748. S S S S I S S S S I S S I S : 14 (7:7) jyotsnā ज्योत्स्ना

1749. S S S S I S S S S I S S I S S : 15 (7:8) chandrasenā चंद्रसेना, chandralekhā चंद्रलेखा

1750. S S S S I S S S S S S S I S S vindhyārū विंध्यारू :14

1751. S S S S I S S kirmīra किर्मीर :7

1752. S S S S I S avoतā अवोला :6

1753. S S S S I kumbhāri कुम्भारि :5

1754. ऽ ऽ ऽ ऽ ऽ : 5 vidyutabhrāntā विद्युद्भ्रांता

1755. ऽ ऽ ऽ ऽ ऽ । । । । । । ऽ ऽ । ऽ ऽ । ऽ ऽ : 19 (5:7:7) puṣhpadáma पुष्पदाम

1756. ऽ ऽ ऽ ऽ ऽ । । । । । । ऽ ऽ । ऽ ऽ । ऽ ऽ phulladāma **फुल्लदाम** :19

1757. ऽ ऽ ऽ ऽ ऽ । । । । । । । ऽ ऽ ऽ : 14 (5:9) asambādhā असंबाधा

1758. ऽ ऽ ऽ ऽ ऽ । । । । । । ऽ ऽ ऽ । ऽ ऽ । ऽ : 19 (5:7:7) chandrabimba चंद्रबिंब

1759. ऽ ऽ ऽ ऽ ऽ । । । । । ऽ । ऽ । । ऽ । ऽ : 18 (5:7:6) kuraṅgikā कुरंगिका

1760. ऽ ऽ ऽ ऽ ऽ । । । । । ऽ ऽ । ऽ ऽ । ऽ ऽ : 18 (4:7:7) chitralekhā चित्रलेखा

1761. ऽ ऽ ऽ ऽ ऽ । । । । । ऽ ऽ । ऽ ऽ । ऽ ऽ : 18 (5:6:7) kusumitalatāvellitā कुसुमितलतावेल्लिता

1762. ऽ ऽ ऽ ऽ ऽ । । । । ऽ ऽ ऽ ऽ ऽ : 14 vāsantī वासंती

1763. ऽ ऽ ऽ ऽ ऽ । । । ऽ । ऽ ऽ līhālarka **लीहालर्क** :12

1764. ऽ ऽ ऽ ऽ ऽ । । । ऽ ऽ । ऽ ऽ : 13 kauḍḍambha कौड्डंभ

1765. ऽ ऽ ऽ ऽ ऽ । । । ऽ ऽ ऽ । ऽ ऽ । ऽ : 16 (4:5:7) komalalatā कोमललता

1766. ऽ ऽ ऽ ऽ ऽ । । । ऽ ऽ ऽ ऽ ऽ ulkābhāsa **उल्काभास**ः :13

1767. ऽ ऽ ऽ ऽ ऽ । । ऽ 8 (4:4) māṇavaka माणवक, māṇavakakrīḍitaka माणवकक्रीडितक

1768. ऽ ऽ ऽ ऽ ऽ । । ऽ । । ऽ ऽ kāsārakrāntā **कासारक्रान्ता** :12

1769. ऽ ऽ ऽ ऽ ऽ । । ऽ । ऽ ऽ : 11 (4:7) guṇāngī गुणांगी

1770. ऽ ऽ ऽ ऽ ऽ । । ऽ ऽ : 9 sundaralrkhā सुंदरलेखा

1771. ऽ ऽ ऽ ऽ ऽ । । ऽ ऽ । । । । । । । । । । । । । ऽ : 22 krauñchā क्रौंचा

1772. ऽ ऽ ऽ ऽ ऽ । । ऽ ऽ । । । । । ऽ : 14 kusumavatī कुसुमवती

1773. ऽ ऽ ऽ ऽ ऽ । । ऽ ऽ । । ऽ ऽ : 13 mattamayūra मत्तमयूर

1774. ऽ ऽ ऽ ऽ ऽ । । ऽ ऽ । । ऽ ऽ ऽ : 14 (4:10) govriṣha गोवृष

1775. ऽ ऽ ऽ ऽ ऽ । । ऽ ऽ । । ऽ ऽ dhīrāvartta **धीरावर्त्त**ः :13

1776. ऽ ऽ ऽ ऽ ऽ । । ऽ ऽ । । ऽ ऽ mattamayūra **मत्तमयूर**ः :13

1777. ऽ ऽ ऽ ऽ ऽ । । ऽ ऽ ऽ ऽ ऽ mattālī **मत्ताली** :12

1778. ऽ ऽ ऽ ऽ ऽ । । ऽ ऽ ardhakṣhāmā **अर्धक्षामा** :9

1779. ऽ ऽ ऽ ऽ ऽ । । sampāka **सम्पाक**ः :7

1780. ऽ ऽ ऽ ऽ ऽ । ऽ ऽ । । । ऽ subhadrāvataraṇi **सुभद्रावतरणि**ः :12

1781. ऽ ऽ ऽ ऽ ऽ । ऽ ऽ । ऽ ऽ : 11 (4:7) śhālinī शालिनी

1782. ऽ ऽ ऽ ऽ ऽ । ऽ ऽ । ऽ ऽ । । । । । । । । । ऽ ऽ । ऽ ऽ । ऽ ऽ : 27 (11:16) mālāchitra मालाचित्र

1783. ऽ ऽ ऽ ऽ ऽ । ऽ ऽ । ऽ ऽ । ऽ ऽ niryatpārāvāra निर्यत्पारावारः :14

1784. ऽ ऽ ऽ ऽ ऽ । ऽ ऽ । ऽ ऽ ऽ ऽ ऽ ऽ ऽ ऽ । ऽ ऽ । ऽ ऽ bhīmābhoga भीमाभोगः :22

1785. ऽ ऽ ऽ ऽ ऽ । ऽ ऽ । ऽ ऽ s̒hālinī शालिनी :11

1786. ऽ ऽ ऽ ऽ ऽ । ऽ hindīra हिन्दीर :7

1787. ऽ ऽ ऽ ऽ ऽ । sāhūti साहूति :6

1788. ऽ ऽ ऽ ऽ ऽ ऽ : 6 vidyullekhā विद्युल्लेखा, s̒heṣharāja शेषराज

1789. ऽ ऽ ऽ ऽ ऽ ऽ । । । । । । ऽ ऽ । ऽ ऽ । ऽ ऽ bhūris̒hobhā भूरिशोभा :20

1790. ऽ ऽ ऽ ऽ ऽ ऽ । । । । ऽ ऽ ऽ ऽ kāladhvāna कालध्वान :14

1791. ऽ ऽ ऽ ऽ ऽ ऽ । । ऽ ऽ । । ऽ ऽ । । kulyāvartta कुल्यावर्त्त :16

1792. ऽ ऽ ऽ ऽ ऽ ऽ । । ऽ ऽ ऽ ऽ līlāratna लीलारत्न :12

1793. ऽ ऽ ऽ ऽ ऽ ऽ । ऽ । । ऽ । ऽ : 13 (4:9) s̒hreyomālā श्रेयोमाला

1794. ऽ ऽ ऽ ऽ ऽ ऽ । ऽ ऽ । ऽ ऽ : 12 (5:7) vais̒hvadev वैश्वदेवी

1795. ऽ ऽ ऽ ऽ ऽ ऽ । nīhārī नीहारी :7

1796. ऽ ऽ ऽ ऽ ऽ ऽ ऽ : 7 ls̒hīrs̒hakarūpā शीर्शरूपक, gāndharvī गांधर्वी

1797. ऽ ऽ ऽ ऽ ऽ ऽ ऽ । । ऽ ऽ ऽ । । ऽ ऽ ऽ ऽ : 18 (9:9) mañjirā मंजिरा

1798. ऽ ऽ ऽ ऽ ऽ ऽ ऽ । । ऽ ऽ ऽ । ऽ ऽ । ऽ ऽ : 18 (5:6:7) siṁhavisphurjitā सिंहविस्फूर्जिता

1799. ऽ ऽ ऽ ऽ ऽ ऽ ऽ ऽ : 8 (4:4) vidyullekhā विद्युल्लेखा, somakānta सोमकान्त

1800. ऽ ऽ ऽ ऽ ऽ ऽ ऽ ऽ । । । । । । । । । । । । । । ऽ : 23 (8:5:10) mandakrīḍā मंदक्रीडा

1801. ऽ ऽ ऽ ऽ ऽ ऽ ऽ ऽ । । । । । । । । । । । । ऽ : 21 (8:5:8) mattakrīḍā मत्तक्रीडा

1802. ऽ ऽ ऽ ऽ ऽ ऽ ऽ ऽ । । । । । । । । । । । । ऽ ऽ : 22 haṁsī हंसी

1803. ऽ ऽ ऽ ऽ ऽ ऽ ऽ ऽ । । । । । । । । । । ऽ । ऽ । । ऽ । ऽ : 26 (8:11:7) bhujaṅgavijrimbhita भुजंगविजृंभित

1804. ऽ ऽ ऽ ऽ ऽ ऽ ऽ ऽ । । । । ऽ : 13 vidyunmālā विद्युन्माला

1805. ऽ ऽ ऽ ऽ ऽ ऽ ऽ ऽ । । । । ऽ । । ऽ ऽ ऽ ऽ ऽ ऽ ऽ । । ऽ ऽ ऽ : 27 (8:11:8) mālāvritta मालावृत्त

1806. ऽ ऽ ऽ ऽ ऽ ऽ ऽ ऽ । । । । ऽ ऽ । । ऽ kāsāra कासार :17

1807. ऽ ऽ ऽ ऽ ऽ ऽ ऽ ऽ । । । । ऽ ऽ ऽ vāṇībhūṣhā वाणीभूषा :15

1808. ऽ ऽ ऽ ऽ ऽ ऽ ऽ ऽ । । ऽ ऽ । । ऽ līlāchandra लीलाचन्द्र :15

1809. ऽ ऽ ऽ ऽ ऽ ऽ ऽ ऽ ऽ : 9 rūpamālā रूपमाला, karpūra कर्पूर

1810. S S S S S S S S S I I I I S I I I I S S I I S S S S tanukilakiñchita तनुकिलकिञ्चित :26

1811. S S S S S S S S S I I S : 12 vikrāntā विक्रांता

1812. S S S S S S S S S I I S S I I I I I S S S I I S pārāvārāntastha पारावारान्तस्थ :23

1813. S S S S S S S S S I I S S S dhīradhvāna धीरध्वान :14

1814. S S S S S S S S S I S S I S S : 15 (8:7) maṇḍūkī मंडूकी, chitrā चित्रा, chanchalā चंचला

1815. S S S S S S S S S S S : 11 mālatī मालती

1816. S S S S S S S S S S S S : 12 vidyādhara विद्याधर, kāñchana कांचन, lakyāṇa कल्याण

1817. S S S S S S S S S S S S S S I S I S S S S aśhokaloka अशोकलोकः :21

1818. S S S S S S S S S S S S S S S : 15 (4:4:4:3) līlālekha लीलालेख, mitra मित्र, jyotis ज्योतिस्

1819. S S S S S S S S S S S S S S S S : 16 brahmarūpa ब्रह्मरूप

1820. S S S S S S S S S S S S S S S S S I I S S S S S S : 25 (4:4:5:12) mantema मंतेम

1821. S S S S S S S S S S S S S S S S S S S S S S S S S S jīmūtadhvāna जीमूतध्वान :26

1822. S S S S S S S S S S S S S S S S S mānākrāntā मानाक्रान्ता :17

1823. S S S S S S S S S S S S S S S S chandrāpīḍa चन्द्रापीड :16

1824. S S S S S S S S S S S S S S S līlālekha लीलालेखः :15

1825. S S S S S S S S S S S S S S saṅkalpāsāra सङ्कल्पासारः :14

1826. S S S S S S S S S S S S S savyālī सव्याली :13

1827. S S S S S S S S S S S S vidyādhāra विद्याधारः :12

1828. S S S S S S S S S S S bhāratī भारती :11

1829. S S S S S S S S S S padmāvartta पद्मावर्त्तः :10

1830. S S S S S S S S S rūpāmālī रूपामाली :9

1831. S S S S S S S S vidyunmālā विद्युन्माला :8

1832. S S S S S S S śhiprā शिप्रा :7

1833. S S S S S S vidyullekhā विद्युल्लेखा :6

1834. S S S S kanyā कन्या :4

1835. S S strī स्त्री :2

1836. S śhrī श्री :1

(b) THE 150 Mātrā-Vṛttas

1837. sugati सुगती :7 = 6 + ऽ

1838. chhavi छवि :8 = 4 + । ऽ ।

1839. gaṅga गंग :9 = 5 + ऽ ऽ

1840. nidhi निधि :9 = 8 + ।

1841. dīpa दीप :10 = 4 + । । । ऽ ।

1842. ahīra अहीर :11 = 7 + । ऽ ।

1843. śhiva शिव :11 = 9 + ऽ or 6 + । ऽ ऽ

1844. tomar तोमर :12 = 9 + ऽ ।

1845. tāṇḍav ताण्डव :12 = । + 10 + ।

1846. līlā लीला :12 = 8 + । ऽ ।

1847. nīta नीत :12 = 9 + । ऽ or 9 + । । ।

1848. ullālā उल्लाला :13 = 10 + । + 2

1849. chaṇḍikā चण्डिका :13 = 8 + ऽ । ऽ

1850. kajjala कज्जल :14 = 11 + ऽ ।

1851. sakhī सखी :14 = 8 + ऽ ऽ ऽ or 9 + । ऽ ऽ

1852. vijāt विजात :14 = । + 13

1853. hākalī हाकली :14 = 4, 4, 4 + ऽ

1854. madhumālatī मधुमालती :14 = 7 + 2 + ऽ । ऽ

1855. sulakṣhaṇa सुलक्षण :14 = 11 + ऽ ।

1856. manamohana मनमारुहन :14 = 11 + । । ।

1857. sarasa सरस :14 = 2 + 5 + 2 + 5

1858. manoramā मनोरमा :14 = ऽ + 8 + ऽ । । or ऽ + 7 + । ऽ ऽ

1859. chaubālā चौबाला :15 = 8 + 4 + । ऽ

1860. gopī गोपी :15 = 3 + 10 + ऽ

1861. chaupaī चौपई :15 = 12 + ऽ ।

1862. jayakārī जयकारी :15 = 12 + ऽ ।

1863. gupāla गुपाल :15 = 11 + । ऽ ।

1864. bhujaṅginī भुजंगिनी :15 = 11 + । ऽ ।

1865. ujvalā उज्वला :15 = 10 + ऽ । ऽ

1866. punīta पुनीत :15 = 10 + ऽ ऽ ।

1867. pādākulaka पादाकुलक :16 = 4, 4, 4, 4 (i.e. ऽ ऽ, । । ऽ, । ऽ । or । । । ।)

1868. padapādākulak पदपादाकुलक :16 = ऽ or । । + 14

1869. chaupāī चौपई :16 = 16 (must not end with ऽ ।)

1870. paddharī पद्धरी :16 = 12 + । ऽ ।

1871. arilla अरिल्ल :16 = 14 + । । or 11 + । ऽ ऽ

1872. dillā डिल्ला :16 = 12 + ऽ । ।

1873. upachitrā उपचित्रा :16 = 8 + ऽ + 4 + ऽ (at least one । ऽ । must be in each line)

1874. pañjhaṭikā पञ्झटिका :16 = 8 + ऽ + 4 ऽ (there must be no । ऽ । in any line)

1875. siṁha सिंह :16 = । । + 10 + । । ऽ

1876. matta samak मत्त समक :16 = 8 + । + 7

1877. viśhloka विश्लोक :16 = 4 + । + 2 + । + 8

1878. chitrā चित्रा :16 = 4 + । + 2 + । । + 7

1879. vanavāsikā वनवासिका :16 = 8 + । + 2 + । + 4

1880. śhriṅgāra श्रृंगार :16 = 3 + 2 + 8 + ऽ ।

1881. rāma राम :17 = 9 + 3 + । ऽ ऽ

1882. chandra चन्द्र :17 = 10 + 7

1883. rājīvagaṇa राजीवगण :18 = 9 + 9

1884. mālī माली :18 = 9 + 9

1885. śhakti शक्ति :18 = । + 7 + । + । । + 3 + । । ऽ or । + 7 + । + । । + 2 + ऽ । ऽ or । + 7 + । + । । + 4 + । । ।

1886. bandana बन्दन :18 = 15 + ऽ ।

1887. purārī पुरारी :18 = 7 + 9 + ऽ

1888. pīyūṣhavarṣha पीयूषवर्ष :19 = 10 + 6 + । ऽ

1889. sumeru सुमेरु :19 = । + 11 + 2 + । ऽ ऽ or । + 9 + 4 + । ऽ ऽ

1890. tamāla तमाल :19 = 16 + ऽ ।

1891. saguṇa सगुण :19 = । + 4 + 5 + 5 + । ऽ ।

1892. narahari नरहरि :19 = 14 + । । । ऽ

1893. diṇḍī दिंडी :19 = 9 + 6 + ऽ ऽ

1894. yoga योग :20 = 12 + 3 + । ऽ ऽ

1895. śhāstra शास्त्र :20 = 17 + ऽ ।

1896. haṁsagati हंसगति :20 = 11 + 9

1897. manjutilakā मञ्जुतिलका :20 = 12 + 4 + । ऽ ।

1898. aruṇa अरुण :20 = 5 + 5 + 5 + ऽ । ऽ

1899. plavaṅgam प्लवंगम् :21 = ऽ + 6 + 7 + । ऽ । ऽ

1900. chāndrāyaṇa चान्द्रायण :21 = 6 + । ऽ । + 5 + ऽ । ऽ

1901. tilokī तिलोकी :21 = 16 + 2 + । ऽ

1902. sindhu सिन्धु :21 = । + 6 + । + 6 + । + 6

1903. santa संत :21 = 3 + 6 + 6 + 2 + । । ऽ

1904. bhānu भानु :21 = 6 + 12 + ऽ ।

1905. rāsa रास :22 = 8 + 8 + 2 + । । ऽ

1906. rādhikā राधिका :22 = 13 + 9

1907. bihārī बिहारी :22 = 14 + 8

1908. kuṇḍala कुण्डल :22 = 12 + 6 + ऽ ऽ

1909. sukhadā सुखदा :22 = 12 + 8 + ऽ

1910. upamāna उपमान :23 = 13 + 6 + ऽ ऽ

1911. hīra हीर :23 = ऽ + 4 + 6 + 6 + ऽ । ऽ

1912. jaga जग :23 = 10 + 8 + 2 + ऽ ।

1913. sampadā संपदा :23 = 11 + 8 + । ऽ ।

1914. avatāra अवतार :23 = 13 + 5 + ऽ । ऽ

1915. sujāna सुजान :23 = 14 + 6 + ऽ ।

1916. niśhchala निश्चल :23 = 16 + 4 + ऽ ।

1917. mohana मोहन :23 = 5 + 6 + 6 + 6

1918. rolā रोला :24 = (odd पद 1, 3) 4 + 4+ 3 or 3 + 3 + 2 + 3

1919. (even पद 2, 4) 3 + 2 + 4 + 4 or 3 + 2 + 3 + 3 + 2

1920. digpāl दिग्पाल :24 = 12 + 12

1921. rūpamālā रूपमाला :24 = 14 + 7 + ऽ ।

1922. madana मदन :24 = 14 + 7 + ऽ ।

1923. śhobhana शोभन :24 = 14 + 6 + । ऽ ।

1924. siṁhikā सिंहिका :24 = 14 + 6 + । ऽ ।

1925. līlā लीला :24 = 7 + 7 + 6 + । । ऽ

1926. sumitra सुमित्र :24 = । ऽ । + 6 + 10 + । ऽ ।

1927. sārasa सारस :24 = ऽ + 10 + 12

1928. gaganāṅganā गगनांगना :25 = 16 + 4 + ऽ । ऽ

1929. muktāmaṇi मुक्तामणि :25 = 13 + 8 + ऽ ऽ

1930. sugītikā सुगीतिका :25 = । + 14 + 7 + ऽ ।

1931. madanāga मदनाग :25 = 17 + 8

1932. nāga नाग :25 = 10 + 8 + 4 + ऽ ।

1933. śhaṅkara शंकर :26 = 16 + 7 + ऽ ।

1934. viṣhṇupada विष्णुपद :26 = 16 + 8 + ऽ

1935. kāmarūpa कामरूप :26 = 9 + 7 + 8 + ऽ

1936. vaitāla वैताल :26 = 9 + 7 + 8 + ऽ

1937. jhūlanā झूलना :26 = 7 + 7 + 7 + 2 + ऽ ।

1938. gītikā गीतिका :26 = 14 + 9 + । ऽ

1939. gītā गीता :26 = 14 + 9 + ऽ ।

1940. sarasī सरसी :27 = 16 + 8 + ऽ ।

1941. s̍hubhagītā शुभगीता :27 = 15 + 7 + ऽ । ऽ

1942. s̍huddhagītā शुद्धगीता :27 = 14 + 10 + ऽ ।

1943. sāra सार :28 = 16 + 8 + ऽ ऽ

1944. harigītikā हरिगीतिका :28 = 16 + 9 + । ऽ

1945. vidhātā विधाता :28 = 14 + 14

1946. vidyā विद्या :28 = । + 13 + 9 + । ऽ ऽ

1947. chuliyālā चुलियाला :29 = 13 + 11 + । ऽ । ।

1948. marahaṭā मरहटा :29 = 10 + 8 + 8 + ऽ ।

1949. marahaṭā mādhavī मरहटा माधवी :29 = 11 + 8 + 7 + । ऽ

1950. dhārā धारा :29 = 15 + 12 + ऽ

1951. chavapaiyā चवपैया :30 = 10 + 8 + 6 + । । ऽ ऽ

1952. tāṭaṅk ताटंक :30 = 16 + 8 + ऽ ऽ ऽ

1953. kukubha कुकुभ :30 = 16 + 10 + ऽ ऽ

1954. ruchirā रुचिरा :30 = 14 + 14 + ऽ

1955. s̍hokahara शोकहर :30 = 8 + 8+ 8 + 4 + ऽ

1956. karṇa कर्ण :30 = 13 + 13 + ऽ ऽ

1957. as̍hvāvatārī अश्वावतारी :31 = 16 + 12 + ऽ ।

1958. tribhaṅgī त्रिभंगी :32 = 10 + 8 + 8 + 4 + ऽ

1959. s̍huddhadhvani शुद्धध्वनि :32 = 10 + 8 + 8 + 4 + ऽ

1960. padmāvati पद्मावती :32 = 10 + 8 + 12 + ऽ

1961. samāna savaiyā समान सवैया :32 = 16 + 12 + ऽ । ।

1962. savāī सवाई :32 = 16 + 12 + ऽ । ।

1963. daṇḍakalā दंडकला :32 = 10 + 8 + 10 + । । ऽ

1964. durmil दुर्मिल :32 = 10 + 8 + 6 + । । ऽ ऽ ऽ

1965. kamand कमंद :32 = 15 + 13 + ऽ ऽ

1966. kharāri खरारि :32 = 8 + 6 + 8 + 10

1967. karakhā करखा :37 = 8 + 12 + 8 + 4 + । ऽ ऽ

1968. haṁsāla हंसाल :37 = 20 + 12 + । ऽ ऽ

1969. madanahara मदनहर :40 = । । + 8 + 8 + 14 + 6 + ऽ

1970. uddhata उद्धत :40 = 10 + 10 + 10 + 7 + ऽ ।

1971. ś́hubhagā शुभगा :40 = 10 + 10 + 10 + 5 + ऽ ऽ ।

1972. vijayā विजया :40 = 10 + 01 + 10 + 5 + ऽ । ऽ

1973. haripriyā हरिप्रिया :46 = 12 + 12 + 12 + 8 + ऽ

1974. atibaravai अतिबरवै :42 = 12 + 9; 12 + 9

1975. dohā दोहा :48 = 8 + ऽ । ऽ + 7 + । ऽ ।; 8 + ऽ । ऽ + 7 + । ऽ ।

1976. dohī दोही :52 = 10 + ऽ । ऽ + 7 = । ऽ ।; 10 + ऽ । ऽ + 7 = । ऽ ।

1977. haripad हरिपद :54 = 16 + 8 + ऽ ।; 16 + 8 + ऽ ।

1978. ullāla उल्लाल :56 = 15 + 13 ; 15 + 13

1979. lakshmī लक्ष्मी :57 = 12; 18; 12; 15

1980. ruchirā-2 रुचिरा-2 :60 = 16 + 10 + ऽ ऽ; 16 + 10 + ऽ ऽ

1981. dhattā धत्ता :62 = 18 + 10 + । । ।; 18 + 10 + । । ।

1982. gāhinī गाहिनी :62 = 12 + 18; 12 + 16 + । ऽ ।

1983. sim;hanī सिंहनी :62 = 12 + 16 + । ऽ ।; 12 + 18

1984. manohara मनोहर :67 = 13 + 13 + 13 + 13 + 13 + ऽ

1985. amritdhuni अमृतधुनि : 144 = six lines of 8 + ऽ । ऽ + 7 + । ऽ ।

1986. kuṇḍaliyā कुंडलिया : 144 = dohā + rolā + dohā where thet hird line of the first dohā is the first line of rolā; and the first word of the 1st dohā is the last word of the 2nd dohā).

CHAPTER 20
THE GREAT HINDI WRITERS
हिंदी के महान साहित्यकार

संस्कृत भाषा की व्यवहारिक लोकप्रीयता के लोप के साथ साथ भारत में महाराष्ट्री (मराठी), शौरसेनी व मागधी भाषाएं मुख्यत: प्रचलित हुई। उनके बाद फिर जो भाषाएं उभरी उनमें से हिंदी साहित्य का जन्म वर्ष सन् 1050 के आस-पास माना जाता है, जब की सन् 1375 तक हिन्दी अपभ्रंश तथा प्राकृत प्रभावों से युक्त थी और उसमें नाथ-साहित्य ही प्रमुख वाङ्मय था।

महाकवि मैथिल-कोकिल विद्यापति के काल से (1375 से) 1900 तक हिन्दी की व्रज और अवधी उपभाषाओं की प्रधानता रही हैं। फिर 1900 के लगभग खड़ी बोली हिंदी साहित्य में प्रतिष्ठित हुई। हिन्दी साहित्य के उदय का काल साधारणतया निम्न लिखित रीति से विभाजित माना जाता है।

ई॰ 650 से 1350 तक आदिकाल। 1350 से 1650 तक का भक्तिकाल। 1650 से 1857 के क्रन्तियुद्ध तक रीतिकाल। 1857 से आज तक का आधुनिक काल। और फिर आधुनिक काल में, 1857 से 1908 तक माना जाता है भारतेन्दु काल। 1908 से 1915 तक का द्विवेदी काल। 1915 से 1938 तक छायावाद काल। 1938 से 1953 तक का प्रगति-प्रयोग काल। और 1953 से आज तक है नव-लेखन काल।

हिन्दी साहित्य प्रवर्तक महापुरुष

गोरखनाथ : (Gorakhnath, about 845)

हठयोग के आचार्य, मत्स्येन्द्रनाथ के शिष्य, आदि-हिंदी-युग के महापुरुष थे गोरखनाथ। इनके उपदेशों में योग, शैव और तन्त्र का सामंजस्य है। गोरखनाथ की चालिस गद्य-पद्य रचनाएं प्राप्त हैं, जिनमें सबदी, पद, जोग, आत्मबोध, ग्यानतिलक, ग्यान चौंतीसा, अभैमात्रा, प्राणसंकली, सिष्यादर्शन, रामावली, नरवैबोध, पंचमात्रा, मछीन्द्र गोरखनाथ आदि हैं। हिन्दी साहित्य सम्मेलन ने नाथ जी का वाणी संग्रह प्रकाशित किया है। इनके सिद्धान्तों का प्रभाव आगे चल कर कबीर दास जी पर पड़ा।

चंदबरदाई : (Chandbardai 1168-1192)

हिंदी साहित्य के पूर्वतम महान् कवि थे वीरगाथाकार श्री चन्दबरदाई भट्ट, जिनका जन्म लाहौर में हुआ था। आप दिल्ली के अन्तिम हिन्दु सम्राट् पृथ्वीराज चौहान के परम सखा और राजकवि थे। समृद्ध काव्य पृथ्वीराज-रासो की रचना इनकी है। जिस समय शहाबुद्दीन पृथ्वीराज को कैद करके गजनी ले गया था उस समय ये भी उसके साथ चले गये। जाते समय उन्होंने रासो अपने सुपुत्र जल्हन को दिया था, जिसने वह पूर्ण किया। पुस्तक जल्हन हत्थ दै, चलि गज्जन नृप काज।

रासो अपने समय की घटनाधों पर सबसे अधिक प्रकाश डालता है। भाषा की दृष्टि से भी इसका विशेष महत्त्व है। वीर भओं की जैसी सुन्दर अभिव्यक्ति इस ग्रंथ में हुई है बैसी अन्यत्र दुर्लभ है। काव्य-चमत्कार की दृष्टि से भी यह ग्रंथ अपनी अपूर्वता रखता है।

इस ग्रंथ की संक्षिप्त कथावतु इस प्रकार से है, मंगलारण, क्षत्रियों की उत्पत्ति, अजमेर के सोमेश्वर का दिल्ली के अनंगपाल तोमर की पुत्री कमला के साथ विवाह, पृथ्वीराज का जन्म, अनंगपाल की द्वितीय पुत्री सुंदरी का कन्नोज के राजा विजयपाल राठौड के साथ विवाह, जयचन्द का जन्म, अनंगपाल का पृथ्वीराज को गोद में लेना, जयचंद को ईर्ष्या होना, पृथ्वीराज का राजसूय यज्ञ, पृथ्वीराज द्वारा संयोगिताहरण, पृथ्वीराज का भोग विलास में लीन होना, शहाबुद्दीन गोरी का हिंदुस्तान पर आक्रमण, पृथ्वीराज के अनेक युद्धों का वर्णन, गोरी के हाथों पृथ्वीराज की अन्तिम पराजय, उसे बन्दी बनाकर गजनी ले जाना, चन्दबरदाई का गजनी जाना, वहाँ पुथ्वीराज की आँखे निकाली जाना, पृथ्वीराज द्वारा शब्दवेध का चमत्कार और गोरी की मृत्यु, पृथ्वीराज और चंदबरदाई का एक-दूसरे को मार कर जीवन-लीला समाप्त करना।

रासो में भाव-भंगिमा के साथ छन्द-परिवर्तन का प्रवाह, काव्य-व्यंजना, चरित्रांकन, वस्तु-वर्णन, रचना-प्रगल्भता एवं शिल्प-सौष्ठव, राष्ट्रीय-चेतना आदि सभी गुण बरदाई की काव्य-प्रतिभा और कल्पना-शक्ति का प्रमाण हैं।

अमीर खुसरो : (Amir Khusro 1253-1325)

अमीर खुसरो संस्कृत, अरबी, फारसी तथा कई भारतीय भाषाओं के ज्ञाता थे। इनकी शेर, पहेलियाँ और रुबाइयाँ लिखने की भाषा हिंदवी है। इनकी पहेलियाँ और मुकरियाँ बहुत लोकप्रिय हैं।

पहेलियाँ : बीसों का सिर काट लिया, ना मारा ना खून किया ।। (नाखून)

मुकरियाँ : रात समय वह मेरे आवे, भोर भये वह घर उठी जावे।
यह अचरज है सबसे न्यारा। ऐ सखि साजन? ना सखि तारा।।

स्वामी रामानन्द : (Ramanand 1299-1410)

कन्नौज के स्वामी रामानन्द जी दक्षिण के आचार्य रामानुजाचार्य की वैष्णव शिष्य परंपरा के होते हुए भी श्रीराम के भक्त थे। राम नाम इनका मूल मंत्र था। आप संस्कृत के प्रकाण्ड विद्वान् थे परन्तु देशभाषा हिन्दी में भी काव्य करते थे। इनके हिन्दी काव्य में रामरक्षा, ज्ञानशीला, योगचिन्तामणि, ज्ञानतिलक आदि ग्रंथ हैं। इनके बारह शिष्यों में कबीर और रविदास भी थे। कबीरदास जी कहते हैं - सतगुरु के परताप से मिटि गये सब कुछ दुःख द्वन्द्व। कह कबीर दुविधा मिटी गुरु मिलिया रामानन्द।

महाकवि विद्यापति : (Vidyapati 1380-1460)

मैथिल-कोकिल श्री विद्यापति का जन्म 1386 में हुआ था। आपका काव्य विद्यापति की पदावली नाम से प्रसिद्ध है। इनकी दूसरी रचना गोरक्ष विजय नामक नाटक है। विद्यापति मूलतः प्रेम और श्रृंगार रस के कवि थे। इनकी यह प्रेम-प्रवृत्ति, श्रृंगार-भावना, सौंदर्य-लिप्सा इनको इनकी इष्ट देवता शिवजी से भी बढ़कर कामिनी दिखाती है। चन्दन चरचु पायोधर रे, ग्रिम गज मुकुता हार। भसम भरल जनि रे, सिर सरसरि जल धार। कुचभय कमलकोरक झल मुदिरहु, घट परिबेस हुतासे। दाड़िम सिरिफल गगन बास करु, शम्भु गरल कठ ग्रासे।।

संत कबीर : (Kabir 1456-1518)

संत कबीर ने रामानंद जी से पायी थी रामभक्ति। उनके विचारों पर शंकाराचार्य के विचारों का पूर्ण प्रभाव था और वेदान्त, उपनिषदों और पौराणिक कथाओं का उन्हें ज्ञान था।

वे ज्ञान का महत्त्व मानते थे अतः वे संसार की स्थिति माया के कारण मानते थे। वे कहते थे कि ईश्वर और जीव का फेर तभी तक है जब तक माया का परदा बीच में पड़ा हुआ है।

संत रविदास : (Ravidas or Raidas)

गुरु रामानन्द जी के शिष्य राविदास (रैदास) संत मीराबाई के गुरु थे। ग्रन्थ साहब में इनके निराकारोपासना संबन्धी पद संग्रहित हैं। इनकी कविताओं में सरलता एवं सरसता पायी जाती है।

प्रभु जी तुम चन्दन हम पानी। जाकी अंग-अंग बासु समानी।।

प्रभु जी तुम वन-घन हम मोरा। जैसे चितवन चन्द-चकोरा।।
प्रभु जी तुम माली हम बागा। जैसे सोनहि मिलत सुहागा।।
प्रभु जी तुम स्वामी हम दासा। ऐसी भगति करी रैदासा।।

गुरु नानक देव : (Guru Nanak Dev 1469-1538)

गुरुनानक देव जी का जन्म लाहौर के तिलवण्डी ग्राम में हिन्दु कुल में हुआ था। आप की कविताएं सरल तथा प्रभावशालिनी हैं। उनका संग्रह गुरु ग्रन्थ साहब में है। भाषा हींदी व्रजभाषा है और कहीं-कहीं पंजाबी-मिश्रित खड़ी बोली है।

रे मन राम सों कर प्रीत।
श्रवण गोविन्द गुण सुनों अरू गाउ रसना गीत।
कर साधु-संगत सुमिर माधौ, होई पतित पुनीत।
कालव्याल ज्यों ग्रस्यो डोलै मुख पसारे मीत।
कहे नानक राम भज ले, जात अवसर बीत।।

भक्तकवि सूरदास : (Surdas 1483-1563)

कुछ विद्वानों का कहना है कि इनका जन्म मथुरा के पास हुआ था और ये आदिकवि चंदबरदाई के वंशज थे। मथुरा में ही उनकी भेंट श्री वल्लभाचार्य से हुई थी और तत्पश्चात् सूरदास जी ने वल्लभाचार्य को अपना गुरु मान लिया था।

सूरदास जी के पिता का नाम हरिश्चन्द्र था और ये जनम से अंधे थे। ये सात भाई थे, जिनमें से छः भाई मुसलमानों के साथ युद्ध करते हुए मारे गए थे। जब घर में कोई नही रहा तो अंधे सूरदास जी भाइयों की खोज में निकले एवं मार्ग में कुएँ में गिर गए। वहाँ श्रीकृष्ण की कृपा से इन्हें नेत्र प्राप्त हुए और ये बाहर निकल आये। परन्तु उन नेत्रों से भगवान् के सिवाय किसी को न देखने की इच्छा से ये फिर अंधे ही रहे।

मीराबाई : (Mira 1498-1547)

मीराबाई का जन्म चौकड़ी नाम के गांव में हुआ था। उदयपुर के महाराणा भोजराज की पत्नी मीराबाई बाल्यावस्था से ही कृष्ण को अपना पति मानती थी। विधवा होनो पर इनका कृष्ण-प्रेम चरम सीमा पर पहुँच गया।

ये कृष्णप्रेमवश नाच उठती थीं और गीतों के स्वरों में अपने आपको भूल जाती

थीं। परिवार वालों के मना करने पर भी इन्होंने कृष्णभक्ति व साधु संगति नहीं छोड़ी। इनकी प्रेमवाणी हिन्दी साहित्य में अपना उपमान नहीं रखती।

गोस्वामी तुलसीदास : (Tulsidas1533-1624)

गोस्वामी तुलसीदास जी को वेद, वेदान्त, उपनिषद्, पुराण आदि का गम्भीर ज्ञान था। अपने समय की सभी परिस्थितियों तथा समस्याओं से वे भलीभाँति परिचित थे। हिंदू धर्म और संस्कृत पर इस्लाम से आया हुआ खतरा और हिंदुओं की आत्म-विश्वास के प्रति निराशा वे जानते थे। परिणामस्वरूप उनका मानसिक क्षोभ बढ़ता जा रहा था। इस अवस्था में तुलसीदास जी ने निर्बल के बल राम का अमृत पिलाकर हिंदु समाज को नव-जीवन दिया।

संत तुलसीदास जी के लिखे हुए बारह ग्रंथ नागरी प्रचारिणी सभा, काशी, द्वारा ग्रन्थावली में दिये गये हैं, वे है – रामचरितमानस (1574), रामनहछू (1586), वैराग्य संदीपनी (1612), बरवै रामायण (1612), पार्वती-मंगल (1586), जानकी-मंगल (1586), रामाज्ञा (1612), दोहावली (1583), कवितावली (1608), गीतावली (1570), कृष्णगीतावली (1569) और विनयपत्रिका (1621)।

दादू दयाल : (Dadu Dayal 1544-1603)

इनका जन्म अहमदाबाद में हुआ था। इनके विचारों पर संत कबीर की छाप है। इनके काव्यों में कबीर और उनके शिष्यों का उल्लेख बारंबार आता है। वे रामभक्त थे। 1556 में अकबर के निमन्त्रण पर वे फतहपुर सीकरी गए और वहाँ अकबर के साथ काफी दिनों तक अध्यात्मिक विषयों पर चर्चा करते रहे।

उनकी वाणी के संग्रह हरडे वाणी और अंगवधू नाम से प्रसिद्ध हुए हैं। इनके अनुयायियों में कवि सुन्दरदास जी का नाम है। इनके शिष्य **सुंदरदास** (1596–1689) जी की भी वेदान्त पुराण आदि के ज्ञानी थे और ब्रजभाषा के कवि थे।

राजा बीरबल : (Birbal 1528-1589)

इस हिन्दी, संस्कृत और फारसी के विद्वान का जन्म कानपुर के पास हुआ था। इनका मूल नाम महेशदास था। वाक् चतुरता और बुद्धिमत्ता इनके महान गुण थे। ये अकबर के दरबार में नवरत्नों में ये एक विख्यात राजा थे। इनकी लेखनी में भक्ति, प्रेम और नीति के छन्द पाये जाते हैं।

जब दाँत न थे तब दूध दियो, अब दाँत भये कहा अन्न न देहै। जीव बसे जल में थल में, तिनकी सुधि लेइ सो तेरिहु लेहै। जानको देत अनाज को देत, जहान को देत सो तोहूँ के देहै। काहे को सोच करै मन मूरख, सोचकरै कछु हाथ न ऐहै।।

गुरु अर्जुन देव : (Guru Arjun Dev 1563-1606)

सिख संप्रदाय के पाँचवे गुरु अर्जुन देव जी ने ही गुरुओं की बानी को गुरुमुखी में लिखवाया था। जहाँगीर ने मुसलमान बनाने के प्रयास में इन्हें जलती कड़ाही में बिठा कर यातनाएं दी थीं और कारागार में डाल दिया था। पाँच दिन गुरु अर्गुन जलते शरीर से तड़पते पड़े रहे किन्तु मन की शांति भंग नहीं होने दी। छठे दिन जपु जी का जाप करते करते प्राण छोड़ दिये। इन्हों ने छः हजार से अधिक पद लिखे हैं। इनकी रचनाओं में गुरु और ईश्वर भक्ति भरी है। इनकी भाषा में हिंदी अधिक और पंजाबी कम है।

महामति प्राणनाथ : (Mahamati Prananath 1618-1694)

इनका जन्म का नाम मेहर ठाकुर था। शिष्यों ने इन्हें परमात्मा स्वरूप प्राणनाथ की उपाधि दी। इनको बाल्यावस्था में ही अध्यात्म का ज्ञान हुआ था और ये पद और साखी जोड़ते रहे थे। इनकी अधिकांश रचना बोलचाल की हिंदी में ही है। इनकी कई रचनाएं सिंधी, गुजराती, कच्छी और अरबी में भी हैं। किरन्तन में इनकी वाणी का संग्रह है। ये बुंदेला राजा छत्रसाल की राजधानी पन्ना में रहे।

गुरु तेगबहादुर : (Guru Tegh Bahadur 1622-1675)

सिख संप्रदाय के नवें गुरु श्री तेगबहादु जी का जन्म अमृतसर में हुआ था। उन्होंने आनंदपुर साहब का निर्माण कराया तथा वही रहने लगे।

औरंगजेब काश्मीरी पंडितों को मुसलमान बनाते जा रहे थे तो इस अत्याचार के विरुद्ध उन्होंने गुरु तेगबहादुर की सहायता माँगी।

औरंगजेब ने गुरु तेगबहादुर को पकड़ कर उन्हें मुसलमान बनाने के लिए अनेक यातनाएं दी परंतु ये धर्म बदलने को राजी नहीं हुए। अंत में औरंगजेब ने गुरु की कत्ल कर दी। उनकी रचनाएं ग्रंथ साहब में हैं। इन्होंने शुद्ध हिंदी में सरल, भावयुक्त पद और साखी रची हैं।

चरणदास : (Charanadas 1703-1782)

चरणदास का जन्म राजस्थान के डेहरा गाँव में हुआ था। पिता मुरलीधर जी के मृत्यु के पश्चात् ये दिल्ली में आ गये। इन्हें बचपन से ही भगवत् दर्शन की तीव्र आकांक्षा थी।

इन्होंने गुरु सुखानंद के पास चौदह वर्ष तक योगाभ्यास किया और अपने अनुयायियों को ब्रह्मज्ञान का उपदेश दिया। इनके पद और साखी सगुण एवं निर्गुण दोनों भक्तिपर हैं। इनकी वाणी सहज, सरल और प्रभावशाली है।

महर्षि दयानंद सरस्वती : (Dayanand Sarasvati 1824-1883)

महर्षि दयानंद सरस्वती जी का जन्म काठियावाड में हुआ था। इनका मूल नाम मूलशंकर था। दयानंद जी ने मुंबई में आर्य समाज का संगठन करते हुए आर्य समाज के पाँचवे नियम में संस्कृत और आर्यभाषा हिन्दी का पुस्तकालय स्थापन करना और आर्य प्रकाश नामक हिंदी पत्र निकालना हिंदु समाज के लिये आवश्यक ठहराया।

लाहौर के संगठन में भी एक उपनियम बनाकर इन्होंने सब आर्यसमाजियों के लिये हिंदी सीखना आवश्यक कर दिया। आपने आर्यसमाज का धर्मग्रन्थ सत्यार्थ प्रकाश खड़ी बोली गद्य हिन्दी में ही लिखा।

संस्कृतके प्रकाण्ड विद्वान् दयानन्द जी को मथुरामें 1874 में हिंदी में बातचीत करते देखकर जवाहरदास जी ने कहा आप यहाँ संस्कृत में भी बातचीत कर सकते हैं, परंतु दायानंद जी ने उन्हें समझाया कि हिंदी में आलाप करने से जन हित अधिक होता है।

भारतेन्दु हरिश्चन्द्र : (Bharatendu Harischandra 1850-1885)

भारतेन्दु जी का जन्म काशी में हुआ था। जब ये दस वर्ष के थे तभी इनके पिता गोपालचन्द्र गिरिधरदास (1833–1860) की मृत्यु हो गई थी।

भारतेन्दु जी ने अपनी केवल 35 वर्ष की आयु में 175 ग्रन्थ लिखे, जिनमें कविता, नाटक, निबंध और कहानी संग्रह आदि सभी क्षेत्र हैं। गद्य में इन्होंने खड़ी बोली तथा पद्य में ब्रजभाषा का प्रयोग किया है।

इनकी कविताएं इष्ट देवता कृष्ण की उपासना, श्रद्धा, शृंगार, सौन्दर्य और प्रेम, हास्य, व्यंग, विनय, आत्म-समर्पण, मातृभूमि का प्रेम, सामाजिक जागरण, हिंदी प्रेम, भाषा का परिष्करण आदि से परिपूर्ण हैं। हिंदी साहित्य में इन्हें युगपुरुष माना गया है।

श्रीधर पाठक : (Shridhar Pathak 1859-1928)

श्रीधर जी का जन्म आगरा जिले में हुआ था। उन्होंने संस्कृत और फारसी में शिक्षा प्राप्त की थी,

परन्तु सरल हिंदी का प्रभाव उनकी रचनाओं पर निश्चित स्पष्ट है। इनकी कविताएं और गद्य रचनाएं व्रजभाषा तथा खड़ी बोली दोनों में हैं। इन्होंने संस्कृत पुस्तकों के अनुवाद किये हैं।

इनकी प्रमुख रचनाएं हैं जगत सचाई सार, मनोविनोद, काश्मीर सुषमा, गोपिका गीत और भारत गीत। इनकी कविताओं में देशप्रेम और प्राकृतिक सौंदर्य होता है।

आचार्य नरेन्द्र देव : (Acharya Narendra Deo (1860-1932)

आचार्य नरेन्द्र देव जी का जन्म उत्तर प्रदेश के सीतापुर नगर में हुआ था। आप ने प्रयाग से संस्कृत में एम्. ए. की। संस्कृत के साथ ही आपने पाली, हिन्दी, उर्दू, फारसी का भी गहन अध्ययन किया। आप काशी हिन्दु विश्वविद्यालय के कुलपति रह चुके हैं। 1937 में उत्तर प्रदेश सरकार ने आपके शिक्षा सुधार कार्य के लिए आपको आचार्य की उपाधि दी। आप हिन्दी के समर्थ लेखक एवं वक्ता थे। आपकी भाषा परिष्कृत तथा परिमार्जित थी।

आपकी समाजवाद पर अनेक प्रसिद्ध रचनाएं हैं तथा ऐतिहासिक और धार्मिक विषयों पर अनेक पुस्तकें प्रकाशित हैं ।

जगन्नाथदास, रत्नाकर : ('Ratnakar' Jagannath Das 1866-1932)

रत्नाकर जी का जन्म काशी में हुआ था। इन्हें प्राचीन संस्कृति, मध्यकालीन हिंदी काव्य, उर्दू, फारसी, अँग्रेजी, हिंदी, आयुर्वेद, संगीत, ज्योतिष तथा दर्शन शास्त्र का अच्छा ज्ञान था। इनकी मुख्य काव्य कृतियाँ हैं उद्धव-शतक, शृंगार-लहरी, गंगावतरण, वीराष्टक और रत्नाकर।

महावीर प्रसाद द्विवेदी : (Mahavir Prasad Dwivedi 1864-1938)

महावीर जी का जन्म जिला रायबरेली में हुआ था। आपने संकृत, हिंदी, बंगला व मराठी भाषाओंका गहन अध्ययन किया। हिन्दी भाषा के अतिरिक्त आपने इतिहास, अर्थशास्त्र, राजनीति, धर्म वैज्ञानिक आविष्कार आदि क्षेत्रों का भी अभ्यास किया।

1911 में आप रेलवे की नौकरी छोड़ कर सरस्वती पत्रिका के अवैतनिक सम्पादक तथा व्याकरण शिक्षक बन कर आगामी बीस वर्ष कार्य करते रहे। इस माध्यम से इन्होंने खड़ी बोली को गद्य तथा पद्य दोनों की भाषा बनाने का आन्दोलन किया। फलस्वरूप काव्य भाषा में खड़ी बोली की प्रतिष्ठा हुई। आपने हिन्दी भाषा का सुसंस्कृत करके गद्य को परिमार्जित एवं प्रांजल बनाया है। आपका साहित्यिक कार्यक्षेत्र के भाषा संस्कार, निबंध लेखन,

आलोचना एवं आदर्श पत्रकारिता आदि चार प्रधान रूप हैं।

महावीर जी मुख्यत: गद्य लेखक ही थे। उनके लेखों के संग्रह रसज्ञ-रंजन और साहित्य-सीकर नाम से प्रसिद्ध हैं। आपकी हिन्दी साहित्यिक सफलता से 1903-1923 का समय द्विवेदी-युग नाम से जाना जाता है। आपके प्रमुख काव्य संग्रह हैं काव्यमंजूषा, सुमन और कविताकलाप। आपके संस्कृत हिंदी अनुवाद हैं मेघदूत, कुमारसंभव, विचार रत्नावली, स्वाधीनता आदि।

अयोध्यासिंह उपाध्याय, हरिऔध : (Hariaudh 1865-1947)

अयोध्यासिंह जी का जन्म आजमगढ़ जिले में हुआ था। उन्होंने स्वाध्याय द्वारा ही संस्कृत, हिंदी, बंगला, पंजाबी और फारसी भाषाएं सीखी थी। इनकी रचनाओं में कविताएं, नाटक, उपन्यास, लेख आदि सभी आते हैं। प्रिय-प्रवास अयोध्यासिंह जी का प्रसिद्ध महाकाव्य है, जिसका आरम्भ प्रकृति वर्णन से है और यह संस्कृत प्रवाह से युक्त है।

इनका दूसरा महाकाव्य है विदेही वनवास, जो शुद्ध साहित्यिक हिंदी में है। इनको हिंदी खड़ी बोली के आदि महाकाव्यकार माना जाता है, जिसमें संस्कृत छंदों की विविधता पायी जाती है। आप गद्य भी बहुत अच्छा लिखते हैं।

आपकी प्रमुख गद्य रचनाएं हैं ठेठ हिन्दी का ठाठ और अधखिला फूल। इनकी अन्य महत्त्वपूर्ण खड़ी बोली की रचनाएं हैं चूभते चौपदे, चोखे चौपदे, वैदेही वनवास और प्रेमाम्बु प्रवाह। इनका रस-कलश व्रज भाषा में है।

मुंशी प्रेमचन्द : (Munshi Premchand 1880-1936)

उपन्यास सम्राट प्रेमचन्द जी का जन्म जिला वाराणसी में हुआ। इनका पूर्व नाम धनपत राय श्रीवास्तव था। इनमें उत्कृष्ट कहानियाँ लिखने की अपूर्व प्रतिभा थी।

इन्होंने लगभग 3000 कहानियाँ लिखी हैं। प्रेमचन्द जी ने कई श्रेष्ठ उपन्यास लिखे हैं जिनमें गोदान, वरदान, प्रतिज्ञा, गबन, सेवासदन, निर्मला, प्रेमाश्रम, रंगभूमि, कार्यभूमि, कायाकल्प आदि हैं। इनके प्रमुख कहानी संग्रह हैं कफन, नव जीवन, प्रसून, प्रेम प्रतिज्ञा।

इनकी रचनाएं उस ग्रामिण जनता का साहित्य है, जिसका जीवन अन्धविश्वास और अज्ञान में बुरी तरह से पिसा जा रहा है। प्रेमचंद जी ने इस जीवन को निकट से स्वयं देखा है।

इनकी कहानियों की लोकप्रीयता इतनी बढ़ी कि फिर ये फिल्म व्यवसाय के लिये भी कहानियाँ

लिखने लगे।

रामनरेश त्रिपाठी : (Ramanaresh Tripathi 1881-1962)

रामनरेश जी का जन्म जिला जौनपुर में हुआ था। इनकी कविताओं पर गांधीवाद का प्रभाव है। राष्ट्रीय कवियों में इनका बहुत सम्मान है। आपकी शैली सरल तथा प्रभावपूर्ण है। इन्होंने देश की प्राकृतिक शोभा का वर्णन सुंदर रीति से किया है। इन्होंने कविता, नाटक, उपन्यास आदि सभी क्षेत्रों में रचनाएं की हैं। आपका हिंदी साहित्य का संक्षिप्त इतिहास एवं आपकी कई बालोपयोगी पुस्तकें और मिलन, स्वप्न, मानसी व पथिक ये चार काव्य प्रसिद्ध हैं। साथ साथ ही आपकी संस्कृत, बंगला व उर्दू कविताएं प्रकाशित हैं।

डा. राजेन्द्र प्रसाद : (Dr. Rajendra Prasad 1884-1963)

राजेन्द्र बाबु का जन्म बिहार के छापरा जिले में हुआ था। आपने पटना विश्वविद्यालय से शिक्षा प्रप्त की थी, एवं परीक्षाओं में आप सदा प्रथम रहे थे।

आप संस्कृत व फारसी के अच्छे विद्वान् थे परन्तु मतृभाषा हिन्दी के प्रति आपकी श्रद्धा अपार थी। बोलचाल की साधारण हिन्दी भाषा अपनाने के कारण आपकी भाषा में प्रवाह था।

आप बारह वर्षों तक भारत गणराज्य के राष्ट्रपति रहे। भारत का संविधान आपकी अध्यक्षता में हुआ था और उसमें हिन्दी को राष्ट्रभाषा बनानो में सर्वाधिक योगदान आपका था।

आचार्य रामचन्द्र शुक्ल : (Ramachandra Shukla 1884-1941)

रामचन्द्र जी का जन्म बस्ती जिले में हुआ। इनकी शिक्षा उर्दू माध्यम से हुई थी, परन्तु इन्होंने उर्दू माध्यम अस्वीकार करके हिंदी का भवितव्य उज्ज्वल करने का ही प्रयास किया, कारण है इनका संस्कृताध्ययन। रामचन्द्रजी काशी में शब्द सागर के सहसम्पादक थे। आप हिन्दी के श्रेष्ठ कवि, निबंधकार एवं समालोचक थे। आपने हिंदी साहित्य का इतिहास, काव्य में रहस्यवाद, रस मिमांसा, बुद्ध चरित आदि पुस्तके लिखी हैं। इनकी गद्य शैली हिन्दी साहित्य में अपना विशेष स्थान रखती है। संस्कृतगर्भित भाषा का प्रयोग इनकी रचनाओं में होता है।

मैथिलीशरण गुप्त : (Maithili Sharan Gupta 1886-1964)

मैथिलीशरण जी का जन्म जिला झाँसी में हुआ। साहित्य जगत में इस राष्ट्रकवि को दद्दा नाम से

जाना जाता था। ये पद्मभूषण अलंकार से सम्मानित हैं।

इनका संस्कृत का अध्ययन गम्भीर था। इनको कविताएं लिखने की रुचि बचपन से ही थी। सरस्वती के सम्पादक श्री महावीर प्रसाद द्विवेदी जी ने इनका काव्य रंग-में-भंग प्रकाशित किया और फिर जयद्रथ-वध नामक काव्यखण्ड प्रकाशित किया। उसके उपरान्त इनके भारत भारती, पद्य प्रबन्ध, चन्द्रहास, तिलोत्तमा, शकुन्तला, पत्रावली, हिन्दू, गुरुकुल, बक संहार, कुणाल गीत, हिडिम्बा वध, अजीत, यशोधरा, द्वापर, नहुष, सिद्धराज, झंकार, साकेत आदि लगभग 40 काव्य प्रकाशित हुए। राम के प्रति इनकी श्रद्धा अटूट थी।

वृन्दनलाल वर्मा : (Vrindan Lal Varma 1889-1969)

डा. वृन्दनलाल जी का जन्म जिला झाँसि में हुआ था। आपके पितामह झाँसी राज्य के दीवान थे और स्वातंत्र्य संग्राम में मारे गए थे, फलस्वरूप आप में सेनानी भावनाएं प्रबल थीं। वर्मा जी ने अनेक ऐतिहासिक उपन्यास, कहानि संग्रह और नाटक लिखे हैं। मृगनयनी, झाँसी की रानी, अमरदेव, महादजी सिंधिया आदि इनके प्रमुख ग्रन्थ हैं।

ये बचपन से ही अत्यन्त भावुक थे। ये एक ज्वलंत देशप्रेमी तथा गम्भीर समाज सुधारणावदी लेखक थे।

आप अचल मेरा कोई में कहते है, हमारा समाज अब भी पिछड़ा हुआ है। उसी समाज के लाज-संकोच में विधवाएं अपने हाड़-मांस को गला-गला कर और जला-जला कर जीवन बिताती हैं। पाखंडियों और धूर्तों की पूजा होती है, पर इन यातनाग्रस्त तपस्विनियों को कोई पूछता भी है?

माखनलाल चतुर्वेदी : (Makhanlal Chaturvedi 1889-1968)

माखनलाल जी का जन्म होशंगाबाद के समीप बावई में हुआ। इन्होंने हिंदी तथा संस्कृत का अध्ययन किया था। वे खंडावा में कर्मवीर नामक राष्ट्रीय सप्ताहिक के प्रकाशक एवं संपादक थे। इन्होंने स्वतंत्रता आंदोलनों में सक्रिय रूप से भाग लिया था। जेल में भी इनकी कलम चलती ही रही थी।

इनकी कविताओं ने देश में नवजागरण किया था। इनकी कविताओं पर राष्ट्रवाद के साथ-साथ रहस्यवाद, छायावाद और प्रगतिवाद का भी प्रभाव है। हिम किरीटिनी और मितरंगिनी इनके कविता संग्रह हैं। साहित्य देवता इनकी गद्य रचना है।

जयशंकर प्रसाद : (Jaishankar Prasad 1890-1937)

जयशंकर जी का जन्म वाराणसी में हुआ था। इन्होंने संस्कृत व उर्दू का गहन अभ्यास किया था। प्रथम ये व्रज भाषा में कविता करते थे फिर खड़ी बोली में कविताएं करने लगे। इनकी कानन कुसुम, करुणालय, प्रेम-प्रसाद आदि प्रारंभिक खड़ी बोली की कविताएं हैं। आँसू, झरना, लहर श्रेष्ठ रचनाएं हैं।

इन्होंने कामयनी नाम का महाकाव्य लिख कर महाकवियों मे स्थान मिलाया। इनके कंकाल, इरावती व तितली नामक उपन्यास और आँधी, प्रतिध्वनि, छाया आदि कहानीसंग्रह भी प्रसिद्ध हैं।

इन्होंने जिस भाँति कविता क्षेत्र में युगान्तर किया उसी तरह से रंगमंच के क्षेत्र में भी युगान्तर का कार्य किया है।

इनके अधिकांश नाटकों की कथावस्तु इतिहास से है और ध्येय है भारतीय संस्कृति को उजागर करना। अत: इन्होंने बौद्धिकता प्रधान, भावना प्रधान तथा सामाजिक नाटक लिखे हैं।

इनके श्रेष्ठ नाटकों में स्कन्दगुप्त, अजातशत्रु, चन्द्रगुप्त, विशाख, जनमेजय आदि ऐतिहासिक रचनाओं नाम है। वस्तुत: जयशंकर जी हिन्दी के सर्वश्रेष्ठ नाटककार हैं।

आपकी संस्कृत युक्त भाषा शैली परिकृत व भावपूर्ण होती है। इन्होंने अभिव्यंजना की अच्छी प्रणाली हिन्दी को प्रदान की है। इनकी गणना छायावदी तथा रहस्यवादी कवियों में की जाती है।

राहुल सांकृत्यायन : (Rahul Sankrityayan 1893-1963)

राहुल जी का जन्म जिला आजमगढ़ में हुआ था। किशोरावस्था में ही विरक्ति पा कर आप सन्यासी बन गये थे और फलस्वरूप आपने बौद्ध धर्म स्वीकार कर लिया था। इसके पूर्व इनका नाम केदारनाथ पाण्डेय था। इन्होंने प्राचीन धर्म ग्रंथों का अन्वेशण किया था। अत: बुद्ध धर्म के उच्च एवं तत्त्विक विचार व निरीश्वरवाद आपकी रचनाओं में होते हैं।

राहुल जी ने कई उपन्यास लिखे हैं। हिंदी व संस्कृत के साथ-साथ ये अन्य कई भाषाओं के मर्मज्ञ एवं विद्वान् थे आप। आपके उपन्यास, कवितासंग्रह तथा कहानीसंग्रह प्रसिद्ध हैं।

विषयानुकूल भाषा शैली इनकी रचनाओं की विशेषता है। आप कहते हैं कि अज्ञान का दूसरा नाम ही ईश्वर है। हम अपने अज्ञान को साफ स्वीकार करने में शर्माते हैं। अत: उसके लिए ईश्वर ढूँढ निकाला गया है।

सूर्यकान्त त्रिपाठी, निराला : (Suryakant Tripathi, Nirala 1896-1961)

सूर्यकान्त जी का जन्म बंगाल के महिषादल जिले में हुआ। इन्होंने हिन्दी, संस्कृत तथा बंगला का अध्ययन किया। इनके विचारों पर स्वामी विवेकानन्द जी के विचारों का प्रभाव है और आपकी कविताओं की गहनता वेदान्त का परिणाम।

कोलकता के समन्वय पत्रिका के आप संपादक रहे। कविता, कहानी उपन्यास आदि सभी क्षेत्रों में आपका नाम उज्ज्वल हुआ है।

आपकी काव्य पुस्तकों में तुलसीदास, परिमल, अनामिका, गीतिका, बेला, अणिमा तथा आपके उपन्यासों में निरुपमा, अप्सरा, अलका आदि प्रमुख हैं। निराला जी जैसे महान कवि थे वैसे ही महान दानी भी थे।

उदयशंकर भट्ट : (Udayashankar Bhatta 1898-1966)

उदयशंकर जी का जन्म इटावा नगर में हुआ। इनके घर में बातचीत संस्कृत में होती थी। उदय जी नें लाहौर में अध्यापन कार्य किया। इन्होंने स्वतंत्रता आंदोलनों मे भाग लिया हुआ था। इनकी अनेक रचनाएं प्रकाशित हैं।

इन्होंने कहानी, उपन्यास, नाटक, एकांकी अदि विविध क्षेत्रों में रचनाएं की हैं। अपितु मुख्यत: एकांकीकार के रूपमें इन्होंने श्रेष्ठता प्राप्त की। पदरे के पीछे नामका एकांकीसंग्रह इनका प्रसिद्ध है। विसर्जन, अमृत और विष, राका, युगदीप आदि इनके प्रमुख काव्यसंग्रह हैं।

पाण्डेय बेचन शर्मा, उग्र : (Pandeya Bechan Sharma 1900-1967)

आप उग्र नाम से जाने जाते हैं मगर एक उग्रवादी रचनाकार नहीं हैं, अहिंसावादी हैं। आप ने खुदाराम की कहानी में कहा हैं -

खुदा अगर खून पसंद करता, तो हमारे बुजू करने के लिये पानी न बनकर खून ही बहाता। गंगा खूनी गंगा होती, समंदर खून का समंदर होता,

खून के फेर में न पड़ो... खुदा खून नहीं पसंद करता।

सुमित्रानंद पंत : (Sumitranand Pant 1900-1977)

सुमित्रानंद जी का जन्म जिला अलमोड़ा में हुआ। इन्हों ने काशी व प्रयाग में शिक्षा पायी और हिंदी, संस्कृरा तथा बंगला भाषाओं का अध्ययन किया।

आप छायावाद तथा रहस्यवाद के कवि हैं।

सुमित्रानंद जी के लगभग 35 काव्यसंग्रह प्रकाशित हैं। उनमें से युगान्तर, युगवाणी, वीणा, स्वर्णकिरण, उच्छ्‌वास, पल्लव, गुंजन, चिदम्बरा आदि प्रमुख हैं। काव्यसंग्रहों के साथ-साथ ही उन्हों ने गद्यसंग्रह, नाटक, उपन्यास व कहानियाँ भी लिखी हैं। ये साहित्य अकादमी पुरस्कार, भारतीय ज्ञानपीठ पुरस्कार व पद्मभूषण अलंकार से सम्मानित हैं। देखिये आपकी भाषा शैली कितनी सुकुमार, सरल तथा मधुर है।

इलाचन्द्र जोशी : (Ila Chandra Joshi 1902-1982)

इलाचन्द्र जी का जन्म अल्मोड़ा में कुमाऊँ राज्य के दीवान घराने में हुआ। एक अच्छे एवं मार्मिक रचनाकार हैं। आपने साहित्य के साथ-साथ कला और विज्ञान का मनोपूर्वक अध्ययन किया। इलाचन्द्र जी श्रेष्ठ कवि, कहानीकार, निबन्धकार तथा उपन्यासकार भी हैं। आपके घृणामयी, सन्यासी और परदेशी नाम के तीन उपन्यास लोकप्रिय हैं।

आप जहाज का पंछी में कहते हैं, कभी-कभी मैं सोचता हूँ कि आज के तथाकथित फ्री-वर्ल्ड में मनुष्य ने मनुष्य को मनुष्य न रहने देने की कसम खा रखी है...। पर अब समय आ रहा है, बल्कि आ गया है, जब आप लोगें की इस संगठित झुठाई, इस सामूहिक भ्रष्टाचार और अत्याचार के विरोध में धरती का एक छोटे से छोटा छिद्र चीख उठेगा और एक-एक कुचली हुई दूब गला कर फाड़-फाड़ कर चिल्ला उठेगी. आप की प्रकृति की रागात्मक वृत्तिया, जीवन का यथार्थ और आत्मानुभूतियों के दृष्टा एवं कवि-चित्रकार हैं।

भगवती चरण वर्मा : (Bhagavati Charan Varma 1903-1980)

भगवती चरण जी का जन्म उन्नाव जिले में हुआ था और प्रयाग में शिक्षा हुई। इनकी कविताओं के दो रूप हैं, एक प्रेम गीत और दूसरा जीवन का हाहाकार। आपने विचार नामक पत्रिका स संपादन किया है। आप सिनेमा के लिये डायलॉग भी लिखते हैं। आपके मधुकण, प्रेम-संगीत आदि काव्य ग्रन्थ और टेढ़े-मेढ़े रास्ते, भूले बिसरे चित्र, रेखा, तीन वर्ष, पतन आदि उपन्यास प्रकाशित हैं। आप श्रेष्ठ कवि, नाटककार, निबंध लेखक, उपन्यासकार और कहानी लेखक भी हैं। आपकी प्रतिभा बहुमुखी है। भगवती चरण जी की भाषा मधुर भी है और तीखी भी।

यशपाल : (Yashpal 1903-1976)

यशपाल जी का जन्म फिरोजपुर में हुआ था और प्रथमिक शिक्षण गुरुकुल कांगड़ी में हुआ। लाहौर में पढ़ते समय ये आप क्रान्तिवीर भगतसिंह तथा सुखदेव जी के संपर्क में आए। तत्पश्चात् क्रान्ति आंदोलन में आपंने आंदोलन में बौद्धिक भूमिका ली।

आधुनिक युग के प्रगतिवादी कथाकारों में यशपाल जी एक प्रमुख स्थान रखते हैं। आपके उपन्यास व अनेक कहानी संग्रह हैं। आपके प्रसिद्ध उपन्यासों में दादा कामरेड, मनुष्य के रूप और झूठ-सच ये तीने विशेष लोकप्रीय हैं। सिंहावलोकन में आप लिखते हैं, मार्क्स को अगर एक पल्टन का नायक बनकर युद्ध के मोर्चे पर जाना पड़ता, तो कैपिटल लिखकर समाजवाद की नींव खड़ी करने का काम किसी दूसरे ही आदमी के कंधों पर पड़ता।

सुभद्रा कुमरी चौहान : (Subhadra Kumari Chauhan 1904-1921)

सुभद्रा जी का जन्म प्रयाग जिले के निहालपुर गाँव में हुआ। इलाहाबाद के 1921 वर्ष के स्वतंत्रता के असयोग आंदोलन के प्रभाव में आपने अध्ययन छोड़ कर राजनीति में भाग कूद पड़ी और फिर बारंबार जेल में जा चुकी। इनकी काव्य साधना के पीछे उत्कट देश प्रेम की प्रभावी शक्ति है। इनकी कविताओं व भाषणों मे सच्ची वीरांगना का ओज और देशभक्ति का अद्भुत प्रभाव प्रकट है। आप का स्थान महिला कवयत्रियों में बहुत ऊँचा है।

सुभद्रा जी का कवितासंग्रह मुकुल नाम से प्रसिद्ध है। इनकी झाँसी वाली रानी और वीरों का कैसा हो वसंत कविताएं देशप्रेमी जनों के हृदतों में कण्ठहार बनकर आग फूँकती हैं। आपकी भाषा सरल तथा बोधगम्य होती है।

जैनेन्द्र कुमार : (Jainendra Kumar 1905-1988)

जैनेन्द्र जी का जन्म अलीगढ़ जिले में हुआ। इनके पिता प्यारेलाल जी का देहावसन हुआ तब ये केवल चार मास के थे। काशी विद्यालय से शिक्षा प्राप्त करके आप गाँधी जी के असयोग आंदोलन में मिल गए और कई बार जेल में गए।

आपका प्रथम लेख अहिंसा है जो विशाल भारत में छपा। सुनीता आपका सबसे अधिक लोकप्रिय उपन्यास है। आपका समय और हम नामक ग्रन्थ गौरवान्वित हुआ है। आपके अन्य उपन्यास हैं त्यागपत्र, कल्याणी, परख, तपोभूमि, विवते, सुखदा, व्यतीत, जयवर्धन आदि। आपके अनेक कहानी संग्रह, निबंध संग्रह तथा नटक भी हैं। मुंशी प्रेमचंद जी के साथ ही आपका उपन्यासकारों मे दर्जा निश्चित् है।

काका हाथरसी : (Kaka Hathrasi 1906-1996)

प्रभुनाथ गर्ग अर्थात् काका का जन्म आगरा के निकट हाथरस में हुआ था। काका ने अपमा व्यक्तित्व संगीत और साहित्य के बल पर स्वयं ही बनाया था। काका एक माने हुए हास्य कवि थे। साथ साथ वे एक अच्छे चिद्धाकार तथा संगीत विद्वान् भी थे। ये मराठी, उर्दू व गुजराती भाषाएं भी जानते थे। उन्हों ने संगीत विशारद, संगीत सागर, तुकन्त कोश और राग कोश नामक चार ग्रन्थ और अन्य 150 संगीत पुस्तकें रची थी और संगीत कार्यालय व संगीत प्रेस स्थापन किए थे। आपको अग्रश्री, ठिठोली पुरिस्कार, कला रत्न, पद्मश्री आदि कई अवार्डस् मिले थे। आप कैनडा में 1984 में आए थे। काका की 1933 में प्रथम कविता थी गुलदस्ता। एन्होंने अपनी कविताओं में सामाजिक, संस्कृतिक, साहित्यिक एवं राजनीतिक रूढिवादिता व भ्रष्टाचार पर प्रहार किया था। उनकी मुख्य रचनाएं हैं काका के कारतूस, काका की मेहफिल, काका के व्यंग बाण, काका का दरबार, काका की चौपाई, काका के चुटुकले, काका की नोक-झोंक, काका की फुलझडियाँ, काका के कहकहे, काका के प्रहसम, काका के कारटून, काका के लव लेटर्स, काका शतक, काका तरंग, काकदूत, हंसगुल्ले, दुलत्ती आदि 42 पुस्तकें।

आचार्य नन्ददुलारे वाजपेयी : (Nandadulare Vajpeyi 1906-1967)

नन्ददुलारे जी हिंदी व संस्कृत के विद्वान् थे। आपने प्रथम पत्रकार की भूमिका चुनी उसके अनन्तर आप ने समीक्षा क्षेत्र में पाँव रखा और उसमें भी सफल हुए। इनकी समीक्षा में बौद्धिकता का प्राधान्य है। आपके अनेक आलोचना ग्रन्थ प्रकाशित हुए हैं। छायावाद के समर्थ आलोचकों में आपका श्रेष्ठ स्थान है।

नन्ददुलारे जी ने काशी नागरी प्रचारिणी सभा द्वारा प्रकाशित सूर-सागर का सम्पादन किया है। आपकी भाषा संस्कृत-बहुल है। समाज और साहित्य में आप चेतावनी देते हैं, अनेक बार समाज की हीनताएं भी लेखकों में तीव्र प्रतिक्रिया उत्पन्न करती हैं और श्रेष्ठ साहित्य के निर्माण में हेतु बनाती हैं। आवश्यक इतना ही है कि कलाकार या साहित्यिक की दृष्टि युग की सामाजिक हीनताओं से आक्रान्त और स्खलित न हो गई हो। ऐसे ही अस्खलित चेता कवि और लेखक स्वप्न दृष्टा कहलाते हैं और अंधकार में प्रकाश के ज्योतिवाही होते हैं।

हरिवंशराय बच्चन : (Harivansh Rai Bachchan 1907-2003)

हरिवंशराय जी का जन्म पवित्र नगरी प्रयाग में हुआ था। घर में छोटे होने के कारण उनको बच्चन (बच्चा) कहते थे। उन्होंने इलाबाद युनिवर्सिटी, बनारस हिंदु युनिवर्सिटी और केम्ब्रीज युनिवर्सिटी

में शिक्षा पाई थी।

इन्होंने 1930 के राष्ट्रीय आंदोलन में भाग लिया था। इनको 1966 में साहित्य अकादमी पारितोषक मिला था और 1967 में पद्मभूशण का सम्मान मिला था। इनको सरस्वती सम्मान, सोवियतलैण्ड नेहरु अवार्ड, लोटस अवार्ड आदि सम्मान प्राप्त थे। इनके सुपुत्र अमिताभ जी एवं अजिताभ जी नें इनका मान और बढ़ाया है।

हरिवंशराय जी नें गीता भाषांतरित की है। इनकी प्रमुख हिन्दी रचना है मधुशाला।

महादेवी वर्मा : (Mahadevi Varma 1907-1987)

महादेवी जी का जन्म फरूखाबाद में हुआ। इन्होंने इलाहाबाद विश्वविद्यालय से संस्कृत में एम.ए. की और वहाँ महिला विद्यापीठ की और साहित्यकार संसद स्थापना की। इनकी भाषा संस्कृत गर्भित है मगर सरल है। इनको आधुनिक युग की सर्वश्रेष्ठ महिला कवयत्री माना जाता है। इन्होंने साहित्यक्षेत्र में छायावादी रचनाकार के रूप में पाँव रखा। आगे चल कर इन्होंने काव्य, तथा गद्य के सभी क्षेत्रों में नए आयाम स्थापित किए। 1934 में इन्हें सक्सेरिया पुरस्कार मिला था और 1942 में द्विवेदी पदक प्राप्त हुआ था। 1943 में मंगलाप्रसाद पुरस्काार एवं भारती पुरस्काार इनको दिए गए थे। 1956 में इनको भारत सरकार ने पद्म भूषण की उपाधि से सम्मानित किया और 1969 में विक्रम विश्वविद्यालय नें डी. लिट्. की उपधि से अलंकृत किया। इनकी प्रधान रचनाएं हैं यामा, नीहार, रश्मि, नीरजा, सान्ध्यगीत, और दीपशिखा। आपके काव्यों मे दीपक एवं प्रियतम की याद ये विषय विशेष रूप से पाए जाते हैं।

हजारी प्रसाद द्विवेदी : (Hazari Prasad Dvivedi 1907-1979)

डा० हजारीप्रसाद द्विवेदी जी का जन्म बलिया जिले में हुआ। इन्होंने संस्कृत का गम्भीर अध्ययन करके काशी हिंदु विश्वविद्यालय से ज्योतिषाचार्य की उपाधी प्राप्त की। उसके उपरान्त एन्होंने शान्तिनिकेतन में कविवर रविन्द्रनाथ ठाकुर जी के साथ कार्य किया। अपने ग्रन्थ के द्वारा हजारीप्रसाद जी ने हिन्दी साहित्य की भूमिका प्रस्थापित की। और गद्य रचना के द्वारा हिन्दी साहित्य को प्रभावपूर्ण भाषा से समृद्ध किया।

भारत सरकार की ओर से ये पद्मभूषण के गौरव से सम्मानित हैं। कबीर, बाणभट्ट की आत्मकथा, चारु चन्द्रलेखा, पुनर्नवा आदि रचनाएं इनकी बहुत लोकप्रिय हैं।

आप एक विद्वान् आलोचक, श्रेष्ठ उपन्यासकार एवं प्रभावी निबन्धकार थें। आपका कहना है कि वृहत्तर जीवन में अस्त्र-शस्त्रों का बढ़ने देना पशुता की निशानी है और उनकी बाढ़ को रोकना मनुष्यत्व का तकाजा है। मनुष्य में जो घृणा है, जो अनायास है, बिना सिखाये, आ जाती है वह पशुत्व का द्योतक है और अपने को संयत रखना, दूसरे के मनोभावों का आदर करना मनुष्य का स्वधर्म है।

रामाधारीसिंह, दिनकर : (Ramadhari Simha, Dinkar 1908-1974)

रामाधारीसिंह जी का जन्म बिहार के मुंगेर जिले में हुआ था। आप बिहार के जाने माने कवियों में प्रथम स्थान रखते हैं।

आप कविताओं के साथ-साथ गद्य भी लिखते हैं, परन्तु आपने क्रान्तिकारी कवियों में जो एक विशेष प्रसिद्धि पाई है वह बहुत कम कवियों ने पाई है।

आपके प्रसिद्ध काव्यों में उर्वशी, कुरुक्षेत्र, द्वन्द्वगीत, रसवन्ति, रेणुका, हुँकार आदि प्रकाशन हैं, इनमें से कुरुक्षेत्र नाम का ग्रन्थ सम्मानित व पारितोषित है।

सच्चिदानन्द हीराचन्द वात्सायन, अज्ञेय : (S. H. Vatsayan 1911-1993)

सच्चिदानंद जी का जन्म लाहौर में हुआ था। क्रान्तिकारी बनकर स्वतंत्रता आंदोलन में चार वर्ष जेल काट चुके हैं। इन्हों ने सैनिक और विशाल भारत नामक दो हिन्दी पत्रिकाओं का सम्पादन किया। 1943 में भारतीय सेना में कैप्टन नियुक्त हो गए। 1947 में प्रतीक नामक प्रयोगवादी पत्रिका चलाई। उसके उपरान्त आकाशवाणी में कार्य किया और बाद में नवभारत टाइम्स पत्रिका का सम्पादन किया।

आँगन के पार द्वार नामक पुस्तक पर आपको साहित्य अकादमी पुरस्कार मिला और कितनी नावों में कितनी बार पुस्तक पर आपको ज्ञानपीठ पुरस्कार मिला। अज्ञेय जी ने कई कहानी संग्रह, उपन्यास, निबन्ध मालाए, और आलोचनाएं लिखी। आपकी मुख्य कृतियाँ हैं आँगन के पार द्वार, भग्नदूत, चिन्ता, हरी घास पर, बावरा, अहेरी आदि। आपको प्रयोगवाद के जन्मदाता जाना जाता है। सच्चिदानंद जी के काव्य में व्यंगात्मकता अत्यन्त सशक्त रूप में है।

बाबा बागार्जुन : (Baba Nagarjun 1911-1993)

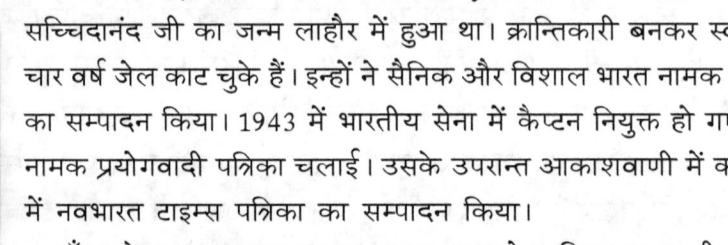

बाबा बैद्यनाथ मिश्रा जी का जन्म बीजर के मैथिल क्षेत्र में हुआ। आप संस्कृत के विद्वान और धर्म के उग्र टीकाकार थे। इन्होंने स्वामी सहजानंद के साथ स्वतंत्रता आंदोलन में भाग लिया था। आपने अपने यात्री उपनाम से मैथिली भाषा में कविताएं लिखनी शुरु की। आप फिर राहुल सांकृत्यायन जी के साथ श्रीलंका गए और बुद्ध बन गए। ततः नागार्जुन के उपनाम से हिन्दी साहित्य लिखने लगे।

आप श्री जयप्रकाश नारायण जी की काव्यवाणी बनकर बीहार आदोलन में सक्रिय

हुए। आपने हिंदी के गद्य तथा पद्य साहित्य को सधन बनाया है।

आपके उपन्यासों में प्रमुख हैं पत्र हीन नंगा गाछ और खिचड़ी विप्लव देखा हमने। आपने कालिदास के नाटक और जयदेव का गीतगोविंद भी भाषांतरित किया है।

भवानी प्रसाद मिश्र : (Bhavani Prasad Mishra 1913-1985)

भवानी प्रसाद जी का जन्म मध्य प्रदेश में हुआ था। आप आचार और विचारों से पूर्णतया गाँधीवादी थे। फलस्वरूप इनके काव्यों मे कथन की सादगी होती है और गहन बात भी अति सरल सीधे तरीके से लिख जाते हैं, मगर वाणी में प्रभाव होता है। जैसे कि निम्न दो पंक्तियों मे ये कितना कुछ कह गये हैं। आज निश्चित हो कि वह असि-धार पैनी है, कि यह मसि-धार पैनि है।

रांगेय राघव : (Rangeya Raghava 1923-1962)

रांगेय जी का जन्म आगरा मे हुआ। इनका मूल नाम तिरूमलै नंबकम् वीरराघव आचार्य था। आप संकृत, हिंदी और ब्रज भाषा के विद्वान् थे। आपको साहित्य के साथ-साथ ही संगीत और चित्र कला में भी प्राविण्य था। आपने केवल कविताएं ही नहीं तो कहानियाँ, नाटक, आलोचना आदि सर्व क्षेत्रों में कुल 150 से अधिक रचनाएं की हैं। आपको 1947 में हिंदुस्थानी अकादमी पुस्कार, 1954 में डालमीया पुरस्कार, 1957 में उत्तरप्रदेश शासन पुरस्कार, 1961 में राजस्थान साहित्य अकादमी पुरस्कार, और आपके स्वर्गवास के पश्चात् 1966 में महात्मा गाँधि पुरस्कार प्राप्त हुआ था।

हरिशंकर परसाई : (Harishankar Parsai 1924-1995)

हरिशंकर जी का जन्म हुशंगाबाद जिले में हुआ था। आपने नागपुर विश्वविद्यालय से हिंदी में एम्. ए. करने के पश्चात् जबलपुर में वसुधा नामक मासिक पत्रिका प्रकाशित की।

आप मुख्यत: समाज सुधारक व्यंग लेखक हैं। राजकीय पाखण्ड और सामाजिक रूढ़िवादी रिवाजों की खिल्ली उड़ाकर आपने सीधा मार्ग दिखाया है।

आप आत्मकथा में कहते है, मैं भारतीय क्लास्किों का शुरु से ही अध्येता रहा हूँ और इनका खुल कर उपयोग करता हूँ। मध्य युग के तुलसीदास, सूरदास, कालिदास आदि के संदर्भ और उद्धरण खूब देता हूँ। बहुत लड़ाइयां लड़ी हैं मैंने इन कवियों के लिए। तुलसी ने खुद जितनी लड़ाई लड़ी होगी उससे अधिक मैंने उनके लिए लड़ी। फिर भी मैं -प्रथम पुरुष एक वचन- का प्रयोग करता हूँ। कुछ व्याकरणाचार्य प्रथम पुरुष को -उत्तम पुरुष- कहते हैं, वे होंगे, मैं नहीं।

मोहन राकेश : (Mohan Rakesh 1925-1972)

मोहन राकेश जी का जन्म अमृतसर शहर में हुआ था। इन्होंने पंजाब विश्वविद्यालय से हिंदी और अँग्रेजी में एम्. ए. की थी। आप भारत विभाजन की पीड़ से दु:खी थे इसलिये समय समय पर आपकी लेखनी में उसका प्रभाव दर्शित होता है।

आप सारिका नामक पत्रिका के सम्पादक रह चुके हैं। राकेश जी हिन्दी भाषा के पहलूदार नाट्य और उपन्यास लेखक थे। आपकी कहानियों में कथाभूमि शहरी मध्यवर्ग की आम जनता प्रायश: होती है।

आपके कथा-शिल्प कौशल्य का सम्मान सहित्य-कला जगत में यथोचित हुआ है। आपको संगूत नाटक अकादमी से पुरस्कार प्राप्त है।

धर्मवीर भारती : (Dharmavir Bharti 1926-1997)

डा. धर्मवीर भारती जी का जन्म इलाहाबाद में हुआ। 1948 में आप श्री इलाचंद्र जाशी जी की संगम पत्रिका के सहसम्पादक बने। 1960 से इलाहाबाद विश्वविद्यालय में अध्यापन करते हुए आपने हिन्दी साहित्य कोश के सम्पादन में सहयोग दिया। फिर आप धर्मयुग पत्रिका के प्रधान संपादक बने।

1972 में आप पद्मश्री की गौरव से अलंकृत हुए। आपने अन्य कई पुरस्कार प्राप्त किए हैं जैसे कि, महाराणा मेवाड़ फाउंडेशन का हल्दी घाटी श्रेष्ठ पत्रिका पुरस्कार, संगीत नाटक अकादमी पुरस्कार, उत्तर प्रदेश हिन्दी संस्थान का भारत भारती पुरस्कार, महाराष्ट्र राज्य का महाराष्ट्र गौरव, बिड़ला फाउंडेशन का व्यास सम्मान, आदि। आपके कई कहानी संग्रह, काव्य रचनाएं, निबंध तथा उपन्यास प्रकाशित हैं। आपके उपन्यासों में सूरज का सातवँ घोड़ा, गुनाहों का देवता और ग्यारह सपनों का देश प्रमुख हैं।

सर्वेश्वर दयाल सक्सेना : (Sarveshvar Dayal Saksena 1927-1983)

सर्वेश्वर जी का जन्म उतर प्रदेश के बस्ती जिले में हुआ था। इन्होंने दिनमान व पराग नामक पत्रिकाओं के संपादन में सहयोग दिया।

इन्होंने बालसाहित्य के साथ-साथ ही नाटक और उपन्यास भी लिखे हैं। इन का सबसे महत्त्वपूर्ण कार्य है नई कविता को एक नया आयाम देना। इस क्षेत्र में आप सर्वोच्च हैं।

सर्वेश्वर जी ने प्रकृति को मानव के साथ मिलाकर अनेक रचनाएं की हैं। वे जीवन की किसी भी परिस्थिति से काव्य रचने की प्रेरणा पाते हैं।

www.ingramcontent.com/pod-product-compliance
Lightning Source LLC
Chambersburg PA
CBHW080943120626
46546CB00010B/2821
* 9 7 8 1 9 8 9 4 1 6 9 5 2 *